Internet Lesbian and
Gay Television Series,
1996–2014

Internet Lesbian and Gay Television Series, 1996–2014

VINCENT TERRACE

McFarland & Company, Inc., Publishers

Jefferson, North Carolina

ISBN 978-0-7864-9805-5 (softcover : acid free paper) ∞
ISBN 978-1-4766-2126-5 (ebook)

LIBRARY OF CONGRESS CATALOGUING DATA ARE AVAILABLE

BRITISH LIBRARY CATALOGUING DATA ARE AVAILABLE

On the cover: Natasha Negovanlis from the *Carmilla* web series
(Vervegirl YouTube)

Printed in the United States of America

*McFarland & Company, Inc., Publishers
Box 611, Jefferson, North Carolina 28640
www.mcfarlandpub.com*

TABLE OF CONTENTS

PREFACE

Internet Lesbian and Gay Television Series, 1996-2014, is the third volume in a multi-volume set of books that examines television programs produced exclusively for the Internet. *Internet Horror, Science Fiction and Fantasy Television Series, 1996–2013* (2014) and *Internet Drama and Mystery Television Series, 1996–2014* (2014) are two prior books, with future titles planned.

An Internet or Web television series (as they are often termed) is a program with a varying number of episodes and patterned after typical broadcast and/or cable series. This process is not new as television did something similar when it first came into a commercial medium of its own in the late 1940s, by copying the format of radio series from the 1930s and 1940s. The Internet is still in its pioneering stages and just as television has progressed, no doubt the Internet will also utilize new innovations.

While television and cable networks have backers to insure professional productions, Internet-produced series are usually financed through fundraising campaigns. Surprisingly, many Internet-produced shows are comparable to what airs on network television. Virtually all Internet series feature unknown but talented performers, and these productions are often labeled "no budget" or "low budget" enterprises. There are a few exceptions in every genre of Internet-produced series, like *Neil's Puppet Dreams* that, even with a top star (Neil Patrick Harris) and a big budget, cannot surpass in quality other web-based series that were made for a few hundred dollars.

While numerous broadcast and cable television series and feature films can be streamed over the Internet, they are "not" produced specifically for that medium and thus *not* covered herein; only series produced specifically for the Internet are chronicled in this book series. This volume focuses on comedy, drama (including crime and romantic dramas), science fiction, horror, variety, and reality series that utilize themes related to the LGBT (Lesbian, Gay, Bisexual, Transgender) community.

Contained within this volume are 335 alphabetically arranged LGBT-themed series from 1996 to 2014, each of which contains: (1) a detailed storyline; (2) episode descriptions (where possible); (3) cast and credits (producer, writer and director, where available); (4) year(s) of production, and (5) commentary. Fifty photographs and an index that also includes individual subject headings for the programs that are specific for lesbian, gay, bisexual, drag or transgender themes, complete the book.

Discovering and researching the programs contained within this book was a challenge as there was simply no one source to go to for a list of shows that fall within this book's purview. Acquiring relevant photographs to illustrate this tome was even more difficult. Every producer that could be found, whether through websites, IMDB Pro, Google, or Bing searches, was contacted. However, much contact information was no longer accurate and many sources never responded. I am grateful to those producers who replied and helped to make the end result visually more appealing.

When it comes to gay-themed series, one will find movie and TV spoofs like *Gay's Anatomy*, *Gay Top Gun*, and *Fagney and Gaycey* (a spoof of TV's *Cagney and Lacey*). Drag-themed series have also presented a wide range of topics like *Chico's Angels* (a send-up of *Charlie's Angels*), *Jeza and the Belles* (a sci fi parody), *Cooking with Drag Queens* (a program on how to prepare meals), and perhaps the most bizarrely entertaining of all: *Drag Queens Reading Obituaries*.

It seems lesbian-themed series are the most predominate in the arena of original web-based entries within the overall genre, and there are private detectives (*Nikki and Nora* and *B.J. Fletcher, Private Eye*), police officers (*Lesbian Cops* and *Lady Cops*), and even time travelers (*Frequency* and *Time Traveling Lesbian*). There are truly erotic tales (*Lesbian Seduction*, *Lesbian Vampires*, and *Vampire Killers*), mainstream TV series extensions (*Watchers: The Virtual Series* [from *Buffy the Vampire Slayer*] and *All My Children*), and even a spoof of the Kardashian family featuring the character *Kam Kardashian* (the long-lost lesbian sister of Kim). There are aliens (*Lesbian Space Invaders*) and cooking shows (*My Drunk Kitchen*), and some that are truly dramatic with a real story to tell—such as *Come Take a Walk with Me*, *Once You Leave*, *Out with Dad*, *Vanessa's Story*, and *The Throwaways*.

For web-based TV shows revolving around offbeat friends, the Internet has given us such fare as *Disappointing Gay Best Friend* and *Sassy Gay Friend*. If you thought only PBS presented programs about gardening, then you haven't seen anything like *My Gay Garden*. And to top it all off there are "gems" like *Homo Thugs*, *Robot, Ninja and Gay Guy*, *Gay Town* and *Drag Becomes Him*. Animated series projects have also produced, with items such as *Geez Louise*, *Girl Crush*, and *Lizzy the Lezzy*. While the majority of the programs contained within this book were produced in the U.S., English closed-captioned foreign-produced series, like *Apples*, *Chica Busca Chica*, *Mama*, *Soy Gay*, and *El Vlog de Greta* are also included.

Internet Lesbian and Gay Television Series is the first and only book of its kind to date to cover this aspect of Internet-based series. It was a challenging but rewarding task and the author would like to thank James Robert Parish for his assistance on this project, along with David Ehrenstein, John Griffiths, and Matthew Kennedy for their input.

Note Regarding Web Addresses: During the process of compiling this book, many official web sites have closed although some episodes still remain on line on sharing sites. These have been listed where the official web site no longer exists. Some others, unfortunately, have been completely taken off line and no text or videos remain. As of May 2015, the following programs can no longer be found although text information is included herein: *Dolls* (foreign version), *Fifty Shades of Girls, Gay and Gayer* (2007), *Girl to Girl, InSight, Justine, LesBros* (2012 talk show version), *Lust of the Vampires* and *My Gay Garden*. This is not to say they are gone forever. With fans posting TV and movie videos every day, these shows could also return to the Internet at a future date.

1 *Absolute Cintron*. youtube.com. 2013 (Comedy).

Stand-up comedy routines by Christian Cintron merge into short sketches that, in most instances, poke innocent fun at the LGBT community. **Cast:** Christian Cintron, David Alfano, Gilbert Garza, Jeremy Bassett, Brooke Trantor, Shulie Cowen. **Credits:** *Producer-Writer:* Christian Cintron. **Comment:** Sort of borrowing the format of the TV series *Seinfeld* (wherein Jerry Seinfeld opened most episodes with a standup comedy bit that led into an episode) Christian Cintron manages to compress standup with a brief skit and achieve a well paced, humorous program that is most enjoyable.

Episodes:

1. The Gay Latino Social Club. A gathering of gay Latinos at a social club is explored.

2. A Fat Superhero? A look at what can happen if an overweight superhero tries to save the day for a victimized female.

3. Christian Video Game. Christian examines what would happen if video games were designed after people.

4. You're Gay Right? A look at how gay people deal with the annoying questions that are often asked about them.

5. Superheroes and Oprah. Christian tests the possibilities of depicting Oprah Winfrey as a superhero for America.

6. Inside Social Media. Christian looks at how the Hashtag (#) has gone too far with social media.

2 *Acting Out*. blip.tv 2012 (Comedy).

A young man named Bogie is gay but believes he must pretend to be straight in order to work. Hollywood, Bogie feels, is a tough nut to crack and being gay and an actor is not the right mix. Being straight offers him better opportunities and the roles that will eventually make him a household name. The program charts his adventures as he pretends

being straight, lives his gay life style and contends with friends who just want to help but just complicate what he is trying to do (all of which is heard through his internal thoughts as situations progress).

Kyle is Bogie's boyfriend, a young man who wishes Bogie would be true to himself and not pretend to

Acting Out. **Series poster art (used by permission of Shane Houston).**

3

be what he is not (although his advice is rarely on target and just complicates his straight life). Bridge and Sadie, Bogie's lesbian friends, try to be helpful and offer advice. Although they deeply love each other, they constantly argue and what advice they give is more tailored to being gay than being straight. Owen is Bogie's best friend, a deliveryman that is more concerned about the economy and his well being than Bogie's problems.

Cast: Brennan Hillard (Bogie), David Tolemy (Kyle), Victoria J. Myers (Bridge), Molly Schrieber (Sadie), Justin Giddings (Owen), Cary Adams (Jackson Powers), John Moschitta, Jr. (Ramshackle), Emily Churchill (Candy Hart), Frank Birney (Warner). **Credits:** *Producer:* Jeff Parke, Shane Houston. **Comment:** Enjoyable saga of a confused young man with good acting and production values. The program has numerous possibilities to continue the story line and encompassing the fast-talking John Moschitta, Jr., as Bogie's agent just adds to the amusement (as not only will he confuse Bogie, but viewers as well with advice that is hard to comprehend [the intent] due to his speedy delivery).

Episodes:

1. The Manager, Part 1. Bogie, believing he is successfully leading a double life, begins his search for a talent manager while finding that advice from his friends is not exactly the right advice to take.

2. The Manager, Part 2. Bogie's efforts to seek Owen's advice (whether or not to tell his manager he is gay), has an adverse effect when Owen learns that his best friend is gay.

3. The Manager, Part 3. Bogie's meeting with a fast-talking agent (Ramshackle) at a diner does not go well when a nasty L.A. bitch (Aureial Sheppers) calls him a "faggot" and shatters his confidence (although his confidence is somewhat restored when a talking magazine cover—that of actor Jackson Powers—offers advice).

4. The Manager, Part 4. Bogie's meeting with Ramshackle shatters Bogie's confidence even more when he leaves the meeting with virtually no idea as to what the meeting was all about. The program's concluding episode.

3 *All My Children.* hulu.com. 2013 (Drama).

The long-running ABC daytime serial (January 1, 1970 to September 23, 2011) revised for the Internet. While the program is a look at the various people who inhabit the Pennsylvania city of Pine Valley, a lesbian story line that was established on the original series in 2001 was carried over here through the lesbian character of Bianca Montgomery (Eden Riegel), the daughter of Erica Kane (a character that was not a part of the web series). On the ABC version Bianca shared her first kiss with Lena (Olga Sosnovska) and it became a media event as it was the first such kiss on American daytime television. As the series progressed, Bianca bestowed

kisses on additional girls and the scenes became increasingly sexual (although considerably tame by today's standards). Bianca's encounters with women became more intense and sexual on the web program but it ended suddenly and situations that were established were never resolved.

Cast: Eden Riegel (Bianca Montgomery), Jill Larson (Opal Cortlandt), Julia Barr (Brooke English), Vincent Irizarry (Dr. David Hayward), Cady McClain (Dixie Cooney), Debbi Morgan (Dr. Angie Hubbard), Darnell Williams (Jesse Hubbard), Thorsetn Kaye (Zach Slater), Paula Garces (Lea Marquez), Lindsay Hartley (Dr. Cara Castillo), Ryan Bittle (Jr. Chandler), Saleisha Stowers (Cassandra Foster), Eric Nelson (AJ Chandler), Jordan Lane Price (Celia Fitzgerald), Denyse Tontz (Miranda Montgomery), Robert Scott Wilson (Peter Cortlandt). **Credits:** *Producer:* Ginger Smith. **Comment:** The program continued in the tradition set by the ABC version with excellent acting and production values.

Episodes: 220 episodes were planned, but only the following list resulted.

1. The Revolutionary Road Home. April 29, 2013.
2. The Nightmare Begins. April 30, 2013.
3. Ghosts from the Past. May 1, 2013.
4. Was It a Boy? Was It a Girl? May 2, 2013.
5. Eyes Wide Open. May 6, 2013.
6. Lessons from the Past. May 7, 2013.
7. Reunited. May 8, 2013.
8. Hung Up. May 9, 2013.
9. A Mother's Nightmare. May 13, 2013.
10. Sinnamon and Spice. May 14, 2013.
11. Stolen Innocence. May 15, 2013.
12. Baptized in That River and Born Again. May 16, 2013.
13. We'll Have Manhattan. May 20, 2013.
14. The Haunted Lullaby. May 22, 2013.
15. Your Every Fantasy. May 27, 2013.
16. Alert the Press. May 29, 2013.
17. Message of Hope. June 3, 2013.
18. Sibling Rivalry. June 5, 2013.
19. Damsel in Distress. June 10, 2013.
20. M.U.D. June 12, 2013.
21. Dead or Alive. June 17, 2013.
22. Out of the Nest. June 19, 2013.
23. Dirty, Sexy Love. June 24, 2013.
24. Pins and Needles. June 26, 2013.
25. Big Bullets and Small Bundles. July 1, 2013.
26. Straight Talk. July 1, 2013.
27. The Law of Passion. July 8, 2013.
28. Danger Becomes You. July 8, 2013.
29. A Mother's Love. July 15, 2013.
30. Secrets and Lies. July 15, 2013.
31. Nightmare on Cedar Street. July 22, 2013.
32. The Mask, the Makeover. July 22, 2013.
33. The Choice. July 29, 2013.
34. What's an Inch Between Friends? July 29, 2013.

35. A Guarded Heart. August 5, 2013.
36. An Enchanted Evening: The Gala Begins. August 5, 2013.
37. Stinky Pinkies and Sabotage. August 12, 2013.
38. Pie, Pitchers and Peanuts. August 12, 2013.
39. That's My Boy. August 19, 2013.
40. Frenemies and Forgery. August 19, 2013.
41. And We Call It Bella Notte. August 26, 2013.
42. Second Chances. August 26, 2013.
43. A Knight to Remember. September 2, 2013.

Note: The program originally aired Monday through Thursday with a Friday recap called *More All My Children* and hosted by Leslie Miller. It later aired new episodes only on Monday and Wednesdays (alternating with the revised *One Life to Live* on Tuesdays and Thursdays).

4 *Alyssa Edwards' Secret.* youtube.com. 2014 (Humor).

Views on various aspects of society as seen through the opinions of drag queen Alyssa Edwards (some of which are shared by the guest drag queens that are listed with their respective episodes). The program is also known as *Alyssa's Secret*.

Star: Alyssa Edwards. **Guests:** Lasanja Estranja, Shangela, Vivienne Pinay. **Credits:** *Producer:* Thairin Smothers, Pete Williams, Blake Jacobs, Adam Asea. **Comment:** Well acted and produced short programs that reveal the "secrets" of an expert on how to deal with the various issues that surround us.

Episodes:
1. Emojis (Alyssa shares her secret on various facial expressions).
2. The Lost Footage (excerpts of not used scenes).
3. Bloopers, Part 1.
4. Alyssa-isms, Part 1 (Alyssa explains how she makes up words).
5. Cats (with guest Lasanja Estranja).
6. Dramatic Limo Story (with guest Lasanja Estranja).
7. Imitations (with guest Lasanja Estranja).
8. Lasanja Estranja's Moment.
9. Alyssa-isms, Part 2.
10. Lady of the Lake (Alyssa recalls a day at a lake when she was a young boy).
11. Sex on the Beach.
12. Tips for the Perfect Summer.
13. Every Tongue Pop (Alyssa explains the pop sound she makes when talking).
14. Alyssa's Boyfriend Marco.
15. Twitter Questions, Part 1.
16. Independence Day Featuring TS Madison.
17. How to Look Picture Perfect.
18. Bloopers, Part 2.
19. Snitch.
20. Alyssa's Birthday with Shangela.
21. House of Edwards with Shangela.
22. When Alyssa Met Shangela.
23. Mother's Day with Shangela.
24. Breaking the Law in Drag.
25. First Kiss.
26. Easter Time.
27. Show Preparations.
28. A Day in the Life of Alyssa Edwards.
29. Earthquake.
30. Bloopers, Part 3.
31. Jamaica Story Time.
32. Business Woman Fish.
33. House of Edwards (behind-the-scenes at Alyssa's home).
34. Last Supper (what Alyssa would do if it were her last day on earth).
35. Valentine's Day.
36. Beyond Belief (Alyssa introduces viewers to her dance studio Beyond Belief).
37. Jet Ski.
38. Driving.
39. RuPaul's Drag Race Season 6.
40. Twitter Questions, Part 1.
41. Happy New Year.
42. Vivienne Pinay's Holiday Takeover.
43. Pearly Gates.
44. Twitter Questions, Part 2.
45. Tongue Popping 101.
46. Vivienne Pinay's Thanksgiving Takeover.
47. Guilty Pleasures.
48. Worst Fears.
49. Vivienne.
50. Vivienne Pinay's Halloween Takeover.
51. Coming Out.
52. Air Travel.
53. Bloopers, Part 4.
54. Accents.
55. Dinner Party.
56. Impressions.
57. Alyssa-isms, Part 3.
58. Prank Call.
59. Alyssa-isms, Part 4.
60. Sex in Drag.
61. Word Association.
62. Bloopers, Part 4.
63. Mirror, Mirror.
64. A Message to Kate Middleton.
65. Top 5 Dating Tips.
66. Alyssa on Dance.
67. Alyssa on Shady Queens.
68. Alyssa on the Orgasm.
69. Honey Boo Boo for a Kardashian.
70. Alyssa on Acting.
71. Amanda Bynes or Lindsay Lohan.
72. Worst Date.

5 *The Amazing Gayl Pile.* gaylpile.com. 2013–2014 (Comedy).

The Ladies' Power Hour, broadcast on the near-bankrupt Shop-At-Home Channel (SAHC for short), is a television program patterned after such successful shopping channels as QVC and HSN. The program airs six days a week and is hosted by Gayl Pile, a presumed gay man who is also the lowest paid employee at the channel. Gayl is the son of Gayl Pile, Sr. (a woman) a big game hunter who was also a show host. Gayl was practically raised on the set (since he was three weeks old) and eventually inherited the position of show host after his mother's passing. Each day, from ten in the morning until twelve noon, Gayl presents female product inventors and beauty and house ware experts in an attempt to sell merchandise and make the station money. Along with the pitches, Gayl upstages his guests, relates anecdotes and tells (bad) jokes all in a misguided effort to become the ultimate home shopping pitchman. But a harsh realization has also entered Gayl's life: he is getting older and life is passing him by. By putting a positive spin on products and show guests, Gayl hides his deep sense of panic and the program charts his efforts to re-invent himself (as an entre-preneur) and become the man he envisions—"The Amazing Gayl Pile, Pitchman Extraordinaire."

J.D. Castlemane is the self-proclaimed Australian "female beauty virtuoso" that co-hosts Gayl's show and on whom Gayl finds an attraction; Renee is the channel's popular model who believes that Gayl's dorky image is definitely hindering her on-air appearance and is determined to change that by seeing to it that he gets fired; the Reverend Dave is the self-righteous man that not only offers unsolicited counsel, but sells shoddy religious items on the channel. Darron, the lowest status member of the Shunt crime family, is the producer who tries to shun as much responsibility as possible (just too much paper work).

Gayl has also written an audio book dedicated to his mother called *Like Mother, Like Son: A Life in Progress* (sells for $39.95); items made for the channel are produced in China by child workers; the station came into being in 1988 and 1-800-Buy-SAHC is its toll-free phone number.

Cast: Morgan Waters (Gayl Pile), Andy King (J.D. Castlemane), Inessa Frantowski (Renee LeMans), Brooks Gray (the Reverend Dave), Leo Scherman (Darron Shunt). **Credits:** *Producer:* Andrew Ferguson, Brooks Gray, Matt King. Morgan Waters. *Writer-Director:* Brooks Gray, Morgan Waters. **Comment:** Canadian produced program where nothing is fully spelled out. There are strong hints that Gayl (and possibly J.D.) are gay (with J.D. also leaning toward bisexual). That aside, it is a well crafted spoof of home shopping channels with very good acting and production values. Everything is done to make the Shop At Home Channel appear real—from the toll free telephone number, the guests hawking their products to the left side bar (of the screen) image telling the viewer the product and its price.

Episodes:

1. Episode 1. Although Gayl seems competent on TV pitching his products, he is seen at home reviewing tapes of his show and not all that pleased. It is also at this time that J.D. is introduced to the audience as Gayl's guest pitchman.

2. Episode 2. While Gayl shows signs of becoming attracted to J.D., he must concentrate on selling J.D.'s latest product: "J.D. Castlemane's Bush Whackers Ultra Absorbent Tampons"—something that is not moving until Gayl talks the Reverend Dave into buying them for him to make J.D. have a sell out of the product.

3. Episode 3. As Gayl recalls incidents about his mother, he must now pitch J.D.'s cream created from kangaroos: "Secrets from the Pouch: Bum and Thigh Cellulite Remover."

The Amazing Gayl Pile. **Poster art from the series (copyright La Rue Productions, Inc.).**

4. Episode 4. Although he is attracted to J.D., Gayl appears to be getting upset that J.D. has overstayed his welcome and is now taking the spotlight away from him.

5. Episode 5. After a night of drinking wine from boxes, J.D. wakes up the next morning in Gayl's bed and learns that Gayl's mother was a hunter and left him a freezer full of wild animal meat.

6. Episode 6. Although Gayl feels J.D. is getting too big for his britches and needs to be taken down a step, he appears on air with him to sell "J.D. Castlemane's Rules Aerobics System."

7. Episode 7. On his show, "The Spiritual Hour with the Reverend Dave," Dave reveals that he dislikes J.D. while Gayl tries to overcome the news that Renee is replacing him as the host of his show for the day.

8. Episode 8. Gayl returns to his show, sporting a flashy new (gay-like) wardrobe on a special presentation: China Appreciation Day (celebrating the fact that all products sold on the channel are made by cheap labor in China).

9. Episode 9. Gayl makes a life-changing decision: he has invested $25,000 to become J.D.'s partner in J.D. Castlemane Industries. A decision he soon regrets when it appears J.D. has run off with the check and Gayl discovers that J.D.'s cellulite cream was responsible for his mother's death.

10. Episode 10. Gayl's life changes for the better when J.D. returns with the not cashed check (claiming the bank wouldn't take it due to poor penmanship) and welcomes him as his business partner. Gayl also announces that he is moving on and that Renee will be taking over the show as the series concludes.

6 American Savage. youtube.com. 2012 (Reality).

On location program that explores subjects related to the LGBT community through first-hand experiences by going to where the stories are and reporting from the scene.

Host: Dan Savage. **Credits:** *Producer-Writer:* Dan Savage. **Comment:** Based on the pilot episode, which appears to be the only episode that was produced, the program is well structured and informative with good on scene production values (the camera is just not turned on and shooting begins but preparation was taken to ensure the scenes are in focus and properly centered on the host and his subject).

Episodes:
1. Pilot. Dan explores the problems of gays in sports by talking to members of the New York City Gay Football League.

7 Angry Old Man & Gay Teenage Runaway. vimeo.com. 2010–2011 (Comedy).

Sobel Altenzorn is an opinionated, grouchy and irascible old man. Lonny is a teenager, a gay who has run away from home to become his own man when his family disapproved of him for what he is. By chance the two meet in a park and begin talking. Pitting the wisdom of the older generation against that of the ideals of the younger generation (whether straight or gay) the program presents a topic with Sobel and Lonny offering their varying opinions on it—Sobel from a straight perspective; Lonny from a gay view point.

Cast: Fred Melamed (Sobel Altenzorn), Lonny Ross (Gay Teenage Runaway). **Credits:** *Producer:* Michael Braun. *Director:* Brennan Shroff. *Writer:* Lonny Ross, Brennan Shroff. **Comment:** The program works well. The characters are perfectly cast and stories short (two minutes or under). It is well acted and the outdoor filming is well executed.

Episodes: Each episode is just a conversation based on the title. *1.* Sandwich. *2.* Oil. *3.* Mets (line up of the N.Y. Mets baseball team). *4.* Marriage. *5.* Immigrants. *6.* Pigeons. *7.* Salad and Pastrami. *9.* The Whole Gay Thing.

8 Any Resemblance. onemorelesbian.com. 2013 (Drama).

Audrey (white) and Maddy (black) are an interracial lesbian couple who have decided that the time has come for them to enhance their relationship by having a child. The program charts the steps that are taken when they find a donor and Audrey is chosen to become pregnant.

Cast: Jen Abrams (Audrey), Maria Bauman (Maddy), Jordan Thomas (Isaac). **Credits:** *Producer-Writer:* Jen Abrams. *Director:* Brian Scott Miller. **Comment:** Smooth flowing story with good acting and directing. It is also somewhat unusual in that superimposed images of women can be seen on background items (like kitchen cabinets) as the situations play out between Audrey and Maddy. The doorway has been left open for the story to continue but it has been sometime since the last episode aired and it now appears unlikely.

Episodes:
1. Logistics. The story line is introduced with Maddy and Audrey realizing they need a child in their life.

2. Insemination. Six months have passed and Isaac has been chosen to become the donor for Audrey to carry the baby.

3. Hopes and Fears. Doubts begin to plague Audrey as she wonders about how her life will change and how it will affect her job if she becomes pregnant.

4. The Test. The concluding episode wherein Audrey learns she is pregnant bringing happiness to her and Maddy but also sadness when they discover that Isaac has been arrested (but for what is not stated).

9 *Anyone but Me.* anyonebutme.com. 2008–2012 (Drama).

Vivian and Aster are 16-year-old high school girls and lovers. They are enjoying a steady relationship until Vivian and her father (Gabe) move from Manhattan to Westchester (about 30 miles away) and into the home of her Aunt Jodie. Gabe, a firefighter suffering respiratory problems as a result of the September 11, 2001, terrorist attacks (where he was actively involved in the Ground Zero search and rescue efforts) felt life would be better for Vivian if she was distanced from what happened in Manhattan and spent her adolescence in a more comforting environment (Gabe's wife had abandoned the family when Vivian was a young girl and he had been raising Vivian alone). Now thrown into a new environment, Vivian is uncertain of her own destiny. She continues her relationship with Aster but conceals the fact of her sexuality from her aunt and her classmates at Clarence High School (as she believes those around her will not accept the fact that she is a lesbian). Stories relate the problems Vivian encounters—from dealing with an aunt who is finding it difficult to become a mother to her, secretly maintaining her love life with Aster and how she deals with the misconceptions she perceived when her "secret" life is slowly uncovered.

Cast: Rachael Hip-Flores (Vivian McMillan), Nicole Pacent (Aster Gaston), Barbara Pitts (Jodie Nevan), Jessy Hodges (Sophie), Alexis Slade (Elisabeth Matthews), Mitchell S. Adams (Jonathan Kerwin), Joshua Holland (Archibald Bishop), Dan Via (Gabe McMillan), Garrett Ross (Sterns), Russell Jordan (Principal Dennis), Amy Jackson Lewis (Jamie), Johnny Yoder (Breck), Helene Taylor (Mrs. Winters), Liza Weil (Dr. Glass), Marissa Skell (Carey). **Credits:** *Producer:* Susan Miller, Tina Cesa Ward, Lida Orzeck. *Director:* Tina Cesa Ward. *Writer:* Tina Cesa Ward, Susan Miller, Scott Alexander. **Comment:** Character-driven story with very good acting and production values. There are kissing scenes (but no nudity) and the program moves right along with touching moments encountered by Vivian and Aster as they attempt to maintain a relationship that appears to be going from good to bad.

Episodes:

1. Heavy Lifting. Vivian and Aster face the prospect of losing each other as Vivian breaks the news to Aster that she is moving.

2. New Alliance. Vivian begins classes at a new school where she meets a fellow student (Archibald) who shares her interest of drawing.

3. Countdown. Vivian and Aster reunite in the city taking in the sights then spending the night together (at Aster's apartment).

4. Vivian + Aster. The scene opens with Vivian and Aster in bed together—but it is not the same as Vivian must once again leave Aster and return to Westchester.

Anyone but Me. Nicole Pacent (left) and Rachael Hip-Flores (photograph copyright by Michael Seto).

5. The Note, Part 1. Aster slowly begins to realize that she must face a new world without Vivian by her side.

6. The Note, Part 2. As Aster devises a way to be with Vivian while at school, Archibald attempts to get closer to Elizabeth, a fellow student.

7. Welcome to the Party, Now Clean Up the Mess, Part 1. Aster, who is practically raising herself (her parents are mostly absent from her life) moves to Westchester and enrolls in Vivian's school.

8. Welcome to the Party, Now Clean Up the Mess, Part 2. Now united again as lovers, Vivian invites Aster to a party to meet her new friends.

9. Out of the Gate. The cast (out-of-character) discuss the events of the prior eight episodes.

10. Enormous Changes at the Last Minute. A school field trip to the New York *Times* in Manhattan (to see the workings of a city desk) finds Vivian and Aster deserting the group for a romantic encounter.

11. The Real Thing. A recap of what has happened so far.

12. Quickly, to the Exit. Elizabeth and Archibald have become close but Vivian and Aster's relationship appears to be facing difficult times.

13. Identity Crisis. Sophie, Vivian's friend, discovers her secret when she sees Vivian and Aster kissing.

14. Girl Talk. Aster and Jodie (Vivian's aunt) spend time together with Aster revealing that she (and Vivian) are lovers.

15. One Step Forward, One Step Back. Vivian confronts Aster about revealing the fact that she is a lesbian to her aunt.

16. The Things We Know. Sophie, understanding Vivian's love for Aster, reveals that she had a romantic encounter with an older man (a teacher named Ben).

17. Date Night. Vivian and Aster attempt to salvage their relationship, which is slowly breaking up now that Vivian's sexuality is known.

18. Naming Things. Vivian, a writer for the school newspaper (*The Gazette*) and Archibald devise a comic strip for the paper that will reveal the lives of students as if they were in an alternate universe.

19. Private Rooms and Public Spaces. Gabe invites Jodie to Manhattan to meet his firemen friends while Aster, having previously been in therapy to control her attitude, returns to her therapist (Dr. Glass) for help in saving her relationship with Vivian.

20. Curtain Up. The first issue of Vivian and Archibald's comic is printed and seen by students as "a lesbian and a black dude trying to save the world" (with Vivian as "The Lesbian Reporter Chick"). Meanwhile, Archibald becomes interested in Elizabeth's acting ambitions by helping her rehearse for a school play.

21. Stick Figures. Vivian, having used incidents from her past to create the comic strip, finds that those memories are now manifesting themselves and causing her to face things she had tried to forget.

22. Far Away. As Aster and Vivian's relationship appears to be on the verge of collapse, Aster feels it is best if she and Vivian stop seeing each other. Shortly after, Aster, now in Los Angeles, meets a college student (Carey) who becomes attracted to her.

23. Something Old, Something New. Sophie's secret comes to light when Ben approaches her in the school hallway, concerned about their one night stand and that if she is okay. Meanwhile, Carey, on a week-long school break, invites Aster to her dorm room. It is at this time that Vivian learns that Ben is Sophie's secret affair.

24. Mapping Home. It is a week later and Aster feels that even though she and Carey were intimate, she still has feelings for Vivian.

25. 2,500 Miles to You. Aster returns to Westchester hoping to rekindle her love for Vivian.

26. We Went Down to Battery Park. Vivian and Aster confront their past to work for a future together in the concluding episode.

10 *Anything Beau's.* anythingbeau's.com. 2011 (Comedy-Drama).

The program opens simply with "Hi, my name is Beau Ratliffe." From that point on, a not-so spectacular view of Beau's life is seen in the form of a video blog. Beau is also gay and "this video blog about my journey and my new life ... is dedicated to a man more visible than most" (being a known writer).

Cast: Eric Durcholz (Beau Ratliffe). **Credits:** *Producer-Writer:* Eric Durcholz. **Comment:** Simple program with Beau talking about what is happening to him; in some cases he goes on location to show exactly what he is talking about. Good video quality and standard production values.

Episode List:
1. Back Home.
2. Opening Credits.
3. Meth.
4. Precious Moments.
5. The Return of Becky Ratliffe.
6. Nest.
7. Everything Goes.
8. B0Mail.
9. Life Sucks.
10. The Writing on the Wall.
11. DIYCSI.
12. The Lab.
13. Title Unknown (Episode has been taken offline).
14. My Evil Twin.
15. Goodbye.
16. "G" Is for Good Times.
17. "F" Is for Fitness.
18. "E" Is for Evansville.
19. "B" Is for Balls.

20. "M" Is for Martin Luther King.
21. "P" Is for Paranormal.
22. Food Stamps.
23. Pit Stop.
24. Headless and Nekked.
25. Drama Storm.
26. Dark Beau.
27. Furry Fever.
28. Prostate Exam.
29. Bird Found!!!
30. Send in the Clowns.
31. Rapture.
32. Beau Ratliffe Is Missing.
33. Beards.
34. Country Rain.
35. Exodus Evansville.
36. I Can't Believe It's Not Meth.
37. Gay Note Unwritten.
38. Lil' Beau Blue.
39. The Weavesnatcher.
40. Shytown.
41. Like 'Em Big?
42. Gorilla Tango.
43. Dust from a Lesbian's Apartment.
44. Death Note/Gay Note Mashup.
45. Pour Some Sugar on Me.
46. Cringe Trailer/Bumper/Teaser.
47. Mount Vernon.
48. Children's Books.
49. Private Dancer at the Funny Spot in Chicago.
50. New Year's Resolutions.
51. Trus$t Fund Baby.
52. Reinvintage.

11 Apples. youtube.com. 2007 (Drama).

Two apartments, both located in the same building in Portugal, provides the basic setting for a look at the lives of several beautiful lesbians, all university students and each seeking romance sometimes with each other, sometimes with women outside of their close-knit circle.

Cast: Patricia Arizmendi (Pixel), Teresa Hernando (Barbi), Saskia Guanche (Doc), Alicia Lobo (Manitas), Gloria March (Ade), Karen Owens (Nanai), Marta Villar (Sam). **Credits:** *Producer:* Amparo Piquer. *Director:* Alfonso Diaz. *Writer:* Veronica Segoviano, Olga Marti. **Comment:** Stylishly filmed program that contains nudity, sexual situations and kissing scenes. Episode one has not been translated into English and is seen with Portuguese dialogue and subtitles. The following six episodes have English captions.

Episode List: *1.* Errores. *2.* Premiere. *3.* Gambito de Drama Rehusado. *4.* WiFi Connection. *5.* Mi Chichi Y Yo. *6.* Outing. *7.* Defectos.

12 Ave 43. youtube.com. 2009–2014 (Comedy).

A spoof of daytime soap operas that is set in the Highland Park section (on Avenue 43) in California and focuses on a number of characters that are, for the most part, anything but normal: Debbie and her roommate Janet; Randy, Debbie's boyfriend; Mike, Debbie's gay brother; Walter, Mike's boyfriend; Shayne, the devious man seeking to destroy Mike and Walter's relationship; Cliff, Janet's older boyfriend, a gay porn star; Viv, Cliff's sister; Fran, Cliff and Viv's mother; Mr. Hakopian, the lonely widower with whom Viv begins a relationship; Ondria, Hakopian's daughter, a young woman who practices witchcraft; Lyle, the man who operates the local prostitution and drug ring (as well as making porno films); Tim, Lyle's henchman (does all the dirty work); Irene and Lotty, the mysterious sisters whose relationship constantly changes; and Pazuzu, Irene's white cat—a feline with a story of his own.

Cast: Chloe Taylor (Debbie), Zoe Perry (Janet), Cody Chappel (Mike), Melissa Denton (Irene), Jonathan Palmer (Cliff), Danielle Kennedy (Fran), Danny Schmitz (Shayne), Cheryl Hawker (Penny), Tom Fitzpatrick (Lyle), Michael Halpin (Walter), Liz Davies (Dierdre Langley), Tad Coughenour (Tim), Gary Holland (Keith), Joe Keyes (Kevin), Abby Travis (Ondria), Jamey Bair (Satan), Andy Steinlen (Pil), Todd Love (Randy), Ava Bozem (Sunshine), Suzanne Lummis (Dahlia), Patricia Scanlon (Lettice), Maria O'Brien (Michelle), Brittany Slattery (Sabine), Dale Raoul (Brenda), Ned Van Zandt (Raymond), John Fitzgerald (Marty), Constance Forslund (Barbara), John Quale (Darvon), Jayne Taini (Viv), Harvey Perr (Mr. Hakopian), Nancy Linehan Charles (Elspeth), Norma Soto (Esmiranda), Robert Scott Crane (TJ), David Bauman (Doyle Landis), Colleen Wainwright (Margo), Diamond Back Annie (Natalie), Mary Scheer (Lotty).

Credits: *Producer-Writer-Director:* Justin Tanner.

Comment: Because the program is not in the proper aspect ratio it takes a few minutes to adjust to the picture (which has characters stretched a bit vertically to fill the screen). Once that is accomplished the viewer is then asked to endure over powering (too close) close ups, the mix of steady filming with its nightmarish shaky camera counterpart and overlook noticeable scene editing. If that can be accomplished an interesting soap opera spoof is presented with a crazy mix of characters that one would not want to meet even in broad daylight in the most crowded of places.

Episodes:

Season 1: Chapters 1 through 11 (June 12, 2009–Nov. 9, 2009).

Season 2: Chapters 12 through 17 (Feb. 23, 2010–June 29, 2010).

Season 3: Chapters 18 through 34 (Sept. 28, 2010–Aug. 8, 2011).

Season 4: Chapters 35 through 43 (Dec. 20, 2011–May 29, 2012).

Season 6: Chapters 51 through 60 (Feb. 9, 2013–Dec. 9, 2013).

Season 7: Chapters 61 through 68 (Mar. 4, 2014–April 24, 2014).

13 *B.J. Fletcher, Private Eye.* bjfletcherprivateeye.com. 2008–2012 (Crime Drama).

Milligan's Bar and Lounge is a business where a pretty but somewhat lonely private detective, B.J. (Beatrix Jean) Fletcher not only hangs out but has called a second home. B.J. is ambitious (when she has to be), charges only eight dollars an hour to investigate cases and has a guardian angel, her friend and lover, Georgia Drew, the bartender who looks out for her because B.J. will not lookout for herself. It appears that B.J. and George (as B.J. calls Georgia) have been lovers for some time as George cares deeply for B.J. and often puts her life on the line to protect her during case investigations. B.J. longs for exciting cases but rarely acquires them, although she attempts to make mundane cases more exciting then they actually are (even if she acquires some bruises doing it). "I want something I can sink my teeth into, one that pays more than eight bucks an hour," she cries. B.J. is also writing a novel based on her cases and carries an audio recorder with her at all times to record her strategy and what happens. Stories follow B.J.'s case assignments with her and George combining their wits to solve each case with as little fanfare as possible.

Cast: Lindy Zucker (B.J. Fletcher), Dana Puddicombe (Georgia Drew), Vanessa Dunn (Jenna Watson), Karim Morgan (Joe Magnum), Natasha Gordon (Marjorie Matlock), Jonathan Thomas (Doyle), Sean Tasson (Louis), Maria Heidler (Mrs. Watson), Patricia Yeatman (Mrs. Drew), Stewart Dowling (Dominic Christie), Kimwun Perehinec (Samantha Steele), Stavroula Logothettis (Katerina Kinsey), Kesta Graham (Christine, the Baker). **Credits:** *Producer:* Regan Latimer, Rochelle Dancel. *Director:* Regan Latimer. *Writer:* Regan Latimer, Alys Latimer. **Comment:** A light-hearted, enjoyable approach to crime solving with a lesbian theme. There are scenes of affection (including kissing). The program is well acted and filmed and the cases interesting.

Episodes:

1. Episode 1. A figure from B.J.'s past—her ex-girlfriend, Marjorie Matlock, hires B.J. to uncover the source of a leak in her office that has been supplying information to her competitors.

2. Episode 2. B.J. and Georgia begin their investigation of case they call "Agatha and Her Leaky Empire."

3. Episode 3. B.J.'s questioning of Marjorie leads her to believe that she is more involved in the case than she is letting on.

4. Episode 4. Just as B.J. and Georgia resolve their first televised case, B.J. finds little time for herself when she is hired by a wife (Marilyn) to discover if her photographer husband (Dominic) is cheating on her.

5. Episode 5. B.J., accompanied by Georgia, begins her investigation of a case they call "Mr. Christie and His Wandering Aperture."

6. Episode 6. Posing as a model, Georgia goes undercover at Dominic's studio in an attempt to get the goods on him.

7. Episode 7. B.J.'s plan to entrap Dominic doesn't go as expected. With Georgia's life now in danger, B.J. asks her friend, police detective Joe Magnum for assistance.

8. Episode 8. Dominic is exposed and the case is solved, but soon thereafter, B.J. acquires something more in line with her sexuality when she takes on the case of "The Little Lost Lesbian: Run, Jenna, Run."

9. Episode 9. B.J.'s attempt to find the missing daughter (Jenna Watson) of a local politician's wife places her and Georgia in a dangerous situation when they become involved in a game of dirty politics.

10. Episode 10. B.J. and Georgia discover they have competition from two men (Doyle, B.J.'s old nemesis, and his partner Louis) who are seeking to find Jenna first (to expose her as a

B.J. Fletcher, Private Eye. **Series logo art featuring Georgia (left) and B.J. (copyright Bee Charmer Productions 2014).**

lesbian and hopefully ruin her father's political career).

11. Episode 11. The case concludes and takes an unexpected turn when Jenna is found and she and Georgia become attracted to each other.

12. Episode 12. Before accepting another case ("Mrs. Lacey and Her Hidden Gems") B.J. and Georgia reflect on their relationship now that another woman has entered the picture (Jenna). After B.J. and Georgia discover that gems were stolen by a bicycle-napping gang, they host a dinner party for the gang in an effort to uncover more information.

13. Episode 13. At the party, B.J. and Georgia's investigation reveals that the gang has an affiliation with the local mafia.

14. Episode 14. B.J. and Georgia's discovery places them in extreme danger. Unknowingly they are being observed by Joe Magnum (who becomes their rescuer).

15. Episode 15. As Jenna and Georgia grow closer, B.J. tackles a case called "Bitter Batter at the Dip 'n' Sip Bakery" (wherein she is hired to find a saboteur whose actions are threatening to close a bakery).

16. Episode 16. As clues to the saboteur's identity become increasingly slimmer, Georgia recruits Jenna's help on the case.

17. Episode 17. Jenna's assistance helps resolve the case but B.J. appears to becoming a bit jealous over her and Georgia's relationship, especially when she learns Georgia and Jenna are going to luncheon with each other's mother (guests Maria Heidler and Patricia Yeatman).

18. Episode 18. The case of "Wheeling and Dealings at the Watson Warehouse" finds B.J. and Georgia becoming involved with the mafia and stolen diamonds.

19. Episode 19. B.J. becomes angered when she learns that Doyle (her nemesis) is responsible for the theft of the diamonds and has put her and Georgia's life in jeopardy.

20. Episode 20. Discovering that Doyle (and his mafia associates) has captured B.J., Georgia and Jenna begin a race against time to save her.

21. Episode 21. With B.J. rescued and the diamonds recovered, B.J. next becomes involved with the case of "The Elusive Husband of Katarina Kinsey" (wherein she and Georgia seek a missing—and elusive husband [Frank]).

22. Episode 22. As B.J. and Georgia continue their investigation, an outside investigator (Samantha Steele) becomes part of the case—and a source of concern for Georgia, whose plans for the future could change her relationship with Jenna and B.J.

23. Episode 23. Finding the elusive husband (Frank) begins to take its toll on B.J. and Georgia as tracking him down has become more of a problem than they previously thought.

24. Episode 24. Georgia's future plans (moving to England) have her a bit on edge during a stakeout in which she and B.J. hope to capture Frank.

25. Episode 25. The concluding episode wherein the case is solved but what will become of B.J. and Georgia's relationship as Georgia prepares to leave for England is left unresolved.

14 *Be Here Nowish.* ora.tv/beherenowish. 2014 (Comedy).

Samantha (called Sam) and Nina, strangers who meet randomly at a party quickly become friends and discover that they have a common goal to change the course of their lives. Sam, straight, is a dating consultant and has just broken up with her boyfriend; and Nina, recently losing her job delivering prescription pills to eccentric clients, is a lesbian. Although Sam can advise men about dating techniques, she cannot seem to hold a boyfriend. Nina, unable to make a commitment, has been living a bit recklessly, hooking up with a different girl each night. Despite the world of differences that define them, they each inspire the other and they impulsively decide to leave New York for Los Angeles to seek a plant medicine ceremony with a Shaman for the guidance they need to re-direct their lives. The program follows their rather outrageous experiences

Be Here Nowish. **Natalia Leite (left) and Alexandra Roxo (used by permission of Alexandra Roxo and Natalia Leite).**

as they experiment with various spiritual practices, attempt to shed their old lives and become a part of each other's new life. **Cast:** Alexandra Roxo (Sam), Natalia Leite (Nina), Adam Carpenter (Clay), Victoria Haynes (Victoria), Christina Jeffs (Christina), Daniella Rabbani (Daniella), Ry Russo-Young (Zoe), Risa Sarachan (Risa), Karley Sciortino (Aurora). **Credits:** *Producer:* Dennis Mykytyn, Natalia Leite, Alexandra Roxo. *Director:* Natalia Leite, Alexandra Roxo. *Writer:* Natalia Leite, Alexandra Roxo, Liz Armstrong. **Comment:** A bit outrageous at times but expertly acted and produced. There are intimate scenes and partial nudity and the doorway has been left open for Nina and Sam to encounter new adventures.

Episodes:

1. Pilot. Sam and Nina meet at a party and quickly become friends.

2. Bob. As Sam attempts to incorporate her own advice for a date, Nina, high after using drugs, ends up in the bathtub with two girls in Sam's apartment.

3. GPO. Sam, unable to abide by her boss's demands, is fired while Nina, meeting with her ex-girlfriend (Zoe) learns about how to change her life through spiritual guidance.

4. Viva Placenta. Nina's decision to hook up with one of her clients (Aurora) costs her a job while Sam, lamenting over the loss of her job, feels she needs a change.

5. The Fish Is Fresh. Sam and Nina agree that they each need a change and head to Los Angeles to find that new beginning.

6. Liquid Gold. Sam and Nina's first experiences as they endure the stress of a spiritual boot camp.

7. Jacqui the Bear. A plant medicine ceremony finds Nina and Sam reliving nightmarish incidents from their past.

8. I Love the Universe. As Nina and Aurora reunite (from episode 4), Sam finds she can attract and apparently keep a man (Clay).

9. Kale Syrup. As Sam and Clay bond, Nina decides that she, Aurora and Zoe need to balance their relationship in a threesome.

10. There and Back Again. Sam and Nina have changed their lives but each also realizes that it is time to move on and, as the program ends, they return to New York to once again reinvent themselves.

15 *Beacon Hill: The Series.* beaconhilltheseries.com. 2014 (Drama).

When her grandfather, Senior Massachusetts Senator William Preston, succumbs to a heart attack, Sara Preston, his granddaughter, a lesbian and a New York City newspaper reporter, returns home to Boston after a six year absence to be with her family: Claire, a mother who finds comfort in alcohol; Eric, her brother; and, to her surprise, William's much younger wife, Evelyn, a woman who is as ruthless as

William. Stories, presented in the serial style of television soap operas (like *All My Children*) portray the events that spark Sara's life—from a former lover (Katherine, now a State Representative seeking a Senatorial seat), political intrigue and the "cat and mouse game" controlled by her grandfather (a staunch Democrat who gets what he wants, no matter what means he needs to secure it).

Other Characters: Senator Tom Wesley, a Republican and William's rival, who is seeking the Presidency; Andrew Miller, Katherine's Chief of Staff, a man with his own political ambitions; Laura Parker, Katherine's best friend and current lover (although Sara's return has stirred old feelings in Katherine); Emily Tanner, a friend to both Sara and Katherine, owns the local coffeehouse; Diane Hamilton is Sara's current lover, the girl who finds herself with a possible rival when Katherine re-enters Sara's life; and Louise Casell, Emily's partner in the coffeehouse.

Cast: Alicia Minshew (Sara Preston), Sarah Brown (Katherine Wesley), Melissa Archer (Evelyn Preston), John-Paul Lavoisier (Eric Preston), Scott Bryce (Tom Wesley), Jessica Morris (Diane Hamilton), Ron Raines (William Preston), Louise Sorel (Emily Tanner), Ricky Paull Goldin (Andrew Miller), Crystal Chappell (Claire Preston), Rebecca Mozo (Laura Parker), Tina Sloan (Louise Casell). **Credits:** *Producer:* Crystal Chappell, Hillary B. Smith, Christa Morris, Linda Hill, Jessica Hill, Ricky Paull Goldin. *Director:* Albert Alarr. *Writer:* Jessica Hill, Linda Hill, Skip Shea. **Comment:** Lavishly produced in the style of network television soap operas with high standards acting and production values. The program is not a copy of or related to a prior CBS series called *Beacon Hill* and has enough intrigue (including the lesbian aspect) to draw viewers to it.

Episodes: Episodes are only available through a pay subscription service and not posted for free on the Internet (titles and descriptions are also not posted).

16 *Becoming Ricardo.* youtube.com/playlist?list=PL3oXBVXj3MywY3o9Exeo09vLejZYCDNMY. 2014 (Comedy).

Jesenia Cruz is a struggling young actress who aspires for greater heights ("a famous non-struggling actress"). *Crime, Law and Justice* is a top rated television series that has put out a casting call for a Latino macho-male lead. Feeling that this is the opportunity of a lifetime, Jesenia decides to audition for the role—as a man. With help from her cousin Sofia, a make-up artist, Jesenia appears like a man and names herself Ricardo Montalban (not to be confused with a real actor with that name, the star of TV's *Fantasy Island*). With some practice, Jesenia actually begins to emulate masculine traits and auditions for—and acquires the role. The program, billed as "It's *Tootsie* meets *I Love Lucy* with more Ricky Ricardo!" explores what happens to Jesenia as she struggles to live two lives and deal with the problems the situation has created—from a crazy ex-boyfriend (Jorge), a female co-star (Vivian) who has fallen in love with her (not knowing she is really a woman), meddling parents (Lydia and Hector) and a cast and crew who are not always sure that Ricardo is the macho Latino he appears to be.

Cast: Jesenia (Jesenia/Ricardo), Sofia Rodriquez (Sonia Cruz), Lisa Velez-Mello (Lydia Cruz), Roman Suarez (Hector Cruz), Junio Teixeira (Steve Castillo), Giorfona Aviv (Vivian Vox), Ron Rivera (Jose Rivera), Nasser Metcalf (Bruce Edwardson). **Credits:** *Producer:* Jesenia. *Director:* Jesenia, Tony Clomax, Davis Wright. *Writer:* Jesenia, Jenni Ruiza. **Comment:** Enjoyable gender-bender sitcom that not only borrows its format from *Tootsie* but most obviously from the TV series *Bosom Buddies*. It is a non-offensive, well acted and produced program that spotlights Latin American performers in a format that is sometimes difficult to sustain if the setting is just not right.

Episodes:

1. In the Beginning. Frustrated that there are few good parts for Latina women, Jesenia decides to change all that by posing as a man to acquire a role on a TV series.

2. I Got the Part. Jesenia acquires the role but now must not only deal with her ex boyfriend, but her meddling parents.

3. First Day on Set, Part 1. Now that she has fooled the casting director, Jesenia, as Ricardo must prove she is a man on the set as the TV program begins shooting its first episode.

4. First Day on the Set, Part 2. What Jesenia thought would be easy turns out to be more complicated than she thought as she tries to perform her role as a man.

5. And Then There Was Steven. Ricardo's sudden popularity has Jesenia struggling to keep up that appearance as a media celebrity while also trying to be herself with a new boyfriend (Steven). The program's concluding episode.

17 Besties for Cash. youtube.com. 2014 (Game).

Two best friends, whether Gay, Lesbian, Bisexual or Drag Queen appear on stage. Before air time, each of the friends was separately asked a series of questions that refer to their lives. On stage, an announcer repeats one of the questions with the object being for each of the friends to match how the other responded. A correct match scores the player $10 with the player earning the most money being declared the winner (the one who knows the most about his or her best friend). **Credits:** *Producer:* Thairin Smothers, Peter Williams, Blake Jacobs, Adam Asea. **Comment:** Interesting variation on *The Newlywed Game* that is well produced and acted and just like the original show, answers are sometimes

shocking. The program is also known as *Couples for Cash*.

Episodes: All episodes are titled "Betie for Ca$h" and are listed as such followed by the performers.

1. Betie for Ca$h: Guinevere Turner and Anna Margarita Albelo.

2. Betie for Ca$h: Chad Michaels and Morgan McMichaels.

3. Betie for Ca$h: Nicole Gemma and Tregg Nardecchia.

4. Betie for Ca$h: Jonny McGovern and Lady Red Couture.

5. Betie for Ca$h: Will Shepherd and R.J. Aguiar.

6. Betie for Ca$h: Darren Stein and Kate.

7. Betie for Ca$h: Miles Jai and Johnny.

8. Betie for Ca$h: Coco Montrese and Ricky.

9. Betie for Ca$h: Adam Asea and Randy.

10. Betie for Ca$h: Blake Jacobs and Stephan Horbelt.

11. Betie for Ca$h: Todd Masterson and Rob Ondarza.

12. Betie for Ca$h: Alyssa Edwards and Laganja Estranja.

13. Betie for Ca$h: Jackie Beat and Mario Diaz.

14. Betie for Ca$h: Colby Keller and Justin.

15. Betie for Ca$h: Raja and Raven.

16. Betie for Ca$h: Mikey Scott and Teddy Margas.

17. Betie for Ca$h: Miles Davis Moody and Gregory Broome.

18. Betie for Ca$h: Calpernia Addams and Andrea James.

19. Betie for Ca$h: Selene Luna and Adam.

20. Betie for Ca$h: Jessica and Hunter.

21. Betie for Ca$h: Phi Phi O'Hara and Mikhael.

22. Betie for Ca$h: Shawn Morales and Robert.

23. Betie for Ca$h: Delta Work and Davey.

24. Betie for Ca$h: Jason Carter and Jason.

25. Betie for Ca$h: Yara Sofia and Rubin.

26. Betie for Ca$h: Raven and Martin.

27. Betie for Ca$h: Vivienne Pinay and Devin.

18 The Better Half. thebetterhalfseries.com. 2013 (Comedy Drama).

Amy and Lindsay are a lesbian couple living in Manhattan. Amy, a brunette, and Lindsay, a blonde, met on a subway train (they made eye contact and it was a love at first sight), dated and later moved in together. Both are self-sufficient although each believes she is working in a dead-end job and has not reached the height of the goals she has set for herself. They also feel that they have become stuck in the same old grind and need to add some excitement in their dull lives. To solve their dilemma, they embark on a series of adventures (experiencing things they have never done before) hoping that it will reignite the spark they had when they first fell in love. The program charts what happens as they begin their quest and attempt to overcome all the hurdles they feel are preventing them from enjoying a lasting relationship.

Cast: Lindsay Hicks (Lindsay), Amy Jackson Lewis (Amy), Adriana DeGirolami (Angel), Katie Hartman (Diane), Todd Briscoe (Sandy), Leah Rudick (Cherry). **Credits:** *Producer:* Christine Ng, Leyla Perez. *Director:* Leyla Perez. *Writer:* Lindsay Hicks, Amy Jackson Lewis. **Comment:** Enjoyable lesbian-themed program with very good acting and production qualities. Both leads, a real-life couple, have a chemistry that spills over from their real lives and onto the screen as anyone can relate to the problems they are facing as they are problems, for the most part, that can be faced by anyone.

Episodes:

1. Going Out. To add some excitement to their lives, Amy and Lindsay plan an evening out with Lindsay's indecision about what to wear to a ladies' bar only setting the scene for a night out that does not exactly go as planned.

2. Sunny Side Up. Believing they are becoming too comfortable with each other, Amy and Lindsay decide to indulge in things they have never attempted before. Their first choice is to visit a karaoke bar.

3. Lesbifriends. Amy and Lindsay join their friends, Angel and Cherry, to discuss matters concerning their next "great" adventure: a camping trip or the Lesbian Cheese Cave.

4. Pure Camp. Having chosen the camping trip, a totally unprepared Amy and Lindsay must now contend with Mother Nature.

5. Early Retirement. Amy's desire to have a child changes the course of her and Lindsay's lives when each feels they are working in dead-end jobs and, unknown the each other, quit at the same time—putting a damper on not only paying the bills but how to afford a baby. The program's concluding episode.

19 *Between Women.* betweenwomentv.com. 2011–2013 (Drama).

Atlanta, Georgia, provides the setting for a look at the lives of a group of African American women (living in what is called the Black Lesbian Community of Atlanta) as they deal with real life problems that could be faced by people of any race or community.

Cast: Amber Jones (Sunny Walker), Onyx Keesha (Allison Young), Toya Sessoms (Winney Rise), Marisa "Dred" Carpenter (Miller Harris), LaShay Donicea (Natalie Hintmore), Dominique LaToy (Rhonda Stephens), Ulia "Noble Julz" Hamilton (Brooke Scott), Tajir S. Hawkins (Mecca Lawson),

Tamika Shannon (Gabby Monroe), Shamonique Mattox (Beautiful Davis), Look Alive (Rae Tyson), Stephen Barrington (Jackson Price), Britt Dias (Alycia Cole), Asa Millar (Porter), Roahmin Murphy (Christian J. Martin). **Credits:** *Producer-Writer:* Michelle A. Daniel. *Director:* Christina Brown. **Comment:** An attractive cast and sexual situations but a considerable amount of profanity and an overabundant use of the annoying shaky (unsteady) method of filming. For some unexplained reason, some cast members yell their lines at one another (apparently to represent shouting) which comes off as rather unprofessional (and annoying). The sound is also bad (most likely due to using only camera microphones) and there are noticeable editing cuts (something that should have been eliminated in post production).

Episodes: Actual episodes appear to have been taken off line although Season 1 Teasers (Episodes 1–11) and Season 2 Teasers (Episodes 1–6) can be viewed on YouTube.com.

20 *Bi: The Web Series.* youtube.com. 2014 (Comedy).

Alex Walker, supporting himself as an artist, is bisexual and having a difficult time adjusting to the fact that he prefers both men and women but is unable to find a meaningful relationship with either as he is constantly drawn to the other if he begins a relationship with one. The program charts Alex's experiences as he struggles to understand and cope with the fine line that exists between maintaining friendships and finding a true love.

Cast: David J. Cork (Alex Walker), Branca Garia (Camille), Glenn Quentin (Kai), Richardson J. Pierre (Damien), Tarron Taylor-Anderson (Julian), Krystine Bailey (Megan), Kadeem Harris (Andre). **Credits:** *Producer:* David J. Cork, Glenn Quentin. *Writer:* David J. Cork. **Comment:** With only a pilot to judge, the program appears well acted and produced. There are sexual situations but for how long the premise can play out before it becomes repetitive remains to be seen.

Episodes:

1. Bi-ography. An introduction to Alex and the situations he faces dealing with his sexuality.

2. Teaser. Brief highlights of what the series is all about.

21 *Black and White.* blackandwhiteseries.com. 2013 (Comedy).

Peter Black is an uptight, easily upset young Caucasian man who lives a comfortable life with a male roommate until that roommate departs suddenly for Scotland for three months without warning and leaves him with a temporary replacement—an off-the-wall apparently gay African-American man named Jamaal. Peter's life is suddenly thrown into a state of chaos and the program explores Peter's efforts to have the peaceful life he once had while attempting to deal with Jamaal's outrageous behavior. **Cast:** Anthony Bergeron (Peter Black), Tory Smith (Jamaal White). **Credits:** *Producer-Writer-Director:* Anthony Bergeron. **Comment:** While not specifically stated Jamaal gives all the indications as being gay—from speech to actions and everything in between. The program is well scripted and it is sort of a more outrageous version of *The Odd Couple* that is also well acted and produced.

Episodes:

1. Knock, Knock, Who's There? Peter's life changes perhaps forever, when he acquires Jamaal as a roommate.

2. The Scariest Doll Ever. While trying to adjust to Jamaal, Peter finds he must also welcome his favorite doll, Tabetha, to the apartment.

3. Message to Grandma Betty. Peter's efforts to make a birthday video for his grandmother are hampered by Jamaal's efforts to become a part of the message.

4. Pickles. Peter and Jamaal have their first "serious" argument when pickles become more than just a pickle.

5. Peter and Jamaal Watch a Movie. Simply attempting to watch a movie together becomes a nightmare when Jamaal constantly distracts Peter with his antics.

6. Driving Mr. White. Peter struggles to deal with Jamaal as a back seat driver when they embark on a trip to find Jamaal's misplaced belongings.

22 Bloomers. bloomersthemovie.com. 2011–2013 (Comedy).

Moxie, a hip Los Angeles–based underwear (or bloomers) company provides the backdrop for a look at the lives of a group of employees (Francesca, Joanna, Ross and Karen) and their friends (Brooke, Vaughan and Clarissa) as they deal with the personal relationships that will change the course of each of their lives.

Francesca, a gorgeous, intelligent and confident bilingual girl from Brazil, is an intimate apparel designer and the maternal figure among her group of friends. She was orphaned as a child in Brazil and raised in Seattle after being adopted by an African-American family. It was here that she befriended Brooke and Ross and together they decided to move to Los Angeles to further their careers.

Brooke is gay and considers himself a loser. He is married to Ross (a heterosexual) and suffers from chronic unemployment (although he later acquires a job at *Wild America* magazine).

Ross, an accountant at Moxie, is, although married to Brooke, a womanizer and has the uncanny knack of falling for impossible women (like Joanna, his Muslim co-worker). Ross was raised by an alcoholic mother and had to fight to get what he wants

and now, as an adult, he feels he has to try harder than anyone else to get his way (and he appears to have no intention of changing his ways).

Joanna is a devout Muslim who was raised by two lesbian mothers. She wears a hijab, prays five times a day and will not consume alcohol or engage in sexual activities. Despite her beliefs, she is obsessed with super heroes, drives a jeep and is a skilled surfer (she loves catching the waves in Malibu on weekends). But being as strict as she tries to be is not always that easy as Ross's persistent attempts to date her have her rethinking who she really is.

Karen, the bra and panty model at Moxie, is a sexy girl with a vulgar vocabulary. She left home when she was 17 years old, doesn't care what other people think of her and has made a career out of the way she looks. She uses what she has (her sexual allure and abrasiveness) to get what she wants, but doesn't realize that what she wants is someone to truly love her for the person she hides beneath the surface.

Clarissa is Karen's estranged sister, a woman who had everything—a husband, money, and a pristine home in Florida until a medical exam revealed she could not have children. Her marriage ended and she lost everything; she is now trying to find herself and hopes to do so by reconnecting with Karen. She soon becomes attracted to women and finds a whole new world opening up to her.

Vaughan, a bartender, was a globe-trotting playboy before he chose to settle down (at least temporarily) in Los Angeles. To him women were just play things—until Francesca became pregnant and he considered the possibility that he may be the father. He has now restructured his life to face the consequences of his actions.

Cast: Fernanda Espindola (Francesca Rosa Tutu), Kirstin Barker (Clarissa Goldberg-Zimmerman), Jay Ali (Vaughn Daldry), Nathan Frizzell (Ross Buchanan), Holly Holstein (Karen Goldberg), Swati Kapila (Joanna Ali-Karamali), Matt Palazzolo (Brooke Matsumoto), Lisa Debra Singer (Yolanda Pissors), Tracey Verhoeven (Dr. Gail Vale), Calico Cooper (Lila Black), Rebecca Brooks (Miranda McNeil), Elizabeth Goldstein (Lisa "Boitano" Tutu), Sean Hemeon (Ken Turnage). **Credits:** *Producer:* Matt Palazzolo, Fernanda Espindola. *Director:* Henryk Cymerman, Tim Russ. *Writer:* Matt Palazzolo. **Comment:** There is a gay and lesbian mix and the program does play quite well with a good story line and excellent acting and production values. The characters are well defined and the program quite enjoyable.

Episodes:

1. L.A. Baby! The friends are introduced with Francesca discovering that she is pregnant but not exactly sure who the father is, Brooke seeking a job and Ross beginning his pursuit of the unattainable Joanna.

2. Have a Little Faith in Me. Ross's persistent efforts to get closer to Joanna has her questioning her

faith while Brooke figures it won't hurt to pray to God for helping in finding work.

3. Sister. Sistah. As Clarissa and Karen become closer, Francesca attempts to deal with her sister, Lisa, who has a drinking problem.

4. Yoko Ono Homo. At an outing to celebrate Brooke's birthday, Ross and Brooke feel it is necessary to consider their "bromance" and whether each is committed to the relationship.

5. Hard to Be a Woman. As Joanna slowly emerges from her shell, she turns to Karen for help on how to deal with the men who constantly pursue them.

6. Being Brave. As Francesca confronts Vaughan about the baby, Brooke finds that his dream job (writing for *Wild America* magazine) is within reach—if he will sleep with the boss (guest Tim Russ).

7. Tiny People. As Vaughan accepts the fact that he is the father of Francesca's baby, the program explores his past encounters with women.

8. Instinct. Ross finally gets his way—a date with the untouchable Joanna—but has difficulty impressing her.

9. Unexpecting. As Brooke begins his first day at *Wild America* magazine, Francesca faces a difficult decision: keep or abort the baby.

10. You're So Hot. Joanna's date with Ross has left her with mixed urges and in an effort to understand them, seeks Karen's advice.

11. Clarissa Explains It All. As Clarissa ventures onto her first lesbian date, she seeks a way to keep it secret from Karen.

12. The Whole Truth. After a wild party Karen awakens to find herself in an alley with no recollection as to what happened. Enlisting Joanna's help, she sets out to find out exactly what happened.

13. On Thin Ice. Francesca's dilemma over her pregnancy continue to haunt her while Karen and Clarissa feel the need to express themselves and become involved in a "who's better at stuff" competition.

14. Demons in the Night. Having made a decision, Francesca confronts Vaughan with her choice to have an abortion. Meanwhile, Clarissa has decided to have another fertility test.

15. The Uncertainty Principle. As Clarissa awaits the results of her test, the Moxie employees prepare for the annual bloomers non-holiday summer party.

16. Mum's the Word. The unexpected arrival of Brooke's mother places Brooke in an awkward situation when she throws a costume party and Brooke must keep her from discovering he has a date with a man.

17. The Book of Bro. In their college days, Ross, Brooke and Vaughan created a series of codes to live by called "The Book of Bro." But as adults living by those codes has become impossible as their pursuit of love has caused them to break every rule.

18. The Heart Is Lonely Hunted. As an axe murder is reported to be on the loose, Joanna's fears are put to the test when she believes that her love for Ross will bring forth the Vatuska, a demon spirit that kills with an axe if she should show signs of regret for what she is doing.

19. Hard to Speak Easy. Karen's plans for a house party go array when the friends decide to embark on a scavenger hunt with the winner receiving a "great night of drinking."

20. Yolanda Get Your Gun. As the company's photo shoot gets under way, Yolanda, one of Vaughan's bitter ex girlfriends, shows up intent on killing everyone. The situation comes to an end with Karen talking Yolanda down but not before Ross is shot and Francesca's water breaks.

21. What on Earth Are We Doing Here? At the hospital it is learned that Francesca gave birth to a girl and Ross will recover. The friends have survived a harrowing ordeal and the program concludes with the possibility of future episodes to further detail events in their lives.

23 *The Bo and Arro Show.* youtube.com/ user/TheBoAndArroSho. 2011 (Reality).

A documentary-like program about a musician (Arro) and a filmmaker (Bo) who have teamed to help other artists (whether straight or gay) find their dream of stardom by starring them in a music video.

Cast: Jeanette Aguilar (Bo), Arro Verse (Arro). **Credits:** *Producer:* Jeanette Aguilar, Arro Verse. *Director:* Robyn Dettman. **Comment:** Billed as "a lesbian web series" although not in the true sense (referring to the stars as they are lovers). The program itself is a bit slow-moving as the women generally just talk about various events in their lives. Music videos are seen (at least in the free episodes) and it is apparent that the camera microphone is being used as when the women team to play a song, it is rather tinny sounding.

Episodes: Episodes are available through a paid subscription service at oml.com. The following episodes are available for free:

1. Season 1, Episode 5. *2.* Season 2, Episode 1: Boo Boo. *3.* Season 2, Episode 2: Ghost in You. *4.* Season 2, Episode 3: Bullies. *5.* Season 3, Episode 3: Promo.

24 *Bob and Andrew.* youtube.com. 2010 (Comedy).

Bob, Andrew and Lauren are friends. Lauren is straight; Bob is gay (having just come out of the closet) and Andrew has switched sides (formally a gay but now straight). Bob is enjoying his lifestyle until Lauren, his co-worker, develops a crush on him but is unaware that he is gay. Bob is not one to face a confrontation and cannot bring himself to tell Lauren he is not interested in her. Instead, he figures he will let Lauren know he is gay without actually telling her (by letting her see him in the company of other men). The program charts what happens when Bob's simple plan becomes anything but and he enlists Andrew to help him achieve his goal (further complicating the situation when Andrew begins to wonder if he made the right choice in becoming straight).

Cast: Bob Woolsey (Bob), Andrew Menzies (Andrew), Lauren Martin (Lauren), April Green (Amy), Tom Belding (Spencer). **Credits:** *Producer:* Keith Opatovsky. *Writer:* Andrew Menzies. *Director:* Darren Borrowman. **Comment:** A well-acted and produced program that needlessly incorporates the use of foul language. The characters are like-able and the story flows smoothly but the possibly of continuing the story appears unlikely as several years have now passed.

Episodes:

1. Pilot. The story line is established as Bob, realizing that Lauren has feelings for him, begins his quest to let her know he is gay without directly telling her.

2. The Date. Realizing that he needs help, Bob asks Andrew to help him deal with Lauren's pursuit of him.

3. The Choice. Andrew begins to question if he made the right choice by becoming straight.

4. The Ex-Girlfriend. Andrew's efforts to reunite with his ex-girlfriend (Amy) backfire when she finds him weird and again dumps him.

5. The Speed Dating. In the first season finale Bob must find a way to deal with Lauren's ever-growing crush on him, a situation that is exposed by Henrietta (Patti Kim), Bob's gossipy co-worker, when Andrew reveals to her that Bob is gay.

6. The Fallout. As the second season begins, Andrew and Bob's friendship appears to be at an end as they have parted company. Bob is now dating another man (Spencer) and Andrew is seeing a woman named Amy.

7. The Meeting. After being apart for a while, Bob and Andrew meet to discuss what has happened since they parted company.

8. The Interview. With his unemployment checks ending, Bob (with Andrew's help) prepares for an interview that lands him a part-time job.

9. The Advice. As Andrew seeks relationship advice from Lauren on how to impress Amy, Bob and Spencer begin preparations on designing a Pride float.

10. Realization. A double date at a night club finds Bob realizing he truly loves Spencer while Andrew is a bit shocked to find the unpredictable Amy actually being nice to him.

11. The Decision. Now that Bob and Andrew have found what appear to be their significant others, they decide to review what has happened and where they are and what they need to do.

12. The Woods. Bob and Andrew have decided that they now need to discuss matters with their mates and do so by planning a relationship confrontation in the woods.

13. The Woulds. The second season conclusion wherein the romantic intervention faces a conflict when Lauren appears and relationships appear to end when Amy believes Andrew has been cheating on her with Lauren and Spencer leaves Bob when he believes he is "bi-curious" and dated Lauren. It concludes with Amy and Spencer leaving together and Bob and Andrew wondering what just happened.

25 Bois: The Web Series. youtube.com. 2012 (Comedy).

"They say if you love someone you will give up everything for them. But if they love you back, they'll never ask you to" is expressed throughout as it follows a group of close friends and the events that spark their everyday lives, especially with the romantic entanglements that each experiences.

Cast: Cucharras Guillory (Champ), Heather Lawerence (Onxy), Trelles Caliste (Romeo), Stepainie Nwami (Detroit), Destiny Hudson (Fresh), Simone Benoit (Tiana), Ashley Brown (Delana), Ashley Debose (Parys), Jennifer Morgan (Farrah), Tamika Davis (Raya). **Credits:** *Producer-Writer-Director:* Brandy Chilo. **Comment:** Like other African-American produced web series that attempt to deal with the gay community, little care was apparently taken before filming to produce a quality program. *Bois* suffers from poor acting, an amateurish, hard to follow, slow-moving story line and poor production values. It does attempt to be a bit different but what probably looked good on paper did not translate well to film.

Episode List: *1.* What Lies Create. *2.* Bad Habits. *3.* If Loving You Is Wrong. *4.* Crossroads. *5.* Truth Hurts.

26 The Boys Who Brunch. theboyswhobrunch.com. 2011–2014 (Comedy).

Each day four gay best friends (Mason, Elliott, Ray and Chad) gather for brunch in a Manhattan eatery. Their time is normally spent chatting about the prior day's events and what they may have planned for that afternoon or the following day. One day Mason changed all that: "I had an idea—something we would have for six days of the week to do—take a dare, like an assignment boys." With all enthused, a dare is presented and each episode charts what happens when each of the friends attempts to complete the challenge and how their lives interact with each other as past (and new loves) complicate matters. The dares are Mason's efforts to discover the answer to something that has haunted him since he met a woman in the park (Marge) who recognized him as being gay without him ever telling her so (she was also married to a gay man for 25 years and still had a happy relationship). Mason's thinking about

#TheBoysWhoBrunch #MoreDrama #MoreSexy #MoreFunny #MoreEverything

The Boys Who Brunch. **Left to right: Evan D. Siegel, Mike Mitchell, Jr., Trip Langley and Joseph Charles Walker (copyright Phylik Productions).**

his relationships was changed and he now wonders if his encounter with Marge was meant to be or was it just a coincidence? His dares are a way of asking a question ("Does everything truly happen for a reason?") and hopefully finding an answer.

Cast: Mike Mitchell, Jr. (Mason Boyd), Trip Langley (Elliott Clark), Evan D. Siegel (Dr. Ray Kirsch), Joseph Charles Walker (Chad Strickland), Seth James (Danny Travers), Sara Lukasiewicz (Jennifer), Jan Leslie Harding (Marge), Matthew Schatz (Jeremy), Joel Robert Walker (Lincoln), Glen Llanes (Ryan), Shane Rodney Lacoss (Guy). **Credits:** *Producer:* Mike Mitchell, Jr., James Papadopoulos, Michael Ray, Brian Robinson. *Director:* James Papadopoulos, Mike Mitchell, Jr. *Writer:* Mike Mitchell, Jr. **Comment:** Well acted and photographed program that has non-offensive sexual situations. The idea is well presented and, although there is a considerable gap between episodes, the overall effect is maintained and the performers remain basically unchanged.

Episode List:
1. The Strangest Encounter. Aug. 26, 2011.
2. Three That Stuck. Sept. 1, 2011.

3. Better Friends Than Lovers. Sept. 8, 2011.
4. We Have an Assignment. Sept. 15, 2011.
5. Everything Happens for a Reason. Sept. 22, 2011.
6. Really Happy for You. Sept. 29, 2011.
7. Anyone Home? Oct. 13, 2011.
8. The Art of Ignoring. Feb. 12, 2014.
9. Only a Test. Mar. 20, 2014.
10. Dear God. April 27, 2014.
11. Crossroads. May 27, 2014.
12. Giant Cliff Ahead. June 19, 2014.
13. Let Yourself In. July 29, 2014.

Note: The following produced episodes have not aired: "The Signs," "Moms and Roses," "One Last Night" and "Optical Illusion."

27 *BoysTown.* boystownshow.com. 2008–2013 (Comedy-Drama).

If there were a place (city or town) that was totally gay or lesbian, it would be the ideal world in which such people could live without fear of rejection from those who view them as strange or weird. Five twenty-something single men (Rick, Chance, Dave,

T.J. and Chris) have found such a place. While they must live with the city's own smattering of "bears, rice queens and gym bunnies" they each have a dream of finding that special someone. The program, adapted from the film *Gaysian* follows a journey not only of discovery, but what each man faces in a world where being gay (even in a gay community) is just as difficult to navigate as a straight or bisexual person in their world.

Cast: J. Hunter Ackerman (Ryan), Albertossy Espinoza (Michael), Jim Patneaude (T.J.), Ricky Reidling (Rick), Jesse Seann Atkinson (Chris), Peter Welkin (Dave), Eric Dean (Jake), Chace Farguson (Chance), Bruce L. Hart (Stuart), Daniel Rhyder (Patrick), Tom J. Mayer (Bain), Florian Klein (Derek), Kyle David Pierce (Tyler), Roxy Wood (Foxxy), Lisa Sanson (Becky), Lena Thomas (Kristi). **Credits:** *Producer:* Ricky Reidling, Michael Coburn. *Writer-Director:* Ricky Reidling. **Comment:** A different approach to presenting a gay-themed series that is well-acted and produced. The available free videos do establish that there are sexual situations and hints that other episodes may present situations that are intended for mature audiences (although a parental warning is not issued).

Episodes: 10 episodes have been produced with only Episode 1 and a trailer (teaser) available to |view for free (the others can only be seen through a paid subscription service). The first episode introduces the main characters living in a gay-friendly world that presents its own share of problems for them.

28 *Breaking Point.* youtube.com/watch ?v=-ROeQRIFK5E. 2011–2012 (Drama).

The lives of a group of friends as they attempt to follow their dreams and how, to maintain their relationships, jobs and even their sanity, must also deal with the triumphs, heartaches and struggles required to do so before they reach their breaking point of human emption. Five women (Crystal, Tory, Dana, Imani and Gabby) are the principal focus of stories. Crystal is a bisexual restaurant owner (and the mother of Aja); Tory, a lesbian, is Crystal's unfaithful girlfriend; Gabby is married to Dennis, a cutthroat mob-connected music producer; Dana, a police officer with a heart of gold, is dating a man named Ben; and Imani is Crystal's straight sister.

Cast: Crystal Coney (Crystal Woods), Olivia Dunkley (Det. Dana Parker), Jessica Tome (Gabby Edwards), Jillian Peterson (Tory Scott), Kyle Steven Templin (Ben Campbell), Dennis Teh (Dennis Edwards), Keena Ferguson (Imani Clarke), Claudia Perea (Lynette Kelly), Cardell Jackson (Victor Brown), Mark Harley (Wes), Wesley Alan Johnson (Tate Kelly), Haile D'Alan (Rick Hubbard), Brian Ceponis (Dr. James Woods), Jordan Preston (Det. Patrick Chase), Joe Komara (Zach Scott), Katrina Nelson (Amber), Essa Thiry (Sheyl Hubbard), Brianna Colleen Marton (Val Brown), Noah J. Smith (T.J.), Etalvia Cashin (Cinnamon), Neto DePaula Pimenta (Emilio), Gichi Gamba (Owens), Kiana Rene (Monica Rhodes), Samantha Sadoff (Aja Woods), Sheilynn Wactor (Chandelier). **Credits:** *Producer:* Caryn K. Hayes, Carolyn O. Jacobs. *Writer-Director:* Caryn K. Hayes. **Comment:** Impressively filmed and expertly acted, but very difficult show to follow with many characters, interconnected stories and numerous plot twists and turns. While first season episodes can be viewed for free on YouTube.com, second season episodes can only be seen via a paid subscription service at JTS.TV. The stories are typical of daytime soap operas like *General Hospital* (intrigue and adult situations) and prove that, with a much smaller budget, a quality program can be produced. The one major flaw with *Breaking Point*, however, is a noticeable audio problem that runs throughout first season episodes. The program is not related to the 1963 ABC series of the same title (as this will also appear when searching the title).

Season 1 Episode List: *1.* Full Disclosure. *2.* House of Cards. *3.* The Return. *4.* Necessary Roughness. *5.* In Too Deep.

Season 2 Episode List: *6.* Unforgiven. *7.* Stand By Me. *8.* Strictly Business. *9.* About a Boy. *10.* Sucker Punch. *11.* Waiting to Exhale. *12.* Catch Me if You Can. *13.* The Trap. *14.* True Colors. *15.* Betrayed.

29 *Breakups: The Series.* breakups.us. 2010 (Anthology).

Improvised stories about people, once in love, who are now facing a crisis that could end their relationship together. Each episode is just a scene that depicts a critical moment in each of the couple's lives as they discuss (sometimes) argue the circumstances that led to the confrontation.

Cast: Cate Freedman (Cate), Timmy Mayse (Timmy), Nicky Margolis (Nicky), Tim Paul (Tim), Paul Jurewicz (Paul), Cecily Strong (Cecily), Andy St. Clair (Andy), Beth Melewski (Linda), Katy Colloton (Katy), Ted Tremper (Ted), T.J. Jagodowski (T.J.), Katie Thomas (Katie), Kellen Alexander (Kellen), Seth Dodson (Seth). **Credits:** *Producer-Director:* Ted Tremper. **Comment:** With the exception of episode 7, which deals with a gay couple, the prior episodes focus on heterosexual couples. Surprisingly, an episode involving lesbians was not made, but perhaps that would have occurred if the program had continued. Considering that the stories are improvised, the actors do an outstanding job of relating their marital difficulties.

Episodes: *1.* Cate & Timmy. *2.* Nicky & Tim. *3.* Paul and Cecily. *4.* John and Linda. *5.* Katy and Ted. *6.* T.J. and Katie. *7.* Kellen and Seth.

30 *Brooklyn Is for Lovers.* youtube.com. 2008–2009 (Comedy).

Brooklyn, New York, provides the backdrop for a look at the lives of five loosely connected young people and their search for love in the present-day world: Casey and Riggles (gay roommates), Annie (bisexual web TV show host), Ashley (butch-type lesbian coffee shop waitress), Dee (straight and Annie's boyfriend) and Ashley, Annie's friend, the woman who introduces her to a whole new world where "black girls are delicious."

Cast: Anne Mistak (Annie), Chris Riggleman (Riggles), Ashley D. Brockington (Ashley), Paul Case (Casey), James Rich (Dee). **Credits:** *Producer:* Zachary Ludescher, James Rich. *Writer-Director:* Shandor Garrison. **Comment:** The program is well-acted and produced but is adult in nature with strong language and sexual situations (a parental warning does appear before each episode begins— "Program intended for mature audiences") but is not restricted.

Episodes:

1. Ass-Trology. Casey and Riggles become roommates as Annie meets and becomes attracted to Ashley. She then surprises Dee by suggesting they have a three-way with Ashley.

2. Losing It. As Casey tries to seduce Riggles (who is addicted to drugs), Dee fears committing to Annie after she misplaces her birth control pills.

3. Third Eye Technique. Dee attempts to add some spice to his love-making to Annie by incorporating advice he learned from a friend.

4. Male Features. Annie's talk about Ashley being a butch lesbian has Dee worried that she may be a he and decides to check further by joining Annie at a bar where Ashley performs a burlesque routine (as he does not want that three-some to be a dude in drag).

5. Gay Seinfeld. Casey, a comedian, roasts Riggles at a gig at Comix while Annie and Ashley are becomingly increasingly closer to each other.

6. Boner's Owner. At a taping of her web show ("Cool and Craft") Dee comes to realize that Ashley may actually be a girl when she and Annie become a bit too intimate during a show taping.

7. Frisky Business. Annie and Ashley have chosen to become lovers with Annie set to spend her first night in bed with her. The concluding episode but the doorway is left open for the story to continue.

Note: There is also a short holiday-themed episode called "Holiday Special from Brooklyn Is for Lovers" that aired on December 21, 2010.

Brooklyn Is for Lovers. Left to right: James Rich, Annie Mistak, Ashley Brockington, Christopher Riggleman and Paul Case (copyright 2015 by Zachary Ludescher).

31 Brothers. youtube.com. 2014 (Drama).

"Do you know a Davyn? Are you an Aiden? These are our friends, our teachers, our co-workers, our husbands, our Brothers" is the series tag line to explore the lives of four transgender (female to male) men living in Brooklyn, New York: Davyn, Aiden, Max and Jack. Jack, previously dating women, has recently begun sleeping with cisgender men (identifies with the gender assigned at birth); Davyn, is contemplating proposing to his long-time girlfriend, Amy; Aiden, the youngest member, is pre-testosterone and seeking to raise the money needed for upcoming surgery; Max, the eldest, is also lacking the money for top surgery but has been on hormones longer than his friends. The program realistically charts the experiences each of the friends face as they slowly attempt to become who they feel they should be, not the sex with which they were born.

Cast: Emmett Jack Lundberg (Jack), Will Krisanda (Max), Hudson Krakowski (Aiden), Jamie Casbon (Davyn). **Credits:** *Producer:* Sheyam Ghieth. *Writer-Director:* Emmett Jack Lundberg. **Comment:** Not a program for everyone as it is quite frank and could be disturbing to some. It is best to avoid the program unless you want to see a realistic look at what it means to be a transgender attempting to cope with life in today's urban society. The program is written and directed by a transgender filmmaker and incorporates transgender actors, making it not only a first for the Internet, but something that has never been done on broadcast or cable television.

Episodes: Thus far only a pilot episode has been released that is basically a realistic introduction to the four leads (presented as masculine and living with asserted gender identity of a male by female assigned-at-birth).

32 Brunch with Bridget. tellofilms.com. 2008 (Talk).

Actress Bridget McManus appears in bed—with a guest ("The hottest queer and queer-friendly stars around") and together they discuss matters important to the lesbian audience, including the stars' lesbian characters, what it's like in Hollywood, and other matters that affect them. Later episodes drop the bedroom setting and have Bridget and her guests seated in a small living room–like setting. Bridget's plush teddy bear, Baby Bridget, assists her as her co-host.

Host: Bridget McManus. **Guests:** Mandy Musgrave, Gabrielle Christian, Lena Headey, Shawn Pelofsky, Elizabeth Hendrickson, Courtney Jackson, Erin Kelly, Elizabeth Keener, Heidi Martinuzzi, Nancylee Myatt, Eden Riegel, Marnie Alton, Shoshona Bean, Carlease Burke, Tina Ceja, Rebecca Drysdale, Karey Dornetto, Poppy Champlin, C. Fitz, Maile Flanagan, Erin Foley, Nisha Ganatra, Julie Goldman, Mariah Hanson, Katie Jawkins, Lisa Rieffel, Page Hurwitz, Eliza Landensohn, Melange Lavonne, Nicole Pacent, Stacie Ponder, Maeve Quinlan, Kate Rigg, Suzanne Westenhoefer, Sandra Valls, Guinevere Turner, Cathy Shim, Gretchen Robinson. **Credits:** *Producer-Writer:* Bridget McManus. **Comment:** Humorous interviews although conducted in a most unusual style. Bridget McManus is relaxed, easy-going and fun to watch. She handles the interviews well and the program is enjoyable and something different to watch.

Episodes: Of the 82 episodes that were apparently produced, only three remain on line:
1. Episode 30: Brunch with Cathy Shim.
2. Episode 73: Brunch with Gretchen Robinson.
3. Episode 82: Brunch with Lisa Rieffel.

Note: Attempts to follow links to other episodes that appear to be on line are not and this message will appear: "Couldn't find that link. But we're on it." There are 14 episodes of *Brunch with Bridget* behind the pay wall on tellofilms.com that can be viewed.

33 Calling in Drunk. webserieschannel.com. 2013 (Comedy).

It can be said that life and love can be seen in different ways by a girl who is straight and a girl who is a lesbian. Two such girls are Sarah (a lesbian) and Loryn (straight) who put that theory to the test in a most unusual way: producing an eight episode program in one day by getting drunk (8 shots and 8 tall drinks) and reasonably trying to discuss "the straight girl vs. gay girl perspective on life, love and alcohol." The program follows their inebriated "journey" to make sense of who they are and where they are heading.

Cast: Sarah Croce (Sarah), Loryn Powell (Loryn). **Credits:** *Producer-Writer:* Sarah Croce, Loryn Powell. *Director:* Lauren Aadland. **Comment:** A most unusual concept to say the least. While the leads are very pretty and like-able, their sequences are very badly edited (jerky and noticeable editing) and can become annoying as the program's flow is not smooth. There is some street language (used as the girls become increasingly intoxicated) and dialogue is a bit difficult to understand at times. The production values are acceptable but the camera work is a bit shaky at times. It is difficult to determine if Sarah and Loryn are really consuming alcohol (or just drinking what could be a juice mix) or just pretending to be drunk. Considering how much alcohol they supposedly consumed, they do not appear as intoxicated as one would expect after "8 shots and 8 tall drinks."

Episodes:
1. Dating. Sarah and Loryn are sober and, as they begin consuming alcohol, discuss the aspect of gay and straight dating.
2. OK Cupid. A few shots later and the girls banter about their loves and the lessons learned.

3. How to Be a Lesbian (and How to Be Friends with One). Sarah and Loryn discuss how they became friends and maintain a platonic relationship.

4. Drinko de Mayo. With alcohol seemingly getting the better of them, the girls try to comprehend the meaning of Cinco de Mayo.

5. Does Size Matter? Sarah and Loryn, now becoming increasingly drunk, discuss the age-old question "does size matter" in sex as well as friendships among women—whether straight or gay.

6. What's Your Cup Size? Not a discussion on breast cup size, but on beer cup size and how one should pour it into a cup (or glass).

7. Drunk Girl Olympics. It's actually "Beer Olympics" with the girls competing in beer opening and beer drinking contests.

8. Vegan vs. Paleo. Eight hours have passed and the girls are drunk—and decide to have a drunk cook-off with Loryn preparing a veggie meal and Sarah a meat-eaters delight.

9. 2 Lesbians 1 Straight Girl. With the first season behind them, Sarah and Loryn decide that a second season of getting drunk over eight episodes would be fun and continue the concept (although billed as "Drunk and Drunker").

10. How to Break Up with Heart. The girls discuss their heart breaks and how each requires satisfaction during sex.

11. Don't F**K with Dinosaurs. A "drunkisode" (as the episode is billed) wherein Loryn and Sarah discuss how to get out of awkward situations with your dignity left in tact.

12. Tricking People into Thinking You're Sober. How to act sober when you are actually drunk is discussed.

13. Sex on the First Date. It appears Sarah and Loryn are more than just tipsy and to help them answer the question of first date sex, they explore the topic with a male guest (voice impressionist Brock Baker).

14. Lesbian Explains Straight Sex. Sarah explains her thoughts regarding straight girl sex while Loryn expresses her views on two girls becoming intimate.

15. Abe Drinking & Ronald Raging. Becoming drunk has become obvious as the girls begin non-sensical ranting and raving.

16. Sobriety Test Fail. Sarah and Loryn agree to a sobriety test—and, as they hoped, fail. With a second season behind them and failing that sobriety test, Sarah and Loryn figure why not and begin a third season of filming eight episodes in one day by progressing getting drunk as the day proceeds.

Note: Seasons 3, 4 and 5 follow the same format and rather than repeat the same situations over and over again, an episode list follows.

Season 3 Episodes: 17. Cubby Rummy Bear Challenge. 18. Twerking in Handcuffs. 19. Awkward Hand Jobs. 20. Alcohol Is Healthy with Meghan Tonjes. 21. Seducing Girls with MaxNoSleeves. 22.

Sexual Encounters of the Worst Kind. 23. Love Our Vaginas. 24. Should You Kiss with Tongue?

Season 4 Episodes: 25. Girls' Thoughts While Watching Football. 26. Babies in Absinthe. 27. How Girls Cheat at Drinking Games. 28. Edward Eggnog Hands. 29. All the Single Ladies. 30. Would You Rather? 31. Drag Queen Makeup. 32. Finale.

Season 5 Episodes: 33. My Drunk Bitchin. 34. Flip Sip or Strip with Jess Lizama. 35. Just the Tip. 36. Are You Drunker Than a 5th Grader? 37. Drunk Heads Up. 38. Drunk Newlywed Game. 39. Drunk Not My Arms Challenge. 40. No Arms Challenge.

34 Capitol Hill. youtube.com/user/CapitolHillSeries. 2014 (Comedy).

Roses Smell (drag queen), not the prettiest woman you have ever seen (bald, beard, moustache; no figure) dreams of life in Seattle, which she believes is the greatest, most beautiful city in the world. She lives in Portland, Oregon, in sort of a hillbilly-like atmosphere and has been raised by her two mean sisters since the death of her mother (who took her own life by drowning when Roses "was a wee child"). Roses has confided in her pet goat that she is about to embark on the greatest challenge in her life and leaves home (as "Seattle awaits me"). A kind motorist, also heading for Seattle, gives Roses a lift when he spots her walking on the road and drops her off in the middle of the city. Immediately, a thief makes off with Roses' luggage, leaving her without money, clothes or a place to stay. Seeing what has happened, a television producer (Tanya) comes to Roses' aid and takes her under her wing, allowing her to stay with her until she can find a job. The following day, life changes for Roses when Tanya finds her a job—as the host of a TV talk show called *Women in the Workplace.* The program charts Roses' adventures as she attempts to follow the words her mother once told her: "No point in living unless you follow every dream." Other characters include George, the chauvinistic TV station owner (harasses female employees); Dottie Pearl, the TV show host who despises Roses for taking the spotlight away from her; Helen Pen Poison, the mystery writer-forensic detective; Mother Terisha, the nun who hates gays and is responsible for "aborting nine gay babies"; and the city's "hunky" Mayor.

Cast: Waxie Moon (Roses Smell), Robbie Turner (Dottie Pearl), Alexandra Cramer (Tanya), Mark Siano (George), Aleksa Manilla (Helen Pen Poison), Brian "Mama Tits" Peters (Cookie), Miss Indigo Blue (Poops), Hannah Victoria Franklin (Sluttonia), Jonathan Crimeni (The Mayor), Syndi Deveraux (Sheriff Johnson), Kaleb Kerr (Cousin Rocky), Nettie Ann Snickle (Mother Terisha), Jennifer Jasper (Sister Malvita), Jewcy That (Michelle). Host: Ben De La Crème. Credits: *Producer-Writer-Director:* Wes Hurley. Comment: While no one is sure exactly what Roses is (a he or a she, but is treated like a she),

Capitol Hill. Robbie Turner (left) and Waxie Moon (© Shaftesbury/Smokebomb Entertainment).

the program comes off as a spoof of not only gender-benders but of 1980s prime-time serials (like *Dynasty*, *Knots Landing*, *Falcon Crest* and most noticeably *Dallas* as the same type of opening theme visuals are used). The program is not only enjoyable from the first episode, but the acting and production values are top rate.

Episodes:

1. Episode 1. Roses Smell leaves home to embark on a new life in Seattle, Washington.

2. Episode 2. Roses' meeting with George nets her a TV talk show called *Women in the Workplace*.

3. Episode 3. Roses' appearance has angered Dixie, the station's biggest attraction, who now fears she will no longer be in the spotlight and vows to change that scenario.

4. Episode 4. As Roses' begins her first show, interviewing Dr. Jen, an evil presence, seeking a human body to manifest itself, enters Dixie's body, intent on killing Roses.

5. Episode 5. A second show causes problems for Roses when its guest, a nun (Mother Terisha of the Holly Hunt Dioceses) talks about her hatred of gays and how she was responsible for "aborting 9 gay babies."

6. Episode 6. The revelation about the aborted babies fosters a police investigation into the Holly Hunt Dioceses with Roses determined to find out exactly what happened.

7. Episode 7. To help Mother Terisha, Roses poses as a gay man and ventures into "gay territory" to discover how the gay community has reacted to the situation.

8. Episode 8. After discovering that the gay community is up in arms, Roses asks Mother Terisha to tell the community that she doesn't hate gays (she was only teasing) and hopefully ease the tension.

9. Episode 9. Roses discovers that Mother Terisha was not teasing and used him in a plot to destroy the gay community by planting a bomb in the bar owned by Roses' new gay friend, Michelle.

10. Episode 10. Roses' efforts to find the bomb, planted in the bar, is successful, but Michelle gives his life to stop its damage by smothering it with his body. Although Roses has temporarily stopped Mother Terisha and her gay murder spree, she also has something else to fear—the demon-possessed Dixie. The first season, concluding episode.

35 *Carmilla*. carmilla.com. 2014 (Horror).

In 1872 Irish author Joseph Sheridan Le Fanu wrote a short story called *Carmilla*, a well-researched work about a beautiful lesbian vampire he based on then existing myths and legends. Being the first such story of its kind, it influenced Bram Stoker to conceive his own, more widely known novel about a vampire (*Dracula*). The original story, set in 19th century Styria, Austria, begins by introducing Laura, a six-year-old girl who lives in a castle with her widowed father, an Englishman retired from the Austrian Service. Being an only child and with no friends to play with, Laura has been tormented by dreams of a beautiful girl entering her bedroom and drawing blood from her through bite marks on her chest. In another part of the country, a girl named Carmilla appears to be experiencing the same type of dream—only she is the girl who appears to Laura.

It is 12 years later when, outside her home, a horse and carriage accident brings Laura face-to-face with the girl in her dreams when she and her father come to the rescue of the carriage riders, Carmilla and her mother. While Carmilla's mother appears to be unscathed, Carmilla has suffered an injury and cannot continue the journey with her mother. Through an arrangement with Carmilla's mother and Laura's father, Carmilla is permitted to reside with him and Laura while she recuperates. Laura and Carmilla become friends but as the days pass, Laura finds herself becoming the object of Carmilla's growing affection for her. Shortly after, when restored family heirlooms are returned to the castle, Laura sees that a 1698 painting of an ancestor named Mircalla Karnstein is the exact image of Carmilla. That night, Laura again succumbs to what she believes are dreams, this time of a cat that enters her room, transforms into a beautiful woman and proceeds to draw blood from bite wounds on her breast. Laura's dreams prove to be anything but as she becomes increasingly ill due to a loss of blood. A doctor, summoned by her father, recognizes the wounds as those made by a vampire and instructs that Laura not be left alone at night. As the story continues, Carmilla is revealed to actually be the woman in that painting, the vampire Countess Mircalla Karnstein and to save Laura, Mircalla must be destroyed. The story concludes with Mircalla's coffin being found and, as Mircalla is destroyed (not only with a stake through the heart but by decapitation and cremation), Laura is released from the spell Carmilla held over her. But is the Countess really dead?

It is 2014 when the web adaptation begins. Laura Hollis is a first-year student at Silas University and pursuing a career as a journalist. She shares a room with a girl named Betty and all is progressing well until they decide to spend a night partying. The following morning Laura awakens to find that Betty is missing and the only explanation is a note, presumably written by Betty that states she has left school to return home. Laura feels that something is just not right when she sees Betty's clothes are still in the room (307) and a young woman named Carmilla suddenly appears to announce that she is her new roommate. Laura immediately becomes suspicious

Carmilla. **Series poster art (used by permission of Smokebomb Entertainment).**

of Carmilla and feels she may have something to do with Betty's mysterious disappearance. Determined to uncover the truth, Laura, assisted by her TA (teaching associate) and current crush Danny, and friends LaFontaine and Perry, begins a dangerous quest to find Betty and expose Carmilla, who is seducing Laura with her hypnotic powers, for what she really is—a lesbian vampire.

Cast: Elise Bauman (Laura Hollis), Natasha Negovanlis (Carmilla Karnstein), Kaitlyn Alexander (LaFontaine), Annie Briggs (Lola Perry), Sharon Belle (Danny Lawrence), Aaron Chartrand (Will), Matt O'Connor (Kirsch), Grace Glowicki (Betty Spielsdorf), Brenton Lalama (Sarah-Jane), Dillon Taylor (J.P.). **Credits:** *Producer:* Christina Jennings, Scott Garvie, Kaaren Whitney (Kaaren Whitney-Vernon), Jay Bennett, Steph Ouaknine. *Director:*

Spencer Maybee. *Writer:* Jordan Hall. **Comment:** A well presented program that adapts the first story about a lesbian vampire and updates it to the 21st century. Not only are the two female leads beautiful, but combine that with vampires and the lesbian aspect and an instant hit is almost guaranteed. The acting is very good and the production values top rate. There have been several movie and television adaptations of the original story and the easiest accessible version is the 1970 feature film *The Vampire Lovers* (released by M-G-M on DVD) that stars Ingrid Pitt as Carmilla/Mircalla.

Episodes:

1. Carmilla. It is three weeks into Laura's first semester when Betty mysteriously disappears and Laura is left to ponder what really happened.

2. Missing. As Laura attempts to get some answers from the school's officials about Betty's absence, she suddenly finds herself with a new roommate—Carmilla.

3. The Roommate. All is not going well as Laura, somewhat uneasy about having Carmilla as a roommate, discovers that she has a number of strange traditions—like pouring blood over her cereal.

4. Freak Out. Positive that Carmilla is no ordinary girl, Laura, with the assist of her friends, begins an investigation to find Betty.

5. Patterns. Although Carmilla explains that she mixed food coloring with corn syrup as a joke to create blood, Laura doesn't accept it and continues her investigation by questioning two girls who disappeared but returned a few days later with no memory of what happened to them.

6. Why Bother. In an effort to alert other students as to what has happened, Laura uploads a video she shot on the school's website.

7. Town Hall. The video, seen by school officials, has no affect on them (as they just dismiss it as nonsense) but Danny, Laura's teaching associate, becomes intrigued and joins Laura in her investigation.

8. Pitsa i Thanato. The video alerts the "bros" of Zeta Omega Mu Fraternity that the "hotties" on campus may be in danger and fosters them to organize a protection patrol, with Laura being their first choice to protect.

9. Nancy Drew. Laura and Danny attempt to come up with a plan to find Betty.

10. The Real Betty. As Laura continues her investigation she believes she is getting close to what is happening and that something sinister lurks at the university.

11. A Visit from the Dean. Realizing that she is stuck with Carmilla as a roommate, Laura makes an effort to understand her, but fails miserably.

12. Evidence. Laura updates viewers as to what has happened so far.

13. I, Spy. Laura confesses that she has been having nightmares that she believes are connected to Carmilla.

14. Research Trip. After visiting the school's foreboding library to do research, Laura is overcome with the feeling that she is the next victim.

15. My Roommate, the Vampire. Laura uncovers the fact that Carmilla is a vampire and now knows for sure her life is in jeopardy.

16. Best Laid Plans. Laura and her friends, LaFontaine and Perry, devise a plan to capture Carmilla and make her confess that she is responsible for the disappearances of girls on campus.

17. It's a Trap. The plan, with Laura dressed as bait to lure Carmilla, works and Carmilla, captured, is tied to a chair in Laura's room.

18. While You Weren't Watching. Although they have Carmilla bound, two additional girls are reported missing, making Laura have second thoughts that Carmilla is responsible.

19. Advanced Interrogation Techniques. The trap reveals that Carmilla is a lesbian and was not trying to kill Laura by her actions, only seduce her.

20. Sock Puppets and European History. Carmilla confesses that she is a vampire, born in 1680 and the daughter of a powerful supernatural mother who requires the blood of young girls. She also laments on the fact that many years ago she lost the girl she loved.

21. Strategic Planning. Laura, Danny, LaFontaine and Perry must now decide what to do with Carmilla—set her free or keep her bound. In an unexpected moment, Carmilla's brother (Will), a vampire also, frees her, telling her their mother is upset that she has been exposed and is on the warpath (to retrieve her). Angry at Laura, Carmilla bites her on the neck.

22. Afterbite. Laura, in a panic that she has been bitten by a vampire, tries to cope with what is happening only to discover from Carmilla, that she too faces the wrath of her mother.

23. We Need to Talk About Carmilla. Carmilla explains that over the centuries she has kidnapped girls for her mother (head of a cult that requires young women for sacrifices) but does not know what happens to make them different when they are freed.

24. Breaking Up (with an Amazon) Is Hard to Do. Danny, upset that Carmilla is free, has it out with Laura, only to reveal that she has romantic feelings toward her.

25. Basic Parasitology. Perry's research reveals that some sought of parasite is responsible for what happens to the girls but is unable to figure out exactly what that parasite is.

26. The Standard Issue. A trip to the foreboding university library nets Laura an ancient book that reveals that in 1874, a similar series of kidnappings occurred.

27. Required Reading. Life is further complicated for Laura when she learns that LaFonatine mysteriously disappeared and a note similar to the one that appeared after Betty vanished was also found.

28. Blame Enough for All. Laura, believing that she is responsible for LaFonatine's kidnapping because the cult could not abduct her, finds comfort from Carmilla and Perry who convince her that she is not to blame.

29. PTSD and Brownies. Laura's fears for La-Fonatine are eased when she reappears the following morning but has no idea where she was or that she was even kidnapped.

30. Monsters, Lies and Videotapes. As LaFonatine learns that she was abducted, she joins with Laura, Carmilla and Perry in an attempt to uncover the strange happenings at Silas University. The first clue comes from LaFonatine's cell phone, which has an audio recording of her kidnapping, but LaFonatine cannot recall any details about why she made it. It reveals, however, that three girls are being held captive but their whereabouts is unknown.

31. Of Hearts and Holy Hand Grenades. Although Carmilla feels uneasy about defying her mother, she seeks a way to destroy her cult by finding a supernatural weapon. Her efforts are sidetracked when her mother possesses Laura's body.

32. Mommy Dearest. Carmilla learns, through her mother's possession of Laura's will, that she is not seeking to kill Laura, but actually save her. If Carmilla will stop Laura from disrupting the sacrificial ritual, she will let Laura live. If not, Laura will become its final victim.

33. Pep Rally. Laura is released from Carmilla's mother's spell but cannot be deterred by Carmilla from her self-imposed mission. Laura, now more determined than ever to expose the cult, approaches the student body to hopefully get help. While the rally is not seen, Laura explains that she was unsuccessful and was hit in the head by a tomato.

34. Don't Go Into the Light. While what happens to Laura is not seen, LaFonatine approaches Carmilla to tell her that she just received a text message from Laura telling her that she is trapped in the basement of an old chapel and to bring stakes. Carmilla deducts that Laura is in the Dudley Chapel in the Lastic Building. Carmilla then leaves saying she is "going to do something stupid." The screen goes to black and reopens to reveal that a battle had occurred and that the cult was defeated—but at what cost? "We won, we actually won," says Laura. "We won but Carmilla is dead."

35. Heroic Vampire Sh**. It is the aftermath of the battle and its details are related by Laura. Laura also laments on the fact that she has lost Carmilla, a girl she once hated but grew to love.

36. Life Goes On. Laura's feelings for Carmilla are apparent, she is hard-pressed to believe that Carmilla is gone until LaFonatine and Perry enter her dorm room with Carmilla—very weak but not dead. Blood that Carmilla had stored in the refrigerator revives Carmilla—and she and Laura share several passionate kisses. Being a vampire actually saved Carmilla and, as it appears they will become lovers, the cast and credits roll with the screen turning to black as they end. Seconds later the scene opens to the dorm room where it is revealed that Carmilla's mother has not been destroyed and will return, leaving the doorway open for another season of episodes to follow.

36 Cat on the Prowl. funnyordie.com/topic/cat-on-the-prowl. 2009 (Comedy).

Cat Davis, a very pretty young woman who calls herself "The Queen of Gay Town," is a lesbian who prowls the streets (in her car) looking for "gay ladies" to interview and get their perspective on what it is like being a lesbian in today's world.

Cast: Cat Davis (Herself). **Credits:** *Producer:* Cat Davis, Kitain Studio. **Comment:** A causal program that is not only well done but informative and interesting as well. Cat Davis is delightful as the host and the program presents interesting tidbits on the girls Cat interviews.

Episode List: Each program's title begins with "Cat on the Prowl" followed by her guests or topic.

1. Cat on the Prowl: That's What She Said.
2. Cat on the Prowl: Eden Riegel.
3. Cat on the Prowl: Lauren Pritchard.
4. Cat on the Prowl: Sandra Grace.
5. Cat on the Prowl: Melanie Hutsell.
6. Cat on the Prowl: Best Bits.
7. Cat on the Prowl: Randi Barnes.
8. Cat on the Prowl: Jenn Colella.
9. Cat on the Prowl: Bobbie Oliver.
10. Cat on the Prowl: Tammy Jo Dearen.
11. Cat on the Prowl: Amy Dresner.
12. Cat on the Prowl: Pamela Ribon.
13. Cat on the Prowl: Fortune Feimster.
14. Cat on the Prowl: Anne Dudek.
15. Cat on the Prowl: Candace Kita.
16. Cat on the Prowl: Jen Kober.
17. Cat on the Prowl: Haviland Stillwell.
18. Cat on the Prowl: Beth Malone.
19. Cat on the Prowl: The Lisps.
20. Cat on the Prowl: Patricia Villetto.
21. Cat on the Prowl: Bridget McManus.
22. Cat on the Prowl: Margaret Cho.
23. Cat on the Prowl: Nate Davis.

37 The Cavanaughs. youtube.com. 2010–2012 (Comedy-Drama).

After two years "of hell," a television pilot called *The Cavanaughs* (starring drag queen Noreen Cavanaugh) is finally completed. It is a comedy-drama about a group of offbeat actors seeking unconventional ways to keep their small theater in Hollywood operational. All hope is riding on a screening to convince network officials it is the show for their network. While the overall plot is good, the fact that each of the characters suffers from some type of neurosis is a turn off and the pilot is rejected. Although disappointed at what has happened, the cast is not defeated. They decide to retool the project and create a new version of the program. A revitalized energy has overtaken the performers and the program charts the process that goes into making a TV series with a particular focus on the cast and how they slowly create a family of their own.

Noreen Cavanaugh, the "woman" for whom *The Cavanaughs* was written, is a flamboyant drag queen actress (man pretending to be a woman) and takes great pride in everything she does. She has a heart of gold and when the new project is begun she becomes like a den mother to her fellow actors.

Bryan, the program's exasperated writer, is gay and has the uneasy job of retooling the program and its characters but is also struggling to overcome the passing of his lover, Shea (who was terminally ill and committed suicide).

Maddie, Shea's sister and Brian's writing and producing partner is a confident woman who cares deeply for her friends and watches over them like they were her own family. She is also a lesbian and cares deeply for an actress on the show (Charley).

Charley, best friends with Maddie, is a chain-smoking actress and secretly a lesbian (she fears revealing her secret will tear her family apart). Charley harbors hidden feelings for Maddie but goes to extreme lengths to conceal it (conflict enters her life when her secret is revealed over the Internet).

Sarah and Mark are actors on the show who share a love-hate relationship. Sarah is a bit quirky and became known through her work in TV commercials; Mark is a successful working actor but too confident as his actions make him appear a bit off-center to those he meets.

Scott, Sarah's best friend is, like Sarah, a good person at heart and hopes to embark on a singing career.

Hope is the producer hired by Noreen to make *The Cavanaughs* happen no matter what it takes to do it.

Cast: Grant Landry (Mark), Cwennen Corral (Maddie), Deborah Estelle Philips (Charley), Adrian Morales (Bryan), Michael Womack (Noreen Cavanaugh), Amanda Broadwell (Sarah), Daniel Rhyder (Scott), Percy Rustomji (Dumas), Mikey Lamar, Ryan Kibby (Shea), Camille Bennett (Hope), Matthew Sergi (Zack), Carla Marie (Charlotte), Lars Slind (Cary), Nathaniel Vincent (Bingo), Emily Sandack (Rebecca), Katie Caprio (Kirsten), Dina Martinez (Herself), Kimberly Fox (Hope), Georgan George (Marlena), Eric Van (Beverly Fairfax), Matthew Trbovich (Zack), Kevin Makely (Justin), Patrick O'Sullivan (Chris). **Credits:** *Producer:* Cwennen Corral, Adrian Morales, Bryon MacDonald, Ryan Kibby, Joshua Gollish. *Director:* Bryon MacDonald, Adrian Morales, Cwennen Corral, Nicole Olmsted, Ryan Kibby. *Writer:* Ryan Kibby, Adrian Morales. **Comment:** A bit of everything: lesbians (Maddie and Charley), gays (Brian and Du-

mas), drag queens (Noreen and Beverly) and straights in a well tuned program that captures the feeling of what goes into the making of a TV sitcom. While the main idea of the program is not original (producing a TV show has been done on such programs as *30 Rock*, *On the Air* and *The Jack Benny Program*) incorporating the gay-lesbian-drag queen aspect does give a whole new perspective on the subject. Searching the program will also bring up a CBS series called *The Cavanaughs* (which also dealt with a family) but they are totally unrelated.

Episodes:

1. Think of Me. A retooled version of *The Cavanaughs* is reborn when the cast decides to give the project a second try.

2. Woman in White. As discussions begin on the project it is learned Charley is a lesbian and her upcoming marriage to Chris (a man) is a pretense to conceal her true being.

3. If Only. Scott believes his singing career may get a jump start when he performs a song written by Bryan; Charley's fears about marrying Chris are beginning to overpower her—is she making the right decision?

4. Half a Moment. As Bryan struggles to overcome a writing block, Mark realizes that he has stalker (Dumas) and Charley, who calls off her wedding, decides she will continue with the show.

5. Stop! Wait! Please! As the deadline for getting the production started approaches, Maddie tries to help Bryan overcome his block and get a script completed.

6. Don't Know How to Love Him. With Maddie's help the script is completed for the show's first episode and a dinner party is held to celebrate. Meanwhile, Dumas confronts Mark (his obsession) and tries to befriend him.

7. Memory. Noreen attempts to learn the reason why two actors (Sarah and Maddie) quit the show (Sarah over a disagreement with Mark; Maddie over her objection to religious jokes in the script).

8. Dice Are Rolling. An uneasy moment for Charley when she and Chris accidentally cross paths; Dumas appears to be upset that Sarah is attracted to Mark.

9. Seeing Is Believing. In an effort to please the show's star (Noreen), Bryan rewrites the script to delete the religious jokes and get Maddie back on board. Meanwhile, Charley is heartbroken that her mother disapproves of her decision to become an actress and is now unsure if she should continue working on the show.

10. Likes of Us. Noreen reveals to her drag queen friend Beverly that she was cast to play Toni in a *Charlie's Angels* spin off called *Toni's Boys* (an actual pilot) but was replaced by Barbara Stanwyck (who played Toni, head of an all male detective agency). Meanwhile a new producer is hired (Hope), who happens to be Maddie's boyfriend's (Justin) ex-girlfriend.

11. Let Me Finish. Mark becomes aware that Dumas appears to be taking a liking to him while Maddie prepares to meet Hope for the first time. Sarah, dismayed by a YouTube posting that she is a terrible actress, finds comfort in Mark as he tries to rebuild her confidence. Realizing that the show could suffer if Charley leaves, Noreen makes a phone call (without Charley's knowledge) to Charley's mother reprimanding her for the situation she has placed her daughter in and demanding that she act like a mother and encourage her daughter.

12. Point of No Return. The first season concludes with a script finally written and the cast preparing for their first table reading (including Charley after a life-changing phone call from her mother).

Note: The remaining episodes continue to depict the troubles faced by the cast and crew as they attempt to get *The Cavanaughs* on the air.

Season 2 Episode List: *1.* The Wine and the Dice. *2.* If Not for Me. *3.* Beautiful Game. *4.* So Much to Do. *5.* Poor Fool. *6.* Dear Old Friend.

Season 3 Episode Titles: *1.* Toast of the Town, Part 1. *2.* Toast of the Town, Part 2. *3.* I Remember. *4.* Let's Talk About You. *5.* Wrestle with the Devil. *6.* Surrender. *7.* Memory of a Happy Moment. *8.* Heaven by the Sea. *9.* Unsettled Scores. *10.* Twisted Every Way.

Season 4 Episode List: *1.* With One Look. *2.* Try Not to Be Afraid. *3.* The Arrest. *4.* Too Late for Turning Back. *5.* Nothing Like You've Ever Known. *6.* Getaway with Anything. *7.* Forgive My Intrusion. *8.* Damned for All Time. *9.* Dead Zone. *10.* An Angel in Heaven. *11.* Once Upon Another Time.

38 The Centre. youtube.com. 2013 (Anthology).

The Centre is a Germany-based home for women founded by Leoni, a Namibian social worker after finding disenchantment with the German Bureaucracy. With the help of a female doctor (Jessi) she befriended years ago in a refugee camp in Lesotho, the two join forces to help women in trouble (apparently lesbians based on available information) with no place else to go.

Cast: Naomi Beukes-Meyer (Leoni), Brigit Stauber (Jessi). **Credits:** *Producer:* Brigit Stauber, Mirya Kalmuth, Lucia Luciano, Julia Stenke, Timalen Jose. *Director:* Amber Palmer, Eddy Balardi. *Writer:* Naomi Beukes-Meyer. **Comment:** German program that has thus far only produced one episode (a pilot) and, without a doubt, the most unusual of all the lesbian series that have been created for the Internet. The program has English subtitles and its subject matter, while different, may also have little appeal to American audiences.

Episodes:

1. I'm Still Down Here. A young woman (Sanaa) seeks help when her love for a German punk girl (Janis) is opposed by her very religious family.

Lucia Luciano stars as Sanaa with Stenke (as credited) as Julia.

39 The Chadwick Journals. youtube.com/watch?v=zMk1C7SCneA. 2008 (Drama).

Chadwick Williams is a journalist who has turned his attention to writing about "MSM" (Men Who Sleep with Men). The situation is also called "The DL" ("The Down Low") and refers to straight men of color who live their everyday lives as heterosexuals (and sometimes married to women) but secretly engage in relationships with gay men. As Chadwick conducts his research, his narration is used to convey the stories of such men (that range from successful executives and street corner hustlers to athletes and happily married men) and how the cross social, economic and cultural boundaries affect their lives. The program is actually a prelude for the second season premiere of the Here! Channel TV series *The DL Chronicles* after a three year hiatus (to sort of reacquaint viewers to the series before its cable premiere).

Cast: Damian T. Raven (Chadwick Williams), Nic Few (Donovan), Ulrich Que (Mark). **Credits:** *Producer:* Deondray Gossett, Sky Gaven, Quincy LeNear, Camrin Pitts. *Director:* Deondray Gossett, Quincy LeNear. *Writer:* Deondray Gossett. **Comment:** Excellent acting and production values that captures your interest from the very beginning (much like its parent series, *The DL Chronicles*, which tells of men of color who lead double sex lives).

Episodes:

1. Donovan. As Chadwick conducts research, he interviews the mysterious Donovan, a man with anger issues who first believes that Donovan hired him for sex, not to be interviewed for a book.

2. Mr. Johnson. As Chadwick continues his questioning, he learns that Donovan, although quite bitter, first became aware that he was gay at age 13 when he became attracted to his math teacher, Mr. Johnson.

3. The Truth Doesn't Matter. Chadwick's line of questioning uncovers inconsistencies in Donovan's stories and Chadwick concludes that Donovan is lying to him.

4. Mr. Turner. The concluding episode wherein Chadwick reveals that he is writing the book for his brother, who was like Donovan and wound up dead.

40 Cherry Bomb. cherrybombtv.com. 2009–2013 (Talk).

Billed as "The Talk Show for Women Who Love Women." Frank discussions and "Celesbian" interviews combine to tackle issues regarding the lesbian community.

Hosts: Dalila Ali Rajah, Gloria Bigelow, Nikki Caster, Tatum De Roeck. **Credits:** *Executive Producer:*

Cherry Bomb. Cast, left to right: Gloria Bigelow, Tatum De Roeck, Nikki Caster, Dalila Ali Rajah (copyright *Cherry Bomb*, photograph by Logan Alexander, www.loganphotos.com).

Dalila Ali Rajah, Bethany Landing. *Producer:* Kimberly Nicole Davis, Mia Domingo, Michelle Hinch. *Writer-Creator:* Dalila Ali Rajah, Bethany Landing. *Director:* Bethany Landing. **Comment:** The program is reminiscent of the daily CBS series *The Talk* for its presentation but its subject matters are strictly geared to a specific audience with provocative subjects and equally shocking and sometimes humorous responses to the questions that are posed.

Season 1 Episodes:

1. Commitment Issues. Making a commitment is discussed with the hosts revealing their own experiences.

2. Dating in the Internet Age. On-line dating is explored with a focus on MySpace stalking and the challenges some women face in being monogamous.

3. Coming Out. A discussion revealing how a girl first realizes she is attracted to other girls and how they should handle it.

4. Gender Roles. The terminology used to describe some lesbians (from "Pillow Princess" to "Stone Cold Butch") is discussed.

5. Deal Breakers. What one should and should not expect in a relationship is discussed.

6. Playa Please. The mysteries of the lesbian "playa" (a girl who is a player) are discussed with tips on how to spot one "and how to tame one."

7. The Polys. Open relationships are discussed and how they can affect some couples.

8. The Ex-Factor. Relationships after a break up are discussed.

9. Green Light Go. The signals to look for to determine what a girl wants, just coffee or a date are explored.

10. Taboos. The hosts discuss the subjects to avoid (from politics to religion) that could affect choices in the bedroom.

11. Gender Roles, Part 2. Gender roles and how they rate on the masculine-feminine scale are explored from a discussion that was begun in episode 4.

12. Urge to Merge. How life changes when two girls move in together is discussed.

13. Meet the Parents. It has to happen sooner or later and when to bring your girlfriend to meet your parents is open for discussion.

14. Bisexual Hurdle, Part 1. Bisexuality in the lesbian community is discussed.

15. Fuzzy Relationships. Comedian Bridget McManus appears in a discussion about whether or not it is healthy to retain a relationship with an ex-girlfriend.

16. Bisexual Hurdle, Part 2. The conversation begun in episode 14 continues with a focus on stereotypes and whether or not a bisexual woman is really satisfied being with just one sex.

17. Cubs and Cougars. Dating outside your age range is discussed (are older women looking for younger women to keep that fountain of youth? Are younger women seeking older women for a more stable relationship?).

18. Too Straight to Date. What happens when a lesbian is attracted to the ever-elusive straight girl is discussed as some lesbians believe some straight girls are lesbians in hiding.

19. Safer Sex. The myths and realities regarding safe sex in the lesbian community are discussed.

20. Getting There. The hosts discuss their personal preferences during intimate moments with their girlfriends.

21. Gay Marriage. Lawyer Chris Wilson appears to discuss the "real" story behind gay marriage in the U.S.

22. Race & Dating. The issues that surround interracial dating are discussed.

23. Long Distance Relationships. How to manage a long distance relationship is discussed with guests Arlan Hamilton (of *Interlude* magazine and "Your Daily Lesbian Moment" blog).

24. Dykeotomy. The program's first male guest (Logan Alexander) and his partner, Hope Wood, discuss their book *Dykeotomy* (a photographic look at lesbians).

25. The Break-Up. The first season concludes with a look at the heartache of breaking up and how to move on.

Season 2 Episodes:

26. Serial Monogamy. The second season begins with Michelle Wolff (Mongo Kiss on the Logo channel series *Dante's Cove*) discussing monogamy, back-to-back and overlapping relationships.

27. The Lesbian Scene. A discussion on how to find "The Lesbian Scene" in one's area is discussed with guest Amanda Deibert (from the web series *Feed*).

28. Valentine's Day. How to celebrate Valentine's Day for a girl and her new love is explored.

29. Living with Your Ex. Guest Jill Bennett joins the hosts for a discussion on the problems and sometimes benefits of a girl living with her ex-girlfriend.

30. A Game of Truth or Truth. A slumber party is held (with the hosts in their pajamas) to answer questions submitted by viewers.

31. Race, Religion and Marriage. Anne Marie Williams, from the Jordan Rustin Coalition, discusses the roles religion and race play within the lesbian community along with the continuing fight for gay rights.

32. What's Up Down There? Sexual health (including how to find lesbian doctors) is discussed with Precious Stallworth, a sex educator from the Los Angeles Gay and Lesbian Center.

33. Cheating, Part 1. Cheating and how it affects relationships is discussed.

34. Cheating, Part 2. The discussion continues with a focus on "Cheating vs. Crushing" and how

the terminology does not always have the same meaning for everyone.

35. Settling in Your Relationship. Latina comedienne Sandra Valls appears to discuss the differences between what is comfortable and what is unacceptable in a relationship.

36. Family Baggage. How bringing excess baggage into a relationship (things passed onto girls by their parents) could affect that relationship is discussed.

37. Truth or Truth, Part 2. Guest Suzanne Westenhoefer joins the hosts to answer questions from a live audience in Palm Springs.

38. The First Time. First time encounters are revealed by the hosts along with their guest, Mariah Hanson of Club Skirts.

39. Loving Too Much. A look at unrequited love (a girl who pursues a girl she knows she can't have) and how it could affect her life (is lusting for her just a waste of time; is it a deterrent from meeting someone she can have?).

40. Dating Women with Children. What a woman should consider before beginning a relationship with a woman who has children or a woman who wants children is discussed.

41. Obsession with Your Ex. A look at how obsessing over an ex-girlfriend or lover can become unhealthy and ruin a new relationship.

42. Sex Play. The second season concludes with a rather startling discussion on sex toys with guest Sarah Tomchesson, a sexual enhancement expert.

Season 3 Episodes:

43. You Call That Sex? The third season begins with guest Andrea Meyerson in a discussion on "So what do you do in bed?" when you are a lesbian.

44. Jealousy. A discussion about how jealousy (no matter what your sexual orientation) can become a huge problem in a relationship.

45. Gay and Religion. Can a person be religious and gay at the same time is discussed with guest Ky Dickens, creator of the film *Fish Out of Water*.

46. Out in the Club. The hosts relate humorous incidents that they have encountered over the years.

47. First Girl Ever. Do women need to "sew some wild oats" before hooking up with another woman is discussed along with the prospect that some lesbians prefer only "first-timers" (being their first love).

48. Is Gay the New Black? A comparison between civil rights for blacks and the fight for equality with the LGBT community is discussed.

49. Following Your Instincts. Comedienne Erin Foley joins the hosts for a humorous discussion on following instincts before and after getting into a relationship.

50. The One. Guest Cathy DeBuono (from the web series *We Have to Stop Now*) joins the hosts for a discussion on whether there is that one special girl or is she just a passing fancy until the next girl shows up.

51. Don't Ask, Don't Tell. Zsa Zsa Gershick, author of the book *Secret Service—Untold Stories of Lesbians in the Military* shares her experiences being a lesbian and in the military.

52. The Butch Mystique, Part 1. A two part discussion on "The Butch Mystique" and how the terminology (often being mistaken for a man) affects such women and how they cope with the life style they have chosen.

53. The Butch Mystique, Part 2. The conversation from the prior episode is continued.

54. Back Burner Relationships. Is there a girl "in the wings" waiting for a girlfriend to screw up so she can move in on that girl? Nicole Pacent and Rachael Hip Flores, from the web series *Anyone but Me* guest.

55. Living Out Loud. Being gay or lesbian in a conservative community is discussed with guest Meghan Hall (from the web series *The Sweet Adventures of Nat and Meg*) who relates her experiences on being a lesbian in the South.

56. Dating Someone in the Closet. The pitfalls of dating someone in the closet are discussed with director Mel Robertson (who also discusses her film, *Queens of the World*, a lesbian love story set in the world of professional soccer).

57. The Butch Mystique, Part 3. "The Butch Mystique" controversy is discussed with guest Rosie Sennett.

58. The Gay-Lesbian Divide. Comedian Jason Stuart joins the hosts for a look at how gay men and lesbians ban together for the cause of equality.

59. It's in the Stars. A discussion, with guest Dani Campbell, about Astrology and can it really affect relationships based on star signs.

60. Dating Out of Your League. Dating out of one's league is discussed as well as should women date within their own league.

61. Pushing Your Buttons. The third season concludes. Guest Skyler Cooper (from the film *The Owls* [Older Wiser Lesbians] by Cheryl Dunye) joins the discussion about emotional triggers and "is your partner pushing them."

Season 4 Episodes: The exact number of episodes in unknown but only six (of most likely 22) episodes remain in line.

1. Episode 8. A discussion on relationships and what the future holds.

2. Episode 9. The issue of whether a girl can be in love with two girls at the same time.

3. Episode 16. How to break up and move on when a relationship appears to be ending is explored.

4. Episode 20. Spending time away from family and devoting time to each other is discussed.

5. Episode 21. Domestic violence in lesbian relationships is discussed.

6. Episode 22. The topic of "best sex ever" is frankly discussed.

Season 5 Episodes:

1. Season 5, Episode 1. How to handle holiday stress when one partner spends time with the other partner's family is discussed.

2. Season 5, Episode 2. A discussion on when it is appropriate for newly formed couples to sleep together without being considered sluts.

3. Season 5, Episode 3. Dealing with each other's anxieties is the main topic of discussion.

4. Season 5, Episode 4. Realizing each other's sexual needs is discussed.

5. Season 5, Episode 5. A discussion based on the book *Five Love Languages* wherein each partner should learn how to give and receive love.

6. Season 5, Episode 6. Bullying is discussed by each of the hosts and how, because of their sexuality, they dealt with the situation.

7. Season 5, Episode 7. The art of wooing is discussed with guest Jacquelyn Kennedy.

8. Season 5, Episode 8. A discussion with guest Sheetal Sheth on the sometimes hidden lives some lesbians must live due to the situations that surround them.

9. Season 5, Episode 9. Lesbian co-dependency is discussed.

Note: In addition to the missing Season 4 episodes, Season 1 and 2 episodes have also been taken off-line.

41 Chica Busca Chica (Girl Seeks Girl). afterellen.com. 2007 (Comedy-Drama).

A look at the lives, loves and personal issues faced by a group of gorgeous women, living in Madrid, Spain, who are also lesbians: Nines, a flirtatious bartender at the local lesbian bar, Chica Busca Chica, who romances every woman she meets although she has an on-again, off-again romance with her boss, Rosi (the editor of a publishing house wherein Nines is hoping to produce a book about a super heroine). Her lame pick-up line, "You have an eyelash on your cheek," grants her the girl she has set her sights on; Ana, a young woman new to the lesbian scene (and desperate for Nines to teach her the techniques of lesbian dating and love); Monica, a judo coach called "The Psycho" at clubs (as she can't quite give up the prospect of losing a girlfriend), and Carmen, a heterosexual who is drawn mostly to women after she discovers she has a cheating boyfriend (Jorge).

Cast: Celia Freijeiro (Nines), Cristina Pons (Monica), Almudena Gallego (Ana), Sandra Collantes (Carmen), Karola Sanchez (Victoria), Paloma Arimon (Rosi), Paco Manzanedo (Jorge), Jimena Fernandez (Michelle), Cristina Camison (Yoyo), Inma Cuesta (Roberta), Maribel Luis (Carla), Isabel Prinz (La Paciente), Eva Pallares (Maite). **Comment:** Premiering on the Internet while the TV series *The L-Word* was still current, *Chica Busca Chica* offered a more focused look at the relationships encountered by the cast. There are sexual situations, numerous kissing scenes and a look at life in a lesbian community outside of the United States. The same can be said for both—the women are gorgeous and the problems they encounter—whether from infidelity to one night stands are the same. The series, with English subtitles, has been re-edited and released to the U.S. under the title *Girl Seeks Girl*. See also *Girl Gets Girl*, a film update of the series.

Episodes: 15 untitled episodes appear but have not been translated (dubbed) into English (some web sites claim there were 13 episodes while others claim 16).

42 Chico's Angels. vimeo. com/5723933. 2010 (Comedy).

A spoof of the ABC TV series *Charlie's Angels*. A mysterious man named Chico has established a private detective organization and hired three (men-in-drag) women (Kay, Chita and Frieda), all police academy failures, as his operatives. To conceal his true identity (possibly a criminal past) he has also hired Bossman to oversee his operations, assist the Angels (his detectives) and keep his identity a secret (as Chico only communicates with his operatives over a telephone) and does not want his true nature revealed. The program charts the cases acquired by Chico's Angels and how, in a style more "feminine" than the original *Charlie's Angeles* (Jill, Sabrina and Kelly) they attempt to solve crimes—in heels, elegant gowns and as bit of sass.

Kay, born in Tijuana, Baja California, is the youngest of 18 children "and the prettiest of them all." Her beauty was so distinctive that it earned her the title of "Miss Tijuana Natural Springs Water" ("The water

Chico's Angels. **Left to right: Kay Seda, Chita Parol, Frieda Lays, Bossman (center) (copyright Shiney Kumquat Productions; photograph by Gabriel Goldberg).**

that springs right through you"). She established a charity called Save the Donkeys, joined, but flunked out of the police academy and finally established herself as a high fashion model. Her stylish good looks and charming personality brought her to Chico's attention when he saw an ad she did for girdles that appeared in the Penny Saver magazine. Kay is self-absorbed, high maintenance and believes she is the not only the prettiest Angel, but the most voluptuous. She is often pursued by "hunky hotties and creepy criminals" and because she also sells Tupperware, her job title reads "Detective/Model/Tupperware Sales Lady."

Frieda, born in Ciudad Juarez Mexico (known as J-Town across the border) was abandoned as an infant and left under the door mat of the convent Las Hermanas de la Madre Guadalupe de los Chavos. She was raised by the convent nuns and was being groomed to join the order until she had an affair with "a handsome churro salesman" and realized she loved sex. But could she give up her decision to become a nun? To test her worthiness, she defrocked a priest (who later became a notorious pimp), left the convent and set out to make a life for herself in society. She drifted into Texas where, with no formal education and few skills, she could only find work where real skills are not required (like dancehall hostess and massage therapists). When Frieda turned to prostitution and was arrested by a vice cop, her life changed for the better when she was sent to jail and befriended a guard. After a sexual encounter, the guard set her up for enrollment at the police academy but her failure to become a rookie set her on a path to re-establish herself in Los Angeles—where she was discovered by Chico and hired as an Angel.

Chita, born in East Los Angeles, is a first generation Mexican-American (her family is from Mexico). Chita dreamed of becoming a ballerina, but being brought up in the ghetto shattered those dreams when gangs ruled and fighting gangs took precedence over dancing. She eventually joined a gang (the Mariposas) and by the age of twelve had become their leader. She soon began selling macramé on the streets to make money but seeing the movie *West Side Story* changed her life. It not only rekindled old memories but got her expelled from the gang when she attempted to pursue them. She enrolled in the Debbie Allen School of Dance but quickly lost her internship when she beat up her boyfriend's boyfriend. Chita's inability to conform to the rules of society eventually got her arrested but also changed the course of her life when, at a police station, she saw a police academy recruitment poster and decided to become a police officer. Her fiery temper caused her expulsion from the academy six months later. While watching the TV series *Candid Camera,* Chico saw a skit gone wildly wrong wherein Chita displayed her fighting abilities and sent show host Allen Funt to the hospital. He felt Chita would make the perfect Angel and hired her. Chita considers herself the smart Angel, is seeking to control her anger issues and fancies herself as the pretty Angel.

Bossman, as he is called, is a long time friend of Chico's ("an old spy buddy"). He was born in Pacoima, California, and had the unique ability to contort his body and escape from anything. He joined the circus, hoping to become a star, but the FBI required his skills and recruited him. He trained to become a Navy SEAL but only rose to the rank of Penguin. Shattered that he could not achieve a higher ranking, he turned to booze and women and one night became so intoxicated that he slipped off an apartment building roof and lost his contortionist abilities when a fire escape broke his fall. When Bossman re-connected with Chico they decided to establish the company with Bossman becoming the liaison between Chico and the Angels (as did John Bosley on *Charlie's Angels*).

Cast: Danny Casillas (Frieda Laye), Oscar Quintero (Kay Sedia), Ray Garcia (Chita Parol), Alejandro Patino (Bossman), Gabriel Romero (Voice of Chico). **Credits:** *Producer:* Danny Casillas, Maria Quintaro, Jerry A. Blackburn. *Director:* Kurt Koehler. *Writer:* Danny Casillas, Kurt Koehler, Oscar Quintero. **Comment:** Drag situations sometimes work and sometimes they just fall flat on their face. Milton Berle used the drag situation to great success on his television series of the late 1940s and early

1950s and the producers have achieved that same rate of success here with a comical, well acted and well-produced program that is truly fun to watch. If *Bosom Buddies* could sustain itself for two years on ABC in the 1980s, *Chico's Angeles* could achieve the same heights as it is TV series worthy. For those familiar with the *Charlie's Angels* theme song you will find that it has been adapted, in part, for the program here (even using, in a way, the same type of opening theme silhouette visuals).

Episodes:
1. Missing Chihuahua. The unthinkable has happened: a ceramic Chihuahua has been stolen from the lawn of a woman (Dora [Cher Ferreyra]) who considers it the last memory she has of her late husband. With little money, she seeks out Chico's Angels and, with her sad story, finds the help she needs with Chico offering his services for free.

2. Steak-Out. The Angels begin their investigation into the dastardly deed.

3. Get Ready for Rumba. Clues lead the Angels to a Ghetto gang (led by Moca [Eden Espinosa]) and a confrontation when Moca denies having the ceramic dog.

4. A Sparkling Finish. While the Angels do take a licking, the dog is recovered as Moca explains that no harm was meant as it was on the list of items to acquire in a scavenger hunt. Believing they have done a good deed, the Angels approach the client and, in the attempt to return the dog it falls, breaks—and reveals the real reason why Dora wanted it back—it hid a cache of stolen diamonds.

5. Ransom and Then Some. Frieda is kidnapped and being held for $100 ransom at the same time a Mexican black market baby operation has been set up.

6. The Price Is Wrong. As Kay and Chita seek Frieda's whereabouts, they uncover evidence that her kidnapping may be linked to the black market operations. Their first clue comes from the envelope in which the ransom note was delivered: it has the street address.

7. Mexican Baby. As Kay and Chita approach the woman of the house (the head of the black market operation) Chita becomes nervous, spills the beans as to what they are up to and causes a confrontation between the woman and Kay.

8. Little Churros. Frieda solves her own kidnapping by paying her male abductor the $100 (which he wanted for women's lingerie) and joins Kay and Chita, who have apprehended the gang leader and solved the case—just when Bossman arrives and informs them of a Mexican black market operation they need to uncover. The program's concluding episode.

43 *Chloe.* youtube.com/watch?v=S-LRIT aHUbI. 2010 (Comedy).

Chloe Sevigny is a woman being impersonated by a man (although the actor playing Chloe does not consider himself a drag queen in the true sense). Through a series of short videos, Chloe's reflections on life are given—from the point of a woman who is actually a man pretending to be a woman. Milton Berle, from his 1948 TV series *Texaco Star Theater* gained great notoriety in skits when he appeared as a woman and the Internet series *Chico's Angels* (see entry) also used the drag queen element to present an enjoyable spoof of the TV series *Charlie's Angels*.

Cast: Drew Droege (Chloe). **Credits:** *Producer-Writer:* Drew Droege, Jim Hansen. *Director:* Jim Hansen. **Comment:** When first viewing an episode, Drew is quite convincing being a woman. It is when viewing episodes back to back that you realize she is a he. The comedy timing is right on and the material covered is well satirized.

Episode List: All episodes feature Chloe against various backgrounds (looks to be filmed using green screen technology) and relating her feelings on the episode's title. *1.* "Independence." *2.* "Birds." *3.* "Easter." *4.* "Horror." *5.* "News." *6.* "Pets." *7.* "The 12 Days of Christmas." *8.* "Sandwiches." *9.* "Reading." *10.* "Exercise." *11.* "Thirty." *12.* "March." *13.* "Valentine's Day." *14.* "Accessories." *15.* "Vacation." *16.* "Barbeque." *17.* "Fr33dom." *18.* "Memorial Day." *19.* "Spring." *20.* "Oscars." *21.* "Manners." *22.* "Holiday." *23.* "Film." *24.* "Toast." *25.* "Comedy." *26.* "Halloween." *27.* "Summer."

44 *Christopher Street TV.* youtube.com. 2006 (Drama).

In Greenwich Village in Manhattan (New York), considered the gay capital of the world, there is a street called Christopher Street and a young man named Christopher Street. Chris, as he is called, was not born in New York but in Memphis, Tennessee, and has recently relocated to Greenwich Village to restart his life. He has chosen to live on the street that bares his name but has also made three friends: Jharemy, Ashton and Shawn, young men, who like Chris, are gay and facing the problems of relationship issues, abuse, and sexual identity crises. The program charts their experiences as they seek acceptance not only in themselves, but from the world in which they live.

Cast: Jared DeWese (Christopher Street), Dwight Allen O'Neal (Jharemy Smith), Dante Sheppard (Ashton James), LaMar Staton (Shawn Leroy James), Nkosi Brown (Derrick Scott), Jamal Bruce (Brian), Lynnette R. Doby (Tracy), Patrick Jones-Roth (CeCe), Eric Joppy (Ian), Julio King (Adam), Elayne Rivers (Rene), J.R. Rolley (Tony). **Credits:** *Producer:* Dwight Allen O'Neal, Steven E. Martinez, Hayward Aaron. *Writer:* Steven E. Martinez, Dwight Allen O'Neal. **Comment:** Filmed on location in New York with a mix of light comedy and drama that attempts to deal with real-life situations. The acting and production values are good

but the series ends unresolved leaving the fate of the characters unknown.

Episodes: Three (of an unknown number of) episodes remain on line: *1.* Christopher Street TV Pilot Episode. *2.* Pumps or Timbs, Part 1. *3.* Pumps or Timbs, Part 2.

Note: In 2012 a proposed spin off called *Christopher Street: Cocktales* was apparently produced but as of January 2015 only a short teaser (trailer) for the series has been placed on-line. Here Jharemy Smith, from the original series, and his straight friend Blaire Knowles, a beautiful young woman, have become business partners in "the hottest gay bar in Manhattan." Jharmey is depicted as a man who can not seem to keep a man while Blaire finds men but not one that suits her. It is difficult to tell from the teaser where the series would head (Blaire turning to women?) but the action appears to be centered on the bar and its clientele with episodes also focusing on the issues facing Blaire and Jharmey. Dwight Allen O'Neal reprises his role as Jharmey but other performers are not credited (nor are production credits given).

45 *Closet Space.* closetspacetv.tumblr.com. 2013–2014 (Drama).

For many gays and lesbians, declaring their sexuality has not been easy, but they have done it and are leading happier lives. But for every one that "has come out of the closet" there are perhaps just as many who are either afraid, ashamed of what others may think of them or still unsure of who or what they are sexually. And one does not have to be an adult to realize that he or she is different; it happens in teenagers and the program explores, through two main characters (Jake and Tara), the problems "queer youth" (as tagged by the program) face as they struggle to find their place in a world that for the most part, does not approve of who they are or what they will become. Jake is a 17-year-old evangelical whose strict religious upbringing has him questioning sexuality while Tara, also 17 but not religious, is a lesbian struggling to hide her "out life" from her conservative family while embracing who she is in the real world.

Cast: Sharae Foxie (Tara), Daniel Robison (Jake), Anny Rosario (Regina), Nina Concepcion (Misty), Becca Leigh Gellman (Sara), Neil Gillen (Aimes), Katarina Hughes (Christy), Kate Romero (Lisa), Vince Major (Pastor Craig), John Stellar (Tad), Jessica Carter Ramsey (Janelle). **Credits:** *Producer:* Ashley McCormick. *Director:* Chanelle Tyson. *Writer:* Karisa Quick, Daniel Robison. **Comment:** Taking a dramatic look (as opposed to a comical look at teens who are gay or lesbian) makes for a provocative series and, while not a solution to the problem, it does shed some insightful light on the subject. It is also told in two different perspectives, that being Jake and Tara are not in the same school or even the same city. Scenes switch back and forth as each deals with a specific situation that they need to deal with. The situations do not always parallel each other, but they are well constructed and presented. While the acting is very good and all the characters well defined, Sharae Foxie is especially delightful as Tara. She is so sweet and so innocent that her presence alone makes the series worth watching.

Episodes:

1. Gran Likes Her Gin. Tara and Jake are introduced in separate settings with each attempting to come to terms with who they are.

2. Hell Is an Eternal Flame Thrower. Jake believes he is all alone in his feelings until he stumbles upon two teenage boys making out in a bathroom and realizes there are others like him. Meanwhile Tara, revealing to her best friend, Regina (straight) feels pressure to express her sexuality rather than hide it by attending a "Tongue" party (mixer for gay, straight and lesbians).

3. Get 'em Tiger. Although reluctant, Tara agrees to attend the mixer—where Regina hopes to hook up with a straight guy but where Tara feels uncomfortable and just not ready for an intimate encounter with another girl. Meanwhile, Jake faces demons of his own when a sermon by a pastor further confuses him as to whether he is gay and if so, does that mean it is a sin? The program's concluding episode.

46 Coffee Talk. *youtube.com/playlist?list=PLoL2kbmYksdOIk1DUZH4v40ds3xeE83bt.* 2013–2014 (Reality).

Two gay college friends (per episode) gather for a cup of coffee to talk about the situations that are affecting their lives at the moment. Light humor mixes with the conversation to make people aware of gay issues in a way that is not only entertaining but informative as well.

Credits: *Producer:* Stefan Pfister. **Comment:** Not a program for everyone as the topics are strictly geared toward a gay audience. Because the program provides a service to its targeted audience, it has been dubbed in several languages and is also close-captioned for the hearing impaired. It is well done and presents what could be just dull talk in an entertaining, non-formal way.

Episodes: Cast members, only identified by a first name, are listed with episodes.

1. Tattoos and Muscles. Marc and Tim discuss their likes and dislikes when it comes to gays who get tattoos and those who showoff their muscles.

2. Football. Cage, a member of the school's football team, and his roommate Larry, discuss the prospect of not coming out (here to the team) that he (Cage) is gay.

3. Dress. Chris and Alex talk about gay dressing and why some gays choose to dress so feminine.

4. My Dad Is Gay. Michael tries to cope with the fact that his father came out of the closet while Brad

contends with a new heartthrob—an older man he met.

47 Come Take a Walk with Me. onemorelesbian.com. 2012–2013 (Comedy-Drama).

"Have you ever heard the saying, 'Take a Walk in My Shoes?'... This is my story and in order to follow it, you have to take a walk in my shoes." These are the opening words spoken by Channing, a young African-American woman born and raised in the small conservative town of Independence, Virginia, as she takes the first steps in redirecting her life by enrolling in college in North Carolina. Here, after acquiring a roommate (AJ), Channing's secret, that she is a lesbian, is revealed and the program follows her journey of self-acceptance with a focus on her loves and the challenges she faces as she prepares to take her place in the world.

Cast: Amber Chloe (Channing), Chasidye Richardson (Kenzie), Nina Lauren (Mira), Katrina Howell (Ka'maya), Jennifer Shannon (AJ). **Credits:** *Producer-Writer-Director:* Mina Minsha. **Comment:** The program is well acted but is difficult to understand at times due to poor audio quality (the first episode, for example, has segments of lost sound altogether). While there is no parental warning, there are sexual situations and vulgar language is needlessly incorporated. The program's intent was "to increase the visibility of queer women of color in the media." Being the first production of Mina Monsha's Lady Luck films, she has achieved that goal with a very vulnerable and like-able protagonist. The story line is very good and Ms. Monsha has chosen to make Channing representative of black women you may see on TV series such as *Girlfriends, Are We There Yet* and *Tyler Perry's House of Payne* although in a more dramatic vein. Just because a woman is African-American doesn't mean she has to be portrayed in an unflattering manner (such as a street bitch with an attitude) or crude as some Internet series portray them. Hopefully, for future endeavors, Ms. Monsha will continue a tradition of portraying African-American women (whether straight or gay) as real women with real problems and not the stereo-typed image some feature films and TV series relish in doing.

Episodes: While episodes are on line, the exact number is unknown. The season 1 episodes that can still be viewed (1–6) begin with Channing enrolling in school and follow her through her junior year. She has been misunderstood and rejected by her family and her struggles with family, friends, finances and faithfulness are explored. Remaining season 2 episodes (2–5) follow Channing as she acquires a job and prepares for graduation.

48 Conversations with My Ex. youtube.com/watch?v=EmszCXjUdJI. 2013 (Comedy-Drama).

New York City provides the setting for a diverse

look at the lives of three ex couples who are also friends: one gay (Michael and Josh), one straight (Janie and Evan) and one lesbian (Dee and Darcy) and the problems each faces in their current and past relationships. **Cast:** Joel T. Bauer (Michael), Maggie Cass (Janie), Hadrian Castro (Bobby), Christopher Kramer (Evan), Erica Linderman (Darcy), Jaygee Macopugay (Dee), Najla Said (Chelsea), Stephen Tyrone Williams (Josh). **Credits:** *Producer:* Blake Drummond, Adam Fitzgerald. *Director:* Adam Fitzgerald. *Writer:* Aubrey Benmark, Michael Matthews, Brian Fountain Murray. **Comment:** Nicely portrayed saga of six diverse people and the relationship problems each faces. The acting and production values are good and the story, which contains non-objective adult situations, flows smoothly from beginning to end.

Episodes:

1. Crossing Paths. The principal characters are introduced.

2. Walking Out. As Dee and Darcy appear to be going their separate ways, Janie and Evan reconnect but only for a sexual encounter.

3. Breaking Away. Dee's life changes forever when she sees that Darcy has found a new girl (Chelsea) while Josh must contend with the fact that Michael has also moved on and Evan with the possibility of losing Janie to a new man (Bobby).

4. Rising Above. Darcy and Chelsea appear to have become a couple while Janie's new relationship takes a turn for the worse when she discovers that Bobby has concealed his health problems from her.

5. Warning Signs. Dee and Darcy, the owners of a Yoga studio, find working together becoming increasingly difficult; Michael continues to have feelings for Josh while Janie struggles to accept Bobby for who he is.

6. Falling Through. The breakup with Michael has caused Evan to turn to alcohol while Darcy and Dee seek a way to work out the problems that now exist at work.

7. Letting Go. The new couple hookups (Darcy and Chelsea; Janie and Bobby; Josh and Jesse) has their ex's realizing it is time to let them go and move on with their lives.

8. Changing Course. In the concluding episode the stage is set for the story to continue with the ex's (Dee, Michael and Evan) apparently accepting the fact that they too must let the past go.

49 *Cooking with Drag Queens.* youtube.com/user/feastoffun. 2014 (Comedy).

Cooking with a comical twist—meals prepared by drag queens. **Host:** Saltina Obama Bouvier (played by Marc Felina), Daphne DuMount (played by Fausto Fernos). Credits are not given. **Comment:** The overall style is reminiscent of TV shows like *The French Chef* and *The Galloping Gourmet* with each meal prepared—and chatter thrown into the mix. The acting and production values are very good and the program is something totally different to watch—no matter how many cooking shows you may have seen. **Episode List:** *1.* Baked Alaska. *2.* Pumpkin Pie. *3.* How to Make Coquito (a Puerto Rico eggnoglike Christmas drink). *4.* How to make Tostones (friend green plantains).

50 *The Courtney Chronicles.* dragaholic.com/2014/07/watch-courtney-chronicles-episode-1-adore-bianca-darienne/. 2014 (Humor).

A tour of America (with visits to Canada) with Drag Queen Courtney Act as the host as she and her guests view the traditional as well as the not-so-common areas of the cities. **Host:** Courtney Act. **Comment:** It was on the TV series *Australian Idol* (the Down Under version of *American Idol*) that a young man named Shane Jenek auditioned but did not make the cut. Not to be discouraged, he created the female alias of Courtney Act, auditioned again and made it through to the finals. Audiences went wild and soon Courtney (still unknown to her fans that she was a man) achieved fame as singer and later became an Australian TV personality before moving to North Hollywood in California. Courtney is an energetic performer and appeared on the sixth season (2014) of the Logo network TV series *RuPaul's Drag Race* and acquired her own show as a result of her appearances. It is hard to believe Courtney is not a real woman when you see her and knowing in advance that she is a he. The program itself is well produced and offers a slightly off-the-wall look at America as seen through the eyes of Courtney and her guests. **Episode List:**

1. Adore, Bianca and Darienne in Chicago, Toronto (for World Pride Day) and New York City.

2. Ben DeLaCreme in Seattle.

3. Cheyenne and Faith in San Francisco.

4. Adore in Vancouver.

5. Brad Loekle on the Atlantis Med Cruise.

6. Conversations with Darienne.

7. Shangela and Courtney in N.Y.C.

8. Behind the Scenes: American Ad Apparel Ad Girls.

9. Crowd Surfing @ Gay.

51 *Cowgirl Up.* onemorelesbian.com. 2011–2013 (Comic Western).

The Double D Ranch is an all-girl lesbian-themed ranch nestled in the heart of the Cochella Valley and "just a stone's throw" away from the resorts, restaurants and shopping centers of a large metropolitan city in California. It is here that gorgeous young women gather to "play cowgirl" and engage in activities such women would not normally be seen doing—from trick shooting to trick riding. The program charts their experiences as cat fighting and making love to each other is also part of the activities. Cricket and Lu are the ranch owners. Among the sexy cowgirls are Savannah, Cricket and Lu's adopted daughter; Dakota, the girl out to win every competition; Maddie, Dakota's best friend, a lesbian with a mean streak; and Robbie, the star of a western TV series called *Spur* who has come to the ranch to learn how to be a real cowgirl and do her own stunts. Rusty and Dee are ranch wranglers; Coon-Ass Kate is the girl who can't see "the lesbian thing" at the ranch and prefers "real dudes." Babe and her associate, Bitsy (a man in drag) are the local law enforcers and, adding intrigue to the story are Maeve and Snapper, con-artists who have secretly learned the ranch sits on top of oil and are now out to acquire the property for themselves.

Cast: Mandy Musgrave (Dakota), Bridget McManus (Babe), Marnie Alton (Abby), Kodi Kitchen (Dee), Melissa Denton (Lu), Linda Miller (Cricket), Shannan Leigh Reeve (Rusty), Kate McCoy (Coon-Ass Kate), Nicole Travolta (Eager Beaver), Niki Lindgren (Jo), Maribeth Monroe (Meredith), Treisa Gary (Sunny Trails), Aasha Davis (Robbie), Butch Jerinic (Chief Morning Wind), Brandy Howard (Snapper), Valery M. Ortiz (Maddie), Maeve Quinlan (Buckshot Betty), Hannah Madison Taylor (Savannah), Matt Cohen (Sheriff Bitsy Calhoun), Pam Pierce (Hooch McCarthy), Nancylee Myatt (The Boss). **Credits:** *Producer:* Nancylee Myatt, Paige Bernhardt, Matt Cohen, Christin Mell, Nicole Valentine. *Director:* Paige Bernhardt, Matt Cohen, Nancylee Myatt, Christin Mell, Courtney Rowe. *Writer:* Paige Bernhardt, Nancylee Myatt. **Comment:** "Wanna see funny and hot girls ridin' horses, shootin' guns and playin' Cowgirl?" is the tag line for an enjoyable girl eye candy series. The girls really appear to be doing their own stunts and the competition sequences, though somewhat campy, are fun to watch. The acting and production values, as with all Tello Film productions are first rate. There are kissing scenes but nothing appears to be too graphic based on the episodes that appear for free.

Episodes: Episodes are available only through a pay subscription service. The following episodes are available for free on the official website.

1. Cowgirl Up: Season 1, Episode 1: The Good, the Bad and the Pretty.

2. Cowgirl Up: Girls Gone Wild: Meredith and Dakota.

3. Cowgirl Up: Girls Gone Wild West: Jo and Eager Beaver.

4. Cowgirl Up Extra: Girls Gone Wild West: Dee and Abby.

5. Cowgirl Up: Girls Gone Wild West: Wrangler Fight.

52 *The Damiana Files.* youtube.com/ watch?v=sRkYyIyqEV8. 2010 (Comedy).

Comical commentary on stories that cover a wide range of topics—from parades and the world of Burlesque to Mardi Gras and home decorating tips by drag queens—host Damiana Garcia and her companion, Barbara Cathy with guests who resemble movie, TV and recording stars.

Cast: Michael Lucid (Damiana Garcia), Mike Rose (Barbara Cathy), Drew Droege (Tanya Roberts), Nadya Ginsburg (Cher/Madonna), Liam Sullivan (Kelly), Gudrun Flaherty (Paula), Jack Plotnick (Evie Harris), Beth Crosby (Jessica), JC Gardiner (Hunter), Willam Belli (Jessica Simpson), Drew Droege (Grimsley), Sam Pancake (Pyotor). **Credits:** *Producer-Director:* Michael Lucid. **Comment:** Clever spoof of entertainment-reporting TV shows (like *Entertainment Tonight*) with drag queens taking center stage (and spoofing name celebrities). An enjoyable program that is truly something different to watch.

Episodes: Of the 33 episodes that were produced, only the following remain on line.

1. Tanya Roberts' Decorating Tips. Former *Charlie's Angels* star Tanya Roberts provides tips on decorating your home.

2. Pageantry, Parades, Pashmina!!! Damaina and Barbara discuss their love of the Mardi Gars. Recording and film star Cher discusses her new film *Burlesque* and her co-star Christina Aguilera.

3. Kelly's Halloween Pointers. Kelly, the "Shoes" and "Let Me Borrow That Top" star tells viewers how to have the ultimate Halloween celebration.

4. Inter-Dimensional Traveler Paula. Spiritual advisor Paula Bouvon Shmooper-Best and her psychic cat Roberto reveal that Damiana has alter egos in other dimensions.

5. Evie Harris' Cabaret Showcase. Gossip reporter Evie Harris receives a visit by Damiana to discuss her upcoming showcase at the Mar Vista Community Center.

6. Thanksgiving with Jessica and Hunter. Fashion divas Jessica and Hunter reveal their latest tips for looking ones best for Thanksgiving and preparing the ultimate turkey stuffing (incorporating vodka and diet pills).

7. A Winters Tidings Processional. Damiana and Barbara comment on Christmas parades and holiday festivities.

8. Jessica Simpson's Christmas Album. A talk about Jessica's new holiday album, "Happy Christmas," leads to a discussion about Jessica revealing incidents from her past romantic relationships and her secret cookie recipe.

9. A Fancy Cat Occasion. A look at felines as Damiana and Barbara attend "The Fancy Cast Occasion" cat show.

10. At Home with Calpernia Addams. Pageant crown winner Calpernia Addams shares her history

of winning beauty contests along with her recipe for "caprsese salad," a food that transforms itself into a strong-mixed Bloody Mary when placed in the refrigerator for five minutes.

11. Easter with Deven Green. Damiana and comedienne Deven Green embark on an Easter egg hunt with a special visit from the Easter Bunny himself.

12. Christmas with Jessica and Hunter. Christmas decorating and fashion tips with divas Jessica and Hunter are explored.

13. Thanksgiving Parade with Damiana and Barbara Cathy. Damiana and Barbara provide commentary for the "A Giving of Thanks and Harvest Promenade" parade.

14. Dishing on *Drag Race* with Pandora Boxx. Pandora Boxx, a contestant on season two of the TV series *RuPaul's Drag Race* shares her feelings about the show and, with Damiana, creates a game called "Cut, Mop or Kai Kai" (wherein the Season 4 contestants of *Drag Race* are evaluated).

15. Tanya Roberts' Hollywood Ghoul House. Tanya appears to promote her new business venture, a haunted Hollywood Bed and Breakfast (Tanya's Hollywood Ghoul House).

16. Damiana and Timmie Brown Celebrate Navidad. Gal pals Damiana and Timmie travel to Mexico to celebrate that country's Navidad holiday tradition.

17. JoJo Savard Forseeing the New. Damiana visits psychic JoJo Savard for a reading to learn what the year 2013 holds in store for her.

18. Making Strong Choices with Grimsley and Pyotor. Traumatizing incidents from Damiana's past are recalled when she visits life coaches Grimsley and Pyotor to learn about their "Strong Choices" therapeutic technique.

19. St. Patrick's Day with Damiana and Barbara Cathy. Damiana and Barbara celebrate St. Patrick's Day by attending the "And Don't You Turn My Brown Eyes Green St. Patty's Day Festival Extravagreenza."

20. Gay Pride Parade. The "Steppin' Out Gay Pride Parade" is seen through the emceeing of Damiana and Barbara.

21. Halloween Parade. Damiana and Barbara's commentary as they host the "All Hallows Scream Haunt & Flaunt Spooktacular."

22. Fourth of July Parade. The "Patriotic Panoply Julybilation and Fireworks Spectacular" parade is highlighted.

23. Madonna's MDNA Interview. Madonna, the Queen of Pop, is interviewed on the release of her new album "MDNA."

24. Easter with Tanya Roberts. Easter traditions are discussed by Damiana and her gal pal Tanya Roberts.

25. Cinco de Mayo with Tammie Brown. Damiana and Timmie celebrate the festive holiday of Cinco de Mayo.

26. Halloween with Tanya Roberts. Tanya shares her tips on how to enjoy "the spooky surprises and marvelous mischief of Halloween."

53 *Dates Like This.* dateslikethis.com. 2012–2013 (Comedy-Drama).

Meg, an openly admitted lesbian, and Alicia, a straight girl, are close friends but not romantically involved with each other. They are both seeking the love of their lives and stories follow that quest in two different ways. In Season 1, Alicia, a down-to-earth girl, tries to just be herself while she seeks that special man. Meg, more inventive, has devised a scheme called "30 Dates in 30 Days" to hopefully find the woman of her dreams. With Meg's 30 Dates system not producing any positive results and Alicia also unable to find a mate, each sets out on a new course to find their special someone in Season 2. Alicia, hoping to reignite her career as a dancer (while working as a bartender) has found romance with a co-worker (Zachary) but a girl named Blake may have awoken feelings in her that she may be bisexual; Meg has several issues to deal with, including a girlfriend from her past (Vera) and her relationship with an older woman (Danielle), a boutique owner.

Cast: Hannah Vaughn (Meg), Leigh Poulos (Alicia), Kathy McCafferty (Danielle), Jessie Barr (Nikki), Rebecca Robles (Blake), Matthew Robert Gehring (Zach), William G. Kean (Scott), Natalie Fehlner (Gwen), Colin Aarons (Owen), Kristen Lazzarini (Vera), Johnny O'Malley (Dave), Keiko Green (Theresa), Jess Ritacco (Lindsay), Katie Hammond (Claire), Jillian Green (Amber), Brittany Anne Oman (Allison), Katie Rose Spence (Jessie), Jill Wurzburg (Norah), Rachel Sussman (Melody), Jenny Donoghue (Kelsey), Amanda Gardner (Stephanie), Samantha Cooper (Jacquelyn), Michelle Polera (Emily), Kiersten Armstrong (Rebecca), Libby Ewing (Dana), Alisha Spielmann (Heather), Devon Buchanan (Rory). **Credits:** *Producer-Writer:* Leigh Poulos, Hannah Vaughn. *Director:* Hannah Vaughn, Leigh Poulos (Season 1), Jessica Solce (Season 2). **Comment:** Meg and Alicia are smartly cast in a well-acted and produced program. There are several kissing scenes. The story flows smoothly from beginning to end and the program is well worth watching.

Season 1 Episodes:

1. Episode 1. Meg and Alicia are introduced as are the first few dates of Meg's "30 Dates in 30 Days" project.

2. Episode 2. As Meg continues her dating spree, Alicia seeks to begin a relationship of her own and hooks up with a man named Scott.

3. Episode 3. Alicia's relationship with Scott appears to be progressing on a positive note while Meg feels a spark when she goes on a second date with Vera.

4. Episode 4. Alicia uncovers a secret about Scott (that he has a child from a prior romance) while Meg tries to deal with a date that is a bit over enthusiastic.

5. Episode 5. As Meg ventures onto a new date

Dates Like This. **Left to right: Jessie Barr, Leigh Poulos and Rebecca Robles (copyright Team Biscuit Films).**

with a girl named Lindsay, Alicia breaks up with Scott when she finds herself unable to deal with his child from a prior relationship.

6. Episode 6. Although Lindsay is ever present on her mind, Meg tests the waters (seeing if Lindsay is her dream girl) by tackling five dates in one day. Meanwhile, Alicia, heartbroken over her breakup with Scott, plans a night out with friends to get over him.

7. Episode 7. As her 30 Days project winds down, Meg tries to get the most out of the last few dates while Alicia seeks a way to repair her relationship with Meg (which had become strained over her neglecting her for Scott).

Season 2 Episodes:

8. Happy Birthday Bitch. It is a year later and Alicia has decided to devote her energies to her career as a dancer while Meg begins a relationship with an older woman (Danielle).

9. Mona Lisas. Meg and Danielle's relationship seems to be progressing well until Danielle begins pressuring Meg into taking it one step further. Meanwhile, Alicia has attracted the attentions of her co-worker (Zachary).

10. Not So Happy Hour. Blake, Meg's best friend, pressures her to tell her more about her mystery girlfriend (Danielle). Later, Alicia invites Danielle to an upcoming concert that will be attended by Meg and worries about how Danielle will

fit into her social circle of friends. It is also at this time that a chance meeting at the bar reunites Meg with Vera, a girl she dated in Season 1.

11. Sorry Ladies. As Meg ponders what to (or not to) tell Danielle about running into Vera, Alicia tries to deal with Blake's increasing attraction to her. Her situation intensifies when Blake, feeling she is being ignored by Alicia, storms out of the bar at the Post No Bills Concert.

12. The Good, the Bad and the Boring. When Meg's encounter with Vera turns out to be better then she expected (as they seem to re-connect), she confides in her friend Nikki that she now has doubts about whom she really loves (Danielle or Vera).

13. Fork and Field. Feeling uneasy over what happened at the bar, Alicia feels she needs to face Blake and discuss her infatuation with her. Meanwhile, Meg's intense feeling for Vera lead Meg to telling Danielle that she needs time to think before moving forward with their relationship. The program concludes with Alicia's confrontation with Blake and an eye-opening experience for Alicia when Blake kisses her and Alicia is left to ponder which love to pursue—Blake or Zachary (who has just confessed his true feelings for her).

54 *Day Drunk Gays.* daydrunkgays.com. 2014 (Comedy).

Bryce, Ean, Mike and Mark are young men, in their early twenties and gay, but not dating each other. They are close friends, meet for brunch, share a drink and talk about life. The conversations that develop are shared with viewers as the friends each try to help the other deal with the issues that affect them, especially those "specific to the modern-day queer men."

Cast: Mark Cirillo (Mark), Ean Weslynn (Ean), Bryce Rankins (Bryce), Mike Callahan (Mike). **Credits:** *Producer:* Ben Simons, Ean Weslynn. *Director:* Ben Simons. *Writer:* Ean Weslynn. **Comment:** Very enjoyable, non-offensive comedy that simply relates brief incidents in the together lives of four friends who are also gay. The acting is very good and the production values and presentation comparable to a TV series.

Episodes:

1. Bruncher. Bryce finds, that being late for his daily brunch with Ean, Mark and Mike, is a no-no as they are becoming fed up with his tardiness.

2. App-Hole. As Mark re-enters the dating scene, he seeks advice from his friends on how to find an app hook-up.

3. Miranda's Wrongs. Encompassing the attributes of the girls from the TV series *Sex and the City*, the friends begin a game of match up as they try to figure out who matches whom.

4. Porn in the Morn. At their breakfast get together, Bryce objects to viewing porn so early in the morning—"We came here to eat, not watch porn."

5. Those Shorts. The guys try to convince Ean that his new shorts are too frilly and not guy shorts but girl shorts.

6. #Soo-Tired. The guys are tired and begin rambling senselessly about everything (for example, "I'm so tired I'm not responding to my Facebook people"; "I'm so tired I'm telling people I'm spiritual but not religious").

7. Beardist. Ean attempts to prove he is not a "beardest" (one who objects to beards) when Bryce and Mark, who wear beards, believe he is not approving of the way they look.

55 Derek and Cameron. youtube.com/ user/brandenblinn/playlists. 2013–2014 (Comedy-Drama).

Derek, age 26, and Cameron, 25, are roommates. Cameron is gay but Derek appears to be straight (a charming ladies' man), although he has thought and fantasized about men but has never been with one sexually. His life changes one day when his fantasies come true and he has an affair with a man—one who is not Cameron (a confident, self-assured gay since he was 15 years of age). Derek's affair with the man (Billy) changes their relationship as Cameron had feelings for Derek but never pursued them because he thought Derek was straight. The program charts the situations that affect Derek and Cameron's life

now that a third man (Billy) has entered the picture.

Cast: Brandon Crowder (Cameron), Thomas H. Adisi (Derek), Eric Colton (Billy), Samantha Stewart (Andrea), Jordan Jones (Michael), Gregory Shelby (Lance), Collin Gaveck (Jared), Mathieu Forget (Jeremy), Julia Kosenevich (Melissa), Zach Gillette (Rufus). **Credits:** *Producer:* William Branden Blinn, Timothy M. Williams, Jack Law, Michael S. Fuller. *Director:* William Branden Blinn. *Writer:* William Branden Blinn. Jordan Firstman. **Comment:** Talkative program that is well filmed and acted but concentrates too much on the situation that arises when Cameron learns of Billy. There is virtually no other story line and the program ends without really resolving the situation.

Episodes:

1. I'm a Guy. Changes confront Derek and Cameron when Cameron discovers Derek is actually gay.

2. You Have to Help Me with This. Derek and Cameron have a life-changing discussion about why Cameron feels Derek crossed the line and gave a false impression he was straight.

3. Identity. The conversation continues with Cameron claiming Derek changed the course of his life for the worse by his actions.

4. Billy. As the program concludes, Cameron is still trying to make sense out of what happened especially since Billy is eleven years younger than Derek.

56 Diary of a Black Widow. youtube.com. 2011 (Drama).

Hope is a young woman who kills without reason. She chooses a victim at random and, while she prefers to seduce them (both men and women) she will also kill them because she has no personal feelings for them and thus has no remorse. Other than an overall assumption of what the series is about, it is not possible to present further information as virtually all information, including reviews and episode descriptions have been taken off line. It is known that Hope has attached herself to another woman (Esperanza) but how is unknown and it is only revealed in the brief web site information that "she may be even more dangerous" than Hope (as she too kills). The one remaining episode on line leaves the viewer with the impression that what set Hope on her killing spree was a dream she had as a child that had intensified over the years and manifested itself into a dark reality when she became a young woman. Searching for the DVD release of the series as well as its feature film version also produces negative results.

Cast: Hannah Townsend (Hope), Shannan Leigh Reeve (Esperanza). **Credits:** *Producer:* Rydell Danzie, Timothy Leigh Reeve, Shannan Leigh Reeve. *Director:* Rydell Danzie, Tomothy Whitfield, Darin Mangan. *Writer:* Rydell Danzie. **Comment:** All episodes, with the exception of "Dreamscape" have been taken off line. Two trailers (numbers 2 and 3) and *Diary of a Black Widow Preview* can also be viewed on line. Based on what is available, the program is well acted and produced but very violent and gory. There are adult sexual situations, kissing scenes and what appears to be partial nudity (trailers are known for not giving away too much). From what can be seen, the series would have been rated TV 14 and on the lines of feature films like *Friday the 13th* but much sexier—and much more interesting to watch.

Episode List: *1.* The Eye. *2.* Vacation. *3.* Demons. *4.* The Apprentice, Part 1. *5.* The Apprentice, Part 2. *6.* Dreamscape. *7.* Empowerment of New Life. *8.* Journey. *9.* Classified. *10.* New Beginnings.

57 *Disappointing Gay Best Friend.* you tube.com/watch?v=nc83NKZcVtY&list=P LD4801D9AE40896C3. 2011 (Comedy).

Tyler is gay, but depressing; Mikala is straight and bubbly. They are best friends and share everything—that is everything Mikala experiences and tells to Tyler. Tyler is a homebody and prefers to do little to move out of his comfort zone and experience the fun side of life (or what Mikala considers fun) through her endless chatter. The reactions and responses Tyler gives to what Mikala is trying to relay to him form the basis of each episode.

Cast: Tyler Coates (Tyler), Mikala Bierna (Mikala). **Credits:** *Producer-Writer:* Tyler Coates, Mikala Bierna. *Director:* Mike Lacher. **Comment:** Delightful program that is short and right to the point (or comical punch line). Many programs in various genres have attempted this type of format (two performers in a stationary setting) and most fail to come across as entertaining. *Depressing Gay Best Friend* is one of the exceptions as it is fast-paced, well written, acted and directed. There is a bit of vulgar language but nothing overly sexual in presentation and one of the better non-offensive gay-themed programs to watch and enjoy.

Episodes:

1. Going Out. "Hey, it's Mikala, and I'm here with my best gay friend Tyler" opens each episode. Here Mikala is all excited about what to have when she eats out but all the droll Tyler can say is "I'll have some Tai and watch Netflix tonight."

2. Lady Gaga. Tyler prefers reading his book rather than listening to Mikala talk about her love of the new Lady Gaga single.

3. Fashion. Mikala is excited to show Tyler her new dress, which she believes makes her look sexy. All Tyler can offer is "It doesn't make you look fat."

4. Vodka. As Mikala talks of her enthusiasm over exotic drinks all Tyler can respond with "I like Bourbon."

5. It Gets Better. Tyler seems to be his usual self-depressed. As Mikala tries to cheer him up with "It gets better," Tyler responds with "What's it's?"

6. B.J. Mikala's talk about sex has her excited—but appears to be a turn-off for Tyler.

7. Brunch. Mikala is excited over a brunch she is going to attend with Tyler and relaying all the fancy foods at her disposal. But when asked what Tyler wants, he responds with "Oatmeal."

8. Fire Island. Tyler is puzzled. Mikala has just returned from the beach at New York's Fire Island with a suntan but wearing sun glasses. When asked why Mikala shows him—she tanned with the glasses on and now the area around her eyes is all white.

9. Date Night. Mikala attempts to help Tyler prepare for a date with her brand of advice and wisdom.

10. Bears and Otters. Curious to know what kind of gay Tyler considers himself, Mikala asks—bear or otter?

11. Hanky Codes. Mikala attempts to explain what the colors of hankies signify to men when a girl wears them.

12. Movie Night. It is Ladies' Night and Mikala is enthused to see a movie called *High Requiem and a Dream* until Tyler spoils the mood by telling her it is a film about heroin.

13. Gay Wedding. Even though Tyler is not dating anyone, Mikala begins planning his wedding wherein she will be the best man.

14. Sex. Tyler leaves the room when Mikala begins talking about sex in the series shortest episode (15 seconds).

15. Musicals. Mikala's enthusiasm over the musical *Cabaret* becomes a turn-off for Tyler as he refuses to sing its theme song with her.

16. Puppy in a Purse. Tyler is not too thrilled by Mikala's latest fashion statement when she appears with a large puppy in a purse.

17. Boyfriend. As Mikala extols the virtues of her new boyfriend, Tyler sets her straight—"He looks like an idiot."

18. Hot Tranny Mess. At a bar Mikala and Tyler met their friend Christian, a transvestite who was crying, and according to Mikala, dramatic. The following day, as Mikala rants on and on about what "a tranny mess she was," Tyler explains why—her mother passed away the day before. The program's concluding episode.

58 *District Heat.* youtube.com. 2014 (Drama).

Washington, D.C., provides the setting for look at the lives of a group of lesbians navigating lives filled with greed, lust, love and hate (and even drugs and criminal activity) with an intent to show that, depending on your position in life, there is a struggle to survive and how temptation plays a role but also how friendship and loyalty can also be a solution.

Cast: T.K. Wyl (Ali), Vaughn Crosby (Kathleen), Keke McCoy (Tinka), Teresa Carroll (Tasha), Komp L'Kade (Krys), Choppa Locka (Choppa), Torrie Wallice (Taylor), Melanie Pino-Elliott (Katie). **Cred-**

its: *Producer-Writer-Director:* Shanova McKenzie. **Comment:** Harsh program replete with foul language, a depressing mood and not very like-able characters. What the producer was trying to achieve does sound good on paper but its execution should have been more relaxed with well-defined characters not characters with little or no appeal or morale. Website information states "the twists and turns are unimaginable as the show takes you through a hurricane of events." Unfortunately, like some other African-American produced programs (straight and gay included) the lowest caliber of such people are profiled and just reinforces a stereotyped view that already exists. Granted, it is an attention-getter, but is it setting the wrong standard for future producers—no matter what race they may be as white and Asian produced programs also have the same distinction as profiling the worst characters possible.

Episodes: Six untitled episodes, labeled *Season 1, Episode 1* through *Season 1, Episode 6* have been produced.

59 *Dolls.* munecoseries.com. 2013 (Drama).

Six beautiful Lipstick-like lesbians (Iziar, Sandra, Patricia, Bea, Makial and Marta) and one gay man (German) have chosen a Freudian psychologist (Eve) to help them deal with the issues that are affecting their individual love lives. The therapy room is the essential setting and allows each of the patients to freely talk about their issues (from sexual identity to gender roles). As secrets are revealed and the participants try to bring order to their chaotic lives, stories relate those experiences with the intent being to make each member see through others experiencing the same or similar circumstance that they can be helped and lead the life they have envisioned without the fear of how their sexuality has (or is) perceived by others.

Cast: Laia Alemany (Eve), Natalia Morreno (Iziar), Inma Olms (Sandra), Maria Velesar (Patricia), Rut Santamaria (Bea), Christina Serrato (Marta), Wanda Obreke (Makial), Bart Santana (German). **Credits:** *Producer-Writer-Director:* Carlota Sayos. **Comment:** Spanish produced program that is expertly acted and produced (has all the qualities of a telenovela, the soap opera–like programs produced for Spanish TV networks like Univision and Telemundo). The program's Spanish title is *Munecos* and while that title does appear on screen, searches will also bring it up under its translated title of *Dolls*.

Episodes: Seven untitled episodes have been produced in Spanish with English subtitles only available on episodes 2–7; the pilot, which establishes the story line, has not been translated and makes it difficult to understand what is happening without knowledge of the Spanish language.

60 *Donksvile's Ghost.* youtube.com/playlist?list=PL96906926CEB63124. 2009 (Comedy).

He was once a human named Donksvile. But as a child he was bullied for being Asian. He also considered himself a part of the in-crowd but when he couldn't join a cool club at school he killed himself. But he has not moved on. He has remained earth bound and apparently "living" the same miserable life he had previously lived. He was misadventure prone then and he is misadventure prone now. Episodes relate brief incidents in the "life" of a ghost who can't seem to do anything right (and who has seemed to have grown from child to adult).

Cast: Dee Jacobs, Jr. (Donksvile). **Credits:** *Producer-Writer-Director:* Matt Bowie. **Comment:** Amusing gem that is lost amid the influx of Internet series. While not totally a gay program, two of the six produced episodes have gay story lines. The acting and production values are very good and the only "special effects" are placing the star in a sheet with eye cutouts and drawn on eye brows. His speech is that of a ghost howling, but it all works for an enjoyable change of pace—but be warned, there is foul language—both in the captions used for Donksvile and the speaking characters.

Episodes:

1. Phone Whore. Ordering a hooker over the phone proves to be a fatal mistake for Donksvile when the woman he believes is coming turns out to be a machine gun wielding killer.

2. Humungous. A take-off on the film *Mad Max 2: The Road Warrior* wherein Donksvile battles the film's bad guy, Humungous over stolen gasoline.

3. Black Magic. Sometime in his life, Donksvile loaned $50 to a demon. Through the use of Black Magic, he attempts to retrieve that loan.

4. Gay Rapist. A gay rapist (A.J. Baldy) will apparently rape anything—including his next victim, a ghost friend of Donksvile.

5. Batman's Revenge. Feeling that the pressures of the job are overwhelming him, Batman seeks the help of a psychiatrist, claiming he sees dead people.

6. Farm vs. Zoo. Donksvile's dreams are anything but normal when he "sees" a war brewing between farm animals and zoo animals.

7. Surprise Porno. A flashback recounts how young Donksvile committed suicide.

8. Batman Attacks. Back to feeling his old self, Batman wages a war on Donksvile and his ghostly companion Johnny Gobs.

9. Gay Rapist Returns. The Gay Rapist is again on the prowl, this time seeking Donksvile.

10. Bestiality Beatbox. Angry that YouTube withdrew his first video, Donksvile seeks a way to prevent them from censoring his latest, which deals with bestiality.

61 *Drag Becomes Him.* dragbecomeshim.com/. 2011 (Reality).

The personality and passion of Jerick Hoffer, an

entertainer who performs as the drag queen Jinkx Monsoon is explored.

Cast: Jerick Hoffer (Himself). **Credits:** *Producer:* Basil Shadid. *Director:* Alex Berry. **Comment:** Typical TV-like documentary style presentation that profiles the actor as he becomes his alter ego. The production values are good and the episodes are slated to be reworked as a feature film documentary scheduled for release in 2015.

Episode List: *1.* Drag Becomes Him #1. *2.* Episode Off Line (Labeled: Private Video). *3.* Drag Becomes Him #3: What It Feels Like. *4.* Drag Becomes Him #4: World on Fire. *5.* Drag Becomes Him #5: Monsoon Season.

62 *Drag Queen Problems.* youtube.com. 2014 (Advice).

Jodie Harsh, an internationally renowned DJ and club sensation drag queen offers advice to drag queens on the various issues that affect them—from how to dress and prepare makeup to how to walk in high heels and how to have sex in drag.

Host: Jodie Harsh. **Credits:** *Producer:* Thairin Smothers, Pete Williams, Blake Jacobs, Adam Asea.

Comment: While specifically geared to a drag queen audience, the program can be of interest to people just curious about how drag queens function in society.

Episode List: *1.* Sex in Drag. *2.* How to Walk in High Heels. *3.* How to Keep Lip Gloss On. *4.* Cat Queen Cat Fights. *5.* Cheating Queens. *6.* Altering Your Voice. *7.* How to Accept Multiple Compliments. *8.* Handbag Essentials. *9.* How Big Is Too Big When It Comes to Hair? *10.* Bloopers.

63 *Drag Queens Reading Obituaries.* you tube.com. 2013 (Comedy).

As obscured as the title sounds, that is exactly what the series presents: a different drag queen for each of the episodes reading an actual obituary over the Internet.

The Readers: Alexis Mendell, Pickles (as credited), Sonja Brooks, Maddox Madison, Loonsey La-Duca, Salty Brine, Penny Lou, Tasha Salad. **Credits:** *Producer:* Amey Goerlich. *Director:* Mike Kelton. **Comment:** Each of the readers simply sits on a chair and faces the camera to relate the obituary. However, mishaps occur—and these are left in as the crew can be heard laughing in the background and the reader herself reacting to what went wrong. It is sort of watching a blooper reel with all that went wrong the actual fun part of the show. The program is a unique, one-onto-itself project as no one has ever thought of turning obit reading into a series. It appears that to showcase the mishaps could have been an afterthought as without them and using a straight-forward reading would have been quite dull and not an audience grabber.

Episode List: Titles are simply the drag queen reading the obituary: *1.* Alexis. *2.* Pickles. *3.* Sonja. *4.* Maddox. *5.* Loonsey. *6.* Salty Brine. *7.* Penny. *8.* Tasha. *9.* Get to Know the Girls. A brief introduction to each of the eight drag queens is presented.

64 *Drama Queenz.* dramaqueenztheseries. com. 2008–2012 (Comedy).

Hoping to further their careers as actors, three friends who are also gay (Jeremiah, Davis and Preston) leave their homes in Queens, New York, and head to Manhattan where they not only become roommates, but each other's life support to survive the traumas of auditioning for roles and finding and dealing with love. Jeremiah is the most enthusiastic friend, full of hope and dreams but plagued by continual bad luck. Davis, the perfectionist, has set his standards for a starring role on Broadway just a bit too high and, despite all the efforts he puts into what he does, he always finds others cannot meet his demands; Preston, the most sensible one of the group, is a realist and knows that the road ahead is a tough one and even more so for gays.

Cast: Dane Joseph (Jeremiah Jones), Kristen-Alexander Griffeth (Davis Roberts), Troy Valjean Rucker (Preston Mills III), Jaylen Sansom (Tristan), Kevin Martinez (Mike), Fred Ross (Donovan), Benjamin Fischer (Trevor). **Credits:** *Producer-Writer:* Dane Joseph, Kristen-Alexander Griffeth, Troy Valjean Rucker. *Director:* Ryan Balar. **Comment:** A well-constructed story that genuinely attempts to explore the problems encountered by three like-able friends. Using black and white sequences during narrated scenes, then switching to color for what happens is different and a nice touch.

Episodes:

1. I Dreamed a Dream. The premise is established as the three roommates are introduced.

2. Unexpected Song. While the thought of stardom is uppermost on their minds, finding romance has also figured into the picture with the roomies each seeking that special someone.

3. Small World. The old saying, "It's a small world," rings true as the roomies make hook ups: Jeremiah and Donovan; Preston with Trevor; and Davis with Diego.

4. A Little Fall of Rain. The roomies wonder if the men they have each met are right as they each deal with compatibility issues.

5. By the Sea. Spending a day at Coney Island (in Brooklyn) finds Davis being swept off his feet by a Russian hunk named Sergey (Jed Resnick), Preston and Trevor becoming closer; and Jeremiah, without Donovan by his side, left to wander the play land alone.

6. Simple Little Things. Following their six-hour get-a-way to Coney Island, Preston finds he and Trevor have bonded; Jeremiah attempting to fix his strained relationship with Donovan; and Davis back

in his reluctant relationship with the controlling Diego.

7. There's Gotta Be Something Better Than This. While Preston and Trevor decide to take their romance one step further, Jeremiah and Davis feel they are now in a rut and need to make changes.

8. Ain't No Party. The season one finale wherein the roomies each learns the value of friendship when they each come to realize why they came to Manhattan and what has happened since hooking up with men who appear to have changed the direction in their lives.

9. And the World Goes Round. The second season begins as the roomies take charge of their lives and hope to get back on track and become actors.

10. That's the Way It Happens. A dispute between Preston and Davis finds Jeremiah reevaluating his purpose and wondering if becoming an actor is what he is meant to do.

11. Money. With few acting jobs and the rent due, the roomies seek ways to raise money.

12. Opening Doors. An audition appears to open a door for Preston while Jeremiah, in a new relationship with Tucker, wonders if he has made the right choice.

13. Make Them Hear You. Preston's attempts to give an outstanding audition backfires and he embarrasses himself (now needs ice cream to overcome the situation); Davis finds that turning to opera may be the break his is looking for in an effort to further his career.

14. Merrily We Roll Along. Each of the roomies takes a time out to look at where they are headed and if they are making the right choice.

15. In My Own Little Corner. As Davis explores the world of opera, the roomies find unexpected guests about to disrupt their lives—their mothers when they decide to pay their sons a visit.

16. Tomorrow. The second season finale finds Davis acquiring a role in an opera and Jeremiah contemplating his relation with Tristan.

17. Everything's Coming Up. The third season begins with each of the roomies attempting to balance work with personal conflicts.

18. Don't Tell Mama. Preston again falls apart at the seams after giving a terrible performance at an audition; Jeremiah finds himself attempting to deal with a little girl's feelings when she sees him kiss another man, calls him nasty and begins crying.

19. Something's Coming. As Preston realizes he must get his life back on track, Davis and Jeremiah meet new possible love interests.

20. I Know the Truth. The roomies recount the past 24 hours of their lives (wherein each had romantic issues).

21. My Favorite Things. A relaxing visit to Central Park is anything but when the roomies each experience something different (Jeremiah realizing he cannot keep a relationship; Davis learning that he must grow up and face life; and Preston believing

he has found a new love, a transvestite named Tranny Boi).

22. Ease on Down the Road. As Jeremiah's hopes for a job are shattered when he is not hired, Preston tries to help Davis find his new love (Tranny Boi) when he suddenly disappears. The concluding episode that leaves the doorway open for the story to continue.

65 *Duder.* duder.com. 2006 (Comedy).

Glen, a gay, and his best friend Ricky (straight) are college graduates living in Brooklyn, New York, but not all that eager to start life as they should. They are enjoying a *Seinfeld* TV-like existence where there is no story and what you do as the day progresses becomes your life—whether it is by oneself or with a group of friends. As press information states, "It's a show about a bunch of duders who just, you know, duder around a bit. It's not the size of the plot that counts, it's how you avoid it at all costs."

Cast: Matt Kirsch (Glen), Alden Ford (Ricky Paulson), Julie Lake (Judy Cakes), Daniel Levine (Paul Gruff), Gregory Kennedy (Gregory), Libby Winters (Lorraine), Justin Noble (Bill), Dru Lockwood (Zev Abrams), Satya Bhabha (Stephen). **Credits:** *Producer-Writer:* Matt Kirsch. *Director:* Katrina Whalen, Ben Kegan, Gregory Kennedy, Jeremy Robbins, Ricky Price, Ryan Iverson. **Comment:** Like-able characters, good writing, acting and directing and stories that are fun to watch. *Duder* is also one of the earliest of the comedy LGBT series and still available to watch. When searching the title as "Duder" some results will come up as "Dudes" but will still direct you to the correct program.

Episodes:

1. Pilot. Introduces the principal cast members in a story wherein Glen proves that drinking can make one do unsavory things—like becoming a racist. Meanwhile Judy, their friend, becomes a hero when, walking by an apartment house, she catches a baby that falls from an open window without a window guard.

2. If Balls Could Talk. A physical exam has Ricky a bit on edge as he fears he may have cancer.

3. The Third Sneeze. Judy appears to suffer from allergies and often sneezes, expecting to hear a "God bless you" when she does. While alone with Ricky, she experiences a sneezing attack and is mortified that Ricky never said the magic words.

4. Lil' Help. As Glen hooks up with a new boyfriend, Ricky finds himself being stalked by his ex.

5. Cat People. Zev's sudden departure leaves Ricky in a quandary—what to do with his cats? Glen comes to the rescue and, although he insists he is not a cat person, volunteers to care for the felines.

6. The Fountain. Ricky and Judy have become close and engage in a sexual act that has both puzzled when Judy climaxes in what is termed "The Fountain."

7. Nice Place. Ricky's reactions when he is invited to see Glen's new apartment.

8. Gregory. A walk in the park by Glen and Ricky unites Glen with his friend Gregory, who immediately assumes he and Ricky are a couple.

9. Who's Paul Gruff? A discussion about their "sexy, manly friend" Paul Gruff has Judy becoming hot and overly anxious to meet him.

10. Welcome Home, Paul Gruff. Ricky and Glen welcome home their long-time friend Paul Gruff.

11. Sex Dream. Ricky becomes a bit uncomfortable around Glen when Gen tells him he had a sex dream about him.

12. Lick Thing. Ricky and Judy discuss the art of turning the pages of a magazine in a typical *Seinfeld*-like story.

13. How Are Your Lives Duder? Paul is back and immediately becomes his obnoxious self when he questions Glen about what it is like being gay.

14. The Toothpaste Incident. *Seinfeld* strikes again when Judy questions the way Ricky brushes his teeth.

15. Glen's Lisp. Glen's sudden development of a lisp has him desperately trying to figure out how he acquired it.

16. Monks Are Hot. Judy's ranting about how Monks are hot has Ricky trying to change the subject and talk about something else.

17. Lost His Swipe. Paul has become terribly depressed and laments to Ricky and Glen how he no longer has the swipe ability (for his metro card) that he had before he left town.

18. Haircut. Ricky has to contend with Glen's ranting about how good he looks with a new haircut.

19. The Epileptic Cat. Ricky finds himself stuck with cat sitting Glen's felines, one of which has epilepsy.

20. More Gregory. Gay talk between Glen and Gregory.

21. Another Door Note. Ricky and Judy had developed a system of leaving each other lovey-dovey notes on their apartment doors. The latest one from Judy finds Ricky revealing that she has broken up with him.

22. Glen and Gruff. A conversation between Glen and Paul is showcased.

23. Duder Announcement. Glen appears to tell viewers that there is only one more episode left before the season concludes.

24. Gray Hairs. Ricky has hooked up with a new girl (Lorraine) who imme-diately notices that, although he is only in his early twenties, he has some gray hairs.

25. The Spoon Revisited. While in Central Park to watch the filming of a new Woody Allen movie, Glen runs into his now famous ex-boyfriend, Stephen and soon has regrets that he and Stephen had broken up.

26. Facebook Faux Pas. As a joke, Ricky posts a message to a friend on Facebook—only to discover from Glen that it was the wrong thing to do (as the friend is mourning the loss of his mother) and seeks a way to delete it.

27. The Other Glen. The concluding episode where, at his improv class, Ricky befriends a classmate named Glen, who may be gay and the perfect mate for Glen.

66 *Dumbass Filmmakers.* dumbassfilm makers.com. 2012 (Comedy).

"Abandoning Our Hopes: A Life Renewed and Lost and Forgotten" is a movie written by Harrison DeWinter, a young man who hopes that his project will help save the environment, battle injustice and promote bisexuality. Harrison, however, is not a producer or knowledgeable in any aspect of filmmaking. He is, even in the eyes of his own mother, a loser. He finds happiness in helping sea turtles find their way to the ocean; hugging big trees ("and even big, big trees") and his film was a love six years in the making. Vicki Moretti, Harrison's producing partner, is an overly organized but lonely young woman. She latches onto the film project with the hope that it will fill the void in her life and win Harrison's love, despite the fact that he is also drawn to men. Enter Bobby Tulane, a handsome ingénue who's the first person to actually understand Harrison's script at a core level, leaving Harrison hopeful, but Vicki feeling threatened and even more alone. The program charts what happens when production begins on a

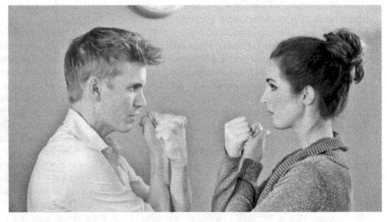

Dumbass Filmmakers. **Hunter Lee Hughes and Melinda Hughes (photograph by Jean Kim).**

film nobody understands and nobody knows what they are doing. Brenda is Harrison's castrating mother; Ricky Blaine is Harrison's vain ex-boyfriend; Scott is a casting director who knows how to play both sides of the fence; Amalia and Nancy are actresses vying for the film's leading female roles; Wanda is Harrison's talent manager. **Cast:** Hunter Lee Hughes (Harrison DeWinter), Elizabeth Gordon (Vicki Moretti), Jimmy Dinh (Scott Fleischman), Justin Schwan (Bobby Tulane), Erwin Stone (Omega), Eric Colton (Ricky Blaine), Denise D. Williamson (Wanda Jones), Dale Raoul (Brenda DeWinter), Barbara Costa (Amalia Sousa), James Lee Hernandez (Rick Rameriz), Melinda Hughes (Nancy Smith), Jared Winkler (Drew Tompkins), Adrian Quinonez (Marco Lorenzo), Ben Wells (Ned Draper). **Credits:** *Producer:* J. Parker Buell, Jason Fracaro, Elizabeth Gordon, Hunter Lee Hughes, Melinda Hughes. *Writer-Director:* Hunter Lee Hughes. **Comment:** The program is well acted and filmed and an enjoyable fantasy look at producing a film—mostly depicting all the problems that are encountered rather than actually getting it made.
Episodes:
1. What's the Story? It took six years, but Harrison has the script for his movie. The problem: it is a muddled mess that is impossible to understand.
2. Do Something. Harrison and Bobby's growing closeness has Vicki becoming jealous and seeking a way to get Harrison for herself.
3. The Rise of Bobby Tulane. Bobby's revelation that he truly understands Harrison's script has Vicki even more determined to sabotage what she sees as a blossoming romance between the two that leaves her out of the picture.
4. Amalia Makes Magic. The choice for a leading lady becomes a battle royal when Vicki tries to "go safe" by choosing Nancy while Harrison prefers the outrageous Amalia Sousa.
5. Scott Stuck in the Middle. As Vicki and Harrison's dispute over a leading actress continues, Vicki's friend Scott, a casting director trying to overcome his shady past, steps in to resolve the situation (as Amalia is chosen).
6. Destruction. With one problem settled another crops up when Wanda, Harrison's manager, informs him that she needs additional financing to continue the movie.
7. Vicki's Power Play. With a leading lady chosen, Harrison now wants Bobby to play opposite her. Vicki, unable to accept him as the male lead, suggests Marco Lorenzo and another battle ensues.
8. The Fall of Bobby Tulane. Vicki's continuing pressure to accept Marco as the leading man forces Harrison to see things her way and drop Bobby as the leading man.
9. Cappuccino Day. Scott continues his search for actors to play roles and convinces Nancy, who lost the lead to Amalia, to play the "part" of a craft

services person and a recovering sex addict (Ned Draper) to "play" the sound engineer. Meanwhile, Bobby is ordered by a surly Vicki to get coffee for the group. Scott then manipulates Bobby into allowing him to "borrow" his mother's credit card.
10. Kung Fu Connection. After devising a plan to continue the film's financing by using his mother's credit card and hiring crew members for free from the pool of desperate actors, Harrison reveals that he has a "Kung Fu" connection to help convince Rick Rameriz (James Lee Hernandez) to serve as cinematographer. Meanwhile, Scott has purchased more than $1,000 worth of goods at the coffee shop for himself. Bobby catches on, but it's too late.
11. Bobby, Harrison, a Credit Card and a Sea Turtle. Wanda's efforts to pre-sell the film have fallen through and Harrison and Vicki must now seek new avenues. Bobby returns with the credit card and admits to Vicki that Scott used it.
12. Known Quantities. The film situation turns bleak when a fraud alert prompts Brenda to lambaste Harrison for using her credit card. Vicki tries to tell him the truth about the credit card, but Harrison can't hear it. With his Plan B attempt now a failure, it appears, in the concluding episode, that the film will never be made.

67 Dyke Central. dykecentral.com. 2012 (Comedy-Drama).

Alex and Gin, classified as butch-type lesbians, are roommates (in their thirties) and part of the vibrant queer community of Oakland. Alex is attempting to sustain her dysfunctional relationship with her girlfriend Jackie, in the face of new life options and the resurfacing of an old flame. Gin is a chameleon whose identity changes with every new interest and tends to lose herself in others. Surrounded by a diverse group of friends who guide, challenge and support them, Alex and Gin struggle to make the right choices and be true to themselves. **Cast:** Tai Rockett (Alex), Giovannie Espiritu (Gin), Comika Ashby (Jackie), Carla Pauli (Fabiana), Amelia Mae Paradise (Molly), Andre Le Blanc (Mario), Tom Paul (Zack), Mahasin Munir (Sol), Ashlei Shyne (Natalie), Therese Garcia (Oli), Rain Dove (Bev). **Credits:** *Producer:* Florencia Manovil. *Director:* Florencia Manovil. *Head Writer:* Florencia Manovil. *Contributing Writers:* Arnetta Smith, Cathy Sitzes. **Comment:** Based on what has been released, it is a promising series that will detail the ups and downs of four friends. The acting and production values are very good. There is a teaser that introduces the remaining episodes coupled with a plea asking for funds to help raise the needed money. There is also a teaser on line that gives a brief look at the series as a whole.
Episodes:
1. Pilot. An introduction to the four main characters: Gin; her best friend and roommate, Alex;

Dyke Central. **Top, cast from left to right: Comika Ashby, Tai Rockett, Giovannie Espiritu, Carla Pauli (used by permission of Florencia Manovil).**

Jackie, Alex's controlling girlfriend; and Fabiana, the newcomer.

2. Taboo. Alex, Gin, and new roommate Fabiana decide to invite people over for a game night during which some of the friends' unspoken secrets are revealed.

Note: While the first two episodes, as listed above are available for free on line, episodes 3, 4 and 5 are available for viewing through purchase on the program's official website. In March of 2015, episodes 6 through 10 became available for purchase.

68 *Dykeotomy.* youtube.com. 2013 (Reality).

Emily and Liz, two very pretty lesbians, host a chat session wherein they answer questions submitted by viewers regarding lesbians.

Host: Emily Lynn, Liz Wyld. Credits are not given. **Comment:** In order for programs of this type to work you need hosts who can work off each other (like a comedy team) as well as present themselves as just regular people. Emily and Liz have accomplished this. They are charming and fun to watch and their style and presentation makes the whole show work. They do share a brief kiss now and then and the discussions are handled with care with a bit of comic overtones to make what could be dull more enticing.

Episode List: Each is a discussion on the topic presented.

1. The Introductions.
2. Bra Burning Lesbians.
3. How to Date in Secret.
4. Lesbian Bed Death.
5. Making Out in Public.
6. Coming Out Stories.
7. Seducing Straight Girls.
8. Seven Terrible Ways to Propose.
9. Breaking Up Just to Cheat.
10. Gay, Straight and In-Between.
11. Is Dyke a Bad Word?
12. Awkward Lesbian Locker Room.
13. The Gay Test.
14. Bisexual Feelings.
15. How to Spot a Lesbian.
16. Is Mulan (cartoon character) a Lesbian?
17. How to Deal with Bullies.
18. The Secret to Becoming Butch.
19. Butch to Feminine Transformation.
20. The Lesbian Test.
21. Lesbians Who Hate Men.
22. If You Like Butch, Why Not Date a Man?
23. How to Dress Like a Guy.
24. Important Update from Dykeotomy.
25. Can Straight Guys and Lesbians Be Friends?

26. Bisexuals and Lesbians.
27. Lesbians Who Date Men.
28. Seducing Straight Girls.
29. How a Butch and a Feminine Get Ready in the Morning.
30. The Glorious Blooper Reel.

69 EastSiders. eastsidersthe series.com/. 2012 (Drama).

An exploration of relationships and fidelity, not only in gay couples, but straight couples as well as seen through the activities of Cal and Thom, a gay couple, and their friend Kathy, a straight girl, and her boyfriend Ian.

Cast: Kit Williamson (Cal), Van Hansis (Thom), Constance Wu (Kathy), John Halbach (Ian), Matthew McKelligon (Jeremy), Stephen Guarino (Quincy). **Credits:** *Producer:* Chrissy Dodson, Kristyne Elizabeth Fetsic, Jonathan Stahl. *Writer-Director:* Kit Williamson. **Comment:** Light comedy mixes with drama in a program that does not focus on the sexual aspects of a relationship but on the efforts of people to solve the problems they have and make a relationship work. The acting and production values are good but due to its gay theme, may have a limited audience.

Episodes:
1. Episode 1. An evening of enjoyment at a party turns to dismay when Cal discovers that Thom has been cheating on him and Kathy, a bit unstable, believes Ian, as nice as he is, is not in love with her (all of which she is imagining).
2. Episode 2. As Cal and Thom's relationship becomes strained when Cal objects to an article Thom has written about their relationship, Jeremy, who is bisexual, sets his sights on Kathy, causing Ian to dissuade him from asking her for a date. The program's concluding episode.

70 Easy Abby. youtube.com/watch?v= PAKGQPiN-JU&list=PLc-afh1yK0_ SynyZdcVFbGSUQt-n49UlZ. 2012–2013 (Comedy-Drama).

Abby is a young lesbian seeking that special girl of her dreams. She is a chronic seducer but does not appear to realize that her aggressiveness is often the reason why she cannot maintain a steady relationship. She works in a bicycle shop, suffers from an

Easy Abby. **The program's poster art (copyright Juicy Planet Pictures).**

anxiety disorder and her world is one filled with neurotic characters. Abby's struggles to make ends meet, deal with the problems of her disorder and somehow find that one special woman are explored in a lighthearted manner.

Cast: Lisa Cordoleone (Abby), Emily Shain (Sara), Laura Chernicky (Eileen), Mouzam Makkar (Danielle), Karmine Byrne (Carolyn), Brian Plocharczyk (Charlie), Leeron Silberberg (Kelly), Lana Smithner (Laura), Fawzia Mirza (Bobbie), Haviland Stillwell (Lydia), Adria Dawn (Angela). **Credits:** *Writer-Director:* Wendy Jo Carlton. **Comment:** There are suggestive romantic encounters coupled with tender kissing scenes but nothing is taken to the point of being too racy even for broadcast TV. The acting and production values are very good and the program, although aimed at a specific audience, can be enjoyed by anyone.

Episodes:

1. Portable Feast. Abby's accidental encounter with a former lover has her wondering if she has what it takes to fall in love when she can not recall the girl's name.

2. Pie's the Limit. As Abby's friends Carolyn and Sara host a dinner party, Abby finds herself talked into a blind date with a woman she actually dated before.

3. Naming the Baby. Abby's date fosters a one night stand while Sara, believing Carolyn is cheating on her, decides to crash at Abby's apartment.

4. Bacon and Legs. Abby tries to cheer up a depressed Sara by introducing her to a group of women at a mid-day brunch.

5. Danish Twist. At a restaurant Abby encounters a girl she once dated, but never reconnected with (they make up for lost time by making out in the ladies' room).

6. Love Monkey. While at work, Abby confides in her co-worker that her mother's arrival has put a damper on her dating life as her mother just doesn't understand her sexual preference.

7. No Fly Zone. With her mother gone and her life seemingly back to normal, Abby finds another distraction when her neighbor, Lydia, interrupts a love-making session to complain that Abby leaves her household garbage on the side of the disposal rather than placing it inside.

8. Martini in the Closet. With Sara still reeling over her breakup with Carolyn, Abby takes her to a lesbian bar—where a stranger (Eileen) makes a play for Sara.

9. Walk Before You Run. After several beers, Sara warms up to Eileen and the two leave the bar together—without Abby.

10. Icing on the Sponge Cake. Abby, tending bar at a wedding reception discovers what making love to an older woman is all about when the bride's mother seduces her and the two have a brief affair.

11. How to Travel Light. Abby hooks up with Danielle, the pretty bartender she met in episode 8.

12. The Meatball Test. After accidentally locking herself out of her apartment, Abby meets her lesbian neighbors (Bobbie and Lydia) for the first time as the program concludes.

71 *Emma Stahl.* onemorelesbian.com. 2010 (Drama).

With organized crime on the rise and terrorist threats becoming more prevalent, the German government organizes a specialized unit composed of its best agents from its various branches of law enforcement. Emma Stahl, a beautiful woman attracted to both women and adventure (but not necessarily in that order) is its top agent. Emma is seductive and her sexuality is her most effective weapon against the enemy. The program charts Emma's case assignments as she not only battles evil, but seduces the women who thrive on breaking the law.

Cast: Meike Gottschalk (Emma Stahl), Gerrit Spangenberg (Emma's partner), Uwe Rapschlaeger (Regie), Matthias Van Denberg (Bornheim), Mira Herold (Fria Bornheim). **Credits:** *Producer:* Sandra Viedot. **Comment:** It appears that only a teaser has been released. It is well acted and produced and shows great potential as being an intriguing series. It is produced in Germany and has subtitles for American audiences.

Episodes:

1. Pilot Teaser. The proposed first story line is established as Emma is assigned to assist local police in uncovering a band of terrorists whose strikes have been killing innocent people.

72 *Empire.* empiretheseries.com/. 2010 (Drama).

Long Island in New York provides the setting for a look at a powerful and wealthy family (the Havens), the owners of the society magazine *Empire* and how they struggle to keep their publishing empire afloat amidst the secrets they hide that could eventually destroy them. While the program is not totally geared to LGBT characters, it does present a storyline revolving around the gay characters of Cane Haven and Jake Harper.

Cubbie Haven is the second born son and currently runs Empire. He is married to Sandra and is the father of three sons, Thomas, Evan and Cane (Thomas and Evan resulted from an affair Sandra had with Cubbie's older brother Arthur). When Cubbie discovered what Sandra had done, he retaliated by sleeping with the family maid (an affair that led to the birth of Katherine; see below).

Ethan Haven, the middle child, has set his goal to prove to his father that he is capable of running *Empire* magazine but living in the shadow of his older brother, Thomas, has put a damper on his goal.

Cane Haven, the youngest of the three brothers, was disavowed by the family when it was discovered he was gay. He works as a private detective and had a relationship with Alex Russo.

Katherine Valentine is the girl who was cared for by Cubbie and Sandra after her mother, a maid to the Havens, died. Unknown to Katherine, Cubbie is her biological father.

Theodora Grant Haven, the daughter of West Coast publishing legend Theodore Grant, is also the widow of Arthur Haven (Cubbie's older brother) and has set her goal to destroy Sandra and Cubbie's marriage—and acquire Empire in the process (a goal set in motion when she discovered that Sandra fathered two sons with Arthur while he was married to her).

Thomas Haven, the eldest of the sons, is the family's black sheep. He was arrested and convicted for statutory rape (a tryst with a 15-year-old male hooker). He served time in prison and later tricked a young woman (Marin Lively) into marrying him. Disgraced by what he had done with his life, Thomas simply vanished and his whereabouts are unknown.

Sandra, Cubbie's wife, is the daughter of a wealthy New England family and met Cubbie while at Harvard.

Marin Lively is the girl who grew up with the Haven brothers (Evan has always been her best friend), but it was Thomas she had been set to marry—until his tryst with an underage male prostitute temporarily ended their relationship. When Thomas was released from prison, he and Marin reconnected and they married—when Marin discovered that her marriage would allow Evan (whom she really loved) to take full control of Empire. Her plan backfired when Evan found out, and angered that Marin and Thomas had married, got even by exposing Marin's teen sister's pregnancy in *Empire* and eventually forcing Marin to leave Thomas and Long Island.

Irving Reed is Cubbie's friend and rival from his college days. He now works as a high-powered attorney (although his practices have him under investigation for fraud and embezzlement) and is married to Kinky (her real name), his second wife, a former stripper.

Colleen Lively, the single mother of Lucy, was a promising actress who traded fame and fortune for marriage to a popular politician.

Lucy Lively, Colleen's daughter, has been pampered by her mother and has ruined her chances of becoming a beauty pageant winner Colleen had set for her by becoming pregnant by her gay best friend (Jake Harper).

Cast: Nick Lewis (Evan Haven), Tina Sloan (Theodora Grant Haven), Kathryn Neville Browne (Sandra Haven), Chris Douros (Thomas Haven), Ryan Clardy (Cane Haven), Richard Flight (Cubbie Haven), Annalisa Derr (Katherine Valentine), Josh Davis (Jesse Jordan), Lise Fisher (Rachel Stone), Christian Barber (Rodney Dillon), Orlagh Cassidy (Colleen Lively), Afton Boggiano (Lucy Lively), Kate Forsatz (Marin Lively), Toby Levin (Jake Harper), Yvonne Perry (Valerie), Harlan J. Strauss (Irving Reed), Mary Leggio (Leslie Reed), Kevin DeBacker (Landon Reed), Heidi Jane Sparks (Kinky Reed), Chris J. Handley (Lance), Morgan Lindsey Tachco (Norma Morton), Molly Bennett (Lisa), Mark Hapka (Trevor), Lauren B. Martin (Bailey), Ellen Dolan (Bag Lady), Von Hottie (Herself), Casey Jon Deidrick (Gabe), Shane Zeigler (Wesley). **Credits:** *Producer-Director:* Steven Slate, Greg Turner, Brian Hewson. *Writer:* Brian Hewson, Craig Turner. **Comment:** Well acted serial-like soap opera whose format has been done numerous times before on television—from 1970s shows like *Beacon Hill* to 2000s *Dirt*. Searching the program will also bring up a 1960s NBC series called *Empire* but the two are not related in any manner.

Episode List: The exact number of episodes is unknown. Below is a list of what appears on You Tube.

Season 1: Untitled Episodes 1 through 10 (July 12, 2009–Aug. 6, 2009).

Season 2: Untitled Episodes 11 through 20 (Sept. 12, 2009–June 29, 2010). Episode 3 is off-line.

Season 3: Episodes 21–28 (Nov. 8, 2010–Jan. 10, 2011). Episode 25 is off-line. Titled episodes are *Bedfellows* (23; Dec. 29, 2010), *A New Normal* (24; Dec. 7, 2010), *Part of the Family* (26; Dec. 20, 2010), *Kiss and Show* (27; Jan. 3, 2011), *Cover Girls* (28; Jan. 10, 2011).

Season 4: Episodes 29–33 (July 23, 2012–Aug. 13, 2012). Titles: *Where's the Party?* (29; July 31, 2012), *Causing a Commotion* (30; July 24, 2012), *Live to Tell* (31; July 30, 2012), *I Don't Give a...* (32; Aug. 16, 2012), *Don't Tell Me* (33; Aug. 13, 2012).

Empire Website Episodes:
1. Season One: The Beginning.
2. Season Two: Sex, Secrets, Secret Rooms.
3. Season Three: Trysts and Takeover.
4. Season Four: Sex, Scandal, Soap.

Note: With the exception of Season 3, which is more of a recap, the other episodes are teasers for the season and what to expect. Actual episodes are not available for viewing.

73 Entangled with You. entangledwith you.com. 2013 (Drama).

A look at the lives of four people seeking happiness but dealing with situations that threatens to destroy their relationships as a couple: Jaliyah and Rocky (lesbians) and Alisha and Craig (straight). Rocky is aggressive and wants a commitment but Jaliyah is fearful of doing so, feeling the time is just not right. Alisha, a trusting woman, and Craig, a bit deceiving, are living together and appear to be happy. Alisha's continual reluctance has Rocky believing they need time apart and leaves her. Discovering that he has a sexually transmitted disease (Gonorrhea) that resulted from an affair he had while committed to Alisha, has Alisha leaving Craig when he decides to tell her, but waited until their anniversary to do so. In a strange twist of fate, Alisha and Jaliyah, total strangers to each other, become roommates. Alisha and Jaliyah, however, find separating is not easy as Craig seeks to win Alisha back and Rocky becomes jealous of her lost love's (Jaliyah) new roommate (Alisha). The program follows the four individuals as they deal with the circumstances of what has happened and try to move on but always realizing that their true loves are still in the picture.

Cast: Loren Lillian (Jaliyah), Kathryn Taylor (Alisha), Jessica Meza (Rocky), Shannan Leigh Reeve (Jen), Al Thompson (Craig), David Spates (Darrell), Vana Bell (Mickey), Crystal Coney (Candice). **Credits:** *Producer:* Caryn K. Hayes, Carolyn

O. Jacobs. *Writer-Director:* Caryn K. Hayes. **Comment:** Although the program ends unresolved, it is well produced and acted. While tame by some Internet series, it does contain adult situations but nothing that is overly graphic.

Episodes:

1. Just Say It. As Alisha and Craig celebrate their anniversary, Craig revels that he has Gonorrhea. Meanwhile Jaliyah is reluctant to give into Rocky's demands of making a commitment.

2. Moving Out, Moving In, Moving On? Rocky feels that she may have been too demanding with Jaliyah and seeks to change that. Meanwhile Alisha and Jaliyah have decided to become roommates.

3. Your Blues Ain't Mine. As Jaliyah and Rocky attempt to move on, they find that leaving the past behind is not as easy as they thought as their ex-s are still a part of their lives.

4. Got 'Til It's Gone. Craig's persistent attempts to win Alisha back are causing more harm than good while Rocky's efforts are making Jaliyha uneasy and having a negative effect on her (affecting her work as a writer). The program's concluding episode.

74 *Everyone Is Gay.* everyoneisgay.com/. 2011–2014 (Advice).

Dannielle and Kristin, two very pretty real life lovers, offer their opinions and try to help people with their problems, most of which are geared to the LGBT community.

Host: Dannielle and Kristin (as they credit themselves). Credits are not given. **Comment:** The hosts work well together and offer advice based on their own experiences. They are dedicated to helping the LGBT community and feel that through their program they can best achieve that goal. To lighten up episodes, Kristin and Dannielle perform a lip-synched song against superimposed backgrounds.

Episode List:

1. Proposal Ideas.
2. Lesbian but Making Out with Boys.
3. 10 Worst Ways to Come Out.
4. Pick Up Truck Love.
5. My Parents Think My Friend Turned Me Gay.
6. Giving Your Number.
7. Identity Bulls**t.
8. Two Girls Love Me.
9. Parents and Pronouns.
10. Gay Guy Love.
11. I Hate Everyone.
12. Pre-Wedding Fights.
13. I Don't Want a Relationship.
14. Gaydar.
15. Offended Religious Parents.
16. Attached Too Fast.
17. LGBTQ Inclusion.
18. Romantic Confusion.
19. Religious Self Hate.
20. Dealing with Cat Haters.
21. Home for the Holidays.
22. How to "Look More Queer."
23. Different Sex Drives, Help!
24. Dealing with Mixed Signals.
25. Scared to Misrepresent LGBTQ.
26. Selfish Bisexuals.
27. My Sister Is Gay, Too.
28. He's Flirting but Has a Girlfriend.
29. Too Young to Know?
30. The Parents Project.
31. Am I Going to Hell?
32. How Do I Tell My Roommate?
33. In Love with a Straightie.
34. Being Vocal About Sex.
35. Feeling Jealous + Looking Too Straight.
36. Being Awkward + Sex Before Marriage.
37. Clothes Shopping + Angry Girlfriend.
38. LGBTQ After College + Prom Ideas.
39. Only Gay Because of Surroundings + Love Notes.
40. Dreams About the Ex.
41. Family Financial Support + Anniversary Gift.
42. Talking Is Hard + Dangerous Flirting.
43. Out to Mom's Family + Friend Zone.
44. Inappropriate Roommate + Funny Ways to Come Out.
45. Commitment + Being Cheated On.
46. Attracted to Androgyny + Cheap Dates.
47. Gay Sisters + Booty Calling.
48. Online Dating + Lesbian Living Arrangements.
49. Gay Wannabe? + Being Shy.
50. Family Mocks My Clothes + Mother-in-Law Trouble.
51. Sexual Confusion + Lesbians Tease Me.
52. Gay Is Gross?! + Talking to Straight Friends.
53. Expanding Gender Identity + Getting Game.
54. Too Soon to Be My Girlfriend? + Anxiety Help.
55. Relationship Confusion + Homophobic Classmates.
56. Is It a Date? + Transitioning Partner.
57. Body Image + Meeting Gays.
58. Poem Romance + Unacceptable Home Environment.
59. Is She Gay? + Friends Meeting.
60. Breaking It Off + Am I Straight?
61. Jealous Girlfriend + OCD and Dating.
62. Being Led On + Saying "I Love You."
63. Coming Out at Work + Rebounds.
64. Talking About Lying + Coming on Too Strong.
65. Prom Dates + Gay and Christian.
66. Explaining Trans + First Kiss.
67. Watching Porn + Helping Insecure Girlfriend.
68. Family-Girlfriend Tension + Friends Say I'm Gay.
69. Explaining Attraction + Navigating Friendships.

70. Teasing a Crush + Slowing Things Down.
71. Age Differences + Protective Parents.
72. Girlfriend Moved On + Effects of an Ex.
73. Talking About Marriage + Friends Being Weird.
74. Body Self-Esteem + Being Misgendered.
75. Snuggling Struggles + Back in the Closet.
76. Dealing with Bullies + Uninterested Parents.
77. Navigating Sleepovers + Offensive Language.
78. Speaking Up + Not Being Out.
79. Straight Girl Love + Living with an Ex.
80. Not Ready for Sex + Name Calling.
81. Might Be Gay? + Anniversary Ideas.
82. Being Sad + Giving Roses.
83. Saying You Love Her + Relationship Regret.
84. Depression + Pronoun Help.
85. Talking about Asperser's + Red Flags.
86. Attracted to BFF + LGBTQ Meetings.
87. Re-Coming Out + Long-Distance Lovin'.
88. Expressing Attraction + Starting to Date.
89. Differing Expectations + Homophobic Employer.
90. Flirting with Women + Convincing Your Parents.
91. PDA Compromises + Navigating Flirting.
92. Allowing Sleepovers + Supporting Parents.
93. Talking About Herpes + Letting Someone Down.
94. Hookups with Friends + Sexual Chemistry.
95. Approaching a Crush + Defining Cheating.
96. Stubborn Girlfriend + Using Sex Toys.
97. Dating Younger + Dealing with Cheating.
98. Drunk Dialing + Ex Leads Me On.
99. Asking Someone Out + Bitch-Ass Hoes.
100. Addressing Sexual Assault + Not "The One."
101. Responding to Homophobia + Questioning Sexuality.
102. Feminism and Sexuality + Is My Crush Gay?
103. Out at Work + Asking Someone Out.
104. How to Re-Come Out + Using Labels.
105. Same Name Drama + More Than "The Lesbian."
106. Getting Over an Ex + Leading Someone On.
107. Gay Dating Etiquette + "Real" Sex.
108. Judgmental Parent + Talking with Family.
109. Long-Distance Relationships + Complicated Love.
110. Talking with Parents + Who Would You Eat?
111. Normal Lesbians? + Y'all Are Quacks.
112. The "Gay Friend" + Being Self-Conscious.
113. Talking to Girls.

75 F to 7th. fto7th.com. 2013 (Comedy-Drama).

Ingrid is a woman who has led a carefree life. She is a lesbian, lives in Brooklyn, New York, and has enjoyed many relationships with other women but has not considered the future. Her years of casual relationships have left her without a steady lover and her sudden realization that she is approaching middle age has her concerned about what steps to take next. Ingrid, who could be considered a butch type lesbian (as opposed to the more feminine Lipstick Lesbian) has set her goal to change her ways and find that one special woman with the program charting her efforts (assisted by her friend Alex) to embrace who she is and deal with her descent into pre-middle-age.

Cast: Ingrid Jungermann (Ingrid), Casey Legler (Simone), Ashlie Atkinson (Alex), Ann Carr (Ann), R.J. Foster (Ron), Elizabeth Gifford (Evelyn), Gaby Hoffmann (Devon), Hye Mee Na (Mel), Amy Sedaris (Kate), Michael Showalter (Ben), Brandi Ryans (Lila), Isaiah Stokes (Alan), Kathleen Wise (Liz), Stewart Thorndike (Dr. Thorndike). **Credits:** *Producer:* Jason Klorfein. *Writer-Director:* Ingrid Jungermann. **Comment:** Light drama mixes with comedy in an attempt to show an older woman facing life in a lesbian community (sort of akin to the adult film industry's glamorizing older women in its series of MILF [Middle-Aged Housewives] series of XXX Videos). The program is well acted and produced and a change of pace in the many lesbian-themed programs on television and the Internet.

Episodes:

1. Off-Leash Hours. The pilot episode that introduces Ingrid and the situation she encounters—helping decide which of the two men she meets better cares for his dog.

2. Tweener. At a Wet Lips (all-girl) softball game in Prospect Park, Ingrid and her girlfriend Alex debate whether or not Ingrid should admit she is a butch-type lesbian.

3. Interchangeable. Feeling a bit lonely, Ingrid hooks up with another girl (Ann) and finds her evening turning from talking to romancing.

4. Family. A visit from Ingrid's aunt (Kate) finds Ingrid becoming uneasy when Kate takes an unexpected and vested interest in her life style.

5. Straight Talk. A conversation between Ingrid and her friend Devon, a mother who loves to flirt, reveals that straight women only seduce lesbians when there is no other option.

6. Gyno. An uncomfortable time for Ingrid when she pays a visit to her gynecologist only to discover her physician has been replaced by a rather unorthodox doctor (Thorndike).

7. Gowanus. Realizing that she has "transphobia" (trouble accepting transvestites), Ingrid talks Alex into helping her overcome her problem by attending a "hip trans party" in Gowanus, Brooklyn.

8. Intersex. Recalling her earlier conversation with Alex, Ingrid finally comes to terms with the fact that she is a butch lesbian.

76 *The Fab Femme.* thefabfemme.com. 2014 (Reality).

A program of "advice, LGBT news, love, politics, gossip, Lipstick Lez and diversity" aimed at the lesbian community to "celebrate you."

Host: Chanel Brown. Credits are not given. **Comment:** While the program's description makes it sound like an *Entertainment Tonight*–like presentation, it is basically just the host and her guest discussing matters. Chanel is a personable host and the program is informative. **Episodes:** Three episodes were produced and each is just a discussion with the host and her women guests.

1. The Fab You: Julia. 2. The Fab You: Stephanie. 3. The Fab You: Kiarra.

77 *Fabulous High.* fabuloushigh.com. 2013 (Drama).

"We want *Fabulous High* to set a new standard for LGBT media" is stated by the program's producers in their series description. While Sierra Mar High (the school seen in the program) may outwardly appear as any high school seen on TV or in the movies, it's student body is skewed more to an "R" rated movie look as opposed to a "G" rated TV profile. Incorporating characters who are straight, gay and lesbian (with the latter two struggling to cope with new sexual identities) as well as those who abuse drugs and alcohol and those that have little or no respect for the law, a picture of what high school life is really about in many cities (and even small towns) is presented. The program focuses on students of different cultures (as well as the stereotypes) and how they not only deal with the pressures of high school life but everyday life and society in general.

Cast: Chris Schellenger (Ryan Woodson), Derek Efrain Villanueva (Jesse Avila), Kimberly Tran (Brooke Lee), Cameron Koa (Cade), Sal Sabella (Dr. Tony Weaver), Jennifer Starr (Elly), Brooke Hutton (Kelly), Kathy Di Stefano (Stacy), Tiffany Glo Malloy (Anita), Price Adam Triche, Jr. (Lalo), Austin Crow (Phil), Barrett Crake (Scott), Taylor Caldwell (Austin), Deidre Lee (Clara), Nancy Henriksen (Maggie Woodson), Iris Taylor (Kay Matsen), Steven Wishnoff (Principal Doug Adams). **Credits:** *Producer:* Derek Efrain Villanueva, Michael Turner, Andrea Krauss, Doug Adams, Renee S. Baltsen, Steven Wayne Kaplan. *Director:* Sean Willis. *Writer:* Derek Efrain Villanueva. **Comment:** Instantly the viewer will see that the program goes far beyond anything high school oriented TV programs like *Saved by the Bell* and *Welcome Back Kotter* ever dared to show or even hint at; even the dramatic *Beverly Hills, 90210*, while somewhat realistic, ventured far from what *Fabulous High* covers in detail: gay and lesbian sexual situations (mostly kissing scenes), drug use, vulgar language, teacher disrespect, break-ing the law and rebellion. Episodes should be preceded by a parental warning for its stark reality but isn't as kids will easily mistake the program for a *Saved by the Bell*–like comedy just by the title. The acting is very good and the production is such that you can feel for some of the students and truly dislike others for what they are doing or what is happening to them. The only complaint would be the use of the annoying shaky camera method of filming, which is not to everyone's liking.

Episodes: Only a pilot film that has been broken down into three parts has been produced. It establishes that one student in particular, Ryan Woodson, the son of a congressman, is the school's main bad boy and will follow him and his friends (Brooke and Jesse) as they navigate high school life.

78 *Fagney and Gaycey.* youtube.com/ watch?v=lTnim91d_KY. 2009–2010 (Comedy).

A take-off on the 1980s CBS TV series *Cagney and Lacey* that dealt with the investigations of N.Y.P.D. detectives Chris Cagney (Sharon Gless) and Mary Beth Lacey (Tyne Daly). While Cagney and Lacey were women, they were not lesbians, just best friends. Ron Fagney and Walter Gaycey are detectives with the L.A.P.D. and, if their last names didn't define them, their actions do as they are not only gay but lovers. Crime is rampant; Ron and Walter appear to be the best detectives on the force and stories relate their efforts to solve unusual crimes in the gayest like manner possible.

Cast: Mike Rose (Det. Ron Fagney), Drew Droege (Walter Gaycey), George McGrath (Lt. Mc-Grath), Andie Bolt (Off. Andie), Amy Procacci (Off. Amy), Brennan Campbell (Off. Brennan). **Credits:** *Producer-Writer-Director:* Mike Rose. **Comment:** Anyone familiar with the CBS series will immediately recognize that the show's musical theme ("The Theme from Cagney and Lacey") has been used here with similar opening visuals. The first episode is reminiscent of a *Cagney and Lacey* opening theme visual where Chris and Mary Beth arrest a flasher. *Fagney and Gaycey* is a clever take-off with good acting and production values but an overabundance of gayness to replicate the friendship that excited between Chris and Mary Beth.

Episodes:

1. Flasher. Ron and Walter seek a deranged flasher who kills people after exposing himself.

2. Baby, Baby, Baby. A series of baby kidnappings in broad daylight has Ron and Walter struggling to figure out who would do such a dastardly thing.

3. Black and Blue. Police work takes second stage as Ron and Walter plan their gay Halloween party.

4. Episode 4. Having solved one case of flashing sort of makes Ron and Walter experts as their next case involves going undercover to find a killer in a flash mob.

5. Episode 5. Tired of being hounded by the relentless Ron and Walter, a deranged killer plots to rid his life of them by luring them into a trap and blowing them up. The program's concluding episode.

79 *Far Out.* youtube.com. 2009 (Drama).

A group of British women, some of whom are lesbians and others that are bisexual, are profiled as they experience life and attempt to cope with who they are and who they want to be with romantically. Billed as "Britain's first-ever Lesbian web series" and "The Lesbian Queer as Folk."

Cast: Grace Wendy Allen (Grace), Faye Hughes (Kat). **Credits:** *Producer-Writer-Creator:* Faye Hughes. **Comment:** All the episodes have been withdrawn from the Internet as well as virtually all text information, including the cast and credits. Based on the only visual evidence that exists (the trailer on the official site and on YouTube), the series appears to be quite provocative and well-acted although with an echoing-like sound track and thick British accents it is difficult to understand dialogue at times. Drama appears to mix with comedy and no specific reason is given as to why the series was taken off-line. The women are very attractive and Grace Wendy Allen and Faye Hughes are the only cast members listed with Faye Hughes also being the creator and writer. There are a number of lesbian web series (for example, *Easy Abby* and *Seeking Simone*) and it appears that *Far Out* is the more sexually explicit of the group.

80 *Fat Guy.* fatguyshow.com. 2011 (Comedy).

Caskey is a young gay man in his twenties. He was born in the Midwest and has journeyed to New York City to further his dream of becoming an actor. He manages to acquire an agent (Susan) and has two best friends (Eva and Kelly) and a problem—he is a bit overweight and somewhat pasty-looking. Although he has his faults, Caskey is determined not to let them deter him from becoming an actor. The program charts his adventures and specifically what happens when he does a billboard ad for a diet pill called DrastiSlim and finds himself embroiled in a scandal when a before shot of him is used with an after shot of a faked slim him—and a warning that use of the pill causes brain cancer.

Cast: Caskey Hunsader (Caskey), Eva Shure (Eva), Andrew Wehling (Greg), Kelly Shoemaker (Kelly), Kristin Maloney (Susan), Lauren Kadel (Kim), Sari Schwartz (Melissa Bennett Mendoza), Jacob Bressers (Susan's assistant). **Credits:** *Producer-Writer-Director:* Caskey Hunsader. **Comment:** "Welcome to the Biggest Series on the Web" is an appropriate tag line for a very enjoyable program with good acting and production values. Choosing to have a "fat guy" as the central figure adds to the

Fat Guy. **Series logo (copyright Upstairs Landing Productions).**

enjoyment as people can relate better to him rather than people who are over-the-top, exceptionally handsome or extraordinarily beautiful as these people do not seem to face everyday problems like "the less fortunate" on TV or in feature films.

Episodes:

1. The Offer. Caskey meets with his agent Susan to discover that she has booked him a photo shoot for a new diet pill called DrastiSlim.

2. The Shoot. After discussing the job with Eva, Caskey appears for the photo shoot but is unaware that the billboard will be faked.

3. The Show. To celebrate the shoot, Eva invites Caskey to one of her show performances and plays cupid by introducing him to Greg.

4. The Date. The billboard has been placed in Times Square but Caskey has yet to see it. Meanwhile, he tells Eva that he and Greg hit it off.

5. The Billboard. Caskey sees the billboard—"I use to hate my Body.... But now I don't. Thanks, DrastiSlim." A before and after photo appears and Caskey, who never even took the pill, gets an uneasy feeling about what has happened.

6. The Aftermath. The billboard has stirred interest but Caskey is fearful and meets with Susan in an effort to stop it from spreading.

7. The Audition. Much to Caskey's surprise, the billboard has producers seeking him and Susan sets him up with a TV casting call that results in disappointment for Caskey when they see he is not the slim Caskey pictured in ads for DrastiSlim and reject him.

8. The Scandal. As TV news woman Melissa Bennett Mendoza reports uncovered evidence that use of DrastiSlim causes brain cancer, Caskey suddenly finds himself being a target of the media—who want the inside story about DrastiSlim.

9. The End. Caskey's world begins to deteriorate around him when Greg, believing that the pill causes brain cancer, confesses that he will not be able to handle the upcoming medical crises and breaks up with him. As the program ends, the scandal has gotten worse—ads for the product are appearing in international magazines.

81 Feed. webserieschannel.com. 2008 (Drama).

Maura Knight is a young woman working as a news blogger for True World, an on-line website. One night, while watching the news on CBN, a story is broadcast covering a beheading in Iraq that shows the incident in graphic detail (the result of someone hacking into the CBN server and releasing the raw, uncut footage). The incident has an adverse effect on Maura and sets her on a path to do something about injustice, beginning in her home town of Los Angeles. Hiding her true identity, Maura posts a video to tell people about the atrocities that are occurring around them and how it needs to be stopped. Her posts soon earn her the name The Vigilante Journalist (also called The Digital Vigilante) and, armed with her camera she begins a one-woman mission to expose the crime and what is really happening on the streets of Los Angeles through the Internet.

Cast: Amanda Deibert (Maura Knight), Sarah Maine (Charlie Hampton), Daniel Miller (Mike Vitorro), Alexandree Antoine (Tanya Edwards), Jennifer Morton (Lisa Dobbyn), Christi Castellande (Bianca), Erin Kelly (Tara), Mike Myers (Mario Carrera). **Credits:** *Producer:* Heroine Films. *Writer-Director:* Mel Robertson. **Comment:** The program is captivating with good acting and production values. Although billed as "A Lesbian Web Series" (as Maura is a lesbian) it is not in the traditional sense as there are no sexual situations. There is vulgar language but it has been edited indicating that producers felt it would play better this way as opposed to leaving it in. Editing might also explain the story line inconsistencies stated in the episode listing.

Episodes:

1. Beheading. Maura is introduced as the CBN newscast of a beheading in Iraq sets her on a path to do something about criminal activity in Los Angeles.

2. Lorna Michaels Exclusive. Maura, in disguise, allows CBN news reporter Lorna Michaels (who dubbed her The Digital Vigilante) to interview her in a further attempt to get her message to the people.

3. Lorna Goes Down. As the interview continues, Lorna is blindfolded and taken to a secret location to see that a digital underground is being formed to expose crime and bring the guilty to justice.

4. Maura's Reality. A flashback explores Maura's life before she became a news blogger to the night of the CBN newscast.

5. On the Fence. Reveals that Maura is sexually attracted to her alluring female coworker, Charlie (and vice versa) and how, after sharing a drink, they are starting to become intimate.

6. Going Down. After working late into the night, Maura and Charlie give into their sexual desires and spend the night together. Unknown to them, they have been observed by a fellow worker at True World.

7. Escape Plan. While it shouldn't matter what Maura and Charlie did together, it causes a ripple at True World and Maura is fired.

8. The Breaks. With bills to pay, Maura finds a job at a restaurant but has not yet resumed her secret alias as The Digital Vigilante.

9. Surveillance. Events will soon change the course of Maura's life. Maura and Tara (a waitress) are alone in the restaurant when two men enter. Maura is in the kitchen when she hears a ruckus and sees the men attempting to rape Tara. Maura, with camera in hand, decides to record what is happening rather than interfere (Tara is saved when a third man, Mike, standing guard outside the restaurant sees what is happening and puts an end to the situation).

10. The Family Problem. While it is not explained exactly how CBN acquired Maura's video of the attempted rape, it is broadcast by CBN and puts Maura's and Mike's lives in jeopardy when one of the men who attempted to rape Tara is exposed as the son of a crime boss—a crime boss who now wants Maura dead and puts a contract out on her.

11. Uninvited Guests. Although it is not made clear how it is known to others that Maura shot the attempted rape footage (especially when she was hiding under a table at the time), Maura and Mike are now on the run for their lives as mob hit men are seeking them (how Mike knows this is also not made clear).

12. Underground. The concluding unresolved episode wherein Maura and Mike attempt to make their way to the underground vigilante headquarters to establish a new base and expose "The Family."

82 FÉMIMIN/FÉMININ. femininfeminin. com. 2014 (Anthology).

Women, whether straight, lesbian or bisexual each face a special set of circumstances. Being lesbian or bisexual is perhaps more difficult as these women are sometimes considered outcasts or just plain weird for what they have encompassed. Women who have embraced the lesbian or bisexual lifestyle are explored in dramatic vignettes with a focus on a particular woman and how she came to be who she is and how she navigates life and love in Montreal, Canada. The women profiled are Lea and Noemie (both single) and their friends, who live as a couple: Celine and Julie, Steph and Sam, Alex and Anne and Emilie and Maude.

Cast: Noemie Yelle (Lea), Macha Limonchik (Celine), Sarah-Jeanne Labrosse (Julie), Eliane Gagnon (Emilie), Eve Duranceau (Steph), Alexa-Jeanne Dube (Alex), Kimberly Laferriere (Anne), Julianne Cote (Noemie), Emilie Leclerc Cote (Maude), Carla Turcotte (Sophie), Marie-Evelyne Lessard (Sam), Catherine Brunet (Sarah), Suzanne Clement (Herself), Helene Florent (Herself), Ariane Moffatt (Herself), Emmanuelle Girard (Karine). **Credits:** *Producer:* Florence Gagnon, Chloé Robichaud, Léonie LeBoeuf, Carolyne Boucher. *Director:* Chloe Robichaud. *Writer:* Florence Gagnon, Chloe Robichaud. **Comment:** The intent to explore lesbian and bisexual women has been done in comedic as well as dramatic form in motion pictures (including explicit adult industry films), television (broadcast and cable) and even on the Internet. *FÉMININ/FÉMININ* attempts to tell a different story by delving into the background of a woman and exploring the incidents that made her become who she is. The path taken to present lesbians in a positive light (rather than focus on the negative aspects that may have also been a part of her life) works well and shows that being gay is not a death sentence but something to embrace if that is the road you feel you should travel. Although subtitles are a distraction (the program is produced in French) stories are well plotted and the acting and photography is excellent. The women are quite attractive and their search for love is depicted in tender moments that can, at times, as in real life, have its awkward moments.

Episodes: The following episode descriptions are reprinted (from the show's press release) as requested by show producer Carolyne Boucher.

FÉMININ/FÉMININ. **Series poster art (copyright Simon Roy).**

1. Lea. The pilot wherein the group of women is presented with a particular focus on Lea and her awkward search for love.

2. Celine and Julie. Céline has recently gotten a divorce and is now facing her new celibate state.

3. Steph and Sam. Steph learns a costly lesson about not taking anything for granted.

4. Noemie. Noémie knows that she is gay. She just hasn't kissed a girl yet.

5. Alex and Anne. Alex mostly doesn't want to ask herself questions, while Anne wants answers.

6. Emilie and Maude. Émilie finds herself homeless and "catless" after her recent separation.

7. Le Chalet (The Country House). The girls reunite for a weekend at the country house.

8. « F/ F ». Every good thing comes to an end.

83 Fifty Shades of Blue. youtube.com/playlist?list=PLYRRQZRmMhXgMK2Yc G9KwPy-MMrOc7fxw 2013 (Action Comedy).

Although it is the year 2013, Frederico Blue and his buddy, Arnoldo, have the illusion they are gangsters and living in the 1950s. Jia and Katja, are their friends, a gorgeous lesbian couple who know the truth about Frederico and Arnoldo: they are morons. Frederico believes that blue is the color and not only dresses in such, but everything associated with him is in blue (even his gun); Arnoldo, on the other hand, appears to thrive on bananas and even incorporates them as weapons. The program, billed as "a test" follows the disillusioned gangsters as they become involved in a plot to retrieve a mysterious suitcase from the real underworld; unknown to them, Jia and Katja are only friendly with them to help them achieve their goal—the suitcase but for themselves.

Cast: Lukas DiSparrow (Frederico Blue), Jordan Adriano Brown (Arnoldo), Suan-Li Ong (Jia), Taly Vasilyev (Katja), Ricky Rajpal (Banana Dealer). **Credits:** *Producer-Writer-Director:* Lukas DiSparrow. **Comment:** Frederico and Arnoldo, although living disillusioned lives, really believe they are gangsters and are not afraid to do what it takes to achieve a goal (even kill if they have too). Based on the two episodes that have been produced, the program shows signs of being a real change from the typical gangster-themed programs of the past. Throwing in two beautiful lesbians, their kissing scenes and some comical action, *Fifty Shades of Blue* could easily become a fan favorite.

Episodes:
1. The Pilot. Frederico and his "left-hand man," Arnoldo begin a dangerous quest—find the culprit who not only stole milk from Frederico's refrigerator but left the oven burning in his kitchen.
2. The Stranger. After questioning several suspects, Frederico and Arnoldo find that they have stumbled onto a case involving the real mob and a missing suitcase. The episode also introduces Arnold's "gun" supplier—the Banana Dealer.

84 Fifty Shades of Girls. funnyordie.com. 2013–2014 (Comedy Anthology).

"50 beds. 50 nights. 50 stories" is the premise as promoted in the program's teaser. Short stories about women and the kind of hook-ups they make are seen in a comedic light with the woman not always coming up with the man (or girl) of her dreams (more of a nightmare she once had).

Cast: Andrea Vicunia (Bella), Antonija Stefek (Anna), Dustin Lemos (Adam), Ray Azemard (Ken), Angela Hu (Kimmy), Ronald Zambor (Him), Adam Ceschin (Jake), Varinia Flores (Lisa), Maruen Murra (Dennis), Maria Pazouros (Kate), Krystina Tasker (Lauren), Daniel Roman (Jake), Anthony Bradford (Carter), Elor Shemtov (Gina). **Credits:** *Producer:* Andrea Vicunia, MJ Caballero. *Director:* Andrea Vicunia, Anastasios Zolas. *Writer:* Jacquci Fanucci, Andrea Vicunia. **Comment:** Enjoyable program with a mix of girl-guy, girl-girl, guy-guy and even guy-killer shorts that are well acted and produced. Of the fifty promoted episodes, only eighteen have been produced and only one remains on line with no explanation as to why the others have been removed. In the view-able episode, "Who Is the Killer? the viewer is challenged to determine which of five people in a bed is the killer—one of two sexy girls? One of two dudes? Or a masked person wielding a knife.

Episode List: All episodes, with the exception of "Who Is the Killer" have been taken off-line.
1. Best Sex I Ever Had. 2. Jealousy. 3. My Heart Will Go On. 4. BMW. 5. The Cuddler. 6. The Movies. 7. Language Problems. 8. 50 First Dates. 9. The Best Friend. 10. Mommy's Boy. 11. Twifight. 12. Wait. 13. Who Is the Killer? 14. Abducted. 15. No Passion. 16. Sex Therapist. 17. Cheat Chat. 18. Oppa Girl/Girl Style.

85 Finding Me. youtube.com. 2007 (Drama).

Spin off from two feature films of the same name wherein the principal character, Faybien Allen was introduced. Faybien is young, gay and stylish and knows the importance of associating himself with the hip people at New York's trendiest spots. While he is good-looking and the nightlife seems to suit him, he is the son of a homophobic father and desperately seeking a more positive direction in his life. The program charts what happens when he encounters new friends (Greg and Lonnie) as his association with them could mean new loves but could also change the course of his life for the worse.

Cast: Ray Martell Moore (Faybien Allen), Ron DeSuze (Faybien's father), Maurice Murrell (Jay Timber), Derrick L. Briggs (Lonnie Wilson), J'Nara Corbin (Amera Jones), Eugene E. Turner (Greg Marsh). **Credits:** *Producer-Writer-Director:* Roger S. Omeus, Jr. **Comment:** Although one can figure out what is going on by sticking with the program, it helps if the feature films have been seen (as the producer just assumes you have seen them and know the plot). The actors do a good job but the production is flawed by very bad sound (camera microphones used) and makes it very difficult to hear what is happening. There are adult situations and vulgar language is used and discretion should be used as some sexual scenes could be disturbing for casual on-lookers.

Episode List: 1. Tell It to Yourself. 2. Worth Searching For. 3. Is That Why You Came Back. 4. What Do We Hope to Hear, Part 1. 5. What Do We Hope to Hear, Part 2. 6. Dynamic Jilted Duo. 7. Not What I Was Expecting. 8. I Just Want to Be. 9. Unfinished Business. 10. The End. 11. 3:58. 12. Episode 101. 13. The Turning Point.

86 Flush the Series. youtube.com. 2014 (Comedy).

On the 1970s TV series *Happy Days*, the loveable motorcycle hood Fonzie (Henry Winkler) had his offices (or headquarters) established in the men's room of Arnold's, a hamburger joint. The idea had not been capitalized upon and bathroom set sitcoms have not appeared on broadcast or cable TV. It took some time and the Internet to re-invent the idea and it has occurred again with *Flush*, this time as a coming-of-age story totally set in bathrooms (at least on *Happy Days* it was an occasional aspect of the series). Here incidents in the lives of four young adults (Lucy, Eliza, Fred and Jack) experience "life" (friendship and intimacy) in private places.

Cast: Natasha Greenblatt (Lucy), Bahia Watson (Eliza), Simon Bracken (Fred), Nadeem Umar Khitab (Jack). **Credits:** *Producer-Writer:* Maisie Jacobson, Natasha Greenblatt. *Director:* Maisie Jacobson. **Comment:** The production gives one the feeling of being in a tight space and it appears the program was actually filmed in bathrooms (as opposed to sets). It is difficult to say for sure, but it appears there will be intimacy between the two female leads but nothing is made clear (whether they are bisexual, straight or lesbians; same gray area with the male stars—are they bisexual?). Being set where it is, it is also difficult to say how long such a concept can last before it just becomes to over-the-top to watch. At the time of publication, a campaign was begun to raise financing for 12 episodes.

Episodes:

1. Trailer. The concept is introduced in a 3 minute and 16 second trailer.

87 Freefall. freefallseries.com. 2013–2014 (Drama).

Atlanta, Georgia, provides the backdrop for a look at the lives of a group of gay roommates (Xavier, Chad and Tony) as they deal with personal relationships, sexual encounters and a dangerous excursion into the darker, criminal side of the Atlanta gay life scene.

Cast: Shamon Glaspy (Xavier), JoVanni (Chad), Dante Simmons (Tyson), Alonzo Fri'zon (Tony), DeAndre Lemans (Nico), Toni Bernard (Ray), Jody Fulton, Jody Ray Vahn (Cameron), Isaiah Green (Saleem), Rico Milan (Myron), J. Troy Richardson (Oliver), Langston John Blaze (Trent), Brandy Grant (Delilah), Lyrik London (Eli). **Credits:** *Producer:* Geno Brooks, Lamont Pierre, Jared Wofford. *Director:* Lamont Pierre. *Writer:* Geno Brooks, Saun Loel, Lamont Pierre, Chris Saunders. **Comment:** Difficult, slow-moving program to follow or even comprehend what is happening. While the creator, Lamont Pierre, states, "We are unapologetically different and committed to diversifying the images of black gay men in media," the intent may have been

good, but the end result is confusing and not well executed. It is a chore just to watch the first episode and if that is accomplished, there is no desire to go any further. *Freefall* is specifically geared to gay black males (with model-like actors and sexual encounters) but its characters fit a stereotyped image as being thugs as opposed to being what they are—gay black men. The program has a depressing feel to it (perhaps induced by a greenish-grey tint in the picture) and numerous, unexplained plot twists do not help move things along. It just adds to the confusion and makes the actors, who are trying to do a good job, seem incapable of handling their roles (sort of beyond their skill as there is simply no character development). There are sexual situations and bad sound makes the production all that much worse (even the lighting is flawed in many scenes).

Episodes: 16 episodes were produced but trying to figure out what is going on and how to present it may not coincide with what the creator had intended or what each individual viewer will interpret. Simplistic, overall plot lines can be seen (like Xavier's dealing with an on-line hook up in the first episode, "Compromising Positions") but as stories progress, what is clear to the show's crew is not clear to viewers. Of the remaining Season 1 episodes, only the following titles remain on line: "Tell Me When It Starts to Hurt" (Cameron attempts to deal with a love hangover; Episode 2), "Learning to Sleep Alone" (Xavier becomes roommates with Chad and Tony; Episode 3), "Fun and Games" (A game of "Truth or Dare" reveals facts about the roommates; Episode 4), "Miami: The Bonus Episode" (The guys embark on a trip to Miami; Episode 11). Episodes 5–10 appear to be off-line. Season 2 consists of five untitled episodes.

88 Frequency. frequencywebseries.com. 2012 (Fantasy).

One night a young clairvoyant (Claire) has a dream about a strange woman (Deanna), a telepath with the ability to travel through time. She sees herself as the woman's lover although she herself is not a lesbian (she is dating Travis, a male police detective). At first Claire dismisses the dream as just a nightmare until the following day, while walking on the street she has a brief encounter with the girl she saw in her dream. The girl however, appears in a ghostly image and soon vanishes, leaving Claire to wonder what happened: was it real or imaginary? Unknown to Claire an encounter she had when she was a young girl would one day change the course of her life. It was the early 1980s and Claire, playing in a park, crossed paths for a brief moment with a young woman (Deanna). Deanna immediately felt a connection to Claire and realized she was to be her future lover. Claire often uses her powers to help the police solve crimes. She is working on a case when Deanna, in another time period (the 1980s) senses that Claire is in danger and uses her ability to travel across time to re-connect with her in the present (2012). Claire is strangely drawn to Deanna and accepts her first as a friend and later as her lover. While it appears that what fate had intended has happened (uniting Claire and Deanna) Deanna also knows their relationship could be destroyed by a mysterious force that, unknown to them, is working through Travis. The program charts the strange events that threaten Deanna and Claire's happiness together and how, with the help of a mystical woman named Jackie, they seek to stop Travis and whatever is controlling him.

Cast: Meredith Sause (Claire DuMurier), Lisa Gagnon (Deanna Shelley), Kat Froehlich (Jackie), Jenn Evans (Susan), Anthony Hughes (Travis). **Credits:** *Producer:* Monique Velasquez. *Writer-Director:* Piper Kessler. **Comment:** The first Internet lesbian fantasy series (with the tag line, "Most importantly, the girl gets the girl"). The program gives the viewer just what he (or she) is looking for—several erotic kissing scenes—coupled with a good story and acting. The plot is quite intriguing and played so that you never can predict what is going to happen next. The kissing sequences (there is no nudity) are quite convincing and the series would be the ideal candidate for the gay cable channels Here! or Logo. Frequency (the producing company) has four additional lesbian web series: *Easy Abby, Girl/Girl Scene, Lesbian Cops* and *Sunny Reign* (see individual titles). Since the story was left unresolved, it does leave the viewer with an interest to see more—not only to find out who or what Travis is, but what happens to Deanna, Claire and Jackie.

Episodes:

1. Episode 1. The main characters are introduced as Claire and Deanna meet physically for the first time.

2. Episode 2. Although she is not a lesbian, Claire becomes strangely attracted to Deanna and the two share their first sexual encounter.

3. Episode 3. As Claire and Deanna begin a relationship, an unknown force, working through Travis, directs a series of murders.

4. Episode 4. Deanna, envisioning a murder, rushes to the scene, where she encounters a mystical young woman (Jackie) who will become instrumental in saving Claire's life.

5. Episode 5. Knowing that Jackie is innocent, but sensing the police will think otherwise, Deanna shelters her from the approaching authorities.

6. Episode 6. With Jackie safe in Claire's home (where Deanna also lives), Deanna meets another girl (Susan) who also envisioned the murder and learns from her that someone she knows is a threat (Travis).

7. Episode 7. As Deanna's love for Claire grows stronger, Deanna senses that not all is right with Travis and he may be the threat.

8. Episode 8. In the 1980s Deanna meets a child—

Claire in the park and realizes she will be her future lover. She also visualizes Travis killing a man and travels to 2012.

9. Episode 9. It is learned that Deanna and Claire have teamed to help injured people with Jackie providing the needed healing (and Deanna erasing the incident form their minds). Deanna reveals that Travis "is out there mucking up the world" (killing) and needs to be stopped.

10. Episode 10. Deanna has a vision of Claire being attacked by Travis, but arrives too late to save her. Jackie, however, is able to bring her back to life at the same time Travis receives a message (from unknown sources) that he failed in his assignment. As Travis returns to complete his task, Deanna kills him (or at least she believes so when he vanishes after being shot). Now, with their presence known by something seeking to kill them, Deanna, Claire and Jackie begin a run for their lives as the series ends.

89 Friday Night Dykes. onemorelesbian.com. 2008 (Comedy-Drama).

A California housing complex provides the backdrop for a look at the lives of four women who are also lesbians: Andrea, Siobhan, Roxie and Geri. While Andrea, Roxie and Siobhan, Lipstick-like (sexy and feminine) lesbians have continual romantic encounters (even among themselves), Geri, not quite as attractive as her three friends, is also seeking romance but with a woman who falls more into her category.

Cast: Maeve Quinlan (Siobhan McGarry), Jill Bennett (Andrea Bailey), Cathy Shim (Roxie Lautzenheiser), Maile Flanagan (Geri O'Flanagn), Elizabeth Keener (Celia Sanderson), Scott Holroyd (Grant L'Entrance), Lisa Long (Nasty Nancy), Linda Miller (Frankie), Elizabeth Gudenrath (Bartender), Tanya Little-Palmer (Foxy), Georgia Ragsdale (Duffy Brennan). **Credits:** *Producer:* Paige Bernhardt, Nancylee Myatt, Maeve Quinlan, Maile Flanagan, Joey Scott. *Director:* Courtney Rowe. *Writer:* Paige Bernhardt, Maile Flanagan, Nancylee Myatt, Georgia Ragsdale. **Comment:** Comedy mixes with light drama in a well-produced and acted series that relates the events that spark the lives of the women with kissing and G-rated sexual situations.

Episodes: 11 episodes have been produced but only the pilot film, which aired on the series *3 Way* remains on line.

1. Pilot. The four principal players are introduced with a particular focus on Geri as she tries to become a part of her friends' lives.

90 Friends and Benefits. friendsandbenefits.tv. 2011 (Comedy).

Four friends (Ben, Calvin, Sophie and Max) and their adventures in Melbourne, Australia, as they each help the other navigate the world of dating in a culture that is continually changing and presenting new challenges to those seeking the perfect mate.

Ben Fitzgerald is 21 years old and gay. He is attending college (business major) and is a bit naïve when it comes to dating as he has just broken up with his boyfriend (Lukas) after two years and believes that on-line dating is the answer to all his problems.

Calvin, 22 years old, is also gay and Ben's best friend (an art major). Although he is very open about his sexuality, he is also very opinionated and Ben's mentor as he begins dating in the single gay lifestyle.

Max, the oldest member of the group (24) is also the most outrageous one and seeks only to have a good time, rarely taking life seriously.

Sophie, Ben's oldest friend (called his "fag hag") is the first person to whom he revealed that he was gay. While Sophie is straight, she respects Ben's choice (and is learning about gay culture through her friendship with him) and tries to help Ben with dating advice.

Cast: Stephen Walden (Ben), Kenny Cheng (Calvin), Pia Prendiville (Sophie), Anthony Jelinic (Max), James Miller (Lukas), Paul de Longville (Alex), Mark Souvannavong (Pete). **Credits:** *Producer-Writer-Director:* Christopher Kam. **Comment:** Australian program that tries to present a realistic view of how gay men deal with the pressures of dating, especially through the Internet. While the particular focus is on younger gay men, it also shows how older gays are affected and tries to bring into focus the real issues such men face. The acting and production is good and, although tagged as a comedy, its themes are realistic with humor used as a way to soften the blow as to what is actually happening.

Episodes:

1. First On-Line Date. After adjusting to the fact that he is now single again, Ben ventures into the world of on-line dating.

2. Criteria. Calvin, a "GAM" ("Gay Asian Male") and his opinionated concept of life, is introduced.

3. Friends on FAB. Max, the sex-crazed member of the group, is introduced.

4. Fag Hag. While the term for a straight girl who is friends with a gay man sounds a bit degrading, So-

welcome to the world of gay dating

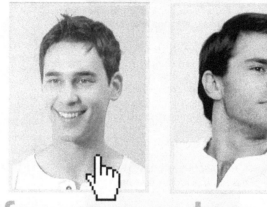

friends and benefits

friendsandbenefits.tv

Friends and Benefits. **Series poster art (used by permission of Christopher Kam, Kameo Media).**

phie is introduced as that straight girl who, while she hates being called a "fag hag" is faithful to Ben and accepts who he is.

5. Couples. Ben's gay couple friends, Alex and Pete are introduced.

6. Morning. A look back on what has happened to Ben as he recalls incidents from his past.

7. Age. The question of whether age matters in a relationship is explored as Ben acquires a date with a man thirteen years his senior.

8. Benefits. Ben, Sophie, Calvin and Max in a discussion about their sexual activities.

9. Safety. As Ben continues his ventures into on-line dating, the subject of safety in doing so is explored.

10. The Club. Feeling that some fun is needed in

their lives, the friends attempt to leave a day's stress behind them and enjoy themselves at a nightclub.

11. One Night Stands. Explores what can happen when, after a one night stand, Ben runs into a man he slept with but has no memory of him.

12. LukasX. Focuses on Ben's reaction when he discovers his ex (Lukas) has also ventured into on-line dating.

13. The Ex. Ben attempts to adjust to the fact that the man he once loved (Lukas) is now seeking someone else.

14. Max's Advice. Max attempts to help Ben deal with the fact that Lukas has moved on without him.

15. Sophie's Talk. Sophie attempts to help Ben cope with the loss of Lukas.

16. Interview. Calvin attempts to help a nervous Ben prepare for his job interview at Plus Bank.

17. First On-Line Hookup. Ben's reactions and efforts to prepare for his first on-line hookup (with Harvey) are explored.

18. Second Date. Having overcome his intimidations about his first date, Ben now prepares for a second one.

19. It's a Small Gay World. An overjoyed Ben introduces his date (Harvey) to his friends but all does not go well when they all offer differing opinions.

20. Pete's Birthday. Ben, Sophie, Calvin and Max join Pete and Alex for a celebration of Pete's birthday.

21. The Moment. The concluding episode wherein Ben and Lukas meet by chance on the street but reconciliation does not happen. As Ben returns to his friends he realizes that he had to figure himself out "and if I don't find love right now, the way I see it I already have three great people in my life who will always be there for me. With friends like these who needs benefits."

91 Gay and Gayer (2007). youtube.com. 2007 (Reality).

Various aspects that affect the LGBT community are discussed.

Hosts: Andy and Brian (as identified). Credits are not given. **Comment:** Very amateurish production with poor picture quality (below today's HD standards) that is mostly hampered by too soft lighting (picture sharpness is noticeably missing). The hosts are very monotone and, while knowledgeable on the topics they cover, their discussions lack the oomph to keep the viewer interested.

Episode List: *1.* St. Louis Pride Parade. *2.* Drag Queens; Sex with Trannies. *3.* Andy and Brian on Gay Stuff. *4.* Misleading Myspace profiles. *5.* The Usual Chit Chat About Gay Stuff. *6.* Dating and Sexual Consequences. *7.* A Holiday for Gays, Heath Ledger, and Bestiality. *8.* Talking About Sex with Ugly People, Lesbians, and the 18–19-year-old Whore Phase. *9.* Dress Codes at Gay Events. *10.* Race Relations and Dating.

92 Gay and Gayer (2013). vimeo.com. 2013 (Comedy-Drama).

Dave and Michael are twins. They may look alike but sexually they are as different as night and day. Dave is gay while Michael professes to be straight but sometimes bisexual. The program, presented as a series of video diaries, explores their varying lifestyles in what are basically scenes of them discussing the various issues they have with each other (from their sex lives to their medical conditions).

Cast: Dave and Michael (as identified). **Credits:** *Producer-Director:* Dan Fry. **Comment:** Strictly geared toward a gay male audience as the characters, especially Dave, are overly (and annoyingly) gay. There is literally no action as the twins just react to what is happening around them. There is brief (but censored) nudity and the program is age-restricted on some sharing sites. Also known as *Gay and Gayer: The Gay-Bi-Straight Web Series*.

Episodes: 12 untitled episodes have been produced that, as stated above, are simply various discussions.

93 A Gay Ass Cartoon. agayasscartoon. tumblr.com. 2014 (Cartoon).

Two African-American gay cartoon characters, K and Mutchy D, explore the LGBT community's culture and lifestyles through their series of short video blogs.

Voice Cast as credited: Kiddo and K (formally known as Mutchy B). Credits are not given. **Comment:** While animated series dealing with gays and lesbians are rare (see also *Lizzy the Lezzy* and *Girl Crush* as two other examples), they do manage to get a message across in a more unorthodox manner as opposed to a live action series. The program portrays its leads as hip-talkers who simply discuss or argue about a topic with animation that is acceptable for the Internet (nothing fancy and nothing that compares to today's computer animated cartoons that are seen on such cable outlets as The Cartoon Network and The Disney Channel).

Episode List: *1.* Virgin Femmes. *2.* Interracial Love. *3.* Partner Still on Ex? *4.* Baby Dykes. *5.* Bad Bitch Complex. *6.* Bad Stud Club. *7.* Not a Stud or Butch. *8.* Sex Toys 101. *9.* Straps and Condoms. *10.* Chat with a Femme, Parts 1 and 2. *11.* K's Gay Ass Poem. *12.* LGBT Internet Dating, Parts 1 and 2. *13.* Black History. *14.* Stud Interview with Mutchy B, Parts 1, 2 and 3. *15.* A Gay Ass—Blooper #1: What Up?

94 Gay/DF. youtube.com. 2013 (Anthology).

A program of varying stories set in Mexico City that attempts to explore and improve the co-existence of the LGBT community with the heterosexual community. Each story focuses on one individual (gay, lesbian, bisexual, transsexual or transgender) and relates personal incidents from the subject's life and how he or she manages to cope with the life path they have chosen. The title refers to Distrito Federal (Mexican Federal District) that permits members of the LGBT community to work in public jobs.

Pilot Episode Cast: Ricardo Gariby (Ricardo). **Credits:** *Producer-Director:* Balam Henera. **Comment:** While the program is an anthology, and most people immediately call to mind such TV series as *The Outer Limits* or *The Twilight Zone*, *Gay/DF* is more styled to a documentary presentation as opposed to a dramatic story with twists and turns. Although only one episode has been produced, it is well photographed and highlights incidents as seen from the profiled subject (with voice-over narration).

Episodes:
1. Ricardo, Transsexual Driver. The pilot episode that explores life as seen through the eyes of Ricardo, a woman-turned-man as he performs his daily job and relates his feelings on sexism, social problems, city violence and the way members of the LGBT community are treated by others.

95 Gay Nerds. gaynerds.tv. 2014 (Comedy).

Ralphie, Sam and Lana are gay but do not fit the typical definition of what their sexuality means. They are literally unable to accept the world in which they live and use pop culture to make sense of everything that surrounds them. The program follows their mishaps as the world of pop culture becomes all too real to them and they often find themselves unable to distinguish fantasy from reality (parodying a TV series or movie).

Cast: Robert Keller (Ralphie), Alexandra Wylie (Lana), Ryan Kerr (Sam). **Credits:** *Producer-Writer-Director:* J.P. Larocque. **Comment:** Well acted and produced parody of not only gay and lesbian characters, but TV shows and movies as well. Although the characters may appear a bit off center, it has to be remembered when watching that their lives have been influenced by pop culture and the only way they can handle reality is to associate it with a movie or TV show that parallels what they are experiencing.

Episodes:
1. Tyrannosaurus Ex. Shades of *Jurassic Park* wherein Ralphie, with the help of Lana and Sam, attempts to break up with his intimidating boyfriend James.
2. The Bat, the Cat and the iPhone. A trying day at work (as a mailroom clerk) finds Lana facing a breakdown while Sam and Ralphie encounter mishap at a masquerade party.
3. Gayliens. Adapting the hunt (for the creature) scene from the movie *Alien*, Lana, armed with her

replica of the pulse rifle from the film, attempts to help Sam find the person who has been stalking him.
4. The Fellowship of Sarah Michelle Gellar. After purchasing a hair clip worn by Sarah Michelle Gellar on the series *Buffy the Vampire Slayer* on e-bay, Lana believes it is cursed and drags Ralphie and Sam on a trip to California to find Sarah and have her remove the curse.
5. Canada's Next Top Bottom. A gay camping trip turns out to be anything but a joyous occasion when Lana, Ralphie and Sam encounter strange occurrences and live a *Blair Witch* type movie experience.
6. 28 Gays Later. Lana becomes infuriated with Sam when he crashes her lesbian get-together and immerses himself in their conversation and becomes like "one of the girls."
7. Rise and Shining. All hell breaks loose when, during a vacation, Ralphie and Sam become trapped in a small cabin and have to deal each other's odd behavior. The program's concluding episode.

96 Gay of Thrones. funnyordie.com. 2013–2014 (Comedy).

Game of Thrones is an HBO series (2011-) about seven noble families engaged in a battle to acquire control of the mythical medieval Land of the Westeros. Episode interpretations can differ based on one's perception of the events that were portrayed. Adapting that concept, *Gay of Thrones* presents a gay interpretation of each episode that also incorporates actual footage from the HBO series to show how such deductions were made. Programs open in a hair salon with a male gay hair stylist (Jonathan) and a client (gay or lesbian) discussing their favorite show with an episode recap begun by the stylist with his clients offering their opinions.

Cast: Jonathan Van Ness (Jonathan), Jeffrey Self (Jeffrey), Alfie Allen (Alfie), Esme Bianco (Ros), Alex Berg, Ross Buran, Todd Fasen, Erin Gibson, Eileen O'Connell, Kristen Rozanski, Margaret Cho, Alison Becker, Bryan Safi, Lilan Bowden, Lucy Davis, Drew Droege. **Credits:** *Producer:* Betsy Koch, Becca Scheuer, Ross Buran, Matt Mazany. *Director:* Erin Gibson, Bradly Schulz, Jeffrey Self. *Writer:* Jack Allison, Alex Berg, Erin Gibson, Bradly Schulz, Jeffrey Self. **Comment:** Amusing idea that, with the incorporation of actual footage from *Game of Thrones* plays well as opposed to just being two characters talking about what happened on their favorite show. The program only covers seasons 3 and 4 of *Game of Thrones* and doing a prequel, so to speak, to cover the first two seasons could have worked just as well even though it would not have been current.

Episode List:
1. All Men Throw Shade. April 13, 2013. The recap of Season 3 of *Game of Thrones* begins.
2. Charisma, Nerve, Talent. April 21, 2013.

3. Serving 100% Better D. April 24, 2013.
4. Fire Is Giving Me Life, Hunty. May 1, 2013.
5. Giving Beat Face. May 7, 2013.
6. The Ratchet Bear. May 16, 2013.
7. Step Into the Light. May 20, 2013.
8. Bye Gurl, Bye. June 4, 2013.
9. Let's Have a Kiki. June 11, 2013. The Season 3 recap of *Game of Thrones* concludes.
10. Gay of Thrones Is Back! April 3, 2014. The second season begins with an overall recap of *Game of Thrones*.
11. The Liar and the Hoes. April 8, 2014. The recap of Season 4 of *Game of Thrones* begins.
12. Two Slores. April 15, 2014.
13. Twerker of Chains. April 22, 2014.
14. Oathwerqer, Bitch! April 29, 2014.
15. Fierce Her Name. May 5, 2014.
16. The Laws of Gay Men. May 12, 2014.
17. Cockingbird. May 20, 2014.
18. The Mounting and the Vagine. June 3, 2014.
19. The Voguer on the Wall. June 9, 2014.
20. Future Legendary Children. June 17, 2014. The program's concluding episode.

97 *Gay Star Trek Phase II.* startrekphase II.com. 2008 (Science Fiction).

During the original run of the TV series *Star Trek* (NBC, 1966–1969) David Gerrold, author of the infamous "Trouble with Tribbles" episode, also wrote an episode that involved gay characters. Paramount, producer of the series, felt the script was inappropriate and rejected it. Years later, when the *Star Trek* spin off, *The Next Generation* appeared (1995), Gerrold retooled that episode ("Blood and Fire") but it too was rejected (although approved by series creator Gene Roddenberry) for being too risqué (the producers feared it would cause a loss of sponsors because parents would complain that their children had seen gay people on *Star Trek*). When the Internet series *Star Trek: Phase II* was launched in 2004 Gerrold saw this as an opportunity to finally get his script produced. During the show's fourth season, "Blood and Fire" was finally seen. In it Ensign Peter Kirk, the gay nephew of Captain James T. Kirk, is granted his request for assignment on *The Enterprise* not so much to be with his uncle, but his boyfriend, Lt. Alex Freeman. As the episode progresses, it is learned that Peter and Alex have made plans to marry and want Captain Kirk to officiate. While the gay characters are treated equally with other characters (alien or human) that have appeared on the various incarnations of the series, it does show that outside pressure forced a gay (or lesbian) aspect of real life to be eliminated from the *Star Trek* universe. Gene Roddenberry believed that everyone is equal regardless of who they are and he tried to convey that concept in every episode without making it obvious (an example being Lt. Uhura [Nichelle Nichols] a beautiful African-American crew member who was treated just like any other crew member with no special attention made of her race or color). But studios and sponsors rule and not even Gene Roddenberry could totally overcome their "wisdom."

Principal Episode Cast: Bobby Rice (Ensign Peter Kirk), Evan Fowler (Lt. Alex Freeman), James Cawley (Capt. James T. Kirk), Ben Tolpin (Mr. Spock), John M. Kelley (Dr. Leonard "Bones" McCoy), Kim Stinger (Uhura), Andy Bray (Chekov). **Episode Credits:** *Producer:* David Gerrold, Gary Evans, Gregory L. Schnitzer, James Cawley. *Writer-Director:* David Gerrold. **Comment:** With all the TV and feature film versions of *Star Trek* it took the Internet to bring the series into modern times with gay characters. The episode appears to have been written to blend the characters in with the other crew members and not make them overly obvious. Unfortunately, the story (running close to two hours total) is stretched and drags, making it less intense than other episodes in the series. While the special effects are good and the alien encounters exciting, the love story aspect could have been edited somewhat to make the inclusion of gay characters more in tune with the concept rather than something that doesn't fit the story. The acting is just passable and that too adds to the feeling that too much focus was placed on Peter and Alex.

Episodes:
1. Blood and Fire, Parts 1 and 2. Peter Kirk is introduced but before he and his lover (Alex) can marry, they are assigned an away mission, headed by Mr. Spock to investigate a distress signal from the Starfleet ship U.S.S. *Copernicus*.

98 *Gay Street Therapy.* tellofilms.com. 2013 (Reality).

Issues that affect the lesbians are discussed— "Those burning questions that you've had but have always been afraid to ask." Each episode is presented from a specific location with the hosts ("non-licensed lesbian therapists") humorously helping the lesbian patrons deal with problems or issues they are facing.

Cast: Julie Goldman, Brandy Howard (Hosts). **Credits:** Producer: Christin Mell. *Director:* Adriana Torres. **Comment:** Based on the available teaser, the on-location presentation is well done and there are attractive girls but other than a glancing look at the advice segment, it has to be assumed the discussions are quite frank and would thus be restricted if the program were available on other sites.

Episodes: Three episodes appear to have been produced but only a teaser for the second episode remains on line for free; the others are available only through a paid subscription service. *1.* Los Angeles. *2.* The Dinah. *3.* Back Lot Bash.

Gay Street Therapy. Series poster art (used by permission of Tello Films).

99 *Gay Top Gun.* youtube.com. 2009 (Comedy).

Parody of the Tom Cruise 1986 feature film *Top Gun* (about students at the U.S. Navy's elite Fighter Weapons School, in particular a cadet named Maverick [Tom Cruise] as he becomes a top fighter pilot). Gays were apart of the service, but their presence not openly admitted. In 1993 the U.S. Military instituted the "Don't Ask, Don't Tell" initiative that allowed homosexuals to serve in the various armed forces. Capitalizing on that aspect for the program, the military established a somewhat less-than-elite unit of gay pilots called "The Other Fighter Weapons School" (called "Gay Top Gun" by its students). Maverick, now a homosexual, and his gay partner, Goose, have attended class and have been promoted to Gay Top Gun. Their assignment, to prevent an uprising and battle Russian pilots over the Indian Ocean is the sub-plot of episodes that focus more on their homeland activities than their battle activities.

Cast: Euriamis Losada (Maverick), Dane Hanson (Goose/Jester), Justin Martelliti (Charlie), Jeff Denton (Iron Man/Viper), Ryan Premesberger (Slider), Chad Skala (Wolfman), James Ferris (West Hollywood), Mike Heim (Johnson), Brian Hamill (Perry),

Henry Foote (Sundown) **Credits:** *Producer:* Jeff Denton, Dane Hanson, Jason Mandel, Joshua Mandel. *Writer-Director:* Dane Hanson. **Comment:** The program has somewhat captured the feel of the feature film and is well acted and produced but goes beyond the film by incorporating strong sexual situations. Because the program also incorporates vulgar language some sharing sights require age verification to view (through an e-mail account).

Episodes:

1. Episode 1. Maverick and Goose (as well as the rest of the squadron) are introduced and told of a mission to fly against the best fighter pilots in the world—for two eight-hour days.

2. Episode 2. Love enters the picture when Maverick falls for a fellow pilot (Charlie).

3. Episode 3. As the squad prepares for a mission, Maverick and Goose's rowdy behavior has its consequences and almost causes them to get expelled from Gay Top Gun.

4. Episode 4. A tragic accident, a pilot being killed in a jet wash (something that never happens) has Maverick and others rethinking what they are doing.

5. Episode 5. Distraught over the death of one team member, Maverick faces a tough decision: whether or not continue with the Gay Top Gun program.

6. Episode 6. In the concluding episode, Maverick has chosen to continue and faces his first assignment—battling the Russians.

100 *Gay Town.* hulu.com. 2008 (Comedy).

Gay Town is, as its name implies, a town populated by gays and lesbians and "the closet" straight people. A young man named Owen is one such rarity in Gay Town—he is straight but must keep his sexuality a secret and pretend to be gay. From as early as he can remember, Owen felt there was something wrong with him ("I never fit in with the other guys"). While boys his age went out for ballet and figure skating, he yearned to play basketball with the girls—and took a beating from other boys for being a non-conformist. As time passed, Owen figured that to live in Gay Town he must pretend to be gay and "got a pretend boyfriend" named Pierce (who actually loves Owen while Owen's attentions are drawn to Lina, a beautiful lesbian who is only his friend because she believes he is gay). As Owen says, "I've always tried to fit in, but you can't hide who you are. I'm an outsider. I'm a straight man living in Gay Town" and stories follow Owen as he tries to do just that—be himself where circumstances just won't permit him to do so.

Cast: Owen Benjamin (Owen), Payman Benz (Pierce Del Mar), Brooke Lenzi (Jen), Jordy Fox (Herbert), Brody Stevens (Mayor Stevens), Andrea Kelley (Annie), Lina Miller (Lina). **Credits:** *Pro-*

ducer: Owen Benjamin, Jesse Shapiro. *Director:* Jesse Shapiro, Todd Strauss-Schulson, Owen Benjamin, Payman Benz, Sam Becker, Greg Benson. *Writer:* Owen Benjamin. **Comment:** Well acted and produced role reversal with a straight person being "the outcast." The program can be watched by anyone (compares to a network sitcom) with some sexual tension between the characters but nothing warranting parental caution.

Episodes:

1. Welcome to Gay Town. Owen is introduced and finds that jobs are scarce as he is constantly being fired for fears that he is straight.

2. Assume the Position. Owen explains that a guy named Pierce claims to be his boyfriend but isn't—"I tried to tell him that I don't like dudes, but he cried and I agreed to it."

3. The Rain-bros. "The Rain-bros, the craziest gay gang in Gay Town," are seen as Owen relives nightmares from his childhood when he was terrorized by them.

4. Born Sinners. As Pierce becomes upset (crying) when he sees Owen flirting with Lina, Owen receives a visit from two "Morman" missionaries who try to persuade him to follow their "religion."

5, 6, 7 and 8: Episodes off line; no descriptive information or titles available.

9. I'm Different. Owen faces still another problem: hiding the fact that he is straight when his father returns to town for a visit.

10. Straight Pride Parade. After being arrested and humiliated for being straight, Owen organizes a Straight Pride Parade for himself and others to come out of the closet.

11. Season Recap. The first season finale that recaps what happened and concludes with Owen rallying all the heterosexuals in Gay Town to march in his parade.

12. What Happened? The second season begins. While alone with Lina, Owen mentions that he had "a dream about her boobs" only to find her slapping his face, exclaiming, "You're straight!" and handed a restraining order.

13. Gay Town on Fire. Owen's parade causes a problem with the gays rioting and torching cars in protest of straights living in Gay Town.

14. The Man. Introduces Owen's gay brother Bruce (with a moustache) as he stands up for his gayness and condemns Owen's straightness.

15. Community Service. Due to his refusal to carry a "fanny pack" (like the men of Gay Town) and conform to the standards of the town, Owen finds himself regulated to community service (as a dog groomer). The situation proves to be more than he expected when he meets Jen, a gorgeous lesbian seeking help in finding her lost pet guinea pig.

16. Small and Bald. Keeping his straightness secret, Owen begins seeing Jen. When Jen learns that Owen and Pierce have broken up (and Pierce is in tears), she sets Pierce up on a blind date with Lance, a gay who likes small bald men (like Pierce).

17. Zip Me Up. Shortly after acquiring a job as a bartender at the town's gay bar, Owen is demoted to restroom attendant for being straight.

18. Back on Track. A straight can't work in a gay bar and Owen is fired. Pierce, unable to make a connection with Lance, is back to the tears (over losing Owen) but in his misery he comes up with "a great idea"—start a boy band called Bun-tastic.

19. Treatment. Believing that he can succeed in Gay Town, Owen hits on the idea of opening a straight bar.

20. A New Start. Owen's straight bar opens at the same time Pierce's band, Bun-tastic makes its Gay Town debut.

21. Finale. As the program concludes, Owen tempts fate by telling Jen, "I like boobs." Jen's response, "I've got two of them," pleases Owen, who is left to wonder should he tell Jen he is straight or continue pretending to be gay.

101 The Gaye Family. vimeo.com. 2010 (Comedy).

The Gayes appear to be a typical African-American family: a father, mother and two teenage children. But they are actually a family that challenges stereotypes: they act gay "but they are as straight as they come." Pervis, the father, is a fashion stylist and sounds gay; Tina, his wife, holds a job with a demolition company; Laura, their daughter, loves sports and dresses like a butch lesbian; and Billy, their son, acts like a feminine gay male but is a diva (a ladies' man). Stories relate the events that befall the family, situations made a bit more complex to resolve as the images they present to the public has them perceived as something they are not.

Cast: Anthony Boyd (Pervis Gaye), Brun Alexandra Drescher (Tina Gaye), Cole (Laura Gaye), Marc J. (Billy Gaye), La Tee (Grandma). **Credits:** *Producer:* Brian Anthony Butler, Norris Young. *Writer-Director:* Norris Young. **Comment:** A surprisingly well acted and produced program that compares to such current syndicated African-American TV series like *Are We There Yet, Tyler Perry's House of Payne* and *Meet the Browns.* It is a non-offensive and well thought out program that should be expanded upon and pitched as a syndicated TV series.

Episodes:

1. Introducing the Gaye Family. The family is seen for the first time as they attempt to have breakfast together and, at first glance, they do appear gay.

2. Episode 2. Just as Pervis arrives home from a frustrating day trying to style First Lady Michelle Obama, Bill announces that he has fallen in love with a girl who looks like Janet Jackson and Tina announces something Pervis regrets hearing: her mother is coming for a visit.

3. Episode 3. Grandma's arrival has Pervis on

pins and needles as they just do not get along with each other (as Grandma says about Pervis, "Something about that boy just ain't right").

4. Episode 4. As tension mounts between Pervis and Grandma, Grandma, on Tina's urging, shocks Pervis by attempting to find ways to please him and end their dislike of one another.

5. Laura Goes to the Dentist. There are kids who eat candy but Laura's extreme over indulgence in the sweets causes anxiety when she develops a toothache and must face the consequences.

6. Billy Comes Home. After leaving home to find himself, Billy returns to the family nest as Sonokio, a member of the religious (and gay-looking) cult Ali Baba.

7. A Very Gaye Vacation. Pervis and Tina embark on a vacation only to have it spoiled when they run into Grandma, who immediately attaches herself to them.

8. The Gaye Family Bloopers. The mistakes made during filming are highlighted in the program's concluding episode.

102 Gay's Anatomy. gays-anatomy.com. 2009 (Comedy).

A parody of the ABC series *Gray's Anatomy* that focuses on three young urologists "who work hard, play harder and touch your private parts for a living." Mark Merriman is a love-sick gay who seems unable to find the perfect man; Jim Gable is a nervous, stressed-out doctor who relieves tension by "giving colonoscopies to the homeless" and Marc Weston finds that dealing with the situations that surround him can only be accomplished by "using cocaine responsibly." The program, also encompassing the silliness of the TV series *Scrubs*, presents a look at an aspect of the medical profession that has not been covered before, although here, in a way that TV or cable would not tackle.

Marc (with a "c") is a graduate of Harvard Medical School and yearns to do his internship in a large New York City hospital. He met Mark (with a "k") during the hospital's interview process and is looking to bond with him.

Jim, a graduate of UC Berkeley, is an eager doctor who dresses in frilly outfits but is eager to "get his hands dirty in the exam room."

Casey is Marc's roommate, a butch lesbian who is on the prowl for a lady lover.

Amy is a neurotic hospital radiologist who seeks to become the best doctor there is. She believes that "her love of cripples" is her proof of leadership qualities.

Eddie is the shy and overly observant doctor's colleague with an eye toward male and female eye candy.

Robin is the mysterious, cocaine-addicted girl who feels like Mark that drugs and good times go together.

Cast: Wil Petre (Mark Weston), Max Jenkins (Jim Gable), Bobby Hodgson (Marc Merriman), Beth Hoyt (Robin Starr), Becca Blackwell (Casey Blunt), Amy Kersten (Amy Campbell), Jim deProphetis (Eddie DeGrazio), Joe Currnutte (Brad Johnson), Meghan Hemingway (Esme Cunkle), Jess Barbagallo (Dyque Vander Goose), Drae Campbell (Shelley Lopez). **Credits:** *Director-Writer:* Karina Mangu-Ward and B. Hodgson. **Comment:** Although the annoyingly unsteady (shaky) camera is used, the program is well done and acted and once viewing it, you will never see medical dramas produced on network TV in the same light.

Episodes:

1. Exciting New Positions. Jim, Mark and Marc compete for a possible opening in a top New York Urology program.

2. Come Out Tonight. Jim scopes out the new urology students by inviting them to his favorite bar for a mixer.

3. Taking It All In. It is the day following the bar mixer and the urology residents begin their rounds while Jim acquires "a front row seat" for his favorite surgery.

4. Unexpected Foursome. Mark and Marc's effort to have an intimate date becomes a group affair when Jim and Casey show up and spoil the moment.

5. Please Be Gentle. Evaluation day at the hospital has the urology team stressed out as each faces judgment by the Chief and their futures are now on the line.

6. Bottoms Up. The first season concludes with Mark surprising everyone with two announcements: he has become engaged to the party girl, Robin and that he is becoming a gynecologist (as he was the only urologist authorized to give pap smears and it changed his medical direction).

7. A Lot to Swallow. The second year of residency begins with Jim, Marc and Mark seeking the position of Chief Resident.

8. Deep Deep Inside. Marc believes that because he has a better knowledge of what causes diseases, he is a shoe-in for Chief Resident. The hospital however, has other ideas and assigns Dr. Brad Johnson the position.

9. Who's Coming Now? In an effort to seduce Jim, Marc invites Jim to dinner; Mark believes he has found a true love when he meets a new intern (Dyque).

10. Urine-vited. Robin and Mark's wedding plan announcement upsets Marc who feels Robin is totally undeserving of him.

11. Gynosaurus Rex. Dr. Shelley Lopez is introduced as the gynecologist that poses a threat to Mark's acceptance into Columbia Presbyterian Hospital as she is up for the same position. Meanwhile, preparations are begun for Mark's bachelor party.

12. Partner Up. The concluding episode that finds Mark calling off the wedding when he discovers Robin is pregnant; and Marc discovering that, after becoming drunk at the bachelor party, he married Eddie.

103 Gayxample. gayxample.net. 2011 (Comedy-Drama).

Spanish produced program that is set in Barcelona and follows the lives of several gay men and women and how they deal with the pressures of being who they are in a world that still does not fully accept them. Combining light comedy with drama, the program explores what they experience from a gay and lesbian perspective: their dreams, hopes, relationships and the problems by families who do not fully accept their sexual choices. The title is pronounced as "Gay-Sham-Pleh."

Cast: Kikki Bonometti (Alex), Maria Boquera (Transeunte), Xavi Mane (Xavi), Babeth Ripoll (Montse), Mireia Sabadell (Alicia), Rafael Tejada (Ivan), Josep Gomez (Lluis). **Credits:** *Producer-Director:* Giuseppe Storelli. **Comment:** Splendid photography and very good acting combine to present a visually appealing series that also contains partial nudity and sexual situations. While it is visually pleasing to watch, episodes are in Spanish with no English translation or subtitles.

Episodes: Ten episodes have been produced and are all in Spanish with the following exceptions (which contain English subtitles):

1. Gayxample: Making of Day 2 (Sub. English).
2. Gayxample: Trailer 1 (English).

104 Geez Louise. geezlouiseshow.com. 2012–2014 (Animated Comedy).

Victoria, sexy, sweet and possessed of a sultry voice is a lesbian and the owner of an all-girl gym called COBB. Cairn, her lesbian, flat-chest sister (compared to the voluptuous Victoria), possesses a deeper voice, is a bit more cautious and loves to eat. Louise, a carefree lesbian, has a somewhat higher-pitched voice and is often mistaken for a man (as is Cairn on occasion). The three women are not only friends but roommates and stories follow their various adventures as they deal with all the problems life throws at them.

Voice Cast: Angela Adams (Cairn/Victoria), J. Adams (Louise). **Credits:** *Producer:* J. Adams, Angela Adams. *Writer-Director:* Angela Adams. **Comment:** Delightful, non-offensive lesbian-themed program that has no sex, no vulgar language and no intimate scenes. It does have well developed stories, intriguing characters and an animation style that becomes increasingly appealing as the episodes play. The stiff-like animation does take getting use to, but that is part of the series charm, especially in the rendition of Victoria (and Maureen) who are the ultimate lesbians while Cairn and Louise are more boy-like (in figure) and even more child-like (especially the mischievous Louise). Angela Adams and J. Adams provide all the voices and you can almost picture the women as they change their voice tones for the different characters.

Episodes:

1. Bird in the Hand. Louise and Cairn try to hide the fact they are lesbians when Cairn mistakenly books them on a nature outing with heterosexuals.

Geez Louise. **Series poster art featuring (left to right) Cairn, Victoria and Louise (copyright Angela Adams, 2011–present).**

2. Cairn on the COBB, Part 1. Victoria, Cairn and Louise meet at COBB, the lesbian gym owned by Victoria.

3. Cairn on the COBB, Part 2. As Victoria and Cairn engage in a face-off, Louise realizes that she is in love with Victoria.

4. Car Tunes & Annie Mae, Part 1. A road trip finds Louise and Cairn becoming stranded in a strange Tennessee town called Gatlinburg when their GPS sends them in the wrong direction.

5. Car Tunes & Annie Mae, Part 2. After a short stay, Louise and Cairn depart Gatlinburg with an unwanted guest—the ghost of an elderly lady.

6. SpaNtaneous, Part 1. The lesbian bar Lezbots sets the scene as Cairn, Louise and Victoria set out for a night on the town.

7. SpaNtaneous, Part 2. While Louise and Victoria enjoy a spa, Cairn sets out to find their missing luggage.

8. Bowled Over 'n Out, Part 1. As Louise and Victoria ponder their relationship, Victoria finds she has become the attraction of a woman called CB (Canadian Bowler).

9. Bowled Over 'n Out, Part 2. As Cairn eagerly awaits to meet her hero, T.S., at an animation/gaming convention, Victoria convinces Louise to engage in cosplay (dressing as a cartoon character).

10. In Front of Everybody? Victoria attempts to deal with the hyper Louise when she becomes an annoyance during a plane flight by treating her like a kid and spanking her in public.

11. Swimmin' with Wimmin. Louise, Cairn and Victoria visit "The Wimmin's Festival of Stuff for Wimmin" only to discover they can't adjust to "the stuff."

12. It's Somebody's Birthd Eh? The New Year (2013) and CB's birthday are celebrated.

13. Get Yaaargh Sweat On! The contest entering Louise finally wins a prize—a "cruise" for three that finds her, Victoria and Cairn aboard a ship that is anything but elegant (especially when it has no engine and its passengers do the rowing).

14. I Can Fix That. With Louise and Victoria back on track, Louise goes a bit overboard in her efforts to look nice for her date with Victoria.

15. The Winery. A tour of a winery works well for Louise and Victoria but not for Cairn, who manages to get herself lost.

16. A Liege of the Their Own. With spring and the softball season arriving, CB plans organizing a team—without Cairn and Louise.

17. Battle of the FemmeBots. Victoria faces her greatest fear—Maureen, her equally gorgeous, childhood rival, who has just returned to town.

18. Sittin' with Louise. Louise becomes a TV addict when she suddenly discovers reality programs.

19. Chip's Ship. Victoria ponders her relationship with Louise when Cairn leaves for a mountain getaway and Victoria finds Louise has no idea how to cater to her needs.

20. Victoria's Secret. A flashback to their grade school days that finds Victoria, Cairn, Louise, Maureen and CB as classmates with Victoria and Maureen realizing that their beauty can get them what they want and, since they each want what the other wants, they will become rivals in later life.

21. LGBT BBQ. To get to know their neighbors a bit more, Louise and Victoria host a backyard barbeque.

22. Halloween Special. Although a bit older than the neighborhood kids, Louise and Victoria decide to go Trick-or-Treating while Cairn remains at home to greet the candy seekers.

23. Lead-Foot Louise. Cairn finds herself becoming a chauffeur when Louise loses her driver's license and needs to go places.

24. It's the Thought That Counts. Louise's belief that Christmas means getting gifts is changed when Victoria explains that it means giving gifts. The results become evident when, on Christmas Day Cairn opens her present from Louise—a bag of restaurant style corn chips.

25. The 7th Map. Cairn, Louise and Victoria embark on a scavenger hunt for a coveted prize but must deal with a cult of Succubus lesbians before claiming it—a cat that Louise believes is the reincarnation of her great, great, great grandmother, Lady Cabindish.

26. Desire's Unfurling Patience. Cairn's experiences as she finds herself talked into caring for Louise's grandmother, Lady Cabindish.

27. Maybe It's French Toast. At a spa get away, Cairn can think of nothing but what to have for breakfast while a jealous CB seeks a way to break up Victoria and Louise's budding romance. The program's concluding second season episode.

105 Generation L: The Road to Mardi Gras. youtube.com. 2011 (Reality).

It is 165 hours until the launch of the 2011 Gay Mardi Gras Parade of Sydney, an annual Australian lesbian party, begun in 2006, that attracts over one thousand followers—"and nobody parties like the gays. So come with me, join our party and meet Generation L." These are the words spoken by Renee, the party's organizer and the program follows a group of real-life lesbians (listed in the cast) as they prepare for Australia's biggest gay event—and what happens before, during and after the festivities.

Cast (as credited): Floss, Kate, Prue, Tania, Yas, Renee, Amber, Patricia. Credits are not given. **Comment:** Although labeled a reality series, it plays more like a regular scripted TV program rather than what the notion of reality brings to mind (capture things as they happen). Although the women are only credited by a first name, they are attractive and handle their roles well.

Episodes:

1. Episode 1. The principal women, a new gen-

eration of lesbians, are introduced followed by a brief history of the Mardi Gras.

2. Episode 2. The girls, gathered at Prue's home, prepare for the Harbour Party event.

3. Episode 3. At the Harbour Party, Tania fears that she will encounter her ex-lover, which begins to damper the festivities for all concerned.

4. Episode 4. Renee discovers that partying is what the Mardi Gras is all about—not an opportunity to mix business with pleasure.

5. Episode 5. At the Gotham Bar, Yas and Hoss discuss their relationship issues.

6. Episode 6. Cameras follow the festivities as the Mardi Gras gets into full swing.

7. Episode 7. As the festivities come to a close, the girls join the official after party at the Oxford Art Factory on Oxford Street.

8. Episode 8. A recap of the 2011 Mardi Gras festivities.

106 Get Out! Of the Closet! funny ordie.com/videos/55bd44d 576/get-out-of-the-closet-episode-1-part-1. 2010 (Comedy).

Billed as an "anti-reality show" wherein an intervention is held to bring gay and lesbians "out of the closet" and face the world as the people they truly are (although the methods incorporated by Natalie "Natty Ice" O'Sullivan and her producer, Barry Gordon Lightfoot, are anything but common as she is mean, doesn't take no for an answer and does whatever it takes to get a closet case into the open). **Cast:** Deb Malone (Natalie O'Sullivan), Kyle Sturdivant (Barry Gordon Lightfoot), Philip Hays (Brian), Rebekeah Dahl (Brian's mother), Marcia Mink (Drag Queen), Sean Stevens (Carlito). **Credits:** *Producer:* Meredith Melville, W. Ross Wells, Jarrod Gullett. *Writer-Director:* Travis Johns. **Comment:** A second series (see also *HA!*) to attempt comedy to bring closeted people into the open. It didn't work very well with *HA!* and the same situation appears here: does it insult the LGBT community or is it truly funny?

Episodes:

1. Pilot, Part 1. Natalie attempts to help a mother bring her son, Brian, out of the closet and into the real world.

2. Pilot, Part 2. Continues the story and also concludes the program with Brian coming to terms with who he really is.

107 Girl Crush: The Animated Ratchet Lesbian Talk Show. girlcrushtv.com. 2013 (Cartoon).

Martika, Jamishiana and Frankoquita (called Frankie) are brash lesbians who host a TV Talk show dedicated to helping such women deal with and overcome problems. While their intent is a good one, the hosts are plagued by numerous problems in their own personal lives and often deviate from a show topic to deal with what is on their plate. Each episode establishes a topic (or at least attempts to) with the hosts prepared to discuss it. Each woman is opinionated, has her own views and to get the upper hand constantly interrupt each other but also manage to enlighten not only themselves, but the viewing audience.

Girl Crush: The Animated Ratchet Lesbian Web Show. **Series poster art (copyright CoquieHughes).**

Voice Cast: Free Lemoi (Martika), Samara Smith (Jamishiana), Basha (Frankquita). **Credits:** *Producer-Writer-Animator-Director:* Coquie Hughes. **Comment:** The women are rude, crude and not drawn as the most attractive African-American lesbians. They use foul language abundantly and to some people, represent the stereo-typed image society has come to expect of certain black women (especially when they degrade each other with street terms like "Ho" and "Bitch"). But that is where the fun lies as creator Coquie Hughes has done in animation what stand-up comedians do all the time on stage—satirize what others may feel is inappropriate or uncomfortable to hear. It is a cartoon and should be viewed as just that—a spoof and nothing more. Episodes are preceded by a parental warning as being rated TV MA (intended for mature audiences). **Episode List:** *1.* Yo First Time Being with a Girl. *2.* Yo First Time Being with a Girl Continued. *3.* First Time and Domestic Violence Continued Again. *4.* Tryna Recap Past Topics. *5.* The Holiday Spirit.

108 Girl Gets Girl. girlgetsgirlthemovie. com. 2014 (Comedy-Drama).

Feature film adaptation of the Spanish Internet series *Chica Busca Chica* (*Girl Seeks Girl*). Nines, a beautiful lesbian has been living in Miami Beach, Florida, for the past nine years and has become a successful illustrator. Life is progressing well for Nines until she is caught cheating on her girlfriend (Rebecca) and life comes tumbling down around her. Feeling that she needs to get her life back together again, Nines returns to her home town of Madrid, Spain, but finds the situation just as complicated there when she becomes infatuated with Carmen, the gorgeous straight best friend of Monica, the woman Nines left behind nine years ago when she felt their decision to have a child was something she could not handle. Nines is eager to seduce Carmen but she is also the almost mother of Candela, the child born to Monica after Nines left on the day they were to be married. The movie plot follows all the intrigues Nines faces as she deals with the past to hopefully find the path she needs for her future happiness.

Nines is a girl who loves being in love. She is a go-getter but she is also unable to make a firm commitment to another girl. Veronica is a lesbian who desperately wants people to love her but she is neurotic and compulsive and those traits make her appear she is just too unapproachable. Sofia, the aggressive business executive, is called "Sofi Please," and seeks a woman to share her life. Lola is a lesbian who appears too serious in her approach to life and it could be the reason why she is having a difficult time finding that special someone.

Kirsten, a beautiful 45-year-old member of the National Rifle Association, is the editor of a woman's magazine (on which Nines worked as an illustrator) and deeply in love with Nines. Although Nines does not share the same feelings, Kirsten has set her goal to capture her heart. Blanca is a straight girl (married to Jorge) and about to give birth. Marta is an actress who has now fully encompassed her life as a lesbian. Javier, divorced from Carmen due to his unfaithfulness, is a man who never wants to grow old or face responsibilities.

Rai is a neo-punk girl who likes women but is angry at the world. Fran is Monica's gay best friend. Gustavo is the man who works with Carmen and has been secretly in love with her for years. Candela is Monica's daughter. Linda, born a man but never happy, now lives life as a transsexual woman.

Cast: Celia Freijeiro (Nines), Cristina Pons (Monica), Almudena Gallego (Ana), Sandra Collantes (Carmen), Maria Botto (Sofia), Sanda Collantes (Lola), Marina San Jose (Blanca), María Ballesteros (Marta), Ismael Martínez (Javier), Sabrina Praga (Rai), Jaime Olias (Fran), Adrián Lastra (Gustavo), Mar Ayala (Candela), Eulalia Ramón (Ana's mother), Estefanía de los Santos (Linda). **Credits:** *Producer:* Sonia Sebastian, Celia Freijeiro, Ana Carrera, Ruth Franco, Alejandro Miranda. *Director:* Sonia Sebastian. *Writer:* Sonia Sebastian, Cristina Pons, Angel Turlan. **Comment:** As of January 2015 the film has not been released. Based on the videos that are on line, it is a very sexy continuation of the original series. The acting is excellent, the cinematography top notch and the girls gorgeous. There are kissing scenes, adult situations and perhaps very brief nudity (judging by what appears in the "Sexy Bath" episode).

Episodes: All are in English with Spanish subtitles.

1. *Girl Gets Girl*: Let's Do This. The film and its characters are introduced.

2. Official Teaser *Girl Gets Girl*. An overview of the project is seen.

3. *Girl Gets Girl* Promo. Cast members appear to ask for help in raising funds to produce the movie.

4. Maria's Sexy Bath. Maria and Celia's sensuous bathroom love scene.

5. Angels and Devils. Maria and Christina debate the prospect on how to pick up women.

109 Girl/Girl Scene. webserieschannel. com. 2010 (Drama).

Kentucky provides the backdrop for a look at the lives of five beautiful women who are also lesbians: Evan, a "serial womanizer" (the equivalent of a male ladies' man); Jessie, a 16-year-old girl who has just come to terms with the fact that she is attracted to other girls; Zoe, Evan's slightly neurotic friend, a woman who is still struggling to overcome a breakup with a woman she truly loved; Maxine, a girl who can attract other women, but is unable to maintain a steady relationship; and Trista, an aggressive woman whose attitude makes it difficult to find someone she feels is her equal. Incorporating tenderness with drama and light comedy, the program explores their lives as each seeks to fulfill her life with another woman.

Cast: Tucky Williams (Evan), Joe Elswick (Jessie), Kate Moody (Zoe), Katie Stewart (Maxine), Roni Jonah (Trista), Lauren Virginia Albert (Ling), Kayden Kross (Avery), Cyndy Allen (Susan), Abisha Uhl (Bender), David Henry (Dan), Santana Berry (Tyler), Eric Butts (Thomas). **Credits:** *Producer:* Tucky Williams, Bill Bassert, Nic Brown, Bill Spanler. *Writer-Director:* Tucky Williams. **Comment:** Although comparisons can be made with the TV series *The L Word*, *Girl/Girl Scene* is a much more dramatic approach. There is some vulgar language, but numerous kissing scenes, and moments of tenderness with genuinely convincing performances by a well-chosen cast.

Girl/Girl Scene. **Series poster art (used by permission of Tucky Williams).**

Episodes:

1. Lovers' Split. Evan, Maxine, Zoe and Jessie are introduced as the four principal characters with Susan, Jessie's mother, and Elliott, Jessie's best friend.

2. A Case of You. As Jessie attempts to tell her mother that she is a lesbian, Zoe seeks to begin a relationship with Maxine.

3. Tired of Sex. A birthday celebration for Jessie becomes a night of tenderness for the girl-hungry Maxine. It is also revealed that Zoe has a younger sister (17-year-old Tyler) and that Zoe suffers from bi-polar depression (and is not consistent when it comes to taking her medication).

4. Chinese Burn. When Susan, Tyler's mother, discovers that Evan is having an affair with Tyler, she informs authorities, hoping to have Evan arrested for seducing a minor. The tables are turned when Susan is informed that in Kentucky sixteen is the age of consent and repressed feelings that she too may be gay are brought to the surface.

5. Help I'm Alive. Although she loves women, Jessie also likes men and feels she and Elliott need time apart when she realizes that Elliott is only interested in her for sex. Meanwhile, Susan comes to the realization that she is attracted to women but finds it difficult to accept that fact.

6. The Flower of Carnage. Evan, concerned over her friend Trista's continual use of drugs, decides to confront her while Susan, building up the needed courage, ventures into a lesbian bar "to check out the dating scene."

7. Psycho Suicidal Girl. As Jessie prepares to attend her high school prom—with three suitors (Evan, Tyler and Elliott), Susan finds an attraction to some of the gorgeous women frequenting the bar.

8. Episode 8. Recaps the prior 7 episodes with a dramatic climax: At Evan's home, Evan and Tyler are kissing when an intruder enters, knocks Evan unconscious and whisks Tyler off to a bedroom. As Evan regains consciousness, she takes a gun from a drawer, enters the bedroom and kills the intruder, saving Tyler's life.

9. Season 2, Episode. 1. As Evan is arrested and questioned by police over the shooting incident, several new women are introduced: Avery, the seductive call girl; Bender, a lesbian addicted to drugs; and Ling, a mysterious Oriental girl.

10. Season 2, Episode. 2. The sexual tensions that exist between Evan, Avery and Maxine are explored.

11. Season 2, Episode. 3. As Bender, infatuated with Ling, makes her move to seduce her, Maxine and Avery begin an intense relationship.

12. Season 2, Episode. 4. Continues to explore the relationship between the characters from the prior episode while Evan, found not guilty of murder, faces a civil lawsuit from the mother of the teenager she shot.

13. Season 2, Episode. 5. Maxine's world begins to take a turn for the worse when she turns to Bender for drugs.

14. Season 2, Episode. 6. Ling's relationship with Bender appears to be over when Ling meets a new girl (Finn) and becomes attracted to her.

15. Season 2, Episode. 7. The concluding episode wherein Ling begins a new relationship, Avery encounters "a quarter-life crisis" and Evan's life takes a new turn when her estranged father re-enters her life and offers her a proposition that will erase the lawsuit and make it appear like it never happened.

110 *Girl Play.* girlplaytv.com. 2013 (Drama).

When the term lesbian is used to identify a woman, images of beautiful, sensual women come to mind (perhaps due to their depiction on TV shows, in feature films and most assuredly in adult [XXX-rated] movies). In real life there are such women but there are also the lesser attractive butch type lesbians and the even more unattractive "masculine-identified women." Asian and Caucasian women are most readily associated with the beautiful sensual lesbian while African-American women are depicted in the less-feminine categories. Credit the adult film industry with portraying beautiful African-American women as sensual lesbians, but for some reason, a majority of web series have chosen to depict African-American women as lesbians in a darker, unflattering light (such as the butch or masculine-like). *Girl Play* attempts to change that image (as producer Aryka Randall states, "It's not reality for all of us") and present African-American lesbians as feminine women who also like to date feminine women. The lives of four such women, living in New Orleans, are explored as they deal with all the issues of life, including finding love and accepting who they are.

Olivia Black, 27 years old, is seeking to establish her own LGBT public relations firm. She is from San Francisco but relocated to New Orleans to attend college. She has recently broken up with whom she considered the love of her life (Tara) and her inability to let Tara go is also hindering her attempts to find someone new.

Tiffany Landry is 25 years old and studying pre-med at Tulane University. While she does date, she feels that she can only attract women who are below her intellectual and financial level and, instead of enjoying a relationship with them, finds herself supporting them. Not wanting to be a mother to such girls, Tiffany has set her goal to find a stable woman with whom she can share an equal relationship.

Marty Gastineau is 28 years old and attending Grad School in New Orleans after graduating from NYU (earning a degree in electrical engineering). Marty is drawn to women who appear to be wealthy and likes the idea of being pampered by a beautiful woman. Her relationships appear to last for only months at a time as Marty feels she must move on with no real idea how to sustain a long-lasting relationship because she hasn't figured out what that one special girl will look like or be like.

April Broussard and Lindsey Jones are a loving couple that plan to be married. April, 28 years old, was born in New Orleans while 32-year-old Lindsey (called L.J.) is a Midwest native. They currently share a house but their relationship is affected by the trust issues each has with the other.

Cast: Ava ReJouis (Olivia Black), Tiffany Anderson (Tiffany Landry), Dre Price (Marty Gastineau), Leslie Bohorquez (April Broussard), Kia Stephens (Lindsey Jones), Bryson Richard (Gabe Landry), Farrell "Mookie" Lockett (Whitney), Rachel Lockhart (Tara), Tamara Thorpe (Renee). **Credits:** *Producer:* Aryka Randall, David May. *Writer:* Neira Hayden, Aryka Randall. *Director:* David May, Jon Gunnar Gylfason. **Comment:** No reason is given as to why the first two episodes are off-line. The series is very well acted and produced and is a different approach to the way African-American lesbians are depicted (as producer Aryka Randall had promised). Well worth watching even though episodes are missing to see how, when care and attention to detail is taken, such series can rise above others of its kind.

Episodes: Four episodes were apparently filmed but only a teaser (trailer) and episodes 3 ("Lesbian Love and Lap Dances") and 4 ("Money Is the Motive") are on line.

111 *Girl to Girl.* onemorelesbian.com. 2012 (Reality).

An attempt to explore the lives of eight up-and-coming young lesbians during a summer stay at a home specially designed to record their daily activities.

Host: Jenna, Tasha and Ashley (as credited). **Credits:** *Producer:* Chloe Anderson. **Comment:** While a series never materialized, promotional videos remain on line. Jenna and Ashley appear in each video and present their idea and how money is needed to finance the project. While the idea immediately sounds like a lesbian version of CBS's *Big Brother* it may have come off as something much more interesting had it been produced. In the "Lessons Learned" episode, Jenna and Ashley are frank and explain the mistakes they made in an attempting to produce a web series when they were not well versed enough to undertake such an endeavor.

Episode List: *1.* Girl to Girl: The Launch. *2.* Girl to Girl: The Explanation. *3.* Girl to Girl: Auditions. *4.* Girl to Girl: Lessons Learned.

112 *Girlfriend Intervention Recap with Shangela.* youtube.com/watch?v=F27E2 HwYoZA. 2014 (Reality).

Girlfriend Intervention is a Lifetime cable series wherein four experts attempt to help restore a woman's confidence (and inner glow) with a complete makeover. Tracy Balan (beauty pro), Nikki Chu ("home and sanctuary guru"), Tiffny Dixon (fashion maven) and Tanisha Thomas (soul coach) are the experts—but did they do a good job? Drag Queen Shangela recaps the prior evening's program commenting on what was done, how it was done and whether with a change here and there it could have been done better.

Host: Shangela. **Credits:** *Producer:* Thairin Smothers, Peter Williams, Blake Jacobs, Adam Asea. **Comment:** Sometimes things the experts do not see or overlook can be seen by a non-expert and it is through those oversights that Shangela makes her comments and suggests what could have been achieved if something was done just a bit differently.

Episodes: Seven recap episodes were produced, each of which has a number (1–7) following the title (for example, "Shangela's Girlfriend Intervention #Recap—Episode 6," "Shangela's Girlfriend Intervention #Recap—Episode 7").

113 *Girls Don't Fight: The Series.* you tube.com. 2012 (Drama).

Starlaina, Angel, Siobhan, Brenda, Jessica and Devin are students at the Taymoore School for the Performing Arts. Starlaina and Angel are lesbians (and lovers) and the school is deceptively deceiving. Beneath its hallowed halls lies a secret student organization called PTA (Post Totem Anthem), a student-led society that maintains order through fear, intimidation and manipulation (sort of psychological warfare). The PTA Raffle, wherein two randomly selected students (one male, one female) face each other in a no rules bout called Fight Night, is the main "entertainment" function of the PTA. Life changes drastically for Starlaina when Angel commits suicide and Starlaina feels she no longer belongs in a world she once loved. Seeing that Starlaina is vulnerable, Jessica, the PTA leader, manipulates her (as well as Siobhan, Jessica and Brenda) into joining the PTA. Still depressed over Angel's death, Starlaina is now faced with the school's dark side and stories follow Starlaina as she and her friends become a part of the fist-fighting world of the PTA.

Jessica actually lives two different lives—the manipulative leader of the PTA and to teachers and parents, the personification of morality and perfection. Jessica feels she is unique and must control the humanity of others and destroy everything that makes a person different from her.

Brenda, in love with Siobhan, is the cute, perky girl everyone loves and adores. She was raised by her brother Mitch and his then girlfriend (now wife) Digna since she was five years old (at which time her mother abandoned the family).

Siobhan, the school beauty, is an unapologetic lesbian who does as she pleases without regard to anyone else's feelings. She is the "school bitch" and the dream girl of every guy—and girl—at the school. Despite her attitude, she is a loyal friend, especially to Starlaina, whom she has known since kindergarten.

Devin is Starlaina's best male friend, the guy who holds the group together and fixes their problems.

Other Characters: Samuel is the dreamboat of the straight girls at the school (and accustomed to girls "throwing themselves at him"); Sebastian is Siobhan's older brother, a senior at the school and somewhat angry with Siobhan as his girlfriend's always become attracted to his sister; Jason is the school genius (IQ of 178) and hates women (stems from his hate of his twin sister, Jessica, whom he feels is hollow inside, exploits men and is the reason why men fail); Benjamin, a guy's man (he is gay), excels in school and does what he wants to do; Lucy, the only girl not in love with Jessica, is the PTA's main fighter, but she is also a girl who is angry at the world and into self-mutilation; Sara, the girl with no respect for authority, feels that the only way she can connect to boys is through sex; Miriam is the school's gossip queen; Mitch is Brenda's older brother.

Cast: Brittany Michelle (Starlaina Hallows), Jacklyn Lisi (Jessica Mooney), Gwyneth Jonnes (Brenda Lively), Mia Topalian (Siobhan Whitney), Mikey Costa-Brown (Devin Mitchell), Jaffrey Amador (Samuel Kilden), Matt Watson (Sebastian Whitney), Kyle Hoy (Jason Mooney), Ryan Foster Casey (Benjamin Abbitt), Naomi Pandolfi (Lucy Cruz), Crystal Yau (Sarah Kaddin), Sarah McAvoy (Miriam Finke), Jeremy Uliss (Mitch Lively). **Credits:** *Producer-Writer-Director:* Mia Kiddo. **Comment:** With only the "Minisodes" trailer to judge by, the program looked well-acted and produced. Only a glimpse of the fighting sequences is seen and it is not really possible to provide any further comment.

Episodes: All episodes have been taken off-line with the exception of two short videos: "Girls Don't Fight Minisodes" and "Girls Don't Fight Cast Interviews."

114 *The Girls Guide.* youtube.com. 2013 (Drama).

Lucy, Victoria and Shaun, friends since high school and now college graduates, are also roommates as they pursue their life's goals. Lucy and Victoria are lesbians (although not dating each other) while Shaun is a straight "dude"—and interested in girls, but not Lucy and Victoria. Victoria is a flirtatious girl and plays the field while Lucy feels more comfortable in a steady relationship. Shaun, like Lucy and Victoria, is seeking a girl and stories follow the three friends as they navigate "the oft tricky road to female affection."

Cast: Christa Anderson (Lucy), Briana Rayner (Victoria), Lucas Blaney (Shaun), Laura Geluch (Jessica), Chelsey Moore (Sarah), Natasha Alexander (Christina), Sean Hewlett (AJ). **Credits:** *Producer:* Tess Calder. *Writer-Director:* Justine Stevens. **Comment:** Very well acted and produced; so much so that you feel as if you are actually watching episodes of a network television series. There are some mild sexual situations and girl-girl kissing scenes.

Episodes:

1. Episode 1. The main characters are introduced in the series pilot film.

2. Episode 2. Lucy, a waitress at Porter's Coffee and Tea House, becomes attracted to a female customer that she later discovers is straight; AJ, Shaun's friend, warns Lucy and Victoria to stay away from his friend, Christina; Shaun fantasizes about meeting the right girl.

3. Episode 3. Lucy, Victoria and Shaun agree that the common areas of their apartment will not be used for romantic encounters while Victoria becomes attracted to a girl named Jessica.

4. Episode 4. As Victoria takes Shaun to a bar in an effort to meet girls, Lucy becomes attracted to a girl named Sarah—while still seeing Jessica.

5. Episode 5. Lucy, believing Sarah is the girl of her dreams, breaks up with Jessica only to later discover that Sarah has a boyfriend and apparently would rather be with him.

6. Episode 6. A party, arranged by Victoria and Shaun to celebrate Lucy's birthday, becomes a rather sad occasion for Lucy when she retreats to her room, lamenting over the fact that she has broken up with Jessica.

7. Episode 7. Realizing that she really loves Lucy, Sarah attempts to see Lucy on the night of her party but is turned away by Shaun; meanwhile, at the party, Victoria becomes attracted to the girl she was told to stay away from—Christina.

8. Episode 8. The concluding episode wherein Sarah, realizing her breakup with Lucy was a mistake, seeks a way to reconnect with her.

115 Girls Like Us. vimeo.com. 2012 (Drama).

Keisha Jackson is a young woman, earning a living as an attorney, but involved in two dramatically different relationships: one with another woman, Zoe (an author) and one with a man, Greg (a gynecologist). At first Keisha is able to handle both affairs, keeping one secret from the other, including her friends and family. But no matter how careful she is, her secret is uncovered by Zoe, who, still wanting to be with Keisha, is now pressuring her into ending

her affair with Greg. On the other front, Greg has been expressing his feelings about marriage and is evenly pressuring Keisha into becoming his wife. The story follows Keisha as she struggles over the biggest decision of her life: be with Zoe, the love of her life, or marry Greg and live the politically correct life.

Cast: Robin Lei (Keisha Jackson), Bethany Stanton (Zoe Baker), Anthony Phillips (Greg Black), Milon V. Parker (Al), Bionca Monroe (Diane Dupree), Nsenga Wilson (Candi Jackson), Dee Dee Bias (Mia), Latanya Lee (Lea). **Credits:** *Producer:* Anike Bay, Kristi Turner. *Director:* Chan Smith, Anike Bay. *Writer:* Anike Bay, Coquie Hughes, Chan Smith. **Comment:** Every source related to *Girls Like Us* calls it either a dramatic series or a web series. In actuality, it is a feature film and the "episode" that is on line is what can be called a teaser (runs a little over 13 minutes of a 74 minute film) to entice watchers to either see or purchase the movie. Although the movie is well written and it does have a very pretty lead in Keisha, its production values are more geared to a web series and do not contain the high production values or acting abilities of an indie (independent) or studio-produced feature film. *Girls Like Us* is an African-American production and is far above others than have been produced for the web (follows in the quality standard established by writer Coquie Hughes in her series *If I Was Your Girl*). While the teaser does not contain nudity, it has an over abundant use of profanity, kissing scenes, some adult situations and domestic violence scenes. The teaser does give an excellent impression of the movie and what to expect and leaves the decision as what to do next totally up to the viewer (there is also a notice at the end of the teaser that reads "View the full movie at movi.es/w2138/19271" but, while a web site will appear, the movie is not available for free viewing).

Episodes:

1. Girls Like Us, Part 1. The story line is established as the secret once held by Keisha slowly becomes the catalyst that will affect the rest of her life.

116 Girls Will Be Girls. funnyordie.com. 2007 (Comedy).

Asteroid, a low budget disaster film of the 1970s; the TV series *Court TV: Celebrities Who Kill* and spokesperson for Dr. Vim's Miracle Elixir are some of the highlights in the career of Evie Harris, a now alcoholic, no-longer-in-demand C-List actress. During her time as a celebrity, Evie had a rival, Marla Simonds, a woman who tried to upstage her at every opportunity (her claim to fame was starring as Chesty on *Fill Her Up*, a spin off [that never actually occurred] from the 1970s actual TV series *C.P.O. Sharkey*). Marla also has a daughter, Varla, who is seeking to follow in her mother's footsteps and become an actress. Life changes for Evie when Marla dies and Varla, desperately in need of money, turns to Evie for help. Although unable to outright give her what she needs, Evie invites Varla to live with her and her roommate, Coco Peru, a not-so attractive spinster who carries an unrelenting torch for the young doctor who performed her abortion several years ago. The program, which encompasses men in drag as women, follows the three roommates as they attempt to live together with the principal focus on Evie and her relentless efforts to reignite a show business career that never had an illustrious moment.

Cast: Jack Plotnick (Evie Harris), Clinton Leupp (Coco Peru), Jeffrey Roberson (Varla Simonds). **Credits:** *Producer:* Michael Warwick, Jack Plotnick. *Writer-Director:* Richard Day. **Comment:** Excellent acting and production values make for an enjoyable drag queen series where the guys as girls are very convincing assuming female roles. The series is adapted from the feature film of the same title and is as good as other series that use the drag queen format (like *Have You Met Miss Jones?*, *Capitol Hill* and *Chico's Angels*).

Episodes:

1. Girl Stalker, Part 1. As Varla announces that her TV series *Busy Girl* is being made into a feature film, it is learned that the women are unknowingly being stalked.

2. Girl Stalker, Part 2. After a discussion in which Varla lambastes the LGBT community, Evie makes her see the error of her thoughts and sets Varla on a mission to find a lesbian and apologize; meanwhile the stalker is revealed to be Evie's demented ex-husband, Bernie, who still can't get over losing Evie.

3. The Jizz Party. Seeing that Coco is not ferrying well in the romantic department, Evie arranges a party (with millionaire guests) in an effort to hopefully find her a husband.

4. Delivering Coco, Part 1. All appears to be normal at Evie's bungalow until Coco's mother (Scott Thompson) arrives for a visit and reveals that she needs a liver transplant. Evie, already the recipient of several such transplants (due to her excessive drinking) devises a plan to get a new liver when she learns that Coco is the donor and she and Coco share the same blood type.

5. Delivering Coco, Part 2. Evie puts her devious plan into action: she subdues Coco's mother, dons a wig and takes her place as the recipient of Coco's liver. The program ends in a cliff hanger of sorts with Evie with a new liver and Coco and Mother attempting to cope with what actually happened.

117 *Girltrash.* ovguide.com. 2007 (Crime Drama).

Tyler and Daisy are beautiful lesbians and lovers who live in Los Angeles and make ends meet through petty crimes (although it is mentioned that Tyler, the tougher of the two, has committed murder). LouAnne Dubois, a flirtatious lesbian who will seduce any woman she admires, is also a criminal and thrives on her talent as a con artist. LouAnne, however, is tired of petty crimes and sets her sights on something bigger—two million dollars, which she steals from Monique Jones, an out-of-control, extremely violent woman who wants her money back—at any cost, no matter who gets hurt (or killed) in the process.

Having known LouAnne from past encounters, Tyler and Daisy again find themselves involved with her when they discover what she has done—not only steal the money but put the blame on them and now Monique is seeking to not only kill her but them as well. Complications set in when Monique, in a plan to bring Tyler, Daisy and LouAnne in the open, kidnaps Daisy's sister, Colby (a lesbian) and her girlfriend (Misty) and threatens to kill them if the money is not returned to her. The program follows what happens as Tyler and Daisy not only attempt to avoid Monique but free Colby and Misty as well.

Cast: Michelle Lombardo (Tyler Murphy), Lisa Rieffel (Daisy Robson), Riki Lindhome (LouAnne Dubois), Margaret Cho (Min Suk), Rose Rollins (Monique Jones), Amber Benson (Svetlana "Lana" Dragovich), Gabrielle Christian (Colby Robson), Mandy Musgrave (Misty Monroe), Maeve Quinlan (Judge Cragen), Jimmi Simpson (Valentine), Joel Michaely (Dryer Guy). **Credits:** *Producer:* Angela Robinson, Alexandra Kondracke, Josh Polon, Rebecca Sekulich. *Writer-Director:* Angela Robinson. **Comment:** The women, including the teenage Misty and Colby, are all very attractive and perform their roles well. The program is filmed in black and white which makes for a different feel as opposed to it being done in color. There is an abundant use of vulgar language and numerous kissing scenes (but no nudity and nothing that borders on pornography) and the program, although tailored to a lesbian audience, can be enjoyed by anyone (just be prepared for the trashy language).

Episodes:

1. Episode 1. Tyler and Daisy are introduced as they contemplate the matters they are facing.

2. Episode 2. LouAnne is introduced as she meets with Tyler and Daisy.

3. Episode 3. Tyler and Daisy discover what LouAnne has done and now all three are on the run for their lives.

4. Episode 4. A flashback to the time Tyler and Daisy first met LouAnne.

5. Episode 5. With no other choice, Daisy and Tyler join with LouAnne to defeat Monique.

6. Episode 6. LouAnne's heist has so angered Monique, a woman called "The Widow Maker" that she connects with a criminal gang to do her dirty work.

7. Episode 7. Unable to find her targets, Monique devises another way to get them: she kidnaps Daisy's younger sister Colby and her girlfriend Misty.

8. Episode 8. When word reaches Tyler and Daisy about the kidnapping, Daisy turns to Tyler for her help in freeing Colby. A plan to use LouAnne

as bait to draw out Monique fails and the girls are back to square one.

9. Episode 9. With no other choice, Tyler and Daisy seek the help of Lana, a deadly assassin.

10. Episode 10. As Misty and Colby attempt to escape from their locked room, Lana begins preparations to get Monique and free Misty and Colby.

11. The Lost Misty Scenes. In 2007, after filming *Girltrash* for 12 days, funds ran out and the series was never completed. This episode consists of unedited and not used footage that focuses on Misty and Colby who, after untying themselves but are unable to escape, turn to each other for comfort (in a sensual kissing scene that is interrupted when they hear someone at the door and prepare to defend themselves. The program ends at this point).

118 *Girltrash: All Night Long.* girltrash allnightlong.com/. 2013 (Musical).

A musical, feature-length version of *Girltrash* (see prior title) that focuses on one night in the lives of the principal characters, from love making to cat fighting, as seen through a series of lively musical numbers.

Cast: Lisa Rieffel (Daisy Robson), Michelle Lombardo (Tyler Murphy), Gabrielle Christian (Colby Robson), Mandy Musgrave (Misty Monroe), Kate French (Sid), Clementine Ford (Xan), Kelly Ogden (Herself), Rose Rollins (Monique Jones), Megan Cavanagh (Officer Margie), Jessica Chaffin (Officer Jackie), Mike O'Connell (Valentine), Malaya Rivera Drew (Lauren), Joanna Canton (Mitchele), Theron Cook (Crisp), Heather Thomas (Nadine). **Credits:** *Producer:* Stacy Codikow, Lisa Rieffel, Angela Robinson, Lisa Thrasher. *Director:* Alexandra Kondracke. *Writer:* Angela Robinson. *Music and Songs:* Killola. **Comment:** Filmed in color (as opposed to the black and white *Girltrash* series) and a surprisingly well done program. Lisa Rieffel, a member of the real life group Killola, and the rest of the cast all handle their acting/singing roles well and the movie makes for a pleasant diversion on the comedy and drama series devoted to lesbians.

119 *Give Me Grace.* givemegracetheseries. com. 2010 (Drama).

A young woman, known only as Grace, appears to lead a somewhat mysterious life. While it is made clear she is a lesbian and in a relationship with another woman (Jolie) her actual life's work is somewhat of a mystery. She appears to be a martial arts instructor but that looks to be her cover as an operative for "The Family," a candle-stein group of women led by Marah, that fulfills contracts of unethical means for clients (exactly what "The Family" is or what they actually do is not clearly stated). The program relates what happens when Grace receives a text message ("You Fail, She Dies") indicating that Jolie's life is in danger if Grace fails and her efforts to not only protect Jolie, but uncover the unknown sender's identity.

Cast: Raelaine San Buenaventura (Grace), Jessica Etheridge (Jolie), Rinabeth Apostol (Ari), Khary Moye (Red), Tiana Salim (Marah), Dana Soliman (Nikki). **Credits:** *Producer-Writer-Director:* Jorna Tolosa-Chung. **Comment:** The program captures your attention from the very beginning (with the text message) and flows into a smooth running, well-acted and produced thriller. It is also a mystery in a way as the released episodes do not fully explain who Grace really is (and how and why she is presumably an assassin) and what "The Family" is all about.

Episodes:

1. Episode 1. The mystery begins—not only of what "The Family" is but who is threatening Jolie's life.

2. Episode 2. Nikki, Marah's ruthless daughter, feels that her mother's leadership is below par and that she should be running the organization in the same treacherous manner of her late father, bringing her in conflict with Grace, who, though fearful of Marah, respects what Marah is accomplishing.

3. Episode 3. Another text message ("Play Nice") is sent to Grace while a sudden death in "The Family" (Marah) by an unknown assassin brings Nikki into power—to run the organization as she sees fit—and find her mother's killer at any cost. The program's concluding unresolved episode.

120 *God Des and She: Never Give Up.* tell ofilms.com. 2009 (Reality).

God Des and She is a queer hip-hop duo that combines hip-hop music with that of pop and soul to produce unique songs that reinforce the fact that being gay (or different) can and should be celebrated. Des God and She hail from Madison, Wisconsin, and had a dream to spread their message beyond the Midwest. They literally packed their bags and ventured onto New York without a plan of attack (so to speak). It was when they appeared on the 2006 season three finale episode ("The Bachelor Party") of the TV series *The L Word* that their career ignited and have since been a strong advocate for a positive influence in the LGBT community. Encompassing a documentary style presentation, the program follows one of their road trips while relating incidents from their personal and professional lives to show how, even though they are "a queer duo," their music is not just for those who are different, but for people in general.

Cast: Alicia Smith (God Des), Tina Gassen (She). **Credits:** *Producer:* Christin Mell, Leah Martel. *Writer-Director:* Julie Keck, Jessica King. **Comment:** The free episode is basically God Des relating how the duo was formed. It is well done and God Des comes off as a down-to-earth young woman who can capture attention just by listening to what she has to say. The production values are comparable to any documentary series produced by network or cable TV and for anyone interested in music, especially in the three genres covered by the duo should check out the free episode as it without a doubt just as captivating as the series as a whole.

Episodes: Five episodes have been produced with only episode 5 available to view for free (the others require a paid subscription account at tellofilms.com to watch). There is also a short trailer (free) that highlights segments of the series.

121 *Going Our Way.* vimeo.com/30974 211. 2012 (Drama).

Next Door is Australia's top-rated television soap opera. It is here that Caz, an unemployed screenwriter, hopes to further her career by acquiring a writer's internship on the show. Her life changes for the better when she applies, but finds competition from Ralph, her life-long nemesis, who is also seeking the same position and who has a much better chance as he already works on the show. The program not only follows the events that spark Caz's life as she and Ralph clash, but her involvement with Matt Doyle, an actor on the show who has fallen for her and the resentment she faces from Saj, her gay friend, who has become jealous that his dream guy (Matt) is seeing Caz.

Other Characters: Rhiannon, a 25-year-old who hopes to change laws, especially traffic, for the safety of the public; and Tobi, a six-year-old, extremely bright child, whose parents are not seen but who lives in the same building with Caz, Saj and Rhiannon in Melbourne, Australia.

Caz is a very gifted girl but not highly motivated and thus not always being able to achieve what she is capable of (especially when she always loses out to Ralph). Following her graduation from college, Caz struck out on her own and moved in with her friends Saj and Rhiannon, but she still remains unmotivated and would rather just watch TV than write it. Her motivation rises when she learns Ralph is applying for an internship and she feels it is now time for her to beat him.

Saj was born in Sri Lanka and moved to Australia when he was a teenager. Although he studied marketing in college, he was interested in filmmaking and met Caz after sneaking into one of her film classes. With no interest in marketing or acquiring a job, he watches films and TV shows and spends his time blogging about them.

Rhiannon, a law student, was raised in a rather unusual environment. After her brother was killed in a car accident, her parents wandered into a world of drinking and drugs and it did change the course of Rhiannon's life as she switched her major from Arts to Law to become a politician and change traffic laws for the better. Her relationship to Caz is closer now than it was when Caz's brother and her brother were friends.

Ralph and Caz have been friendly enemies since grade school and he has made it a goal to be the best at everything, especially when it comes to Caz. While Caz has the same goals as Ralph, he is far more motivated and Caz always comes in second. He works as a runner (gopher) on *Next Door* and secretly runs the show's fan forum.

Matt, the principal star of the show, is a simple guy who finds himself competing for Caz against a different kind of competition: Ralph, but not in the normal sense as Caz is now totally focused on getting the internship and finally beating Ralph at something. Information on Tobi, "child genius," is marked "Classified" and nothing is revealed.

Cast: Donna Pope (Caz), Lauren Wade (Rhiannon), Matt Young (Matt Doyle), Sajeeva Sinniah (Saj), Tobi Johnson (Tobi), Gordon Boyd (Ralph), Thomas Bulle (Jay), Don Bridges (Al), Clara Pagone (Liz), Chris Chalmers (Eddie). **Credits:** *Producer:* Jessica Brajoux, Fiona Eloise Bulle. *Director:* Jessica Brajoux, John Erasmus. *Writer:* Fiona Eloise Bulle, Thomas Bulle, Dean Watson. **Comment:** An amazingly well produced and acted program that was, according to the producer, made for $18 ("We entered a competition to create our own web series and win $50,000 ... but we were unsuccessful. We didn't take this as a setback, rather a challenge ... we tried to make one for as little money as possible. By gathering a talented group of people and finding a few friends with equipment, we managed to make this web series for $18"). Maybe the networks could take a lesson and see that enormous amounts of money are not needed to produce an enjoyable program.

Episodes:

1. Episode 1. Saj and Rhiannon talk Caz into "stalking" the stars of their favorite soap opera.

2. Episode 2. While seated in a bar waiting for the cast to appear, Caz learns of an internship position on the show.

3. Episode 3. As Caz ponders over a decision as whether or not apply for the internship, the roommates prepare for a visit from Rhiannon's hippie parents.

4. Episode 4. Caz decides to apply for the internship—only to discover that Ralph has applied for the same position.

5. Episode 5. Saj becomes jealous when he learns that his heart throb, Matt, has asked Caz out on a date.

6. Episode 6. Caz and Matt's date is anything but common when Caz's clumsiness makes it appear that the two can never be an item—which delights Saj as he now feels he may still have a chance with the show's star.

7. Episode 7. Caz finds herself in a compromising situation when she attempts to sabotage Ralph's efforts—and gets caught by Matt.

8. Episode 8. Caz receives the news she has been hoping for (the internship) and she and her friends celebrate at the Felix Bar, where it all began. The first season concludes.

9. Episode 9. The second season opens with Caz, now with a new job and a new home, still wondering if she can get out from under Ralph's shadow, now that he too has been offered the internship.

10. Episode 10. Eddie, Caz's brother arrives unannounced, putting a damper on her fresh start as he appears to be looking for a place to stay while he works out his personal problems.

11. Episode 11. Saj's inability to accept Caz and Matt as a couple, has him acting strangely and Eddie wondering what kind of men his sister is dating.

12. Halloween Special, Part 1. Caz, Saj and Rhiannon decide to celebrate Halloween with a spooky party.

13. Halloween Special, Part 2. As the party gets underway, Caz feels all is not right when strange things begin to happen.

14. Episode 14. As Caz begins to help write *Next Door* Matt finds Rhiannon becoming attracted to him.

15. Episode 15. At a *Next Door* staff party, Caz finds herself caught in the middle between Saj and Matt when Saj makes a play for him.

16. Episode 16. The concluding episode wherein Ralph realizes that what he has been doing to Caz over the years was wrong and attempts to apologize and make friends; Caz responds with "Let's just say friendly" leaving the doorway open for additional episodes.

122 *Gold Stars.* goldstarsshow.tumblr.com. 2014 (Comedy).

Cassie and Anna are lesbians and roommates (but not lovers) who work as freelancers—doing whatever type of odd job that comes their way to make money. The girls share a two bedroom apartment in Brooklyn, New York, and their efforts to get by on what little money their enterprise nets is the focal point of stories.

Cast: Lane Moore (Cassie), Molly Knefel (Anna), Katie Compa (Carol), Hilary Warburton (Ghost Girl), Brittany Connors (Elyse), Chen Drachman (Yael). **Credits:** *Producer-Writer-Director:* Lane Moore. **Comment:** Delightful comedy with the only problem being the last episode wherein background noises make dialogue difficult to understand. There is no nudity or foul language and only the last three episodes deal with the lesbian aspect of the series. Lane Moore and Molly Knefel are nicely cast as each plays well off the other (sort of like a female "Odd Couple" but without the neatness or untidiness). The episodes, short as they are, flow smoothly and have television quality-like production values.

Episodes:

1. The Foot Job. The girl's acquire their first job but it is not a pleasant experience for Cassie when she reports back to Anna (exactly what the title means is not explained, nor is anything seen regarding it).

2. The Couch Guy. Hoping to show Cassie she appreciates all she is doing for her, Anna presents her with a gift (a rather cheap bracelet that immediately breaks when Cassie looks at it).

3. S**T Job. Cassie expresses her doubts about taking a job to become part of a weird study of her bathroom regularity.

4. Craigslist Roommate Search. Anna's theory that she and Cassie need a third roommate has them encountering an assortment of weirdoes when they make a Craigslist posting.

5. Housewarming Party. As Anna and Cassie throw a housewarming party to meet their neighbors, Cassie has an encounter with a most unusual guest—the ghost of a girl who once occupied the apartment.

6. But You Don't Look Gay Enough to Be a Lesbian. Although Cassie is just as pretty and sexy as Anna, she finds herself trying to figure out why Anna continually gets hit upon by girls and she doesn't.

7. Cool Girls. In an attempt to attract a girl who hates her (Carol), Cassie buys some marijuana, thinking smoking weed together will bond them.

8. Awkward Date. Cassie's first date with a girl she just met (Elyse) becomes awkward when Anna makes herself a part of their activities. The program's concluding episode.

123 *Good People in Love.* wardpicturecompany.com. 2011 (Drama).

Carolyn and Max are a couple about to be married and to celebrate the occasion invite their best friends, Sarah and Scott and Beth and Anna to an engagement party. Sarah and Scott have differing views on marriage, especially those involving gay and lesbian couples. It is a time in New York City when the equal rights marriage bill has been passed and Scott and Sarah set out to explore their points on love and marriage by using the party's other two couples as guinea pigs in their little experiment. The program charts what happens when Scott and Sarah's manipulative actions cause more concern than just acquiring answers.

Cast: Rachael Hip-Flores (Sarah), Heather Leonard (Carolyn), Steven Alexander (Max), Megan Melnyk (Anna), Renee Olbert (Beth), Jesse Wakeman (Scott). **Credits:** *Producer-Writer-Director:* Tina Cesa Ward. **Comment:** Network TV–like drama with good acting and production qualities. There is some vulgar language and kissing scenes. The program flows smoothly from beginning to end.

Episodes:

1. Setting the Table. Sets the scene as the party guests arrive and Scott and Sarah begin preparations to manipulate their friends.

2. A Drink Before Dinner. Beth and Anna's attempts to make love are not so secretive when Sarah realizes what they are up to.

3. Main Course. At dinner, the conversation turns a bit ugly when hidden feelings are revealed.

Good People in Love. **Left to right: Rachael Hip-Flores, Megan Melynk, Renee Olbert, Jesse Wakeman (copyright Ward Picture Company, Inc.).**

4. Left Over. Continues from where the prior episode left off with Beth and Anna relating their feelings about each other—and now not so sure they are the perfect couple.

5. Call It a Night. While Anna and Beth seek to resolve their differences, Carolyn and Max have a confrontation when Max reveals that, although he loves Carolyn, she is very manipulative and it could impair their future happiness together. The program's concluding episode.

124 *Gossip Boy.* gossipboyseries.com. 2011–2013 (Drama).

Gossip Girl TV series title switch that charts, in soap opera like form, the lives of several gay young men living in Los Angeles: Jairus, an 18-year-old who leaves an unloving home (being raised by an aunt and uncle) to live his life as an open gay with a stranger he met over the Internet (Nathan); Mat, heartbroken after breaking up with his lover after a five year relationship who is set on a new path by his therapist: right life's injustices as a means of moving on; and Jordy, a troubled youth Mat takes under his wing in an effort to reconstruct his own life.

Cast: Daniel Landroche (Jairus Moore), Christopher Sams (Nathan Cross), Matt Brough (Jordy), Kevin Farias (Mat), Angela Henderson (Rhonda Morgan), Matthew Arnett (Devin Potter), Collin Chute (Travis), Sterling Price (Erik), Ryan Shaughnessy (Zain), Jennifer Monce (Kara), Kelly Kemp (Faith), Jodi Carol Harrison (Aunt Darlene), Kelli Joan Bennett (Bea), Bobby Gold (Luthur), Paige Morrow Kimball (Lisa Moore), Jonah Blechman (Narrator). **Credits:** *Producer:* Jason Lockhart, Linda Fulton, Paul A. Storiale, Adam Lloyd, Justin Michael Stevenson, Robert Mitchell. *Director:* Paul A. Storiale, Bree Pavey, Robert Mitchell, Charlie Vaughn. *Writer:* Paul A. Storiale, Bree Pavey. **Comment:** Exceptionally well-acted and produced program. The characters are very believable and the situations, while true-to-life, are not overly done and dragged out; they are dealt with honestly and swiftly, making for a smooth flowing transition from situation to situation.

Episodes:

1. It Gets Better. Establishes the story line as Jairus, turning 18, moves to Hollywood to be with Nathan.

2. Friends and Family. Jairus moves in with the older Nathan but feels the situation getting a bit uncomfortable when he realizes Devin, Nathan's friend, is becoming jealous.

3. Changing Paths. As Jairus and Nathan talk Jairus discovers that Nathan has not been totally honest with him about being monogamous. Mat, Nathan's friend, is seen consulting a therapist after he and his lover of five years have just broken up.

4. I Want You. As Rhonda and her boyfriend, Erik, discuss their future relationship, the recluse Jordy is introduced.

5. The Mysterious Man. It appears that Rhonda and Erik's relationship will come to an end as Rhonda is reluctant to move to accompany Erik in

his new job. Her revelation that she is pregnant appears to be the glue that will keep what will now become a long-distance relationship together.

6. OMG. As the tension between Nathan and Devin grows, Devin makes a play for Jairus, hoping to make Nathan jealous.

7. Caught in the Rookie Jar. As Nathan confronts Jairus, telling him that he has had sex with other men and does not love him, he is surprised to hear that Jairus was also not faithful to him.

8. Delicious Proposal. After Rhonda and Jairus spend the day together to talk about what has been happening to them, Devin appears to Jairus to ask him out on a date.

9. I Lied, to Be Honest. Realizing that Jairus is the only hope she has for keeping Erik, Rhonda tells him that she lied about her pregnancy but now needs his help—to get her pregnant ("he will never know it is not his") as she needs to be with him.

10. Reverse Karma. The first season concludes with Jairus taking charge of his life and leaving Nathan for what he hopes will be a better life without him.

11. One Year Down. The second season begins with Jairus, Rhonda and Devin now living together; the lesbian couple, Faith and Kara are introduced as the owners of the Romano Café.

12. The Secret. A complex story is set up that is resolved in the last episode. It appears that Rhonda had a brother (Charlie) who was kidnapped by his babysitter but never found. The sitter turns out to be Lisa Moore, Jairus's mother and Jairus was that kidnapped child. When Darlene, Lisa's sister, threatens to reveal what had happened, Lisa kills her, hoping but failing to keep her secret. When the truth comes out Jairus becomes part of his actual family again.

13. Hot Guy Down the Hall. Jairus turns his attention to becoming a writer by enrolling in a class; Faith and Kara open their cafe; Rhonda prepares to meet "The Hot Guy Down the Hall" (Luthur).

14. Episode 4/10 (Untitled). Nathan and Jairus, known for making the club scene, have been replaced by Devin and Nathan as the clubbers since Jairus and Nathan broke up. Jairus is seen preparing to write a story as a class assignment.

15. Marriage Equality. Kara and Faith, although living together for eight years, have reached a point in their relationship where everything seems to be causing a problem. Hoping to find answers, they seek the help of a therapist. Nathan, moved by the story Jairus has written, believes it is time he came out of the closet and tell his parents he is gay.

16. Hot Potato Salad. Having been at odds with her father for several years, Rhonda returns home to make amends; meanwhile, Jairus receives a call from a classmate (Travis) asking him out on a date.

17. Lesbians Are Cool. Believing that a child is needed to save their relationship, Kara and Faith begin a search to find a donor; Rhonda's parents ap-

pear not to be thrilled over that "Hot Guy Down the Hall" when they believe she and Erik were meant to be together. The situation becomes more uncomfortable when Erik returns from his trip.

18. Tricky Travis. Kara and Faith have decided on a donor—Jairus; now to convince him. Meanwhile Travis, who thought he was straight, now doubts his sexuality as he is becoming attracted to men as well as women (perhaps begun when he made that phone call to Jairus in episode 16). Rhonda's reunion with Erik has her suppressed feelings for him returning; so much so, that she accepts his proposal of marriage (she and Luthur remain friends).

19. Charlie. As Kara and Faith find that Jarius is willing to become the donor they are seeking, they agree on taking a trip (later seen as a trip induced by drugs). Travis's inability to clearly see his present situation has him contemplating suicide.

20. Everything Happens for a Reason. The concluding episode that finds Travis is about to kill himself and Nathan being charged with murder (killing Devin. Other than a brief police station scene wherein Nathan is accused of the crime, nothing else is given). Ten months pass and Rhonda and Erik are now parents and Jairus has made a decision to move on with his life and head to the Midwest as the program ends.

125 *The Grass Is Pinker.* thegrassispinker. com. 2012 (Comedy).

A group of young people and their efforts to navigate life—as gays and lesbians and the problems each encounters when they try to hook up with people of the same sex and for some, as they deal with a former lover who just won't let go. It's not "The Grass Is Always Greener," it's "The Grass Is Always Pinker on the Other Side."

Mya is shy and sweet and looking for the perfect girl to be her mate. Zoe is the new girl in town and just trying to fit in and a hook up with a girl. Joseph is very flamboyant, fun-loving and straight forward (he tells it like it is).

Nick is Joseph's lover, a young man who thinks he knows it all (he's also very stuck-up). Lisette is the bitch of the group, a selfish girl who, once she finds a girl to love wants that girl to love no one else but her.

Chris is Lisette's girlfriend, a smooth-talking, easy-going flirt. Jackie is Zoe's opinionated friend; Ned is Mya's recently retired father; Mr. Downey is the manager of True Buy, a technical support center.

Cast: AnToni Logan (Mya), Cherise Quimby (Zoe), Destiny Wheeler (Lisette), Stephen Rollins (Joseph), Yarek Kaczmarzyk (Nick), Kim Armstrong (Jackie), Tony Lyn (Ned), Teri Grijalva (Chris), Chris Rodriguez (Mr. Downey). **Credits:** *Producer-Writer:* AnToni Logan, Cherise Quimby. *Director:* Cherise Quimby. **Comment:** Based on the video information that is still on line, the acting and production values are good and there appear to have been kissing scenes (judging by the second promo). The "Milk Moustache" episode revolves around Joseph attempting to set Mya up on a date.

Episodes: Only one episode ("Milk Moustache") remains on line with three promotional videos: "The Grass is Pinker: Extended Promo," "The Grass Is Pinker: Promo 1" and "The Grass is Pinker: Promo 2."

126 *The Grinder Guide.* youtube.com. 2013 (Reality).

Australian produced program that follows a group of gay men as they encompass the abilities of "Grindr," a hook-up app. Whether it is to make friends, the starting point for a date, or just a hook-up for sex, the consequences of each application is seen to show viewers the pros and cons of the ubiquitous social network program for gay men.

Cast: Joel Allen. Paul Colebrook, Jack Colwell, Dan Murphy, Senthorun Raj, Sergio Rebelo, Nathan Valvo, Justin Wee. **Credits:** *Producer-Director:* Damien Dunstan. **Comment:** With good production values and a personable cast of real-life gay men, the program is not for everyone as its concentration is on the gay community and its approach to "Grindr." It is interesting to see how the app works—and how it can be both a blessing and a nightmare for those who choose to encompass it.

Episode List: *1.* The Grinder Guide Pilot. *2.* Sex. *3.* The Profile Pic. *4.* Race. *5.* The Date. *6.* The Aftermath. *7.* Body Image. *8.* Finale.

127 *The Grove.* thegrovetheseries.com/. 2013 (Drama).

The marriage of two beautiful lesbians, Cordelia Nicolette "Nico" Moynihan and Ivy Rose Rodriquez, sets the stage for a look at life in The Grove, a town on the Central Coast of California. It was founded in the early 19th century by members of the Moynihan family, Irish settlers who planted almond trees on the hundreds of acres of baron land that would eventually become known as The Grove. Over time other families had settled there, including the Kincaids, who acquired land from the Moynihan's but eventually sold portions off to develop new ventures. Once friends, the families are now in a battle to acquire as much land as possible to plant almond trees and a look at the differences and similarities of both families are depicted.

Cordelia is an auto mechanic and the daughter of Doyle Monihan, the owner of the Grove Tavern and Inn. Ivy, a baker, first met Nico when she came to her bake shop for her famous sweet bread; Ivy is later employed by Doyle at the tavern. Lauren is Doyle's daughter, an entertainment lawyer and Nico's half-sister; Sean is Lauren's brother and now head of the

Moynihan family almond business. Patrick "Paddy" Kincaid is the man responsible for destroying almond groves to develop an office park and his mini-mansion. Gloria is Patrick's spoiled socialite wife; Maximus, called Max, is Patrick's homophobic son, "the bad boy about town." Marigold is Patrick's selfish, spoiled daughter; Prissy is Patrick's mistress (and proud of it); Katherine, called Kitty, is Patrick's niece, an activist and political fund raiser; Jonny Chavas is the foreman of Doyle's almond groves.

Cast: Crystal Chappell (Nico Moynihan), Jessica Leccia (Ivy Rodriquez), Jordan Clarke (Patrick Moynihan), Beth Maitland (Gloria Moynihan), Christian LeBlanc (Max Moynihan), Nadia Bjorlin (Marigold), Bobbie Eakes (Katherine), Peter Reckell (Jonny), Linsey Godfrey (Poppy), Judi Evans (Prissy), Harrison White (Bobby). **Credits:** *Producer:* Crystal Chappell, Christina Morris, Michael Sabatino, Hillary B. Smith, Paul Barber, Karen Wilkens, Susan Flannery. *Director:* Karen Wilkens, Susan Flannery. *Writer:* Crystal Chappell, Michael Sabatino, Paul Barber. **Comment:** Although only a pilot has thus far been produced it sets the stage for a serial-like presentation that will show the intrigues that exist between the two families. There are sexual situations (especially between Nico and Ivy) and the sexual chemistry between Crystal and Jessica is the highlight of the program.

Episodes:
1. The Grove Pilot. The saga of the Moynihan and Kincaid families begins as the wedding between Nico and Ivy becomes the catalyst that will bring to light (via flashbacks) the past indiscretions that haunt both families.

128 *Ha! The Web Series.* youtube.com. 2009 (Comedy).

HA (Homosexuals Anonymous) is a Christian fellowship wherein people share their feelings about the gay lifestyle and attempt to overcome their homosexuality. Such a center in Florida, run by Bruce, "an ex-gay" and attended by one person in particular, Roger, is the center of attention as Roger, an Evangelical Christian struggles to deal with his plight—being mistaken for a gay when he feels he is straight although the situations he encounters make him believe he is gay. Flashbacks are used to explore Roger's life as he desperately wants to discover who he is.

Cast: Robert W. Evans (Roger), Bruce Vilanch (Bruce), Rebecca Flinn (Angela), Dawn Didawick (Mama), Ryan Hill (Ryan), Brian Kirchoff (George), Scott Nevins (Pastor Bob), Perry Laylon Ojeda (David), Charles Shaughnessy (Dr. Morberley), Jonathan Sharp (Sasha), Lisabeth Harris (Brenda), Bobby Wise (Bobby), Damon Kirsche (Laramie). **Credits:** *Producer-Writer:* Perry Laylon Ojeda. *Director:* Larry Raben. **Comment:** While the program is intended to be a comedy, it can come off as an insult to gays and lesbians as its presentation is skewed to curing such people of their "addiction." Bruce Vilanch, genuinely a talented writer and comedian (as proven by his stint on *The Hollywood Squares*) comes off as rather over-bearing and not fun to watch as he oversees the HA center (he just does not seen to have the compassion needed to help people suffering from serious sexual identity problems). Overall the production is well filmed and adequately acted although the choice to set most of the "action" in the center was not a good choice as the acoustics makes the sound hollow at times and difficult to understand. See also *Get Out! Of the Closet!* for a similar program.

Episodes:

1. My Name Is Roger. Roger is introduced as he attends his first meeting at HA.

2. That's My Mama. Roger attempting to tell his mother that he may be gay is seen in a flashback.

3. Yogi & Boo Boo. Center leader Bruce shares his experiences being a born again heterosexual.

4. Hit Me George. Center members are treated to a guest speaker who reveals his experiences as a recovering gay.

5. Episode Removed from the Internet.

6. I Know What You Did Last Summer. Roger recalls (via a flashback) his summer at an all boys camp.

7. Not Your Average Bear. Roger learns how men "of a different persuasion" are viewed by others.

8. The Little Polar Bear. As a class assignment Roger reads a story he wrote as a child that reveals traces of him thinking he may be different.

9. Laramie. The class is treated to a guest singer (Laramie), a cowboy-like ex gay who entertains with songs of hope of overcoming their shame.

10. I Want My Mommie Dearest. Roger attempts to deal with a visit from his mother.

11. I Love You, Mommie Dearest. Roger's worst fears are realized when his mother learns of his love for men.

12. Boo Boo Makes Yogi. A reference to the Hanna-Barbera cartoon characters Yogi Bear and his companion Boo Boo Bear wherein Roger reveals his feelings about attending an all-male yoga class.

13. The Dinner. Roger faces another fear—inviting his boyfriend to his mother's house for dinner.

14. Dr. Morberly. The dinner party has startling consequences for Roger: he discovers that his father was gay.

15. The Gospel According to Pastor Bob. A pastor's speech at the center appears to be further confusing Roger as to whether he is really gay or not.

16. No Going Back. The concluding episode wherein Roger graduates and is declared an ex-gay—but is he really as the episode ends?

129 *Half Share.* half-share.com/the-web-series. 2011 (Comedy).

New York's Fire Island Pines is a real retreat for gay men during the summer (Memorial Day to Labor Day). Because rooms are expensive a system called Half Share exists for those who cannot afford their own room. In Half Share, if you do not bring your own roommate you are anonymously paired with someone you may or may not like. The summer months of the year 2011 are explored as a group of gay men gather for what they hope will be a time of hookups as well as fun in the sun.

Ito, a drunk who collects antiques and lusts after elderly men, is the housemother. Michael Yes and Michael No are a bitchy dysfunctional couple that appear to thrive on alcohol; Harold, a Park Avenue lawyer, is a drug-addicted, sex-crazed, semi-crossing diva; Mac is the out-of-towner (retreating to New York after a breakup) who is teamed with Lex, a man who is his complete opposite. While Mac is laid back and unaccustomed to life in a big city, Lex is a man of the world who drinks, smokes pot and seeks fun anyway he can. He also sees Mac as a challenge and he and the other housemates join forces to see that Mac, "the fish out-of-water" becomes one of them before the summer is over.

Cast: Alec Mapa (Ito), Jack Plotnick (Michael Yes), Sam Pancake (Michael No), Jesse Archer (Lex), Kyle Spidle (Mac), Kevin Morrow (Harold), Marcus Shane (Wee), Joey Dudding (Brandon), Robin Byrd (Robin), Marc Alan Austen (Silver Fox). **Credits:** *Producer:* Peter A. Cross, Mich Lyon, Jesse Archer, Sean Hanley. *Writer-Director:* Jesse Archer, Sean Hanley. **Comment:** Originally produced as a pilot for a TV series that was rejected by both broadcast and cable networks for being just too risqué. The producers then brought it to the Internet where it aired along with a Kickstarter.com campaign to acquire the money to produce additional episodes. It appears, being that the pilot was produced in 2011 that the campaign had failed. The program itself is different and one can see why, with its edgy material it was rejected as a normal television series. The acting and production values are excellent and it is a fun look at a group of gays, especially the only normal one (Mac) on what is called "The Island of Misfit Boys" (a take-off on the song, "The Island of Misfit Toys" from the TV special *Rudolph the Red-Nosed Reindeer*).

Episodes:

1. Pilot. The story line is established as Mac arrives on the island, is teamed with Lex and encounters his first adventure: getting drunk to overcome the fact that he lost his watch, the last reminder of his recent breakup.

130 *#Hashtag: The Series.* hashtagtheseries.tumblr.com. 2013 (Comedy).

The program is billed as "A Queer Web Series for the Mainstream." Andersonville, a small town in Chicago, is home to Skylar and Liv, best friends who are lesbians but not dating each other. Each is also addicted to the social media to find that someone special: Skylar, a struggling stand-up comic, is Twitter obsessed while Liv, a dog lover and book aficionado, is an avid Instagram user. Adapting the concept of on-line dating, but presenting it in a totally new light, the program explores what can happen when dating goes to the extreme and can open the doorway to covert flirting (as way of getting to know a potential love interest) but can also reduce ones dating life to on-line interactions.

Cast: Caitlin Bergh (Skylar), Laura Zak (Liv), Marnie Alton (Tash), Kate Black-Spence (Rose), Remy Maelen (Emily), Amy Thompson (Miriam), Pete Navis (Ben), Anji White (Heather), Amy Dellagiarino (Melissa). **Credits:** *Producer:* Julie Keck, Christin Mell. *Director:* Jessica King, Christin Mell. *Writer:* Caitlin Bergh, Laura Zak. **Comment:** Based on the trailers, the program is well acted and produced. Whether to purchase the episodes is basically based on what the viewer can ascertain from the teasers.

Episodes: Only two teasers are available on line for free (episodes can only be viewed through a paid subscription service).

1. #Hashtag Official Trailer. Presents a good look at what the series is about.

2. #Hashtag Insta Trailer. A brief look at the program is presented.

#Hashtag. Series poster art (used by permission of Tello Films).

131 *Have You Met Miss Jones?* youtube. com. 2012–2013 (Comedy).

Angelina Jones, a somewhat mentally unstable widower in her thirties, works as a low level Hollywood gossip reporter. She (a man in drag) is also the mother of Joe, a gay teenager for whom she is seeking to find a mature father-figure. In an effort to find a man who can change Joe's life around, Angelina joins a speed dating service (Miss Lolly's) and the program charts all the mishaps Angelina encounters—not only from off-the-wall dates, but from the seemingly unstable people that are also a part of her life: Connie, her foul-mouthed, married-to-the mob mother; Jake, the devout Atheist; Christian, the recovering heroine addict; Kelly, a deviant who believes Angelina may be a transgender; and Double D, the celebrity transsexual mafia hit man now a part of the FBI's Witness Protection Program.

Cast: James Di Giacomo (Angelina Jones), Patty McCormack (Connie Campolitarro), Dot-Marie Jones (Miss Lolly), James Kyson (Jake), Art LaFleur (Limo Lou), Ilia Yordanov (Joe Jones), Greg Bryan (Double D), Bunny Levine (Minnie LaValla), Ugo Bianchi (Father Gallo), Cleo Anthony (Kelly), Louis Trent (Christian Glam Rocker). **Credits:** *Creator:* James Di Giacomo, David D. Mattia. *Executive Producer:* James Di Giacomo, David D. Mattia. *Producer:* James Di Giacomo. *Co-Producer:* Taras Kotliar. *Associate Producer:* Tom Shell, Ricki Maslar. *Writer:* David D. Mattia, James Di Giacomo. *Director:* James Di Giacomo, Tom Shell. **Comment:** From the catchy opening theme vocal to the closing scene in the last episode, the program flows smoothly from beginning to end. The acting and production values are very good and accepting the fact that a man plays Angelina and that devilish kid (Patty McCormack) from the 1956 feature film *The Bad Seed* has grown and now has a potty mouth should not deter anyone from enjoying something truly different when it comes to comedy programs.

Episodes:

1. Versatile. Although Angelina believes speed dating is the best means by which to find a husband, Joe voices his objections that such a venture is just a waste of time.

2. Atheist. A speed date that pairs Angelina with an atheist (Jake) is explored.

3. Cakes and Cookies. Angelina's date with Jake becomes more of a problem than Miss Lolly had anticipated and finds that she must intervene before each kills the other.

4. Area 51. Miss Lolly believes she has found the perfect date for Angelina—Double D, the low-ranking mafia hit man that is anything but desirable to her.

5. Who's Troy Donahue? While she doesn't have enough misery already, Angelina finds even more when her unconventional mother and her chauffeur (Lou) arrive at her home in Burbank and immediately begins showering Joe with affection—something she never shows Angelina. Troy Donahue, a 1960s actor, is best known for his role on the TV series *SurfSide 6* while Patty McCormack, a child actor from the 1950s, is perhaps best known for her film role in *The Bad Seed* and Anne on the TV series *The Ropers*.

6. All About That Gay Stuff. As Connie and Joe Bond, Angelina learns that she has psychological flaws that are preventing Joe from leading the lifestyle he prefers.

7. Smoke and Vodka. Too much Vodka has Angelina cozying up to Double D while Connie seems intent on carrying out her plan to remove Angelina and Joe from the hell hole in which they live.

8. You'll Get Yours. As all seems as normal as can be expected at Angelina's home, Connie comes to the rescue when an intruder breaks in, showing Joe that she is more than just "a potty-mouthed grandmother." Meanwhile, Angelina and Double D have had one too many drinks and spend the night together.

9. The Housekeeper. The following morning, when Double D arrives at Angelina's apartment, he is met by Connie who reveals that he is really Diane Delasante, a transsexual Mafia hit man now in the Witness Protection Program. The confrontation, however, has tragic consequences when Double D suffers a heart attack and Connie must call in "The Housekeeper" to dispose of Double D.

10. Drano "The Finale." The Housekeeper, Minnie, arrives and with her necessities (garden lime, Drano, bleach and a large plastic bag) proceeds to dissolve Double D in Angelina's bathtub. Meanwhile, as the program concludes, it is left unresolved as what will become of Angelina and Joe—will Connie achieve her goal? Will Angelina find a man to turn Joe's life around? Will Double D's demise mean trouble for Connie?

Have You Met Miss Jones? Poster cover art featuring James DiGiacomo as Miss Jones (used by permission of James Di Giacomo).

132 *Heet Gras (Hot Grass).* heetgras.nl. 2010 (Drama).

Dutch produced series that revolves around a girls' football (soccer) team but especially Sam, a beautiful 16-year-old lesbian who is drawn to fifteen-year-old Roxy, the team striker. Being the first lesbian-themed series made in the Netherlands by two young filmmakers (Sia Hermanides and Alieke van Saarloos) the program follows the traditions set in American-made lesbian series as it not only focuses on the relationship that develops between Sam and Roxy but on their struggles as teenagers in a rapidly changing world.

Cast: Tamara DaFies (Sam), Dina Abadir (Roxy), Sinem Kavusi (Selma), Susan Visser (Anneke),

Manoushka Zeegelaar (Shirley), Mustafa Akkurti (Kazim), Mohammed Chaara (Coach Cain), Cecile Sarfo (Noelle), Sydney McCartney (Priscilla), Karim El Guennouni (Jaccomo). **Comment:** well done program with an attractive cast and good production values. Although the English subtitles distract from the visual aspects of the program the message that homosexuality exists in young people is clearly presented. It is also interesting to see how a program produced in the Netherlands (and the first of its kind for that country) handles such a topic; the producers felt it was time to represent lesbians in their media (as gay men and bisexual women were already well represented).

Episodes:

1. Heet Gras Pilot. The story line is established with the program ending without resolving issues. The pilot originally aired in July of 2010 and a fundraising campaign was begun to continue the series. It is unlikely, now that four years have passed, that any additional episodes will be filmed. The pilot has since been taken off-line.

2. Heet Gras Teaser. Although the pilot is no longer available, a well-done teaser can still be seen that gives the overall concept of the series (with English subtitles).

133 He's with Me. youtube.com. 2013 (Comedy).

A look at the lives of four modern-day men and how they deal with the situations that confront them: Martin Adams (gay), a critic for the *Village Voice*; Ted Adams (gay but pretending to be straight), an advertising executive; Benny (gay), a real estate broker and hopeful cabaret performer; and Eddie (straight; a police officer married to Val).

Cast: Jason Cicci (Martin Adams), Bradford How (Ted Adams), Darcie Siciliano (Val), John Thomas Cramer (Eddie), Ryan Duncan (Benny Costa), Veronica Reyes-How (Henny Hernandez). **Credits:** *Producer:* Jason Cicci, Sebastian La Cause. *Director:* Sebastian La Cause. *Writer:* Jason Cicci. **Comment:** While the overall attempt is comedy, there are dramatic moments (like Eddie preparing to become a father) and the two mix well for an entertaining and well produced and acted series.

Episodes:

1. Stalling. The pilot episode wherein Martin and Ted (both with the surname of Adams, but not related) meet for the first time at Val and Eddie's wedding.

2. Take Me Out. Realizing that Martin and Ted have made a connection, Val tries to move the romance along by urging Martin to reach outside his comfort zone so as not to lose Ted.

3. Mandate. Martin and Ted each receive advice on how to prepare for their first date together at a Yankees baseball game. Meanwhile, their friend Benny has arranged for Martin and Ted to attend an art exhibit.

4. Sexy Things. While Ted and Martin appear to bond at the art exhibit, Val and Eddie encounter difficulty when they see the painting of a nude woman (not shown to the viewer) and begin arguing over just what was the artist thinking.

5. High Rise High Noon. As Val and Eddie seek a new apartment, they find help from Benny non-too-helpful when he presents them with high rise dwellings somewhat out of their price range.

6. Dude. Ted, who pretends to be straight, fearing his family will discover he is gay, begins to worry when his father drops by and fears what he will think of his friendship with Martin.

7. Ball Busting. Eddie, a police officer, is wounded in the line of duty while Ted appears to become attracted to his co-worker, Henny, when she helps him resolve a work-related problem (and thus ignites feelings that he may be bisexual).

8. Real Babies. After a night of drinking, Martin wakes up in bed with someone he never would have expected—Benny. Val, pregnant by Eddie, fears telling him as she believes he is not ready for fatherhood.

9. Jealousies and Jobs. As Martin suffers from writer's block Val reveals she is pregnant to Henny. Meanwhile, Ted's continual infatuation with Henny begins to put a strain on his relationship with Martin.

10. Danny Boy. On advice from Henny, Val tells Eddie that she is pregnant; Benny seeks Ted's help in preparing his cabaret act; and, as Ted realizes he loves Henny, he proposes marriage, ending his relationship with Martin. The program's concluding episode.

134 The Hinterlands. hinterlandsthemusi cal.com. 2013 (Musical Drama).

Paul is 16 years old and gay. He "lives in the middle of nowhere," is scrawny, plans on becoming a theoretical physicist and is not only shunned by others at his high school but bullied as well. In the first Internet series to tackle the serious, true life issue of gay bullying, *The Hinterlands* focuses on Paul (in particular) and how, with thoughts of suicide ever present on his mind, he tries to deal with what is happening (especially his sexuality) as he journeys up the rocky path to adolescence, made more difficult by what he has chosen to become.

Cast: Connor Russell (Paul MacIntyre), David Andrew Anderson (Gus), John Bolton (Paul's father), Andrew Brewer (Jake Carlton), Zoe Considine (Janie), Erin Dilly (Paul's mother), Caitlin Kinnunen (Bobbi Jo), Brianne Wylie (Margie), Keith Maxwell (Gym teacher). **Credits:** *Producer:* Annie Cull, Kat Ramsburg. *Director:* Brandon Ivie. *Writer:* Michelle Elliott, Danny Larsen. **Comment:** While real issues are covered in a well produced program, it is also unique in that the story is told as a musical with the situations that Paul (and others like him) encounters being professed in song rather than inner thought narration. It is different, especially in a gay-themed program and well worth watching whether gay, lesbian or straight as bullying is not just "a gay thing." The actors perform their roles very well (performing and singing) and the production values are top rate. While the program is worthy of a TV or cable broadcast, the creators felt "that kids need to be able to access a story like this from the safety of their own laptops, iPads and smart phones. And kids in the real hinterlands are the most in need of a project like this, as some communities are highly intolerant of gay, lesbian, bisexual and transgender kids."

Episodes:

1. The Hinterlands. Paul is introduced as the viewer gets a first-hand look at how bullying takes place in a high school.

2. Go Team Win. While brainy, Paul is also agile and, hoping to fit in, attempts to become a member of the volleyball team.

3. Stupid Me. Becoming a team member had Paul believing it would change his life. Although he is a very good volleyball player, his being gay cannot be suppressed or stop the bullying.

4. The Boy They'll Never Know. Bullying is just not restricted to Paul's school. It happens everywhere and when Paul hears that bullying caused a boy (Ethan) in a nearby town to take his life, Paul feels that he must do the right thing and pay his respects.

5. Like It Here. In the neighboring town, Paul, by Ethan's gravesite, reflects on his own life's experiences being bullied.

6. Worthy. As Paul prepares to leave town he meets an older man (Ethan's school bus driver) and learns, through a conversation, how bullying affected Ethan's life.

7. Supernova. With a new attitude about life after speaking to the bus driver, Paul faces his fears and returns to school to stand up to those who are destroying his life.

135 *Home Wrecker Houseboy.* youtube. com. 2007 (Comedy).

It is a time when the world has changed and bad things happen to good people and where villains embellish the rewards of their treachery. Being good is a strike against you and such people find that becoming evil is the only way to survive. Spoofing those who are good and achieve their wealth through legitimate means, the program incorporates a gay theme and charts the lives of several less-than-desirable bad people: Morgan, "a snake" who lies, cheats and destroys anyone who gets in his way of getting what he wants; Steve, a good apple "with a rotten past" who betrayed his true love to save his own hide; Derek, the town's most prestigious businessman who

is now "the village chum"; and Benny, the man who had the perfect life until he turned into a junkie.

Cast: Cameron Zeidler (Benny), Jeremy Lucas (Steve), James Masotto (Derek), Tyler Kamerman (Morgan), Brad Murphy, Kevin Fortney, Joe Palmiotti, J. Andrew Heyl, Jeffrey Wylie, Bill Quade, John Anthony Cirillo. **Credits:** *Producer:* Tim Dumas, Kevin Richey. *Writer-Director:* David LeBarron. **Comment:** Very well acted and produced but geared totally to a gay male audience. Strong sexual situations prevail throughout the series and, for reasons that are known only to the producer, episodes do not contain cast or credit information. A special cast video exists that gives such information "in response to viewer requests to see the cast." Although the producer claims this video is really not to his liking (production) it is well done and follows the presentation of *The Young and the Restless* TV series opening to introduce the cast (still images over superimposed images).

Episodes: 43 of 50 episodes appear to remain on line (the exact number of produced episodes is stated to be 50, but some web sites only host half as many while others less than 10). Each of the episodes is untitled but labeled by initials and a number (for example, HH 3, HH 4, HH 30, etc.).

136 *Homo Thugs.* youtube.com. 2012 (Comedy).

Big Thug and his sidekick, Little Thug are African-American homophobic, closeted gangsters who won't admit to the fact that are gay (even though they are turned on by men of any color). They talk about how they are not gay, but can't refute the fact that they even dream about men. Stories follow Big and Little as they go about their daily lives commenting on this and that but their actions, especially when it comes to not admitting they are gay, makes you realize they are—even if they will not admit it.

Cast: Kevin Barnett (Big Thug), Jermaine Fowler (Little Thug). **Credits:** *Producer:* Bodega Cat Sanchez. *Director as credited:* Kenji. **Comment:** There is vulgar language, Big and Little perform their roles expertly and the program is meant to be nothing more than a deliberate exploration of the stereotyped male black gay-would-be gangster. Enjoyable, well written and produced program that is worth watching just for something different when it comes to a portrayal black gay men.

Episodes:

1. Soft in the Paint. Big and Little are sitting on the stairs of an apartment building and rambling, telling each other they are not gay—until a mucho man passes and has you thinking otherwise.

2. Tip Drill. Big and Little, while eyeing some handsome men, still insist they are not gay.

3. Get Dick or Dis Tryin'. Big and Little are trying to convince themselves they are not gay until they see a hunky dude exercising, become excited—

but are still convinced they are not gay. The program's concluding episode.

137 *The Horizon.* youtube.com. 2009–2013 (Drama).

Sydney, Australia, provides the backdrop for a story detailing the life of Jake, an 18-year-old young gay man from a small town (Bega) and his experiences in the big city when he leaves home to hook up with whom he believes is the love of his life, AJ, an older man who, unknown to Jake is "the resident man-whore of Oxford Street" (Sydney's gay strip).

Cast: Jake Andrew Perry, Alistair Cooke, Paul Layton (Jake), Jay Duncan, Indigo Felton (AJ), Patrick James (Wilma/Dennis), Sam Davis Harris, Mathew Clarke (Micky Rose), Rebecca Sunshine, Sarah Louella (Millie), Adam George (Saxon).

Credits: *Producer:* Mark Benko Ure, Christian Taylor, Brian Cobb. *Director:* Boaz Stark, Mark Benko Ure. *Writer:* Boaz Stark. **Comment:** Nicely produced but very strong adult-themed program. The acting is very good and the stories are well thought out and presented (although last season episodes are the most risqué, especially dealing with the idea of unprotected sex). The program bills itself as "the most successful online series made out of Australia and the most watched gay web series in the world" (supposedly over 22 million views by July 2014 "and growing by 40–60,000 views a day").

Episodes 1–8, 2009: The principal characters are introduced as Jake, a naïve 18-year-old, leaves home to hook up with AJ, a 28-year-old he met on a gay Internet social site. Jake's first experiences are profiled as he discovers AJ is rather flamboyant and sleeps around (although Jake soon finds romance with Chris, AJ's ex-lover but still his roommate) and befriends and becomes roommates with Wilma, a caustic drag queen.

Episodes 9–16, 2012–2013: As AJ continues his quest to sleep with as many men as possible, Jake wants to maintain a strict relationship with him and is fearful of following AJ's reckless path. The situation changes, however, when Jake and AJ spend the night together and AJ vows to remain faithful. Micky and Millie, Jake's friends from his home town (Bega) are introduced. Unknown to Millie, Micky is bisexual (had a previous affair with Jake) and, as the story unfolds, hooks up with AJ, causing a rift in AJ's relationship with Jake. Background information on Dennis is also given, showing how he chose to become Wilma when his parents rejected him as their son for being gay. Vincent Day plays Dennis as a boy with Nick Day and Belinda Giblin as his parents.

Episodes 17–24, 2013: The relationship between Dennis (as Wilma) and his mother is explored as he tries to reconnect with her after his father's death. Jake and AJ have parted company with AJ hooking up with a new love (Saxon) and Micky, realizing that he loves Jake, reveals that he is gay when Millie catches him working as a "gay rent boy" to make money. The season concludes in a rather unprecedented manner with Micky lobbying for the right to have unprotected sex but perhaps realizing he was wrong when a medical exam reveals he has HIV.

138 *Hungry for You.* youtube.com. 2010 (Comic Strip).

"Do you like vampires? How about lesbian and bisexual vampires?" is the tag line for an unusual presentation (told in comic book panels) about a beautiful young woman (Lucia Von Hagen) and her induction into a world of the living dead. For Lucia, an up-and-coming rock musician, it happened one night at a swinger's party (called "a casual key party") when she became attracted to Petras De Carlo, an alluring woman that unknown to Lucia, is a vampire. Lucia, drawn to Petras, finds herself unable to resist her and the two kiss. Suddenly, Lucia feels pain as Petras, with fangs drawn, bites her on the neck and kills her. Now, with Lucia's blood as part of her blood, Petras takes a knife, cuts her hand and, as blood flows from her palm, places it over Lucia's mouth. The blood flows into Lucia's mouth and she is brought back to life—as a vampire. The program ends with Lucia not fully aware as to what happened but told by Petras that she can never return to the life she once lived.

Voice Cast: Deborah Stewart (Lucia), Amanda Majkrzak (Petras), John Peterson, Kim Hoke, Teri Maher. **Comment:** Although the program uses still comic panels with balloon dialogue, it is well presented and is literally like reading a comic book with music playing in the background. The characters are well drawn and the story intriguing although with four years having elapsed since the last episode played, it is doubtful the story will continue.

Episodes:

1. Episode 1. Lucia, attending a swinger's party, is drawn to the beautiful Petras.

2. Episode 2. Having lured Lucia to her, Petras begins the process of turning Lucia into a vampire.

139 *Hunting Season.* hunting season.tv. 2012 (Comedy).

Alex is young (20) single and gay. He is smart and successful and works as a blogger at the media news and gossip company Gawker. After work, however, Manhattan becomes his playground and his experiences with his friends becomes the basis for his Internet series of blogs that anonymously detail his rather crude and careless activities in the gay community.

Cast: Ben Baur (Alex), Walker Hare (Lenny), Marc Sinoway (Tommy), Jack Fever (Nick), Jake Manabat (TJ), Tyler French (Reese), Kate Geller (Lizzie), Brit-Charde Sellers (Shania). **Credits:** *Producer:* Jon Marcus, Stephanie Meurer, Rose Troche.

Director: Jon Marcus. *Writer:* Adam Baran, Jon Marcus. **Comment:** There is no doubt the program was inspired by the gay television series *Queer as Folk.* While *Queer* was a ground-breaking endeavor, it was also well done and careful as to what it depicted. *Hunting Season* goes one step further with gratuitous nudity and vulgar language. The program originally aired on logo.com in a censored version (digitally blocked nudity) while an uncensored version aired on huntingseason.tv. The censored version was then seen on vimeo.com (without parental warning).

Episodes: Eight untitled episodes were produced. One episode can be viewed for free on YouTube.com (surprisingly without restriction) and the entire, uncensored series is only available through a paid subscription service on huntingseason.tv.

140 Husbands. husbandstheseries.com. 2011–2014 (Comedy).

In 2011 the federal government passed an amendment that granted marriage equality for gay and lesbian couples. Eager to celebrate what has happened, a gay couple (Cheeks and Brady) travel to Las Vegas only to become intoxicated and, in a drunken stupor, unintentionally marry. While the marriage is legal, Cheeks, a well-known actor, and Brady, a major league baseball player, were not ready to make such a commitment but find they must now stay married to save their careers as a public divorce would disappoint their fans and ultimately destroy their careers. While the program focuses on the problems the newlyweds face, it explores some problems that could also enter any marriage showing that whether the union is gay, lesbian or straight, it takes two people, working together as a team to make the marriage work.

Cast: Brad Bell (Cheeks), Sean Hemeon (Brady Kelly), Alessandra Torresani (Haley). **Credits:** *Producer:* Brad Bell, Jane Espenson, Jeff Greenstein. *Director:* Jeff Greenstein, Eli Gonda. *Writer:* Brad Bell, Jane Espenson. **Comment:** Enjoyable program with very good acting and production values. The characters are very like-able and the program flows smoothly from episode to episode. Although it has been stated that *Husbands* is the first such program to focus on a gay married couple, it is not so as the concept dates back to television in 1974 when the ABC series *Hot L Baltimore* presented a gay couple (although not married as the amendment did not exist) as well as a lesbian character long before any other show.

Episodes:

1. Waking Up in Vegas. A flashback is used to relate how becoming drunk at a celebration for marriage equality led to an actor and ball player marrying.

2. We Can't Be Married. As news of the marriage hits the media, Cheeks and Brady decide that to protect their careers, they need to stay married.

3. Being Britney. Brady and Cheeks attempt to deal with all the publicity that is resulting from their "drunken Vegas wedding."

4. A Decent Proposal. As the newlyweds ponder the situation, Brady does the right thing and proposes to Cheeks, signifying that they will remain married.

5. IDEHTW. As Cheeks and Brady prepare to leave Las Vegas and return to Los Angeles, Haley, Cheeks' best friend, arrives to find out just what happened.

6. Haley, the Life Coach. Realizing that Cheeks and Brady have no idea what they doing or how to sustain a marriage Haley volunteers her services as their life coach.

7. Normal People. With one decision made, moving into Cheeks' home, the newlyweds contemplate on just what else they must do to present themselves as a normal married couple.

8. The Together Thing. Taking their marriage one step at a time, Brady and Cheeks next create a bond of trust together.

9. Instant Love. Haley attempts to bond Cheeks and Brady even further by presenting them with something to care for together—Jack Russell Mix, a dog.

10. Return of the Zebra. Haley's help is proving not so helpful when Brady and Cheeks begin arguing about equal rights in a relationship when Brady is authoritative and Cheeks is just the opposite.

11. Winky Face. Seeing that Brady is upset by his lack of enthusiasm over spreading the news about their marriage, Cheeks solves the issue by releasing information to social networking sites.

12. Appropriate Is Not the Word. It is the newlyweds three week anniversary and each is preparing for their biggest test to date: appear in a televised interview to talk about a photo Cheeks posted of him and Brady kissing (as such a picture could destroy Brady's career do to a morality clause in his contract).

13. The Straightening. The episode focuses on the interview with Vic Del Rey (Jon Cryer) with Brady trying to protect his career despite a teammate's (Mekhi Phifer) advice that he should end his relationship with Cheeks and look out for himself.

14. A Better Movie of What We're Like. The released photo has positive effects when Brady learns it has gotten him an endorsement deal.

15. I Do Over, Part 1. With the situation improving, Brady and Cheeks decide to have a private ceremony and re-declare their vows in front of family and friends.

16. I Do Over, Part 2. Before the ceremony begins, Claudia (Amy Acker), Brady's ex-fiancée, shows up, implicating that he "switched sides" while Brady's father, after along talk with Brady, consents to let him marry whomever he chooses.

17. I Do Over, Part 3. The marriage takes place with Brady's mother (Beth Grant) and father (Michael Hogan), who were having marital difficulties,

seeing that they too may be able to settle their differences and remain together.

18. I Dream of Cleaning, Part 1. In order to become a "typical housewife" for Brady, Cheeks persuades his neighbor, Parker (Elaine Carroll) to cook and clean the house.

19. I Dream of Cleaning, Part 2. When his neighbor Kajal (Janina Gavankar) drops by, Cheeks reveals that the ideal lifestyle is not staying at home while Brady works, but he does it because he feels Brady deserves it.

20. I Dream of Cleaning, Part 3. The series concludes with Brady and Cheeks revealing that each has gotten other people to do wifely things (Brady had persuaded a friend to do the grocery shopping) and that the charade needs to end and they can become a real couple.

141 Hustling. hustling.tv. 2011–2013 (Drama).

Ryan Crosby, a successful adult bisexual film star and male escort (working under the name Rod Driver) had it all—when he was in his twenties and thirties. Now, at 40, clients are few, adult film roles are just as few and the thrill of pornography has lost its appeal. Realizing that he has reached a turning point, Ryan suddenly sees life in a different light and begins to wonder what he has accomplished and what lies ahead. With dwindling resources and no job prospects, Ryan consults a career counselor for help. Although Ryan is an excellent cook he fails to see this as an alternative; instead, lacking the self-confidence and self-worth to believe in himself, he ventures back into the world in which he feels safe— sex. During one such film Ryan meets a makeup artist (Liv) who changes the course of his life and makes him see what he is actually capable of achieving. The program charts Ryan's regression than transformation as he learns that being middle age doesn't mean you can not move on and accept other challenges.

Cast: Sebastian La Cause (Ryan Crosby), Jessica Press (Liv), Daphne Rubin-Vega (Rosa Juarez), Andrew Glaszek (Jay), Mara Davi (Charlie), Sharon Washington (Lena), Gary Cowling (Mitchell Getz), Gerald McCullouch (Geoffrey), Kevin Spirtas (Joel), Wilson Cruz (Dr. Gabe Bermudex), Gail Herendeen (Lorraine Munson), Brian Keane (Franco La Rock), Facundo Rodriquez (Julien Massi). **Credits:** *Producer-Writer-Director:* Sebastian La Cause. **Comment:** Intended for mature audiences with sexual (gay) situations and vulgar language. The acting and production values are excellent and a parental warning is stated before each episode begins.

Episodes:

1. Pilot: Let's See How You Like It. Ryan, realizing that he needs a change in his life, visits a career counselor (Mitchell Getz), but becomes somewhat evasive when he asks about his job history.

2. Deep End. Finding little help from the counselor, Ryan, assisted by his friend Jay, attempts to do an on-line job search.

3. New Information. Ryan's decision to work on a film for Franco La Rock brings him in contact with Liv, a sexy makeup artist who will soon change his life.

4. Dead. As Ryan prepares himself for a scene, he and Liv start to become friends.

5. Now or Never. Having found inspiration from Liv, Ryan returns to his counselor while also taking advice from Jay.

6. Ibitha. As Ryan and Liv become closer, Ryan begins thinking about using his cooking skills and getting out of the porn industry.

7. A Hard Bargain. Ryan takes the first step and acquires a job as an apprentice to an established personal chef (Geoffrey).

8. The Flow. As Ryan and Liv's relationship grows closer, Ryan reveals incidents about his past life.

9. Old Habits. As his old habits begin to manifest themselves, Ryan has difficulty focusing on his new job.

10. After Taste. As Ryan tries to reconnect with his estranged mother (Lena), Geoffrey becomes increasingly attracted to Ryan.

11. Chairo Pacea "O." Ryan's landlady, Rosa, offers him some cooking advice while Lena tries to understand where Ryan's love of cooking came from.

12. Open Door. Ryan continues his escort activities and begins to wonder if he is bisexual now that he and Liv are close.

13. Hunger Pangs. As Liv and Ryan deal with relationship issues, Ryan finds himself getting close to his film co-star (Julien).

14. G and T. Now that he and Liv are close, Ryan tries to tell Jay about it (as it will affect their relationship).

15. Laundry. Ryan meets with his mother's psychiatrist after he learns that she attempted suicide and gets more than he bargained for when she makes him see more clearly where his life is headed when he reveals that his mother never approved of his porn star life.

16. Chateau Margaux, Part Uno. As Rosa continues to show Ryan cooking techniques, Ryan considers opening his own restaurant.

17. Chateau Margaux, Part Deux. Ryan continues his efforts to open his own restaurant while at the job with Geoffrey, Ryan meets his new assistants Olivia and Cherry. Meanwhile Ryan discovers that Liv has a secret life—in love with another man (Joel) and yearns to become his trophy wife.

142 I Can't Think Straight. youtube.com. 2011 (Drama).

In 2008, the independently produced feature film *I Can't Think Straight* introduced the characters of

Tala, an upper class Jordanian of Palestinian descent and Leyla, a Muslim (from South Asia). The women, both of whom are lesbians, live in London, England. Tala, outgoing and spirited, has just launched her own magazine; Leyla, quiet and sensitive and hoping to become a writer, is dating Tala's best friend and business partner (Ali). The film depicts how two women from very different backgrounds must face new challenges, most importantly, breaking the long-held traditions that each family holds dear, including the concept that marriage is between a man and a woman and nothing else.

In 2011, an Internet fund-raising campaign was launched to turn the film into a web series. Promotional videos were produced to raise the funds and continue the story of Tala and Leyla with a more intense look at their lives and the challenges they face. Although it appears that a series was never made, the promotional information is still on line and makes it appear that such a series exists. As of December 31, 2014, the actual program has not appeared.

Cast: Lisa Ray (Tala), Sheetal Sheth (Leyla), Antonia Frering (Reema, Tala's mother), Dalip Tahil (Omar, Tala's father), Rez Kempton (Ali). **Credits:** *Producer:* Kelly Moss, Hanan Kattan, Mervyn Wilson, Lisa Tchenguiz. *Director:* Shamin Sarif. *Writer:* Shamin Sarif, Kelly Moss. **Comment:** The cast represents the roles that would have been carried over into the series at the time. The videos that appear on line show selected scenes from the film and are very well done with good acting and outstanding cinematography (no doubt to also be carried over to the series). There are kissing scenes and adult situations but no nudity.

Episodes:

1. I Can't Think Straight Web Series Launch Video. Shamim Sarif and Hanan Kattan (the director and producer) appear to present their series idea to potential backers.

2. I Can't Think Straight Video Blog. Samim and Hanan continue their plea for backers to help finance the project.

143 *I Hate Tommy Finch.* tellofilms.com. 2012 (Drama).

An intimate look at two life-long friends (and lesbians), Stephanie and Alyssa, from ages 8 to 35 as they contemplate the events of their lives—from

I Hate Tommy Finch. **Series poster art (used by permission of Tello Films).**

their first meeting to coming to terms with their sexuality. The program is actually a play that, during a Chicago performance, was filmed and reedited into an Internet series.

Cast: Nicole Pacent (Stephanie), Shannan Leigh Reeve (Alyssa). **Credits:** *Director:* Jessica King, Christin Mell. *Writer:* Julie Keck, Jessica King, Christin Mell. **Comment:** Five episodes were produced that basically break the play down into five acts of discussion. It is well acted with sometimes touching insights given as the women look back on their lives. There are minimal sets (as it is a filmed stage play) and the intimacy of a play is captured—even over the Internet.

Episodes: Available only through a paid subscription service. On-line, free episodes are as follows: *1.* Bosom Buddies. *2.* Birthday Wish. *3.* Teaser: Lip Gloss. *4.* Teaser: Sleepover Sneaks. *5.* Sneak Peak: Age 21. *6.* A Sneak Peak of I Hate Tommy Finch. *7.* I Hate Tommy Finch Trailer.

144 I Love Dick. outlicioustv.com. 2013 (Comedy).

A parody of the 1950s CBS TV series *I Love Lucy*. It is 1955 and a young gay couple, Mickey and Dick, have just rented an apartment (for $75 a month) from their female landlords, Fran and Edy. Mickey is the "man of the house" (so to speak) and based on the Ricky Ricardo character on *I Love Lucy* (as Mickey too is in show business). Dick, his more girly-like lover (based on Lucy Ricardo, Ricky's wife) yearns for a career in show business (like Lucy) and is regulated to caring for the apartment while Mickey works.

It is also a time when gays and lesbians were not readily accepted and for Mickey, being gay could be a strike against him. Rather than spoil any chances at acquiring acting jobs, Mickey pretends to be straight with Dick being just a guy he shares an apartment with. Fran and Edy (the stretched equivalent of Ricky and Lucy's landlords, Fred and Ethel Mertz), happen to be lesbians and are unaware that Mickey and Dick are gay (and vice versa). Stories relate the events that befall a gay couple in a time when being gay is not accepted and how they deal with the situations that could expose their "secret."

Cast: Jeremy Lucas (Mickey), Michael Ciriaco (Dick), Sarah Gaboury (Edy), Patricia Villetto (Fran). **Credits:** *Producer:* Tony Jeris, Brian Pelletier. *Writer:* Tony Jeris. *Director:* Brian Pelletier. **Comment:** Amusing, well-done spoof of *I Love Lucy* with very good acting and production values. The program is filmed in black and white and even has a laugh track to represent a live studio audience (a rarity in Internet shows). The program is also squeaky clean and worth checking out for a modern take on an old TV sitcom.

Episodes:

1. Episode 1. The story line is established as Mickey and Dick move into their new apartment.

2. Episode 2. As Mickey and Dick settle in, Mickey receives word that he has an audition for a TV sitcom pilot called *Mother Tells All*, making Dick a bit jealous.

3. Episode 3. Mickey's audition turns out to be a bit unusual as the casting director is gay and appears to want him.

4. Episode 4. Realizing that Mickey left his script at home, Dick rushes to the audition to find Mickey and the casting director in a compromising situation (mistaking an improvised scene for something else).

5. Episode 5. Mickey, realizing that Dick is upset, attempts to explain what happened and save their relationship.

6. Episode 6. Mickey receives word that he acquired the role of Robby on the show but Dick believes he was hired so the casting director can have his way with him.

7. Episode 7. Seeing that Dick is upset, Edy and Fran invite Dick to join them and their "girlfriend"

Jean for a night of bowling. Unknown to Edy and Fran, Jean is actually a man—and has eyes for Dick.

8. Episode 8. Dick, believing Jean is a woman, uncovers "her" secret when Jean tries to seduce him.

9. Episode 9. *Mother Tells All* premieres but an argument follows that has Mickey and Dick dividing the apartment in half.

10. Episode 10. To help Dick with the housework, Mickey hires a male maid—and Dick quickly finds himself falling for him.

11. Episode 11. With the apartment back to normal and Dick's infatuation with the maid a thing of the past, Dick becomes upset when Mickey forgets their one year anniversary.

12. Episode 12. The concluding episode wherein Mickey fears, that if he reveals he is gay, it will cost him acting jobs.

145 I Luv U But.... iluvyoubut.tv. 2012 (Comedy-Drama).

"I love my mother," Mouna says, "But I can never tell her I'm gay; she'd kill me or she would make herself sick and die and I killed her. I don't want to break her heart, but I'm 35 and the only way to get out of the house is in a wedding or a coffin." "What about me," Sam, Mouna's friend, contends, "I am a man and my parents are still telling me what time I have to be home by and they are constantly pushing chicks in my face to get married. There is no way my parents could accept my being gay." Such is the dilemma faced by Mouna and Sam. They have concealed their sexuality from their strict families but have "come out of the closet" to their friends. Fearing their family would never accept who they are Mouna and Sam marry for convenience but continue to live a lie as they pursue their search for a mate. Mouna and Sam are Arab-Australian (born in Australia) and being sexually different is something that Arabs generally keep secret and do whatever it takes to keep that sexuality a secret. The program shows how culture, family and honor play a role in the gay and lesbian communities in strictly religious families and how two people attempt to circum navigate tradition and not be ostracized for doing so.

Cast: Abbey Aziz (Mouna), George El Hindi (Sam), Alissar Gazal (Mouna's mother), Rose Souaid (Sam's mother), Sash (Sash, Mouna's girlfriend), Paul Capsis (Receptionist), Rhys Bobridge (Sam's boyfriend), Neil Singleton (Bare-Chest Boy/Salesman), Alice Ansara (Hot Femme), Jacqui Greenfield (Orgy Girl 3), Ludwig El Hadda (Cousin Ludwig). **Credits:** *Producer:* Alissar Gazal, Darine Eljarrar (Season 1), Megan McMurchy (Season 2). *Writer-Director:* Fadia Abboud (Season 1&2), Peter Polites (Co-Writer, Season 2). **Comment:** Abbey Aziz is captivating as Mouna, especially in the first episode. The cast is well chosen and the story line flows smoothly from beginning to end. The production is television quality and a program well worth watching for an enjoyable, non-offensive lesbian-gay mix.

Episodes:

1. I'm Gay and I Have to Get Married. The charade begins as Mouna and Sam marry to conceal the fact that they are gay.

2. I Want the Big Room. An argument ensues over who should get the bigger bedroom when Mouna and Sam rent their first apartment.

3. You Gotta Get Out of Here My Mother Is Coming. An unexpected visit from Mouna and Sam's mothers has Sam scrambling to get his sleepover date out of the house.

4. Do You Have to Wash His Undies? Sash, yearning for Mouna to spend more time with her and less time performing wifely duties (like laundering) attempts to convince her it is possible to break the mold—just like she did when she came out and left her strict family.

5. Get Outta My Bed. Another predicament for Sam as his mother decides to visit just as he is entertaining a male friend.

6. Be Quiet, I've Got a Date Coming. As Mouna begins romancing her girlfriend (Sash), Sam is nagged by his mother to get Mouna pregnant so she can have a grandchild.

7. Did You Have to Get Married, Cuz? Through a visit by Sam's cousin Ludwig it is learned he believes Sam did the right thing as he told his parents he was gay and life has never been the same.

8. Please Have Children Before I Die. Mouna faces her turn when her mother pleads with her to have children.

9. You Can't Go Out Dressed Like That. At a gay night club Mouna meets an old (straight) friend, Nadine (Nisrina Aminc) but does not acknowledge Sash as her girlfriend, fearing her secret will come out. Angry at Mouna for not revealing who she really is to Nadine and frustrated with Mouna leading a double life, Sash breaks up with her.

10. You're Living a Lie. Although Mouna is heartbroken over Sash leaving her, she feels she must move on and find someone new.

11. I Want to Live. As Mouna and Sam visit their mothers, they become the sounding board as their problems are dumped on them.

12. There Is an Equity to Orgies. Mouna's thoughts as she contemplates an orgy with three other girls.

13. Life Goes on Without You. Recalling what her mother said (from episode 12) and still longing for Sash, Mouna begins to realize, now that her mother is a widow, that, like her mother, she has to move forward.

14. Delete That Video. Mouna appears on her mother's favorite cooking show to help chef Ali Baba (Alissar Gazal) prepare a meal.

15. Can We Watch My Show Together. Sam has found a new boyfriend (Rhys Bobridge) and seeks a way to keep the relationship going.

16. Condoms Are Not One Size Fits All. The irresponsible Sam fears he may have contracted HIV and now nervously awaits the test results.

17. I Don't Want These Dishes. Mouna and Sam have their first domestic quarrel.

18. I Luv U. At pool party given by Ali Baba, Mouna begins to remember the good times she had with Sash and starts lamenting over the fact that they are no longer together. In the house

I Luv U But. **George El Hindi and Abbey Aziz (used by permission).**

Mouna spies an Aladdin-like lamp and rubs it. A puff of smoke emerges, materializes into a genie (Abbey Aziz in a dual role) and wishes she and Sash were together. The program concludes with Mouna's wish apparently granted as she returns to the party to reclaim Sash.

146 Ice Queens. vimeo.com/89874887. 2014 (Comedy).

In 1994 Olympic figure skaters Tonya Harding and Nancy Kerrigan were competitors at the Lillehammer Games. Weeks before their face-off, Tonya's then husband (Jeff) hired a goon (Shane) to take out Nancy (by injuring her knee) to ensure that his wife would win. The plan looked successful at first, but Nancy quickly recovered and achieved a silver medal, bringing disgrace to Tonya. To commemorate the occasion, drag queens from the Logo TV series *RuPaul's Drag Race* recreate the incident in a way that it has never been seen before.

Cast: Willam Belli (Tonya Harding), Morgan McMichaels (Nancy Kerrigan), Delta Work (FBI Agent), Colby Melvin (Jeff Gillooly), Yara Sofia (Oksana Baiul), Christopher Adames (Shane Stant), Vivienne Pinay (Reporter). **Comment:** Tonya is really the center of attention with her actions being the most satirized. The acting is very good and the production itself is entertaining from beginning to end. *Ice Queens*, which was produced by Logo TV,

is the first such TV series that simultaneously premiered across linear TV, the web, mobile, and social (LogoTV, LogoTV.com, the LogoTV app, Facebook, Twitter, Instagram and Vine).

Episodes:

1. Tonya Harding. The evil plan is hatched to take out Nancy.

2. Favor. Tonya's husband hires Shane to do the foul deed and whack Nancy across her knees.

3. Drag. Tonya witnesses the take out and now has high hopes of winning the women's figure skating competition.

4. Who Did It? Nancy, seen holding her knee, pleads to know who did it and "Why, why, why?"

5. You Better Talk. The FBI quickly apprehends a suspect—but are having a difficult time making him talk.

6. Meat Lover's Pizza. A recovered Nancy now competes against Tonya for Olympic prestige.

147 If I Was Your Girl: The Web Series. webserieschannel.com/if-i-was-your-girl/. 2012 (Drama).

A profile of two lesbian couples and the incidents that both weaken and strengthen their relationships: Lynn and Stacia and Rhonda and Toi. Lynn is a successful corporate executive who sees Stacia as a sexual plaything (her "girl toy") while Stacia, fifteen years younger than Lynn, is hopelessly in love with

If I Was Your Girl. Left to right: Marquita Temper Brooks, Alana Mike, Dana Guest and Rondala Kelly (copyright Coquie Hughes).

Lynn and remains with her hoping to change the way Lynn sees and treats her. Rhonda and Stacia became friends while serving time in prison and have remained so. Rhonda is the typical butch lesbian who needs to control her lover, as she does with Toi, who to keep Rhonda as her lover, accepts the consequences. The program explores each of the women— the domineering Lynn and Rhonda and the complacent Stacia and Toi and how their lives intertwine and how, despite their differences, they are there for each other in times of need. The program is adapted from the feature film *If I Was Your Girl.*

Cast: Dana Guest (Lynn), Marquita Temper Brooks (Stacia), Rondala Kelly (Rhonda), Alana Mike (Toi), Toy McNeely (Neena). **Credits:** *Producer:* Coquie Hughes, Jeremy Jones. *Writer-Director:* Coquie Hughes. **Comment:** The program is tailored to African-American audiences. It is one of the very best of such programs and worth watching to see how time and care can accomplish a realistic program that does not delve into depravity. There is partial nudity, sexual situations and vulgar language and the four leads do a good job in representing their characters.

Episodes: Only 4 of ten episodes were produced. According to the producer "Production has been cancelled indefinitely for the *If I Was Your Girl* project. I apologize to our fans that we were unable to present episodes 4–9 which explains what led to the bizarre yet international presentation of episode 10. Never-the-less, thank you for your support." Episodes 1, 2 and 3 have been edited to form an 87 minute movie while the concluding episode just continues to follow incidents in the lives of the women.

148 *Imaginary Bitches.* youtube.com/user/ImaginaryBitches. 2008–2009 (Comedy-Drama).

Catherine is a rather mean young woman, very greedy and selfish and very demanding. Heather, called "an anxiety whore" by Catherine, is a bisexual, perky, rather nice but too promiscuous (she also yearns to have sex with TV's *Hannah Montana*; a.k.a. Miley Cyrus). Jennifer is as beautiful as Catherine and Heather but more of a down-to-earth girl. She is a lesbian and in love with her creator, Eden. Catherine, Heather and Jennifer all have one thing in common—they are girls created in the mind of (and can only be seen by) Eden, a beautiful, slightly self-conscious young woman who feels neglected as all her friends are in a relationship. When loneliness got the better of her, she created Catherine, Heather and Jennifer as companions, someone to talk to—but the "girls" evolved into "Imaginary Bitches" and cause Eden more problems than she had before she created them. The program relates the situations that occur—and how Eden handles them as Catherine, Heather and Jennifer become more real than imaginary to her. Lizzie, Brooke and

Imaginary Bitches. **Series poster art (used by permission of Andrew Miller).**

Connie are Eden's closest friends while Jessalyn, a friend to Eden at first, becomes more of her nemesis as stories progress (especially when it is revealed that she is a lesbian).

Cast: Eden Riegel (Eden), Brooke Nevin (Brooke), Elizabeth Hendrickson (Lizzie), Connie Fletcher (Connie), Jessalyn Gilsig (Jessalyn), Angela Trimbur (Angela), Michael Daniel (Cassady), Megan Hollingshead (Shannon), Brittany Ishibashi (Brittany), Sam Page (Riley). **Credits:** *Director:* Andrew Miller. *Writer:* Andrew Miller, Nichole Millard, Jeffrey Poliquin, Bo Price, Kathryn Price, Sam Riegel. **Comment:** Enjoyable program with very good acting, writing and production values, made especially appealing with Eden Riegel as Eden as she is so natural that she makes you believe she is really talking and reacting with someone as opposed to speaking into thin air (the "bitches"). As it stands now, it would make a good transformation to a network (or cable) television series as all aspects are already in place for one to start.

Episodes:

1. It's Not Easy Making Imaginary New Friends. Following a date that Eden is anxious to tell her girlfriends about but finds no one will listen, she creates Catherine as a means by which to relate her daily happenings.

2. The Dirtier Isn't Always Better. When Eden's friend, Lizzie, doesn't invite her to a couples' party, Catherine voices her objections, calling Lizzie a terrible friend. Unable to deal with Catherine's accu-

sations, Eden creates Heather as a means to defend Lizzie.

3. Where Were You When Eden Got Drunk and Puked All Over Me and Lizzie. When Brooke, Eden's friend, discovers Eden's "friends," and fears losing her to them, she confronts them to win Eden back.

4. A New Leper in the Colony. Eden's life appears to be improving when she is invited to a single's party but encounters a real bitch—Jessalyn, her nemesis, who could put a damper on her happiness.

5. It's Totally What You Think. Eden discovers she is not the only one living with imaginary friends when Eden meets a man (Mark) with his own imaginary life.

6. Help Dr. James Help You. On Brooke's advice, Eden visits her psychiatrist, Dr. James (James Kee) only to discover he is more out of touch with reality than she is.

7. A Spiritual Bitch Bath. Catherine and Heather step in to help Eden see that Brittany, a spiritual guru she and Brooke trust, is a fraud.

8. Sexy Secret Santa. Catherine, Heather and Jennifer seek a way to get rid of Connie, Lizzie and Brooke when they crash their Secret Santa Party with Eden.

9. Porn Star Priest. Catherine, Jennifer and Heather find their existence threatened when Connie convinces Eden to have a priest (Charlie Kiznik) exorcise them.

10. Imaginary Bridezilla. Eden's "bitches" are delighted when Lizzie, breaking up with her boyfriend, has too much to drink and has a dream wherein she marries but sees herself as a "bridezilla."

11. Only Crazy Girls Quife. The "bitches" come to Eden's rescue when she falls for a man that just doesn't seem right for her.

12. Three Bitches Is an Imaginary Crowd, Part 1. Jennifer helps Eden create an on-line dating profile that, like Jennifer, has Eden seen as a lesbian.

13. Three Bitches Is an Imaginary Crowd, Part 2. The program concludes with Eden encountering Jessalyn's hostility when Eden meets a girl on-line and arouses Jessalyn's jealous streak.

149 *In Between Men.* inbetweenmen.com. 2010–2013 (Comedy-Drama).

Dalton, Dane, Benjamin and Massimiliano are four men living in New York City. Although they are friends and gay, they believe they live in an in-between world, one that is not gay (as they can not relate to the clichés that define it) and one that is not straight (as dating or living with the opposite sex is beyond comprehension). Each of the friends is a successful professional and each relies on the other for support in times of need. The program follows their experiences, their hookups and the problems they encounter living in their self-created in-between world.

Cast: Nick Matthews (Dalton Fuller), Ben Pamies (Benjamin Reed), Chase Coleman (Dane Sullivan), Margot Bingham (Kendra Sharpe), Michael Sharon (Massimiliano Costa), Sidney E. Wright (Kyle Leary), Mark Tallman (Brian Sharpe), Max Ryder (Jacob Ross), Kaolin Bass (Jeremy), Dan Stern (Paul), Ron Nummi (Bill), Noam Harary (Andrew Reed), Jennifer Gelfer (Sharon Curtis), Drew Moerlein (Cayn), Sharina Marton (Michelle), Susan Slotoroff (Abigail). **Credits:** *Producer:* Jennifer Gelfer, Quincy Morris, Christina DeHaven, Sidnei Beal III. *Director:* Jennifer Gelfer. *Writer:* Quincy Morris. **Comment:** The story line reads well, sounds like a great idea but the presentation lacks the oomph seen in the text. While the production values are top rate, the writing is well-below par and, even though the actors are competent, the poorly chosen dialogue presents a truly stereotyped view of gay life (as not all gay men [or women] are overly successful in business and not all gay men [or women] are constantly involved in sex and clubbing). Of all the characters, it can be seen that Dalton is just too stiff and Massimiliano, the wealthy Italian with English as a second language, has an accent that can make one cringe as it is that unreal. Anyone familiar with the series *Sex and the City* will immediately get the feeling that *In Between Men* is a male version of it just by its copied opening narration style. One may also question why hip-hop music is used as the theme when it has no relevance to the actual show. The program can be looked upon as a spoof of gay life but it can not be taken seriously as an actual representation of gay life in a city.

Season 1 (2011) Episode List: *1.* Pride and Prejudice. *2.* It Takes 2. *3.* Business As Un-Usual. *4.* Secrets and Ties. *5.* Muscles and Manbags. *6.* Trouble in Paradise.

Season 2 (2013) Episode List: *1.* Dying to See You. *2.* Under the Big Top. *3.* The Gang Bang's All Here. *4.* Arts and Aircrafts. *5.* Kind of a Big Deal. *6.* La Familiar, Part 1. *7.* La Familiar, Part 2. *8.* Two for One. *9.* Wake Up Call.

150 *In the Deep.* youtube.com. 2012 (Comedy-Drama).

London's East End provides the backdrop for a look at the intimate lives of five friends: Emilia, Riley, Ade, Rene and Wesley. Emilia is a lesbian; Ade, Rene and Wesley are gay; and Riley is straight. Although only two episodes have thus far been produced the program appears to not only explore their lives and loves, but the secrets they are hiding from themselves and each other.

Cast: Denver Isaac, Olu Ubadike, Luke Wilson, Zebulun Delisser, Gareth Andrews. **Credits:** *Producer-Writer:* Joseph A. Adesunloye, Joy Gharoro Akpojotor. *Director:* Joseph A. Adesunloye, Vins Blake. **Comment:** The program is tagged as "a queer web series of people of color" and is expertly acted and produced (television quality values) in England. Although there are no sexual situations in the produced episodes, there is considerable vulgar language and language that is a bit hard to understand at times due to British accents. Being a program that airs world-wide, it would have been a nice touch if the producers matched the players with their characters. While they may be known in England, they are total unknowns in the U.S. and who plays who is always more acceptable to on-lookers.

Episodes:

1. Episode 1. The pilot episode that gives a brief introduction to the five regulars: Emilia is drawn to Riley even though she has a boyfriend; Ade is struggling with not only being gay but British-Nigerian; Wesley is torn between seeking love or being swept off his feet by someone; and Rene, a fun-loving, carefree individual who must learn to grow up and accept who he is.

2. Episode 2. Emilia is seen preparing for a fund raiser while Rene is shocked to see someone (not shown who) when he answers a knock at the door.

151 *In the Loop.* youtube.com. 2009 (Reality).

"Girls are fine but boys are better!" opens a program about real life incidents in the lives of three gay friends (Albert, Alex and George) and how they deal with the real-life issues they encounter alone or together.

Cast: George, Albert and Alex (as credited). **Credits:** *Producer-Director:* Ryan Yezak. **Comment:** Although the program purports to be a real-life look at the three men, the men act like the girly stereotyped gays giving the program an unnatural feel and making it look more like something that is scripted rather than natural (unless the leads are feminine-like gays). Other than that, the production values are typical of a low budget production.

Episode List: *1.* Pilot. *2.* Fool for Love. *3.* My Life Would Suck Without You. *4.* Oh My Husband, Part 1. *5.* Oh My Husband, Part 2. *6.* My Heart Is on E. *7.* Working It Out. *8.* Tom. *9.* Marching On. *10.* New Year's Eve. *11.* Suspect. *12.* Death Becomes Her. *13.* The Stolen Date. *14.* Bloopers.

152 *In the Moment.* inthemoment.tv. 2008–2013 (Drama).

Reality presented as soap opera to detail the lives of gay men and the decisions they make (mostly sexual) living in the City of West Hollywood. The program is intended to be an awareness factor, to enlighten and educate not only its target audience but anyone, whether gay, lesbian, bisexual or straight about HIV prevention.

Cast: John Bryant (Carlos), Pete Scherer (Shawn), Sammy Sheik (Edgar), Jesse Lewis IV (Stephen), Desi Jevon (Ricky), Nigel Campbell (Kyle), Patrick J. Nicolas (Paul), Kapule Ravida (Mike), Michael Redford Carney (Brandon), Matt McConkey (Billy), Janora McDuffie (Shelby), Levi Fiehler (Adam), Jull Weber (Danny), Jesse Lewis (Stephen), Bradley Estrin (Eric). **Credits:** *Producer:* Dave O'Brien, Marc Cittadino, Andy Dugan, Michelle Kramer. *Writer-Director:* Dave O'Brien. **Comment:** The program is produced by the Los Angeles Gay and Lesbian Center and the City of West Hollywood. Although the presentation follows that of TV soap operas like *Days of Our Lives*, the message about precaution is often made clear. The acting and production values are good and, despite its depressing overall feeling, the program is informative.

Season 1 (2008–2009) Episode List: *1.* The New Guy. *2.* The Mistake. *3.* The Bad News. *4.* Point of Attack. *5.* Connections—Sort Of. *6.* New Beginnings. *7.* Separations. *8.* Tempting Proposals. *9.* Cleaning Up Images. *10.* Resolutions of Sorts. *11.* Setting Things Right for Now. *12.* Someone Like You. *13.* Testing, Testing.

Season 2 (2009–2010) Episodes: All episodes have been taken off line (including titles).

Season 3 (2010) Episode List: *1.* Light and Dark. *2.* Tumbling Down. *3.* Come Together.

Season 4 (2012–2013) Episode List: *1.* Three Times Before Breakfast. *2.* I Thought I'd Be Alone Forever. *3.* You're a Big Boy. *4.* Don't Base Your Life on a Madonna Song. *5.* Sex Was Getting a Little Boring.

Season 5 (2013) Episode List: *1.* Are You Listening to Me? *2.* How Much More Intense. *3.* Into Black Guys. *4.* Small Family Thing. *5.* Major Life Changes. *6.* Real and Enduring.

153 *InSight.* youtube.com. 2008 (Crime Drama).

Guin Marcus, a lesbian and detective with the Los Angeles Police Department, is a woman who possesses a unique gift: a psychic ability to not only envision the future but see how a crime was committed. Fearful of losing her job, Guin conceals her abilities from her fellow officers, including her partner, Cheryl Jones. While Guin can physically see how a crime was committed, her clairvoyance also allows her to have sensual visions of passion wherein she is making love to other women, especially fellow officer April Reece. Guin has accepted who she is although she constantly struggles to control what she is able to do. The program charts Guin's case investigations as she incorporates her psychic abilities to solve crimes but also find a way to balance the two lives she has created for herself. See also *The Seer*.

Cast: Deborah Stewart (Guin Marcus), Amanda Majkrzak (Cheryl Jones), Emma Lynch (April Reece), Ryan Gawel (Capt. Briggs). **Credits:** *Producer-Writer:* Linda Andersson, Sara Marx. *Director:* Linda Andersson. *Narrator:* Sara Marx. **Comment:** Based on the only video information that remains, a short trailer, the program is well acted but appears to have been filmed in soft focus (not as sharp as HD). There are sexual situations and kissing scenes (although abbreviated for the trailer) and what appears to be intriguing cases for Guin to solve.

Episodes: Eight episodes were produced but have been taken off line (including titles and descriptions. "This Video No Longer Exists" will appear).

154 *Intersection.* intersectionseries.com. 2009 (Drama).

Time passes quickly and a group of friends, no longer the dreamers they once were, have reached a new stage in their lives—the realization that what they hoped for 10 years ago has not happened and they must now accept who they are and what they did achieve. The program relates the incidents that affect each of the friends (listed below) and how what they hoped to achieve and what has actually become of them.

Darlene is a talented actress with the uncanny ability to empathize (step into someone else's shoes and feel what they are feeling). Unfortunately, for Darlene, her gift leaves her with emotional problems that she has not yet fully figured out how to handle. Darlene attended college in New York and appeared in a number of regional plays based on the works of such playwrights as Shakespeare, Chekov and Ibsen but never anything that is comparable to a Broadway production. Although frustrated, Darlene has vowed to remain in New York to reach the heights she knows she is capable of despite the fact that producers are not breaking down her door. She also feels, that being a lesbian, she can never find satisfaction in a relationship as her empathetic abilities make it difficult for her to be herself (she instinctively becomes involved with the emotions of whom she dates and herself becomes vulnerable).

Denton, a few years older than Cindy, teamed with her to form the underground's first music scene couple. It was the early 2000's and they appeared to be made for each other. He was quite talented and provided the support and encouragement that Cindy needed at that point in her life. But Denton felt it was time for him to start a family but knew Cindy would not give up her career to do so. After expressing his feelings to Cindy, they amicably agreed to break up. Cindy sought her own goal while Denton would later marry and begin a family. Neither regrets what happened and are still close friends.

Hal, born in the Midwest, worked as a software developer in Manhattan for 10 years before quitting what he considered a boring, dead-end job to get in on the ground floor of a start-up company.

Iris, born on Long Island, majored in psychology in college and later acquired a teaching certificate (she is now a high school history instructor). She dated Hal and has dreams of beginning a family.

Karen, a former actress and theater school graduate had a few off Broadway roles but after 1,001 auditions Karen realized it was fruitless to continue and quit acting to acquire a non-theatrical job. She is dating an actor (Vince) and hopes to one day settle down, marry and raise a family. Although it appears, at times, that Karen regrets the decision she has made, it seems she enjoys reliving her acting career through Vince.

Lynda is a yoga instructor whose dreams of becoming a professional dancer were cut short by a debilitating injury. When her dream was shattered Lynda was at a loss as what to do next. She tried everything from waitress to cosplay (dressing up as cartoon characters at trade shows) but nothing appealed to her until she found a love of yoga—first as a student, then instructor and finally the owner of her own studio. Dating at the present is not on her agenda as she is still trying to adjust to her new life.

Megan is Cindy's older sister, a girl who, during grade school knew what was expected of her—good grades to lead to college and a good job. Megan's enthusiasm never influenced Cindy and Megan realized as they both grew up that Cindy, although talented, would never achieve the same success as her. Megan cares for Cindy and still tries to instill her values in her and knows she will succeed in convincing Cindy that life can be better (a corporate job, a family and life in suburbia) than chasing pipe dreams.

Nathaniel, born in New Hampshire, believes music is the most important thing is his life and everything else including relationships, take a back seat. Nathaniel began writing his own songs in middle school but never considered it a paying career until 10 years after, while working for a Wall Street firm he realized the wheeling and dealing did not give him the satisfaction he received from song writing. He quit his job and has now put all his energies into a music career.

Vince, a graduate of the American Academy of Dramatic Arts, is steadily employed as a commercials actor although he is also in demand as a stand-in for feature films and TV programs. Vince lives for the moment and is not ready to settle down, a life-style that cost him a three-year relationship with Karen, who wanted to begin a family and live in suburbia.

Casey, named by his parents after their favorite poem about baseball ("Casey at the Bat") is a graduate of Farmingdale State College (on Long Island in New York) and played baseball on the school's team, but never pursued that goal any further. Instead, he headed to Manhattan, acquired a job as bartender, married (and divorced) shortly after and is currently happy as he is, tending bar.

Cast: Becca Ayers (Cindy), Cotton Wright (Darlene), Merritt Minnemeyer (Karen), Gabe Silva (Hal), Jessica Stone (Lynda), Jeffrey Lamar (Nathaniel), Jessica Henson (Iris), Joe Mihalchick (Vince), Stephen Ott (Jeff). **Credits:** *Producer:* Jonathan Betzler, Nicolas Bernardine. *Director:* Jonathan Betzler, James Minihan, Minnie Tran, Ricard Atkinson. *Writer:* Kelly Jean Fitzsimmons, Jim Cairl. **Com-**

ment: A well chosen cast in a light drama with good acting and production values. While the idea is not new (the TV series *Friends* will come to mind) *Intersection* is different in that it looks at what was hoped for as opposed to what has been achieved and how hope for something swiftly fades as one grows older.

Episodes:

1. March 4, 2009. The various cast members are introduced to viewers.

2. March 5, 2009. Explores the career choices the friends have made, including Karen and Nathaniel, who have made the most dramatic changes.

3. Thursday, March 5, 2008. Stories of past incidents are revealed as the friends meet at a bar for a get-together.

4. March 6, 2009. As Karen begins her new job, Darlene's audition doesn't quite go as well as she had hoped.

5. Monday, March 16, 2009. Darlene, as she takes a temp job, and Lynda, as she begins a new business are profiled.

6. Friday, March 27, 2009. Jeff becomes increasingly obnoxious as he and Karen accompany Cindy on an outing to meet a musician.

7. Thursday, April 2, 2009. Hal is the center of attention as he institutes some rules in his company.

8. Thursday, April 2, 2009. Cindy's life becomes a bit more complex when her sister (Megan) comes to visit.

9. Friday, April 3, 2009. Cindy and Megan's efforts to reacquaint themselves have each experiencing some mishaps when they have a bit much to drink.

10. Friday, April 3, 2009. Megan decides to return home while Jeff, seeking an apartment, finds help from Hal in looking for one.

11. Friday, April 10, 2009. Cindy finds her career on the rise when she collaborates with a fellow musician.

12. Friday, April 10, 2009. Lynda's date is explored as Jeff continues his search for an apartment.

13. Saturday, April 11, 2009. The program concludes by presenting a series of events in the lives of the friends.

155 *Into Girls.* intogirlswebseries.com. 2013 (Anthology).

Dramatic vignettes that explore the lives of several women: Alice, Sam, Tess, Chelsea and Jasmine, who are lesbians; and Morgan, who is straight and how each affects the other's life.

Cast: Melanie Rothman (Alice), Christine Lee (Sam), Krystine Summers (Kayla), Emerald Sullivan (Jasmine), Nelcie Souffrant (Stephanie), Sarah Miller (Morgan), Annalisa Chamberlin (Chelsea), Sam Glovin (Alex), Jin Kim (Herself), Mackenzie Wyatt (Herself). **Credits:** *Producer:* The Fourth Wave. *Writer:* Jin Kim. **Comment:** Enjoyable, non-offensive series (for its lesbian themes) that is well acted and produced. Topics range from meeting over the Internet through Skype ("Skype Sex"), a girl revealing to her parents that she is a lesbian ("Meet the Bockers") and sex toy shopping ("Babeland").

Episodes:

1. Is This a Date? Although Sam and Tess are attracted to each other, Sam begins to doubt Tess's feelings for her when they go out on a date and Tess is anything but romantic.

2. The Purchase. Alex and Chelsea find that, after purchasing a sex toy, it is not right for them and must now try to figure out how to return it.

3. The Naked Roommate. Episode removed from the Internet.

4. Girlfriends. Although they have been friends for some time, Alice cannot hold back any longer and attempts to seduce her straight best girlfriend Morgan.

5. Butthole. Episode removed from the Internet.

6. Danielle. A young woman (Danielle), whose mother is not aware of her sexuality or her lesbian-themed poetry, ponders whether or not to recite one of her poems at her mother's upcoming wedding when she is asked to do so.

7. Dick. An obnoxious young man, who cannot accept lesbians, brings out the worst in Laura when she faces him and defends her sexuality.

8. Ready, Set, Go. Continues from episode four with Alice now even more determined to have Morgan as her lover.

9. Meet the Bockers. An awkward situation arises when Chelsea brings her girlfriend (Alex) home to meet her parents.

10. This Is a Date? Sam and Alice embark on their first date—then ponder what they should do.

11. Morning After. A date shared by Sam and Alice is explored.

12. Snapback. Feeling that her appearance is preventing her from finding the perfect girl, Jasmine goes a bit overboard in a make-over to increase her chances.

13. Grool. Sam and Alice embark on a second date in a sequel to episode 11.

14. Skype Sex. A text-messaging hookup unites Alice with Kayla.

15. Navigate. Jasmine, a recent high school graduate, begins questioning her sexuality and whether she still likes girls when she feels attracted to men and begins dressing more like them.

16. Babeland. Alex and Chelsea attempt to buy a sex toy at an adult store (Babeland).

17. Coming Out. Alice faces her biggest challenge—telling her parents she is a lesbian.

18. Separate Paths, Part 1. Chelsea and Alice's relationship suddenly changes when Chelsea returns from a trip to California (to New York) and tells Alice that she has been offered a good job but may reject it to be with her.

19. Separate Paths, Part 2. Chelsea and Alice ponder their future together following Chelsea's announcement.

20. Dear Alice. Explores what could be the end of Morgan and Alice's relationship when Morgan announces she is moving to L.A. The program's concluding episode.

156 *It Could Get Worse.* itcouldgetworse. tv. 2013–2014 (Comedy).

Jacob Gordon, an actor who is also gay, feels his career is just about to come to an end when he is asked to audition for a Broadway musical called *The Ice Queen* and his hopes are renewed. The exhilaration is short lived when he learns that his co-star is Veronica Bailey, a notoriously temperamental stage star who is not only difficult to work with, but known for being a diva that gets her way or it's no way at all. Jacob's frustrations do not stop there, they only begin there. He is in a floundering relationship with Philip and his parent's, especially his mother (Judy) just doesn't understand his life choices. To make matters worse, his parent's have just separated and his father (Leo) has moved in with him, hampering his relationship with Philip. A struggling actor about to land the role of his dreams and what happens as he not only deals with Veronica, but all the other annoyances that happen to be a part of his hectic life.

Cast: Wesley Taylor (Jacob Gordon), Gideon Glick (Philip Klein), Alison Fraser (Veronica Bailey), Adam Chanler-Berat (Ben Farrel), Mitchell Jarvis (Sam Atkinson), Brennan Brown (Rich), Richard Poe (Leo Gordon), Nancy Opel (Judy Gordon), Bryce Ryness (Hank), Hannah Nordberg (Sadie), Blake Daniel (Colin), Jennifer Damiano (Stacy), Brandon Espinoza (Keith), Tony LePage (Ned), David Rossmer (Perry), Andre Ward (Kendrix), Stephanie J. Block (Jenny). **Credits:** *Producer:* Paula Marie Black, Jesse Stalnaker, Mitchell Jarvis, Wesley Taylor, Paris Remillard. *Writer-Director:* Mitchell Jarvis, Wesley Taylor. **Comment:** Well acted and produced look at a young gay man (Jacob) and how show business affects those around him when, at times, he must pretend to be straight to acquire roles. Some web sites list as many as 18 episodes for this series (due to a listing of episode highlights as actual episodes with the same information repeated three different times) but there are actually only nine.

Episodes:

1. Give 'Em Hell for Me, Kid. Jacob's audition for the musical lands him the job but appears to be the catalyst that is threatening his relationship with Philip.

2. He Sounds Like a Girl. Jacob's enthusiasm over acquiring a co-starring role is dampened when he discovers that the notorious Veronica Bailey is the star.

3. Lighten Up. Jacob's life continues on a downward spiral as Philip is becoming more distant and his parent's separation can only mean more trouble entering his life.

4. Let Down Your Hair. Jacob's father (Leo) takes up residence in his apartment; Sam, Jacob's eccentric agent becomes impressed with his one-man show; feeling he needs help, Jacob seeks a therapist.

5. Terrible People. Jacob acquires the romantic lead opposite Veronica as rehearsals for the play begin—just as he is about to end his relationship with Philip and begin a new one with Ben, a fellow actor.

6. Uncharted Territory. When Ben announces that he is moving back to Los Angeles, Jacob decides to join him, hoping the West Coast will provide the kick start his career needs.

7. Straight Offer. As Ben, Jacob and Sam (Jake's agent) settle in, Jacob becomes jealous when Ben is offered a film role.

8. Too Much Candy. Jacob's sudden addiction to on-line hookups appears to be a catalyst that will test his and Ben's relationship.

9. Fate. As Jacob lands a role in a film opposite film star Joseph Vincinelli, he runs into his ex-boyfriend (Philip) and, as the program concludes, wonders if the career choice he made was the right one.

157 *It Gets Betterish.* itgetsbetterish.com. 2011 (Comedy).

Eliot and Brent are gay men in the 21st century and trying their best to navigate life in a world that expects, among other things, an obsession with Lady Gaga, flamboyance and immaculate attire. While gay, Eliot and Brent are not lovers (only friends) and only emulating a stereotypical gay life style as they detest Lady Gaga and are struggling to live their chosen lifestyle to the fullest while encountering all the annoyances that attach themselves to gay men (like orgies and straight women who seek that perfect "gay best friend"). In essence, the program profiles two gay men who could be perceived as odd and the complications that arise when Brent, a closeted transgender, reveals that he is pregnant.

Cast: Eliot Glazer (Eliot), Brent Sullivan (Brent), Nicole Byer, Michael Hartney, Ann Carr. **Credits:** *Producer:* Seth Keim. *Director:* Randy Foreman. *Writer:* Eliot Glazer, Brent Sullivan. **Comment:** Although the program ends unresolved regarding the pregnancy issue (other than Brent dreaming of giving birth) it is still an enjoyable program to watch. Although episode 8 is the most offensive (excessive amounts of vulgar language—although it is bleeped) other episodes have curse words left untouched. Why? The acting is good and the overall production well executed.

Episodes:

1. Drag Queen. Believing they can enhance a party to which they have been invited, Eliot and

Brent find providing the entertainment not that easy a task when they attempt to hire a drag queen.

2. Lady Gaga. Eliot and Brent attempt to convince all concerned that while everyone loves singer Lady Gaga, they hate her as the megastar has taken the gay queen title away from performers such as Madonna and Cher.

3. Gay Republican. Eliot and Brent's confrontation with a bar patron when they discover he is not only gay but something they despise—Republications.

4. Pregnant. Eliot is shocked when Brent reveals that he is a transgender and has become pregnant by another man.

5. Karaoke. Eliot and Brent perform songs in a seemingly unrelated episode as they make their way around the city.

6. Party Monster. At the Le Taint Bar, Eliot and Brent encounter Rudy, Eliot's high school classmate, a man who is "so gay" (purposely stereotyped) that his actions become an embarrassment to him in front of Brent.

7. Orgy. As Brent's pregnancy progresses, he and Eliot ponder a choice they have to make: attend an orgy or their friend's baby shower.

8. Fag Hag. At a dinner party Eliot and Brent meet a straight girl (Shuana) who is seeking the status of having a gay best friend. Shuana, however, is so revolting (in language and manner) that Eliot and Brent contend that "not every gay dude wants to be a straight girl's best friend" and attempt to avoid her (with little luck as she has attached herself to them).

9. HIV AIDS Test. The friends face their worst fears when they agree to take an HIV test in the program's concluding episode.

158 Jack in a Box. jackinaboxsite.com. 2009–2012 (Comedy).

Ticket Universe is service whereby theater patrons can purchase tickets by telephone for their favorite shows. One such employer is a man named Jack. He possesses a BFA degree in acting but he has no life skills. He is also gay and with few, or at times, no acting jobs, he was forced to find a job and took one as a ticket seller as it involved no physical activity and, in a way, has kept him in touch with the theatrical world. But it is not the world he wants. He is often mistaken for a woman over the phone ("I'm a sir, not a ma'am") and his patience has worn thin over the years dealing with people who are even more unstable than he is. The job has left Jack with anger issues and his love of the theater has turned to hate of the theater and the program follows Jack's efforts to navigate the life he now leads, made bitter by the fact that he is growing older and no longer the mild-mannered, easy-going, theater-loving person he once was.

Cast: Michael Cyril Creighton (Jack), Beth Cole (Becca), Katina Corrao (Suzie), Lusia Strus (Gloria), Desiree Burch (Jill), Becca Blackwell (Kris), Paul Thureen (Drew), Mary Testa (Jack's mother), Alison Frazer (Aunt Heidi), Cole Escola (Drew). **Credits:** *Producer:* Michael Cyril Creighton, Jim Turner. *Writer:* Michael Cyril Creighton. *Director:* Jim Turner, Marcie Hume. **Comment:** A very good program idea that is ruined by truly annoying and bad camera work. Not only is the unsteady (shaky) camera method used, but it is coupled with unsteady back and forth panning (from character to character as they speak) and just as unsteady in-and-out zooming on characters' faces. What effect the director was seeking is unknown as the whole production is more of a turn off than something to watch. If you can overlook the camera work, the acting and writing are excellent and the program quite enjoyable as Jack just struggles to survive each day.

Episodes:

1. The Receiver. An introduction of sorts as Jack is seen answering phones and becoming increasingly angry dealing with customers.

2. The Alpha Actor. Jack's daily break routine (enjoying a cigarette and cupcake away from his office box), is interrupted when he meets Simon (Patrick Heusinger), an old acquaintance he rather not meet again.

3. The Evaluation. A rather non-caring Jack faces an evaluation by his boss Becca who has become concerned about his haphazard work styles and phone attitude.

4. The Student. Jack attempts to deal with Ricki (Jackie Hoffman), a college student (and his least favorite customer) as she seeks to finagle him out of a show ticket.

5. The Rave. Jack becomes depressed over the career he should have had when he reads a rave review of the incest musical *Bros of Desire*.

6. The Mother. Becca finds Jack's work response not to her liking when she sees that he will let the phone ring until he finishes a bagel but drop everything to answer a cell phone call from his mother.

7. The Co-Worker. As Jack prepares for an audition, he finds his efforts complicated when Becca assigns him an assistant named Suzie.

8. The Friend. Prudence (Mary Louise Burke), one of Jack's very special customers, attempts to brighten up his typical dreary day on the job.

9. The Change. Jack feels that a change is needed and he must distance himself from his continual dependence on his box. He does so by quitting with a goal to re-invent his acting career.

10. The Agent. Now, unemployed but somewhat enthusiastic, Jack reestablishes contact with his agent, Gloria, a sexy, man-crazy, deep-voiced woman who is not that comfortable handling the unpredictable Jack.

11. The Lunch. With money tight, Jack is skimping and saving and what has happened to him becomes evident when he meets with a wealthy friend named Millie (Hannah Bos) for lunch and he pays for a cupcake with a roll of pennies.

12. The Family. Jack faces criticism from his mother and Aunt Heidi who have more compliments about Lady Gaga then they do of him.

13. The Roommate. While it is just a coincidence, Jack needs help with paying the rent and acquires a roommate named Jill—a girl who finds Jack a bit unstable.

14. The Interview. While it is not an acting job, Jack prepares for an interview as a receptionist at a high-end boutique marketing firm.

15. The Buzz. Jack's women problems are explored—from his roommate to his agent.

16. The Reunion. Jack again clashes with his former, boss, Becca, when she appears at the same audition at which she hopes to acquire a role.

17. The Return. Learning that Becca no longer works for Ticket Universe, Jack returns to his old job (and box and cupcake and cigarette break) but under a new boss named Kris.

18. The Victim. Gloria acquires Jack a role—playing the victim (an adult "baby" in diapers) in a play.

19. The Visit. Now working alongside Suzie, Jack figures he must get to know her better and accepts an invitation to visit her apartment where he finds she is a bit off-the-wall and living with a pregnant roommate.

20. The Surprise. Jack is again faced by his mother and aunt, this time with her friend Dawn (Julie Halston)—all in an effort to bond over the TV series *The Real Housewives*.

21. The Testosterone. Although women are not his forte, Jack feels he must bond with his new boss (Kris) if he is to continue his manipulative work habits.

22. The Advice. Jack acquires a date (with Drew) and seeks (the not so helpful) advice from Millie and Jill as to how he should act.

23. The Date. Jack and Drew embark on what could be considered a date from hell replete with sexual tension, nervous laughter and horrendous jokes. But Jack appears to be happy.

24. The Breakup. Jack meets with Gloria, thinking she has acquired him a job, but finds her terminating their business relationship when she tells him her inability to have a sexual dream about him (as she does with other clients) means she can no longer represent him.

25. The Compromises. Now without an agent, Jack realizes that for any relationship to work there has to be compromises and sets out to change his controlling ways so as not to lose Drew.

26. The Staff Meeting. At a Ticket Universe staff meeting, a new employee (Beau) is introduced but Jack is more concerned over two other things: why Suzie has an orange juice drink without the pulp and who will take possession of that last donut on the table.

27. The Pest. A computer malfunction finds Jack attempting to bond with Kris and wondering just who (or what) Beau is when he appears to be getting a bit too familiar with him.

28. The Snake. Gloria reconnects with Jack and offers him a job (playing the role of a diabetic man) but also manipulates him into taking voice lessons to improve his singing skills.

29. The Grilling. Jack and Drew have bonded and Jack believes his mother and Aunt Heidi should meet him. As Drew gets the third degree, he learns that his widowed mother has made her own hookup with another man.

30. The Bonding. A look at what happens when the box office closes for the night: Jack, Suzie and Beau bond over drinks.

31. The Future. The concluding unresolved episode wherein Jack ponders his future when he is offered a promotion at Ticket Universe, but accepting could put a dent in his acting career.

159 *Jenifer Lewis and Shangela*. youtube.com. 2012 (Comedy).

RuPaul's Drag Race is a cable television series hosted by drag queen RuPaul wherein aspiring drag queens vie for a chance at stardom. One such contestant is Shangela Wadley and singer-actress Jenifer Lewis, seeing potential in Shangela, takes her under her wing and the scripted program follows Jenifer as she mentors the up-and-coming performer (who, until she becomes a star, resides in the basement apartment of Jenifer's Hollywood mansion).

Cast: Jenifer Lewis (Herself), D.J. Pierce (Shangela Wadley). **Credits:** *Producer:* Jenifer Lewis. *Director:* Mary Lou Belli. *Writer:* Mark Alton Brown, Dee LaDuke. **Comment:** Delightful program that plays much better than website information leads you to believe (a star helping a newcomer to achieve success in a reality-like program). The program is like a sitcom with Jenifer and Shangela playing perfectly off each other as the teacher and the student. Jenifer's "potty mouth" actually adds to the comedy as Shangela can get on anyone's nerves and Jenifer is no exception. She plays the role expertly and the whole concept just works to produce a program worthy of a television or cable broadcast (although dialogue will have to be bleeped).

Episodes:

1. Pilot. Jenifer begins her mentoring of Shangela by using her experience in the film *Hereafter* to instill in her the motivation needed to act.

2. Recognition. Trouble looms at the Lewis mansion when a delivery man recognizes D.J. (without makeup or in costume) as playing Shangela but fails to know who or what a Jenifer Lewis is.

3. Gold Earrings. While searching for her missing gold earrings, Jenifer comes to realize that Shangela needs to develop her own identity and not impersonate pop stars like Beyonce on stage.

4. Mouse. The unthinkable happens—a mouse has invaded Jenifer's 2.3 million dollar home and,

being deathly afraid of mice, has to rely on D.J. to rid her home of the varmint. The program's concluding episode.

160 Jeza and the Belles. youtube.com. 2011 (Science Fiction Comedy).

When their lives are threatened by thugs, the three Belle (drag queen) sisters (Badora, Sue-She and Jeza) are transported to the realm of Eusta, Drag Queen of the Galaxy, where they learn she is unhappy with the planet Earth, its violence and crime and that she plans to destroy it. Pleading by the sisters to spare the planet changes Queen Eusta's mind and she gives them the opportunity to save Earth by eliminating evil. If they succeed, the planet will be spared; if not, it will be destroyed. To help them in their mission, Eusta presents each of them with a special piece of jewelry. Badora receives a bracelet that allows her to move swiftly through time; Sue-She possesses a necklace that makes her fierce and agile; and Jeza is awarded a ring that makes her a sorceress and able to control minds. Making their mission even more difficult, is an evil villainous named Smelva, a (real) woman who emits a fish odor, surrounds herself with her army of legal male prostitutes and has defied Queen Eusta to conquer the universe. The Belle sisters are returned to Earth to first defeat the thugs that threatened them then to combine their powers and rid the world of evil before Queen Eusta destroys the planet.

Cast: Jeza Belle [Billy Canyon] (Jeza Belle/Queen Eusta), Sir Honey Davenport [James Clark] (Badora Belle), Tara Miso Rice [Danart Ros] (Sue-She Belle), Gina Jarrin (Smelva). **Credits:** Producer: Billy Canyon, Cee Canyon. Writer-Director: Billy Canyon. **Comment:** Very well acted, television-quality production that even incorporates a sitcom-like laugh track (not needed, but something different in an Internet show). The sisters are outlandish (especially in their hair styles) and the program is enjoyable from beginning to end.

Episodes:

1. Drag Queen Heroes. The story line is established as the Belle sisters meet Queen Eusta for the first time.

2. Uhhh.... No Fishy. Smelva makes her first appearance and becomes a serious threat to the Belle sisters as they must now also stop her reign of terror.

3. The Boy Is Mine, Part 1. An attempt by the sisters to stop a bank hostage situation has unexpected results when each falls for the handsome kidnapper (Darwin Reina)—a trap set by Smelva to capture them.

4. The Boy Is Mine, Part 2. The sisters have fallen for the trap set by Smelva and must now find a way to extradite themselves in the concluding episode.

161 Jillian's Peak. jillianspeak.com. 2014 (Drama).

Jillian Thomas is a very pretty African-American woman that appears to be living the American Dream. She has a good job as a photographer, a lovely home in Detroit and is married to Keith. As long as she can remember, Jillian had been taught to follow her dreams and achieve happiness. But lately Jillian has been overcome with feelings that everything is not right in her life. Her relationship with Keith has been floundering and she has been haunted by feelings that have her questioning her sexuality ("Am I a Lesbian?"). Unable to live under her present situation, and feeling the need to find the truth, Jillian moves to New York City and in with her best friend from college, Gail, a self-assured lesbian. The program explores Jillian as she embarks on a journey of self-discovery to once and for all find what truly makes her happy.

Cast: Jillian Thomas (Herself), Lisann Valentin (Gail Ramos), Hector Hicks (Charles James), Hope Garley (Lucille James), La Rivers (Victoria James), Vince Edgehill (Pastor Johnson), Karen Goldberg (Candice Myers), Sheena Williams (Sherricka White), Grant E. Harvey (Keith Thomas). **Credits:** Producer Danielle Johnson, Charzette Torrence. Writer: Preston Edwyn, Arthur Graham. **Comment:** Judging by the trailer that is available, the program is well acted and produced and presents an African-American woman in a much more positive light (very attractive and not a foul-mouthed street bitch) than has been portrayed on most other African-American lesbian series.

Episodes: 12 episodes have been produced but not released as of January 2015.

162 Joni and Susanna. afterellen.com. 2008 (Comedy).

Joni is a beautiful lesbian and friends with Susanna, an equally beautiful straight girl. Although Joni is attracted to Susanna, she realizes she cannot have her and has set her sights on finding that special girl. Susanna is seeking the perfect man but, like Joni, having a difficult time connecting with the right person. The program follows their efforts to help each other find that special someone and what happens when their efforts often sabotage what they are trying to accomplish for the other.

Cast: Joni Lefkowitz (Joni), Susanna Fogel (Susanna), Bridget McManus (Bridget), Stephanie Escajeda (Stephanie), Ginger Haggerty (Ginger), Terrie Haggerty (Terrie), Julia Miranda (Julia), Jaime Reichner (Jaime), Dave Richman (Dave), Mariah Robinson (Mariah). **Credits:** Producer: Susanna Fogel, Joni Lefkowitz, Erica Kraus. Director: Susanna Fogel. Writer: Susanna Fogel, Joni Lefkowitz. **Comment:** The program is well acted and produced and the episodes are humorous as Joni and Susanna are like "frenemies" with their good intentions always back firing and causing more innocent harm than good.

Episodes:

1. Party. At a friend's birthday party, Joni and Susanna each spot someone they would like to meet—but they need each other's help in doing so.

2. Gym. Jamie, the girl Joni met at the party, invites Joni and Susanna to her gym for a little more than just exercising.

3. Comedy. Guest Bridget McManus appears as Joni and Susanna (and Dave, her date from the party) attend Bridget's stand-up comedy act.

4. Stable. Joni and Bridget appear to have made a connection at the club and with Susanna tagging along Bridget accompanies Joni to meet her mother.

5. Brunch. Complications arise when, during brunch with Joni and Susanna, Bridget runs into her ex-girlfriend.

6. Mall. In an effort to help Joni get her mind off Bridget (who seems to have reconnected with her ex), Susanna takes her mall shopping.

7. Joni and Susanna Go to Jack-in-the-Box. Seated in a car, Joni and Susanna just talk to each other while driving to Jack-in-the-Box for lunch.

8. Joni and Susanna Look for a Parking Space. Having reached their destination, Susanna, the driver, seeks a parking space.

163 Judys. webserieschannel.com. 2013 (Comedy-Drama).

Macen, Harper, Ezell, Vaughn and Carvin are five gay friends living in what is called Gay Atlanta. Each of the men has a distinct personality and each is there for the other in times of need. The program relates incidents in their daily lives as they not only interact with each other but those who are also a part of their inner circle. **Cast:** De'Von Forbes (Macen Givens), Casey Hamilton (Harper Campbell), Corey Pope (Carvin White), Ryan Pitts (Ezell Frasier), Terry Evidence (Vaughn Mitchell), Meredith Monroe (Marissa Moore). **Credits:** *Producer-Writer:* Casey Hamilton. *Director:* Casey Hamilton, Briana Hightower. **Comment:** Based on the pilot episode, a much more down-to-earth, non derogatory look at a group of African-American gay men. Unlike other harsh series that profile gay black men, *Judys* looks to be a more talkative profile with the friends finding both joy and sorrow as they help each other navigate life in the gay community.

Episodes:

1. Spring Summer Feelings. The pilot episode that introduces the friends, especially Macen, seen sleeping in bed with a woman then setting out to explore his feelings—is he gay or bisexual?

2. Promotional Teaser. A look at the program and what to expect is presented.

164 Julian. youtube.com/playlist?list= PLd8TF7E0vwKnzGYT1YDjMggvTvzNn qrBd. 2013 (Drama).

Julian is a 16-year-old boy living in Germany. Like other teens his age, he attends school, has friends, dates a girl and does not always get along with his parents. But Julian, like few others his age, is also struggling with his sexuality when he suddenly becomes attracted to boys. With doubts now filling his mind, is he gay or bisexual, the program explores Julian's efforts to discover who he is and come to terms with that decision despite what his friends and family think.

Cast as credited: Anton B. (Julian), Justus B. (Dennis), Florian Muller (Philipp), Kevin W. (Marc), Jania Engelhardt (Sarah), Giasmina Talman (Lara), Maik Scholz (Reggie). **Comment:** German produced program wherein the closed captioning feature must be activated for the English subtitles. It is smartly photographed and well acted and, despite the distraction of having to read what is happening, it appears that a true depiction of what some teenagers face, whether male or female when they are unsure of their sexuality, will be explored (possibly in the same manner as the series *Out with Dad* [see entry] did in exploring the life of a high school girl dealing with her coming out as a lesbian).

Episodes: Eight episodes are mentioned as being produced but only the series pilot film is on line and establishes the story wherein Julian suddenly becomes aware that he is "different" when he becomes attracted to another boy.

165 Justine. justineseries.com. 1996 (Drama).

Justine DeMarco is a woman who has achieved her dream of becoming an actress. But for Justine the road to success was not an easy one. She was born in Iowa and yearned to be an actress. Her activities in high school and college revolved around the school's theater companies which, in a way, trained her as an actress. But for Justine, small town productions were not the life she was seeking. With what money she had saved and with a strong determination, Justine ventured onto Hollywood to seek her dream of fame. It was shortly after, when her finances became low and she needed work that she found a job as a waitress at a bar. It is here that she befriends the bartender (Madison), the daughter of the bar owner (Bruce) who instantly becomes attracted to her (hinting that Madison and possibly even Justine are lesbians). Unlike Justine, who is more of a homebody, Madison is a party-like girl and introduces Justine to a world she has never known before: clubbing and mixing with the higher ups in society. Being a small town girl, Justine has reservations about what is happening and feels she needs to concentrate on her acting career. But it is at one of Madison's clubbing ventures that Justine's life is changed when she meets a theatrical agent seeking "a special girl" for a film role. The agent sees that something special in

Justine and, after learning she is an actress, sets her up on an audition. The door has been opened and the program charts Justine's journey to stardom, a road filled with both joy and sorrow and friendship, as Madison also becomes a part of her life. **Cast:** Justine Sanford (Justine), Amber Marks (Madison), Stanford Shields (Bruce). **Credits:** *Producer:* Justine Sanford. **Comment:** A pioneering series that is both sentimental and a bit brazen for is time. The lesbian aspect was hinted at with Justine and Madison being lovers but it was never stated as fact. There are no kissing scenes (only hugging between Justine and Madison) and not a mention of the word lesbian. The picture quality is only fair but the acting is in line with a network TV series.

Episodes:

1. Meet Justine. Following a brief look at Justine's world in Iowa, the program begins her journey as she ventures onto Hollywood.

2. Justine and Madison. While looking for a job Justine meets Madison for the first time.

3. Justine, Madison and Bruce. Justine not only finds a helping hand from Madison, but from Bruce, the bar owner who offers her a job.

4. Justine and the Side Job. Needing extra money, Justine takes a job as a singing telegram girl—only to arrive at the wrong address and be mistaken for a stripper at a bachelor party.

5. Justine and Her First Break. A night out with Madison has an unexpected result when Justine meets an agent seeking "a special girl" for a film.

6. Justine and Her Light on Broadway. Justine's performance is a standout and has critics taking notice of her singing and acting ability.

7. Justine and Her Rise to Fame. A fast paced episode that quickly establishes Justine's rise to fame while also focusing on her continuing (and close) relationship with Madison.

8. Justine and Her Awards. Highlights of Justine's growing success are highlighted with hints that she and Madison have become more than just friends.

9. Justine Finale. In the concluding episode, Justine's career appears to be only just beginning and what lies ahead is unknown. "Life is a kicker," says Justine. "You never know what to expect. Suppose I didn't follow my dream, what would have happened to me? Would I have met Madison? Would I have become an actress? I wonder."

166 *K & A.* karlyandalex.com. 2014 (Comedy).

Boston provides the setting for a tale of two dysfunctional friends, Karly (straight) and Alex (a lesbian) and the problems each encounters—co-dependent on the other and each seeking to find the perfect mate—but not with each other. **Cast:** Audrey Claire Johnson (Karly), Ashley Elmi (Alex). **Credits:** *Producer:* Audrey Claire Johnson, Katie Shannon, Mike Madden. *Writer-Director:*

Katie Shannon. **Comment:** Enjoyable comedy with good acting and production values. The characters are very like-able and the sexual situations acceptable; the use of vulgar language is really not needed as gutter talk does not enhance scenes.

Episodes:

1. The Herpes. Worried over the fact that she may have an STD, Karly drags Alex to the gynecologist to learn about sexually transmitted diseases.

2. K & A Do Nice Stuff for People. Karly and Alex experience "the joys and sorrows" of community service when Karly suggests, "We should do something nice for someone."

3. DeTox. Karly and Alex, addicted to alcohol, decide to see how long each can go without taking a drink.

4. 50 Shades of K & A. Rather intimate episode wherein Karly and Alex experiment with sexual toys with Alex finding, that because she is a lesbian, she cannot receive the same satisfaction as Karly.

5. Intervention. When Karly and Alex realize they are too dependent on each other, they decide to hopefully resolve the situation through an intervention.

167 *Kam Kardashian.* kamkardashian. com. 2012–2014 (Comedy).

While the world believes that only Kourtney and Khloe are the sisters of Kim Kardashian, there is actually a fourth sister, the fictional Kameron (called Kam), an alluring woman who was disowned by the family when a sex tape scandal (involving Kam and Marcia Clark, the prosecutor in the famous O.J. Simpson murder trial) revealed that Kam was a lesbian. Cut off financially and evicted from the Kardashian home, Kam had no choice but to fend for herself and now survives mostly through petty crimes. Kam is proud of the fact that she is a lesbian, has a girlfriend (Mary Hollis) and has one ultimate goal: to once again become a part of the Kardashian family. The program charts her attempts, assisted by the slightly unbalanced Mary, as she finds re-inserting herself into the Kardashian brand is not as simple as just claiming she is a Kardashian. (It is revealed that the Kardashian family had knowledge of the sex tape and when it was learned that Kim became pregnant by a man named Tom Greene and not her husband, they leaked the tape to the media to take attention away from Kim and place it on Kam.) **Cast:** Fawzia Mirza (Kam Kardashian), Mary Hollis Inboden (Mary Hollis), Joel Kim Booster (Joel), Mark Raterman (Himself). **Credits:** *Producer:* Fawzia Mirza. *Director:* Ryan Logan. *Writer:* Fawzia Mirza, Brittany Ashley, Joel Kim Booster, Mary Hollis Inboden, Mia Horberg, Ryan Logan, Jackie Migliore. **Comment:** An enjoyable spoof the Kardashian family, especially Kim, with very good acting and production values. Fawzia Mirza is very convincing as Kam and can make you believe that

Kam Kardashian. **Mary Hollis Inboden (left) and Fawzia Mirza (used by permission of Fawzia Mirza).**

she could actually be a Kardashian and not just an actress playing a role.

Episodes:

1. The Gay One. While in a bar, Kam begins drinking and lamenting over the fact that the sex tape was leaked by her family to the TV program *TMZ*.

2. Haircut. Feeling that a change is needed, Kam decides that a new hair style may do the trick.

3. BFF. Mary, who likes to pretend she is a Mermaid attempts to offer Kam advice on dating—stop the one night stands and find a steady girlfriend.

4. Hustlin'. A glimpse of Kam's hustling expertise is explored when she helps a stranded motorcyclist, learns he is engaged and attempts to sell him a wedding ring.

5. Xmas Special. Kam and Mary reflect on the old year (2012) and look forward to the New Year.

6. Orange You GLAWD. Kam finds herself in a precarious situation when she is abducted by Agent Stone (Beth Stelling) of GLAWD (Gays and Lesbians Achieving World Domination), a top-secret gay rights organization to become the face of a gay revolution. But first she needs to be reformed and her image white-washed.

7. First Date. In an attempt to find Kam a steady girlfriend, she is set up on a date with a girl (Keli Simpkins) who treats the date like a job interview to see if Kam has the qualifications to be her girlfriend.

8. One Night Stand. Mark, Kam's friend, gets more than he bargained for when he shows up at Kam's apartment and catches Kam making love to his fiancé.

9. Internment. Joel, the intern at GLAWD assigned to change Kam, finds the job a bit more challenging than he (or Agent Stone) had imagined. But slowly, Kam appears to be changing her style.

10. Fan Fiction, Part 1. Kam and Mary begin a search for an author who has written *Kim in Court*, an on-line chronicle that credits Kim as having a torrid lesbian affair with Marcia Clark, not her.

11. Fan Fiction, Part 2. Meeting with the book's author (Kandy Kardashian) in an attempt to set the record straight, Kam not only discovers that she is a long-lost Kardashian sister, but there are many other sisters that are unknown to the world.

12. Therapy. To hopefully overcome her abandonment issues, her lust for Marcia Clark and her need to find stabilization in her life, Kam seeks the advice of a therapist.

13. Fashion Forward. In the concluding episode Kam's life appears to be improving for the better as she attempts to launch her own fashion line.

168 Kelsey. blip.tv. 2013 (Comedy-Drama).

Kelsey, a pretty, openly admitted lesbian, is seeking the love of another woman but her tendency to point out her faults (like talking too much and her weird sense of humor) before she can even get to know another girl is almost always an immediate turn off and Kelsey continually finds herself alone. After numerous breakups Kelsey comes to realize that being a bit-off-the-wall is more of a hindrance than an asset and sets out to change her quirky ways and become a new woman. Although her intentions are good changing becomes a problem and Kelsey is about to give up until she hits on the notion of asking her friends, Samantha, Rowan and Tyrone for help. The program relates the drama, chaos and mishaps that occur as Kelsey attempts to become someone she is really not in her quest to find the perfect woman for herself. Also known as *This Is Kelsey* and *Kelsey: The Series.*

Cast: Nicole Yannetty (Kelsey), Sharina Martin (Samantha), Daniel K. Isaac (Tyrone), Brennan Taylor (Rowan), Lauren A. Kennedy (Joanne), Richard Bird (Leroy), Gina Primavera (Jen), Charlotte Simpson (Shane). **Credits:** *Producer:* Christina Raia, Kelsey Rauber. *Director:* Christina Raia. *Writer:* Kelsey Rauber. **Comment:** Subtle drama mixes with comedy to detail the efforts of a slightly awkward woman as she seeks romance. Nicely acted and well produced and worth checking out for a different approach in a lesbian-themed web series.

Episodes:

1. Palette Cleanser. Kelsey is introduced in a rather unflattering manner: seen with a bruised lip after being dumped not so tenderly by an ex-girlfriend (Shane).

2. Don't Hit Send. Feeling that the Internet may be the place to find a mate, Kelsey also discovers that she is rather uninformed when it comes to computer dating.

3. www.dating? Kelsey faces a drawback when she learns that Shane has moved on and is now seeking romance with another woman.

4. Shopping in Groups. Kelsey seeks the advice of a friend (Joanne) to help her write an on-line dating profile.

5. A Best Friend's Birthday. Kelsey's habit of relentlessly rambling is explored after she acquires a computer date.

6. U-Haul-er. Kelsey confides in her friend (Tyrone) about her computer date and how it never turned into a one-night stand.

7. Hanging Out Without. Kelsey discovers that her best friends are having a secret affair.

8. Bluffing. A poker party thrown by Kelsey reveals incidents in the lives of Kelsey and her friends.

9. Drive Through. A ride in Tyrone's new car turns out to be anything but pleasurable when Kelsey and her friends become cramped for space.

10. Making Things Work. The concluding episode finds Kelsey, now in a relationship with Joanne, discussing events of the past few months.

169 Ken. webserieschannel.com. 2013 (Comedy-Drama).

Ken, a born-again Christian, has just broken up with his girlfriend Stephanie and feels his whole world is now crashing down upon him. One night, Ken walked into a bar to have a drink. The following morning held a shock for Ken when he woke up in bed with another man and not only had him ques-

tioning his religion (he considers himself a man of God), but his sexuality—is he gay (and it took getting drunk for his suppressed preference to surface)? The program charts the events that now spark Ken's life as he attempts to figure out just who and what he really is—gay, straight or bisexual.

Cast: Jarret Janako (Ken), Krystal Farris (Stephanie), Yarc Lewinson (Paul), Leigh Ann Rose (Jessica), Travon McCall (Duke). **Credits:** *Producer-Writer-Director:* Eddie Griffith. **Comment:** Quite realistic, well played and produced African-American program dealing with problems that actually exist. The program is set away from the bedroom and is more of a personal look at the torture Ken faces as he struggles to determine who he is—"I'm a man of God—sacrificial and Holy Ghost filled.... I'm not someone who gets drunk and has sex with men.... I'm going to Hell."

Episodes:

1. Pilot. The story line is established as Ken realizes that, after a night of drinking, he may also be attracted to men as well as women.

2. Confrontation. Ken's revealing what happened to Stephanie finds him encountering her anger when she feels he cheated on her and her dreams of a life with Ken are now shattered. When Ken is unable to convincingly explain to Stephanie that what happened was a one-time thing, she leaves him.

3. Climax. It has been several months since the incident and Ken has been avoiding church and most of his friends. Still unable to re-connect with Stephanie, Ken seeks help from a friend (Paul) hoping to solve his dilemma. Meanwhile, Stephanie, a nurse, is seeking to find another man as she wants "to become a wife, mother and grandmother" and believes that cannot be achieved with Ken.

170 L.A. Girls. webserieschannel.com. 2013 (Comedy).

A parody of the HBO series *Girls* that focuses on Shoshana, Marnie, Hannah and Jessa four women who are also friends and navigating life in Los Angeles. While the program is mostly a comical look at the mishaps the women encounter, it also hints on the fact that Marnie may be a lesbian (or at least bisexual) and that Ray and Elijah are gay. Shoshana is a level-headed girl with a heart of gold; Hannah is an unemployed actress struggling to make ends meet; Marnie dates men but is thought by some to be bisexual; Jessa, like Marnie, has no real character development, and her scenes involve her adoption of a South African child (whom she later loses in a park after getting drunk). Adam, Hannah's friend, works as an adult film star extra; and Elijah is a male model.

Cast: Tiffany Ariany (Shoshana Shapiro), Rya Meyers (Marnie Michaels), Kylie Sparks (Hannah Horvath),Victoria Bullock (Jessa Johansson), Carl Gambino (Adam Sackler), Zachary Haven (Knick

Knack), Kyle Colton (Ray Ploshansky), Michael Collins (Elijah Krantz), Erich Lane (Charlie Dattolo). **Credits:** *Producer:* Tiffany Ariany, Matt Blessing, Kylie Sparks. *Director:* Matt Blessing. *Writer:* Tiffany Ariany, Matt Blessing. **Comment:** Very well acted and photographed program that does not require you to watch the HBO series to enjoy it. The lesbian and gay aspects are not really pursued and story lines are abruptly ended without resolving issues. There is a bit of foul language.

Episodes:

1. Judaism Nepotism. Life changes dramatically for Hannah when her parents, upset that after two years she has not made it as an actress, cut off her financing, leaving her with no money and no job.

2. I've Got Knick Knack in My Pants. Life again throws Hannah a blow when a doctor's visit reveals she has an STD.

3. Is Everyone Gay? Hannah's quest to discover who gave her the STD leads her to the conclusion that everyone she knows is gay.

4. This Isn't Breaking Bad. The STD story line is dropped (with no conclusion) as Hannah, desperate for money, takes a job dealing drugs on the street (spoofing, in part, the TV series *Breaking Bad*).

5. Mirrors. The concluding episode wherein Hannah's drug operations seem to be paying off until Adam sees what she has become and appears determined to change her life around; while Marnie, spied upon by her boyfriend, accuses her of being a lesbian and sleeping with Hannah.

6. L.A. Girls Blooper Reel. Various outtakes culled from the series five episodes.

171 *Ladies Lust Love.* youtube.com. 2012 (Drama).

A proposed series (thus far only a pilot has been produced) about lesbian, bisexual and straight African-American women from all walks of life and how they deal with the situations that surround them.

Cast: All performers are credited only by a first name as follows: Carresha (Autumn), Sharinna (Brandy), CK (Carman), Alisha (Carter), Jasmine (Angel), Kasha (Kerri), Nikki (Jayla), Ashley (Stacey), Yoshi (Chris). **Credits:** *Producer-Writer-Director:* Bonnie Janelle. **Comment:** Very talkative, slow-moving concept that apparently never went further than a pilot episode. The annoying shaky camera method of filming does not help the story nor does noticeable editing. There are mild sexual situations, some traces of street language and badly presented kissing scenes. Rather than frontal views of kissing, the audience is presented with views that obstruct the kiss (like shooting the scene from the back of the head of one girl while she kisses another girl). There is also a noticeable buzzing sound in some scenes and the overall project, while good on paper, is just poorly executed to film. What to expect

was posted as "Lesbians, bisexuals, insecurity [insecure women], down low, confused, party girls, drinkers, deceitful [women], hustlers, etc. You will be able to relate to one of these women. Straights are welcome." The statement presents two thoughts: what kind of audience was the producer seeking and what kind of women are in the "etcetera." category.

Episodes:

1. Pilot. Introduces the women and somewhat establishes a story line but exactly what is unknown as "This is a pilot. Changes have been made accordingly."

172 *Lado C (Position C).* ladocserie.com. 2013 (Comedy).

Spanish produced program set against the background of Buenos Aires that relates incidents in the lives of six life-long friends (Mia, Zoe, Esteban, Lucas, Rita and Bautista), each very different from the other as they navigate life in a changing society.

Mia, 24 years of age, is a free-spirit but afraid to make a commitment and is thus uncertain what the future holds when it comes to marriage and a family. She earns a living as a fashion photographer and prefers to photograph men as "women drive me crazy." She considers Esteban to be like the brother she never had (although they share a love-hate relationship) and Lucas was her prior boyfriend.

Bautista, proud of the fact that he is 25 but looks 22, is somewhat vain and not only considers himself a great friend, but "a great lover." He is an actor, hoping for that big break, but nearly broke as he continually takes on pro bono short films. He is also gay and says, "Men are like potato chips, you can not eat just one."

Rita, 25 years of age, is also uncertain about her future. She has a Master's degree in Ecology but has not yet pursued a job in that field. She believes in astrology as the stars hold the answers to millions of questions but the smog of the city prevents her from seeing them clearly and getting the answers she needs.

Lucas is 24 years of age and considers himself a ladies' man ("They say each woman is different, so I am a bachelor in tourism"). He has a passion for video games and claims there isn't a game he hasn't played. Lucas also says that "if you thought gamers had no sex you are wrong."

Esteban, a 24-year-old journalist whose passion is reading books ("even though they say I do not belong to the generation that reads books"). He and Lucas are roommates and it is revealed that Esteban is bisexual.

Zoe, recently returning to Buenos Aires to be with her friends, claims "that a lady never reveals her age" but is within the 22–25 age range. She loves traveling (although she has a fear of flying), movies (she has a tendency to dress as a character she admires) and holds a secret (later revealed) that she is a lesbian.

Cast: Federico Araujo, Juan Dujo, Kiara Sanders, Leandro Staffa, Romina Lucia Escobar, Mary Viau. **Credits:** *Producer:* Benjamin Landaburu, Juan Dujo. *Writer-Director:* Juan Dujo. **Comment:** Very little information remains on line and the program is not blessed with the most pleasing translation from Spanish to English. There are no cast and character match-ups and based on text information alone, the program is difficult to comment upon as no indication is given as to what type of rating it would have or if it contains nudity, sexual situations or even vulgar language.

Episodes: All episodes have been taken off-line. Although episodes 1 ("Pilot 1—The Big Day") and 2 ("Rider 2—Transgaysor") are listed on the program's website, they are not able to be viewed (the still scene that highlights each episode will remain stationery).

173 *Lady Cops.* afterellen.com. 2009 (Drama).

Lady Cops is a fictional television series about Jo and Sienna, female police officers who are also lovers. Mikki Majors plays the role of Sienna and Lara Lancaster is Jo. While they are lesbians on screen, in real life Mikki and Lara are straight and are anything but lovers as they despise each other. The program explores incidents in their off-screen and on-screen lives with the intent to not only spoof the numerous crime dramas on TV but poke fun at the lesbian community as well.

Cast: Liz Vassey (Mikki Majors/Sienna), Christina Cox (Lara Lancaster/Jo), Donna Scott (Winter Kole), Rob Moran (Brick Schlouse). **Credits:** *Producer:* Maeve Quinlan, Nancylee Myatt. **Comment:** Well acted and produced program that focuses more on Mikki and Lara's activities as police officers and lovers than their off-screen lives. The program is a spin off from episode six (*Lady Cops*) that aired on the anthology series *3Way*.

Episodes:
1. Lady Cops: Brotherly Love. Jo and Sienna investigate a case involving the murder of a young woman who died from booze, pills and a blow to the head. The pilot and only episode that remains on line.

174 *The Legend of Sprada.* youtube.com. 2011 (Comedy).

Unable to achieve her dream of becoming a super star in England, Sprada (a drag queen) elects to try her luck elsewhere and chooses the United States. In Chicago, which she now calls home, Sprada acquires a new best friend, Dixie Lynn (a drag queen) and an agent, Walter Bastardman ("the 'd' is silent") and a new hope to become a mega super star. The program charts Sprada's adventures as becoming that international super star takes more than just being

talented, beautiful and eager especially when her agent specializes in casting females in movies and TV series that require corpses (being seen only covered in a sheet).

Cast: Spencer Gartner (Sprada), Dixie Lynn Cartwright (Herself), Bill Larkin (Walter Bastardman), Dave Camp (Oscar), Claire Kander (Lizzie), Brandon Vejseli (Landon Skankefski). **Credits:** *Producer-Director:* Brandon Vejseli. *Writer:* Brandon Vejseli, Steve Macy, Spencer Gartner, Dixie Lynn Cartwright. **Comment:** *Chico's Angels* is one example where programs about drag queens work. *The Legend of Sprada* is another one. It is very enjoyable with good acting and production values. Although the doorway had been left open to continue the story, it appears that now that four years have passed, additional episodes will not be produced.

Episodes:
1. Coming to America. The saga begins as Sprada leaves England for Chicago.

2. Box of Hair. Sprada's first meeting with her agent is not all that encouraging, until she meets Dixie Lynn, the woman who takes her under her wing to help her achieve her dream.

3. Tops and Bottoms. Dixie Lynn begins Sprada's make over with a new wardrobe that is more in line with the sexy clothes she wears.

4. I Know What I'm Doing. With Dixie Lynn's help, Sprada prepares for her first high fashion photo shoot.

5. Really Proud. The big day arrives and Sprada does her best to prove she is a natural at the photo shoot.

6. Paycheck. The photo shoot produces some stunning photos but the paycheck Sprada receives is anything but delightful ($11.10) when she learns that in addition to Walter's 69 percent commission there are such fees as chair sitting and door opening.

7. Short a Waitress. Seeing that Sprada is upset and needs money, Dixie Lynn secures her a job as a waitress in a coffee shop.

8. Hello World. Footage of Sprada before she came to America is seen when her old cell phone pictures and videos are recovered.

9. Nailed It. Thrilled that Walter finally got her an audition for a TV show, Sprada performs for producers by singing the song "On the Good Ship Lollipop" and acquires the role—that of a corpse covered in a sheet.

10. Rock Your World. The break Sprada has been waiting for comes when she meets Oscar, the man who becomes so infatuated with her that he becomes her sugar daddy.

11. Some Other Bimbo. Sprada, believing she is Walter's only client, finds disenchantment when she discovers he has another client and prefers her over her.

12. Grand Slam. As Sprada begins to have doubts about her dream ever coming true, she is visited by

three other drag queens that also have Oscar as a sugar daddy and Walter as an agent but are bitter over the fact that she has taken their corpse jobs away from them. As the program concludes, the drag queens kidnap Sprada leaving Dixie Lynn, Oscar and Walter to wonder why but most importantly, how to get her back.

175 *Lesbian Cops.* youtube.com/playlist? list=PLC6F4857FFFD58223. 2011 (Crime Drama).

Tori Jones, a Lipstick Lesbian (feminine) and Rashida Thompson, a butch type lesbian, are police detectives and partners that investigate crimes associated with robbery and homicide. Tori, while good at her job, had a penchant for losing male partners through tragic circumstances during case investigations. To resolve a problem (who to team with Tori) it was decided to assign her a female officer as it is believed Tori would become more responsive to protecting her partner and vice versa. Whether the experiment will work is unknown as teaming two women who are also lesbians is something that has never been done before. In the presented story Tori and Rashida attempt to solve the drug-related murder of a teacher at Hamilton Elementary School.

Cast: Gena Shaw (Det. Tori Jones), Krystal Marshall (Det. Rashida Thompson), Thomas Jones (Chief Wilson), Dane Reade (Det. Frank Martin), Casey Nelson (Off. Casey), Suzanne Quast (Virginia Cunderson), Shawn G. Smith (Dustin Brown). **Credits:** *Producer:* Firouz Farhang, Jessica Matthews, David Aslan, Aaron Burnett. *Writer-Director:* Firouz Farhang. **Comment:** A very vulgar program that uses an over-abundance of foul language. The acting and production values are good, but the attempt to mix crime drama with comedy falls flat; obscene words simply do not turn drama into comedy. The lesbian match-up is also hard to fathom (the women are just not compatible) and having a superior (Wilson) belittle a subordinate (Tori) for her sexual preference is a poor stab at comedy (as it too does not work—even if Tori lashes back with her dose of foul language). The concept is said to be "an action-packed cop drama inspired by movies like *Death Wish, Lethal Weapon, Bad Boys* ... and anything else that kicks ass!" It fails to meet those standards and there is no nudity, kissing or scenes of affection between Tori and Rashida in the episodes. There is also no parental warning (the episodes can also be viewed on sharing sites like YouTube) although two versions of the episodes have been released: "Uncensored" and "Censored" (which contains bleeped foul language). *Lesbian Cops: The Movie* was made and has also been released on DVD.

Episodes:

1. I Hate Drugs, Part 1. Tori is teamed with Rashida after her prior partner, a recent rookie school graduate, is shot.

2. I Hate Drugs, Part 2. A case begins as Tori and Rashida investigate the death of a school teacher.

3. We've Got Solid Evidence. The suspects in the case are questioned.

4. Not Again. Tori and Rashida become close for the first time when Rashida tries to help Tori overcome her feelings that she has hit rock bottom.

5. I Heard Crazy. Tori, back on her feet aggressively pursues clues to find the killer.

6. Why's He Beeping. Tori and Rashida continue their investigation as the series concludes.

176 *The Lesbian Game Changer Video Series.* youtube.com. 2012 (Advice).

A program designed especially for lesbians wherein the host attempts to help such women "get unstuck, get happy and create love in your life today" by exposing "Three Hidden Keys to Lasting Love and Happiness."

Host: Mary Gorham Malia. **Credits:** *Producer-Writer:* Mary Gorham Malia. **Comment:** Based on the teaser, the program is a casual presentation that attempts to help women embrace their sexuality and find happiness while doing so.

Episodes: All episodes have been removed with only a short teaser remaining that explains the show's concept.

177 *Lesbian Love.* onemorelesbian.com. 2012 (Reality).

"Lacey met Jessica. They fell in love.... And now they have to figure out.... Lesbian Love" are the visuals that open the program. Through discussions among themselves and with guests from the lesbian community, matters that relate to such women are explored with hopeful solutions given by the end of each episode.

Host: Lacey Stone, Jessica Clark. **Credits:** *Producer:* George Stoll. **Comment:** With the only video information being the one remaining episode, the program has a very relaxed format with the hosts making their guests feel right at home. The production values are comparable to any TV talk show and the program no doubt provided a service when originally broadcast.

Episodes: 135 episodes were produced but only episode 134 ("Back in the Saddle Again") remains on line and, with guest Nikki T, Lacey and Jessica discuss how to get back in the game after a breakup.

178 *Lesbian Seduction.* twilightwomen. com/twilightwomen-indices/lesbian-seduction-series.html. 2009–2014 (Anthology).

Erotic stories wherein women seduce and make love to other women. Each story listed is composed of several episodes and other than a very brief meeting of the women involved, there is virtually no dialogue as the concentration is strictly on the affection the women share with each other.

Cast: Ann Ampar, Robin Joy (and as credited) Mara, Catherine, Tiffany, Cindy, Marie, Gina, Tasha, Monique. **Credits:** *Producer:* Twilightwomen.com. *Director:* Div For'e. **Comment:** The most erotic of the lesbian web series. There are abundant (and long) kissing scenes coupled with partial nudity and very sensuous stories. The program is careful not to cross the fine line between hard core and soft core pornography and remains just within the limits of the soft core category. The programs are age restricted, well-acted and photographed and shows that vulgar language, depraved characters and stereotyped gay images are not needed to make a program about gays, lesbians or transgender.

Episodes:

1. Anna's Lesbian Seduction. Anna seduces a young woman who comes under her mysterious powers of attraction.

2. The Bedroom. In her bedroom, a woman awards her lover satisfaction through punishment.

3. Love and Kisses. An episode wherein kissing scenes are the predominate factor.

4. Depraved Desires. Although they are tender with each other, two women indulge in sexually activity that is a bit out-of-the-ordinary.

5. Boots. An older, experienced woman asserts her control over a younger woman for a night of sexual pleasure.

6. Fifties Beat. A nostalgic story set in the 1950s and featuring women in lingerie typical of that era, making love.

7. Descent. A seduction as depicted through an encounter by two young women.

8. Sauna. Two women seduce another woman in a sauna in a tamer scene that has been done in Triple X rated films of the past.

9. Massage. Like the new trend in adult films (matching older women with younger women) a scene is played out wherein a young, inexperienced secretary is seduced by her older, more experienced employer.

10. Cindy and Mara. Two young women are profiled as they seduce each other.

11. Lazy Afternoon. Features Ann Ampar attempting to seduce Robin Joy with Robin showing what she will and will not do.

12. The Room at the Bottom of the Stairs. Two women seduce each other in a secret room in a large mansion.

13. Dancing. An older woman attempts to seduce a younger woman who is reluctant to open up to her.

14. Absent Mistress. A young woman attempts to conceal her affair with another woman from her domineering mistress.

15. Playing Roles. Two women experiment with role playing in their sexual encounter.

16. Secret. Tender kissing takes center stage before two women engage in their actual love-making.

17. House of Shame. The program's overall theme is changed for an episode that focuses on submission between three women.

18. Kings X. Ann and Robin's affair with a third woman (Marie) is showcased.

19. Ann's Pleasure. A casual conversation between Ann and Robin becomes something more intense when they become lovers a short time later.

20. Bruised Bottom. Ann Ampar teases and flirts before the camera in a solo performance.

21. Whip. Ann and Robin find they have an onlooker (Monique) and indulge in a sensual encounter that soon has Monique aroused and eager to join in.

22. Slow Burn. Ann and Robin are featured in a scene that features sensuous kissing.

23. The Visit. A second episode set at the House of Shame, this time featuring Catherine and Tiffany in a love-making session.

24. Bonded. Ann and Robin are again featured as a couple whose attempts to bond to each other are seen through their love-making encounters.

25. Rope. Ann Ampar in a second solo performance this time seducing the audience in light bondage.

179 *Lesbian Space Invaders.* youtube.com/channel/UCALM0oDZOi6Rq-cORq9BAQHA. 2010 (Comedy).

Femgina is a planet in an unknown galaxy that is ruled entirely by women. Men appear not to exist and technology has advanced to a point where Femgina's lesbian citizens can use estrogen powered ships to travel through time and space. It is the year 2069 and the Scientific Council has deemed it necessary to begin an exploration of other planets in the galaxy. Exploratory groups are formed with each party assigned to study a specific planet. One such group consists of Zelda (the captain), Lou Lou (the medic), Tawny (maintenance engineer) and Blurfy (navigator). Their assignment: search the universe for a new source of pelvic devices to satisfy their queen. The program charts their haphazard efforts when they land on the planet Earth and encounter men for the first time.

Cast: Kathy Betts (Zelda), Tierza Scaccia (Tawny), Jessica Londons (Lou Lou), Cameron Esposito (Blurfy), Marsha Mars (Avery), Nicki Shields (Crazy Cat Lady), Kerry Norton, Rosemary C. McDonnell, Jen Bullock. **Credits:** *Producer-Writer-Director:* Christine Collins. **Comment:** There are no special effects; there is no nudity, no kissing, no foul language and no graphic sexual encounters—but it is produced in black and white! The acting and production values are good with comedy thrown in as the women encounter life on Earth although some will be disappointed in the lack affection between the Lesbian Space Invaders and their encounters with Earth women.

Episodes:

1. Caught Between a Rock and a Hot Spot. The women begin their quest to satisfy their queen.

2. You Know They Do Aliens, Don't You? As their ship's fuel becomes depleted, the women must land on a forbidden (to them) planet called Earth and find a source of estrogen.

3. And I Thought They Were Crazy on Planet Femgina. As the women explore their new surroundings, they encounter a man for the first time, become involved with a group of female Bible worshipers and find shelter with the Crazy Cat Lady (who believes her plush cats are real).

180 Lesbian Tea Basket. queerfatfemme. com. 2010 (Reality).

Aspects of the lesbian community are discussed by the host (sometimes accompanied by a guest) over a cup of tea (as the host has a passion for tea and says, "So grab a cup of tea, cozy up to your computer and enjoy!").

Host: Bevin Branlandingham **Credits:** *Producer-Writer:* Bevin Branlandingham. **Comment:** It's not high tech (just a camera pointed at the host on a set) but it is informative—both on aspects that affect lesbians and on the pleasures of tea.

Episodes:

1. Celestial Seasonings Sugar Cookie Sleigh Ride.

2. Twining's Citrus Spice Sunset (Mackenzi and Regan guest).

3. Allegro's Rooibos Vibrations (with guest Macy).

4. Yogi's Rest & Relax Sampler (with guest Erin Bunny).

5. Allegro's Thirst Tamer (with guests Miss LEZ 2010, and Drae Campbell).

6. Magic Fruit Tablets and Yogi's Breathe Deep Tea (with guest Elisabeth).

7. Trader Joe's Pomegranate White Tea.

8. PG Tips (with guest Austin Femme Mafia Mistress Jessie Dress).

9. TSalon's Silence Red Tea.

10. Maple Tea (with guests Alix and Jen).

11. Stash Lemon Ginger with guest Wyatt Riot.

12. Celestial Seasonings Red Zinger (with guest Leslie Medlik).

13. Spike's Coffee and Tea Hippie Iced Tea.

14. Whole Foods Get Gorgeous Tea (with guest Bird La Bird).

15. Consolation Tea (with guest Leslie and Chavon).

16. Lipton's Herbal Ginger Tea and Sunbeam's Electric Tea Kettle.

17. Making You Own Gifty Lesbian Tea Baskets.

18. Tea Accessories for All Ages.

19. Hope, Tea and Chalkboard Mugs.

20. The Gossip, Beth Ditto, Rishi Iced Tea with Guest Host Bridget Sweetz.

21. Womb Tea Made by Witches.

22. Episode Taken Off-Line.

23. Sleep Tea.

24. Episode Taken Off-Line.

25. High Tea at the Palace Theater.

26. Birthday Lake Tea.

27. Woodstock Tea Shop, Orange White Chocolate Black Tea.

28. Grandmother Reviews Oh Canada from David's Tea.

29. Teavana's Youthberry Wild Orange Blossom Blend.

181 Lesbian Vampires. twilightwomen. com. 2010–2012 (Erotic Horror).

A dimly lit, foreboding chamber called the Vampire Den provides the eerie setting. It is here that beautiful, sensual women who are not only vampires but lesbians gather to engage in a night of sexual ecstasy with one another as each requires a thirst for female blood. Each episode explores a covet gathering and the lust that ensues.

Cast: Ann Ampar, Robin Joy. **Credits:** *Producer:* Twilightwomen.com. *Director:* Div For'e. **Comment:** Very risqué program that contains mild amounts of blood (as the girls draw it from each other) coupled with kissing and caressing scenes. The girls are very scantily clad and very brief, partial nudity can be seen.

Episodes:

1. Night Pickup. An innocent appearing Laundromat provides the setting for a young woman to be seduced by a female vampire and drawn into her sensuous web.

2. The Feed. Four women, eagerly anticipating a night of sexual pleasure, make their way into the Vampire Den to take part in a sensuous orgy of love and blood.

3. Monique's Story. A young woman, drawn to a seductive female vampire, finds her life about to change forever when she succumbs to the temptation of the Vampire Den.

4. Karen's Story. As two sensuous lesbian vampires (Ann and Robin) make love, a mysterious woman (Karen) becomes infatuated with Robin, seeking to steal her away from Ann.

182 Lesbros. youtube.com/playlist? list=PLRaNjmaMzBZhEfbB_lFEncxZeED 8SP-mO 2012 (Comedy).

"One straight guy and one gay girl, best friends forever—Lesbros" are the program's opening theme lyrics as it introduces Luis, who is straight, and Vickie, a lesbian, best friends ("lesbros") who try to help each other navigate the world of dating, relationships and the daily stresses of life.

Cast: Luis M. Navarro (Luis), Vickie Toro (Vickie). **Credits:** *Producer:* Erika Cervantes, Linda Yvette Chavez, Emily McGregor. *Director:* Emily

McGregor. *Writer:* Luis M. Navarro, Vickie Toro. **Comment:** From the catchy theme song to the last bars of its closing theme, *Lesbros* is a charming, well-acted and produced series that is well worth watching. Vickie and Luis are into each other, but not in a romantic way and each story is just a look at a brief incident in their daily lives.

Episodes:

1. Sex Ed. Luis tries to ease Vickie's insecurities about dating a girl she just met when she fears a second date may lead to more than just hand holding and something more intimate—something she is not yet ready to tackle.

2. Our Gang. Vickie and Luis surprise each other with identical bracelets and decide they should form their own gang—the Lesbros.

3. Exercise. When Luis and Vickie read an article that states many people are obese they decide to create their own exercise video to help—"The Lesbros Righteous Workout."

4. Doma. With Luis believing his life is in a lockdown and Vickie afraid to give of herself to another girl, they attempt to help each other deal with their romantic issues.

5. Haircut. Luis believes Vickie's shoulder-length hair may be the reason why her love life is suffering and decides she needs a haircut.

6. Butchest. The haircut Luis performed now makes Vickie look like a butch lesbian—something she first dislikes but soon accepts.

7. Comic-Con. Vickie and Luis recall a day of enjoyment when they attended a Comic Con convention and their friendship bonded.

8. Spooning. Vickie and Luis attempt to comfort each other over dates that didn't go well for either of them.

9. Secret Handshake. Luis and Vickie decide that they need something to bond their relationship—a secret handshake.

10. Threesome. Vickie and Luis attempt to set their lesbian friend Emily (Emily McGregor) up with a co-worker they call "Lesbian Co-Worker" (Suzy Pasqualeto) and learn that match-making is not their forte.

11. Dopplebros. In a take-off on the term Doppelganger (a person's evil twin) Vickie accompanies Luis to his ear, nose and throat doctor only to encounter an "evil" version of themselves in the waiting room—lesbros who are their complete opposite.

12. Marriage Equality. Vickie and Luis discuss wedding plans—her dream of a Harry Potter-themed affair while Luis extols his visions of a *Star Wars* wedding.

13. Muffins. As Vickie prepares to enjoy her morning muffin, Luis relates his disgust of them ("over-baked cupcakes").

14. Happy Movember Love, Lesbros. Luis feels, that for once in his life he must make a statement and proceeds to grow a moustache.

183 LesBros. youtube.com. 2012 (Talk).

Real life friends (and lesbians) Mary (a psychology major) and Maddie appear in a vlog (from their college dorm room) to relate their feelings on being lesbians and to help other women learn about and deal with the problems of being gay.

Cast: Other than introducing themselves by a first name, there are no last names given for Mary or Maddie (who are also assumed to be the producers as credits are not given either). **Comment:** Both women are quite attractive and have a genuine audience appeal. While the production is well lit a stationery camera is used and only medium views of the women are seen with Maddie (to the left of the screen) sometimes being partially out of camera range (only right side portions of her face are seen) due to the aspect ratio of the production (a wider lens setting should have been used).

Episodes:

1. LesBros Pilot. Mary and Maddie discuss the differences between the more feminine Lipstick Lesbian and the more masculine Butch Lesbian.

184 LESlieVILLE. youtube.com/playlist ?list=PLo1pwAmevlN6uPvaqpVqzjVg32Tu 3Oljw 2013 (Drama).

Sera, Gwen, Ona and Laura are lesbians and each is involved in the other's life: Sera, recovering from a broken relationship with Gwen, has become attracted to Ona. Unknown to Sera, Ona is involved in a relationship with Laura. As Sera takes the first steps to meet Ona, her life is thrown into a whirlwind of uncertainty when Gwen returns to her and she again finds herself being drawn to her. Ona too is faced with concerns of her own as she is dating Laura but has become attracted to Sera. In soap opera–like fashion, the program follows the decisions each woman must make as their romance blossoms but at what cost to the women who really love them.

Cast: Samantha Wan (Sera), Tiffany Claire-Martin (Ona), Jenna Harder (Gwen), J.M. Frey (Casey), Sarah Grace (Jeri), Meghan Campbell (Laura). **Credits:** *Producer:* Nadine Bell, Stephen Leck, Russell Winkelaar. **Comment:** Tenderly portrayed saga of women in love and what happens when uncontrollable events enter the picture to change the bliss each hopes to find. Nicely acted and well produced, the program is an insightful look at women navigating the world between lust and true desire.

Episodes:

1. Sight. The four women are introduced with Sera becoming attracted to Ona (who is dating Laura).

2. Getting to Know You. Unaware that Ona has been dating Laura, Sera attempts to get to know Ona by asking her out on a lunch date.

3. The Great Debate. Gwen, Sera's former lover, re-enters her life while Ona arouses Laura's jealous streak when she tells her about Sera.

4. Shoes, Shoes, Shoes. With eyes only for each other, Sera and Ona continue their blossoming romance and embark on a shoe shopping spree.

5. Birds of a Feather. While helping her friends, Jeri and Casey with their wedding plans, Sera fantasizes about her own wedding to Ona.

6. The Great Debate Redux. With Gwen back in her life, Sera is now torn between Gwen and Ona.

7. Close Quarters. As Sera and Ona spend more alone time together, Sera finds herself becoming deeply attracted to Ona and finding it difficult to keep their relationship platonic.

8. Jill and Jill Went Up a Hill. At a party given for Jeri and Casey, Ona becomes jealous when she sees Sera and Gwen together.

9. The Morning After. The party winds down—with Sera and Gwen reliving old times by having a romantic encounter.

10. A Few. Although it appears that Sera and Gwen will reconnect, Ona confronts Laura about her feelings for Sera. The program's concluding episode.

185 *Let's Do It Together.* youtube.com. 2014 (Comedy).

"This is a story of love—the beginning, the middle and the not-so fairy tale ending" is heard as the program begins to introduce two beautiful lesbians: Lily Watts, a free-spirited young woman and Nicola Green, a religious woman in denial over her sexuality (and dismayed by the fact that her parents strongly oppose the path she has taken). It is the year 2009 when, at a party, Lily and Nicola meet for the first time and immediately find an attraction to each other. As time passes they date, fall in love and marry. In 2013, life for Lily and Nicola is anything but the blissful relationship they once shared as circumstances beyond their control have led to them divorcing. The program charts their lives together—from their first meeting to the breakup and to a chance encounter a year later after each has gone their separate way.

Cast: Cassie Ghersi (Nicola Green), Jade Kilburn (Lily Watts). **Credits:** *Producer:* Steve Golin, Larry Kinnar. *Writer-Director:* Cathy Ghersi, Jade Kilburn. **Comment:** While there are kissing scenes and adult situations, the primary focus remains on the breakup and the incidents that can turn happiness into tragedy. The acting is very good but the production values lack at times. There is a loss of sound during the concluding minutes of Nicola and Lily's chance encounter in the last episode (sort of ruins the tender atmosphere that had been established). Some scenes are also dark and hard to make out while other scenes have a green-blue-purple tint that is more of a distraction (especially when the girls are kissing) than a statement.

Episodes:

1. Episode 1. Lily and Nicola are introduced as a seemingly happy couple whose lives are soon seen deteriorating with circumstances that neither can handle.

2. Episode 2. Lily's addiction to prescription pills coupled with Nicola's inability to be honest not only with herself but those around are the catalysts that end their relationship.

3. Episode 3. As Nicola composes a poem to help her overcome the heartbreak she feels, flashbacks are used to highlight dates each has had in the past. A flash forward reunites Lily and Nicola at Coney Island where they are reunited in a chance encounter and, while each still appears to be attracted to the other, it was a relationship that was never meant to be. Nicola concludes the program: "'What happens when you have to face that person you once loved? Do you ignore her like it never happened? Do you give up trying to become friends?" As Nicola and Lily once again walk away from each other, Nicola adds, "But how long before you actually forget?"

186 *Let's Talk Lesbian.* youtube.com/ watch?v=f_vpblVm5Zc. 2013 (Reality).

Several African-American lesbians discuss topics relevant to the lesbian community in various locations as opposed to a talk show studio setting.

Cast as credited: Street Poet, Nae, Charm, Miek, Tre, Morgan, Samone, Taylor, Maghony, Chase, Tae. **Credits:** *Producer:* Street Poet, Jacque "Venom" Gochett, Speak on It Ent. **Comment:** Matters that affect lesbians are tackled—but in ways no talk show ever attempted—at various locations with the hosts often arguing among themselves about what are the correct and incorrect aspects of the topic. The program comes off as rather harsh in that the women do argue (and use vulgar language) and presents itself as more of a staged production rather than an unrehearsed reality program. There are some sound problems, especially in outdoor scenes (like wind blowing into the microphone thus making it difficult to understand what is being said) but overall the women handle themselves well and the production itself is well done.

Episode List: *1.* The Meet and Greet. *2.* Friends. *3.* Raising Kids. *4.* Lesbians in Church. *5.* Domestic Violence. *6.* Cheating. *7.* Touch Me Not. *8.* Marriage. *9.* Bisexual.

187 *Lez-B-Honest.* onemorelesbian.com. 2011–2013 (Drama).

An African-American production that, set in Palm Beach, Florida, explores the lives of a group of lesbians and the problems each encounters not only in their relationships with one another but in the community in which they live.

Cast as credited: Alex (Brandi), Portia (Channie), Chanel (Trish), Ashley (Shannon), Tye (Christina), Reese (Charmaine), Shawna (Star), Misha

(Roxii), Jade (Sunny), Que (Nore), Keisha (Bella), Omar (Roberto), Shalesse (Lovely). **Credits:** *Producer-Writer:* Dacia Mitchell, Shannon Todd, Tonica Freeman. **Comment:** The program attempts (and succeeds in showing that) such women (labeled here "queer women of color") do come in different shapes and sizes and that the situations portrayed in the program do actually happen and not glamorized to make them seem more than they actually are. Unfortunately, with the good also comes the bad. There is virtually no character introduction and trying to figure them out can become a bit confusing. The sound is also poor at times, making it difficult to understand what is being said (most likely due to the use of camera microphones only). There is an over-abundant use of vulgar language (giving the impression that "queer women" constantly curse), kissing scenes and the traditional adult situations (girls in bed or making out together). The program is also a bit out of aspect ratio (images are stretched a bit to fill the screen from top to bottom). It is also a mystery as to why the entire cast (on screen and elsewhere) only credit themselves with a first name.

Episodes: Two seasons of programs were produced, but only 10 untitled episodes (from Season 2) remain on line along with the following "extras":

1. I Need Cover by: Lez-B-Honest 2.0.
2. Ice Challenge Accepted by Storm of Lez-B-Honest 2.0.
3. Lez-B-Honest Cast Members 2.0.
4. Lez-B-Honest Booking Promo.
5. Lez-B-Honest Bow Ties vs. Stilettos Club Promo Video.
6. Lez-B-Honest Behind the Scenes Photo Shoot.
7. Lez-B-Honest Round Table.
8. Lez-B-Honest Season 2 Bloopers.
9. Lez-B-Honest Presents "50 Shades of Blue" Season Finale Viewing Party.
10. Lez-B-Honest A Word with DJ Storm and Shawn.
11. Spoken Word by Brandi of Lez-B-Honest.

188 Lez Be Proud. thefabfemme.com. 2011 (Reality).

Dawn and Debbie and Kristie and Lauren are lesbian couples who live in the Texas Bible Belt and proud of who and what they are. The women have agreed to open their homes (and lives) for the world to see and the program relates the events that befall each of the women as they share their hopes, struggles and faith.

Cast (as credited): Dawn, Debbie, Kristie, Lauren. **Credits:** *Director:* Ravi Kiran, Sean Anderson. **Comment:** The program is rather candid with what appears to be a true representation of what it is like to be a lesbian and living in the Bible Belt (where such lifestyles are not readily accepted). The program follows the format of broadcast TV and cable

reality series (like *The Real Housewives*) with the subjects reacting to situations, facing the camera to give opinions and confronting the issues that surround them.

Episodes: Five episodes were produced and all are on line with the exception of number two. Each is rather long (more in tune with a TV or cable show) and follows the women through the various events that affect their daily lives.

189 Lighthouse. lighthousewebseries.com. 2014 (Reality).

A look at the lives of several young women living and working in Atlanta: Mona, Amanda, Andrea and Chrystal. Mona is a Private National/International Investigator with "a fashion savvy equal with street swag." Amanda, called Gio, is the daughter of Brooklyn crime boss, possesses "suave swag" and owns McGregor House, a shelter for abused and drug-addicted women. Chrystal is a firefighter and in an interracial relationship with Andrea. The program, billed as a lesbian web series, is set in Washington, D.C., and explores the issues the women face, including same sex dating, sex and drug abuse, domestic violence, transgender and homophobic discrimination and human sex trafficking.

Cast: Mona Reed, Amanda G. Armanii, Andrea Garner and Chrystal Forest. **Credits:** *Producer-Writer:* Lea Pearson. **Comment:** The program is more like a message to women than an entertainment presentation as it deals with real-life issues and attempts to address them as realistically as possible.

Episodes:

1. Follow the Light: Lighthouse Web Show Q&A. Not an actual episode in the normal sense (but the only visual information that exists) and more of an introduction to what the series will entail.

190 Lindsey's Loft. youtube.com. 2013 (Drama).

Events in the life of Lindsey, a pretty African-American lesbian as she reacts with the people that surround her in her everyday life.

Cast: Ivy Lindsey (Lindsey). Other cast members are not credited. **Credits:** *Producer-Writer:* Ivy Lindsey. **Comment:** The posted information states that the presented episode is "for promotional use only" and indicates that a series will be made (although it also appears that one or two episodes have already been made as scenes were pulled from them to make the clip footage). It is very difficult to judge the merits of the series as the clip episode runs only two minutes and thirty-eight seconds. Ivy is very pretty, the acting good and the scenes chosen well filmed. There also appears to be nudity, but a title card placed over Ivy's breasts block the viewer from really seeing anything.

Episodes:

1. Clips. Several scenes are presented in a promotional reel from a proposed series.

191 LIPS. flovinger.com. 2012–2013 (Comedy-Drama).

Synopsis: reprinted by permission of Flo Vinger. "LIPS" is a loosely scripted rockumentary. London and Didi are two seasoned chick rockers who refuse to give up their Hollywood dreams of money, fame and an endless supply of other chicks. Their dream is to play at the biggest lesbian event of the year, the Dinah Shore weekend. On their rise to fame, a manager/barista books them not so glorious gigs, like a Bris ... what could possibly go wrong? "If you have never heard of us," says London, "then you must not live on the planet Earth."

Cast: Flo Vinger (London), Vivi Rama (Didi), Marlyse Londe (Tangent Queen, Helen), Elaine Hendrix (Herself), Ashley St. Pierre (Tangent Queen, Doris), Hana Mae Lee (Endora), Christine Lakin (Rocker Chick), Sheetal Sheth (Rousaura), Debra Wilson (X-Girlfiend), Brian Jay Ecker (Bubba), Lita Lopez (Barista), Bernardo Verdugo (Armondo), Catherine Waller (Snaps), Amber Tisue (Amber). **Credits:** *Producer:* Flo Vinger, Brian Jay Ecker, Kate Tobia. *Director:* Flo Vinger, Chad Callner. *Writer:* Flo Vinger, Brian Jay Ecker. **Comment:** A well acted and produced program with a slightly different approach to series encompassing lesbian characters. There is plenty of eye candy and kissing and comical mishaps as the band struggles to achieve their dream.

Episodes:

1. Chicks with Licks. Bubba, LIPS' biggest fan and mediocre film maker, begins an assignment making a rockumentary of the band as they seek stardom.

2. Dinah or Bust. Helen and Doris sign on as Tangent Queens (backup lesbian eye candy as LIPS has a lesbian following) while Didi hires a manager (Fiona) with a gambling problem (in high school she was known as "Sticky Fingers Fiona").

3. The Love Itch. As it is revealed that Bubba has deep feelings for London, a ghost from Didi's past—Armondo, enters her life.

4. Trickery. It is revealed that Didi ruined Armondo's life by sleeping with his fiancé and now he seeks revenge—by getting her deported.

5. Working for Tips. Fiona's bookings are anything but typical as she has LIPS' performing first at a Bris then a funeral. The first season concludes.

6. Audition This! The second season begins with the group preparing to perform at Coacehlla.

7. Lips or Bust. LIPS performs the song "If You Were a Booger" for potential band mates at an audition.

8. Elaine Hendrix Won't Take No for an Answer. As film and television actress Elaine Hendrix displays her musical abilities for the band, London and Didi show they are more interested in her breasts than her lack of musical talent.

9. Debra Wilson Faces Off with London. London and her ex-girlfriend (Debra Wilson) cross paths again but neither is happy to see the other.

10. Snaps and Gino. As two young women, Snaps and Amber audition for the band, London hires Gino, a would-be Mafia gangster, as their manager.

11. Swept Off Her Combat Boots. As Helen fantasizes about having London, Rousaura is the one who sweeps London off her feet. Meanwhile Gino takes over the band.

12. Rousaura Rocks London's World. It is a love at first sight for London when she sees Rousaura, a sexy dancer.

13. Lip Locked. As London and Rousaura become closer, Helen is tricked into making out on camera.

14. Dreadlock Lap Dance. London's relationship with Rousaura intensifies after Rousaura gives London a sensual lap dance.

15. Ur the Opposite of That. Now inspired by her infatuation with Rousaura, London writes her first love song—"Ur the Opposite of That."

16. Love Hurts. Bubba's love for London angers his girlfriend, Endora, a woman involved in voodoo and black magic, who is determined to change Bubba's feelings about London.

17. You're in My Personal Space. London's fascination with Rousaura takes her into a world of lust and love that she has never before experienced.

18. Barbie's a Lesbian. As

LIPS. Season 2 series title card (copyright 2014 Stretch Productions).

Endora continues to test Bubba's love for her, a girl (Doris) sets her sights on Helen.

19. R.I.P. Fiona. Although London is unsure of her love for Rousaura, Rousaura continues pursuing her. Meanwhile, Endora attempts to use her voodoo powers to destroy London.

20. The Ultimate Kiss. With London still being pursued by Bubba, London herself is unsure of her feelings until Rousaura pins London in a closet and gives her "the kiss of her life."

21. Here Today, Gone.... Today. When Snaps makes a move on Doris and she is exposed as being a lesbian, Doris tries to come to terms with her once hidden sexuality; meanwhile, as the second season ends, London finds a note that reveals Rousaura has left the country, making Bubba believe that he now has a chance to be with London (forgetting that Endora is still seeking to "hang London by her toenails and staple her legs together").

192 *Little Horribles.* littlehorribles.com. 2013 (Comedy-Drama).

Amy is a 27-year-old lesbian living in Los Angeles. She is pretty, a bit overweight and appears to envy the more glamorous and seductive lesbians she encounters. She is looking for a relationship with another woman but finding that special person presents its own share of problems. She is not seductive, she does not pretend to be something she is not and she is a bit shy when it comes to approaching beautiful women. With those strikes already against her, Amy tries to navigate the lesbian scene and find the romance she is seeking.

Cast: Amy York Rubin (Amy), Ann Carr, Leslie Korein (Emily), Ilana Glazer (Lindsey), Echo Kellum (Paul), Ana Cristina Mayer (Herself), Misty Monroe (Girl), Sophia Mayer Pliner (Herself), Hannah Victoria Stock (Hannah), Cynthia Stevenson (Amy's mother), Tom Virtue (Amy's father). **Credits:** *Producer:* Amy York Rubin, Issa Rae. *Director:* Amy York Rubin, Bridget Palardy. *Writer:* Amy York Rubin. **Comment:** There are a few kissing scenes, but no nudity or intense sexual situations. The program is well acted and produced and the episodes are just the right length so as not to stretch out a situation and make it boring. The concluding episode leaves the doorway open for future encounters for Amy as she seeks that one special mate.

Episodes:

1. Sexual Activity. Amy's hopeful romance with a new girl goes from good to bad when the girl breaks up with her.

2. LMFAO. At work, Amy begins a computer chat with a fellow worker (Lindsey) that looks promising but later fizzles out.

3. Date. Amy secures a date with an attractive girl whose sole ambition in life is to become a florist.

4. Road Rage. Explores the problems Amy encounters when she becomes stuck in a traffic jam.

5. Stunning. Amy becomes depressed when she sees a girl she likes being seduced by a gorgeous lesbian.

6. Member. A look at Amy's family—from a mother who isn't quite sure if Amy is a lesbian or bisexual; a father who doesn't seem to care and a kid sister who knows exactly who Amy is.

7. Bathroom Mirror. In the ladies room at a local bar, Amy encounters two lesbians who give her advice on how to attract a woman.

8. Armrest. On a plane flight, Amy finds herself dealing with a crying baby, an annoying little boy and a gorgeous mother that arouses feelings within her.

9. Basketball. Since all the conventional ways to meet a girl appear to be failing, Amy joins an all-girl basketball team hoping for something more than just shooting baskets.

10. Oldies. Amy finds that even as she tries to enjoy her favorite pastime, watching movies at the Silent Movie Theater, she encounters sympathy from the elder patrons who wonder why she is at the theatre alone.

11. Spinning. Amy's decision to not purchase fast food at a drive through causes problems when she begins arguing with two female customers over the fatty content and high calorie count such foods contain.

12. Two Parties. Amy's luck may have changed when she attends two parties on the same night as the program concludes.

193 *Lizzy the Lezzy.* funnyordie.com/lizzy thelezzy/webseries. 2006–2014 (Cartoon).

Lizzy is an animated stand-up comic. She is a lesbian (and proud of it) and "talks about lesbian stuff, coming out of the closet and homophobia." She is not the prettiest of girls, has virtually no figure and appears rather drab looking. Lizzy says, "My basic outlook on life is that being gay is fabulous and homophobes are stupid." In a rather unusual format (even for TV and cable), Lizzy presents her stand-up comedy acts as well as an occasional song as she also loves to sing about being a lesbian. Lizzy, who is called "The Lezzy Professional Lesbian" has some unique friends (Nic the Bi-Chick, Danny the Tranny, Stan the Macho Man and Kate the Straight) that are also a part of her act.

Voice Cast: Ruth Selwyn (Lizzy). **Credits:** *Producer-Writer-Animator:* Ruth Selwyn. **Comment:** The animation is well done as is the mix of live action and animation (for example, when Lizzy joins singers Bria and Chrissy for the song "We Are So Very Gay"). While the subject matter (and language) is adult-themed, accompanying visual material is G-Rated. The series originally aired on Myspace.com.

Episode List:

1. Sex with Your Ex?!

2. We Are So Very Gay.

3. New Lesbian Dating App.

4. WTF Russia?!

5. Orange Is the New Black.

6. #Proud to Love a Bisexual!

7. Homophobia for Dummies.

8. I've Met the Girl of My Dreams.

9. Homophobes, Homophobes, Why Are You So Silly?

10. I Love Being Gay.

11. Transgender Day of Remembrance 2012: Vikki-Marie's Story.

12. Free Meditation Session with Lizzy the Lezzy.

13. Love Is Love.

14. I Kissed a Bisexual and I Licked It!

15. How to Be a Lesbian Stud!

16. A Lotta Lezzy Lovin'!

17. Let's Wipe Out Homophobia!

18. Menstrual Blues.

19. God Made Me to Do It!!

20. Lizzy Auditions for the L Project.

21. S**T Guys Say to Lesbians.

22. Lizzy's Christmas Karaoke: Rockin' Around the Christmas Tree.

23. Lizzy's TitBits: You Bring Out the Animal in Me.

24. Lizzy's TitBits: You're Hot.

25. Lizzy's TitBits: I Fancy You.

26. Lizzy's TitBits: Lesbians Are Fun!

27. Lizzy's TitBits: There Are Lesbians Everywhere.

28. Lizzy's TitBits: Dykes on Bikes.

29. Lizzy Meets Shashabil Forte the Drag King.

30. Gay's Cause Earthquakes.

31. Pray Away the Gay.

32. Happy Birthday Wipeout Homophobia on Facebook!

33. Lizzy at the L Beach Lesbian Festival.

34. Straight Men (Who Want a Three-Some with Lesbians).

35. First Lesbian Kiss!

36. Being a Single Lesbian.

37. Coming Out of the Closet.

38. It's a Girl! The Birth of Lizzy the Lezzy.

39. Ask Lizzy: Arielle's Three-Some Dilemma.

40. Size Matters!

41. Free Tampons.

42. Happy New Year.

43. Christmas Is Gay.

44. Thong! Does My Ass Look Big in This?

45. It Gets Better!

46. Bed Intruder?

47. Secret Bonus Video!

48. Been for a Cervical/Pap Smear Test Lately?

49. Lindsay Lohan in Jail!

50. I'm a Lesbian! A Song for Lesbians.

51. Lizzy the Lezzy Stand-Up Comedy on the Sundance Channel!

52. My Bad Romance.

53. I'm Proud!

54. I'm So Hot for You!

55. Let Constance McMillen Take Her Girlfriend to the Prom!

56. Valjazzling: How to Valjazzle Your Valjayjay like Jennifer Love Hewitt!

57. New Year's Resolutions!

58. Lizzy's 12 Days of Christmas! Merry Christmas Everyone.

59. Marriage Equality/Gay Marriage?!

60. Teacher, Teacher, Gimme a Lecture! Lizzy the Lezzy Gets Laid, The Book Launch, Part 1.

61. Lizzy's Singing in the Shower! The Book Launch, Part 2.

62. Cupid, Cupid, You're Really Stupid! The Book Launch, Part 3.

63. Protest After Shooting Attack at LGBT Youth Club—2 Dead.

64. Lesbian Addict!

65. Lesbian Tongue Twister.

66. Goodbye *L Word*.

67. Batwoman Is a Lesbian!

68. Happy Valentine's Day!

69. Gay & Lesbian Siblings!

70. Fight the H8! Equal Rights for All!

71. Happy Halloween!

72. The American Elections.

73. Lizzy the Lezzy Does Gay Israel.

74. Me and My Creator Ruth on TV!

75. Lizzy the Lezzy Is Waiting for Your Phone Call!

76. Lizzy Meets a Girl in a Lesbian Bar.

77. Lizzy the Lezzy Animated Stand-Up Comedy in German!

78. Lizzy the Lezzy in Hebrew!

79. Lizzy the Lezzy Stand-Up Comedy in French!

80. Lizzy the Lezzy Stand-Up Comedy in Spanish!

81. Remembering Lawrence King (Larry).

82. Lesbian!

83. Merry Christmas from Lizzy the Lezzy.

84. National Coming Out Day 2014!

85. Is Homosexuality a Temptation from the Devil?

86. Lizzy the Lezzy and Gary the Gay, Episode 1.

87. Lizzy the Lezzy and Gary the Gay, Episode 2.

88. Happy Easter! Lizzy the Lezzy and Gary the Gay.

89. One Night Stands: Lizzy the Lezzy and Gary the Gay.

90. Lizzy's *L Word* Season 4 Recap.

91. A Song for My Exes!

92. For the Blind! (Lizzy performs a routine in a blindfold for blind people).

93. For the Deaf/Hard of Hearing.

94. Lizzy's *L Word* Recap, Seasons 1, 2 & 3.

95. Sex Toys.

96. Straight Girls!

194 Log Jam. youtube.com. 2012 (Comedy).

The Log Jam is the hippest gay Republican bar in Chicago. It is also the hangout for three friends—Arnold, Betsy and Phil, gay conservatives seeking love and understanding in a liberal gay world. Arnold, currently unemployed (dismissed from his job as a government contractor for the Blackwater project) is seeking what he calls "Mr. Hard Right." Betsy, an investment banker, considers herself a power lesbian and has set her goal to get the Republican Party to recognize that she and others like her have the right to choose the lovers of their choice without the backlash that same sex relationships cause. Phil, a powerful CEO also seeking that perfect mate is a man with a passion for family values but tormented by his inner demons—his lust for exotic fetish play. As the friends meet each day at the bar, Nancy Reagan, the drag queen bar owner, dispenses advice regarding life and love and the program relates the incidents that befall Arnold, Betsy and Phil as the advice given is not always the right advice to follow when it comes to their love lives.

Cast: Andy Eninger (Phil), Becca Levine (Betsy), John Loos (Arnold), David Cerda (Nancy Reagan), Katy Colloton (Linda the Moderate), Lisa Linke (Gillian), Brett Mannes (Rich). **Credits:** *Producer-Writer:* John Loos. *Director:* Ward Crockett. **Comment:** While most of the action takes place within the bar, the stories are well plotted and nicely acted. The production values are good and the only objection would be the use of foul language, which was not really needed.

Episodes:

1. Minority Outreach. The main characters are introduced along with Nancy Reagan, the bar owner.

2. The Billionaire. Arnold believes he has found the man of his dreams, a gay billionaire (Brett Mannes) until he learns, that in return for drinks, Arnold must play a horse and be ridden by the cowboy-drunk billionaire.

3. Ladies' Night. Betsy's effort to enjoy a Ladies' Night with her lesbian friends turns into a disaster when Gillian, her ex-lover, appears and sets her sights on reclaiming Betsy.

4. The Liberal. Phil believes he has found the man of his dreams until he discovers he is a liberal and opposed to everything he stands for as a Republican.

195 Love Bytes. lovebytestheseries.com. 2013 (Comedy-Drama).

Jade, Michael and Stacey are friends who share an apartment. Jade, a 26-year-old videographer, is a

Love Bytes. Left to right: Emily Rose Brennan, Adriano Cappelletta and Billie Rose Pritchard (used by permission of Tonnette Stanford).

lesbian and looking to have as much fun as possible before settling down with the woman of her dreams. She is a vegetarian and a passionate advocate for animal rights. Jade, attracted to girls for as long as she can remember, is a Virgo and a bit picky when it comes to dating and prefers women who are more eccentric than normal. Michael, a strong believer that money can often spoil relationships, is gay and looking to become a trophy husband by finding a man who is rich and will spoil him. Until that time comes he avoids dating men who are poor fearing he may fall in love and ruin his dream. He is 27 years old, has the astrological sign of Leo and works as a receptionist. Stacey, 28 years old and single, is straight and dreams of settling down, having a family and living in a cottage in the country. She is a Pisces, works as an artists' representative and finding the man of her dreams is much more difficult than she imagined as she has a tendency to meet men who are anything like what she pictures. The program follows their mishaps as each ventures into the world of dating with each seeking that special someone that neither seems able to find.

Cast: Emily Rose Brennan (Stacey), Billie Rose Pritchard (Jade), Adriano Cappelletta (Michael), Bec Irwin (Samantha Fox), Dave Halalilo (Adam). **Credits:** *Producer:* Tonnette Stanford, Emma McKenna. *Writer-Director:* Tonnette Stanford. **Comment:** British produced, delightful lesbian-gay mix series. The characters are very well executed and likeable with excellent writing and directing. There are sexual situations, kissing (mostly girl/girl) and a well thought out and executed program.

Episodes:

1. Herpes of the Lips. Jade believes she is in seventh heaven when she begins dating Samantha Fox, a sexy lesbian D.J. while Michael finds his life turned upside down when he responds to an on-line dating opportunity and finds the man faked his profile and is actually a despicable dud.

2. Justin Beaver. Hoping to glamorize herself for a night out on the town with Samantha, Jade borrows Stacey's valuable ring and later, while making love to Samantha, manages to lose it "in the most unusual (and intimate) of places." With Stacey demanding her ring back and Samantha in a panic, Michael steps in to resolve the situation by performing an emergency ring extraction. Due to its mature subject matter, the episode is restricted on YouTube and requires proof of age to watch (using an e-mail account).

196 Love, Lies and Lesbians of Mobile. youtube.com. 2013 (Reality).

A profile of several women, all lesbians, who reside in Mobile, Alabama. The principal women are Mello, a stripper (and, just by her looks, the most pleasing to watch), Calondra, a hair stylist; Bigg Bizz, a professional photographer; Looney, a woman who loves to drink and party (as she says) and Ra Lynn, the mother of a young daughter.

Cast as credited: Mello, Calondra, Bigg Bizz, Ra Lynn and Looney. Credits are not given. **Comment:** A program totally geared to an African-American audience. There is an abundance of foul language and, while the photography is acceptable, the sound is hard to understand at times due to outdoor filming and using what appear to be only camera microphones. The women that were chosen are not the most pleasing to watch and do not represent what many people associate as being lesbian (the feminine "Lipstick Lesbian" as depicted on TV shows like *The L Word*). These women are harsh-looking, foul-mouthed and give the impression that the more feminine lesbians do not exist in Mobile. A mix of both types would have been a wiser choice.

Episode List: *1.* Episode 1. *2.* Episode 2. *3.* Problem. *4.* Support. *5.* Finale.

197 The Lovers and Friends Show. youtube.com/watch?v=oUKUwvEbmXw. 2008 (Drama).

An exploration of the Latina and African-American lesbian community as seen through the experiences of Lisa, a young med student who has just come to terms with the fact that she is a lesbian; Kai, her best friend, a girl with a heart of gold, who is dealing with relationship failures; Tori, an entertainment columnist; Yasmin, an outspoken political activist; Mercedes, a social-climbing magazine editor and Dre, a butch-type lesbian who has had several lovers and is still seeking that one elusive woman.

Cast: Kendall Starr (Lisa), Shakelia Tharpe (Dre), BeBe Brunswick (Yasmin Reynolds), Kissa Jo (Sasha Reynolds), Nicole Pina (Tori Ramirez), Marlaina Law (Kai Whitaker), Christy Rodriquez (Mercedes), Mona Lisa (Julia Hernandez), Martina Mehta (Christina Miller), Kelvin Brown (Keon Whitaker), Julian McKay (Jamal). **Credits:** *Producer-Writer-Director:* Charmain Johnson. **Comment:** The first Internet series to be totally focused on women of color who are also lesbians. Unfortunately, what could have been a more romantic entry and a real tribute to Latino and African-American lesbians comes off as a rather crude, poorly produced program complete with vulgar language, poor acting and a grainy-like picture. The women are, honestly, just not appealing, even in their sexual encounters. It appears to be an attempt to focus on harsh reality as opposed to tenderness, romantic stories and compassionate love scenes.

Episodes: 36 untitled episodes were produced and have since been released on DVD. What remains can be sampled on YouTube under the search title "The Lovers and Friends Show." The series is also known as *Lovers and Friends* but searching this title will not bring up the episodes and may lead you to the 1974 CBS series *Paul Sand in Friends and Lovers.*

198 LSB: The Series. onemorelesbian. com. 2013 (Drama).

Rome, Italy, provides the backdrop for a look at the lives of a group of Italian girlfriends and how they not only deal with the issues of homosexuality in their country, but the problems of navigating the pressures of everyday life. Nicki, an aspiring photographer, is the principal character. She has returned to Rome from a trip to London to reconnect with her friends. While beautiful, she is superficial, flirtatious and is quite irresponsible as she jumps from one relationship to another. Nicki also appears hard and judgmental and seems to have an answer for everything. Filomena, in love with love, is an aspiring actress, looking for that perfect girl to spend the rest of her life with. She has a bubbly personality and is the one who can ease the tensions that arise among her group of friends. Benedetta, a shy girl from a Catholic family, is a college student and a bit perplexed about her sexuality (as she still does not fully understand her attraction to girls herself). Giulia, Nicki's best friend, is a practicing lawyer who is not only honest but generous and stubborn. Martina is Giulia's lover, a student of psychology at college. She is from a small southern town and moved to Rome two years ago. Martina has not revealed her sexuality to her family or friends at school and is also cheating on Martina with a girl named Judy. **Cast:** Connie Lentino, Denise Sicignano, Chiara Aliverinini, Stefania Capece, Samantha Silveitri, Gianluca Lovono, Agata Cecconi. **Credits:** *Producer-Writer-Director:* Geraldine Ottier, Floriana Buonomo. **Comment:** Expertly acted and produced Italian program that, while a lesbian series, does not concentrate on kissing or love-making sessions. It is more of overview of what problems and situations such young women encounter for who they have chosen to become. **Episodes:** 12 untitled episodes were produced in Italian. Episodes are identified by number (for example 1X12, 2X12, 3X12, etc.) and are closed captioned but the icon must be activated to view.

199 Lust of the Vampires. lustofthevampires-webseries.com. 1998 (Horror).

One night after leaving a night club, two women (Angelique and her lover, Amber) are attacked by a mysterious woman, a powerful vampire known as the Countess Sabrina, and left for dead. Amber, drained of her blood by Sabrina, does not survive, but Angelique, barely alive herself, recovers but is no longer the fun-loving, globe-trotting society heiress she once was. She has been transformed into a vampire but for reasons that she cannot explain (perhaps her DNA chemistry) she has not come under Sabrina's control and can think and function for herself. She also has only one thought: kill Sabrina for taking the life of her beloved Amber, a sit-uation that becomes even more devastating to Angelique when Amber rises from her grave and Angelique must kill her (by a stake through the heart) to stop a killing spree controlled by the Countess. The program, which contains nudity and very suggestive girl/girl love scenes, follows Angelique as she begins her quest—seducing lesbian vampires (all of whom were lesbians before becoming victims) and extracting what information she can from them about the Countess (and where she is hiding) before she kills them (by driving a stake through their hearts. Angelique carries a small oblong case with her that contains pointed stakes and a hammer-like object). **Cast:** Nicole Galiardo (Angelique), Madison Gorman (Amber), Sabrina Leigh (Countess Dracula). **Comment:** A very early Internet horror series that was no doubt influenced by the WB series Buffy the Vampire Slayer that expanded upon the lesbian character of Willow (Alyson Hannigan). Only the three principal performers receive credit. There is virtually no text information available on the series and the exact number of episodes is unknown (only four could be found). The production values are acceptable (it is obvious that it was shot on video tape) and the acting is quite good. The three main performers are beautiful and do appear nude suggesting that the program could be a soft core adult film that had been re-edited into a web series. While Angelique is depicted as a loving vampire (she is soft and gentle with her victims), Sabrina is vicious, seducing her victims then violently draining them of their blood—something she needs to do to prove her power to rule (which could also mean Angelique's demise as she is not prepared to encounter such a vampire). Based on what can be seen, the program is very much like the made-for-video film *Muffy the Vampire Slayer*. **Episodes:**
1. The Countess. A flashback reveals the incident that changed the course of Angelique's life when she and Amber were attacked after leaving a night club.
2. Angelique. Angelique learns that a powerful vampire, known only as the Countess, has risen from her grave and is responsible for killing Amber and turning her into a vampire.
3. The Oath to Destroy. Bitter and vengeful, Angelique vows to destroy the Countess and begins her quest by seducing the female vampires who have infiltrated the lesbian community (for victims) for information. Unknown to Angelique, the Countess has become aware of her actions.
4. A Love to Destroy. Hoping to use Angelique's love for Amber against her, Sabrina resurrects Amber in a plot to have her destroy Angelique.

200 Lyle. lylemovie.com. 2013 (Thriller).

Leah and June are a lesbian couple and the parents of a toddler named Lyle (given birth to by Leah). With Leah now expecting her second child (a daughter), she and June begin looking for a new apartment and stumble across one that seems to fit their ever need. While the apartment appears like a dream to June, Leah soon becomes unnerved when she spies a mysterious pregnant woman on the street and a chill runs up and down her spine. Although mystified as to why, Leah dismisses it as just nerves until she sees Lyle talking to someone she cannot see and that same chill returns. Is what is happening to Lyle connected to that pregnant woman she saw? The program, billed as a lesbian version of the film *Rosemary's Baby*, establishes, by the two released episodes, that something evil is lurking but exactly what is not revealed (site information states that the remaining seven episodes will disclose that Leah will discover that her fears are real as she will encounter a satanic cult seeking her child).

Cast: Gaby Hoffmann (Leah), Ingrid Jungermann (June), Rebecca Street (Karen), Michael Che (Threes), Kim Allen (Taylor), Eleanor Hopkins (Lyle), Christaine McCloskey (Diane), Margaux Whitney (Margaux), Charly Esterly (Charly). **Credits:** *Producer:* Alex Scharfman. *Writer-Director:* Stewart Thorndike. **Comment:** Former child actress Gaby Hoffmann (from the TV series *Someone Like Me*) stars in a well produced and acted program that, judging by the first two episodes, will not only be a suspenseful series but one that will well be worth watching. A mystery is established almost immediately and draws the viewer right in. The shortness of the episodes allows for situations to unfold swiftly and keep your attention, thus avoiding all the unnecessary filler material needed to stretch scenes if they were produced for broadcast TV or cable.

Episodes:

1. Episode 1. As Leah and June settle into their new apartment, Leah discovers that one of the rooms had been previously used as a nursery but all such evidence had been sealed over with new wallpaper.

2. Episode 2. Leah and June's first night together is a restful one but Lyle's strange behavior the following morning and Leah's seeing that a new tenant (the pregnant girl) has become her neighbor, has her believing something is just not right.

201 *Make a Hot Girl Laugh*. youtube.com. 2014 (Game).

A very beautiful (and busty) girl appears on stage opposite two male comics (originally one gay and one straight) who, according to the announcer "is totally out of their league." With their best material, and within a thirty second time limit, each of the comics must make the girl laugh. At the end of the time, the hot girl reveals which comic did the trick and made her laugh the most.

Comment: Originally titled *Make a Hot Girl Laugh: Gay Guy vs. Straight Guy* but that concept was dropped to also accommodate straight comics.

The girls chosen for the subjects are very sexy and do show considerable amounts of cleavage (if not for the decency standards of youtube.com and its producing company, comedy.com, the girls would have appeared topless). The idea is not original as a syndicated series called *Make Me Laugh* appeared on broadcast TV and The Playboy Channel (with topless girls) and used similar formats. The program itself is well done and entertaining and the girls make for eye candy viewing.

Episodes: There are no regulars (and credits are not given). The performers are listed with the episode on which they appeared.

1. Lost in the Translation. *Comics:* Mark Ellis and Julius Sharpe. *Girl:* Talli Huntkins.

2. Me Sophia Horny. *Comics:* Mike Faverman and Tom O'Keefe. *Girl:* Sophia Lin.

3. Best Chest in the West. *Comics:* Shawn and Randy. *Girl:* Brooke Long.

4. Kylah Kim Possible. *Comics:* Ben Gleib and Owen Smith. *Girl:* Kylah Kim.

5. Bosom Buddy Holly. *Comics:* Al Berman and Tom Clark. *Girl:* Holly Weber.

6. Sophia Lin and Bare It. *Comics:* Eric Edwards and Jordan Morris. *Girl:* Sophia Lin.

7. The Breast of Times. *Comics:* JT Jackson and Sean Green. *Girl:* Holly Weber.

8. Here Titty Titty. *Comics:* Brandon Tyra and Ngaio Bealum. *Girl:* Stacy Hayes.

9. Quinn It to Win It. *Comics:* Claude Stuart and Dan Gabriel. *Girl:* Jenny Quinn.

10. Brooke But Don't Touch. *Comics:* Clinton Pickens and Dave Hanson. *Girl:* Brooke Long.

11. How the Breast Was Won. *Comics:* Adam Hammer and Adam Devine. *Girl:* Kylah Kim.

12. Jiggle All the Way. *Comics:* Adam Hunter and Blake Anderson. *Girl:* Jenny Quinn.

13. Racy Stacy. *Comics:* Jeff Hanson and Mark Serritella. *Girl:* Stacy Hayes.

14. Body Paint by Numbers. *Comics:* Dan Annic and Timothy Knapp. *Girl:* Krista Simmonson.

15. Brazilian Everywhere. *Comics:* Kenny Kane and Adam Richmond. *Girl:* Talli Huntkins.

16. Miss February. *Comics:* Josh McDermitt and Paul Morrissey. *Girl:* Michelle McLaughlin.

202 *Mama, soy Gay (Mom I'm Gay)*. youtube.com. 2013 (Anthology).

"Hi, I'm Paula and this is my story. Today's the day I tell my mother who I am. She doesn't know it yet, but today I'm telling her.... I like girls." Paula, a very pretty teenage girl, opens the program with those words and her mother (Gloria) does not take it well; in fact, one could say she looses it, as she can not accept what has been revealed to her and immediately says, "What did I do wrong? Why me?" As she rants and raves, she places the blame on Paula playing with Barbie dolls as a child—"Barbie's are to blame for this. It was that gigantic-titted, hard-ass doll." Thus is the situation Paula faces as she sets out to live the life she has chosen, apparently receiving the support of her brother (Humberto) but objection from her conservative mother and an uneasy road ahead as she faces friends and other family members. Thus begins the first story in a proposed series that will explore various young people struggling to cope with such inner conflicts as "Am I a lesbian?" "I like boys," "I'm gay," and "I never had a boyfriend or girlfriend."

Cast: Sofia Elliot (Paula), Julia Calvo (Mother), Nicholas D'Agostino (Humberto). **Credits:** *Producer:* Sofia Elliot, Aldana Arotce, Mariela Alfaro. *Writer:* Sofia Elliot, Mariela Alfarp. **Comment:** The Spanish program is well produced and acted and uses light humor to convey dramatic issues. Sofia Elliot is so captivating as Paula and Julia Calvo so hysterical over the news that the two combine to make a very enjoyable first episode.

Episodes:

1. Mother Plant. Paula builds up the courage to tell her mother that she likes girls.

203 *McManusLand.* onemorelesbian.com /tello/webseries/mcmanusland/. 2011 (Comedy).

The Bridget McManus Half-Hour Comedy Hour is a variety show hosted by comedienne Bridget McManus on the "low rent" gay TV network ICON. Bridget has expectations of reaching great heights in the entertainment world but her only claim to fame has been her low rated television series (which airs on the second Wednesday of every month at 3:30 a.m.). While the show does give Bridget some hope of achieving fame, her world comes crashing down around her when she receives a cancellation notice and finds her dreams are shattered.

Bridget is a lesbian and married to Karman, a level-headed woman who has supported her through her numerous efforts to become a star. While losing her show is a blow, Bridget has not been defeated. She has her own ideas about how to play "the fame game" and the program follows her slightly delusional efforts (and reveals her inner workings) to achieve her dream—no matter how many times she encounters rejection.

Cast: Bridget McManus (Bridget), Karman Kragloe (Karman). **Credits:** *Producer:* Bridget McManus, Adriana Torres. *Director:* Adriana Torres. *Writer:* Bridget McManus. **Comment:** Bridget McManus is an absolute delight and her scenes pampering her dog (Taffy) are truly comical. The entire program is well acted and produced and, while there are brief moments of tenderness, the program's focus is on Bridget and the set-backs she encounters trying to reignite her career.

Episodes: While season 1 is available for free, season two is available only through a paid subscription system at the program's website.

Season 1:

1. I Am Oprah. Bridget's plans for fame are put on hold when she receives word that her series has been put on hiatus.

2. Fat Action. Although heartbroken, Bridget has high hopes of achieving her dream by seeking a role in a super hero TV series called "Fat Action."

3. Secret Agent. Acting alongside an overweight super hero doesn't pay off and sends Bridget on a quest to find an agent and hopefully better roles.

4. The End of a New Beginning. Hoping to convince the heads of the ICON network that her show should continue, Bridget prepares 16 new scripts only to find that ICON has permanently cancelled her show.

Season 2: Continues the story line with Bridget determined to achieve her dream and Karman, inspired by Bridget's enthusiasm, rekindling a dream of her own (from high school): starting her own rock band, Peg Leg.

204 *Megan and Meghan.* webserieschannel. com/megan-and-meghan/. 2012 (Comedy).

Megan (long blonde hair) and Meghan (shorter blonde hair) are friends who live and work in Chicago. They are very pretty, love vodka and Diet Coke, have an insanity for wearing wigs and seek what appears to be only fun. But are they gay? Megan feels she may be a lesbian (or bisexual) as she kissed a girl and really liked it. Meghan, on the other hand, believes she is straight although she has a knack for falling for men who are gay. The program relates events in the lives of Megan and Meghan as they navigate life in a big city.

Cast: Kiley B. Moore (Megan), Leah Raidt (Meghan). **Credits:** *Producer-Writer:* Joseph W. Reese. *Director:* Joseph W. Reese, Colin Sphar. **Comment:** It doesn't matter if you can't tell which Megan is Megan and which Meghan is Meghan (although the episode descriptions will help you determine the difference) as the program is delightful either way. The episodes are very short (under three minutes) and being as such makes you wish they were somewhat longer as Kiley B. Moore and Leah Raidt are a delight to watch.

Episodes:

1. Katy Perry. As Megan revels that she kissed a girl and enjoyed it, Meghan tries to figure out why she seems to attract gay men.

2. Serenity. Meghan, excited about the new lower back tattoo she has just gotten, shows Megan, telling her it is Asian for Serenity. Megan douses Meghan's happiness when she tells her it doesn't mean Serenity, but "thank you" leaving Meghan to ponder what that means.

3. RuPaul. After a night of drinking Megan learns from Meghan that the woman she shared a drink with was not a real woman but a drag queen again instilling in Megan that she may like girls (when she

can tell when a girl is a real girl). The title refers to Logo TV's *RuPaul's Drag Race* TV series.

4. Bastian. While Megan and Meghan apparently have some sort of job (not stated) Megan calls Meghan to embark on an adventurous quest: find day jobs.

5. Lost Phone. Meghan resorts to a public access computer in a diner to e-mail Megan that she lost her cell phone and is unable to call her.

6. D.I.Y. Megan seeks a way to get Meghan out of the house and join her for some fun after she began planning her wedding (even though she has no boyfriend) and embarked on a D.I.Y. (Do It Yourself) furniture-building project.

7. Kesha. After another encounter with a man who turns out to be gay, Meghan feels she needs some answers (why she is attracted to gay men) and seeks the advice of a gay couple (William Von Vogt, Matthew Sherbach) she encounters in a park.

8. Bears. Meghan, overly excited to show Megan the new Bears dress she bought to wear to an upcoming football game, does so only to hear from Megan, "That's only a jersey with a belt on it" plus a remark that the short jersey is revealing that she forgot to wear anything under it. In a comical sequence, Meghan, who carries panties in her handbag, proceeds to put them on in public (there is a very noticeable edit here indicating that either Meghan had already been wearing panties and they were not supposed to be seen or she literally forgot and the scene edited for decency).

205 *Melody Set Me Free.* youtube.com. 2010–2014 (Comedy-Drama).

Patience O'Brien is a young woman (drag queen) who has dreamed of becoming a singer (although her mother opposes her doing so). When the opportunity arises for Patience to become a contestant on an *American Idol*–like television program (and hopefully impress KKQueen, the [drag queen] owner of a record label), she achieves her goal and signs onto KK's label. But what Patience had conceived as an enjoyable career turns out to be just the opposite when she discovers that KK seeks only to become the top label by producing "nasty songs" and the nastier the better—something that deeply bothers Patience as she detests singing about sex. But she is under contract and can't quit and the program relates her experiences in an industry that has turned her dream into a nightmare.

Cast: Kalup Linzy (Patience O'Brien/KK Queen), Theodore Bouloukos (Faith), Lawanda Hodges (Eve), Dwight Allen O'Neal (Chasity), Reginald L. Barnes (Isaac), Humberto Petit (BT), Andrienne Filleaudeau (Grace Jackson), Jobz Cameron (Hope Jones), Chrystal Claire (Mama), Darold Cuba (Daniel), Josh Sandler (Sunshine), January LaVoy (Summer). **Credits:** *Producer:* Richie Hill, Kalup Linzy. *Writer-Director:* Kalup Linzy. **Comment:** For

reasons that are not explained, series creator (and star) Kalup Linzy overdubs all the character voices. He does a very good job as the synchronization is right on but if you are not aware of this, the characters appear to move a bit slowly (to allow for precise dubbing). Unfortunately, after the first episode, the voice-over dubbing becomes quite obvious and becomes more of an annoyance than an artistic statement. While the music industry is known to be a cut-throat business, no holds are barred to show that it is just that and newcomers, no matter how talented they are, must face the facts and somehow make their own inroads to achieve success.

Season 1 Episode List: *1.* Return to the Battlefield. *2.* Past to the Future. *3.* Family Union, Part 1. *4.* Family Union, Part 2.

Season 2 Episode List: *5.* No Longer Me. *6.* Daughter, She's Yours. *7.* Get Rid Of. *8.* Flashback to Shoot. *9.* Faded to Black. *10.* Everything Has Changed. *11.* Mushy Wushy. *12.* Conversations Wit De Churen, Part 1. *13.* Conversations Wit De Churen, Part 2. *14.* Two Down, One Woke.

Season 3 Episode List: *15.* All About the Head. *16.* Dates. *17.* Babies, Engagements, Parties. *18.* Chokin' Reality. *19.* Run It in a Deep Hole. *20.* Conversations Wit De Churen: Me, Me. *21.* KK Queens Survey.

Season 4 Episode List: *22.* We Kiki, the only episode released as of October 2014, features actor Macaulay Culkin as P and his efforts to convince KK Queen to sign up his band, The Pizza Underground.

206 *Mission: Rebound.* missionrebound.com. 2010 (Comedy).

Cloie and Vera are friends. Although Cloie is a lesbian and Vera is straight, they have a non-sexual relationship with each other. Vera accepts Hayley as Cloie's lover and Cloie accepts Malcolm as Vera's boyfriend. Hayley and Malcolm also know each other and all hell breaks loose when Cloie catches Malcolm having sex with Hayley. The couples separate and, while they have been burned by their respective lovers, Cloie and Vera plot to get even. The program follows two scorned women and the path they take when they attempt to rebound.

Cast: Vera Miao (Vera), Cloie Wyatt Taylor (Cloie), Malcolm Barrett (Malcolm), Thea Brooks (Hayley), Adalgiza Chermont (Ada), Jesse Torrilhon (Jesse), Karey Dornetto (Heather). **Credits:** *Producer:* Vera Miao, Cloie Wyatt Taylor, Micki Poklar. *Director:* Gigi Nicolas. *Writer:* Vera Miao. **Comment:** The program, while well acted, is a bit hard to see at times due to poor lighting. There are adult situations and vulgar language is used but overall it is an amusing series and different when it comes to lesbian and straight mix series.

Episodes:

1. Ho-Mates. The three-year friendship between

Cloie and Vera faces its biggest hurdle when Malcolm (Vera's boyfriend) beds Hayley (Cloie's girlfriend).

2. Cuddle Ditch. The first taste of revenge occurs at a party where Vera and Cloie show their ex's they can move on.

3. Astro-Stalker. Vera attempts to get Cloie back into the dating scene via on-line dating (with a girl named Heather) while Vera has a confrontation with Malcolm over what has happened.

4. Tour de Pants. At a BBQ she is attending with Cloie, Vera finds herself in a quandary when she is asked to "come over to the Dyke side but is not sure she is ready to give up men for women, especially since she still has hopes of making up with Malcolm. The program's concluding episode.

207 *Momma'z Boi.* youtube.com/watch ?v=l52z01cH3VQ&list=PLf9vC4eyvVvvC wdq8fDHA6kbZS2-fqueR. 2013–2014 (Comedy).

Michael King is a young man with a secret: he is gay. Lin King is his mother, a woman with her own little secret: she is bisexual, but has chosen to live life as a lesbian. Donte' Wallace is a gay and Michael's secret boyfriend. The program explores what happens when both Michael and Lin reveal who they are sexually with a behind-the-scenes look (the hook ups and sexual activity) at the gay life style in Atlanta, Georgia.

Cast: Nijae Lopez (Michael King), Kevin Mines (Donte' Wallace), Jae Patterson (Lin King), Macc Rivera (Alex Santos), Poerik Soulja (Darnell Chambers). **Credits:** *Producer:* Lyriqal Blyss, Nijae Lopez, Kevyn Mines. *Director:* Lyriqal Blyss. *Writer:* Nijae Lopez, Kevyn Mines. **Comment:** The title is correct as is (no reason given for that "z"). It is an African-American production and tries very hard to extol the fact that Atlanta is a welcoming city for gays but fails on virtually all levels with the most disappointing being the amateurish acting coupled with an equality amateurish story line (both come off as simply bad). The camera work is also very non-professional. Many scenes are badly lit and the sound quality poor and often hard to understand (like in the first episode, where a beeping noise from a smoke detector with a weak battery is heard). Better character development could have helped greatly as would the use of external microphones (relying only on the camera microphone is obvious and is the culprit for the poor sound; background noises can also be heard because of it). Credit has to be given for trying as there are shows (in other genres) that are far worse.

Episode List: *1.* A Mother's Love. *2.* First Time. *3.* Russian Roulette. *4.* Skin, Part 1. *5.* Skin, Part 2. *6.* Crazy Week. *7.* Déjà vu. *8.* One and Only. *9.* Puppy Love. *10.* Genesis.

208 *Morgan McMichaels' Living for the Lipsync.* youtube.com. 2014 (Variety).

Morgan McMichaels, a contestant on the second season of the Logo cable TV series *RuPaul's Drag Race*, presents drag queens lip-synching new and classic songs.

Host: Morgan McMichaels. **Credits:** *Producer:* Thairin Smothers, Pete Williams, Blake Jacobs, Adam Asea. **Comment:** Enjoyable program that shows the talent some drag queens have for impersonating famous celebrities—and how they would be seen performing a song.

Episode List: *1.* Pink and Missy Elliott. *2.* Ligly Azalea and Alanis Morissette. *3.* Kylie Minogue and Janet Jackson. *4.* Britney Spears and Lil' Kim. *5.* Miley Cyrus and Madonna. *6.* Michael Jackson and Pitbull.

209 *Mugs: The Web Series.* mugsthefilm. com. 2013 (Comedy).

Kevin appears to be a typical high school student but he is far from what is considered typical. He is the son of a single mother whose addiction to alcohol placed his upbringing in the hands of his cross-dressing housekeeper, Ramon. While it appears Ramon's orientation has had no effect on Kevin, Kevin finds his world spinning out of control when he acquires a summer job at a local coffee house (Mugs) and finds its patrons are anything but normal (all a bit quirky). His fellow employee, Charlie, is openly gay and their boss (Rosie) is an eccentric. Suddenly, taken out of his comfort zone and introduced to a world that he has never known before, Kevin realizes that how he was brought up was not normal and he is now unsure of who he is and who he wants to be. The program charts Kevin's efforts to navigate a world he cannot fully comprehend and discover who he really is.

Cast: Brian Kane (Kevin), Michael Howell (Charlie), Gio March (Ramon), Mamie Morgan (Rosie), Laina Burgess (Darcy). **Credits:** *Producer:* Zac Underwood, *Director:* Mckenzie Figueiredo. *Writer:* Kyle Taylor, Z.T. Underwood. **Comment:** For some reason, producers believe that using abundant amounts of foul language makes for good comedy. It doesn't. The acting and production values are very good and the story, although unresolved (it appears Kevin will follow a gay path) leaves the doorway open for the series to continue.

Episodes:

1. Kevin Gets a Job. Kevin is introduced as Ramon urges Kevin to get a job for the summer and his choice is anything but a wise one when he is hired to work in a coffee shop.

2. Kevin Gets Accused of Thieving. Kevin's first day on the job finds him befriending Charlie but also being accused of a theft—stealing co-worker Darcy's jalapeno string cheese and $20.

3. Kevin's Play Date. Kevin and Charlie begin to find an attraction to each other much to Darcy's dismay, who has become curious about their relationship.

4. Kevin Gets Into a Fight. Rosie forbids co-workers from dating and confronts Kevin and Charlie about their relationship.

5. Kevin Gets Involved in Drama. Seeing that Kevin and Darcy are not compatible with each other, Rosie assigns them a shift wherein they must work together and hopefully get to like each other.

6. Kevin's Discovery. With Darcy again being robbed, Kevin becomes a sleuth of sorts and spots Rosie stealing the money Darcy had hidden in the coffee shop.

7. Kevin Makes Up. Following the altercation from episode 4, Kevin and Charlie make up and appear to becoming close again.

8. Kevin Sees Something Crazy. After Darcy again accuses Kevin of stealing from her, Kevin drags Charlie along on a stakeout for the backup evidence he needs to prove Rosie is the thief. The program's concluding episode.

210 My Best Gay Friends. youtube.com. 2012 (Comedy-Drama).

Vietnamese produced program that is set in Ho Chi Minh City and follows the lives of three young gay men sharing an apartment: Khoa, a college student who was forced out of his family to live independently; Rje, the operator of a food market stall (selling a rice vermicelli pasta); and Doi, the roommate with an unknown, mysterious past. The overall focus of episodes is a look at how young people adjust to living on their own for the first time and how they deal with their sexual encounters (which also focuses on the lesbian, bisexual and transgender characters listed after the three leads).

Cast: Huynh Nguyen Dang Khoa (Khoa), Tran Nguyen Kim Han (Rje), Ngo Xuan Nhat (Nhat), Minh Thanh (Thanh), Tran Bao Bao (BB Tran), Tong Minh Khang (Tony), Magic Quyen (Khoa's mother), Cindy Thai Thai (Herself). Credits: Producer-Writer-Director: Huynh Nguyen Dang Khoa. Comment: The program's Vietnamese title, *Bo ba di thoa*, is roughly translated as *The Bitchy Trio* but has been reassigned the name *My Best Gay Friends* for English-speaking countries. It is actually a statement by the producer to bring to light the LGBT community in Vietnam through three housemates in a more realistic way than the negative portrayal of gays in Vietnamese feature films and TV series. As the producer stated, "It's not right. I'm gay and I see my life as very normal. That's why I want to bring true images of homosexuals to everyone to change their perspective on us." The program itself is well produced and acted but is not dubbed in English and the closed captioning feature must be activated to understand what is happening.

Episodes: Eleven of fifteen planned but untitled episodes are on line. Each is tagged with the series title followed by the season and episode number (for example, My Best Gay Friends—Bo ba di thõa S01E 02 [Season 01 Episode 2], My Best Gay Friends—Bo ba di thõa S01E 11).

211 My Brother's Keeper. youtube.com/ user/mybrotherskeepertv.   2006–2012 (Drama).

The gay communities of Atlanta, Los Angeles, Miami and New York City are explored via thinly-connected stories about a group of gay men with a focus on the social, political and personal issues each subject faces. It is not so much about being gay, but the real-life issues such men face (from bipolar disorder and homelessness to co-dependency and unemployment) and how they deal with both their sexuality and the world that surrounds them.

Cast: Hubert Mitchell (Shakil), Chandia Brennen (Tionne), James Bland (Malik), Sandra Nicole (Juanita), Shelah Marie (Dorian), Melissa Coakley (Asia), Nyjo Brennen (Dallas), Samora Suber (Tori), Jessica Pizer (Leslie), Ivy Cohen (Rosemary), Shamon Glaspy (Xavier), Valentine Loman (Calvin), Jared Wofford Darius, (Aaron), Chris Saunders (Xen), Montrel Miller (Kyle), Victor Boneva (Rafael), Geno Brooks (Lawrence), Eric Cash (David), Ami Lavender (Robin), Tiffany Black (Kayla), Muhammad Mujahid (Jermaine), Chyna Irizarry (Brandy), Valentine Loman (Calvin), Tamario Fletcher (Miles). Credits: Producer: Lamont Pierre, Jared Wofford, Samora Suber, Nyjo Brennen, Geno Brooks, J. Suk Paige.

Director: Lamont Pierre, Shelah Marie. Writer: T.J. McIntyre, Lamont Pierre. Comment: A model program other potential African-American producers should follow as a template for how to make a relevant web series. Characters are well-developed and story lines properly thought out and presented. While it can become depressing at times (it is a slice of reality) the production is outstanding for the subject matter it covers. Season three episodes weave stories about gay characters into those of straight characters thus only four third season episodes are actually about Calvin and Xavier, the principal players (episodes 1, 4, 11 and 12).

Season 1 Episodes: 4 Untitled Episodes.

Season 2 Episodes: 4 Untitled Episodes.

Season 3 Episodes: 1. A Home for Calvin. 2. Rex's Forte. 3. Tionne, Interrupted. 4. Calvin's Burden. 5. The Taming of Maxine. 6. Kyle's Demons. 7. Malik Opens Up. 8. Juanita's Mission. 9. The Reoccurrence of Dallas Wright. 10. Leslie's Freedom. 11. Xavier's New Life. 12. Dorian's Choices. 13. The Shenanigans of Rosemary and Neal.

212 My Drunk Kitchen. blip.tv/My-DrunkKitchen. 2011–2014 (Comedy).

A program of meal preparation—with a lesbian

hostess who loves to drink and, as she becomes increasingly drunk, attempting to make the dish a recipe calls for.

Host: Hannah Hart. **Credits:** *Producer-Writer:* Hannah Hart. **Comment:** It's not *The French Chef* or *The Galloping Gourmet* but it is a clever, well-executed take on cooking shows that are now flourishing on cable stations like The Food Network and The Cooking Channel. Hannah is a delightful host (whether sober or drunk) and the episodes quite amusing. It might be advisable not to follow Hannah's directions as what you may come up with will most assuredly not be to your liking.

Episodes:

1. Butter Yo S**t. Hannah begins her program by consuming wine and attempting to make a grilled cheese sandwich.

2. Let's Mac Out. Baking macaroni and cheese (from the store-bought box) becomes a bit more complex when Hannah mixes beer with wine.

3. Omelet You Finish. Being a bit drunk works well for Hannah when she prepares a dish she believes is an Omelet.

4. Not Easy Bake Oven. Turning her attention to making cookies, Hannah discovers that a recipe as simple as cookies is much more complicated when drunk and not her expertise.

5. Smashed Brothers. Inspired by the character of Mario (from the Mario Brothers video game) Hannah dresses as the character to prepare, in a drunken stupor, Italian-style meatballs.

6. Brunch? What Food Makes a Good Brunch? Hannah believes it is pancakes and proceeds to prepare them.

7. Tacos. Tacos seem easy enough to make until Hannah creates a new drink—"Jargaritas" (mixing margaritas in a mason jar).

8. Ice Cream? Someday. Making home-made ice cream is not complicated but Hannah proves it is when the chef indulges in too much wine.

9. Latkes. Hannah proves that drinking Vodka does not fare well with preparing a Russian dish called Latkes.

10. Poutine. Hannah's show takes to the road where, in Canada, indulging in native drinks does not go well while attempting to make Poutine.

11. Candy Hand. Hannah discusses Halloween in an episode that finds her not drinking, but indulging in candy.

12. Pizza. Preparing pizza is a bit easier when the crust is store bought. You simply add the sauce and toppings and bake. But, as Hannah discovers, that becomes an impossible task when drunk.

13. Meat Pie. How to make a meat pie? While drunk, Hannah prepares one with turkey as the filling.

14. Raw Vegan Cheesecake. Feeling she needs help to make a cheesecake, Hannah invites her friend, Hilm Rawn—for drinks and ideas.

15. MRE's. Feeling the need for some fresh air, Hannah heads out to her back yard to drink and prepare MRE's (Meals Ready to Eat).

16. Quesadillas, Part 1. Preparing a cheese quesadilla becomes a bit of a challenge when Hannah mixes Russian Sake with tequila shots.

17. Quesadillas, Part 2. As her drinking becomes more persistent, Hannah feels using a low carb tortilla shell will make the perfect quesadillas—maybe so, but not when intoxicated.

18. Macaroni Salad. Some pasta, mayonnaise and perhaps celery and chopped carrots do make a good macaroni salad—but not when drinking and you require the help of a friend (guest Grace Helbig).

19. My Drunk Chicken. What to do with beer and a roasting chicken? Hannah knows—"Beer Can Chicken."

20. PHO'ed. Pho is a Vietnamese meal that requires following a recipe. But when drinking does following a recipe matter? Hannah proves it does.

21. O'Onion Rings. As simple as making onion rings sounds, Hannah's impaired-by-drinking processes finds her deep frying an onion slice along with lasagna and a cookie.

22. Shepherd's Curry. While visiting England, Hannah devotes her show to the country's various cultures by creating a Curry Spiced Shepherd's Pie.

23. Toast. Can anything be easier than making toast? It can when drunk and Hannah demonstrates just how tough making toast entrees can become.

24. Cake in a Jar. Inspired by mail order pastries, Hannah shows how to create what she calls "Cake in a Jar" that can be shipped across the country.

25. Tuna Melt. As Hannah has somewhat of a meltdown and confesses that her show is a bit off-center she proceeds to make a tuna casserole dish using pickles.

26. F.M.L./Thick Mint. Girl Scout Cookies are delicious but Hannah believes she can make a better Thick Mint Cookie (but not when impaired by alcohol).

27. Melting Pot. With a road trip planned, Hannah decides to make her viewers happy by preparing a special meal to celebrate their individual cultures—placing food native to that city in a large pot and see what develops.

28. Shamrock Shake. Hannah teams with her friends Grace Helbig and Mamrie Hart to prepare a drink called Shamrock Shake.

29. Fish Fingers and Custard. Guest Chris Hardwick helps Hannah prepare a British dish called Fish Fingers with Custard.

30. Flan Girl. Guest Tyler Oakley joins Hannah to prepare flan—but not with traditional fillings like caramel or chocolate.

31. SF Bread Bowl. Hannah begins her road tour and on her first stop prepares homemade bread.

32. Rough New York Cheesecake. Having had "great" success in the past with making a cheesecake, Hannah gives it a second, even less successful shot with a New York style cheesecake.

33. Fourth of July. Some apples, cinnamon, sugar and a pie crust go beyond Hannah's comprehension when she attempts to bake an apple pie to celebrate the Fourth of July.

34. Food 52. What to do with a watermelon and gin? Hannah knows—make a watermelon gin cocktail.

35. Burning Man. Hannah prepares (or tries to) boxed Italian meals.

36. Elaborate Thanksgiving Special 2011. The program departs from its normal format to showcase a video of a cat grooming a dog.

37. Holiday: Gingerbread. What started out as a project to make a Gingerbread House becomes less likely as Hannah's intoxication has created a Gingerbread Rabbi.

38. Holiday: Chocolate Shuffle. With Valentine's Day approaching Hannah's efforts to make a chocolate soufflé result in that being scrapped for chocolate dipped orange slices.

39. Filled Cheese Redux. Guest Shane Dawson joins Hannah to celebrate St. Patrick's Day via rum and coke drinks.

40. American Strudel, Part 1. With the pastry shell not rolled out, ingredients that can't be found and using the wrong type of apple, Hannah makes her version of an apple strudel.

41. American Strudel, Part 2. The prior episode continues with Hannah seemingly enjoying her non-traditional strudel.

42. Silent Movie. Preparing breakfast cereal—done in a tradition as if it were a silent film of the early 1920s.

43. Birthday Cake. Grace Helbig joins Hannah to make a reasonable-looking birthday cake for their friend Jenna Marbles.

44. Nachos. It tastes good and can be purchased as a snack—but can Hannah make a better Nacho snack? With alcohol as her guide, it is a most unusual Nacho.

45. Storm of S'mores. Hannah shows how to pass the time of a stormy day by combining a cookie with a marshmallow to make s'mores.

46. Caramel Apples. Sounds simple—put an apple on a stick and dip it in melted caramel. For Hannah, however, she requires and receives help from actress Felicia Day to prepare various candied apples.

47. My Hung Over Kitchen. Hannah attempts to provide tips on dealing with a hang over—but filming it when she is hung over.

48. Thanksgiving for Juan. Hannah shows how to prepare a special meal using a Cornish game hen, potatoes and bread stuffing.

49. Baked Corn Dogs. Guests Hank Green, Mamrie Hart and Grace Helbig join Hannah to prepare corn dogs. Sounds easy enough—if you have the sticks to place on the frankfurters (here Hannah makes them into muffins).

50. Super Bowl Special. With the big football game approaching, Hannah prepares variations on the traditional pig-in-a blanket.

51. My Hung Over Kitchen. Although intoxicated, Hannah attempts to prepare a breakfast burrito while offering viewers a tour of her kitchen.

52. Sea Bass. Fish and wine do not mix well when Hannah attempts to prepare a sea bass dinner.

53. Dick Taters. How to combine mashed (while smashed) potatoes with cut up frankfurters to create an easy family dinner.

54. Banana Cream Pie. With help from Robin Roemer, Hannah attempts to make a banana cream pie.

55. The Hartwhich. Guest Jamie Oliver joins Hannah to create "meatballs cut in half and stuffed with goodies."

56. Childhood Dreams. Hannah shows how to make a sandwich she enjoyed as a child: peanut butter and jelly with potato chips placed between the slices of bread.

57. Thirty (First) Year Old. Hannah attempts to make a birthday cake for her guest, her sister Naomi on her thirty-first birthday.

58. Red, White and Booze. To celebrate the Fourth of July, Hannah shows how to prepare a dish that uses watermelon, feta cheese and blueberries.

59. Untitled. While not the easiest dish to make, Hannah tackles crepes.

60. Popcorn Pretzel. With melted caramel, Hannah proceeds to make popcorn covered pretzels.

61. Pop Fickle. Using an ice try and mixing cranberry juice, vodka, lemonade and a flavored ice drink to make a Pop Fickle.

62. Eggplant Parnassian. An eggplant and cheese combination that requires something Hannah does not have—a sober mind to prepare properly.

63. Turkey Bacon Bits. Realizing that she is continually drunk and burdened by hangovers Hannah devises a hangover remedy—turkey bacon (as its salt content will cure that hangover, or so she says).

64. Fried Avocado. It sounds easy—if you can get the pit out of the avocado, slice it and have a frying pan.

65. Drunk in the Kitchen. Hannah celebrates the third anniversary of her show by making a grilled cheese sandwich.

66. Grapes of Wrath. Hannah demonstrates how to make homemade grape jelly in 10 easy (if you are sober) steps.

67. Brownies. Mary Louise Parker joins Hannah to make brownies.

68. Mission: Im-pasta-ble. Hannah's final show of 2014 wherein she demonstrates how to make home-made ravioli.

Note: Second season episodes (2012) feature a series of videos called *Coming Out* wherein Hannah talked about her sexual orientation.

1. So. This Is Me. Hannah discusses coming to terms with who you are.

2. Nervous. Hannah reveals what it is like to be

attracted to a straight girl but knowing you can't have her.

3. Straight People. A Valentine's Day program wherein Hannah relates incidents from past relationships.

4. Marriage. Gay marriage is discussed.

5. The Closet. Hannah reveals what it was like to be in "the closet" and how difficult it was for her to "come out."

213 My Gay Family. vimeo.com. 2011 (Comedy).

Australia's Gold Coast provides the backdrop for a look at two gay men, Dan and Johan, as they leave their home in London and embark on a new life and adventures adjusting to the cultural and political change of the Land Down Under. Accompanying them in their journey are Thyme and Holly, dogs (highland terriers) who comment on the actions of their masters through off-screen human voices.

Cast: Dan Fry (Dan), Johan Venter (Johan). **Comment:** An unusual gay series that is basically the two friends encountering a situation and attempting to deal with it. It is well acted and filmed and has nothing offensive about it. It is produced in Australia and the situation using vocal thoughts for the dogs dates back to the 1950s TV series *The People's Choice* wherein a basset hound provided commentary.

Episodes:

1. Learning. After settling in Dan takes it upon himself to teach Johan how to drive a car.

2. Dull as a Dishwasher. The guys try to figure out the complexities of their new automatic dishwasher.

3. A Date with Gym. Dan and Johan enter a gym—and try to figure out the equipment.

4. Cracked Lens. It's a sunny day—and a cracked lens on a pair of sun glasses fosters Dan and Johan to purchase a new pair.

5. Erecting a Pole. A day at the beach is not all that enjoyable as Dan and Johan struggle to assemble a tent.

6. Silence is Brown. Dan and Johan attempt to enjoy the solitude of their beach front home over a cup of coffee.

7. High Kite. Seeking to find something different to do, Dan and Johan attend a kite show.

8. Ummm Ommm. With mostly comments by the dogs, Dan and Johann take up meditation.

9. Male Scrubbers. Dan and Johan decide to redecorate and begin by painting the walls.

10. The Parrots. While Dan and Johan continue painting, the dogs become fascinated by several parrots that have flown into their backyard.

214 My Gay Garden. vimeo.com. 2013 (Comedy).

"Come with me and you'll see the whole world through my gay garden" are the opening theme lyrics

that introduce Archibald Coxman, a horticulturist whose garden is his life—and love. Through theme specific topics, Archibald treats his viewers to the ins and outs associated with caring for and loving your garden.

Cast: Michael Rivkin (Archibald Coxman), Leslie Newton, Jack Back, Chris Parnel, Kevin Chamberlin, Christen Sussin. **Credits:** *Producer:* Michael Rivkin, Rick Darge. *Director:* Rick Darge. *Writer:* Michael Rivkin. **Comment:** Unusual to say the least. Well acted and produced spoof of PBS and cable gardening shows that cleverly presents an alternate to normal planting and caring for a garden.

Episodes:

1. Lime Tree. Archibald explains how to start your own garden beginning with the planting of a lime tree.

2. Snails. A snail expert shows Archibald how to rid the garden of the leaf-eating pest. As posted "No snails were harmed in the making of this episode."

3. Pies. Fruit trees and bushes are discussed with a keen insight as to which ones make the best pies.

4. Vernon. It's a sad day in the gay garden when Archibald attempts to prune his favorite tree, Vernon, but Vernon refuses to let him do so.

5. Root. The nightmare of plant and tree roots come under fire as Archibald attempts to explain how some are needed and others must be cut away.

215 My Gay Roommate. youtube.com. 2012–2014 (Comedy).

Nick, a young man just beginning his freshman year at college, shares a dorm room with James. Nick is gay, James is straight and the program charts their experiences as they navigate life living in the same world but experiencing life in two totally different worlds. First season episodes focus on Nick, as a college freshman, living on his own for the first time. The second season, set away from college, follows Nick as he returns home for the summer break and reacquaints himself with friends and family. Third season episodes find Nick, now unsure about the direction his life is taking, deciding to take a year off and explore his options in New York City, including finding a new roommate.

Cast: Noam Ash (Nick), Philip Lockwood-Bean (James), Heather Peterson (Nick's mother), Drew Paramore (Ed), Matthew Christian (The Cowboy), Yessenia Rivas (Eduarda), Melis Aker (The Princess). **Credits:** *Producer:* William Gerber, Danielle Bryant, Demi Marks. *Director:* Austin Bening. *Writer:* Noam Ash, Austin Bening, Sam Korda. **Comment:** Typical Internet production with good acting and production values. The characters are like-able and the story, although compete for each season, appears to be in search of a format as its three different settings make it feel like three different series.

Season 1 Episodes: Six untitled episodes were produced.

Season 2 Episodes: *1.* The Art of Manscaping. *2.* The Lemonade Stand. *3.* Mommy Bootcamp. *4.* Breaking Tradition. *5.* Uncle Buck.

Season 3 Episodes: *1.* Next Top Roommate. *2.* The Bigger Man. *3.* Coming Out. *4.* Touched By an Angel. *5.* All Good Things. *6.* Coital Logistics.

216 *My Lesbian Friend*. youtube.com. 2013 (Comedy).

Three years ago, two young women, Keara and Kathleen, became roommates but it was not until recently that Kathleen revealed to Keara that she not only likes girls "but I'm attracted to them." It takes a few seconds for Keara, who is straight, to realize that Kathleen has just admitted that she is a lesbian but not romantically attracted to her (which pleases Keara for a few seconds until she asks—"Why not!"). While the answer to that question is not revealed, Keara and Kathleen are still the best of friends and share a plutonic relationship. Society, however, sees such a situation as two young women living together as not just friends, but lovers. Keara and Kathleen are each seeking that special someone and the program tackles a situation that has often been played in gay-themed series, but infrequently on lesbian-themed programs: a best friend situation (with all the highs and lows that Keara and Kathleen encounter as they navigate a dating life but not with each other).

Cast: Keara Doyle (Keara), Kathleen McKeown (Kathleen). Credits: *Producer-Writer:* Thyna Catamara, Keara Doyle, Kathleen McKeown. *Director:* Thyna Catamara. Comment: The program is very well acted and produced. Keara and Kathleen are both quite attractive and the storyline is very well constructed. Other than the one episode on YouTube there is virtually no other information on line to explain the series concept or the number of episodes produced. It appears that even though the available episode is labeled number seven, it could actually be the pilot and made to look like more episodes were produced but have been taken off line.

Episodes:

1. Barbecue. At a backyard barbecue, talk about lesbians upsets Keara who lashes out against her

The Neighbors. Series poster art (used by permission of Tello Films).

friends for making fun of them and implying that her friendship with Kathleen is something to be ashamed of not cherish.

217 *The Neighbors*. youtube.com/playlist? list=PL3PHB4Tt_zFI2f_Tn2Ws_KHhQS fzyeyNa 2013 (Comedy).

A spin off from *Roomies* (see entry) that continues to relate events in the lives of two women, friends Sam and Alex as they pretend to be lovers to keep a dream apartment housed in a gays only residence.

Cast: Julie Goldman (Sam), Brandy Howard (Alex), Kelly Beeman (Sally), Hannah Aubry (Tammy), Emily Peterson (Tami). Credits: *Producer-Director:* Christin Mell. *Writer:* Julie Keck, Jessica King. Comment: The program retains all the charm of the original series and is also well acted and produced. While only three short episodes appear on line, the doorway has been left open to continue the story line with the girls struggling to overcome the numerous situations that could threaten their exposure. A similar concept was presented on the TV series' *Bosom Buddies*, *Occasional Wife* and *Ned and Stacey* although using lesbians for *The Neighbors* is a more interesting idea and has a far greater appeal than two guys pretending to be women (*Bosom Buddies*) to keep an apartment or two single people (a man and a woman) pretending to be married and sharing an apartment to fool others and achieve a goal (*Occasional Wife* and *Ned and Stacey*).

Episodes:

1. The Thinnest Walls. Continual noise from the apartment of their neighbors, Tammy and Tami, has Alex believing they are making love while Sam believes it must be something else as Tammy and Tami are sisters and would not be making love to each other; Alex believes differently and tries to convince Sam that it happens.

2. The Laundry Room. In the laundry room, Alex spies Tammy and Tami acting overly sexy with each other—but each time Sam turns around to look the sisters appear to be normal.

3. Being the Baguette. During a trip to the grocery store Alex and Sam run into Tammy and Tami who are becoming affectionate in public. A curious Alex asks how they maintain their relationship and is surprised to hear it is through games like hopscotch, which they even play in their apartment (hence the noises heard by Alex and Sam).

218 Neil's Puppet Dreams. youtube.com. 2012–2013 (Comedy).

Neil Patrick Harris is an actor who like most people has dreams when asleep. But unlike virtually everyone else, when Neil dreams he dreams about puppets—puppets that are alive and representative of "people" he encounters in his daily life (including "puppet sex and nudity" and drag queens). Neil also has the "ability" to fall asleep anywhere at anytime and it is through those sudden sleep experiences that the viewer sees first hand what happens when one dreams of puppets. Neil lives with his life partner David Burtka and opens each episode with "Hi, I'm Neil. I sleep a lot and when I dream, I dream in puppet."

Cast: Neil Patrick Harris (Himself), David Burtka (Himself), **Voices:** David Massey, Colleen Smith, Allan Trautman, Donna Kimball, Nathan Danforth, Victor Yerrid, Brian Henson, Brian Clark, Spencer Liff, Mykell Wilson. **Drag Queens:** Willam Belli, Matthew Sanderson. **Credits:** *Producer:* Janet Varney, Neil Patrick Harris, Brian Henson, Seth Laderman, Chris Hardwick, David Burtka. *Director:* Kirk R. Thatcher. *Writer:* David Burtka, Brian Clark, Neil Patrick Harris, Michael Serrato, Kirk R.

Thatcher, Janet Varney. **Comment:** The program is produced in association with Muppet creator Jim Henson's company "Alternative Henson." It is a television quality production with excellent writing and acting. It is also a unique idea and with some editing, it could make a good network or cable special.

Episodes:

1. The Lullabye. Many people dream of falling. But for Neil, that fall is accompanied by flying puppets and an illustrative song.

2. Doctor's Office. A routine trip to see his doctor turns nightmarish when the human doctor (Nathan Fillion) transforms into a puppet physician and is astounded to discover that humans like Neil are "built" differently than puppets.

3. The Restaurant. In a restaurant Neil falls asleep to see that he is a waiter in an establishment run by some off-the-wall puppets.

4. To Catch a Puppeteer. Being the only human in his dreams, Neil finds he is the target of the Puppet Police when he becomes a wanted felon called "The Puppeteer" for molesting puppets (placing his hand in their back to operate them).

5. Dream Bump. Neil's dreams become a bit outlandish when they not only include puppets, but dancers and drag queens.

6. Alien Abduction. Doing what he does best—falling asleep, Neil experiences a dream come true—being abducted by aliens and probed.

7. Bollywood. An elaborate well choreographed episode with Neil performing in a Bollywood-type musical.

219 The Newtown Girls. thenewtowngirls. com. 2012 (Comedy-Drama).

Scarlet, a very pretty lesbian living in Newtown in Sydney, Australia, is seeking the girl of her dreams. Although Scarlet has dated several women, finding that one special girl has evaded her. The program explores the obstacles Scarlet faces—from ex-girlfriends, complicated relationships (including one with her best friend Alex) and virtually anything else that can complicate her life as she turns to pretending she is someone she is not to find the right girl.

Cast: Debra Ades (Scarlet), Renee Lim (Alex), Kylie Watson (Veronica), Kate Austin (Kym), Elizabeth Gibney (Lexie), Sontaan Hopson (Nicki), Shalane Connors (Rachel). **Credits:** *Producer:* Natalie Krikowa, Ann Pilichowski. *Director:* Julie Kalceff, Emma Kelite, Imogen Dall, Spencer Harvey. *Writer:* Julie Kalceff, Natalie Krikowa. **Comment:** Australian produced program that combines elements of drama and comedy in an enjoyable program that is nicely acted and produced.

Episodes:

1. I'm Home. Introduces Scarlet as she returns to Newtown from a year-long trip in South East Asia (to get over a breakup with Kym) and begins preparations to re-enter the dating scene.

The Newtown Girls. Left to right: Kylie Watson, Renee Lim, Kate Austin and Debra Ades (photograph by Shana Turner © Zenowa Films, 2011).

2. Dress Up. Feeling that she needs some help getting back in the game, Scarlet seeks the advice of her friend Alex.

3. The Justin Bieber Look. After becoming intoxicated during a date and losing a potential lover, Scarlet realizes that she must change her ways if she is ever going to find her dream girl; she begins by acquiring a new wardrobe.

4. The Puppy Episode. Scarlet turns to Internet dating but finds she too is unlucky there when her inbox remains empty. She then hits on the idea to get a puppy "because lesbians love puppies."

5. Juicy. After failing with the puppy trick, Scarlet joins the Newtown Lesbian Book Club (run from Veronica's bookstore, where Scarlet is also employed)—but has trouble trying to read the required book in time for the weekly discussion.

6. Balls. Scarlet manages to bluff her way at the book club gathering, meets some girls and even encounters hits on the Internet. She also learns that lesbians like sports and figures to become a sports enthusiast to attract one.

7. It's a Date. Scarlet secures a date for the first time in a year with "a hot chick" (Lexie).

8. Super Green. As Scarlet seeks a way to impress Lexie, Alex tries to convince her that she should be herself and not put on airs to impress her.

9. At the Vanishing Point, Part 1. Scarlet believes

she has found the perfect mate in Lexie until doubts are raised when her ex-girlfriend (Kym) returns.

10. At the Vanishing Point, Part 2. Scarlet's feelings for Kym are rekindled when they meet and now Scarlet must choose between a new love (Lexie) and an old love (Kym) in the concluding episode.

220 *Nikki and Nora.* tellofilms.com. 2013 (Crime Drama).

Nicole "Nikki" Beaumont and Nora Delaney, lovers and former detectives with the N.O.P.D. (New Orleans Police Department) have combined their sleuthing abilities and now operate as private detectives. The women are roommates and reside at 213 Toulouse Street. Each was born in New Orleans and each has a unique perspective about the town in which they live, especially the French Quarter, which (for the series) is laden with crime and secret identities that require "the touch of the velvet hammer" (seductive women) to solve and uncover. Being lovers appears to have been the main reason why Nikki and Nora resigned from the police department (just not acceptable to some). Becoming private detectives is their way of "solving your problems" and "fixing what is broken." The program follows their efforts to solve crimes while at the same time dealing with the personal issues their relation-

Nikki and Nora. **Left to right: Liz Vassey, Christina Cox, Janina Gavankar (used by permission of Tello Films).**

ship creates in a time when such relationships are still not accepted. Also known as *Nikki and Nora: The N&N Files.*

Cast: Liz Vassey (Nikki Beaumont), Christina Cox (Nora Delaney), Armin Shimerman (J. Hewitt Kemp), Jim Beaver (Arliss Fontenot), Janina Gavankar (Lea Sadina), Kitty Swink (Dottie Reid), Ian Castleberry (Ace), Holis Hannah (Celia South), Tess Harper (Mary Delaney), Charlie Hoffacker (Det. Muhammed Al-Sidr), Thayer Abigail Lund (Abby), Candice L. Preston (Det. Kendall Clark), Shannan Leigh Reeve (Det. Riley Morgan), Aasha Davis (Violet Craig), Wallace Langham (Carl Mottenberg). **Credits:** *Producer:* Paige Bernhardt, Christin Mell, Nancylee Myatt, Liz Vassey, Christina Cox. *Writer-Director:* Nancylee Myatt. **Comment:** A well-produced and acted program that has its roots in an unaired 2004 network TV pilot film called *Nikki and Nora: Lady Cops.* The pilot was pitched to the now defunct UPN network but was rejected for its lesbian theme. It was leaked to the Internet and received numerous hits on YouTube suggesting to producer-creator Nancylee Myatt that such a series could be produced but in a different medium. A trailer was created followed by four episodes and an open doorway for more stories to follow. The actual pilot storyline (a murder investigation) was recreated for the web series (the exception being that Nikki and Nora were police officers with the Special Crimes Unit of the N.O.P.D. and that their relationship was not actually stated but

obvious they were lovers. Even though lesbians have been featured on broadcast TV—and in more suggestive scenes than presented in *Nikki and Nora* it can only be assumed UPN executives were reluctant to showcase women as lovers at the time). Had the pilot sold, it would have been the first crime drama with lesbian protagonists as lead characters. Liz Vassey and Christina Cox are expertly cast as the lovers and one may find that some scenes are very dark and difficult to determine what is happening. There are scenes of affection between Nikki and Nora as well as brief kissing sequences but nothing as compared to girl/girl scenes on such TV shows as *The L Word.*

Episodes:

1. Episode 1. Nikki and Nora investigate the death of a young woman (Elizabeth Turner) who was apparently killed by someone she knew.

2. Episode 2. Nikki and Nora question Elizabeth's brother, Peter, learning that she had dated several men, including a wealthy man who began stalking her after their breakup.

3. Episode 3. A coroner's report reveals that skin fragments had been found under Elizabeth's fingernails. To add to the tragedy, she was also beaten but did put up a struggle as her left shoulder was dislocated and her lung punctured. It is also revealed that she had been raped.

4. Episode 4. Clues lead Nikki and Nora to suspect that a police officer (Codell) is the culprit as he has a violent temper and was dumped by Elizabeth.

But to prove it becomes the problem as the series concludes.

221 *No Man's Land.* youtube.com. 2012 (Reality).

A home improvement–like program with two very pretty lesbian hosts (Anne and Shelly) and how-to videos on decorating and designing as the women, just acquiring their own apartment in Brooklyn, New York, use their expertise as decorators to transform their home into a do-it-yourself project.

Host: Anna and Shelly (as credited). Credits are not given. **Comment:** While not on the scale of the PBS TV series *This Old House* or any HGTV re-modeling projects, Anna and Shelly make redecorating as simple as possible using items that can be found in any hardware store with tips on doing it on a budget—and as green as possible. Anna and Shelly are dating each other and, while they remain feminine, they do take on messy chores like painting and plastering. The program is well done and informative, especially for novice young women interested in a woman's touch when it comes to repairing or re-modeling one's home. There is also an adult X-rated film series called *No Man's Land* (beautiful lesbians making love) and this may come up in searches if the words "web series" are not added after the main title ("No Man's Land Web Series").

Episodes:
1. Meet Shelly and Anna. The women introduce themselves and what to expect as the series progresses.
2. Painting a Wall.
3. Earth Day Subscriber Saturday.
4. Gallery Wall.
5. Anna and Shelly in Puerto Rico.
6. Mother's Day Gift Idea: DIY Indoor Herb Garden.
7. Reused Items with Molly Austin.
8. Shelving Unit with Allison Oropallo.
9. Storage Ideas with Franchesca Ramsey.
10. Fourth of July at the Fort Greene Flea Market.
11. Viewer Comments.
12. Moving Tips.
13. Tools.
14. DIY (Do It Yourself) Closet.
15. Viewer Comments 2.
16. Bedroom Makeover Surprise.
17. Tuesday Top 5: Female Design Bloggers.
18. DIY Mason Jar Lanterns with Anna's Mom.
19. No Man's Land: Tuesday Top 5—Photo Displays.
20. Viewer Comments 3.
21. Reupholstering with Grace Bonney.
22. Beach House Décor Drinking Game.
23. Viewer Comments 4.
24. Tuesday Top Five: Christmas Decorations.
25. Ikea Hacks.

222 *No Shade.* noshadeseries.tumblr.com/. 2013 (Comedy-Drama).

New York City provides the backdrop for a look at the lives of four diverse friends: Noel, a young artist raised in a strictly religious family by a homophobic mother, who has left his home in Brooklyn to live his life as an open gay; Eric, a promiscuous Manhattan bar manager; Danielle, a make-up artist who is also a transgender woman; and Kori, an unemployed dance teacher. As each struggles to live, date and love they must also deal with their personal demons and navigate a more difficult road to achieve their goals for being who and what they are (like Danielle encountering Tran phobic harassment and documentation issues; Noel's bout with parental and religious condemnation; Kori's efforts to overcome gay bashing and Eric's addiction abuse).

Cast: David Brandyn (Noel Baptiste), Terry Torro (Eric D. Stone), Donnie DuRight (Kori Jacobs), Tamara Williams (Danielle Williams), Chantel Rogers (Patricia Baptiste), Jon Rentler (Joe). **Credits:** *Producer-Director:* Sean Anthony. *Writer:* Sean Anthony, David Brandyn, Terry Torres, Donnie DuRight, Tamara Williams. **Comment:** The program is a notch above other African-American programs that focus on gays in that it has better acting and production values (more like something that would play on the Logo or Here! cable channels). Unfortunately, like others of its kind, it uses frank sexual language as well of its share of gutter talk, and one should be prepared for that before watching. There are also sexual situations but no parental warnings or attempts to block the series (that is, an e-mail account to verify age is not required).

Episode List: *1.* No Shade Pilot. *2.* When Opportunity Knocks. *3.* No Roaches. *4.* Penetration and Sin. *5.* Poppin on a Handstand. *6.* Insensitive B*tch. *7.* Fight the Hate. *8.* Trans-cending. *9* The Shade of It All. *10:* S**T Gets Real.

223 *Normal Gays.* normalgays.tumblr.com. 2013 (Comedy).

"Don't be weird, be normal" and "normal gays talking about normal things" are the program's tag lines that explain the simple premise: two gay men just talking or doing normal things.

Cast: Matt McLean, Tommy Do. **Credits:** *Producer-Writer-Director:* Tommy Do. **Comment:** An interesting concept but rather vaguely presented. It would be nice to have background information on the two characters to give the viewer some insight as to who they are (you get the impression they are drag queens by the first episode). There are no sexual situations and each under two-minute episode is just talk with little or no action.

Episodes:
1. Episode 1. A bit difficult to figure out exactly who the main characters are as no introduction is

given and two men are only seen putting on makeup and preparing to dress as women.

2. Episode 2. A discussion ensues over whether or not to paint the bedroom.

3. Episode 3. What is legal and what is illegal is discussed.

4. Episode 4. What not to do when you enter a gym to exercise (here, not talk to each other).

5. Episode 5. How a gay man can make a pretty straight girl look gorgeous.

6. Episode 6. International news stories are the topic of discussion.

7. Episode 7. A discussion of the book *Moby Dick* is presented.

224 Not Looking. funnyordie.com/not looking. 2014 (Comedy).

A spoof of the HBO series *Looking*. A young man named Parker has been in Los Angeles for three years and has accomplished nothing that is worth talking about. He is gay and his love life has been just as unrewarding. His gay friends, Colby, Danton, Shayne and Rodrigo all seem to be progressing well in the dating game and Parker believes he should stop looking for Mr. Right and just settle into the life he is now leading. The program follows events in the lives of the friends, especially Parker when a girl enters his life (Tina) and gives him a new outlook to seek that perfect man.

Cast: Jason Looney (Parker), Justin Martindale (Colby), Jeremy Shane (Shayne), Drew Droege (Danton), Jai Rodriquez (Rodrigo), Jes Dugger (Tina). **Credits:** *Producer:* Jason Looney, Karen Liff, Jon Robert. *Director:* Jason Looney. *Writer:* Jason Looney, Drew Droege, Justin Martindale, Jeremy Shane. **Comment:** Simple, non-offensive tale of five gay friends with good acting and production values. There is nothing offensive and the program flows smoothly from beginning to end.

Episodes:

1. Episode 1. Parker is introduced along with his friends Colby, Shayne, Danton and Rodrigo.

2. Episode 2. Colby and Rodrigo have a falling out when Colby believes Rodrigo cheated on him.

3. Episode 3. Danton's faked on-line dating profile earns him a series of disastrous dates with men who also lied about who they really are.

4. Episode 4. Lance Bass guests as Shayne's ex-boyfriend, Robby, who has returned to surprise Shayne; meanwhile, as Rodrigo moves on, Danton begins falling for Parker and the unexpected also happens to Parker when he runs into a girl he knows (Tina) and Danton believes he is leaving him for a woman.

5. Episode 5. Parker's encounter with Tina leads Danton to believe that Parker is cheating on him with a girl; Shayne once again says farewell to Robby as they cannot mend their relationship and Parker confesses to Tina that he is gay, but hopes they can still remain friends. The program's concluding episode.

225 NYC Glitters. youtube.com. 2011 (Comedy).

As a child Joe fell in love with the feature film *The Muppets Take Manhattan* ("I wanted to hang out all day with Kermit"). Years later, now living in Philadelphia with his male lover, Joe happens to catch his favorite movie on TV and memories of how he felt as a child rush back, making him again wanting to hang out with Kermit in Manhattan. On impulse, Joe leaves his small apartment and lover and moves to Manhattan, where he believes he can find the life he has been seeking. He has since made several friends (gays Steven and Josh; and Taylor and her boyfriend, Michael) and the program charts their experiences as they seek to fulfill their hearts desires, especially focusing on Joe "as my real adventures begin."

Cast: Joe Harris (Joe), Sarah Pribis (Taylor), David McEniry (Seth), Kevin Beckett (Josh), Graham Halstead (Steven), Christof Lombard (Marcus). **Credits:** *Producer-Writer-Director:* Joe Harris. **Comment:** Only a pilot film has been produced and it is not only well acted and produced but cleverly written (has a nice witty touch to it). While nothing major has been established (like what the friends do for a living or how they met) the doorway is left open for that and many other issues to be addressed should the program continue (it is hinted that Taylor is a dancer and Josh is pursuing a musical career).

Episodes:

1. Deal Breakers. The pilot film introduces the friends as they meet in Central Park for a picnic lunch and discuss the circumstances that relate to couples breaking off relationships.

226 Old Dogs and New Tricks. odnt.tv. 2011 (Drama).

A program that probes the question "Does (sex) life end for gay men as they approach 50" as seen through the activities of four such men: Nathan, Al, Brad and Ross. Nathan is a successful talent agent; Brad is a singer whose only claim to fame is that he had a hit song in the 1980s and has turned to the world of Internet dating; Al, nicknamed "Muscles," is a personal trainer at a gym called WeHo; and Ross is a former TV star of the 1990s who has settled into a gay marriage where his husband appears to be having a more successful career than him. As each of the men, living in West Hollywood, California, nears that 50th birthday, their feelings regarding middle age and what the future holds (sexually) is explored as they now navigate a strongly youth-obsessed culture.

Cast: Leon Acord (Nathan Adler), Curt Bonnem (Brad King), Jeffrey Patrick Olson (Al "Muscles"

Carter), David Pevsner (Ross Stein), Amanda Abel (Lydia Lasker), Bruce L. Hart (Nelson Van Eddy), Rutanya Alda (Barbara), Mo Gaffney (Jolene Sherman), Kathryn Leigh Scott (Lily Anne Carter), Thom Bierdz (Bobby Burton), Patrick Bristow (Dr. Keebler), Doug Spearman (Neal Kelly), Terri Garber (Dr. Ashley). **Comment:** Well acted and produced program that does contain some vulgar language and adult sexual situations (each episode is preceded with "The Following Is Intended for Mature Audiences, Viewer Discretion Is Advised"). Veteran TV actresses Terri Garber and Kathryn Leigh Scott (who gained notoriety from the 1960s TV series *Dark Shadows*) appear on the program.

Episodes:

1. Pilot. The regulars are introduced as Nathan recalls how the four became friends.

2. It's My Party. As Nathan begrudgingly prepares to celebrate his 50th birthday, his friends try to cheer him up with stories of their sexual conquests over the past 24 hours.

3. And I'll Whine if I Want To. Nathan begins to feel his age when he runs into a man with whom he had a long-forgotten one-night stand while Al feels he has finally found his Mr. Right (Bobby).

4. Stuck in a Jam. Al, Ross and Brad's efforts to cheer up Nathan do not seem to be working as Nathan now feels he is living an empty life; Ross appears to be having martial issues while Al believes he has too much in common with Bobby.

5. Strange Bedfellows. As Nathan seeks the help of a psychologist (Dr. Keebler) to overcome his feelings of self pity, Ross seeks a way to deal with growing compatibility problems in his marriage to Neal.

6. Topsy Turvy. Ross and Neal fail to resolve their differences while Nathan hooks up with someone that could change his life—Damian.

7. Bottoms Up. Ross finds himself temped by a younger man; Al and Bobby's relationship begins to fall apart; although dating the younger Damian, Nathan begins to feel his age.

8. It's Noel Coward Time. Brad becomes infatuated with porn star Rod Rodriquez (Zay Rogue) while Ross and Neal find overcoming their differences even more difficult.

9. Mood Swings. Nathan's efforts to break off with Damian becomes more difficult than he thought when Damian appears to not want to let go; Neal's frequent absence continues to fuel the fire between him and Ross; Brad begins to rethink his relationship with Rod.

10. Big Fat Gay Wedding. At a gay wedding, guest star Greg Louganis (Dirk) is introduced as a former notorious circuit boy who has chosen to settle down (with Nelson) while Ian Buchanan guests as a photographer (Christoph) who has eyes for older gay men, especially Nathan.

11. Bad Reception. As their friend Lydia, a cabaret performer, sings at Nelson and Dirk's wedding, Christoph makes his approach on Nathan.

12. Best Laid Plans. Christoph's efforts to impress Nathan apparently fail as he still has feelings for Damian; Al and Bobby plan a romantic weekend while Ross decides to look into Internet hook-ups.

13. Date Night. As Al and Bobby's romantic weekend get-away is anything but romantic, Nathan and Damian attempt to explore and understand the differences in each other's world.

14. Skinny Lady Sings. As Lydia debuts her cabaret act, Brad, Nathan, Ross and Al deal with the issues that they are currently facing.

15. Last Gasps. The concluding episode wherein Al tries to rekindle the flame between him and Bobby; Brad and Rod attempt to make a re-connection; Ross and Neal attempt to overcome the barriers that are separating them; Nathan seeks help in his relationship from a new therapist (Dr. Ashley).

227 *Once You Leave.* onceyouleave.com. 2011–2012 (Drama).

After serving two years in the Peace Corps, a young woman (Kayla) returns to her home town to re-connect with her former babysitter and the girl she yearned for but never dated (Rachel). Kayla and

Once You Leave. **Poster art from the series (copyright For Now Productions 2012, courtesy Nate Locklear).**

Rachel were only five years apart and, after building up the courage to confess her love to Rachel, Kayla found rejection. Heartbroken and unable to deal with the situation, Kayla joined the Peace Corps. As time passed Kayla realized that running away was not the answer and chose to return home. But just as Kayla had changed, so had those she left behind. Not only had her college friends moved on but so had Rachel, leaving town for a job as a live-in caretaker in another city (Salado). Desperate to find Rachel, Kayla embarks on a quest that ends in tragedy when she learns that Rachel apparently committed suicide (her body was found in a river) as there were no signs of foul play. Kayla cannot fully accept the fact that Rachel took her own life and begins a lone journey to discover the answers to the questions that are now haunting her and, along the way, somehow find herself and build the courage she needs to face the future.

Cast: Kayla Olson (Kayla Marshall), Jacki Brinker (Rachel Perkins), Johnny Anderson (John Anderson), Cynthia Schiebel (Mary Anderson), Eric Anschutz (Tim Squires), James Jackson Leach (Jon-Michael Perkins), Rae Petersen (Linda Taylor), Jerry Carroll, Jr. (Tunde), Mark Wilson (Ronnie Caulters), Nathan Harris (Kenley), Samantha Ireland (Molly), Lyndsey LeJeune (Abby), Nate Locklear (Ben Langley), Indigo Rael (Awenasa). **Credits:** *Producer:* Nate Locklear, Kayla Olson, Jason Massey, Anita Garza, Michael Hale, Samantha Ireland. *Director:* Nate Locklear. *Writer:* Nate Locklear, Kayla Olson. **Comment:** Captivating program that is expertly acted and produced (television quality production). The program contains nudity and adult situations but the presentation varies depending on where it is watched. The official site and sharing site Vimeo.com present the uncensored version as the producer originally envisioned the series. YouTube.com airs a censored version (blurred nudity) to comply with its community standards policy. Episodes 3, 8 and 9 are the affected episodes and are labeled "NSFW" (Not Safe for Work"). The program incorporates some vulgar language and its cinematography is captured in a very raw and hand-held style that may cause uneasiness for viewers not accustomed to the process (which can be seen on television in programs like *Modern Family*, *N.Y.P.D. Blue* and *The Closer*). There is nothing wrong with the process, it just takes getting use to (as producer Nate Locklear related, "The handheld style was used to pit Kayla against her environment. The motion is often chaotic to show how Kayla's world is not stable and ready to crumble at any time"). The episodes are each over 20 minutes long but the story flows smoothly and nothing is stretched to fill that time frame. *Once You Leave* is not like other lesbian-themed programs and filled with kissing and/or adult situations. It is a young woman's quest to accept what has happened and find a way to move on. And it works.

Episodes:

1. You Can Never Go Home Again. The story line is established as Kayla, the daughter of an alcoholic mother, returns home after a two year absence to re-connect with Rachel.

2. A Change of Plans. When Kayla learns that Rachel has moved to Salado to find work, she begins a quest to find her. Her journey comes to a tragic end when she learns from Rachel's employers (John and Mary Anderson) that Rachel has died, her body found floating in a river.

3. Saturn Return. Spending the night in the room once occupied by Rachel, Kayla, deeply affected by Rachel's death, sets out on a quest to find out why she killed herself. Her journey begins by seeking out Rachel's brother, Jon-Michael (Kayla later learns through Rachel's blog that her world came crashing down around her and she did not know where to turn. Apparently no one saw the signs that she would take her own life. Further, more detailed information regarding Rachel's plight can be found at http://rachelperkinsblog.blogspot.com).

4. Rite of Way. As memories of her past with Rachel continually haunt her, Kayla finds herself trying to cope with Rachel's loss.

5. Tunde et le Feu. Rachel was Kayla's plan for her future happiness. As boredom sets in while waiting out a storm, a look at Kayla's two-year absence is seen as a Peace Corps volunteer.

6. Battered Suitcases. As Kayla continues her road trip, she stops to help a mother (Abby) and her child (Camden) stranded by an inoperable car. The tables are quickly turned when Kayla is robbed by a teenager at a rest stop.

7. I Would Run. Kayla, without money, wanders into town and manages to secure a job as a diner dishwasher. It is here that she meets Ben, the cook, a man with as much disillusionment as her (hiding from the past and running from the future as he too lost a girl who was the hope of his life).

8. Animal Kingdom. A flashback to a time when Kayla and Rachel were younger, here pretending to be animals, coupled with Kayla's determination to find her estranged father. On the way, she encounters a girl (Molly) and spends the night with her.

9. Sunset. While Kayla is a lesbian, she discovers that Molly is bisexual when her boyfriend catches them in bed and throws Kayla out. Flashbacks of Kayla and Rachel are again seen as Kayla hits the road in search of her father.

10. Rachel. Kayla's quest to find Rachel's brother (Jon-Michael) has come to fruition but it may also hold the key to another mystery surrounding Rachel's death when Kayla learns he had a crush on her and was jealous that she (Kayla) was infatuated with Rachel. Could Jon-Michael have killed Rachel to acquire Kayla for himself?

11. Sunrise. As Kayla continues her journey, seeking her father, she reflects on what has happened and what she plans to do.

12. Building Sandcastles. Kayla's meeting with her father reveals that he left her with her mother because he felt he could not raise her and that was the best solution. She also sees that her father lives in squalor (in a trailer park) and recalls that, as Rachel said, "You can never go back once you leave." The program concludes with Kayla, still reflecting on Rachel's loss but determined to move on and hopefully find someone as special as Rachel was to her.

228 1 Guy, 2 Gays—The Sitcom That Has Not Aired Yet. youtube.com. 2011 (Comedy).

Robert and Mitchell are gay and roommates and desperately in need of a third roommate to help pay the rent. To hopefully solve their problem they place an ad on CraigsList and get a response from a young man named Mark. Mark appears to be what they are looking for except for one vital question—is he also gay? With the premise set, two gay roommates and one who may or may not be gay (as he shows no indication of being either straight or gay) the program relates the incidents that befall each of the guys—with Robert and Mitchell seeking to discover if Mark is one of them.

Cast: Tim Fratt (Robert), Mike McCarthy (Mitchell), John Sulcido (Mark/Jay), Brittani Plavala (Julie), June Fratt (Gram). **Credits:** *Producer-Writer:* Rene DeLeon. *Director:* Robert Urquieta. **Comment:** While the idea is a bit different, the program encompasses an annoying laugh track that ruins the entire production; it is obvious that the laugh track was inserted after the episode was filmed as the characters unknowingly talk over the faked laughter without a pause to allow what is said to be heard. While the laugh track situation has been toned down dramatically on television, *1 Guy, 2 Gays* is a throwback to TV's earlier days when that annoying laugh track could be heard on programs like *The Patty Duke Show*.

Episodes:

1. Pilot. With Mark moving in, Robert and Mitchell devise a plan to have their friend Julie check him out to see if he is gay or straight.

229 Oops. youtube.com. 2011 (Drama).

The West Midlands in the United Kingdom provides the setting for a look at several lesbians living in its urban community and the problems they face in their daily lives.

Cast as credited: Bea (Rochelle), Racheal (Racheal), Thaossa Sweets (Tekevsa), Nathenie Reid (Edge), DJ Jigga (Pappa). **Credits as listed:** *Producer:* Natalie May-Wolfe, ST Media. *Director:* ST Media. **Comment:** When something is about to happen—usually romantically—"Oops" is seen (in a banner on the screen) as well as heard verbally by the character experiencing the situation. There are the needed "Oops" to tone down sexual situations and the filming is good but the program suffers from bad sound (camera microphones make it hard to understand the dialogue at times). The production is also a bit dark and, instead of cutting back and forth between characters talking, the panning method is used, which can become annoying as the camera moves across the screen from left to right then right to left until the scene is completed.

Episodes: The number of produced episodes is unknown. Only five untitled episodes, which can only be seen on Youtube, remain on line.

230 Orange Is the New Black. netflix.com. 2013–2015 (Drama).

Piper Chapman is a young bisexual woman, sentenced to 15 months in Litchfield Prison for criminal conspiracy (her involvement in drug trafficking). Piper, the daughter of Carol and Bill Chapman, was raised in an upper middle class family, graduated from college but made a wrong decision in life when she met Alexandra, called Alex, a lesbian at a bar and began a romantic and adventurous relationship with her. Piper was soon reeled into Alex's world of trafficking for an international drug cartel. But it was not the life for Piper and she and Alex parted ways—but not before Piper had come under the radar of authorities. As Piper changed her life for the better and began a promising relationship (with Larry), her past comes back to haunt her and she is charged as an accomplice to money laundering and drug smuggling. Piper accepts her punishment, hoping to pick up her life with Larry after her release, and begins her new life as an inmate (coincidentally, in the same prison where Alex is also serving time). The program charts Piper's life in prison with flashbacks detailing the lives of the inmates and personnel (some of whom are exploitative and corrupt) who also reside within the penitentiary.

Other Inmates: Tiffany "Pennsatucky" Doggett (accused of murder), Dayanari Diaz (drug dealing), Galina "Red" Reznikov (Mafia affiliation), Nicky Nichols (drug abuse), Poussey Washington (selling marijuana), Yvonne "Vee" Parker (drug supplier), Brook Soso (political protester), Rosa Cisneros (bank robbery), Claudette Pelage (murder and human trafficking), Tasha "Taystee" Jefferson (dealing drugs), Yoga Jones (manslaughter), Sophie Burset (credit card fraud), Gloria Mendoza (SNAP fraud), Sister Jane Ingalls (trespass on a nuclear facility during a protest), Blanca Flores (theft), Carrie "Big Boo" Black, Suzanne Warren, Mercy Valduro, Maria Ruiz, Jimmy Cavanaugh, and Angie Rice (offenses not revealed).

Prison Staff: John Bennett, Scott O'Neill, B. Moskovitz, Wade Donaldson and Wanda Bell (Corrections Officers), Sam Healy (Counselor/Corrections Officer), Joe Caputo (Warden's assistant),

Natalie Figueroa (corrupt executive assistant to the warden), Joel Luschek (Electrical systems manager), Igme Dimaguiba (Nurse).

Cast: Taylor Schilling (Piper Chapman), Laura Prepon (Alex Vause), Taryn Manning (Tiffany "Pennastucky" Doggett), Dascha Polanco (Dayanara Diaz), Uzo Aduba (Suzanne Warren), Kate Mulgrew (Galina "Red" Reznikov), Natasha Lyonne (Nicky Nichols), Lorraine Toussaint (Yvonne "Vee" Parker), Michelle Hurst (Miss Claudette Pelage), Danielle Brooks (Tasha "Taystee" Jefferson), Constance Shulman (Yoga Jones), Laverne Cox (Sophie Burset), Selenis Leyva (Gloria Mendoza), Beth Fowler (Sister Jane Ingalls), Laura Gomez (Blanca Flores), Lea DeLaria (Big Boo), Jessica Pimentel (Maria Ruiz), Patricia Squire (Jimmy Cavanaugh), Julie Lake (Angie Rice), Matt McGorry (John Bennett), Joel Marsh Garland (Scott O'Neill), Pedro H. Mojica (B. Moskovitz), Brenden Burke (Wade Donaldson), Catherine Curtin (Wanda Bell), Michael Harney (Sam Healy), Nick Sandow (Joe Caputo), Alysia Reiner (Natalie Figueroa), Matt Peters (Joel Luschek), Kaipo Schwab (Igme Dimaguiba), Kimiko Glenn (Brook Soso), Barbara Rosenblat (Rosa Cisneros), Emma Myles (Leanne Taylor), Diane Guerrero (Maritza), Abigail Savage (Gina Murphy), Lolita Foster (Eliqua Maxwell), Jason Biggs (Larry Bloom), Pablo Schreiber (George Mendez), Lauren Lapkus (Susan Fischer), Yael Stone (Lorna Morello), Robert Stanton (Murray Kind), Madeline Brewer (Tricia Miller), Tracee Chimo (Neri Feldman), James McDaniel (Jean Baptiste), Deborah Rush (Carol Chapman), Todd Susman (Howard Bloom), Lori Tan Chinn (Chang), Vicky Jeudy (Janae Romano), Maria Dizzia (Polly Harper), Annie Golden (Norma Romano). **Credits:** *Producer:* Jenji Kohan, Sara Hess, Liz Friedman, Lisa Vinnecour, Michael Trim, Gary Lennon. *Director:* Michael Trim, Andrew McCarthy, Phil Abraham, Uta Briesewitz, Jodie Foster, Constantine Makris, Matthew Penn. *Writer:* Piper Kerman, Jenji Kohan, Sian Heder, Sara Hess, Nick Jones, Lauren Morelli, Marco Ramirez, Liz Friedman, Tara Herrmann, Gary Lennon. **Comment:** Very harsh program that portrays life in a women's prison with a particular focus on Piper and how she must learn to accept and become a part of a strict system. The acting and production values are top notch and the characters convincing in their roles. There are sexual situations, nudity and vulgar language and the hope of one woman as she waits for the day she will be released and returned to the outside world. The program, based on the novel *Orange Is the New Black: My Year in Prison* by Piper Kerman, is also the first such program to feature a real trans-gender woman, Laverne Cox, as a transgender character (Sophie). It also features Laura Prepon (from *That 70s Show*), Kate Mulgrew (*Star Trek Voyager*) and Todd Susman, a television character actor with numerous credits. Actress Jodie Foster has come on board as a director (of Season 1, Episode 3, "Lesbian Request Denied" and Season 2, Episode 2, "Looks Blue, Tastes Red"). Television itself has presented several series using the background of a women's prison (*Prisoner: Cell Block H*, *Women in Prison* and *Dangerous Women*) but none as explicit as "*Orange*" although for its time in 1980, the syndicated Australian series *Prisoner: Cell Block H* was quite realistic (even in its subtle lesbian hints).

Episodes:

1. I Wasn't Ready. Piper begins her prison sentence with a flashback sequence depicting her life before prison when she discovers that Alex is also an inmate.

2. Tit Punch. Although Piper and Alex are no longer lovers, Piper finds herself being hit upon by a lesbian inmate known as "Crazy Eyes."

3. Lesbian Request Denied. Piper, aware of Crazy Eyes' intentions, rejects her and moves in with another cellmate (Claudette); a flashback sequence explores Sophie's world and how she committed credit card fraud to finance her sex-change operation. This episode is directed by actress Jodie Foster.

4. Imaginary Enemies. Piper's relationship with Claudette is explored as she is assigned to work with her in the electrical shop. A flashback sequence depicts how Claudette came to be imprisoned: by killing a man who abused one of her employees in her housekeeping business.

5. The Chickening. It is revealed that an inmate (Alex) informed authorities about Piper; Claudette applies for an appeal to her case; Red, the kitchen cook, offers a gift to the inmate who can capture a stray chicken that had wandered into the compound.

6. WAC Pack. As Piper has a confrontation with her mother (Carol), Larry believes there is a story here and sets out to write about Piper's incarceration. Piper, asked to run in an election for head of WAC (Women's Advisory Council) refuses—but is placed on the ballet by a prison staffer (Sam).

7. Blood Donut. As Piper tries to again get closer to Alex, she finds that her appointment to WAC has infuriated another inmate (Tiffany) who had wanted the position. Meanwhile, Red is propositioned by a guard (Mendez) to help smuggle drugs into the prison.

8. Moscow Mule. A flashback depicts Red's involvement with the Russian mafia, while Piper, again becoming close to Alex, feels slighted that Larry's published article is full of inaccuracies.

9. F**ksgiving. Thanksgiving at the prison finds Mendez using Red's connections to smuggle drugs into the prison and threatening her life if she doesn't cooperate. A flashback sequence to Alex's past shows that she was raised in a lower economic environment (than Piper) and how she became involved with the drug cartel. Alex and Piper continue to become close, especially after they perform a sexually arousing dance during a show.

10. Bora, Bora, Bora. A look at how the program "Scared Straight" works when juveniles arrive at the

prison to get a dose of what lies ahead for them if they do not straighten up. One juvenile in particular, Dina, is profiled as Piper tells her that the most frightening part of incarceration is not the walls that confine you but having to come face-to-face with who you are. Meanwhile, Mendez's drugs cause the death of an inmate (Tricia), threatening an investigation that could expose him.

11. Tall Men with Feelings. Fearing a federal investigation, prison authorities cover up Tricia's death and make it appear she committed suicide. Meanwhile, Larry's appearance on a radio program angers inmates, especially Crazy Eyes and Claudette, when he negatively speaks about them, but praises others (like Red) for the good job they are doing. Later, when Piper admits to Larry that she loves Alex, Larry tells her that it was Alex who turned her over to authorities.

12. Fool Me Once. Larry's radio interview causes unforeseen problems when a journalist inquires about sudden spending cuts when the prison had just received increased funding. Meanwhile, Piper confronts Alex and learns that she was hurt and turned her in when Piper dumped her. Hoping they are still lovers, Alex confronts Piper: "Nest with Larry or travel with me and be prepared for anything."

13. Can't Fix Crazy. The concluding first season episode wherein it is revealed that Piper has chosen Larry over Alex; however, when Larry visits Alex, hoping to tell her to stay out of Piper's life, he learns that it was Piper who rekindled their relationship and that his inability to make a serious commitment is responsible for Piper's actions. After reflecting, Larry ends his relationship with Piper and Piper attempts to return to Alex.

Season 2 Episodes:

1. Thirsty Bird. Piper flown to Chicago to testify against Alex's drug king, finds herself facing perjury charges when she is caught lying under oath (in a plan by her and Alex to deny knowing the drug king, fearing his revenge).

2. Looks Blue, Tastes Red. Flashbacks reveal incidents in the life of an orphaned girl, Tasha (now called Taystee) as she came under the wing of a drug dealer (Vee) and learned all the wrong aspects of life. This episode directed by Jodie Foster.

3. Hugs Can Be Deceiving. Larry hopes to use Piper in a story about possible corruption involving the prison's finances.

4. A Whole Other Hole. As inmates Big Boo and Nicky engage in a contest to see who can bed the most female prisoners, Red activates the old greenhouse—not so much for growing plants but to use its drainpipes as a means of smuggling goods into the prison.

5. Low Self Esteem City. Tension between the Latina women (led by Mendoza) and the blacks (led by Vee) are reaching epidemic proportions with a fix needed before a turf war erupts.

6. You Also Have a Pizza. Larry asks Piper to be a mole and secure what information she can on what is happening to the monies allotted to the prison.

7. Comic Sans. A prisoner's (Jimmy) escape puts an extra strain on the guards as they have now beefed up their patrols and inspections, placing the prisoner's under even more scrutiny and stress.

8. Appropriately Sized Pots. Rosa's troubled past is explored via flashbacks as Piper, although enjoying the special privileges she has been given, is facing resentment form others.

9. 40 oz of Furlough. Red and Vee's tumultuous history is seen through a series of flashbacks as Piper is given a furlough to attend her grandmother's funeral.

10. Little Mustachioed S**t. Vee's attempts to muscle in on Red's operations fail. Meanwhile, as the guards step up their patrols to find the contraband source, flashbacks are used to detail more in the history of Piper and Alex.

11. Take a Break from Your Values. A hunger strike threatens to expose prison conditions (which are deplorable) and made even worse when a nun (Sister Ingalls) joins in.

12. It Was the Change. The situation between Red and Vee continues to worsen until Red attempts to strangle Vee with plastic wrap and is unable to actually kill her. Vee, realizing that Litchfield has changed them, ends the tension by making peace with Red.

13. We Have Manners. We're Polite. The concluding episode wherein Piper finds the evidence she needs and presents it to the warden (and not Larry). Rosa, learning she has only 3-to-6 weeks to live, seizes upon an opportunity to steal a van and escape, hoping to enjoy her remaining time away from prison. As Sister Ingalls puts an end to the hunger strike, Vee, using the greenhouse drainpipes for her escape, meets a seemingly deadly ending when she is struck by the van driven by Rosa.

Season 3 Episodes: Scheduled for release in 2015: *1.* It's the Great Blumpkin, Charlie Brown. *2.* I'm a Bitch Because I'm Sad. *3.* Sometimes Bad Things Happen to Bad People. *4.* The Great Hate F**k. *5.* Kids: Yum! *6.* Offended but Okay. *7.* Back to the Rape Well. *8.* Use Your Tears as Lube. *9.* Heroin Robin Hood. *10.* The Rapiest Pap Smear. *11.* Gay Feet. *12.* Never-Ending Rumspringa. *13.* Hot for Janitor. *14.* Great Service, Lovely Scent.

231 *Orange Juice in Bishop's Garden.* orangejuiceinbishopsgarden.com. 2006–2015 (Drama).

To most students, the Bishop's Garden crew is a family where the majority of students have known each other since middle school. It is a place where friends are made for life—and because of the bonds built, few could fathom being friends with anyone else. It is the 1990s, and episodes detail not only the events sparking their lives (especially lovers Sarah and Gwen), but also the fashion, culture, and lore of the series' setting, Washington, D.C.

Note: Series creator Otessa Ghadar personally requested that her overall series description be included with the entry. It is as follows:

You know that summer, right ... the summer where EVERYTHING changed? *Orange Juice in Bishop's Garden* (OJBG) is that summer. And Bishop's Garden is the place where it all happens. It's the summer of '94 and naive and rebellious teens are engaging in all kinds of underage tomfoolery. Think grunge, Doc

Orange Juice in Bishop's Garden. Ellen Winter (left) and Katie Foster ("Summer of '95," episode 5 copyright 20/20 Productions, all rights reserved).

Martens, raves, the invincibility of youth, and epic first loves.

OJBG details the lives of a group of teenagers navigating high school and growing up in DC during the 1990s. It's all about teen magic—creating new and marvelous mischief with best friends, listening to mix-tapes and reading Sassy magazines, missing the last Metro, and getting stuck miles from pay phones. Accompany the young heroine, Sarah, as she gets herself into idle summer misbehaving, love triangle betrayals, and friendship fall-outs.

Most importantly, these are the summers where an unexpected romance between two teen girls, Sarah and Gwen, begins to blossom.

These are their days of youth, full of honest beginnings, where everything in life is insatiably tried for the first time. They will delight in new experiences, not thinking of consequences or that certain episodes of their lives will be irreparable, unchangeable. "Do you like me? Yes or no." Love will at times seem simple—other times, awkward, full of anxiety, complicated beyond comprehension. But it is unimaginable to them that time could do anything to diminish the intensity of their feelings.

All the teens will have their unique drama—whether with failed-yet-exemplary parents, clumsy self-discovery, or glorious heartbreak—and they will cling to their friendships to get through it all. They'll find relief, secrecy and rebellion through going to raves. Careless and carefree, they are timeless teenage renegades on the search for meaning and identity. They'll set each other up and tear each other down. They'll crash house parties and realize that sometimes in life, there are no "do-overs." They'll steal cars, candies, and hearts. They'll make you wish you were a teen again.

Venture into Bishop's Garden and remember what it feels like to have your whole life ahead of you! Let teen raucousness rage on.

The epic "Sarah & Gwen" love story develops and spans throughout 7 total seasons. It is this romance that sparked a following for the web series and its creator, Otessa Ghadar. The story is part recollection, part urban legend, and part pure fiction—but completely inspired by the author's memories of growing up in Washington, D.C., and the enchantment of her youth.

The Students:

Sarah, 15, was born on March 9, is a Pisces, loves the colors maroon and green and coffee is her favorite flavor of ice cream. She finds comfort in nature, photography and literature and cherishes her friendship with Kris, Roxanne, Beth, Maggie and Jake. "The Bishop's Garden crew is my family; a group that, for the majority, has known each other for years. But when I meet Gwen, an older girl from school, and started seeing her as more than a friend, everything changed. All of the different images people think I'm supposed to uphold only make me realize that, sometimes, I don't even know myself. But when I'm with Gwen, I feel like I can create my own image of who I really am: a totally badass and fearless girl in love."

Gwen, a Capricorn (born January 1), goes crazy over bubble gum flavor ice cream and lavender is her favorite color (she claims her talent is touching her tongue to her nose). "I'm the confident, outgoing girl of the group. Once Sarah and I officially began dating, everything felt spectacular. But when Sarah makes plans to go off to college and I realize that I'll be the loser still stuck at home, serving coffee to yuppies in the coffee shop, I freak out. And even though I love Sarah, I up and leave for New York to make a name for myself."

Alex, the newest arrival (from Rhode Island) hopes to become a journalist. Mango sorbet is her preferred ice cream choice. She loves cooking, the color aqua blue and was born on July 1st (making her a Cancer). Her claim to fame is that she can make "the best frittata anyone has ever eaten." She also says, "I'm all about Italian food, starry nights, and writing the next big story. Anyone who tries to diss my food, my friends or my ideas, will have a big problem to deal with."

Ryan, born April 6 (Aries) is fond of the color red, loves vanilla ice cream and considers himself the life of any party. He recalls that his fondest memory of Bishop is "kissing Yasmine during the spin the phone game. Love a conquest."

Chloe, born November 15 (Scorpio), loves rum raisin ice cream but has no favorite color. She is a ballet school drop out and has a knack at carpentry ("I have made Adirondack chairs"). "Elusive and intriguing (and occasionally rebounding with Sarah), I'm the girl everyone wants to know, but no one seems to understand. I was totally into Adrian, but his seriousness and focus is kind of weirding me out. I'm beginning to think that it's not just him because I keep getting distracted and sabotaging things ... like hooking up with lots of girls on the sly."

Tamsin, favorite colors green and black, is a Gemini (born May 21) and dark chocolate is her preferred ice cream flavor. Being the undefeated video game champion of *Teenage Mutant Turtles* is her claim to fame. She likes horror movies and if she can't be a rock star, she will settle for a career as a writer.

Libby, is an independent girl who says "Please don't call me Liberty. My Mom only uses my 'government name' when I am about to be grounded." She was born on February 3rd ("Which means I am an Aquarius baby!"), loves the color purple ("Not the movie, but the actual color"), keeping the peace, concerts "and all the other stuff hippies partake in." As she says, "Love, Peace and Chicken Grease."

Drew, born July 8 (Cancer) loves strawberry ice cream and the color Navy blue.

Rob (real name Robin), is a Sagittarius (born December 10) and red is his favorite color. He has his own band (The Skullions) and loves to play at wild parties.

Remi (real name Remington) is a health nut (prefers frozen yogurt over ice cream) and is an Aquarius (born February 4). Silver/chrome is his favorite color. He says "Some people call me Tinkerbell" and he is into "the new stuff like raves."

Maggie, an Aries (born April 18) loves chocolate chip cookie dough ice cream and the color magenta ("Oh, and mustard yellow too"). "Here's the scoop," she says, "I love Bishop's Garden and my gal pals. Sarah is my best friend in the whole wide world!" She likes long walks in the park, a good book and a night out on the beach with that special someone. She also says, "Maggie, Mags ... even the dreaded Margaret are what I go by, but you can, and will call me Maggie!"

Strawberry Shortcake, born in July (Cancer) is fond of the colors pink, rose and magenta and says," Your Majesty, Her Royalty, Your Highness, or just Queen. Whatever it is you feel like calling me.... I am the Queen of the rave scene."

Cassandra, a Taurus (born May 8) likes the color sunset orange and says, "My parental units are still stuck in the 60s and don't believe in the formal ed-ucational system, so I'm home-schooled." She is living a Spice Girls wannabe world after having performed in a band and will take risks and try things she does not feel comfortable with. "When it comes to people, I'm outgoing and protective of my friends. When they get hurt, I arm myself with some truth, major mojo and tarot cards."

Davis, born July 5 (Cancer), loves neapolitan ice cream and the color neon orange. He claims he can build anything out of Legos.

Colin, born September 13 (Virgo) likes the color orange and chocolate chip ice cream. "I would say I can be a bit of an extremist at times, but it's only because I feel I have to protect myself and the ones I love. I make it clear that I am not your friend until you earn that title, and you can't just approach me in any kind of way. This attitude can cause some tension between me and my best friend, Slake, and my baby sister, Kris, who's technically my step-sister. But, I'm not a total buzz kill. I know how to have fun: I'm just not pressed like the rest."

Yasmine, a Pisces, was born on March 7 and tin roof banana split is her desert choice (she also likes the color—not the movie—purple). She considers herself the most popular girl in school ("I mean everybody wishes they were me. I have the cutest clothes, the cutest hairstyles, the cutest accessories, the nicest house. Who could ask for more?"). "There's not much to say about me except I like guys; guys like me, and a lot of girls are jealous of me. Okay, I know this sounds a little full of myself, but I'm a nice girl. I'm not a Drama Queen, like Maggie. I'm really chill and I love to have parties. So if you ever see me hanging around, don't be afraid to say hi!"

Kristina, a Taurus (born April 26) loves rocky road ice cream, the color yellow and says, "I'm pretty quiet and shy around people I don't know very well; so making friends isn't always easy for me. Once you get to know me, I'm super friendly and a completely loyal and devoted friend."

Brianna, who loves peach ice cream and bright colors, is an Aquarius (born February 17) and has set her sights on becoming a rapper.

Slake, a Gemini (born in June) is a ladies' man (his favorite color is whatever a girl's eyes are) and mint choco chip is his favorite flavor of ice cream. "I know, like, five chords on guitar, but if anyone asks me if I play an instrument, I always say I'm kind of a virtuoso. There's a couple things people like to know about me: yes, my hair is naturally curly, and yes, you can touch it. Colin and I go way back, and that story stays between him and me."

Travis, favorite color red, is a Sagittarius (born December 20), He likes chocolate ice cream. "Okay, here's what you need to know about Travis. Think of me as a facilitator. See, I know safe is boring. So I got ahead and raised the stakes. If nothing's safe, then nobody's bored. I'm always down to get down and when I'm around, you can be absolutely sure that you're gonna have a story to tell tomorrow."

Laura, born November 2 (Scorpio) loves the color black and dark chocolate chunk ice cream. She is a Goth girl, can play bass and is considered "the scary but cool girl in black." "I'm the quiet, moody, and somewhat scary girl who always wears all black. But I promise I'm not that scary. I'm friends with everyone in the group, except Yasmine. She's way too full of herself."

Roxanne, a Virgo (born September 19) loves the color pastel pink and orange sherbet ice cream. She can knit and is loyal to her friends, charming and a free-spirit. "I'm the only child of the wealthy Grey Family and because my father battles alcoholism, and my mother is obsessed with being a socialite, I've grown up quickly. At times, my maturity contrasts with my friends, but I try to use it to hold everyone together. I've made my friends my family, especially Beth, Sarah, Kris, Maggie, and Yasmine."

Fumkie, born May 6 (Taurus) is fond of the color green and peanut butter cup ice cream. As she says, "Hey what's up you guys, this is Fumike. I'm an 18-year-old, fun loving individual. I love eclectic vintage clothes and take a lot of pride in my style. I love music! Hanging out with my friends and such. My friends are like my life. They are basically the coolest people I know."

Adrian, a 22-year-old bike messenger hangs out with the teenage students. He is a Libra (born October 5), likes vanilla ice cream and the color burnt umber.

Sam, a young man with no apparent goals says of himself, "I'm too cool to be tied down by anything: labels, girlfriends, dumb drama. My days are spent cruising in my 1986 Red Thunderbird and checking my pager that is near constantly blowing up. My latest life dilemma: whether I'm feeling Jackie, SUPER hot and mysterious, or Alex, all brooding and moody. God, my life is so tough. Gotta bounce.... Mahalo!"

Cast: Ellen Winter (Sarah Roberts), Katie Foster (Gwen Ennis), Rachel Peters (Alex Anders), George Ross (Ryan Whistler), Storm Garner (Chloe Bastion), Kristin Rogers (Tamsin English), Donnis Collins (Liberty "Libby"), DeAndre Baker (Drew Wilson), Albert Tholen (Rob), Orla Conway (Remington "Remi" Davis), Aleca Piper (Maggie Frederick), Desirae Zentz (Strawberry Shortcake), Sarah Hirsch (Cassandra), Roberto Carmona (Sam), Clayton Pelham (Colin Mitchell), Le'Asha Julius (Yasmine Barhum), Verity Allen (Kristina Mitchell), Billie Krishawn (Brianna Lewis), Jesse Swire (Slake Ostler), Andrew Cohen (Travis Kauffman), Hannah Goldman (Laura Mortison), Laura Long (Roxanne Grey), Antonio Tillman (Fumike Okoye), Roberto Carmona (Sam), Nick Libowitz (Adrian Johnson).
Credits: *Producer-Writer-Director:* Otessa Ghadar.
Comment: The acting and production values are very good and the characters and story lines well developed. It is a change of pace from what a number

of student-oriented web (and television) series have done, in that it is a surprisingly pleasant diversion from the rest.

Episodes: Following is a season-by-season listing of episode titles. All of Season 1 episodes have been taken off-line with the exception of a 2 minute and 38 second recap.

Season 1 Episodes:
1. Orange Crush.
2. Will You Be There Tonight?
3. Boys Night Out.
4. Yasmine's House.
5. Misery in McMansions.
6, 7, 8. Midnight, Hunter's Moon, Parts 1, 2 and 3.
9. Fleshy Ears.
10. Operator.
11. Whisper Down the Lane.
12. Brutus and Caesar Will Have Their Revenge on DC.
13. The Secret Halloween Easter Egg.

Season 2 Episodes:
1. Have a Good Summer.
2. Hearsay, Rumor & Scuttlebutt.
3. Carly's Birthday.
4. L+T & S+G.
5. Do You Like Me?
6. Yes or No.
7. Not Your Training Bra.
8. You're My Needle and I Found You.
9. Poor Cinderella.
10. Trouble in Paradise.
11. The Lunar Landing.

Season 3 Episodes:
1. The Friend Percent.
2. Escape to Candyland.
3. Cavort in the Borg.
4. Doors of Perception.
5. Worst Day Ever.
6. Best Served Cold.
7. Something to Put in Your Hat.
8. A Simple Answer.
9. Ding Dong Ditch.

Season 4 Episodes:
1. Sarah Live! At Comet Ping Pong Tonight.
2. C Is for Clandestine.
3. Ask Me Anything.
4. Paradise Found.
5. Break Up or Stay Together.
6. The Recruit.
7. Freshman at Beach Week Music Video.

Season 5 Episodes:
1. Summer of '97.
2. The Audition.
3. What the Cards Hold.
4. Signed, Sealed & Delivered.
5. Trial Expired.
6. Go Fish.
7. Fairytale in the Supermarket.

Season 6 Episodes:

1. Summer of '97 Continues.
2. Brought to You By the Letters DXM.
3, Have You Seen My Friends?
4. Berries, Cream and Untold Dreams.
5. Taking Out the Trash.
6. Table for Two.
Season 7 Episodes:
1. There's More Than One of Everything.
2. The Dust Bowl.
3. Gordon's Dilemma.
4. The Giant Mumbles in His Sleep.
5. Firehook.
6. GOA.
7. Not St. Elsewhere.

232 *Other Men.* othermenseries.tunblr.com. 2014 (Drama).

It has been one year since Jerry, a young gay man, had moved from a small town to Toronto, Canada, to pursue an English degree at college. It is revealed that a playwright (Hank) had not only taken him under his wing but had become his lover. Exactly what will develop is unknown as only a pilot has been produced and it basically deals with Jerry reflecting on his first year as he sought to find a place for himself in "Toronto's queer community."

Cast: Nathan Carroll (Jerry), Jonathan Nathaniel (Odie), G. Kyle Shields (Hank). **Credits:** *Producer:* Adam Klymkiw, Illya Klymkiw. *Director:* Stephanie Coffey. *Writer:* Ben Ladouceur. **Comment:** The program is well produced and acted but does contain vulgar language. Information regarding the plot has been given based on the episode; the producer states: "It is hard to say just how the plot will develop. Will the entire series take place within one year, or will we see Jerry move on from his reflection? One thing is for sure: there's little of the sassy wit of stereotyped gay humor we've become accustomed to in many web series.... It is a refreshing and dramatic twist on the genre."

Episodes:
1. Pilot. Establishes a story line that places Jerry in college but what direction actual episodes will take is unknown (continue the flashback situation or place Jerry in the present and detail his life as a gay in college).

233 *The Out Crowd.* theoutcrowd.tv. 2013–2014 (Comedy-Drama).

Marshall, a young man living in New York City, is a twenty-something late bloomer in admitting the fact that he is gay. He has suppressed all his feelings and must now, for the first time face life "being out" while trying to fit in. The program follows his struggles as he seeks not only love but success, acceptance and friendship as well.

Cast: Liki Wright (Marshall), Maribel Martinez (Lina), Hzekial White (Raquan), Ashton Pina (Nan-

tucket). **Credits:** *Producer-Writer:* Liki Wright. *Director:* Ashton Pina. **Comment:** Enjoyable mix of comedy and light drama with good acting and production values (although some scenes in the third episode are dimly lit). Although the program ends unresolved, the doorway has been left open for the story to continue.

Episodes:
1. The First Time. Marshall is introduced and begins to realize that the only difference between who he is (gay) and what he is not (heterosexual) is perspective. It is also his first time getting dumped then getting drunk as an after effect.
2. A Night in Nantucket. Marshall attempts to wiggle his way out of a sticky situation when he hooks up with a man he later discovers is everything he detests.
3. No Fats, No Fems. To hopefully jump-start his faltering love life, Marshall joins an Internet dating site—with a profile composed by his friend Lina that is really not him. The program's concluding episode.

234 *Out with Dad.* outwithdad.com. 2010–2014 (Drama).

Rose Miller, the 15-year-old daughter of freelance graphic designer Nathan Miller, lives in Toronto, Canada. Rose's late mother was named Sarah and her best friends are Vanessa and Kenny. Rose appears to be a typical girl until she finds that she has become attracted to Vanessa (and Vanessa to her) and they share a first kiss together. The program explores what happens to Rose when she comes to realize she is drawn to girls and how the situation affects the people who are close to her.

Claire is the lesbian who later becomes close to Rose; Alicia is Kenny's girlfriend; Angela is Nathan's romantic interest, a realtor; Johnny is Nathan's gay friend and advisor; Dave is an architect and Nathan's work partner; Theresa is Vanessa's mother; Steven is Vanessa's father; Jacob is Vanessa's younger brother; Marion is Claire's mother; Ted is Claire's father; Brian is Claire's brother; Matthew is Vanessa's older brother; Fatima is Matthew's wife. See also *Vanessa's Story*, the spin off series.

Cast: Kate Conway (Rose Miller), Will Conlon, Jonathan Robbins (Nathan Miller), Lindsey Middleton (Vanessa LeMay), Catherine Medrek (Claire Daniels), Corey Lof (Kenny), Laura Jabalee (Alicia Van Haren), Kelly-Marie Murtha (Angela), Darryl Dinn (Johnny), Wendy Glazier (Theresa Le May), Robert Nolan (Steven LeMay), Jennifer Kenneally (Marion Daniels), Andrew Kinos (Ted Daniels), Daniel Solokhine (Brian Daniels), Neil Silcox (Matthew LeMay), Afshan Golriz (Fatima Le-May).**Credits:** *Producer:* Jason Leaver, Eric Taylor, Kara Dymond, Rebecca Rynsoever, Josh Ary. *Writer-Director:* Jason Leaver. *Composer:* Adrian Ellis. **Comment:** Well-acted, written, directed and produced program that honestly deals with a sensi-

Out with Dad. Jonathan Robbins and Kate Conway (copyright JLeaver Presentations, 2014).

tive topic and how it affects teenage girls. While there are kissing scenes, they are tastefully done and the situations encountered by Rose are also handled with care. A fourth season of episodes is in production and will no doubt follow in the tradition set by the prior episodes.

Episodes:

1. Rose with Vanessa. Rose is introduced as she shares her first kiss with Vanessa then becomes a bit confused as to what has just happened.

2. Out to Lunch. When Rose's father suspects that Rose may be a lesbian, he seeks advice from Johnny, his gay friend, on how to deal with the situation.

3. Movie Night with Dad. As Rose begins to realize what is happening and that she prefers girls, Nathan attempts to bond with Rose in an attempt to open up about her sexuality.

4. Party Out. At a party Rose believes her secret may be revealed when a friend notices she is dancing with Vanessa rather than a boy.

5. Blind Date with Nathan. As Rose's party continues, Nathan meets Angela on a blind date set up by Johnny for him. Hoping to get some advice, Nathan reveals his beliefs about Rose to Angela.

6. Tea with Dad. The party ends, Nathan's date ends and Rose and Nathan conclude the day by discussing their night out over a cup of tea.

7. Chemistry with Vanessa. As Rose and Vanessa study for a chemistry exam, they each find they are sexually attracted to the other.

8. Out with Kenny. In an attempt to build up the courage to tell her father about her liking girls, Rose practices first by revealing her secret to best friend Kenny. Season one concludes.

9. Out with Dad. As season two opens, Rose builds up the courage and reveals her sexual preferences to her father.

10. Asking Out Alicia. When Rose notices that Kenny has become attracted to Alicia (their schoolmate) she helps Kenny work up the courage to ask her for a date.

11. Having It Out. Theresa, Vanessa's close-minded mother, fears for Vanessa when she discovers that Rose is a lesbian and, hoping to protect her from the "evil" that Rose has become, forbids her to hang out with Rose.

12. With Jacob and Vanessa. The situation between Vanessa and Rose has Vanessa's parents arguing while Jacob, Vanessa's younger brother, fears losing her like his older brother Matthew (who was "pushed away" for marrying a Muslim girl named Fatima).

13. Striking Out. As Vanessa tries to come to terms with her mother's demands, Alicia begins to fear Rose (not knowing she is a lesbian) and her continual involvement with Kenny (as they are just best friends).

14. Working It Out. With the situation between Rose and Vanessa becoming increasingly troublesome for all concerned, Nathan again seeks Johnny's help, this time being advised to attend a PFLAG (Parents, Family and Friends of Lesbians and Gays) meeting.

15. Out with PFLAG, Part 1. Rose, believing PFLAG could help, joins with Nathan and Johnny and attends a meeting.

16. Out with PFLAG, Part 2. At the meeting, Rose befriends a woman (Claire) facing the same challenges.

17. Chatting with Claire. Rose and Claire's attraction to each other appears to be drawing them closer together.

18. The Museum Outing. Rose, excited about her new friendship with Claire, invites Kenny to meet her at work (at the Scarborough Historical Museum in Toronto).

19. Out with Doubts. An uncomfortable situation arises for Rose when, at a café with Claire, she meets Vanessa and her suppressed feelings for her begin to surface again.

20. Out of Mind. Realizing that seeing Vanessa has changed Rose, Claire attempts to help by getting Rose to open up about her. Season two concludes.

21. Starting Out. The chance meeting at the café has also affected Vanessa, who is now finding it difficult to keep away from Rose. Meanwhile Rose has accepted an invitation from Claire for dinner at her house. Season 3 begins.

22. Dining In & Out. As Rose meets Claire's family and prepares for dinner, Nathan finds that Angela is upset that he has not told Rose about his relationship with her.

23. Storming In & Out. Although Claire is older than Rose, they are sexually drawn to each other and begin kissing—only to be caught by Claire's father and ostracized.

24. Swashbuckling Adventures of Making Out. A date at the movies for Rose and Claire becomes more than just watching a film (*Pete Winning and the Pirates*) when they begin kissing. Unknown to Rose, a classmate is spying on her.

25. Outed. The following day at school Rose faces the unkind consequences of her movie night with Claire when word starts spreading about what happened and that Rose is a lesbian.

26. Out with Song and Dance. Claire tries to help Rose deal with the situation at school and Vanessa, desperate to be with Rose, runs away from home. In a unique twist, situations are presented in song and dance (and very well done) to celebrate Rose's coming out. See *Vanessa's Story* for the episodes dealing with Vanessa from this point on.

27. Hanging Out. After spending an enjoyable day together on Toronto Beach, Rose and Nathan return home to learn from Vanessa's distraught father, that Vanessa has run away and her whereabouts are unknown.

28. Going Out. As Rose, Kenny and Claire try to make sense out of what Vanessa has done, Nathan prepares for a date with Angela. By chance, Rose and Claire run into Nathan and Angela at a sidewalk café. It is Rose's first meeting with Angela and the four agree on a double date.

29. Double Date with Dad. While the double date appeared to be a bit awkward at first, it turns out for the best when Rose believes Angela is the perfect girl for her father. But for Rose, it also brings back memories of her feelings for Vanessa.

30. Pushed Out. The situation at her Catholic school becomes increasingly difficult for Rose when she encounters the wrath of Brittany Robinson, a school Queen Bee. In the girls locker room Brittany refuses to have Rose near her while she and several other girls change clothes and orders that she leave. A confrontation ensues with Brittany pushing Rose to the floor, calling her "a lesbo" and kicking her in the stomach.

31. Stressing Out. Although she attempts to keep secret what happened at school from her father, Nathan feels something is troubling Rose and believes attending another meeting at PFLAG may help her deal with it.

32. Out with PFLAG, Part 3. Various stories are related by the PFLAG members as Rose tries to deal with what is now happening (being bullied) and Nathan seeks to learn what is truly bothering her.

33. Out with PFLAG, Part 4. The meeting results in Nathan learning that Rose had been bullied at school and, as the two have a heart-to-heart talk, Rose's friends, Claire, Alicia and Nowmee (Harprett Sehmbi) discuss the possibility of forming a Gay-Straight Alliance at their school.

34. Getting It Out. Rose builds up the courage to face what has happened between her and Brittany and seeks help from the school principal.

35. With Family and Friends. Having seen first hand what Rose is experiencing, Nathan faces his own parents and tells them that their grandchild is a lesbian. The third season concludes with plans to celebrate Rose's upcoming birthday.

Note: There are also a series of twelve videos wherein Rose relates incidents from her childhood in a series of short videos.

1. Rose's Video Diary #1: My First Video Diary.

2. Rose's Video Diary #2: School Days.

3. Rose's Video Diary #3: Changing Relationships.

4. Rose's Video Diary #4: My Pen Pal Penny.

5. Rose's Video Diary #5: Inspiring Bravery.

6. Rose's Video Diary #6: My Dad Is Seeing Someone.

7. Rose's Video Diary #7: Being LGBT in Catholic School.

8. Rose's Video Diary #8: Perfect Moment.

9. Rose's Video Diary #9: First Memory.

10. Rose's Video Diary #10: Body Issues.

11. Rose's Video Diary #11: Chai Latte.

12. Rose's Video Diary #12: The Spaghetti Scoop Conspiracy.

235 The Outs. theouts.squarespace.com. 2012 (Comedy-Drama).

Brooklyn, New York, provides the backdrop for a look at the lives of two gay men (Mitchell and Jack) and their straight best friend Oona. The story begins with Mitchell and Jack ending their long term relationship (unable to work out their differences) and seeking to move on (although it is evident they still have feelings for each other). It then proceeds to focus on their (and Mitchell's roommate Oona's) efforts to navigate the dating scene, find that special someone and just figure things out.

Cast: Adam Goldman (Mitchell), Hunter Canning (Jack), Sasha Winters (Oona), Michael Hanson (Keith), Jordan Barbour (Owen), Tommy Heleringer (Scruffy), Kate Dearing (Amy), Shawn Frank (Russell), Alaine Livingston (Beth), Philip Taratula (Ty). **Credits:** *Producer:* Adam Goldman, Amelia Keiser, Amanda Warman, Joanna Gurin, Melissa Tapper-Goldman, Jack Jackson. *Director:* Adam Goldman. *Writer:* Adam Goldman (story by Adam Goldman and Sasha Winters). **Comment:** While some may be offended by the excessive use of vulgar language, the program is well acted and produced. The characters of Mitch and Oona are especially appealing: Mitch for his vulnerability and Oona, for the hidden insecurities she tries to hide through sexual encounters but inevitably affect her search for the perfect man.

Episodes:

1. State of the Union. The three principal characters are introduced with Jack seeking to build up the courage to embark on a first date after his breakup with Mitchell.

2. Whiskey Dick. At a reunion party for her high school classmates, Oona persuades Mitchell to pose as her boyfriend to make her ex boyfriend, Tucker (Aaron Matteson), jealous. It works in a way as Oona hooks up with a classmate named Russell.

3. Moon River. As Mitchell tells Oona that the only thing he has to look forward to is the party she is planning to throw, he retreats to his apartment to listen to every version of the song "Moon River" that he can find on the Internet.

4. Fun Party. Mitchell's life takes a turn for the better when he attends Oona's lavish party but over indulges in alcohol and finds it necessary to call Jack for help in getting home.

5. F**king It Up. As Mitchell recovers from his drunken stupor, he realizes that he needs Jack back in his life and sets his goal to overlook what has happened and win him back.

6. Significant Others. Mitchell's pursuit of Jack is proving fruitless as Jack feels comfortable with a new hookup. Meanwhile, Oona seeks Mitchell's help in dealing with Russell, who is not the overly romantic man she would like.

7. Over It: The Outs Chanukah Special. The concluding episode that is set during the Christmas-Chanukah season and relates incidents in the lives of Mitchell, Oona and Jack as they reflect their lives and the relationships they have made.

236 The Peculiar Kind. thepeculiarkind.com. 2013 (Reality).

Unscripted interviews and conversations are used to candidly explore the lives and careers "of queer women of color."

Cast as credited: Ivette, Murielle, Jade Foster, K.C., Sara, Mila. *News Segment Host:* Kimberley McLeod. **Credits:** *Producer-Director:* Alexis Casson, Mursi Layne. **Comment:** Informative, well-done program that while geared to the African-American woman, explores issues that can affect any race.

Episode List: *1.* Party Etiquette. *2.* Gender Roles. *3.* For Hire. *4.* Where I'm From. *5.* Pillow Talk. *6.* Queers in the Media. *7.* Church vs. State: A Look at Family and Religion. *8.* Artist Spotlight. *9.* AfroPunk Fest Recap. *10.* LGBT Homeless Youth.

237 People You Know. peopleyouknowthe series.com. 2014 (Drama).

"No one can tell you how your life will be once you are on your own. You have an idea that you imagined all your life" and following that idea forms the basis of the series as a group of people, who have become like a family, are profiled as they seek everything they ever wanted—from money, power and love and what happens when the unexpected enters the picture "and you lose control of your life and your surroundings and your family are ripped apart. How can you handle it? Who can you depend on?"

Lucas Marquez is a venomous, master manipulator (of people's emotions) who will use whatever means possible to get what he wants, most importantly becoming head of a powerful public relations firm.

Monty St. James is a brilliant psychologist whose passion for helping others often prevents him from pursuing his own goals.

Jenna Naidu is an over-achiever and has to be the best at what she does; second best is something that is not in her vocabulary. She is devoted to the ones she loves and can be considered the voice of reason among her friends (and lovers).

Mia St. James is presented as "The Dream Girl," the girl who has that girl-next-door persona and is not only every guy's fantasy but the obsession of every girl that sees her. She is very intuitive and can pick up on the subtle differences in her surroundings and in the people she meets.

Patrick Carter, called "The King of the Great White Way," is an older gentleman who has seen his share of happiness and tragedy and is now determined to guide the younger generation on a path that will let them avoid the mistakes he has made.

Reese Adams is a party animal (first to arrive and the last to leave) whose deep-rooted insecurities often place him in uncomfortable situations that often cause him nothing but trouble.

Billy Bennett, born in Australia and raised in England, left home following "harrowing circumstances." He relocated to New York City where he incorporates his street smarts to survive.

Christian Torres is a brilliant defense attorney who, although he longs for a 1980s-like fantasy life and happy endings, is described as "a cut-throat Cuban wolf in the courtroom, but a puppy in his daily life."

Brady Campbell is a voracious reader and the program's HGN (Hot Gay Nerd). His intellect and physique, he feels, will bring "all the men to his yard."

Emma Young, called "The Fallen Angel," is an infectious girl with a vivacious rocker-like attitude who can command attention wherever she goes.

Cast: John Dylan DeLaTorre (Lucas Marquez), Baltimore Russell (Monty St. James), Jaime Elise Summers (Mia St. James), Salma Shaw (Jenna Naidu), Chris Costa (Christian Torres), Aaron Schoonover (Reese Adams), Blaine Pennington (Brady Campbell), Danielle Leaf (Emma Young), Lee Mitchell (Billy Bennett), Jevon McFerrin (Steven Jackson). **Credits:** *Producer:* John Dylan DeLaTorre, Baltimore Russell. *Director:* Rob Margolies, Michael D. Akers. *Writer:* John Dylan DeLaTorre, Baltimore Russell. **Comment:** Although the actual episodes are not available for free, watching the series teaser gives one a good idea of what the program is all about. It is well produced and acted and, in soap opera–like fashion, will detail the triumphs and tragedies that each of the main characters faces, including gay, lesbian and straight relationships.

Episodes: Episodes are available through a paid subscription service. The following videos can be viewed for free:

1. Episode 3 Preview: Moving On.
2. Episode 4 Preview: Mixed Signals.
3. People You Know Interview with Aaron Schoonover.
4. People You Know Interview with Salma Shaw, Part 1.
5. People You Know Interview with Salma Shaw, Part 2.
6. People You Know Interview with Blaine Pennington, Part 1.
7. People You Know Interview with Blaine Pennington, Part 2.
8. People You Know Interview with Chris Costa, Part 1.
9. People You Know Interview with Chris Costa, Part 2.
10. People You Know Interview with Jaime Summers, Part 1.
11. People You Know Interview with Jaime Summers, Part 2.
12. People You Know: Official Series Trailer.
13. People You Know: Pilot Preview.

Episode List: *1.* I Do, I Don't, Part 1. *2.* I Do, I Don't, Part 2. *3.* Moving On. *4.* Mixed Signals. *5.* Follow Your Bliss. *6.* Let's Do Brunch.

238 *Perks the Musical.* blip.tv/perks/perks-pilot-5291172. 2011 (Musical Comedy).

Courtney is a beautiful young woman who has become the obsession of a tech-savvy gamer named Josh. Josh, however, is too shy to even approach Courtney and just admires her from afar. When Darwin, Josh's gay best friend, realizes that Josh's infatuation with Courtney is dulling his gaming senses, he decides to help and together they devise a means by which Josh can impress Courtney—by writing a musical to express his feelings for her based on her favorite book *The Perks of Being a Wallflower*. Encompassing the style of a Broadway production, the program tells a love story through song and dance as Josh attempts to win the love of Courtney—before he loses her to Matt, the man who also has set his sights on her.

Cast: Allison Strong (Courtney), Alex Wyse (Josh), Alex Brightman (Darwin), Paul Cereghino (Matt), Arden Myrin (Miss Pilgrim), Ghana Leigh (Librarian). **Classmates:** Kristine Hsia, Mitch Dean, Derek St. Pierre, Felicia Blum, Brittney Lee Hamilton, Ravi Roth, Anich D'Jae, Howah Hung, Noah Zachary, Antonio Addeo, Jessica Angleskhan, Carrie Salmon, Aaron Riesebeck, Koe Popson. **Vocalists:** Alex Wyse, Allison Strong, Alex Brightman, Paul Cereghino, Hayley Podschun, Anich D'Jae. Kendal Hartse, Mitch Dean, Derek St. Pierre, Felicia Blum, Brittney Lee Hamilton, Ravi Roth. **Credits:** *Producer-Writer:* Tom Diggs. *Director:* Bill Oliver. *Music:* Jason Michael Snow. *Lyrics/Choreography:* Mishaela Faucher. **Comment:** Off-Broadway and up-and-coming Broadway performers are featured in a lively production that is somewhat lost on the Internet as it requires the resources of a broadcast or cable network to be appreciated (virtually all other forms of entertainment work well on the Internet, but musicals, rare as they are on the Internet, feel out of place and more geared to a television broadcast). Allison Strong has appeared on Broadway in *Bye Bye Birdie* and *Mama Mia*; Alex Wyse in *Lysistrata Jones* and Alex Brightman in *Wicked*. Anyone familiar with the song *Johnny Angel* (by Shelley Fabares of *The Donna Reed Show*) may associate *Perks* to it as it told the story of a girl who fantasized about a boy who didn't even know she existed.

Episodes:
1. Perks (Pilot). Josh has fallen head-over-heels in love with Courtney but is unable to approach her until he and his friend Darwin devise a way—write a musical based on her favorite book.
2. The Making of Perks. A look at the choreography used for the program by choreographer Mishaela Faucher.
3. The Making of Perks—Actor's Advice. A second look at the making of *Perks* by actors Brittney Lee Hamilton, Felicia Blum, Howah Hung, Anich D'Jae and Carrie Salmon.

239 *Plan V.* youtube.com. 2009 (Drama).

Argentina provides the setting for a foreign-produced version of *The L Word* that explores the life of a gorgeous, 30-year-old lesbian (Ana) with a rocky romantic life and the changes that occur in her life when she meets a captivating girl (Laura), falls deeply in love with her then discovers she is her brother's (Martin) girlfriend. As Ana contends with her share of problems, both romantic and personal, the program also focuses on her close-knit group of friends—Flor, a party girl, and Mara and Pato (a couple).

Cast: Lorena Romanin (Ana), Sofia Wilhelmi (Laura), Diego Gentle (Martin), Serrana Diaz (Mara), Maruja Bustamante (Pato), Gael Rossi (Dario), Gaby Bex (Flor), Martin Lavini (Ezequiel), Armenia Martinez (Zulma), Mariana Otero (Emilia). **Credits:** *Producer:* Sofia Wilhelmi, Maria Solari. *Director:* Maruja Bustamante, Lorena Romanin. *Writer:* Lorena Romanin, Sofia Wilhelmi, Maruja Bustamante. **Comment:** While America's *The L Word* stood for "Lesbian" Argentina's *Plan V* stands for, according to the producer "Vagina." The produced episodes have English captioning, are lavishly filmed and very well acted. It is also a known fact that Spanish-language programs, such as the soap operas produced for Univision and Telemondo, incorporate only the most beautiful women and most handsome men. This is not the case here as the cast is average-looking and, while there are sexual situations, the annoying shaky (unsteady) method of filming does not help move things along; it proves to be just the opposite as scenes of people talking to each other do not have to bob up-and-down and from side-to-side (unless the intent is to make one a bit nauseous).

Season 1 Episode Titles: *1.* Es Obvio. *2.* La Que Duerme Con Chicas. *3.* No Robaras, Parte 1. *4.* No Robaras, Parte 2. *5.* Es Lo Que Parece. *6.* Cuando es No, es Yes. *7.* No se, te Estoy Levantando. *8.* Perdon, no Puedo. *9.* Alfrolatino 2005, con Vibrador. *10.* Que Haces, Laura? *11.* Lo Dejamos Aca?

Season Two: Twelve untitled episodes simply marked as "Season 2, Episode 1," "Season 2, Episode 2," etc.

240 *Planet Unicorn.* youtube.com/watch?v=L6UWR0kSFcE. 2007 (Cartoon).

It is the year 2117 and life has changed dramatically for some children for as young as the age of eight they have come to realize that they are gay. Shannon is one such boy and while attracted to other boys he also has a fascination with unicorns, the mythical horse with a horn on its forehead. One day life changes forever for Shannon when he finds a magic lamp and is granted three wishes. A fur coat and a flying car encompass his first two wishes, but for that last wish, he asks for a planet populated by unicorns, three of which he befriends and names Cadillac, Feathers and Tom Cruise. The program explores Shannon's experiences on Planet Unicorn as he and his friends learn lessons about life.

Voice Cast: Mike Rose (Shannon/Cadillac), Drew Droege (Feathers), Tyler Spiers (Tom Cruise).

Credits: *Producer:* Mike Rose, Tyler Spiers. **Comment:** Amusing program that explores life through unicorns. The animation is a bit stiff and does not compare to the standards set by cartoons produced for broadcast or cable TV (even in those produced in the 1960s for Saturday morning TV).

Episodes:
1. Episode 1. Shannon meets the unicorns for the first time after making his third wish.
2. Episode 2. As Shannon learns about unicorns, the unicorns learn about expressing emotions through him.
3. Episode 3. Shannon and the unicorns encounter their first adventure when they make a trip to the sea.
4. Episode 4. The sin of vanity threatens to destroy the friendship between the unicorns.
5. Episode 5. The unicorns become jealous when Shannon makes a new friend and fears losing him to someone else.
6. Episode 6. The unicorns learn about Christmas when they take the place of Santa's reindeer while the reindeer explore Planet Unicorn.

241 *Portraits.* youtube.com/watch?v=L6UWR0kSFcE. 2014 (Comedy-Drama).

Brazilian-produced program that looks at the lives of five young gay men and women as they deal with the issues of their sexual orientation in a society (whether here or abroad) that doesn't always accept them for who they are; their experiences are the "Portraits" through which others facing the same circumstances can learn to accept who they are.

Cast: Victor Corujeira, Luna Kruschewsky, Marcos Barreto, Mirella Matteo, Albert Elliot Lira, Daniel Becker, Jorge D'Santos, Clarissa Napoli, Josy Luz, Ricardo Albuquerque, Marcelo Dantas. **Credits:** *Producer-Director:* Raphael Garden. **Comment:** Sexual situations, brief, partial nudity and excellent acting highlight a well-produced foreign series that provides a sensitive look at both gay and lesbians, some of whom conceal their secret while others are openly admitted. The program is in Portuguese and the closed captioning feature needs to be activated to see English subtitles. Its original title is *Retratos* but its translated title *Portraits* will also come up in searches.

Episode List: *1.* Retratos 1×01—Alex e Théo (Gay Series). *2.* Retratos 1×02—Lara e Pietra (Gay Series). *3.* Retratos 1×03—Levítico 18:22 (Gay Series). *4.* Retratos (Portraits)—Gay Series—Teaser.

242 *Prettyboy.* prettyboywebseries.com. 2013 (Reality).

Billed as "a real-life look inside of being a lesbian in today's world," the program explores, through a group of African-American lesbians, their struggles after coming "out of the closet."

Host: Ruth Carter. *Cast as credited:* Brandi, Nic, Ink Poison, Kid, Chili, Unique, Shavina, Stacy, Kay-Kay, Aja, Desi. **Credits:** *Producer:* Kim Monday. **Comment:** Only a teaser appears to remain on line and from it one can see that it is an interview-like program and encompasses off-center images of its subject (as Chili, in the teaser, is favored to the right of the screen) and varying lighting effects (from dark to light and soft to harsh).

Episodes:

1. Teaser. A short overview of the program that features a young woman named Chili.

243 *The Pride and Pretense of Eirik.* you tube.com. 2011 (Comedy).

The conversation held between a gay young man (Eirik) and his gay friends (one per episode).

Cast: Jeffrey Self (Eirik), Jim Hansen (Jim), Ben Campbell (Ben), Tom DeTrinnis (Tom). **Credits:** *Producer:* Jeffrey Self, Jim Hansen. *Director:* Jim Hansen. *Writer:* Jeffrey Self. **Comment:** A simplistic program that showcases Eirik as he discusses a matter with a friend. The presentation is well done with good acting and short, right-to-the-point stories.

Episodes:

1. Eirik and Jim. Eirik questions Jim as to why he never responds to his twitters.

2. Eirik and Ben. Eirik and Ben discuss eating and what people consume.

3. Eirik and Tom. Eirik talks to Tom about his fascination with a handbag he saw in a store and how he was compelled to buy it.

244 *Producing Juliet.* producingjuliet. com. 2013–2014 (Drama).

Rebecca Welles, a corporate executive, and Laura Gordon, an actress, are in love but also in an open relationship with a third girl (Michelle). Rebecca and Laura's relationship appears to be a happy one although Rebecca feels somewhat neglected as Laura is more focused on her acting career than on her. One night, after attending Laura's performance in a play called *Comforts of Home* at The Secret Theater, Rebecca meets Juliet Bello, the play's struggling author. As Rebecca becomes friendly with Juliet, she believes she has found a new focus in life and impulsively decides to resign from her job to produce Juliet's second play (*When I Imagined You with Me*). As Rebecca comes to know Juliet, she learns that Juliet has feelings for, but has never become romantically involved with Evan, her gay friend (currently in a relationship with a man named Henry). Evan has feelings for Juliet but is unable to accept the thought of becoming her lover. Rebecca, although in an open relationship, desires more attention from Laura; Juliet must come to terms with her feelings for and relationship with Evan; and Evan must choose between Juliet and Henry. The program relates the choices each must make to achieve the happiness each desires.

Cast: Alisha Spielmann (Rebecca Welles), Rachael Hip-Flores (Juliet Bello), Jenny Grace (Laura Gordon), Andy Phelan (Evan), Betty Kaplan (Andrea), Stacey Raymond (Michelle), David Drake (Henry), Chinaza Uche (Jacob Aarons), Kevin Sebastian (Richard Nichols). **Credits** *Producer:* Tina Cesa Ward, Rochelle Dancel, Allison Vanore. *Writer-Director:* Tina Cesa Ward. **Comment:** Exceptionally well acted and produced drama with a story line that flows smoothly from beginning to end. The cast is well chosen and each plays their role to perfection.

Episodes:

1. Producing Juliet Pilot. The story line is established as Rebecca meets Juliet for the first time.

2. Necessary Condition. As Rebecca makes a life-changing decision to resign from her job and produce Juliet's second play, an intimate look at her and Laura's relationship is also seen.

3. The Play's the Thing, Part 1. Rebecca's new venture has Laura wondering how this will affect their relationship while Evan fears he will lose Juliet forever.

4. The Play's the Thing, Part 2. As Evan confronts Juliet about her play he learns that it is literally about her and how she is desperately struggling to find a way to move on without him (as he can't have her and his boyfriend, Henry); meanwhile as Rebecca commits herself to producing Juliet's play (and acquires the help of Andrea, the theater producer), Laura begins the first move to rekindle her romance with Rebecca.

Producing Juliet. **Series title card (copyright Ward Picture Company, Inc.).**

245 Prop 8: The Web Series. youtube.com. 2009 (Comedy).

Comical vignettes that explore what could happen if your rights were stripped away and, in essence, the government controlled your very life, including what you can but mostly cannot due. It is also pokes fun at the LGBT community as each episode concludes with a character saying, "At least the gays can't get married."

Cast: Benny Fine (U.S. Agent 1), Rafi Fine (U.S. Agent 2). Other cast members are listed with their respective episodes. **Credits:** *Producer-Writer-Director:* Benny Fine, Rafi Fine. **Comment:** Each episode strips away a part of the California Constitution, especially Proposition 8 (taking away same sex marriages) in short episodes that are more frightening (if such a thing could happen) than comical. The acting is very good and the episodes just the right length as not to become over indulgent on the subject being tackled; they are straight and right to the point. Although episodes geared specifically to the LGBT community had not yet been produced, such stories would have been told and a good example as to what would have happened can be seen by what transpired in the "Religion" episode.

Episodes:

1. Religion. A young couple (Bard Fletcher, Sara Fletcher), enjoying the freedom of religion are approached by the Government Agents and told it is now against the law to enjoy religious freedom.

2. Military. The U.S. Army is now in control and can do as they please—including taking over your home if they so desire. *Cast:* Woody Tondorf (Husband), Lindsay Stidham (Wife), Lisa Schwartz (Daughter).

3. Slavery. The Proclamation that freed slaves is overturned as a white couple (Maxwell Glick, Katie Locke O'Brien) seeks to hire a black maid (Dayyanah Coleman)—but without pay as she will become their slave.

4. Murder. If they government seeks your property and you refuse to forfeit it, agents have the right to kill you for it. Scott Chernoff and Andy Goldblatt play the couple facing the agents and the loss of their home.

5. Stripped. A young woman (Lisa Schwartz), seeking a job at a company confronts a male-chauvinist boss (Rafi Fine) who not only sexually abuses her but refuses to give her the job because she is a woman (she ends the episode by saying, "At least the gays can't get married").

246 Q: The Series. youtube.com/play list?list=PL80E795A2CA818B44. 2011 (Comedy-Drama).

Although billed as "a comedy series about a group of queers" it is more of a dramatic look at a group of college friends with differing sexual preferences: Nicole and Jessica (lesbian couple), Kate (bisexual), Brian (straight), Zach and Alex (gay couple), Andy (lesbian) and Elijah (gay).

Cast: Steven Leone (Zach), Jordan Lee Knape (Kate), Corinna Nunn (Andy), Luke Muldar (Brian), Marvin Bernard (Alex), Justine Hope (Nicole), Nina Rekhviashvili (Jessica), Drexel Heard (Elijah). **Credits:** *Producer-Writer:* Julia Elizabeth. *Director:* Isaiah Everin. **Comment:** Well acted and filmed (by Columbia University students) but very slow-moving with virtually no action. Why it was labeled a comedy is a mystery as there is nothing funny about the problems gays, bisexual and lesbians encounter in society, especially a closed one like college. While there is some foul language, the program focuses mostly on the hookups made by the various characters although nothing is presented that is overly graphic.

Episode List: *1.* First Friday. *2.* Breaking the Binary. *3.* Going Out. *4.* Awkward. *5.* Hot Box in the Circle of Trust. *6.* Identity. *7.* Bi-Curious Blunder. *8.* Boyfriend.

247 Queen Dad. queendad.com. 2013–2014 (Comedy).

By day Monty Ellis works as a plumber. By night he is Flora, a popular drag queen at The Malebox, a Vermont gay bar run by Betty Hunter. Monty is also gay but at one point in his life, he was straight and did marry (Susan) and had a child (Jack) that he abandoned at birth (in Texas). Years later and unknown to Monty, Jack has begun a search to find his father and meet the man who deserted him. One night, as Monty is returning home from the bar, he sees a stranger asleep on his sofa. The stranger, it turns out is Jack, Monty's 17-year-old son. The program relates a father and son's efforts to reconnect with one another and of Jack's efforts to accept Monty for who he is when he discovers the dual life he is leading. Nick is the bouncer at the bar; Henry is Monty's bisexual friend.

Cast: Sean Moran (Monty Ellis/Flora) Matt Parisi (Jack Ellis), Ethel Goldstein (Betty Hunter), Jon van Luling (Nick Dinoto), Ben Ash (Henry Collins), Vivian Jordan (Susan Ellis), Berta Briones (Dr. Briones), Marc Bouchard (Chipper). **Credits:** *Producer:* Don Bledsoe, Berta Briones, Sean Moran, Arnold Wetherhead. *Director:* Sean Moran. *Writer:* Don Bledsoe, Sean Moran. **Comment:** Good idea but the pacing is a bit slow, making the program feeling like it just drags. While the acting and production values are good, foul language on Jack's part sort of ruins the overall feeling of the series.

Episodes:

1. Drips Are a Drag. The story begins as Jack seeks to find the father who abandoned him at birth.

2. Meet Jack and Jameson. Monty, surprised that Jack has found him, begins the process of acquainting himself with his son.

3. No Homo. Jack, offered a job by Betty at the club, learns that his father has a lover (Henry).

4. Halloween Bashed. Realizing that Jack is not too enthusiastic about totally reconnecting with Monty, Betty intervenes and tells Jack that he must make a choice—either accept him or head back to Texas.

5. Testosterone Trouble. A visit to the doctor spells bad news for Henry when it is learned he has cancer. Meanwhile, Jack is surprised by a visit from his mother Susan when she suddenly turns up at the bar. The program's concluding episode.

248 *Queens.* queenstheseries.com/. 2010 (Comedy).

John is a young man, living in a small Midwestern town whose life seemed just perfect—until his girlfriend left him and broke his heart. Unable to deal with what has happened John packs his bags and moves to New York City. But Manhattan is the big city and John is unable to handle its fast-paced life style. Unable to go home again, John moves to Queens, New York, and becomes roommates with Benjamin and Willy, gays who are living together but not involved with each other. A bit naïve about city and gay life, John must now contend with the antics of Benjamin and Willy, two off-the-wall gays who are anything but helpful as he seeks to restart his life.

Cast: Cary Mitchell (John), Andrew Waffenschmidt (Benjamin), Sam Albertsen (Willy), Meghan Sinclair (Danielle). **Credits:** *Writer-Director:* John Gebhart, Dure Ahn. **Comment:** The program, billed as "A comedy about living in Queens," is well acted but does contain vulgar language. There are no sexual situations and the primary focus is on John as he attempts to deal with Benjamin and Willy's antics.

Episodes:

1. Spandex Party. The story line is begun as John moves in with gay roommates Benjamin and Willy.

2. John's Gay Date. At a bar, John meets a man, begins a conversation and the man pays for the drinks. When Benjamin and Willy learn about the date and what happened, they tell John that he had drinks with a gay man.

3. Willy Wants an STD. A television commercial for STD's prompts John to get tested—along with Willy.

4. Fag Hag. When John meets Danielle but is unaware that she is Willy's "Fag Hag" (straight girl who is friends with a gay man), he finds Willy becoming jealous when he learns John asked her out on a date. The program's concluding episode.

249 *Queens of Drag: NYC.* youtube.com. 2010 (Reality).

A look at the real lives of men who perform as drag queens—from their choice to becoming a drag queen to the make-up preparations to the acts they have created for their characters.

Host: Bianca Del Rio (played by Roy Haylock). Credits are not given. **Comment:** Interesting concept that goes behind-the-scenes to present an insiders view of drag queens. The program is well presented as well as informative.

Episodes:

1. Sherry Vine. Played by Keith Levy, a singer who often impersonates Lady Gaga.

2. Lady Bunny. Real Name is not given. She is the founder of Wigstock, the largest drag festival in the world.

3. Bianca Del Rio. Played by Roy Haylock, a professional costume designer (makes his own character gowns).

4. Hedda Lettuce. Played by Steven Polito, who is distinguished by her green and blonde hair (hence her name), a stand-up comedienne.

5. Acid Betty. Played by Jamin Ruhren (who appears with Epiphany [Calen Tomaszewski]), both of whom are performers.

6. Peppermint. A singer but only credited as Kevin.

7. Dallas DuBois (Played by David Logan), a singer-dancer, and her guest Logan Hardcore (played by Logan Slaughter), a performer.

250 *Queer Duck.* icebox.com. 1999–2006 (Cartoon).

Adam Seymour Duckstein (a gay duck) better known as Queer Duck since he came out of the closet and revealed to the world that he is gay, works as a nurse and is the son of Jewish parents (a mother who is in denial that Adam is gay and a diabetic father). He has two siblings, an older straight brother (Lucky) and a lesbian sister (Melissa). Also a part of his immediate life is Little Lucky, his seemingly bicurious nephew and Steven Arlo Gator, Adam's significant other (who is nicknamed Openly Gator). Radio talk show host Laura Schlessinger (drawn here as a considerably less-attractive woman than she really is) is Adam's nemesis for her negative attitude toward the gay community. Adam, like any heterosexual person (or animal in this case) would just like to live the life he has chosen without all the misconceptions and hatreds that are associated with it. Adam, however, likes to gossip about anything that interests him, intrude where he is not wanted and stories follow all the pitfalls that Adam encounters simply because he cannot mind his own business.

Voice Cast: Jim J. Bullock (Queer Duck), Kevin Michael Richardson (Openly Gator), Billy West (Bi-Polar Bear), Maurice LaMarche (Oscar Wildcat), Estelle Harris (Adam's mother), Tress MacNeille (Dr. Laura). **Credits:** *Producer-Writer:* Mike Reiss. *Director:* Xeth Feinberg. **Comment:** The earliest of the animated gay series that has suggestive content but strays from sexual situations and vulgar language. The program uses flash animation that is well done but is not as sophisticated as animation currently seen on cable TV (cartoons produced for broadcast networks have virtually disappeared, especially since the CW, the last holdout on airing Saturday morning cartoons, abandoned the decades-old practice in October of 2014). The stories are amusing and so much so that the Showtime cable channel picked up the series for a run in 2002.

Episodes:

1. I'm Coming Out. In honor of National Coming Out Day, Adam decides he must take a stand and reveal the fact that he is gay.

2. Fiddler on the Roofies. Adam, who is afraid to admit to his nephew that he is gay, struggles to deal with the situation when Little Lucky finds his collection of gay video tapes.

3. Oh Christ. Unable to comprehend their son being gay, Adam faces an exorcism-like encounter by his parents to make him "normal."

4. Queer Doc. Adam's efforts to pull a prank on Dr. Laura backfire when she grabs a shotgun and seeks his hide.

5. B.S. I Love You. Adam, obsessed with singer Barbra Streisand, attempts to attend one of her concerts but is seen as a threat, tackled by her security guards and tossed into jail.

6. The Gayest Place on Earth. A theme park geared to gays becomes a nightmare for Adam when his efforts to impress a gay sailor lead him into a confrontation with that sailor's significant other.

7. Gym Neighbors. Adam's kidding about Gator's large behind has negative results and sends Gator, accompanied by Adam, to a gym to lose that extra weight.

8. Queer as Fowl. Adam, bored by the ceremonies at a funeral for a friend, decides to liven up things by turning the occasion into a gay disco party.

9. Wedding Bell Blues. After being frightened by Dr. Laura, who appears as a gremlin outside the plane on which Adam is flying, Adam proposes to Gator—only to find his excessive vow list the catalyst that makes marriage impossible at this time.

10. Ku Klux Klan and Ollie. The episode explores Adam's encounter with a clan opposed to gays and a revelation that he is not alone in the life that he has chosen as history itself is littered with gay figures.

11. The Gay Road to Morocco. A spoof of the Bob Hope-Bing Crosby "Road" pictures of the 1940s (and seen in black and white) wherein Adam and Gator perform songs as they travel to Morocco and encounter animated versions of Bob Hope, Bing Crosby and a sultan named Abu Ben Dover.

12. Quack Doc. A flashback to Adam's hatching is seen as he, Gator, Bi-Polar Bear and Oscar Wildcat visit a psychiatrist (Dr. Ben Swine) to help each of them cope with the various problems they are facing.

13. Oscar's Wild. Animated versions of Joan Rivers and Jack Nicholson appear in a story wherein

Adam and Gator, attending a boring Academy Awards ceremony, decide to add excitement by tearing the theater apart.

14. A Gay Outing. As a Cub Scout leader, Adam finds a camping trip outing with his nephew more than just roasting marshmallows over the camp fire when Little Lucky finds his copy of *Out Magazine* and begins asking him questions about it.

15. Radio Head. Dr. Laura appears to again taunt Adam and Gator—only this time, while they are hosting a radio program, to come out of the closet herself.

16. Tales of the City Morgue. Three short stories: Adam's obsession with *Yentl* (a Barbra Streisand film); Oscar's creation of a Frankenstein-like creature; and Bi-Polar's hope that he will be abducted by aliens to become a breeder.

17. Homo for the Holidays. As Adam and his family celebrate the December holidays, guest Openly Gator finds himself the target of Adam's father to arrange a date for him with Adam's gay sister Melissa.

18. Bi-Polar Bear and the Glorious Hole. Without food and money and believing he can find a meal at Oscar's home, Bi-Polar becomes stuck in Oscar's doorway when he attempts to enter but is a bit too large around the middle.

19. Santa Claus Is Coming Out. A Christmas season spoof with Adam meeting the real Santa Claus after he begins playing songs that out Santa as being gay.

20. Mardi Foie Gras. In the concluding episode, Adam's efforts to rid his life of Dr. Laura by placing a voodoo curse on her backfires and causes him to drink—so much so that he wakes up the following morning in bed with a woman and wondering if he could now like females.

251 QueersLand. youtube.com. 2012–2013 (Comedy).

Breeze and Rainbow are "hippy power lesbians"; Cyan and Magenta, are diva, fashion style setters; Xanax and his best friend, Tamazapam, are bisexual teenagers; and Barry, a wanna-be drag queen and his boyfriend, Thomas are the profiled "QueersLand" people who appear in separate brief skits that present that stereotype view of what such people are like in the mind's eye of many people (although the situations presented could be real, they are greatly exaggerated to present a "mocumentray" style presentation).

Cast: Leah Pellinkhof, Rhys Emmett Rathbone, Aveena Anthony, Carita Gronroos, Joseph J.U. Taylor. **Credits:** *Producer-Writer:* Leah Pellinkhof, Rhys Emmett Rathbone. **Comment:** Two actors (Leah Pellinkhof and Rhys Emmett Rathbone) convincingly play six different characters in an amusing, well-produced Australian program. While gays, lesbians, bisexual and drag queens are the brunt of the satire, it is typical of the comedy presented on TV series like *Monty Python's Flying Circus* and *Little Britain* (simply harmless fun).

Episodes:

1. Episode 1. "Welcome to QueersLand, Darling" begins the series with a first look at the six main characters.

2. Episode 2. The recurring characters, Maureen (a plain-looking lesbian seeking the girl of her dreams) and her homophobic brother Chook are introduced along with Blain, a gay soap opera star and his manager Cynthia, who is struggling to keep Blain's "gayness" in the closet.

3. Episode 3. As Maureen prepares for a blind date, Cyan (gay) and Magenta (a lesbian) extol the virtues of beauty by creating "Fugly No More," a school "for people far-less attractive than us."

4. Episode 4. Cynthia's struggles continue as she tries to prevent Blain from revealing he is gay and ruining his career; Maureen's blind date arrives—a much older, not-so-attractive woman; Breeze and Rainbow discuss their living situation in a commune-like setting; Thomas tries to offer support to Barry as he prepares to enter the world as a drag queen.

5. Episode 5. Xanax and Tamazepam explain how their parents are affecting who they want to be; Blain has taken Cynthia's advice about staying in the closet, but his inner gayness wants to manifest itself; Cyan and Magenta teach their class about the allure of accents.

6. Episode 6. Maureen's beliefs that all lesbians look like the women on the TV series *The L Word* have been shattered since meeting her blind date (Shaz); Barry and Thomas face a huge problem—what name should drag queen Barry have; Breeze and Rainbow have left the commune and are now living together, basically to get away from Rainbow's ex, the seemingly deranged Mangroves.

7. Episode 7. Xanax (and her friend Syd) and Tamazapam (and his friend Vada) make out; Cyan and Magenta appear in their first TV commercial extolling their school and how Fugly No More can get you more of what you want if you transform from ugly to gorgeous (well almost gorgeous).

8. Episode 8. Maureen discovers that Shaz attended school with her mother—but feels that she is the woman she has been seeking; Blain feels he must show the world who he is despite Cynthia's efforts to stop him; Barry and Thomas have come up with the perfect name for drag queen Barry—Tora Hyman; Breeze and Rainbow share the reason why they left the commune as disturbing visual images of the unstable Mangroves are seen. The program's concluding episode.

252 The Randy Rainbow Show. randyrainbow.com. 2013 (Comedy).

Randy Rainbow (his given name) is an openly gay

Jewish man who earns a living as an actor, writer and comedian. He has produced a number of YouTube videos that highlight his comedic style and has also produced a five-episode web series that encompasses one aspect of his videos: his knack for staging fake interviews with famous people by incorporating real audio and/or video footage of those people via telephone conversations, cardboard like images or still photographs.

Host: Randy Rainbow. **Credits:** *Producer-Writer:* Randy Rainbow. **Comment:** The program can be watched and enjoyed by anyone as it is not specifically geared to a gay audience (more of a mainstream audience). Randy is delightful and although only five short episodes appear as a series, there are many other videos that can be enjoyed on YouTube by typing "Randy Rainbow" in the search mode.

Episodes:

1. Two Minute History of Gay. Randy performs a song that praises those who have encompassed being gay.

2. Jeremy Irons Marries His Son. Randy laments on the fact that all his gay friends are marrying and he is not even gay dating.

3. Jodie Foster Lesbian Matchmaking. In a conversation with his mother, Randy relates that he has established a company called Randy Rainbow Lesbian Matchmaking. A client then arrives, actress Jodie Foster (seen only from the back of her head) and Randy attempts to find her a date (but finding she is not the most cooperative of people).

4. Randy's Fling with Pope Francis. Randy has a surprise for his mother—he is bringing Pope Francis, whom he met on the web site Christianmingle.com over for Passover dinner. Randy also performs a song-and-dance number with the Pope.

5. What's Up Biebs? Randy tries to ease the tension singer Jason Bieber is experiencing over the rumors that persist in his life.

253 The Real Girls' Guide to Everything Else. therealgirlsguide.wordpress.com. 2010 (Comedy).

Rasha is a free-lance journalist whose writings reflect her political, lesbian and feminist outlooks. When her views are deemed too controversial and her agent threatens to drop her if she doesn't change her style, Rasha decides to see life from a different perspective and pretends to be a "glitter-wearing, shoe-obsessed, Cosmo-drinking straight girl." With the help of her girlfriends (Sydney, Angie, Liz and Vanna) for guidance Rasha enters whole new world and reflects, through her writings, how the world is seen through the eyes of a straight girl.

Rasha, who earns a living as a journalist, is hoping to write a book called *The Women's History of Afghanistan*. She enjoys exposing corruption and if she could, she would save the world. Rasha dislikes body glitter and prefers to shop at the men's section of The Gap. She last read the book *The Shock Doctrine.*

Sydney is an apartment house manager who also earns a living as an artist-graphic designer (her current project is "growing out body hair to use in an installation piece"). She last read the book *Variations in Red: An Artist's Guide to Painting with Menstrual Blood* and loves bargain basement and yard sales and anything her girlfriends, Rasha and Vanna consider donating to Good Will.

Angie is a girl who likes puppies, bunnies, kitties and anything ending in an "e" sound as well as anything on which she can put her name. She is a nurse although she has aspirations to become an actress. Her style of clothing is anything pastel (hopefully with rainbow or teddy bear designs) and print scrubs for hospital duty. She last read the book *Love, Lunch and a Macy's Sale: A Girl's Guide to Getting Mr. Right Portfolio.* She is currently involved in two "thought-provoking" projects: organizing her headband collection by color and creating a vision board from back issues of *People* magazine.

Vanna, the lead singer of an indie rock group called Fashionista/IT Consultant, enjoys fixing other people's fashion mistakes (she is currently involved in a project to change Rasha's male-like fashion style). She dislikes fanny packs and believes shopping "is really a form of tithing. I like to think of it as giving back to the community both financially and aesthetically." She last read the book *How to Create Minions and Improve Your Friends.*

Liz, a publishing house book editor is also a lesbian and dreams of marrying Rasha. She is somewhat like Elaine Benes (from the TV series *Seinfeld*) as she too is obsessed over punctuation. While her clothing style is vintage 1920s to the 1950s, she also likes to cook, arrange flowers and read (her last book was *My Big Fat Lesbian Wedding*). **Cast:** Robin Dalea (Rasha), Reena Dutt (Sydney), Nikki Brown (Vanna), Carmen Elena Mitchell (Angie), Jennifer Weaver (Liz), Bruno Oliver ("Big"), Meena Seredib (Nusheen), Mike Datz (Bartender), Anna Khaja (Aliyah). **Credits:** *Producer:* Carmen Elena Mitchell, *Director:* Heather de Michele, Reena Dutt, Jennifer Weaver. *Writer:* Carmen Elena Mitchell. **Comment:** Truly enjoyable comedy romp with excellent acting and production values. It is witty and well written and shows that, although it was produced for the Internet, it has the qualities that could make a good broadcast or cable series.

Episodes:

1. Love, Lunch and a BOGO Sale. The story line is established as Rasha conceals her lesbian sexuality to do what her agent wants—write "chick lit" (literature reflecting the common everyday woman).

2. TrueLoveAlwaysForever.com. To begin her new life, Rasha enters the world of heterosexual dating and discovers that straight men are attracted to her.

3. When Alie Vera Isn't Everything. Rasha's delve into the straight world has Liz upset, fearing she will lose Rasha to a straight dude.

4. Boys, Burqas and Bunions. While Liz continues to fear that Rasha is going "to switch sides," Rasha finds help with her book when one of her dates ("Big") accompanies her to Afghanistan.

5. Covering Your Ass: Afghan Style. In Afghanistan Rasha meets with her cousin Nusheen (Meena Serendib) and through a contact Big has with the Taliban leader Habib (Ronobir Lahirr) Rasha feels she will get the information she needs for her book—despite the fact that she is in a war zone and her life is constantly in peril.

6. A Girl's Guide to Covering War Zones. It has been some time since Rasha has returned from Afghanistan and she has written a book based on her experiences in the war-torn country called *A Girl's Guide to Covering War Zones.* To help celebrate the release of her book, Rasha, Angie, Liz and Vanna meet for lunch and aspects of Rasha's experiences are discussed as the program ends.

254 *Rent Controlled.* tellofims.com. 2014 (Comedy).

Heather and Jennifer are lesbians and lovers who appear to be happy until they decide to rent an apartment and move in together. It takes less than twenty-four hours for them to realize they are not compatible and feel it is best to break up. But they also realize they have a problem: they must still live together as neither one can afford to break the lease. Jennifer appears to be fine with the arrangement but Heather is a bit more worried as she finds that she still longs for Jennifer. "In her former life, she was either a porn star or a Kardashian," says Heather of Jennifer (while she says of herself, "Hi, I'm Heather. I guess you can say I'm a hopeless romantic"). The program follows Heather and Jennifer as they each attempt to move on—with the help of their friends: Kyle and Lauren, and Ted and Carla, straight couples; Helga ("Likes women"), Anna ("Hot stuff"), Karen ("Mature lesbian lawyer") and Bianca ("Jail bait").

Cast: Heather Dean (Heather), Remy Maelen (Jennifer), John Loos (Ted), Abby McEnany (Carla), Dan Wenzel, Jr. (Kyle), Anji White (Lauren), Jax Turyna (Bianca), Bex Marsh (Karen), Charlita Williams (Anna), Natasha Samreny (Helga). **Credits:** *Producer:* Christin Baker. *Director:* Julie Keck, Jessica King. *Writer:* Heather Dean. **Comment:** As with all Tello Films productions, excellent production values and top notch acting. A free on-line trailer gives a good indication as what to expect in terms of kissing scenes and adult situations—all of which are expertly handled and sensitively presented.

Episodes: Seven episodes have been produced, all of which are only available through a paid subscription service. See also *Til Lease Do Us Part* for a similar program.

255 *Ring My Bell.* youtube.com. 2014 (Comedy).

Various drag queens appear in a simple set setting, seated at a desk with an orange telephone to respond to a telephone call that is presumably made by a viewer to answer the questions he or she may have about them.

Credits: *Producer:* Adam Asea, Blake Jacobs, Thairin Smothers, Pete Williams. **Comment:** Perfectly centered picture; steady camera; clear image and well-presented advice program with some of the bloopers that occur left in.

Episodes: The performers are listed with their episodes.

1. Courtney Act.
2. Rom Gross.
3. Jonny McGovern.
4. Will Shepherd and R.J. Aguiar.
5. Darren Stein.
6. Miles Jai.
7. Coco Montrese.
8. Ben DeLa Crème.
9. Regan Fox.
10. Jeffrey Self.
11. Paul Zahn.
12. John Polly.
13. Colby Keller.
14. Venus D. Lite.
15. Miles Davis Woody.
16. Detox.
17. Johnny Scruff.
18. Big Freedia.
19. Ongina.
20. Serena ChaCha.
21. Jiggly Caliente.
22. Tatianna.
23. Jimmy James.
24. Jessica and Hunter.
25. Love Connie.
26. Kelly Mantle.
27. TS Madison.
28. Josh Flagg.
29. Mimi Imfurst.
30. Pandora Boxx.
31. Billy B..
32. Selene Luna.
33. Karrine Steffans.
34. Candis Cayne.
35. Damiana Garcia.
36. Noah Levy.
37. Marc Malkin.
38. Vivienne Pinay.
39. Phi Phi O'Hara.
40. Bradford Shellhammer.
41. Calpernia Addams.
42. Casey Jane Ellison.
43. Vivienne Pinay, Shangela and Alyssa Edwards.
44. Manila Luzon.
45. Wendy Ho.
46. Carmen Carrera.
47. Gregory the Gray Ghost.
48. Madame LaQueer.
49. Daniel Franzese.
50. Holly Woodlawn.
51. Chris Crocker.
52. RuPaul and Lauren Harries.
53. Mathu Andersen.
54. Shannel.
55. Alyssa Edwards.
56. Sharon Needles.
57. Chad Michaels.
58. Victoria PorkChop Parker.
59. Shawn Morales.
60. Jason Carter.
61. Roxxxy Andrews.
62. Jinkx Monsoon.
63. Alaska.
64. Tammie Brown.
65. Deven Green.
66. P'Trique C'est Chic.
67. Latrice Royale.
68. Angelyne.
69. Sonique Love.
70. Delta Work.
71. Raja.
72. Santino Rice.
73. Gloria Shuri.
74. Yara Sofia.
75. Raven.
76. Bobcat Goldthwait.
77. Cheri Woods.
78. Layla.
79. Johnny and Kooks.
80. Rex Lee.
81. Clint Catalyst.
82. Cutest Dog in the World.
83. Dr. Bomgay.
84. Nelson Aspen.
85. Scotty Brown.
86. Peter Paige.
87. Sean Conroy.
88. James St. James.
89. Kato Kaelin.
90. Kim and Jordan.
91. Matt Temple.
92. Miss Coco Peru.
93. Leslie Hall.
94. Nelson Aspen.
95. Perez Hilton.
96. The UkuLady.
97. Shane Klingensmith.
98. Dungeon Majesty.
99. Micah McCain.
100. Norman Korpi.
101. Jack Plotnick.

102. Andy Cohen.
103. Ethan Mechare.
104. Punk Bunny.
105. Ray Richmond.
106. World of Wonder Halloween.
107. Amy Alkon.
108. Justin Jorgensen.
109. Wash Westmoreland.

256 Risa and Christina: Available. risa andchristina.com. 2011 (Comedy).

They hug, often dress alike, snuggle up with each other, give each other flowers and gifts and insist, despite what they do, "we are not lesbians." Risa and Christina are the women who are not lesbians but are thought to be so by their parents (and possibly anyone else who might know them). While being a lesbian is nothing to be ashamed about, Risa and Christina insist they are heterosexual and need to do something to prove it. Their decision: join OK Cupid, an Internet dating site wherein women seek potential suitors. But will it prove to their mothers that they are straight? The program follows Risa and Christina as they each seek a male mate and what occurs when they do find a likely prospect but go totally overboard in attempting to learn all about his likes and interests.

Cast: Risa Sarachan (Risa), Christina Jeffs (Christina). **Credits:** *Producer-Writer:* Risa Sarachan, Christina Jeffs. *Director:* Louis Gruber, Risa Sarachan, Christina Jeffs. **Comment:** Although only Risa and Christina appear, they handle their roles well. Not only are they attractive but the mishaps that occur as they prepare to meet never seen dates are well done and make each episode very enjoyable. Whether or not Risa and Christina are lesbians (or bisexual) is never revealed.

Episodes:

1. A Note to Our Mothers. To prove to their mothers that they are not lesbians, Risa and Christina join an Internet dating site.

2. The CEO. It appears that once a suitor is found, they will each compete for his affections. Here they attempt to learn all about energy drinks when they find a CEO of such a company.

3. The British Bloke. A potential Englishman suitor has the girls attempting to learn everything about British culture.

4. The Preschool Teacher. Going back to their school day memories as Risa and Christina prepare to meet a preschool teacher.

5. The Private Investigator. How to impress a private detective is the question as the girls seek the ins and outs of detective work.

6. The Film Buff. A hit on a horror film buff becomes a bit spooky when Risa and Christina watch one too many fright films in an attempt to impress him.

7. The Politician. Risa and Christina emerge themselves in the political system to impress a politician.

8. The Asian Guy. Unfamiliar with Asian culture, Risa and Christina go a bit overboard trying to learn more for a potential love connection.

9. The Doctor. Risa and Christina believe marrying a doctor is the answer and proceed to explore the field—by playing the electronic game "Operation."

10. The Straight Man. An Internet hit has Risa and Christina wondering if the prospect is gay or straight as his profile could read either way.

11. El Guapo. The girls fantasize about marrying a man from a foreign land.

12. The Neighbor. Risa and Christina seek the attentions of their new neighbor.

13. Southern Gentleman. In an attempt to impress a man from the South, Risa and Christina immerse themselves in learning southern cooking.

257 Robot, Ninja and Gay Guy. youtube. com/results?search_query=robot%2C+ninja+and+gay+guy+. 2009–2010 (Comedy).

Gay Guy (as he is called) and Chad are roommates and lovers until Chad, fed with Gay Guy and the pathetic life he leads decides to end the relationship and move on, giving him no advance notice of his moving out. Unable to afford the rent on his own, Gay Guy places an ad on CraigsList.com seeking a new roommate. Ninja, as he is called, becomes his first response but before he can say yes or no, there is a knock at the door and Robot, a human-looking android also applies for the roommate position. Gay Guy's indecisiveness earns him two new roommates and a truckload of problems as he must deal with a gentle Ninja with a secretive past and a Robot curious to learn about the human world (exactly where Robot came from or who created him is not revealed). Three roommates, three differing lifestyles and the situations that develop as Gay Guy, Ninja and Robot each seek to lead separate lives and not intrude on the other's privacy.

Cast: Travis Richey (Gay Guy), Ryan Churchill (Robot), Brian Giovanni (Ninja), Phil Brown (Chad). **Credits:** *Producer:* Rob Wood, Travis Richey. *Director:* Rob Wood. *Writer:* Eric Loya, Travis Richey. **Comment:** Broadcast TV or basic cable-ready series with excellent acting and production values. Each episode flows smoothly from start to finish and the Ninja's disappearing and reappearing—and Gay Guy's reactions are truly well done (and funny).

Episodes:

1. The Robot Situation. Intrigued by Robot and how human he acts, Gay Guy seeks a way to find out if he is really a robot.

2. Origin Story. How Gay Guy acquired Ninja and Robot as roommates are seen in a flashback episode.

3. The Party. Now that he is stuck with Ninja

and Robot, Gay Guy decides to celebrate and throw a party.

4. New TV. Ninja and Robot's accidental breaking of Gay Guy's TV while play fighting forces Gay Guy to buy only what he can afford—an old analog set.

5. Field Trip. Gay Guy accompanies Ninja to the local comic book store to return a book and is surprised to see that his former lover, Chad, is the salesman.

6. First Halloween. Gay Guy decides to throw a Halloween party to help Robot understand the human tradition of celebrating Halloween.

7. Gay Guy's Not Here. After Ninja locks Gay Guy out of the apartment following an argument, Gay Guy struggles in vain to talk Robot into letting him back in, but, unfortunately, Robot can't comprehend what wanting to come back in or open the door means.

8. Jealousy. Robot seeks to learn what jealousy is all about when he comes home with his own gay friend and proceeds to make Gay Guy jealous.

9. Game Night. Gay Guy, Ninja and Robot decide to play board games and institute a game night tradition.

10. Ninja Training. Feeling a need to better himself, Ninja consults the wise and elder Lil' Ninja in an effort to find his deeper inner self.

11. Mr. Furper. Before acquiring his new roommates Gay Guy was annoyed by his snooping landlord, Mr. Furper. Things haven't changed—the nosey Mr. Furper has again invaded Gay Guy's life, this time curious about Ninja and Robot.

12. Recurrence. Gay Guy, often annoyed by Ninja's ability to move swiftly from one place to another, seeks to find out where he goes when he disappears. While trying to figure that out, Chad makes a sudden reappearance in Gay Guy's life leaving the doorway open to explore a possible rekindling relationship in the concluding episode.

258 Rods and Cones. wifey.tv. 2014 (Comedy).

Carole, a lesbian, and Mitzi, a bisexual, are art school graduates and out of work. They are $80,000 in debt (student loans) and desperately seeking a way to keep their heads above water. When they learn of a competition called "The Woman's Comedy Contest" in Los Angeles they decide to enter (with their "Hot Mom Act") and hopefully win the "Big Cash Prize." While they are not the only contenders, they most fear George and Bess, called "The MILfies," performance artists in their thirties hoping to win the grand prize by pretending to be "Mommy Comics." The program charts the situations that result as Carole and Mitzi attempt to win the top prize. **Cast:** Beth Lisick (Carole Murphy), Tara Jepsen (Mitzi Fitzsimmons), Erin Markey (George), Jibz Cameron (Bess). **Credits:** *Producer:* Lagueria Davis,

Kurt Keppeler. *Writer:* Tara Jepsen, Beth Lisick. *Director:* Laurel Frank. **Comment:** Although the series has not been released (as of Jan. 2015) it appears to be an enjoyable comedy outing just by the brief video information that has been made available. The main leads (Carole and Mitzi) are delightful and play off each other quite well (like a well-oiled comedy team) and their competition, George and Bess are the type of villains that you love to hate.

Episodes:

1. Rods and Cones: A Proposal. A 44-second preview of what the series is all about. Available on YouTube.com.

2. Rod and Cones Trailer. A 62-second preview of the series that is only available on viemo.com.

259 Role Play Gay. youtube.com. 2013 (Comedy).

Sketches that attempt to deal with subjects that affect gays through the role playing of the program's stars (who appear as characters germane to the topics they are discussing) as they debate issues. They also state: "PLEASE NOTE: These are roles we take on, and we believe it's okay to make fun of yourself and others, with your tongue in your cheek and no malice! It's all light hearted fun-ay!!"

Cast as credited: Dan and Johan. **Credits:** *Producer-Director:* Dan Fry. **Comment:** Australian produced program that cleverly tackles a topic through humor. It is amusing and had the program taken the other route (straight discussions or debates) it would not have the same impact nor be as enjoyable.

Episodes:

1. Episode 1. Gay men in the army are discussed with Dan as a gregarious American camp queen and Johan as a straight-acting butch South African colonel who believes gay men are not army material.

2. Episode 2. Dan and Johan as gay dog lovers—one who has an eight times champion; the other a mangy mutt that has never been entered in a show.

3. Episode 3. A look at split personalities through Gay Lad Dave and his alter-ego Camp Michael, a jet set go-go dancer/escort.

4. Episode 4. Coming out of the closet is explored with Dan as an Essex cockney man who is married with children and has just come out and Johan as a pompous gay man who detests gays who wait so long to declare themselves.

5. Episode 5. Mike and his alter-ego Dave cross examine each other in a discussion on gay and gayer.

6. Episode 6. Dan portrays a married man-gay wannabe who must decide if he should indulge his wife's fantasies and watch and perform gay porn.

7. Episode 7. A look at gays and the film industry through a Hollywood producer named Mr. X.

8. Episode 8. Dan and Johan explore the problem of whether it is best to play it safe and remain monogamous or being promiscuous but careful about it.

9. Episode 9. A debate on an old, but existing law in Queensland, Australia called "The Gay Panic," which stands in court as strong defense if a man has murdered a gay man because he felt physically threatened. Here Dan is a drippy hypochondriac and Johan a very jovial cheesy geek who doesn't deal with politics.

10. Episode 10. A debate on what gay marriage means in 2013. Dan appears as an erratic priest who is not sure about anything while Johan appears as a French priest who has strong opinions on gays and marriage.

260 *Roomies*. tellofilms.com. 2013 (Comedy).

Sam and Alex are best friends who, although lesbians, are not dating each other. Each is in a relationship and each has their heart broken when their lovers abandon them. By chance, Sam and Alex re-connect at a bar and when each learns the other is seeking an apartment, they decide to become roommates but must pretend to be a couple when they fall in love with what turns out to be a "gay only" apartment. The program follows the pitfalls they encounter as they attempt to find romance (with other girls) and keep their true life a secret. See also *The Neighbors*, the spin off series.

Cast: Julie Goldman (Sam), Brandy Howard (Alex), Kelly Beeman (Sally), Hannah Aubry (Tammy), Emily Peterson (Tami), Caitlin Bergh (Cait), Abby McEnany (Sue Fox), Jim Bennett (Dave), Deborah Craft (Tess), Noelle Lynn (Mallory).

Credits: *Producer-Director:* Christin Mell. *Writer:* Julie Keck, Jessica King. **Comment:** A bit like the TV series *Bosom Buddies* (wherein two males posed as females to keep an apartment). The acting, story line, and production is top rate and worthy of a network or basic cable presentation.

Episodes:

1. Long Time No See. After breaking up with their respective partners, old friends Sam and Alex re-connect and decide to become roommates.

2. Waterbugs. Sam and Alex find an apartment but to keep it they must pretend to be a couple.

3. Do You Feel Me? Sam and Alex agree to the charade and must not only convince their landlady (Sue Fox) they are lovers, but their "super cute" neighbors, Tammy and Tami.

4. Sex Addiction Is Real. The charade appears to

Roomies. **Series poster art (used by permission of Tello Films).**

be working but the pretence soon takes its toll on Alex, who cannot see other girls when she is in "love" with Sam.

5. Strange Bedfellows. Having made it clear to Alex that she must not crack under the pressure seems to work at first—until the girl that broke Alex's heart and dumped her returns—and threatens to expose the charade.

261 *Rose by Any Other Name*. facebook. com/RoseByAnyOtherNameTV. 2009 (Comedy-Drama).

Rose is a very pretty young woman who is leading a comfortable life as a lesbian until a chance meeting with a heterosexual man named Anthony stirs feelings in Rose that she may be bisexual when she finds herself uncontrollably attracted to him. Rose believed she had her life all planned out—to meet and marry the girl of her dreams but now a man has entered the picture and placed serious doubts in her mind as to her sexual orientation. Feeling that she needs an answer, Rose begins a relationship with Anthony to discover the truth about herself. The program relates that courtship with an attempt to show that regardless of gender, people can and do fall in love with each other and what may feel right for the moment may not be the answer in the long run.

Cast: Stephanie Reibel (Rose), Kyle Schickner (Anthony), Fay Wolfe (Veronica), Jamie Michaels (Holly), Steph Davis (Chris), Cathy DeBuono (Renee), Kristen Howe (Jo), Oren Skoog (Eric), Jay Burns (Marc), Jonte LeGras (Chris), Tannalee Moore (Vanessa). **Credits:** *Producer:* Heather Hollin, Sam Jones, Derek Leininger. *Writer-Director:* Kyle Schickner. **Comment:** The lead actresses are excellent in their performances when they act with each other but something gets "lost in the translation" (so to speak) when they intermix with the male performers (the chemistry the girls share with each other is lost). The program is well produced but there is no reason given why, when the website is still open, the episodes can no longer be watched ("This Video Is Private" will appear).

Episode List: Of the 11 episodes produced, only the following six titles are listed on line. *1.* A Pair of Star-Crossed Lovers. *2.* And Thou Art Wedded to Calamity. *3.* Enter the Friends. *4.* Thy Head Is Full of Quarrels. *5.* O! I Am Fortune's Fool. *6.* You Shall Confess That You Are Both Deceived.

262 *Royal Sabotage.* royalsabotage.tumblr. com. 2012 (Comedy).

Royal Stevenson is 20 years old, gay, unemployed (a master at avoiding work), carefree and living in Los Angeles off money he somehow manipulates from his wealthy family. His life consists of having fun—from bed hopping to drinking without thinking of the consequences. While the type of work Royal does is not stated, he does have a sexy associate named Beau Bardot (a woman) and a best bud, Vegas, and through their eyes, Royal's playful road to self destruction is comically depicted.

Cast: Kingsley Benham (Royal Stevenson), J.J. Wienkers (Vegas Smart), Lindsey Moore Ford (Beau Bardot), Alexis Victoria Bloom (Lily/Rose), Patrick Gomez (Antonio Fuentes), Grant Sloss (Grant Tucker), Fuller Huntington, Jr. (Sean Little), Granison Crawfird (Jason Black). **Credits:** *Producer:* Kingsley Benham, J.J. Wienkers, Alexis Victoria Bloom, Kimberly Eaton, Patrick Gomez. *Director:* Alexis Victoria Bloom, Patrick Gomez. *Writer:* Kingsley Benham, J.J. Wienkers. **Comment:** Very fast moving program that is well acted and produced. Episodes are very short (under 3 minutes) and a lot happens but reduced to just what happens

and nothing else. A bit disappointing at times as it looks like stretching just a bit would have made the episode even better than it is.

Episodes: Only 6 of 24 produced episodes are on line.

1. Pilot. At his "You Got Fired Party," Beau seeks a way to approach Royal to learn if she will still get paid as his associate.

2. You Can Party Foul. Following the wild party, Vegas, who is straight, tries to figure out if he had sex with a woman or a man as his hangover is preventing him seeing a clear picture.

3. Bruthas and Sistas. Royal returns home and a brief look at his sisters, Lily and Rose are seen (although Royal has trouble telling which one is which). It is revealed, as Royal believes, they are both "married to black men": Lily who still lives in Los Angeles (and is), and Rose, living in New York "with a white man from South Africa."

4. I Will Always Smell You. Royal is shocked to learn that his ex-lover (Antonio) has moved on and found someone new.

5. The Old Man and the Teeth. Royal, claiming to be an expert pool player, shows Beau his latest game winnings: an old man's false teeth which he took as payment when the debt couldn't be paid.

6. Arsenic and Old Lays. Royal arranges a roast for Vegas, complete with all the "insulting" compliments he can think of at their favorite bar, Hot Milk.

263 *RuPaul Drives.* youtube.com/playlist? list=PLhgFEi9aNUb1DqfC6XA5syJmZT p1uDRiY. 2013 (Reality).

RuPaul, the Drag Queen host the Logo TV series *RuPaul's Drag Race* takes on the role of a chauffeur and as he drives a special guest around Hollywood (with no planned destination) each comments on various aspects of life.

Star: RuPaul. **Credits:** *Producer:* Thairin Smothers, Pete Williams, Blake Jacobs, Adam Asea. **Comment:** Although skewed toward a drag queen audience as the host and most of his passengers are drag queens, the program is well done and gives an insightful look into aspects of the people who hitch a ride.

Episode List:

1. RuPaul Drives.... Victoria PorkChop Parker.

2. RuPaul Drives.... Sharon Needles.

3. RuPaul Drives.... Vivienne Pinay.

4. RuPaul Drives.... Alyssa Edwards.

5. RuPaul Drives.... Manila Luzon.

6. RuPaul Drives.... Chad Michaels.

7. RuPaul Drives.... Shawn Morales and Jason Carter.

8. RuPaul Drives.... Tyler Oakley.

9. RuPaul Drives.... Henry Rollins, Part 1 and 2.

10. RuPaul Drives.... Courtney Stodden, Parts 1 and 2.

11. RuPaul Drives.... Agnez Mo.
12. RuPaul Drives.... Chris Crocker.
13. RuPaul Drives.... Daniel Franzese.
14. RuPaul Drives.... Kat Von D.
15. RuPaul Drives.... Marianne Williamson.
16. RuPaul Drives.... Cassandra Peterson ("Elvira, Mistress of the Dark").
17. RuPaul Drives.... Taylor Dayne.
18. RuPaul Drives.... Kristen Johnston.
19. RuPaul Drives.... Michelle Visage.
20. RuPaul Drives.... Lucian Piane.
21. RuPaul Drives.... Lohanthony.
22. RuPaul Drives.... Chi Chi LaRue.
23. RuPaul Drives.... Iggy Azalea, Parts 1 and 2.
24. RuPaul Drives.... Olivia Newton John, Parts 1 and 2.

264 *RuPaul's Drag Race Fashion Photo RuView.* youtube.com/watch?v=IzYEQa0i OZY. 2014 (Variety).

RuPaul's Drag Race is a Logo television series wherein drag queens compete in various beauty-like contests. Raja and Raven, two former contestants appear to critique the queens who appear on the program, sort of a Mr. Blackwell (famous fashion critic) fashion critique but geared to women who really aren't women.

Host: Raven (episodes 1–30), Raja (episodes 1–11; 13–25), Tatiana (episode 12), Morgan McMichaels (episodes 26, 27, 28), Delta Work (episode 29). **Credits:** *Producer:* Adam Asea, Blake Jacobs, Thairin Smothers. Pete Williams. **Comment:** Well produced program that while aimed at fans of the RuPaul series, has appeal for others as it is interesting to see how drag queens see other drag queens (just like how men and women see other men and women).

Episodes: All episodes are untitled. Episodes 1 through 22 have the series title with an episode number (for example, "RuPaul's Drag Race Fashion Photo RuView with Raja and Raven, Episode 3." The exception is episode 12, which teams Raven with guest Tatianna). The remaining 8 episodes are titled as follows: 23. Holiday Drag Bowl. 24. Reunited Red Carpet, Part 1. 25. Reunited Red Carpet, Part 2. 26. Raven and Morgan McMichales, Part 1. 27. Raven and Morgan McMichales, Part 2. 28. Raven and Morgan McMichales, Part 3. 29. Raven and Delta Work: Thanksgiving. 30. The Lost Footage.

265 *Sassy Gay Friend.* youtube. com. 2010 (Comedy).

Suppose it was possible to go back in time and change the destiny of people (both real and imaginary) who had contemplated killing themselves. Would history (and literature) be changed? As a doomed person is about to meet an unkind end, a sassy gay friend appears to talk them out of what is about to happen and set them on a different path.

Typical of each program is this example from the episode "Eve." Eve (from the Biblical Adam and Eve) is seen about to pick an apple from a tree. A narrator is heard: "Meet Eve from the Bible. She is about to eat the apple and be blamed for the fate of mankind. This fate could have been avoided if she had a Sassy Gay Friend" (who then appears to say, "What are you doing? What, what, what are you doing? followed by his efforts to set her on a different path).

Cast: Brian Gallivan (Sassy Gay Friend). **Credits:** *Producer:* Mark Krenlen. *Director:* Joshua Funk. **Comment:** Absolutely delightful program to watch. The acting and production values are top rate and each episode is a humorous look at what would happen if an intervention were held—even if it was by a "Sassy Gay Friend" you didn't know you had.

Episodes:
1. Cyrano de Bergerac. Sassy Gay Friend attempts to convince Cyrano to romance the lovely Roxanne on his own and not hide the fact of his large nose.
2. Way Off Base. Sassy Gay Friend gives a crash course in baseball.
3. TMI About Relationships. Sassy Gay Friend discusses relationship problems.
4. Royal Pain. Royal Weddings are discussed by Sassy Gay Friend.
5. Macbeth. Lady MacBeth (Jean Villepique) receives a visit from Sassy Gay Friend right before she would become insane following her husband's killing of the King.
6. Great Expectations. Miss Havisham, from Charles Dickens' *Great Expectations* receives a visit from Sassy Gay Friend as she is about to take her life.
7. It Gets Better. Sassy Gay Friend reveals some information regarding himself.
8. The Giving Tree. Literature's *The Giving Tree* (by Chill Silverstein) is about to be cut down when Sassy Gay Friend arrives to save it from a woodman's ax.
9. Eve. Eve (Milynn Sailey) is about to eat the forbidden apple when Sassy Gay Friend appears to set her on a different path.
10. Othello. Desdemona (Mary Beth Monroe), from Shakespeare's *Othello* receives a warning when Sassy Gay Friend appears to tell her of her husband's plot to kill her.
11. Romeo and Juliet. Just as Juliet (Stephanie Allyne) is about to kill herself, Sassy Gay Friend arrives to tell her she can go on without Romeo.
12. The Odyssey. Odysseus, from Homer's *The Odyssey* has just disembarked from the Trojan Wars and is set to begin his ten-year journey back home. Sassy Gay Friend appears to see that he returns home in far less time.
13. Hamlet. Ophelia (Colleen Foy) from Shakespeare's play is about to take her own life when Sassy Gay Friend arrives to change her thinking.
14. Black Swan. Nina (Madeline Walter) from the feature film *Black Swan* is heartbroken over her

inability to achieve perfection at ballet and about to die when "What, what, what are you doing? It's only ballet, get over it…"

15. Way Off Base. Baseball receives center stage from Sassy Gay Friend.

16. Henry VIII. Just as Henry VIII is about to behead his wife Anne Boleyn for her inability to give him a male heir to the throne of England, Sassy Gay Friend appears to convince him to stop his murderous ways.

17. Sassy Gay Friend Uses Foul Language. Sassy Gay Friend takes a look at the game of basketball.

266 *Scissr: A Lesbian Web Series.* scissr webseries.com. 2013 (Drama).

Scissr is a lesbian bar in Brooklyn, New York, and the gathering place for four beautiful women (Aviva, Corey, Emily and Niamh) who met, oddly enough, through an iPhone app. Each is seeking that girl of her dreams and the program charts their experiences as they each set out to accomplish their goals.

Aviva has just come to terms with her sexuality and "has come out of the closet." She lives in the East Village, is 22 years old and "seeking a serious relationship."

Niamh not only feels she is in a dead-end job but her love life is just as empty. She is 27 years old, lives in Williamsburg and is "seeking relationships."

Emily, 24 years old, lives in Bushwick and is, as she says, "seeking whatever." The "whatever" is an equally beautiful woman she hopes to impress and make a commitment with; not a woman only interested in one-night stands.

Corey, having just broken up with her lover (Caitlin), is 22 years old and looking for someone new.

Cast: Lauren Augarten (Aviva), Paulina Singer (Corey), Kelly Sebastian (Emily), Jamie Clayton (Niamh), Holly Curran (Eloise), Daniel Thompson (Mikey), Alisha B. Woods (Sam), Stephanie Begg (Caitlin), Taylor Blakin (Taylor). **Credits:** *Producer:* Lauren Augarten, Marshall Thompson, Teri Murphy Thompson, Stephanie Begg, Josh Mawer. *Director:* Josh Mawer, Stephanie Begg. *Writer:* Lauren Augarten. **Comment:** Well photographed (one can see care was taken), acted and produced program. While there is some vulgar language, the women are all very attractive and perform their roles well. It is a lesbian-themed show but deviates slightly from other such programs in that it attempts to profile such women in "a more realistic world, where gay women come in a multitude of colors, shapes, and sizes." And it achieves that goal.

Episodes:

1. Pilot. The main characters are introduced as they meet and get to know each other.

2. Trailer. Highlights from the first episode are presented with a sneak peak as what to expect in future episodes.

Scissr: A Lesbian Web Series. **The Ladies of Scissr (left to right:) Kelly Sebastian, Lauren Augarten, Jamie Clayton and Paulina Singer (photograph copyright by Patrick James Miller [www.patrickjamesmiller.com]).**

267 Second Shot. secondshottv.com. 2013 (Comedy).

Dot Collins, the owner of a gay bar (Dot's Hole in Morton, Ohio) embarks on a whaling expedition only to lose her life when the ship sinks. Kat McDonald, a young woman living in Miami, and a former employee of the bar, is summoned to Morton for the reading of Dot's will. While each of the bar employees are expecting that one of them will inherit the bar, it is Kat who is the most shocked when it is revealed that she has been left the bar. Kat, who had become famous as a pro soccer player but lost that fame when she cost her team a world championship decides to continue the tradition set by Dot (as her career has been on a downward spiral ever since—spokes girl for Glow and Go Discount Cosmetics then sales counselor at a sports wear company). The program relates the problems that befall Kat and her staff as they not only attempt to get along with each other, but run "the only gay bar in three counties." Ty, a beautiful lesbian waitress (who has had made love to more girls than she can remember), Linda, the bar karaoke singer, Jodi, the bartender, and Martin, the gay bartender assist Kat. Allison is Kat's ex-girlfriend (who is now married to a police officer named Paulie); and Krystal is Jodi's younger, flirtatious sister.

Cast: Jill Bennett (Kat McDonald), Amanda Christensen (Allison Silva), Maile Flanagan (Jodi Munson), Minnie Jo Mazzola (Ty Rosenfeld), Maia Madison (Linda Boonkowski), Matthew Scott Montgomery (Martin Honeycutt), Joe Crowley (Paulie Silva), Zoe Perry (Krystal Munson). **Credits:** *Producer:* Jill Bennett, Annie Price, Rebecca S. Katz, Maia Madison, Dara Nai. *Director:* Annie Price. *Writer:* Claudia Cogan, Yvette Foy, Maia Madison, Dara Nai, Jason Romaine, Tammy Lynne Stoner, Jill Bennett, Nancylee Myatt, Maile Flanagan. **Comment:** The program contains all that is necessary for a great TV sitcom—from acting to production values but thus far only three episodes have emerged. There are kissing scenes but nothing sexually graphic, as just when something interesting looks to be happening, Kat and Allison are interrupted.

Episodes:

1. You Can't Go Home Again. So Why Am I Here? The story line is established as Kat returns home and learns she has inherited a gay bar.

2. If It Ain't Fixed, Don't Break It. As Kat expresses her opinions that the bar needs to change its image to attract younger patrons (other than the 40s crowd it now has) Kat is reunited with her former lover (Allison), who is now married to a man (Paulie). Meanwhile, Krystal has appeared at the bar, angering Jodi, who can't deal with Krystal's flamboyant style.

3. Heat? What Heat? Just as a heat wave hits Morton, Linda devises a song and dance act for the bar called The Dot's Hole Review. Meanwhile, as Martin dreams that Paulie is his boyfriend, Kat and Allison have become attracted to each other and make out in the concluding episode.

268 Secret Girlfriend. youtube.com/watch?v=BoQvf3z9i_k. 2007–2008 (Comedy).

Are you a girl and do you have a secret girlfriend? Are you a guy and do you have a secret girlfriend? Depending on who is viewing (straight, lesbian, gay or bisexual) the lone girl who appears in each episode speaks directly into the camera and address you as if you were her lover and talks about something in your non-existent relationship. Each episode runs under two minutes and there are six girls, each with a differing personality, designed to attract a particular type of person: Carmen (an alluring tease), Jackie (a girl addicted to sex), Katherine ("it-girl starlet"), Mandy (intense, artistic and "crazy"), Sarah (the cute girl next door type) and Topaz (the aggressive, sultry Russian beauty). Unfortunately the women do not receive credit. In 2009 the Comedy Central cable channel retooled the idea a bit and created its own version of the series. Still using the title *Secret Girlfriend*, the program stars Alexis Krause as Mandy, Sara Fletcher as Jessica, Michael Blaiklock as Sam, Derek Miller as Phil and you (the viewer) as You. You have a secret girlfriend named Jessica, two best friends, Sam and Phil and a crazy ex-girlfriend named Mandy. As you try to just live your life and interact with your friends you find your life is plagued by Mandy—a girl who won't let go (or go away) no matter what you try to do to discourage her and move on. And the more you anger her, the worse it is for you.

Credits: *Creator:* Jay Rondot, Ross Novie. **Comment:** While the idea of talking directly to the camera dates back to 1950 on TV with *The George Burns and Gracie Allen Show* it is still quite effective and presents a more intimate one-on-one basis. The program has no cast or credits listed and virtually all on-line information relates to the 2009 *Secret Girlfriend* TV series that evolved from the web program and not the web series.

Episodes: 20 episodes were produced but only 4 episodes and two trailers remain on line.

1. Secret Girlfriend Promo 1 (brief sequences with several different girls).

2. Secret Girlfriend Promo 2: Jessica.

3. Secret Girlfriend: Topaz.

4. Secret Girlfriend: Jessica.

5. Secret Girlfriend: Mandy.

6. Secret Girlfriend: Katherine.

269 Secrets. afterellen.com. 2010 (Comedy).

Everyone has secrets and everyone who has them

hopes they never come to the surface. Adapting the format of a daily television soap opera, but only incorporating the recap aspect of those programs, the hidden secrets that affect the lives of a group of people—and how they struggle to keep their hidden demons secret are told (focusing on the highlights of what each scene would entail) as opposed to an actual episode.

Cast: Ellen Epstein (Shayla), Karen Springer, Andrea Boyer (Pam), Maureen Aducci (Margie), Tina Johnson (Gayl), Sabina Batalman (Amber), Sebastian Stuart (Philip), Collin Knight (Raquan), Seth Bodie (The Lips), June Wilson (Spooner), Polly Williams (Wynonna), Ilya Tacevich (Lana), Miranda Knox (Jessica), Georgia Gladden (Shavonne), Crystal Waters (Carrie), Ali Sherman (Logan), Matt Chapuran (Cooper), Steve Kleinedier (Jerrald), Nathaniel Fink (Kyle), Daniel J. Bermington (Frank), Megan Summers (Tish), Marjorie Zohn (Dr. Jewison), Christina Cannon (Noreen). **Credits:** *Producer-Director:* Faith Soloway, Lian Brownell. *Writer:* Faith Soloway. **Comment:** A unique idea that is well presented and acted. With only hints of gay, lesbian and transgender characters, one can only imagine what would have developed if the program were presented as a regular series. Even in its abbreviated form, it is still enjoyable. NBC attempted such an idea in 1971 with a pilot film called *The Shameful Secrets of Hastings Corners* (starring Hal Linden) and nothing has since been attempted until the Internet and *Secrets*.

Episodes: Each episode opens with "This week on *Secrets*" followed by a very brief look at what happens based on the titles.

1. Episode 1 Recap: *The Potluck* (Shayla becomes upset when she finds traces of ham in her vegetarian baked beans). *The Engagement Party* (Margie, fearing her nieces and nephews will discover she is a lesbian, introduces her lover, Gayl, as her traveling companion). *Raquan's Late Night* (Philip, Raquan's lover is becoming upset that he spends more time with his Hommies than him).

2. Episode 2 Recap: *Tish's Homecoming* (Tish returns home from the hospital suffering from amnesia). *The Dinner Party* (Raquan struggles to make it through one of Philip's boring dinner parties). *Dr. Jewison's Crisis* (Feeling it is unethical for a doctor to fall in love with her patient, Dr. Jewison terminates her therapy sessions with Noreen).

3. Episode 3 Recap: *Rachel's Roommate* (It is Thanksgiving and Rachel's grandmother is not all that happy when she sees her granddaughter with her female lover). *Rekindling Tish* (Tish is still trying to deal with her amnesia). *Raquan's Moment of Truth* (Philip meets Raquan's Hommies for the first time).

4. Episode 4 Recap: *Steven's Resolution* (Steven finds his New Year's resolution not to watch porn only lasting 20 minutes). *The Custody Battle* (gays Jerrald and Cooper argue over who should get custody of the dog, Cocoa, they shared when they were

a couple). *Spooner's Repeat Customer* (at the Diesel Garage, run by lesbians Spooner and Pam, Pam becomes jealous when a persistent female patron [Lana] sets her sights on Spooner).

5. Episode 5 Recap: *Spooner's Super Bowl Party* (Spooner throws a Super Bowl party for her lesbian friends). *Dante's First Birthday* (Dante's first birthday is celebrated by his two lesbian mothers, Carrie and Logan). *Alone Time* (Philip and Raquan finally get some time alone).

6. Episode 6 Recap: *The Oscar Party* (Jerrald acquires a job as a living statue at the Oscar ceremonies). *Shavonne Showdown* (Philip, who is white, and Raquan, who is black, face the wrath of Shavonne, Raquan's sister, who does not approve of their relationship as lovers). *Dante's Bedtime* (Carrie becomes concerned over Logan's obsession with Dante).

7. Episode 7 Recap: *A New Player in the Game* (Spooner and Lana appear to be a couple until Pam, with a new girl in her life [Aphrodite] sparks Spooner's jealous streak). *At Mama's Bedside* (Raquan feels he must tell his dying mother about his lover, Philip). *Joan's Old Bandmate* (Joan finds herself recalling past memories when she performs a song with her band).

8. Episode 8 Recap: *Jessica's Dad* (Jessica tries to overcome an embarrassing moment when her transgender father makes an appearance before her friends at school). *One Long Rehearsal* (Joan faces numerous challenges as she seeks songs for an upcoming performance). *Frank's Encounter* (Frank feels that he and his lover, Kyle are beginning to drift apart).

270 *Seeking Simone.* seekingsimone.com. 2009 (Comedy-Drama).

Simone Selkin is an actress with a minor role on the television series *CSIS: Forensic SWAT*. She lives in Toronto, Canada, has a best friend, Audrey (an English teacher) and is looking for romance with another woman. Being attractive and a lesbian does not always mean she will attract the right girl as she has not yet found her ideal mate. To solve her dilemma, Simone permits Audrey to create an online profile for her (under the name "Spicy Lime") and stories relate Simone's encounters with a varied group of women—from one that could be her dream girl to those who could be her worst nightmare.

Cast: Renee Olbert (Simone Selkin), Anna Chatterton (Audrey), Kiran Friesen (Caramel Kiss), Sara Gilchrist (Sylvia Grihm), Zoie Palmer (Rebecca), Michelle Girouard (Elisa), David Bronfman (Stone), Mike McPhaden (Leslie), Liz Pounsett (Gina), Evalyn Parry (Betti). **Credits:** *Producer:* Renee Olbert, Rosemary Rowe. *Director:* Naomi Jaye. *Writer:* Rosemary Rowe. **Comment:** Charming series with acting and production values comparable to any television program in the same genre. There are scenes of intimacy between Simone and the women she encounters (kissing) but nothing graphic.

Episodes:

1. Single Lesbian Psychos. Simone, new to the world of Internet dating, mistakenly allows Audrey to create her profile, and winds up with something that is not really her.

2. Please.... Please Stop. Simone's profile acquires her a first date—with a girl (Elisa) who appears normal—until her true nature (a crack-head) reveals itself.

3. Hammer Toes. Simone's profile brings her in contact with a lovely musician—a girl whose music is her life and with whom Simone finds nothing in common.

4. A League of Her Own. The passive Simone finds a challenge to her life style when she meets Caramel Kiss, an aggressive woman who immediately seduces Simone, causing Simone to realize such women are out of her league.

5. Dirty Birds. Simone's sexual encounter with Caramel Kiss has her rethinking her approach to women when she auditions for a role in the courtroom drama *The Albatross Appeal* and finds herself attracted to the show's gorgeous producer.

6. Free Tibette! When Simone learns that her character on *CSIS* is to be shot and she will be out of a job, Simone makes a play for the writer (Tibette) hoping to seduce her into keeping her job on the show.

7. Tippi Hedren's Slutty Daughter. In an attempt to find Simone the right woman, Audrey surprises her with a blind date—a girl (Sylvia) who immediately becomes attracted to Simone; so much so that Simone abandons her principals of not sleeping with a girl on a first date to make love to her (Tippi Hedren is an actress best known for her role in the Alfred Hitchcock film *The Birds* although she has nothing to do with the episode).

8. Heat of Passion. Simone realizes that she should have remained true to her principals when she finds Sylvia wants to begin a steady relationship with her.

9. Dread Carpet. At an awards ceremony, Simone finds that her relationship with Sylvia is becoming a media issue.

10. Leslie. Feeling that it is best, Simone and Sylvia decide to break up. The episode ends unresolved as a new woman enters Simone's life—an accountant named Leslie, a girl Simone chooses on her own.

271 *The Seer.* youtube.com. 2008 (Crime Drama).

"What do you see when you close your eyes? I see life and all its dimensions" says Guin Marcus, a former police detective turned private investigator who uses her sixth sense (to see what others can not) to solve crimes. "I'm on a path I did not choose but sometimes life just decides for you and you've got to play along." Guin (a lesbian) is currently a partner with Annie Finn (Marcus and Finn, Private Investigators) and, during her time on the police force was romantically involved with her then partner, Detective April Reese—a girl who comes back into her life after a two year absence (it was her affair with April that, as she says, "crossed the line" and changed the direction of her life). The program's only story line explores Guin's efforts to find Jeremy Rains, a psychopathic killer and the complications that ensue when he kidnaps Dee (Guin's current lover) as bait to lure Guin and dispose of her (as she is the only one who can prove he is the killer). See also *InSight*, a prior series featuring the Guin Marcus character.

Cast: Deborah Stewart (Guin Marcus), Michelle Tomlinson (April Reese), Landall Goolsby (Jeremy Rains), Vincent DePaul (Det. Burnette), Shant'e Reese (Annie Finn), Patricia Melone (Dee), Maria Falgione (Samantha). **Credits:** *Producer:* Linda Andersson, Chris Bebel, Teri Maher, Deborah Stewart. *Writer-Director:* Linda Andersson. **Comment:** The program, while well acted, appears to be a copy from a VHS tape as the video quality is bit poor. There are kissing scenes and sexual situations and the story flows smoothly from beginning to end. The plot plays a bit like the recurring story line on NBC's *Profiler* series wherein a killer used the same tactics to lure his pursuer to him.

Episodes:

1. Episode 1. The story line is established as a young female jogger is killed and the police suspect that a psychotic (Jeremy Rains) is the culprit.

2. Episode 2. Guin, hired by the police to help capture Jeremy, finds that she can not only see Jeremy as the killer—but he can see her as the only person who can stop him.

3. Episode 3. A flashback to Guin and April as lovers while police officers is seen while in the present, Jeremy kidnaps Dee (Guin's lover) sending Guin on a desperate search to find her before it is too late (the program concludes with Jeremy dragging Dee into a building and Guin closing in).

272 *Sez Me.* sezme.com. 2013 (Children).

"There's so many ways to be, there's so many you's and me's, sez me" is the motto of a program that attempts to acquaint children with and help them understand the LGBTQ community. Ultra Charmin, a drag queen, is the host and the program encompasses colorful animation, sound effects and an unscripted segment between a child and an adult as its teaching tool. A child, chosen by the producer from a diverse family (e.g., gay, lesbian or single parent) interviews an adult who represents a non-traditional gender (e.g., drag queens, feminine men, masculine women) in an effort for children to learn by asking questions about their subjects.

Cast: Jeff Marras (Charmin Ultra), Michelle

Matlock (Parker Pumernickle), Audrey London (Herself). **Credits:** *Producer-Director:* Mor Erlich. **Comment:** A beautiful pixie (*Pixanne*), a mouse (*The Mickey Mouse Club*), a slapstick comedian (*The Soupy Sales Show*), a scruffy Old West coot (*The Gabby Hayes Show*) and even a Muppet frog named Kermit (*The Muppet Show*) have hosted television series for children in fantasy-like presentations. *Sez Me* surpasses those programs and tries to be as real as possible in its aim to create a dialogue about those who may appear different or queer to children. The presentation is well done and the children chosen as interviewers are knowledgeable about the LGBTQ community and their insights could help other children acquire a better understanding as to why some people are different.

Episodes:

1. *Sez Charmin and Duy.* Jeff Marras is interviewed by a child (Duy) to introduce viewers to Jeff's life as a drag queen.

2. *The Weivretni.* The title refers to Interview spelled backwards and focuses on a conversation held between Charmin and a young girl (Aubrey) as they talk about gender, friends and family.

3. *Charmin's Angels—Sez Cypress and Eve.* Highlights of an interview conducted by a young girl (Cypress) of guest star super model and DJ Eve Salvail.

273 *She Life.* shelifeseries.com. 2014 (Drama).

The activities of a group of diverse African-American lesbians are profiled as they deal with issues—from romantic encounters to cheating to deception—issues that can also be encountered by members of any society or here, as defined by the program's tag line: "Real issues found in the LGBT Community."

Cast as credited: Trap Dinaro (Trap), Star (Maya), Cassandra (Charm), Toshiba (Loren), Shante (Star), Lou (Lou), Maria (Staxx), Tozie, C.J., Ashley, Lyric, "Harm," Latte. **Credits:** *Producer-Writer-Director:* Cassandra German. **Comment:** Viewer comments (as seen on YouTube) have mostly been harsh ("confusing program; it appears to have no plot"; "bad writing"; "needs better lighting"; "terrible acting"; "bad sound"). In all honesty, those comments are true but examining what has been produced could also be positive. The actors are not professionals and it appears they are ad-libbing at times (perhaps following a plot outline). Taking this into consideration, and comparing it with other such programs (like *The Lovers and Friends Show*), *She Life* is much better (just in the attractiveness of some of the girls alone). What the program needed was an introductory episode to acquaint viewers with the main girls, which may have made it easier to figure out who is who and what is going on. As it stands now, it is confusing and it does need better lighting (as some scenes are very dark). The unsteady (shaky) camera does not enhance anything and is just plain annoying here (there are also some out-of-focus scenes that also hinder the production). Most of the actors do a good job handling their roles and what the producer was trying to achieve can be seen in

Sez Me. Series poster art (copyright Sez Me, 2014; all rights reserved).

various scenes. It would have also been nice to credit the performers with full names as opposed to what appears on the screen. There are mild sexual situations, kissing scenes, and for whatever reason, an abundant use of vulgar language. Overall, for an amateur, apparently no or low budget program, it does have problems but it is also trying its best to be something different and bring to light—in a realistic way, what is happening to African-American lesbians in today's society.

Episode List: *1.* World Premiere of *She Life* Episode 1. *2.* She Life Episode 2. *3.* She Life Episode 3.

274 She.Likes.Girls. youtube.com. 2011 (Drama).

She Likes Girls (without the dots) is a 2007 anthology video that encompassed six lesbian themed stories. One of the stories, "The Uninvited," had been taken out of the video and placed on line in 2011 in what appeared to be the beginning of a web series that would have incorporated videos from other sources to create an Internet lesbian series.

Cast: Katie Boyle (Shelley), Heidi Sulzman (Mattie). **Credits:** *Producer:* Dylan Robertson. *Director:* Louise Runge. *Writer:* Louise Runge, Heidi Sulzman. **Comment:** "The Uninvited" left the doorway open to continue the story and perhaps, if episodes had been produced for the web series, it would have followed Mattie's pursuit of Shelley. Being that four years have now passed since the episode was produced, it is doubtful a series will emerge. The episode itself is well crafted and a bit eerie as you can never tell what Mattie is up to. The production values are also high caliber.

Episodes:

1. The Uninvited. Shelley and Mattie are very attractive young women who live in the same apartment complex but are strangers to each other—until Mattie finds an attraction to Shelley and begins stalking her. At first Shelley thinks nothing of it, especially when Mattie saves her from a choking incident but then finds herself becoming uneasy when she senses not all is right with Mattie.

275 Simple Events. simpleevents.tumblr. com. 2012 (Comedy-Drama).

Leanne Wright, an 18-year-old bisexual teenager (although more interested in girls), has just enrolled in college (in the city of Hamilton). She is pretty, energetic and following in the footsteps of her father (hoping to become a doctor). While she is taking pre-med courses she sometimes doubts she has chosen her career goal and feels it was thrust upon her. Attending classes and meeting new people is not a problem for her, but acquiring money is as she is living off what her scholarship pays and she soon finds that it is not enough (and, if she drops out or fails,

she will have to immediately pay off the scholarship). On her first day in Hamilton, she meets Grace Burns, a political science major who offers to help her with her luggage and help her out financially— by offering her money if she will passionately kiss her in public. With only $20 to her name, Leanne agrees. She not only kissed a beautiful woman (as she exclaims) but has made a new friend and stories chart Leanne's experiences, more comical than dramatic, as she begins her first year of college at Mc-Master University.

Matt is Grace's 17-year-old boyfriend, a member of the school's hockey team; Joshua, 18 years old, is Matt's brother; Ravi is Grace's overprotective gay friend, a 19-year-old who fears Leanne and Grace will become a couple and he will lose his best friend; Amanda is Leanne's roommate, a sexy girl with a knack for finding mishap.

Cast: Kate Stephen (Leanne Wright), Katie Hill (Grace Burns), Michael Patricelli (Matthew Cote), Mike Desmond (Ravi Patel), Melissa Height (Amanda Sampson), Erich Szpytma (Joshua Cote). **Credits:** *Producer:* Linda Mitton. **Comment:** Smooth flowing story with enjoyable characters, some kissing and a bit of comedy thrown into the mix. The acting and production values are good and a worth-while program to watch.

Episodes:

1. Pilot. Introduces Leanne as she meets Grace (wearing a rubber chicken hat) and is offered money if she will kiss her in public.

2. Jersey. In a panic because he loaned his lucky jersey to Amanda, Matt seeks a way to recover it before hockey practice.

3. A Party. Leanne attends her first party with Grace—only to see that things are getting out of hand when alcohol is introduced.

4. Charity. As money problems still plague her, Leanne sets her sights on figuring ways to earn some without breaking the law. The program's concluding episode.

276 Single_Never_Married. WillPTV.com. 2013 (Comedy).

Deon is a young woman who has written a successful book about love, relationships and dating. In reality, however, she is not only unlucky in love but her book expertise appears to work for everyone but her. Deon, a lesbian, hails from Texas and has a dog named Violet. To most people, a dog is just a dog; but to Deon, Violet is like the sister she never had. She obsesses over Violet and apparently fails to realize that her obsession is seen as just plain weird to her dates and an immediate turn off to all except Max, her next-door neighbor who truly loves her but feels he has no chance with her as she is not interested in men. The program charts Deon's continual attempts to find the girl of her dreams (maybe even any girl at all) and Max's efforts to not only remain her friend, but possibly her lover (after five years of trying, he has not given up hope).

Cast: Lauren Hamilton (Deon), Monique Gelineau (Charlie), Tracy Mazyck (Max), Violet (Violet). **Credits:** *Producer-Writer-Director:* Angela Burris, Lauren Hamilton. **Comment:** Very enjoyable lesbian-themed program with very good acting and production values. Deon is so in love with the dog that she can't see that her obsession with Violet is the reason for all her problems—all of which adds to the fun and, being that the series ends with Deon thinking she has found the right girl, leaves the viewer to wonder what will become of Max, but most importantly, what will become of Violet once she realizes there is a stumbling block to her finding happiness.

Episodes:

1. Can I Get a Hug? As Deon attempts to get closer to her date, she finds her efforts to no avail when Max enters and causes the girl to leave. But not to worry as Deon finds comfort in pampering Violet when she rejects Max's advances.

2. Massage Me. Deon's date appears to be going better than she had hoped for—until she realizes the time and must get Violet to bed.

3. Me or Your Dog! Deon's efforts to get closer to her girlfriend (Charlie) take a turn for the worse when Charlie wants to become intimate but Deon can't pull herself away from Violet.

4. I'm in Love! Violet has ruined another relationship; Deon is dissatisfied working as a temp and feels that life may be better back in Texas. As she is about to follow her instinct, she meets a sexy new co-worker (Jessica) and sets her goal to make her the one. The program concludes at this point.

277 *Sintillate Studios.* webserieschannel. com. 2010 (Comedy).

Naughty Nannies and *Probing Felicity* are two of the many X-rated films produced in Australia by Sintillate Studios, a video company that makes titles for "the adult connoisseur of sex." But what appears in their videos is only "the good stuff." What happens during the making of such "classics" is never meant to be seen by the public as making such films is not always as easy as it looks—hook up a guy and a girl or a girl with another girl (or any combination) and point a camera and shoot. It is what happens that you do not see in the making of X-rated adult films that is shown—with all the backstage drama and none of that "good stuff." Felicity and Carly are sisters; Brad is Carly's boyfriend; Justin and Sterling are actors; Alisha is the ditzy starlet; Jizz is the eccentric director and Rose is the neurotic producer.

Cast: Siobhan Novello (Carly), Karly Ann (Felicity), Craig McDonald (Justin), Marcus Hall (Brad), Kate Kelly (Alisha), Joseph O'Neill (Sterling), Christie Sistrunk (Rose), Charlie Handcock (Jizz). **Credits:** *Producer:* Bec Darling, Gary Sewell.

Director: Gary Sewell. *Writer:* Amy Costello, Tina McKimmie, Siobhan Dow-Hall, Gary Sewell. **Comment:** Delving into such territory as X-rated films is risky as what they present and what decency laws permit on broadcast and basic cable TV are limited. With the Internet it is just the opposite although some sites do have decency standards and restrict what can be shown. The producers of *Sintillate* Studios have taken that into account and created a PG-rated version of an X-rated topic. While there are sexual situations (including girl/girl love scenes) nothing is really offensive as such scenes as depicted here have been seen on various broadcast TV series with even more boldness. The acting is very good and placing that behind-the-scenes turmoil that occurs is something really different to see.

Episodes:

1. The Sound of My Prick. A porn parody of *Mary Poppins* (including a clever variation on the original title song) finds stars Alisha and Felicity about to make love as Alisha performs her song.

2. Angry Lesbian Prisoners. The lesbian scene progresses but turns ugly when Felicity and Alisha appear unable to get along with each other and complete the scene.

3. Vaginas for a Vote. Studio heads fear trouble when their latest film is threatened by feminist protestors.

4. Sex Education with Miss Titwank. Felicity and Carly embrace for the worst when their mothers, becoming suspicious of their occupations, pay a visit to the set.

5. Cockadile Cumdee. With funding on his latest film running dangerously low and he is unable to hire a male actor, Justin elects to star in a gay porn film himself.

6. Arse-tralia. A backdoor-themed movie has Felicity and Alisha at odds over the leading role while the third leading actress, Rose, faces all the fallout.

7. Carly the Vampire Layer. Carly gets the leading role in a *Buffy the Vampire Slayer* spoof but her boyfriend, Brad, is not so enthused by her new role.

8. Shakespeare in Latex Gloves. An acting coach attempts the impossible—teaching the cast the Bard's words for a Shakespearian porn-theme flick.

9. Service My Pipes. The Boss takes over as head of the studio, forcing Jizz to perform his off-camera prowess on camera.

10. Tower-In-Her-Fur-Now. The cast joins forces to save the financially-strapped Sintillate Studios in the concluding episode.

278 *Skin Deep.* skindeeptheseries.com. 2012 (Drama).

A promotional video for a proposed series that was to focus on the gay community in Atlanta, Georgia, but not through family, co-workers or friends, but on six characters (three black, three white) who are anonymous to each other.

Rod is a middle twenties-aged white male who works nights as a club dancer to supplement his small earnings as a professional kick boxer (which often causes him to question his sexuality). While he is not currently in a relationship, he finds himself more comfortable dating white men. He lives with a straight man named Keith and respects Keith's relationship with his girlfriend Sadie.

Lawrence, a black male in his late 20s, is well educated and recently came out to his family that he is gay only to find that they literally disowned him (cutting off all his finances). Although he has enough money to support himself for a short time, he is struggling to make a career choice and find a good-paying job. Although Lawrence is proud of his heritage, he finds an attraction only to men of different races.

Whit, a mid-thirties white male, is a sales representative who was raised in a conservative upper middle-class family. He has not yet come out to his family (as he was raised as a strict Catholic and thus feels guilty about his being gay. This also affects his dating life as he is not comfortable revealing who he is and he prefers meeting men on line or in sex clubs).

Tyrone, a black male about 22 years old, has recently moved from a small Georgia town to begin work as a fireman in Atlanta. He comes from a very religious family and has had little interaction with the white community and associates only with black men. Tyrone is also a bit wet behind the ears, having just come to full terms with his sexuality, and is dangerously drawn toward "thuggish" men.

Paul, an older white male (48 to 52 years old) is a private investigator whose clients include straight women hiring him to spy on their husbands (thus causing a conflict of interest for him). Paul is in a steady relationship and marriage plans are in the making.

Gregory, a 40–45-year-old black male, has been in an interracial relationship for several years. He is an activist for the Black Gay Community and works as counselor for troubled youths. Gregory is not attracted to a man because of skin color (he finds all races attractive) and often finds dislike from other black gays for his choice of lovers.

Cast: K.C. Morgan (Whit), Max Guhtmc (Rod), Dess Epps (Tyrone), Denerick Lindsay (Marcus). Performers for the roles of Paul and Lawrence had not yet been cast. **Credits:** *Producer-Writer-Director:* David Summers. **Comment:** Based on what is available it appears to be a well scripted idea that mixes white and black gays in separate scenarios that all have a common thread—"I want to be loved." The teaser is being shopped (presented to various producers) in the hopes of acquiring the financing to produce an actual series for regular TV or the Internet. As the producer states: "The footage you see here is presented as a teaser to the series. This footage is being used as marketing material to present to net-

works, directors and production companies for consideration to their programming options. We have not filmed any episodes for viewing due to budgetary restraints. Sponsors to help us achieve that goal are welcome."

Episodes:

1. Promotional Teaser.

279 *Skin: The Web Series.* youtube.com. 2013 (Drama).

Renee Best, age 20, is Biology major in her junior year at Bennett College. Simone Donovan, age 20, a sophomore at Bennett and majoring in psychology, lists her hobby as stalking and her computer as her best friend. Corie Reeves, a 20-year-old business major at Bennett is best friends with Renee and claims that talking is her hobby. Munchie, as she is called, is 21 years old and a Culinary Arts major at the University of North Carolina in Greensboro. Her best friends, she claims are chefs and eating is her hobby. Skylar Donovan, Simone's older sister (25) has a Masters degree in Bio-Medical Science and currently attends the Morehouse School of Medicine. She claims shopping is her hobby and money her best friend. Tonya Green, age 21, is a senior majoring in Social Work at Bennett University. Jamie Peters, a Communications major at Bennett, is 22 years old and best friends with Tonya. Joseph Collins, a 22-year-old Political Science major at North Carolina A&T, is the only male character that interacts with the women.

Renee, a lesbian, is not looking to hook up with anyone for the moment until a mysterious girl named Tonya Williams connects with her on CollegeChat.com. The two begin corresponding and, while Tonya is only seen in a picture she has posted, it appears that a fondness for each other is developing; so much so that after two months Renee has fallen in love with her (the viewer is also kept in the dark as to who Tonya is as her identity is always obscured). The program relates what happens as Tonya's messages to Renee cause her to become curious as to who Tonya is and what results when Renee meets her mysterious lover—a girl who is nothing like her photo or who she pretended to be, but a deranged girl seemingly out to kill her.

Cast: Brittany Gardner (Renee Best), Janae Peats (Tonya Green), Charlotte Jones (Munchie), Dominique Mackey (Skylar Donovan), Steven Neal (Joseph Collins), Quisha Walker (Corie Reeves), Alexis Small (Jamie), Adrienne Mavritte (Simone Donovan). **Credits:** *Producer:* Racquel Bethea. **Comment:** The program opens with a warning that meeting someone on line and getting attached does happen—but what happens when the person in the picture is not the person you thought she was? A mystery is immediately set up when Renee connects with Tonya and, while not the high caliber of a major motion picture or TV series, *Skin* manages to keep you curious in a well-paced, well-acted and produced program that does not drag or fail to solve the mystery.

Episodes:

1. Episode 1. The main characters are introduced as Renee connects with a girl named Tonya on the Internet.

2. Episode 2. It has been two months since Renee and Tonya met on line and are falling in love but it appears that they live far apart and this could hamper their relationship. Meanwhile, a girl named Simone receives an unexpected visit from her sister (Skylar) who immediately sees that Simone is acting a bit strange and complains that she has not taken her medication.

3. Episode 3. As each message from Tonya to Renee becomes more and more of a puzzle to her, Renee begins snooping and finds that the Tonya Green on campus, whom she thought was her Tonya, is not and that someone has stolen her identity and is pretending to be her. Unknown to Renee, she is being stalked by the mysterious girl pretending to be Tonya.

4. Episode 4. In the concluding episode Renee is lead into a trap by the fake Tonya, who is revealed to be Simone (the real Tonya's roommate), wielding a razor-blade like weapon and dead-set on killing Renee.

280 Skye's the Limit. onemorelesbian. com/skyes-the-limit-season-1-episode-1. html. 2012–2013 (Drama).

Samaya Beauvais, called Skye, is a young woman living in Washington, D.C. She has just been laid off from her job (following her return from vacation) and we learn in an opening speech, "I am a writer with a hell of a story to tell." Skye is also a lesbian and what has happened in her life over the past six months forms the basis of the episodes. In flashback-like sequences the incidents that not only affected Skye, but her older "baby" cousin (Cassie), work wife (Taylor), Taylor's boyfriend (Tyler), Bryn and Marisol, Skye's friends (with Marisol pushing Skye to pursue a writing career), Ronnie, Skye's Howard University friend and Jay, Skye's former girlfriend.

Cast: Shauntice Wyatt (Samaya "Skye" Beauvais), Samantha Lynn Grier (Cassie Beauvais), Breeze Bennett (Taylor Saint-James), Carlton Jones (Tyler Smith), Zuri Prior-Graves (Jalayna "Jay" Dandridge), Jessica Pierce (Marisol Millan), Romy Simpson (Maya), LaRita Massey (Mutha Indigo), Crystal Cornish (Jasmine Saint-James), Sheena Styles (Bryn Daniels), Mel Williams (Samantha "Sam" Wainwright), Kenecole Blake (Tracy Brown), Lyrikk Mashairi (Kendra Jameson), LaPorschia Dephyne (Gina "DJ Got Damn"), Jordyn White (Robin Davis), Thomas A. White (Jacob Davis), Katrina Wheeler (Toni Toussaint), Marly Mattison (Brenda Santos). **Credits:** *Producer-Writer-Director:* Blue

Talusmah. **Comment:** A well acted but involved program with too many characters and trying to figure out who is who and how they are connected makes it difficult to follow. The characters are, to say the least, diversified but stretching out who they are (that is, only glimpses are given regarding their backgrounds) makes more for confusion than anything else (the intent appears to be revealing little by little as episodes progress) but holding the viewer's interest could be lost. Just like with network and cable TV, programs that tend to be different and present "thinking" (so to speak) most often do not make it. With the many distractions involving Internet TV—from pop-up ads to the website's surrounding graphics, attention can be easily lost and capturing it is not easy with programs that require thinking outside the box. The production values are good but there appears to be some inconsistency in the story. It is told through Skye's experiences but it leaves one to wonder how she can relate certain details when she was not apart of those incidents.

Episode List: *1.* Skye's the Limit: Pilot Episode. *2.* Trapped in the Closet. *3.* Tongue Tied. *4.* Coming to Dinner, Part 1. *5.* Coming to Dinner, Part 2. *6.* Rockin' Robin. *7.* Mercury in Retrograde. *8.* Feasting in Scraps. *9.* T.G.I.F.

281 The Slope. vimeo.com/user7692596. 2011–2012 (Drama).

Park Slope in Brooklyn, New York, provides the backdrop for a story about Desiree and Ingrid, a real-life lesbian couple and the problems they face and attempt (but fail) to overcome to save their relationship. Desiree is more attractive and feminine (people say she looks like Sandra Bullock) while Ingrid, happy the way she is, appears a bit older and more masculine looking (as she wears little makeup and is not one for fancy clothes).

Cast: Desiree Akhavan (Desiree), Ingrid Jungermann (Ingrid). **Credits:** *Producer-Writer-Director:* Desiree Akhavan, Ingrid Jungermann. **Comment:** A true-to-life story of two women who were lovers but have since gone their separate ways. The women are instantly like-able and they encompass their roles well. There are no nude or kissing scenes and only one brief sexual situation. There is some offensive language (referring to street-slang for female body parts) and dialogue appears to be ad-libbed in some episodes (when the girls talk about their pasts). Overall the program is well done and a bit different than other lesbian-themed web series.

Episodes:

1. Miserable Animals. Desiree and Ingrid are introduced for the first time as Ingrid adopts a stray dog (a Husky).

2. Pretty People. Desiree and Ingrid discuss their appearance and how other people see them.

3. Queer Programming. While walking the dog, Ingrid runs into a bisexual friend and must endure

her endless chatter about a TV soap opera called "The Real Albert" (about gays and lesbians).

4. Bottoms Up. Desiree and Ingrid talk frankly about lesbian positions during sex.

5. It Gets Better. The women relate incidents from their past lives.

6. Open Dialogue. It is shown that arguments between the two will eventually break them up. Here, Desiree tries to convince Ingrid to become intimate with a straight couple to experience something different.

7. Harnessing Jeff. Ingrid's efforts to avoid a male friend while walking the dog fail and she is subjected to his endless chatter about going to the dentist.

8. Outtakes. An outtake from an episode is showcased as season one concludes.

9. Taking Spaces. The start of season two begins with Ingrid finding herself being hit on by a man and Desiree talking about relationships with her friend Anna (Anna Rose).

10. Revolving Door. A woman (Ann Carr) becomes attracted to Ingrid and attempts to seduce her, placing Ingrid in a difficult situation as she is dating Desiree.

11. Primary Care Giver. To bond their relationship, an enthusiastic Desiree tries to convince a reluctant Ingrid that they should consider adopting a baby girl.

12. Pride and Prejudice. Ingrid is shocked to discover that her gay friend Markus (Markus Kirschner) is opposed to lesbians and can't accept the fact that Ingrid is one when she reveals it to him.

13. The 5 Stages of Grief. Desiree and Ingrid's continual disagreements cause them to call off their relationship after one year.

14. Conversation Theory. As Desiree meets with her friend Kai (Beverly Whittemore), a lesbian gone straight, and her boyfriend, Mike (Pedro Gomez Milan) she continually talks about Kai's lesbian affairs in what appears to be an attempt by Desiree to win Kai's heart and turn Mike off to dating a former lesbian.

15. Fashion Forward. Desiree's attempt to move on with her life is not as easy as she thought as she still has feelings for Ingrid.

16. Miserable Best Friends Who Used to Be Together. Desiree and Ingrid meet to discuss their joint possessions—including the dog. It concludes with them unable to resolve their differences and agreeing not to see each other again (and the dog—both leave and the dog is torn with which one to follow home).

282 Social Animals. vimeo.com. 2011 (Comedy-Drama).

Three young women (Sarah, Riley and Kate), their male friend (Tom) and their efforts to overcome their seemingly directionless (and rather boring lives) as they try to help each other find the still unknown happiness they are seeking.

Riley is a glamorous girl who is drawn to other women but whom you would never suspect of being drawn to yard sales and involved in "dumpster diving" activities to acquire the "treasures" that someone else may have tossed away. She is also adventurous and always there for her friends in the time of need.

Thom had dated Kate, but when they realized they had nothing in common, they mutually agreed to break up but remain friends. Although Tom is straight, he contends that "dudes are boring" to hang out with and delights with his female "hangout friends."

Kate has not moved on and lives in the same neighborhood in which she grew up. She is an only child and "hates most people, including her friends" (a result of being secretly attention starved). Because her situation has not changed since she was a child, she has settled into her uninspired life and admits that she is just too lazy to meet new people.

Sarah, born in New England, is a flirtatious girl who grew up in a household with an abusive and alcoholic father. Although she hangs out with two women, she is straight but has a weakness for falling for older men in uniform. Her one principal fault could be considered her attempts to project her outlooks into the people who surround her—an effort to make up for the lack of affection at home from her father.

Cast: Riley Rose Critchlow (Riley), Kate Heckman (Kate), Sarah Erin Roach (Sarah), Thom Shelton (Tom). **Credits:** *Producer-Director:* Erin Weller. *Writer:* Kate Heckman, Erin Weller. **Comment:** Well-acted and produced and, although there is more comedy than drama, an enjoyable program to watch.

Episodes:

1. Perry's Party. The friends discuss the prospect of attending a friend's birthday party—something they finally agree on despite the fact that the girl, Perry (Allison Fields) is a flake and throws child-like parties.

2. Let's Get Physical. When Riley feels that she may be putting on weight, Tom agrees, forcing Riley to seek an exercise program—until actually pursuing one takes more ambition than she has.

3. Adventures in Babysitting. Sarah's job as a babysitter requires the help of her friends when she is left in charge of a wild child. The program's concluding episode.

283 Spin the Bottle. spinthebottle.com. 2012 (Comedy).

Six friends, while always a bit tipsy from too much alcohol, attempt to help each other deal with sex, relationships and life itself. Perry and Roy are a gay couple; Liv (Roy's sister) and Leeza are straight girls; and Bobby (married) and Chad (who prefers to be called "The Chad") are straight best friends.

Cast: Matthew Barnard (Roy), Emma Payne

(Leeza), Jeff Castle (Bobby), Joshua Christian (Chad), Kate Reavis (Liv), Raychel Espiritu (Kylie), Reena Shah (Justine), Matt Palazzolo (Perry), Vaz Andreas (Steve), Chase Hinton (Adam), Joe Chacon (Jose), Jessica Bay (Jules). **Credits:** *Producer-Director:* Fred Germany. *Writer:* Matthew Barnard. **Comment:** Non-offensive, well acted and produced program that mixes straight characters with a gay couple (Roy and Perry). The cast is attractive and stories, while short, are right to the point although stretching some by a minute or two would have made some scenes not feel so rushed.

Episodes:

1. Episode 1. The six friends are introduced with a revelation that Bobby is planning to get a divorce (believing his wife [who is never seen] is cheating on him).

2. Episode 2. While Leeza seeks to find Liv a date, Chad begins preparations for Bobby's divorce party.

3. Episode 3. Roy and Bobby's plans to open a gay wine bar called Rope, hit a snag when Bobby, not sure he should sign his divorce papers, prompts Roy to put things on hold until Bobby makes up his mind.

4. Episode 4. Chad's attempts to flirt with a girl at work (Kylie) but fails miserably.

5. Episode 5. As preparations continue for the divorce party, Liv brings a date to the party (Steven) who is believed to be gay by his dress and actions.

6. Episode 6. Things become uncomfortable for Bobby when he catches Leeza in a compromising situation with Chad while Roy and Perry venture into the kitchen to see Steven kissing a girl and realize their "gaydar" was wrong.

7. Who's the Man? Simplistic episode wherein Justine, Bobby's niece and Leeza's friend, reveals that she rates the men she dates on a scale from one to nine, stunning Chad and Bobby.

8. The Fidelity Test. As Bobby begins to wonder if his wife really cheated on him or not, Justine suggests he enact "The Fidelity Test"—hook his wife up with "a hot guy" and see what happens.

9. Virgin Alert. When Chad discovers that his younger brother, 21-year-old Adam has not made it with a woman, he sets his goal to change all that by setting him up with Bobby's wife.

10. All on Tape. The encounter Chad set up for Adam has a surprising twist when Chad has it secretly recorded and reveals Bobby's wife was again unfaithful.

11. Can I Go Now? As Justine describes how she rates men, Liv comes to realize that what Justine rates as a one or nine does not mean the same thing to her as she holds a different set of standards when it comes to dating.

12. I Banged Her. As Bobby musters up the courage to sign the divorce papers, Justine introduces her friends to her new love, Jose.

13. Big Dick. Leeza, who writes a dating column

is asked to change its direction from telling what to do on a date to what not to do as she, like many girls, is in a dating slump. Meanwhile the big day is nearing and Roy and Perry are ecstatic about the opening of their bar.

14. Big News. Leeza's life takes a dramatic turn for the better when her editor requests that she turn her column into a series of dating books.

15. That's Not a Hanger. Leeza appears to be out of her dating slump—but her sexual encounters with a man is secretly watched by Chad and Bobby.

16. Bartender or Go-Go Boy. In the concluding episode Leeza relishes in her efforts to help Roy and Perry by choosing Go-Go Boys for their gay bar.

284 Spy Queens. youtube.com. 2014 (Comedy).

"They're three career criminals with a shot at freedom. Now they're working for the Feds who put them away. Bad girls gone good" is the opening of the teaser for a program about three felon drag queens played by Larraine Bow (arrested for computer hacking), Britney K. O'Day (a cat burglar) and Ruby Monroe (charged with assault and battery) who are recruited by the FBI and offered a pardon if they will use their unique skills to help them solve sensitive cases. Borrowing elements of the TV series *She Spies* (which used the same three [real] girl concept as well as the same opening theme words) and *Charlie's Angels* (wherein three [real] girls received orders over a speaker phone from their mysterious employer) *Spy Queens* cleverly combines elements of both series (not to mention films like *James Bond* and *La Femme Nikita*) to relate their adventures as they try to become good, receive their pardons and capture the bad guys (even if they happen to be drag queens).

Cast: Larraine Bow, Britney K. O'Day, Ruby Monroe, Felicia Forrester. **Credits:** *Producer-Director:* Ephram Adamz. **Comment:** Although the TV series and feature films mentioned above may be familiar to you, you have never seen them like this before. Using drag queens puts a whole new twist on the concept (like *Chico's Angels* [see entry] did with *Charlie's Angels*) and makes for an enjoyable program to watch.

Episodes: Episodes have not yet been released and thus far only a short teaser is available that barely highlights aspects of the series.

285 Starting from... Now. startingfrom nowtv.com. 2014 (Drama).

Hoping to achieve her dream of becoming a graphic artist, a young woman (Stephanie Fraser, called Steph) moves from her country home in Australia to the big city (Sydney) when she acquires a job with a large graphics company. Steph, a lesbian, is somewhat naive and now lives with her childhood friend, Kristen and Kristen's live-in girlfriend Darcy. The situation becomes a bit awkward when Steph and Darcy are drawn to each other and Steph is not only faced with problems at work (prove her abilities within three months or face termination) but at home where her attraction to Darcy could destroy her relationship with Kristen if she should pursue it.

Cast: Sarah de Possesse (Steph Fraser), Lauren Orrell (Kristen Sheridan), Rosie Lourde (Darcy Peters), Bianca Bradey (Emily Rochford), Linda Grasso (Trish Faulkner). **Credits:** *Producer-Writer-Director:* Julie Kalceff. **Comment:** An Australian serial that is well acted and produced. The story line is well presented and the women chosen for their roles are very appealing and can draw you right into the story (especially Steph, who is so sweet, but so naïve at times, that you feel for her as she faces life away from her natural environment). Those not familiar with seeing Australian produced movies or TV shows may find the accents a bit hard to understand at times but do not let that deter you from seeing just how good foreign-produced programs can be.

Episodes:

1. Episode 1. Steph is introduced as she moves in with Kristen, meets a girl at a bar (Darcy) then discovers Darcy is Kristen's live-in girlfriend.

Starting from... Now. Series poster art (copyright Common Language Films).

2. Episode 2. Steph's dream job turns out to be more of a bust when she reports to work and is told she has three months to prove herself or face termination. The good thing: she befriends Emily, the gorgeous office manager (who appears to have become instantly attracted to her).

3. Episode 3. At home, as Steph broods about her day at work, she not only finds a sympathetic ear in Darcy but sees that she and Darcy are becoming increasingly attracted to each other.

286 Steam Room Stories. youtube.com. 2010–2014 (Comedy).

A group of men, gay, straight and bisexual, seated in a steam room and wearing only towels, discuss various matters that, for the moment (the particular episode) are of vital concern to them.

Cast: Chad Olson (Trevor), Ben Palacios (Blair), Joe Fidler (Beau), Tamario Fletcher (Shane), Christopher S. Reid (Chris), Steve Snyder (Ross), Adam Bucci (Adam), Justin Clark (Hunter), Michael Poursh (Mike), Jess Welch (Carson), Josh Wise (Josh), Peter DiVito (Tony), Cedric Jonathan (Cedric), Lee Amir-Cohen (Brad), Paris Dylan (Paul), Israel Korn (Luke), Jason E. Thomas (Jake), John Suazo (John), Burke McLain (Burke), Pablo Hernandez (Pablo). **Credits:** *Producer:* J.C. Calciano, Nicholas Downs. *Director:* J.C. Calciano. *Writer:* J.C. Calciano, Nicholas Downs, Steve Snyder. **Comment:** While an all male cast appears, the program is not totally geared to a gay audience. Anyone can enjoy the discussions held by the men. The acting is good and the production values just as good.

Episodes:

1. Kissability. David finds that his lack luster date has unforeseen consequences when his date posts pictures of that date on Facebook.

2. Private Texts. David, finding a cell phone in the steam room, upsets Hunter when he begins reading its sexy messages.

3. You Know You Want Me. A new steam room member has David and Hunter sizing him up.

4. Was That You? An unpleasant odor has the steam room regulars trying to figure out its source.

5. My Nephew. Brad's penchant for showing too many pictures of his nephew has the other steam room members questioning his motives.

6. Steamed Sack. Ross finds the steam room a bit overwhelming and, much to the surprise of the others in the room decides to drop the towel and steam nude.

7. The Porn Star. Hunter becomes overly excited when he believes his favorite male adult film star has entered the steam room.

8. New to Hollywood. With a hope to become an actor, Christian leaves the group to further pursue his career.

9. Childhood Memories. David and Hunter reminisce about their childhood.

10. Glitter. David relays aspects of his night of wild partying to the boys.

11. Watch This. The guys couldn't care less as Hunter shows off his new watch.

12. Peeping Tom. Ross attempts to post a candid picture he took of a member in the steam room across from theirs.

13. Is It Gay? Ross's strange behavior has Brad believing he may be gay.

14. Gay Date #1. As Valentine's Day approaches, Hunter asks David out on a date.

15. Gay Date #2. The guys learn about David and Hunter's date the following morning.

16. Donna the Dominatrix. Ross, thought to be gay, isn't when he tells the guys about his new girlfriend, a Dominatrix.

17. Obama's Health Plan. Aspects of the proposed Obama Health Plan is discussed (the episode aired May 12, 2010).

18. Mob Connections. The guys learn that Ross's family is connected to the mob.

19. Justin Bieber's Disguise. Hoping to attract both guys and girls, Hunter begins dressing like singer Justin Bieber.

20. Hunter's Grudge. The guys decide to relax and just enjoy the steam for a change.

21. Celebrity Sex Encounters. The guys are "treated" to endless chatter as Ross and David tell them about their hook up with Lindsay Lohan, Hugh Jackman and Paul Rudd.

22. The Gayest Underwear. Ross and David discuss what could be considered "the gayest underwear on the planet."

23. Naughty Girls Ass Dial the Guys in the Steam Room. Ross vents his dismay with a girl he dated to the guys.

24. Best Gay Pick Up Lines. The guys use their best lines to befriend a new stud in the gym.

25. Drunk at the Christmas Party. A night of drinking at an office Christmas party is discussed.

26. Is It Gay Too? What does and does not constitute gay behavior is discussed.

27. Justin Bieber and Miley Cyrus 18th Birthday Count-Down Apps. The guys find an app that will alert them when their favorite underage stars, Miley Cyrus and Justin Bieber, will turn 18.

28. Sneak Peek in the Steam Room. The guys discuss body piercing.

29. A Boner in the Steam Room. The guys notice that a new member has become turned on by them.

30. Tom Cruise's Gay One Liners. The guys again use their favorite pick up lines to impress a new member of the gym.

31. Sarah Palin Runs for President a Year Early. Some of the guys change from Democrat to Republican when they believe Sarah Palin is the right choice for President of the U.S.

32. I Don't Think It's Gay. The straight and gay guys of the group discuss their differences.

33. What's Your New Horoscope Sign? Each of the guys try to figure out their astrological sign is when it is revealed that a 13th Astrological sign has been discovered.

34. Ashton Kutcher Audition. One of the steam room regulars gets a break when he is asked to audition for a role in an Ashton Kutcher movie.

35. Straight Guys That Like to Gay Flirt. An argument ensues between the straight guys over which one of them gets attention from the gay studs in the gym.

36. My Cousin the Rent Boy. The hazards of becoming a rent boy are explored.

37. The 9-inch Italian. A new Italian stud has the guys eager to get to know him better.

38. Is That Yours? A sex toy found in the steam room has the guys quizzing each other as to who owns it.

39. Happy Finding. The straight guys discuss ways of relieving stress without cheating on their girlfriends.

40. Everyone Is Gay. Steam room member Paul has come to a conclusion that everyone he knows is gay.

41. Facebook Pictures. What not to post on Facebook comes under advisement by the guys.

42. Meeting Normal Guys. The guys begin a discussion on how "uncool" stuck up people are.

43. Merry Christmas. Although the holiday is nearing, the guys are not in such a festive mood.

44. Stuffed in the Steam Room. The guys probe the discovery of a teddy bear they find in the steam room.

45. Getting Some Ass. Ross and Beau discuss their latest dates.

46. Worst Pick Up Lines. To be fair, the guys now discuss the worst pick up lines.

47. Gay Chicken. With nothing better to do, the guys play a game of gay chicken.

48. Sex with Siri. The guys experiment with the iPhone 4gs with Siri site.

49. Do I See a Nut. The guys discuss how and how not to wear their towels in the steam room.

50. Single on Valentine's Day. The guys relish in the fact that it is Valentine's Day and they are single and without mate worries.

51. Last Texting. The guys try to solve the problem of being a last texter.

52. What Turns Women On? The guys discuss what turns women on—and off.

53. ComicCon Comic Convention. The guys discuss "the hot dudes" they saw at the ComicCon Convention.

54. Gym Commandments. The guys discuss the rules that must be followed if they are to share a steam room together.

55. The Easter Bunny. A discussion is held on the true meaning of Easter.

56. The Gay Hankie Code. Just as women have a hankie code (colors telling men certain things) so do guys and the gay code is discussed.

57. Pussy Whipped. The guys discuss sexual acts in an episode that is more adult-themed than prior episodes.

58. The Gay Audition Movie Kiss. The art of movie kisses is discussed.

59. Not So Magic Mike. After seeing a performance of male stripper Magic Mike, the guys discuss the prospect of becoming strippers.

60. Otters, Cubs and Bears, Oh My! Gay labeling by the guys comes under discussion.

61. Masturbation Tips. The guys discuss the various techniques of masturbation.

62. Touch Yourself. Self examination is discussed.

63. Best Views in the Gym. The guys discuss which areas of the gym provide the best views of the hot guys.

64. Shirtless Singing. A not-so entertaining "treat" as the guys begin singing in the steam room.

65. A Not Gay Halloween. With Christmas and Easter tackled in prior episodes, guys decide to lament on Halloween.

66. Where the Boys Are. Taking a hint from the Connie Francis song "Where the Boys Are," the guys decide to check out the gym for where the hot guys gather.

67. Gaydar List. A discussion on what sets off a gay guy's gaydar (able to spot another gay).

68. I'm Not Gay. Is acting gay a hidden sign that a guy is gay is discussed.

69. How's Your Sister? Family secrets are revealed by the steam room guys.

70. Wanna See My Tattoo? The guys show off their tattoos to each other.

71. Valentine's Day. It's Valentine's Day 2013 and this year the guys discuss their big plans for the night.

72. What's Your Tail Tally? Each of the guys relates how many hook ups he has made.

73. Gay Pride. The straight guys reveal their strategy for picking up girls at a Gay Pride Parade.

74. St. Patrick's Day. The guys gather in the steam room to celebrate St. Patrick's Day.

75. Checking Out Hot Guys. Why gays checking out hot guys bods is considered "ungay" is discussed.

76. Easter Baskets. With Easter of 2013 approaching the guys talk about their favorite part of the celebration.

77. Manscaping. The guys talk about their daily routines including grooming tips and advice.

78. Butt Chugging. While it would appear to be dangerous, steaming while drunk, the guys do just that as each shows up drunk for their daily steam.

79. Premature Ejaculation. A frank discussion is held between the gay and straight members of the steam room.

80. Pirating Porno. The guys hit on an idea to become rich and famous by making their own cell phone porno video.

81. Gay Sex with Straight Men. A discussion is held on how gays hook up with straight men.

82. Do You Moan During Sex? The guys reveal what sounds can be heard during their sexual encounters.

83. The Gay Make-Out Test. When the straight guys hear that working out makes you gay, they decide to take the make-out test to see if either one of them is gay.

84. The 80s Are Back. With trends changing all the time, the guys discuss the 1980s look and how it has made a comeback.

85. Gay Drinking Games. The guys engage in some steam room drinking games.

86. How Do You Know You're Gay? The guys discuss the things that actually make one gay.

87. Bucket List. Each of the guys reveals what he has achieved sexually.

88. Panty Raid. The guys discuss the differences between boxers and briefs.

89. Gay Birthday. The guys plan a celebration of their gay birthday (the day they came out of the closet).

90. Boys in the Bathhouse. Steam room or bathhouse? The issue of which is better comes under discussion.

91. High School Reunion. Ben prepares for his high school reunion—and all set to show off his fantastic physique.

92. No Homo. The gay guys attempt to show the straight guys they are not "gay gay" but act like straight guys.

93. Damn Hipsters. The guys discuss breaking the steam room rules of not smoking by lighting up cigars to thank viewers for their support in making the program possible.

94. The Virgin. A newcomer to the steam room finds he is a virgin when the guys tell him the rules he must obey to maintain proper steam room protocol.

95. Trixie in the Steam Room. When Trixie, the world-famous transgender singer, enters the steam room, Blair seeks a way to impress her and hopefully perform a duet with her.

96. Give Your Girlfriend a Hand. Unable to make headway with his current girlfriend, Ben seeks the guys help in impressing her.

97. Truth. To help the time pass in the steam room the guys begin commenting on the YouTube videos they hate.

98. Straight Advice for Gay Marriage. The straight guys give their gay buddies advice on gay marriages.

99. Turning Gay. After a newspaper article reveals that working out can turn people gay, the straight guys decide to test the theory.

100. Pornstache Rides. Straight dude Ben relays his feelings that a "pornstache," (moustache) such as the guys in adult films wore in the 1980s, will be the key he needs to impress the chicks.

101. Your Bud's Baloney. With nothing else to really talk about, the guys decide to size each other up by using body parts.

102. Explode. The guys discuss working out in the gym.

103. Man Love on Valentine's Day. Two straight dudes argue over the idea of exchanging Valentine's Day gifts to each other—one says it's okay; the other says no way.

104. Twerking It. The guys learn that exercising at home by "twerkercizing" is better than working out in the gym.

105. A Scruffy Celebrity. Celebrity status comes to the steam room when Johnny Scruff joins the guys.

106. What So Great About Vaginas? Why straight dudes only go for women is put up for discussion.

107. Boy Bunnies. The guys talk about sexy boy bunnies as Easter approaches.

108. Tom Daley and Gay Face. Can a person's face indicate a guy is gay is discussed by the steam room guys.

109. Hot Guys Are the Most Insecure. The issue of whether compliments to straight guys by gay guys make them insecure is discussed.

110. Twink in the Steam Room. The gay regulars eye a new member as he enters their steam room session.

111. Bisexual Power. Ben and Christopher discuss whether or not bisexual existed in mythology.

112. Ethnic Stereotypes. The guys discuss that one should not be judged by how they dress.

113. Gay Birthday. A celebration in the steam room as one member celebrates his birthday—not the day he was born but the day he discovered he was gay.

114. Ball Slips. When a towel slips a yellow Smiley Face appears to prevent the viewer from seeing anything they shouldn't. The guys discuss this version of censorship in the concluding episode.

287 Steel River. youtube.com/playlist?list=PLH2LbReElEJmIqtquBQfzMukEwhrk7Mp9. 2013 (Drama).

Four gay men (Terry, Ivan, Addison and Kadoe) residing in Atlanta, Georgia, are followed as they navigate life as they are now living it, not as they envisioned it would be when they were younger. Principal focus is on Terry, a singer who calls himself "a mainline R&B performer" and his struggles, not only in the cutthroat music industry, but with the men in his life. **Cast:** Emani Williams (Terry), Brandon Anthony (Ivan), Horatius Croom III (Kadoe), Cort King (Addison), Wesley Adams (Shelton), Andrea Carter (Brenda), Karris Jordan (Will), Jordan King (Dex), Chances Williams (Rontae), Luckie Andrews (Greg), Courtney Maki (Michelle), Ayalanda Butler (Tiffany), Brittany Bracket (Paris), Malcolm Spears (Tyrone). **Credits:** *Producer:* Tyrell Lewis, Mello Dyme. *Director:* Henderson Maddox. *Writer:* Jermaine Kamell, Tyrell Lewis, Mello Dyme. **Comment:** An African-American production that prob-

ably looked good on paper but just did not translate well to film. The production values are just as poor as the acting. There are audio problems (low sound making what is happening hard to understand), difficult to follow story lines and characters that come and go with apparently no connection to one another. The sexual situations are not the most pleasing to watch, especially the scenes with male-female hookups as the men are at fault here (they are just so distasteful they become unpleasant to watch). While the program's pacing leaves a lot to be desired, it does start off on a good point in that it does establish characters and what appears to be the principal story line (Terry and his singing career) but quickly spirals downward as it tries to show and do too much without really thinking things through. Had better pre-production planning taken place, *Steel River* could have become a lot better than what has materialized. **Episodes:**

1. Man in the Mirror. Quickly establishes Terry as "a mainstream R&B singer" although he is gay and the conflicts that are slowly destroying his life, especially his controlling manager (Shelton).

2. Rejection. Terry is now touring with the group CHANCE and has the possibly acquiring a recording contract with O'Hara Records.

3. Addiction. As two of the men, Kadoe and Rontae become closer, Terry, dissatisfied with his recording contract, is released from it but without his love of music to guide him, appears to be lost as what to do next.

4. Three's a Crowd. While Terry seeks what to do next, Will confronts Michelle over her sadistic ways while Addison, Ivan and Kadoe decide to drown their sorrows with alcohol.

5. Time Heels All Wounds. Desperate to find love, Ivan attempts an on-line hook up but only finds rejection (he then finds comfort from his mother, Brenda, who tries to ease his pain).

6. The Shock Attack. The concluding episode wherein Terry attempts a career comeback; Rontae has hooked up with a new love (Greg), and Ivan again seeking the love he needs to sustain his life.

288 Straight Up Gay. afterellen.com. 2014 (Comedy).

Alison, a lesbian, and Brenden, straight, are friends. While it is sometimes said that a straight male cannot be friends with a lesbian (and vice versa) Alison and Brenden have broken that mold and it is through their eyes that each learns about sexuality, gender identity and everything else that divides the two sexual identities (sort of a lesbian's guide to discover how gay males form friendships with straight women and make their own friendships with straight men). By using a comedic approach, the program also focuses on Alison and Brenden's experiences, being young singles (in their twenties) and navigating the dating scene—helping each other and presenting a perspective from both angles (although it can come to a situation where both are longing for the same girl).

Cast: Alison Levering Wong (Alison), Brenden Gallagher (Brenden). **Credits:** *Producer-Writer:* Alison Levering Wong, Brenden Gallagher. *Director:* Dan DeLorenzo. **Comment:** *Will and Grace* TV series parody with a lesbian twist (as *Will and Grace* focused on the gay character Will who was best friends with straight girl Grace). The acting is very good and the overall production is television series quality.

Episodes:

1. The Barista. While in a coffee shop, a waitress gives both Alison and Brenden the impression that she is interested in them, leading Alison and Brenden to find out who she really prefers. The waitress is not credited.

2. Brenden's Cousin. While it is a shock to Brenden but a delight to Alison, a visit by Brenden's cousin Taylor leads to the discovery that she is a lesbian. Taylor is not credited.

289 Street Behavior. streetbehavior.com. 2012 (Drama).

Life in any city, but especially New York, can be trying for anyone, whether straight, gay or bisexual. Encompassing the gay culture of the city and focusing on a group of such people, but in different age groups, a realistic look at how they deal with various issues (love, religion versus sexuality, concealing who they really are) is presented with a particular underlying message that gays also exist in a world considered only straight.

Cast: Christian Frazier (Angelo Martinez), Drew Khandi (Javonni Anderson), Richard Morgan (Jonathan James), Yaku Quillakasha (Jeffrey Lonon), Roman Anthony (Thomas Nash), King Carter (Shawn Delany), Naysimone Crews (Stacey Tolliver), Demi Davis (Erica Watkins), Ariana Fekett (Layla Roberts), Cedric Jones (Reginald), Toni Jay (Kevin Delaney), Bobbi Owens (Lynette James), Dewayne Queen (Tyqui Clark), Francisco Vegas (Serapis Love), Rj Veney (Lionell Graham), Shoshanna Withers (Kyrah Henry). **Credits:** *Producer-Writer-Director:* Rj Veney. **Comment:** At first glance the program appears to be badly acted and produced. The characters appear crude and despicable and the directing only acceptable. Keep watching. It takes a few minutes to adjust to the gritty, realistic presentation. The intent by the producer to achieve his goal can be seen as the program is about street behavior and the interactions of gays (including lesbians) not only with one another but the rest of the world. It is what happens and how it happens is presented here. There is strong language, adult situations, partial nudity and a real feel for what happens—all of which should be taken into account before watching as there are no warnings on episodes before they begin.

Season 1 Episode List: *1.* Secrets. *2.* Bad Habits. *3.* Pain. *4.* Consequences. *5.* Revealed. *6.* Anger. *7.* Deception. *8.* Instinct.

Season 2 Episode List: *1.* New Beginnings. *2.* Deceit, Part 1. *3.* Deceit, Part 2.

290 Studville TV. studvilletv.com. 2013 (Comedy-Drama).

Riley is "The Player," an architect in a large firm and successful at virtually everything she does. Anise, called "The Doctor," is an entrepreneur and the owner of her own production company; she is also a Sunday school teacher. Channing, the hopeless romantic (looking for the ultimate fairy tale), is a former women's basketball standout turned fire fighter. Shaneen, called "The Kid," is a school teacher and athletic coach who is considered the most naïve member of the group—both in life and love. Four lesbian "studs" and their journey through life, seeking love but encountering all the heartaches that accompany it and how, through their close ties they help each other deal with not only the bad times, but the good times as well.

Cast: Toni Fields (Channing), Shawn Taylor (Riley), Champ Champ (Shaneen), Faurice Bobby Harley (Anise), Lenor Arielle (Serenity), Alexius Elayne (Morgan), Ameer Jewell (Alyssa), Nikki Kanai (Hope), Onyx Keesha (Autumn), Ivy Morae (Taylor), Melissa Poe, Brittany Rice (Brandi), Iana Skye (Seven), Cinque Tang (Tatum), Jordan Spencer (Lydia). **Credits:** *Producer:* Sheri Johnson. *Director:* Sheri Johnson, Steven Thompson. *Writer:* Rob Fox. **Comment:** African-American themed program that tries hard to rise above others of its kind that are rather crude. There are suggestive sexual situations (nothing is really seen) and it does take a bit of watching to adjust to the characters as it is a "hood" series and the ladies are somewhat over-the-top (especially Shaneen with her annoying, bitchy attitude and Channing, although sweet, who is much too promiscuous, always wanting to bed a girl five minutes after she meets her). Riley, on the other hand is too trusting, and it causes her grief while Anise is very indecisive—married to Lydia but seeing Autumn and not sure whom to be with. The acting is acceptable and the overall production (visual quality) very good although there are noticeable edits (when cuts are used to transition scenes) and dips in the sound (as well as the musical soundtrack overpowering dialogue).

Episode List: *1.* Pilot. *2.* 'Til Death Do Us Part. *3.* A Crack in the Ying and Yang. *4.* Things That Make You Go Hmmm. *5.* A Storm Is Coming. *6.* Real Recognizes Real. *7.* Intervention. *8.* Let It Burn. *9.* The Great Divide. *10.* Un-Copasetic. *11.* The End Is Just the Beginning. *12, 13* and *14:* Untitled episodes. *15:* The Johnson Story. *16:* Catch 22. *17:* The Third Degree. *18.* The Seepage. *19.* The Charade. *20.* Prelude to Diss.

291 Submissions Only. submissionsonly.com. 2010–2014 (Comedy).

Penny Reilly is an aspiring young actress hoping to become a Broadway star. She is optimistic, talented as a singer and dancer, and full of energy. As she experiences the ups and downs of what it takes to make it on Broadway, the program, which encompasses musical numbers, relates the events that spark her life as she auditions for plays: *Iron Dog, Intersection, Mean Girls, Piñata Party* and *Jeremy's Fort*. While the program focuses mainly on straight characters, Penny's closest friend, Tim Trull, the head of a casting agency, is gay as is Steven Ferrell, Penny's agent and Tim's ex-boyfriend and Cameron, an actor.

Other Characters: Gail Liner is Tim's secretary; Aaron Miller, an actor, is Penny's on-and-off romantic interest; Linda Avery is the flirtatious stage director; Serena Maxwell is Aaron's girlfriend (a Broadway star); Raina Pearl is a Broadway actress and Penny's roommate; Nolan Grigsby is the eccentric Broadway director; Randall Moody is Tim's reader; and Agnes Vetrulli is an off-the-wall actress who replaces Randall as Tim's reader.

Val Reilly is Penny's mother; Don Martin is Val's second husband and Penny's stepfather; Donny Rich is the uptight casting associate; Andy Edmond is the music director; Adorable Girl (as she is called) is the actress who appears to know everyone; and Eric Hennigan is the actor on whom Penny has a crush.

Cast: Kate Wetherhead (Penny Reilly), Colin Hanlon (Tim Trull), Stephen Bienskie (Steven Ferrell), Lindsay Nicole Chambers (Gail Liner), Santino Fontana (Aaron Miller), Max von Essen (Cameron Dante), Anne L. Nathan (Linda Avery), Donna Vivino (Serena Maxwell), Asmeret Ghebremichael (Raina Pearl), Jared Gertner (Randall Moody), Marilyn Sokol (Agnes Vetrulli), Wade McCollum (Nolan Grigsby), Patrick Heusinger (Eric Hennigan), Beth Leavel (Val Reilly), Rick Elice (Don Martin), Andrew Keenan-Bolger (Donny Rich), Annaleigh Ashford (Adorable Girl), Jeffrey Kuhn (Andy Edmond). **Credits:** *Producer:* Joanna Harmon, Jeff Croiter, Michael Croiter, Teon Cromwell, Jen Namoff, Tom Rice, Jack Sharkey, Kevin McCollum. *Writer-Director:* Andrew Keenan-Bolger, Kate Wetherhead. **Comment:** Well acted and produced look at Broadway and the frustrations that go along with producing, auditioning and starring in a play. First season episodes, which aired on YouTube, are good but improve technically as the series progresses (although second and third season episodes can only be seen on BroadwayWorld.com).

Episodes:

1. Old Lace. Penny is introduced as she returns to New York from Los Angeles and immediately acquires a job as a reader for Tim as he begins casting several short plays.

2. 165 Flies. As Penny reconnects with her friends Eric and Raina, she is talked into attending an acting class that, while ridiculous, allows her to make a connection with a fellow student (Aaron). Meanwhile, Linda consults with Tim about casting a new play called *Iron Dog*.

3. Intersections. Penny acquires a job as an understudy for the play *Intersections* but becomes annoyed when its leading man, Eric, becomes more interested in flirting with the leading lady (Serena) than giving his all to the play.

4. You're So Bad. As Penny and Aaron become readers for *Iron Dog* Steven meets Cameron, the gay actor who captures his fancy.

5. Mean Like Me. A program of auditions: As Penny auditions for *Iron Dog* and *Mean Girls* (a touring production), Aaron attempts to tell her that he is giving up acting to attend law school.

6. Somethin' Else. At a party for potential investors for *Iron Dog*, Linda discovers that Tim is gay and that Steven has hooked up with a new love (Cameron). Penny also discovers that while she auditioned for *Iron Dog*, she acquired a role in the musical *Mean Girls*.

7. Harness Malfunction. A mishap on stage, causing Penny to sprain her hip, forces her to leave *Mean Girls* and return to Manhattan where she learns that she may have a chance at *Iron Dog* as the play is being recast.

8. Gay Gardens. In the Berkshires, where Tim has traveled to check on a play he cast, he, Steven and Cameron spend an uneasy day together when they become trapped in Cameron's summer home during a storm.

9. ⅔ Memorized. As Tim teams with director Nolan Grigsby, Aaron, who has just broken up with Penny, joins Steven's casting agency, apparently giving up his plans to become a lawyer. Meanwhile, all is not well with Penny when her parents visit and her stepfather, an actor, gets a call back from and audition and she doesn't.

10. The Miller-Hennigan Act. After auditioning for the musical *Pinata Party* Penny decides that she no longer will date actors when she leans that Aaron is now seeing Broadway star Serena Maxwell.

11. Y'all Were Great. It's opening night for *Iron Dog* and the cast becomes dismayed when the reviews are anything but flattering.

12. Woof. The day after effects of bad reviews as experienced by Serena, Penny, Tim, Randall, Gail, Steven but especially Nolan, whose directing methods caused the play's downfall.

13. The Growing. Although he feels his methods are far above every other director, Nolan continues his process. Meanwhile, Penny auditions for the role of the crippled sister (opposite Serena) in the play *Jeremy's Fort* when she learns *Iron Dog* is closing.

14. Another Interruption. As Penny acquires the role in *Jeremy's Fort*, Tim realizes that he has feelings for Nolan and seeks to get closer to him.

15. Petit Sweet Ending with N. As Penny begins rehearsals for *Jeremy's Fort*, Randall books a six month gig as a cruise ship entertainer and Aaron, undecided about his future, leaves the city.

16. Having Foresight. *Jeremy's Fort* could be headed for tough times when a leaked video to the Internet shows the director lashing out against the artistic director; Raina heads to Los Angeles when she receives a role in a TV pilot film; and Agnes finds a job as Tim's new reader.

17. Box of Dirt. Aaron's decision to again become a lawyer leaves Serena heartbroken while the leaked video causes the director to be fired and replaced by Linda Avery.

18. Expectations. The program's gay characters take center stage with Steven and Cameron as well Nolan and Tim reassessing their relationships.

19. Very Meta. Rehearsals for *Jeremy's Fort* resume while Gail contemplates making a career change.

20. Dangerous Anesthesia. The concluding episode wherein Gail decides to become a casting director and the cast prepares for the opening of *Jeremy's Fort*.

292 *Sunny Reign.* girlsmoove.wix. 2012–2013 (Crime Drama).

Sunny and Reign are lovers and con artists who thrive on devising small scams—nothing big and nothing that will get them caught (at least they hope). When Sunny and Reign have a falling out and each goes their separate way, a con worth a half-million dollars reunites them—not only as thieves but as lovers. The program charts their efforts to parlay a series of small scams into one complex hustle that will net them a small fortune.

Cast: Blaxx Casanova (Sunny), Kream Stalleion (Reign), Trice McKinney (Sway), Lorena Dali (Nelly), Tramaine Renee (Wiz), Bradford Haynes (Savage), Chantaille Elkerson (Dreya), Davinchii Woods (Marco). **Credits:** *Producer:* Bradford Haynes, Tramaine Renee. *Writer-Director:* Tramaine Renee. **Comment:** Fast-moving story with good acting and production values. The program, which contains vulgar language, is also unique in that it presents a lesson on how a scam (or racket) is performed and how one can protect themselves from it (sort of like the 1950s TV series *Racket Squad*).

Episode List: *1.* Friendly Reminders. *2.* Choose Wisely. *3.* Learn to Adjust. *4.* Revamp the Team. *5.* Become the Connect. *6.* Confuse Reality. *7.* Run Game. *8.* Drive Slow (The Finale).

293 *Surely Undecided.* bluelightpictures.com. 2012 (Comedy).

While in a park just trying to soak up some sun, Claire, a 17-year-old high school girl, is struck by a stray golf ball hit by a gorgeous young woman who becomes instantly attracted to her when she goes to retrieve the ball. Claire is a bit taken aback, not knowing exactly what to think of the girl, especially when she tells her that she thought she was a lesbian ("I'm pretty sure you're gay"). Claire's life seemed to be progressing smoothly until the girl's remark started her thinking about her sexuality. "Am I gay?" To further complicate the situation, her brother, Liem, who had witnessed what happened, tells her that he believes she is gay and sets Claire on a roller coaster of emotions—"do I like men or women?" Stories follow Claire as she seeks the answer to who she is sexually—a situation made more complicated by her parents, who, after learning from Liem what had transpired in the park, are dead set on proving she is not a lesbian.

Cast: Maddison McClellan (Claire), Lindsay Norman (Amber), Brett Hardin (Liem), Rosa Nichols (Mom), Richard Houghton (Dad). **Credits:** *Producer:* Vu Nguyen, L. Courtney Thorpe, Derrick Granado. *Director:* Vu Nguyen. *Writer:* Vu Nguyen, Richard Houghton. **Comment:** Unfortunately only three short episodes where produced and leaves the viewer wanting more. Maddison McClellan is delightful as Claire, so much so that you not only want to see more of her, but what happens to her—is she a lesbian? Is she bisexual? Is she straight? Answers that may never be revealed as it has been over two years since the last episode was produced. The acting and production values are top rate and, due to the program only just establishing itself, there are no kissing scenes or adult situations.

Episodes:

1. Claire-Fixation. The story line is established when a stray golf ball awakens feelings in Claire that she may be a lesbian.

2. The Parents. Dinner is not all that normal when Liem reveals to his parents what happened and that Claire is a lesbian (which she denies—but can't convince her parents otherwise).

3. The Blind Date. Pop arranges a blind date for Claire with a boy (who turns out to be an obnoxious nightmare) with the following words: "You go out on that date but don't come back gay." The program ends unresolved but leaves the doorway open for further episodes.

294 *The Sweet Adventures of Nat and Meg.* discoversweet.com. 2009 (Reality).

Lesbian culture in various cities and small towns in the U.S. is seen in a video diary compiled by a real life lesbian couple (Natalie and Meghan).

Host: Natalie Gregory, Meghan Hall. **Credits:** *Producer-Writer-Director:* Halle Sherwin, Natalie Gregory, Meghan Hall. **Comment:** Natalie and Meghan are an adorable couple that, based on the only video information that exists, perform their tasks well as hosts. While there is a little play between them, they do present their topic as thoroughly as possible within the time restraints allotted for each episode.

Episodes: Only one episode, "The National Equality March" remains on line and presents highlights of the event that occurred in Washington, D.C., on October 11, 2009.

295 *The Switch.* welovetheswitch.com. 2012 (Comedy).

Erwin is a transgender and has made a tough decision to come out of the closet and appear as he feels he should, a woman named Su. The decision has drastic consequences when it costs Su, an upwardly mobile software company manager not only her job but her apartment when all sides see her as a freak and not right for either her company or her landlord. As Erwin, Su was playing it safe. He was lonely and had no social life. As Su, Erwin has found a new outlook on life and is going to make the best of it she can. But until that time comes, Su has little money, no place to live and must crash at friend's homes until she can re-establish herself in the business world. The program follows Su as she sets out to live the life she wants to live despite the numerous problems that go along with being a transgender (it also establishes the notion that if Su cannot make it in her new life in "East Vancouver's Queer Underground," she may revert to again becoming Erwin).

Cast: Julie Vu, Domaine Javier (Su Phan), Amy Fox (Chris), Kent S. Leung (Russell), Susan Van Zaig (Sam), Abbey Spracklin (Toni), Ahmed Muslimani (Nate), Vincent Viezzer (Zoey), Chance Kingsmyth (Phil), Bobbi-Jean Charlton (Barbara). **Credits:** *Producer:* Amy Fox. *Director:* Ryan Elias, Vanessa Taro. *Writer:* Amy Fox, Shevon Sinsh, Wren Handman, Susan Chev. **Comment:** The program is an Internet first as its entire cast is composed of transgender performers. The original pilot is well performed and acted and the program itself is quite enjoyable and would have no doubt been an interesting project to watch had funding been made to produce additional episodes.

Episodes:

1. Test Pilot. The original concept for the series is presented as described above with Julie Vu as Su. There is also a trailer that has Domaine Javier playing the role of Su in what appears to have been a casting change but it is really not possible to tell how much of the original story line was also altered, if at all. Julie Vu appears sexier and prettier than Domaine Javier's interpretation of the role. There is no reason given why the change was made (Julie Vu appears in the pilot as well as in the "See the Cast" section of the web site while Domaine Javier appears in a trailer and is only mentioned as playing the role in "The Help to Make The Switch Happen" text that appears).

296 *Tanya X.* tanyax.com. 2010–2011 (Erotic Adventure).

The Bureau of Knowledge, Intelligence and Nonstandard Investigations (B.I.K.I.N.I. for short) is an organization run by the beautiful Director Martin and whose agents use sex as their main weapon. Tanya X, as she is called, is a gorgeous B.I.K.I.N.I. agent who finds women just as pleasing as men and uses her sexual abilities to foil evil wherever it exists. The program charts Tanya X's latest assignment: break up a counterfeiting ring run by Big Balls Parker, owner of BB's Nightclub, and his busty associate Knockers, fiends who will stop at nothing to flourish in the world of criminal activity.

Cast: Beverly Lynne (Tanya X), Christine Nguyen (Sandy Bottoms), Kylee Nash (Knockers), Monique Parent (Director Martin), Randy Spears (Cooper), Evan Stone (Big Balls Parker), Billy Chappell (Tony Baritone), Eric Masterson (Newton, Jr.), Robert Don (Ricardo). **Credits:** *Producer:* Rob Pyatt, Beverly Lynne, Dean McKendrick, Steve Fry, Brian David. *Writer-Director:* Dean McKendrick. **Comment:** With the exception of under 30-second episode previews on YouTube, the series has been taken off-line. The program is a spin off from the feature film *The Girl from B.I.K.I.N.I.* and features nudity and soft-core sexual situations (especially between Tanya and other girls). The series plays like the movie and is very adult-in-nature (although the situations are humorously presented).

Episodes:

1. Jungle Fever. Just as she completes an assignment in the Amazon jungle, Tanya X returns to headquarters where she is assigned to break up a counterfeiting ring.

2. Is It Fake? A she prepares for her assignment Tanya X is equipped with sex-themed weapons.

3. Ye Olde Sex Shoppe. At a sex shop Tanya X meets with (and makes love to) undercover CIA agent Sandy Bottoms for information on BB.

4. Big Balls and Knockers. Armed with the information she needs about BB and Knockers, Tanya X begins the next phase of her assignment.

5. Fraternization. In her meeting with Director Martin (which is more than just talk) Tanya X believes going undercover to infiltrate BB's Nightclub may be the best tactic.

6. An Old Flame. A complication sets in when Tanya X learns that her former boyfriend, FBI Agent Cooper has also been assigned to the case.

7. Hitting the Mattresses. With Cooper as her partner on the case, Tanya begins the assignment by meeting with mobster Tony Baritone for training on how to act like a gangster (and deceive BB).

8. Lap Dance at BB's. As Tanya practices her 1930s movie-like gangster moves, Tony sets the stage with BB to meet Tanya X (in her disguise as Angie Paluzzi).

9. Tanya X Meets Big Balls. With the stage set,

Tanya X (as the mobster Angie) prepares to meet BB for the first time.

10. Libido Enhancement. Director Martin gets some action of her own as Newton, Jr. (B.I.K.I.N.I.'s weapons creator), shows her his latest sex weapons.

11. Truth or Dare. Tanya X's meeting with BB goes well—until the truth serum she places in his drink to get him to reveal his counterfeiting plans are foiled when Knockers consumes it.

12. It Ends in a Smokin' Hot Three-Way. In the concluding episode Tanya X nabs BB and Knockers—but not before a sexual encounter precedes the arrest.

297 *Tha Life Atlanta.* youtube.com. 2014 (Reality).

A realistic look at the lives of several gay black men living in Atlanta with a particular focus on their clubbing activities and how each seeks that significant other. **Cast as credited:** Alex, Arden, Brodney, Chuck, Dean, Marcel, Mehran, George Smith. **Credits:** *Producer-Director:* George Smith. **Comment:** Strictly geared to gay men of color as it is not a show for everyone. The production values are very good including the sound (wireless microphones were used to achieve better quality than relying on the camera microphone, which produces poor audio in certain situations). It is difficult to say where future episodes are headed based on what has thus far been released. The title, *Tha Life Atlanta* is correct but using "That" in searches will also bring up the title. **Episode List:** *1.* New Beginnings. *2.* Turn Down for What? *3.* Fix It Jesus. *4.* Movers, Shakers and Fakers.

298 *That Gay Guy.* youtube.com. 2014 (Comedy).

Daniel, as the theme says, "Is a gay guy we know and love." Daniel is personable and appears to have accepted his sexual orientation well until he hits middle age and experiences that dreaded "middle age crisis." Now he has feelings that he has not accomplished what he was capable of but had he made the right choice sexually? Adding to his frustration is his boyfriend and roommate, an unemployed, drug-addicted video game playing addict. The program depicts the chaos that ensues as Daniel tries to find meaning and balance in his life while not only dealing with his boyfriend, but the pressures of his job (working for a corporation that builds deadly weapons for the military and thrives on wars). **Cast:** David Nance (Daniel), James Kazan (Boyfriend), Scott Swan (Slutty Friend), Truong Swan (Asian Friend), Rob Hamm (Shawn), Twany Arnold (Peepers), Scott O'Neill (Mr. Blakely). **Comment:** Short, right-to-the point episodes that tackle the subject facing Daniel in a well thought-

out manner. The acting and production values are good and, for some unknown reason, some characters are not given an actual name. **Episodes:**

1. Episode 1. Hoping to determine if he is possibly bisexual, Daniel accepts a blind date with a younger woman (Alder Sherwood).

2. Episode 2. As Daniel begins to take his frustrations out on his co-worker (Shawn) over his dismay for working for a company that kills people, he finds himself being called into the boss's (Mr. Blakely) office and ordered to take a vacation until he can again think clearly.

3. Episode 3. Life finally seems to be progressing for Daniel until he discovers a gray hair and panic sets in.

4. Episode 4. A second panic attack for Daniel—what to do when he discovers that his boyfriend is cheating on him? The program's concluding episode.

299 *That's What She Said.* twssonline.com. 2010 (Comedy-Drama).

Five close friends (Nicole, Rae-Anne, Babette, Leslie and Shin) and their efforts to navigate life in Los Angeles.

Nicole Tran, nicknamed "Nic," is a slightly awkward young woman, born in Ohio and making the transition to life in California after a broken romance (with another woman) set her on the path to not face her problems, but run away from them. The L.A. lesbian scene is something totally new to Nicole and has opened up a new world of opportunities for her.

Rae-Anne Constantino, called "Rae," is Nicole's roommate, a caring girl and the glue that holds the friends together. She and Leslie work at a West Hollywood flower shop that is owned by Rae's family. Although she is attracted to other women, Rae prefers to be called "SGS" (Straight Girl Syndrome), as it depicts her problem of falling for women who are straight as opposed to being gay (as is her current involvement with Christina, who is straight).

Babette "Baby" Liu is the flirtatious, fun-loving girl who often gets herself overly involved in romantic situations that require the help of her friends to overcome. Babette, friends with Rae-Anne since high school, doesn't intentionally mean to find trouble but her efforts to seek fun with other women just mushroom into situations that get out of hand.

Leslie Park, an activist who will involve herself in any cause she feels worthy of, is an advocate for equal rights and what she calls "queer rights." Though as forceful and outspoken as she is, Leslie has a tendency to fall for gay men.

Shin Tanaka is a woman whose past is unknown and who prefers to keep it that way (it is best if one does not ask). She is mysterious, passionate about photography and has a difficult time expressing her emotions and tends to suppress them. Shin has an "in" with the "in crowd" lesbian scene but she never lets her encounters reach a point where she cannot control them.

Cast: Vicky Luu (Nicole Tran), Allison Santos (Rae-Anne Constantino), Claire Kim (Leslie Park), Narinda Heng (Shin Tanaka), Annigee (Babette Liu), Antoinette Reyes (Chloe), Aspen Clark (Cecilia). **Credits:** *Producer:* Pearl Girl Productions. *Director:* Vicky Luu. **Comment:** Although billed as a "Queer Asian American Web Series," it is about lesbians and is better than its billing leads one to believe. Comedy mixes with light drama to relate events in the lives of the friends with good acting and production values. It is also one of the very few programs devoted to profiling Asian American lesbians and worth checking out (another example being, though in a more dramatic vein, *Give Me Grace*).

Season 1 Episode List: Episodes are no longer on-line. *1.* Just Friends. *2.* Body Language. *3.* On-Line Dating. *4.* The Valentine's Day Edition. *5.* Post Holiday Stress Disorder. *6.* Self Love. *7.* How to Break Up. *8.* Losing the Relationship Weight. *9.* Episode #1.9. *10.* The Makeover Show. *11.* Five Dollar Dates. *12.* Pheromones and Attraction. *13.* Celebrity Mail. *14.* The Five Senses. *15.* Dopamine and Pair Bonding. *16.* Long Distance Relationships. *17.* Episode #1.17. *18.* Good Conversation. *19.* How Not to Break Up. *20.* Answering Fan Mail.

Season 2 Episodes: Only four untitled episodes (2–5) remain on line: *2.* That's What She Said—S02E02 (Season 2 Episode 2), *3.* That's What She Said—S02E03, *4.* That's What She Said—S02E04, *5.* That's What She Said—S02E05.

300 TH3M (THEM). youtube.com/playlist?list=PL8jT7i-2JF7KZ17uE712NQLnsK_7I-vtA. 2011 (Comedy-Drama).

Seven diverse women are profiled (Ali, Cameron, Jasmine, Nicole, Robbi, Toni and Traci) with a look at how their dreams of acceptance, success, sex and love affect and test their bond of friendship.

Cast: Constance Anderson (Nicole), Bethany Ford (Jasmine), Tana Matthews (Ali), Chantel Sings (Traci), Mysnikol (Cameron), Elle Richards (Robbi), Carmen Richardson (Toni), Octavia Wright (Anija), Kara M. Greshwalk (Monica), Andrea Ivy (T'Asia), Traci Kerney (Sheila), Scott Carson (Bob Meyer), Nicole Kruex (Sasha), Obuatawan Holt, Jr. (Jason), Christian Johnson (Marty). **Credits:** *Producer:* Angela Barrett, Tye Green. *Director:* Shannon McCarville, Tyler Jensen, Rachel Nelson, Paul von Stoetzel. *Writer:* Tye Green, A.J. Cameron Pollard, Julia Hamilton. **Comment:** Well done and acted program whose episodes are somewhat long (over 30 minutes each). There is partial nudity, foul language, kissing scenes and adult sexual situations but (other than certain dialogue) nothing that is really offensive. The program does mix lesbians, bisexual and straight characters with Monica and Traci's encounters being the most provocative.

Episodes:

1. Love? What's That? The women are introduced with each revealing her goal to achieve success.

2. I'm So in Lust with You. T'Asia (a lesbian) becomes jealous when Traci (bisexual) secures a date with a man; Cameron and Nicole begin to feel the strain of their 13-year relationship; Toni finds herself falling prey to the advances of a woman she has been trying to avoid (Sheila) and Monica, hoping to rekindle Jasmine's love for her, invests in her and Ali's clothing line.

3. Maybe Women Aren't a Good Idea. As their relationship ends, Cameron seeks the love of another woman while T'Asia, fearful that she may lose Traci, sets out to win her back. Meanwhile, Traci's lustful pursuit of women, while she is in a relationship with Robbi, appears to be the catalyst that will end their relationship.

4. Just a Little Bit Longer. Cameron, apparently in love with both Nicole and Ali, is having difficulty choosing one over the other; Jasmine and Traci, unknowingly dating the same man (Marty) are unaware that he is playing both of them; Ali's hook up with a girl named Tre reaches a turning point when Tre's sexual fetishes are more than Ali can handle; Toni and Robbi's relationship appears to be at an end when Toni's inability to remain monogamous has Robbi thinking it is best they break up; and Monica's fantasies about sleeping with Traci becomes a reality. The program's concluding episode.

301 Three: A Web Series. youtube.com/user/3webseries/videos. 2014 (Comedy).

Layla, Tanner and Jason are best friends but each with a different sexual preference. Layla is straight, Jason is bisexual and Tanner is gay. Layla and Tanner live together while Jason resides in his own apartment. Unknown to Layla and Tanner is that the man they are both dating is their Jason, who has managed to keep his affair with both of them from each other. The program charts what happens when Layla and Tanner discover that they are both unknowingly dating the same man and the steps they take to resolve the situation: engage in a three-way with the winner being chosen by Jason (the one he would rather date).

Tanner is not the most common of men (not that he is gay) but because he not only perspires in all uncomfortable situations, but he is addicted to a nine-to-five job. Layla, who suffers from a medical disorder wherein she cannot be alone or live alone, is considered a "biatch" in every sense of the word. She enjoys sex, eating (even more than sex) and spending money. Jason, an intellectual artist, enjoys sky diving and reading political best sellers. He also engages in sex with men and women but can never be sure who he is the most comfortable with.

Cast: Lucas Omar (Tanner), Amber Sym (Layla),

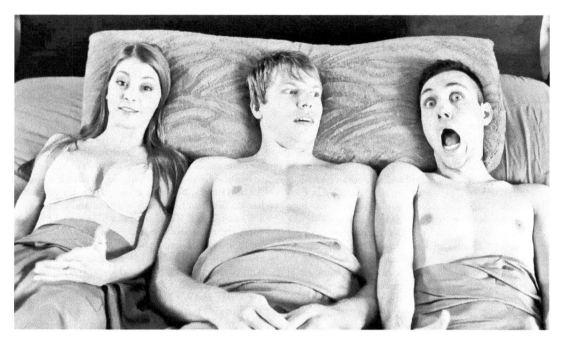

Three: A Web Series. Left to right: Amber Sym, Andrew Sturby and Lucas Omar (used by permission of Lucas Omar).

Andrew Sturby (Jason). **Credits:** *Producer:* Joshua Moody, Todd Yonteck, George Petrick, Lucas Omar. *Writer-Director:* Lucas Omar. **Comment:** Too short will be your immediate reaction. The premise is good and the characters well thought out and presented. Layla is the perfect opposite for Tanner (sort of like a male-female version of *The Odd Couple*) with Tanner falling prey to the more over-powering Layla, a girl who appears to get what she wants by nagging. The acting is very good and the production values comparable to any TV sitcom.

Episodes:

1. The Proposal. It is revealed that both Layla and Tanner are dating the same man—but are unaware of it.

2. Jason # 1 and #2. The charade is uncovered when Layla and Tanner realize they have been dating the same Jason.

3. Bloody Tampons. Layla tries to convince Tanner to have a three-way competition in order to discover which of them Jason prefers.

4. Avocados. Although it is against his better wishes, Tanner agrees to Layla's game and the competition begins at Jason's apartment.

5. I Wanna Mate. As the evening pushes on, Layla and Tanner recall some uncomfortable moments on past dates with Jason.

6. Clitoris Trophy. The party has adverse effects when it appears that Jason chose Tanner, leading Tanner and Layla to arguing and seemingly ending their relationship after 10 years.

7. Spank You. The big moment has arrived—

both Layla and Tanner perform a striptease for Jason (with Layla the more sensuous) in an effort to capture Jason's affections.

8. Disney Jail. As Layla and Tanner begin arguing over who Jason should choose, an upset stomach forces Layla to leave the room, leaving Jason to get closer to Tanner.

9. Creme Brulee. Season 1 concludes with Layla, now feeling better, returning to the bed with Jason and Tanner and, while the three are eating creme brulee, the unthinkable happens—Jason's mother arrives unannounced and is surprised to see her son in bed with a woman as well as another man.

302 The 3 Bits. the3bits.com. 2013 (Comedy).

Madison, Henry and Roman Bits are siblings and each has a story to tell. In a rather unusual twist on other Internet series, each sibling has his or her own three episode program incorporated within the overall title. Madison is portrayed as a housewife and mother, hooked on drugs, who relates her feelings about life via a blog. Roman's segment is that of a lesbian attempting to readjust her life, going from drug dealer to a legitimate job as a gardener (as the series tag line states, "Roman used to deal weed now she pulls weeds") and Henry, the youngest sibling, as he explores the gay life.

Cast (Roman Segment): Margaret Singer (Roman), Lola C. Albright (Kelly), Mila Myles (Taz), Marla Mindelle (Jill), Atong Arjok (Pussy Baby),

Cole Escola (Henry Bits), Hugh Sinclair (Dad Bits), Lynn Laurence (Mom Bits), Macauley Devun (Burger). *Note:* Although IMDB.com and other sources credit movie and TV actress Lola Albright (TV's *Peter Gunn*) as playing Kelly, it is not the same actress.

Cast (Madison Segment): Erin Markey (Madison Bits-Mozzarella), Margaret Singer (Roman), Emily Davis (Jane).

Cast (Henry Segment): Cole Escola (Henry Bits), Evan Hoyt Thompson (Wayne), Jeremy Jordan King (Marcus), Jimmy Brooks (Jeff). **Series Credits:** *Producer:* Robert Profusek, Jonathan Parks-Ramage. *Writer-Director:* Margaret Singer, Max Profusek. **Comment:** An enjoyable program that runs the gambit from being intimate ("Roman") to just plain obscure ("Madison"). The Roman segment is the most sensual, with nudity and tender scenes between Roman and her girlfriend (Kelly). Henry's outlook on life is the most relaxed segment while the Madison entry's first episode is a bit shocking. Each of the leads performs their roles quite well and believable in the characters they portray. The production values are also very good and the gay-lesbian-straight mix works well without any one segment over-powering the other.

Roman Episodes:

1. Episode 1. Roman is introduced as she decides to give up her drug dealing operations to concentrate on her job as a gardener but finds her girlfriend, Kelly (a law student) not-too-enthused as she feels it is not a lucrative job.

2. Episode 2. Complications set in for Roman—not only from her family's attempts to celebrate her birthday (where Madison is hoping for "a lesbian party") but from her old crew, who have stolen a pound of dope from a rival operation.

3. Episode 3. Although Roman and Kelly have been intimate, Roman has never seen Kelly totally nude. In an attempt to remedy the situation, Roman manipulates a love-making session allowing her to see everything—and finds herself shocked when Kelly becomes totally upset and leaves her. But for good?

Madison Episodes:

1. Episode 1. Madison opens her segment with "Hello fans, this is Madison" and proceeds to show her fans how to connect with their babies. She demonstrates by placing a white substance (coke) on the baby's stomach and snorting it.

2. Episode 2. Hoping to give her fans a different perspective on life, Madison and her guest, her sister Roman, indulge in a discussion about women's issues and differing lifestyles.

3. Episode 3. Madison concludes her segment when she and her best friend, Jane, chat about life in general and what they hope to achieve.

Henry Episodes:

1, 2 and 3. Each is basically a look at Henry and his friends and how they adjust and accept the gay lives they have chosen.

303 *Three Way.* tellofilms.com. 2008 (Comedy).

Young Doctors Who Cry is a television soap opera on which Siobhan McGarry plays the role of a doctor's wife. She is married to Dirk LaBonte, an aging motion picture action star and is enjoying a life of luxury until their marriage collapses and Siobhan finds herself nearly broke and retaining only her beloved dog Mojo (who dies a day later) in the divorce settlement. Although Siobhan is straight there are hints she may be bisexual as she is overly attracted to her best friend since childhood, Roxanne, whom she calls Roxie ("because she's my rock"). The divorce has left Siobhan financially strapped and emotionally scarred and Roxie becomes Siobhan's lifeline when the two move in together. Life is progressing well for Siobhan and she appears to be recovering emotionally until her world is again shattered when Andrea, Roxie's girlfriend (and lover) also moves in with them (creating sort of a female version of the TV series *Three's Company*). Further complicating Siobhan's life is Geri, Roxie's ex-girlfriend who again wants to become a part of Roxie's life. The program charts the events that spark the lives of all four women, especially Siobhan as she seeks a life of serenity, happiness and maybe sexual experimentation.

Cast: Maeve Quinlan (Siobhan McGarry), Jill Bennett (Andrea Bailey), Cathy Shim (Roxie Lautzenheiser), Maile Flanagan (Geri O'Flanagan), Donna W. Scott (Winter Kote), Elizabeth Keener (Celia Sanderson), Liz Vassey (Mikki Majors), Christina Cox (Lara Lancaster), Kristy Swanson (Leslie Lapdalulu), Bridget McManus (Rhonda Rapid Delivery), Gabrielle Christian (Cindy Shimms), Linda Miller (Frankie), Elisa Dyann (Jamie). **Credits:** *Producer:* Paige Bernhardt, Nancylee Myatt, Maeve Quinlan, Joey Scott. *Director:* Mary Lou Belli, Courtney Rowe, Nancylee Myatt, Robert Ben Garant. *Writer:* Paige Bernhardt, Maile Flanagan, Nancylee Myatt, Maeve Quinlan, Georgia Ragsdale.

Comment: Maeve Quinlan is delightful as Siobhan as she tries to make sense of everything that happens around her. The other cast members are just as good and the story line flows smoothly (even though there is a gap in the free episodes). The production values are TV quality; there are kissing scenes and a bit of profanity but overall a charming, non-offensive program to watch.

Episodes:

1. Let the Gaymes Begin, Part 1. As Siobhan introduces viewers to the life she now leads, another blow shatters her emotionally: her role on the soap opera has been reduced to that of a brain-dead woman who does nothing but lie in a hospital bed.

2. Let the Gaymes Begin, Part 2. With Roxie and Andrea as her housemates, Siobhan slowly begins to learn how lesbians act when she joins them and Geri in a game of guessing lesbian celebrities from verbal clues.

3. Let the Gaymes Begin, Part 3. When her dog Mojo's ashes are accidentally delivered to ex hubby Dirk's home by mistake, Siobhan devises a plan to retrieve them with Andrea, Roxie and Geri as her partners in crime.

4. The episode has been taken off-line but apparently introduces Celia, Andrea's ex-girlfriend, who causes more emotional problems for Siobhan when she re-enters Andrea's life.

5. Fatal Distraction. Continuing events established in the prior episode, it appears Roxie is becoming extremely jealous that Celia has begun hitting on Andrea while Geri believes she is being stalked by Leslie, a gorgeous lesbian that appears to be a bit unstable.

6. Lady Cop. Siobhan's life suddenly changes for the better when she acquires an audition for a female police officer in a Lifetime network TV series called *Lady Cop*. All is progressing well with her housemates helping her study her lines until she auditions, gives producers the impression she is a lesbian and they change the direction of the series to focus on two lesbian cops as opposed to a male-female team. The worst part: Siobhan is not hired.

7. Psychodrama. Having six free therapy session certificates, Siobhan decides to cash them in and see a therapist for help. Siobhan's living situation so excites the therapist that it soon becomes a situation where the therapist invites Andrea and Roxie to the sessions to learn about lesbian love-making with Siobhan's problems inconsequential.

Note: The above episodes are available on line for free. Other episodes, available through a subscription service, include *Siobhan Sizzles*, *Rhonda Rapid Delivery*, *What's for Dinner*, *Friday Night Dykes* and *The Dinah Monologues*. In all, twelve episodes have been produced as well as twelve "confessional extras" (airing in late 2014 and early 2015).

The Throwaways. Series poster art (used by permission of Tello Films).

304 *The Throwaways*. tellofilms.com. 2012 (Drama).

For some, being gay or a lesbian is more of a curse than a declaration of who they are. Some find acceptance while others are considered weird and just not acceptable as a part of society. Olivia, a 17-year-old girl, is one such person, a lesbian whose family strongly disapproves of who she is. Olivia was the perfect daughter. She attended church, studied hard, never broke a curfew and had planned to attend Brown University. She never used drugs, never drank and even got along with her siblings. However, when her parents uncovered her sexuality, it was beyond their comprehending and literally disowned her when her mother caught Olivia and a girl "study buddy" engaging in more than just books. To hopefully "cure her of the disease" it was decided to send Olivia to an institution in Utah "to fix her." Defiant, Olivia ran away and, on her seemingly endless journey to find herself, met Dorsey, a girl in the same position, who introduced her to a group of other such "Throwaways," misunderstood young women who have banned together to create their own little community. As Olivia adjusts to her new world she quickly learns that a darker side to society exists (a counter-culture of violence, crime and drug abuse) and that she must navigate it to survive—and hopefully make her way back home one day. The program follows Olivia's experiences as she and others like her struggle to enjoy a life with the girls they love no matter what others think.

Cast: Ashley Andersen (Olivia), Kate Black-Spence (Dorsey), Molly Pan (Jazzlyn), Hannah Aubry (Rynn), Mia Jones (Mia), Kristin Bennett (Olivia's aunt), Rocco Cataldo (Bill), Butch Jerinic (Olivia's mother), Michael Marsh (Olivia's father), Bridget McManus (Fiona), Ashley Nguyen (Nancy), Fawzia Mirza (Jayne), Jacqueline Salamack (Amy), Rachel Shapiro (Andrea), Luca Marsh (Bailey). **Credits:** *Producer:* Jessica King, Christin Mell. *Director:* Jessica King. *Writer:* Julie Keck, Jessica King. **Comment:** Based on the only available episode, the program is well acted and produced. Ashley Andersen is appealing as Olivia and the story itself appears intriguing.

Episodes: Only episode 4 ("Room for One More") of 10 produced episodes and a teaser for the series remain on line.

305 *Til Lease Do Us Part.* youtube.com/playlist?list=PLY8g4moKhkwm-evU-phVbABBgpbU12lCm. 2014 (Comedy).

Mikka, a bisexual, and Shannon, a lesbian, are roommates and lovers. But as incidents creep in and put an end to their relationship they find, that although they have broken up, they still need to live together to fulfill the terms of their apartment lease, which still has six moths to run. While it appears Shannon has gotten over Mikka, Mikka finds it much more difficult to let Shannon go. The program charts what happens when Mikka and Shannon attempt to find new loves but discover that living together with an ex is not the most inviting of situations when it comes to finding that significant other.

Cast: Hannah Hogan (Mikka), Joanne Sarazen (Shannon). **Credits:** *Producer:* Adrianna DiLonardo, Sarah Rotella. *Director:* Sarah Rotella. *Writer:* Adrianna DiLonardo. **Comment:** Although it is not related to the Tello Films series *Rent Controlled*, the plot is similar as it deals with the same situation (lovers breaking up and having to live together). The acting and production values are network television quality. The situations are well played and the program well worth watching.

Episodes:

1. Episode 1. Mikka and Shannon have broken up but choose to still live together to full the commitment requirements of their lease.

2. Episode 2. It is the following day and Mikka and Shannon are still trying to adjust to living together as singles without becoming sexually attracted to each other.

3. Episode 3. Dating becomes a bit uncomfortable for Shannon when she brings home a date (Reese, played by Giainne O'Flynn) and Mikka proceeds to make herself part of that date.

4. Episode 4. Mikka has a date with Eduardo (Rodrigo Fernandez-Stoll) and Shannon a second date with Reese. The problem: they both wind up using their apartment for a non-planned double date.

5. Episode 5. The double date does not go well as both Eduardo and Reese find that trying to date a girl when she still lives with her ex just won't work.

6. Episode 6. The six months are up and Mikka and Shannon can now go their separate ways. But do they? As the episode ends, Mikka and Shannon kiss and say to each other, "Should we renew the lease?"

306 *Time Traveling Lesbian.* afterellen.com/time-traveling-lesbian. 2009 (Science Fiction).

While stocking DVD's in the video store where she works (Reel Life), Rebecca Drysdale notices one marked "Recommended by Carl." Rebecca is a lesbian and a member of an improvisational group but as of late, has not had many dates. Curious by the DVD that she found, Rebecca plays it and learns that in the year 2319 scientists have developed a means of time travel. But it is also a time when something sinister called The Leak is seeking to control time travel to alter past history for diabolical means. The image on the DVD identifies himself as Carl and his purpose is to recruit a lesbian to return to the past to fix the events that have been altered by The Leak. Rebecca was chosen as she is anonymous and could best serve their purposes. Although reluctant at first, Rebecca becomes intrigued and agrees to become Carl's Time Traveling Lesbian. Stories follow Rebecca as she journeys back in time—not only to set history on its proper course but seduce the historic beauties that are a part of those time frames.

Cast: Rebecca Drysdale (Herself), Drae Campbell, Hanna Cheek. **Credits:** *Producer:* Bryan Carmel. *Director:* Brendan Colthurst. *Writer:* Rebecca Drysdale. **Comment:** The stories are sexy and play well with gorgeous girls for Rebecca to encounter. There are kissing scenes (no nudity) and the program is a good candidate as a TV series for the Here! or Logo cable channels. While its one fault would be the continual (and needless) use of foul language, its episodes are humorous, fun to watch and will leave some viewers wanting more.

Episodes:

1. Studio Fifty.... Whore? Although the episode opens with "Last time on Time Traveling Lesbian," there was actually no last time. It establishes the storyline as Rebecca finds the DVD and is faced with a decision—whether or not to become the unseen Carl's agent.

2. Sappho's Sacrifice. Rebecca is equipped with a wrist communicator (to contact Carl and vice versa) when she agrees to become his agent.

3. When in Rome. Rebecca journeys back to Ancient Rome to stop an imposter of Apollo from preventing the fall of the Roman Empire.

4. Hats. Rebecca's life comes into peril when The Leak become aware of her activities and believes she is a threat to their goals.

5. Dangers of Improv. A plan by The Leak to bring notoriety to Rebecca finds Rebecca returning to the past to reverse her now famous world-wide celebrity status to once again become anonymous.

6. Summer of Love. Rebecca's time traveling experiences have allowed her to encounter and make love to many beautiful girls (although only kissing is seen). Carl's worst fears come to light when Rebecca falls for a girl in the 1960s and wants to remain with her. She learns that if she chooses to remain in a time period not of her own, history will be changed (as here, where if she remains, The Leak plan to set the women's movement back 10 years will succeed).

7. 12 Monkeys. As Rebecca prepares to be whisked back to the Old West days of Kate Winslett, she is sidetracked when she feels something is not right.

8. To Be Cunt-inued.... Get It? Never Mind. Rebecca's feelings grow stronger when Carl assigns her to return to the days of Genghis Khan but Rebecca discovers something else. She spies two of The Leak conversing with a computer and hearing Carl's voice. Have her travels been for the greater good or has Carl planned something else for her? The episode ends in a cliff hanger.

307 *Tough Love.* toughloveseries.tumblr. com/. 2013 (Comedy).

An "Odd Couple" parody that is set in Queens, New York, and depicts events in the lives of two roommates as they navigate life: Blaire, a disorganized lesbian in denial (sort of like a female Oscar Madison) and Steven, her uptight, obsessive best (and gay) friend (an elaborate spoof of Felix Unger). **Cast:** Steven Bell (Steven), Blaire Mackenzie Wendel (Blaire). **Credits:** *Producer-Writer:* Steven Bell, Blaire Mackenzie Wendel. *Director:* Cody Ball. **Comment:** Well acted and produced program that does a good job of transposing the Oscar Madison and Felix Unger type of characters into a lesbian-gay mix. Each episode is complete in itself and stories most enjoyable.

Episodes:

1. Weight Loss. When Blaire complains that she may be at risk of becoming morbidly obese, Steven decides to use tough love and convince her to lose weight by exercising (which upsets her more than initially helping her).

2. Personal Space. Steven and Blaire attempt to find some space of their own while sharing an apartment that does not permit personal space.

3. Meditate on This. Steven's efforts to mediate are a catalyst that may end his friendship with Blaire when her numerous distractions prevent him from doing so.

4. Rage Quilt. Steven and Blaire arrange a game night with Scrabble the game of choice—and Steven determined to win and retain his Scrabble championship.

5. Don't Panic. Steven's efforts to get a good night's sleep become anything but when Blaire begins suffering from a series of panic attacks.

6. Lady Lessons. Believing that the Internet may hold the key to finding a girl, Blaire (with Steven's help) attempts to compose an on-line profile.

7. Barbie. Blaire recalls some unpleasant childhood memories when she and Steven decide to engage in "coloring book hangout time" (to get in touch with their inner child).

8. Jealousy. Although she is a lesbian, Blaire becomes increasing jealous when Steven begins ignoring her and paying more attention to the new man he met. The program's concluding episode.

308 *Trainers (2012).* youtube.com/watch ?v=ul2UJQ4-HV4. 2012 (Comedy).

John, who is straight, and Justin, who is gay, are friends and roommates but not lovers. They work as trainers in a corporate gym but due to stupid mistakes each has been fired: John for having sex with a gym patron; Justin for calling a patron fat. Rather just sit around and wallow in self pity, John and Justin decide to start their own business as trainers from their apartment on Fulton Avenue. The program charts their mishaps as they try to avoid the situations that caused their termination and run a gym as the experienced trainers they believe themselves to be. **Cast:** John Francis O'Brien (John), Justin Mortelliti (Justin), Laura Jean Salerno (L.J.), Adam Meyer (Adam), Kevin Daniels (Kevin), Rebakah Tripp (Elizabeth). **Credits:** *Producer-Writer:* John Francis O'Brien. *Director:* Cameron Thrower. **Comment:** Only a pilot film has thus far appeared and it is well made and acted. While there is foul language it is not possible to tell how the romantic situations that would involve John and Justin would play out. John appears to be a lecherous ladies' man (will go after any girl, no matter how thin or fat) while Justin appears to be a bit classier and will not jump into bed with the first man he sees.

Episodes:

1. Is It Hard? The pilot episode that establishes the premise as described above.

309 *Trainers (2013).* trainersshow.com. 2013 (Comedy).

In a city (Los Angeles) with numerous gyms, one stands head and shoulders above all others as not only being the best, but the only one that can offer a physique building experience called The Technique. The establishment is the Sweat L.A. Gym and while it may have prestige, it lacks business and is on the verge of closing its doors. The program relates the efforts of the staff to somehow save their beloved gym by acquiring paying customers but not kill each other in their efforts to do so.

Reggie is the gym manager, a man who eats, sleeps and breathes the gym. Mandy, a trainer, is an actress with an ultimate goal to become a TV star (her clients are her second priority). Al, who wishes people would call her Alexandra, is a trainer who is also a lesbian (although she has not yet come out) and conceals her relationship with her girlfriend (Lara). Eddie is the egotistical trainer who believes he is the best trainer he has ever known (his claim to fame is that he once did 2,107 squats without a break).

Kaylie is a front desk greeter who wishes she could be more alluring. Samson is the body builder who held the Mr. America and Mr. Universe titles (he pines for Kaylie but his Finnish accent makes everything he says incomprehensible and has Kaylie in a daze). Jin, a Caucasian adopted by Asian parents, is a martial arts expert who believes he is Asian and speaks with an Asian accent. Julio, the Latin lover with the perfect physique (and in love with himself), developed a training procedure called The Technique (he also moonlights as a stripper for Hunks of Hollywood). Scott is Kaylie's front desk associate. Paige is Scott's bitchy girlfriend.

Cast: Jason Kelley (Reggie), Selah Victor (Mandy), Shannon MacMillan (Al), Aubrey Mozino (Kaylie), Michael Onofri (Eddie), Pasi Schalin (Samson), Adam Burch (Jin), Dominic Rains (Julio), Brandon Jones (Scott), Natalie Lander (Paige), Meredith Freen (Lara), Clarke Kohler (Henry), Eileen Fogarty (Rhonda), Kim Kendall (Marie), Alan Blumenfeld (Kleinberg), Allison Summers (Anorexic Allison). **Credits:** *Producer:* Selah Victor, Michael Onofri, Alexa-Sascha Lewin, Tony Muscio. *Writer:* Selah Victor, Michael Onofri. *Director:* Alexa-Sascha Lewin. **Comment:** Well developed program with very good acting and production values. There is some vulgar language and brief (blurred) nudity but nothing graphic. Because of his accent, Samson's dialogue sequences are seen with subtitles.

Episodes:

1. The Predicament. Realizing that finances are lacking, Reggie announces that the gym may close if something is not done to attract customers.

2. Julio. It is thought that a fitness super star may be the answer to their problems so Julio, developer of The Technique, is hired to hopefully turn things around.

3. O.M.G. As Al comes out of the closet and admits that she is a lesbian, Mandy goes overboard in her efforts to impress a movie producer; Reggie announces that, due to financial problems, the gym will be closing (the concluding episode).

310 *Transparent.* amazon.com. 2014 (Comedy-Drama).

Mort Pfefferman is divorced and the father of three children: Sarah, a woman seeking passion in a loveless marriage; Ali, a girl with no ambition who apparently lives off her family; and Josh, a record producer. Mort also has a secret: his alter ego, Maura, the woman he wants to become. The program opens at the dinner table where Mort is planning to tell his children that he is a transgender but that aspect is put on hold as flashbacks are incorporated to explore Mort's past, his married life and the circumstances that led to him realizing that he was meant to be a woman.

Cast: Jeffrey Tambor (Mort Pfefferman), Amy Landecker (Sarah), Gaby Hoffmann (Ali Pfefferman), Melora Hardin (Tammy), Abby Ryder Fortson (Ella Novak), Kiersey Clemons (Bianca), Judith Light (Mom), Rob Huebel (Len), Alexandra Billings (Davinia), Lawrence Pressman (Ed), Alison Sudol (Kaya), Alyvia Alyn Lind (Grace), Noah Harpster (Francis), Emily Robinson (Teenage Ali), Cleo Fraser (Young Ali), Makenna James (Young Sarah), Zander Faden (Young Josh). **Credits:** *Producer:* Jill Soloway, Andrea Sperling, Jennifer Corey. *Director:* Jill Soloway. *Writer:* Jill Soloway, Michael Fitzerman-Blue, Noah Harpster. **Comment:** Well-acted, produced and written program that incorporates transgender performers in supporting roles. Jeffrey Tambor's genius at characterizations excels here as he interprets a man dealing with the issues that are not only going to affect his life, but those of his family as well. The idea, though, is not new and has been used on television series like *Sisters*, *Parenthood* and *Brothers and Sisters*. The program also spotlights Judith Light (from the TV series *Who's the Boss?*), Gaby Hoffmann (from the TV series *Someone Like Me*), Melora Hardin (most notably Adrian Monk's wife on the TV series *Monk*) and Lawrence Pressman (numerous TV roles).

Episode List: *0.* Original Pilot. *1.* Revised Pilot. *2.* The Letting Go. *3.* Rollin'. *4.* Moppa. *5.* Wedge. *6.* The Wilderness. *7.* The Symbolic Exemplar. *8.* Best New Girl. *9.* Looking Up. *10.* Why Do We Cover the Mirrors?

311 *True Trans with Laura Jane Grace.* on.aol.com/show/true-trans-518250660.288/518451031. 2014 (Reality).

An exploration of the world of transgender men and women as seen through the cross-country travels of Laura Jane Grace, an American musician (singer, songwriter, guitarist) who founded the punk rock band Against Me! Each episode features Laura Jane talking to a guest and discussing issues from coming out to transitioning to the hardships such people face.

Host: Laura Jane Grace. Credits are not given.

Comment: Laura Jane, born Thomas James Gabel in 1980 and married to visual artist Heather Hannoura (since 2007) had suffered with gender identity problems since childhood and came out as a transgender woman in 2012. Laura Jane is the front woman for the band Against Me and one of the most visible transgender music stars. The band's song, "True Trans Soul Rock" served as the basis for the series. The program is well produced and hosted and should provide a service to the transgender community as do such programs geared for the lesbian and gay communities.

Episode List: *1.* Growing Up. *2.* Gender Diaspora. *3.* Finding Trans. *4.* Not Alone. *5.* Coming Out. *6.* Transitioning. *7.* Resilience. *8.* Relationship. *9.* Transparenting. *10.* Acceptance.

312 *Twenties*. youtube.com. 2013 (Comedy-Drama).

"Hattie's Humble Opinions" is a web program hosted by a very pretty African-American woman named Hattie. She is a lesbian, expresses her thoughts but receives very few Internet hits. She is also unemployed and thanks to her girlfriend, Nia, she has a place to live (sharing her apartment). But Hattie also has another problem—she is in love with an emotionally damaged straight woman (not seen) who appears not to share the same feelings about her. Like Nia, and her friends Marie, Ben, Lauren and Chuck, Hattie is in her twenties and attempting to navigate young adulthood and society at large (a situation made more difficult for Hattie as she is not as ambitious or outgoing and is hoping to become a success over the Internet).

Cast: Courtney Sauls (Hattie), Ashley Blaine Featherson (Marie), Nia Jervier (Nia), Brandon Bell (Ben), Marque Richardson (Chuck), Lenne Klingman (Lauren). **Credits:** *Producer:* Queen Latifah, Shelby Stone, Sakim Compere. *Director:* Justin Simien. *Writer:* Lena Waithe. **Comment:** Smartly produced and acted with a very engaging lead. While the off-line episodes also focus on Hattie's friends, they depict her evolvement into a more secure adult and how she achieves the success she sought over the Internet when she changes her style to that of a real person with real problems (and how lost she feels) as opposed to just randomly talking about life.

Episodes: Four episodes were produced. With the exception of a four part pilot film (that establishes the story line and characters) its other three episodes have been taken off line.

313 *Twenty-Five*. watchtwentyfive.com. 2013 (Comedy).

After graduating from high school, three friends, Beryl, Jimmy and Taylor, parted ways to begin the next phase of their lives: college. Two years after graduating, the friends re-connect in New York City with the program chronicling the journey each has (and will) take as they navigate life as adults.

Beryl is an aspiring actress and struggling to make her mark on the world. She has been in a relationship with a man she met in college but is unsure if they have a future together. Jimmy (gay), is an Internet blogger (although he considers himself a writer), still single and looking for his significant other. Taylor, a teacher (for the Teach For America program in Missouri) has relocated to Manhattan hoping to find a better job and a place to call home. Oakley is the man Taylor meets in Central Park and with whom she begins a relationship; Kyle is Beryl's gay friend (whom she met in yoga class) that Jimmy has a difficult time accepting; Kendall is a bit-off-the-wall girl who becomes Beryl's rival in everything.

Cast: Brennan Caldwell (Jimmy), Jordy Lievers (Beryl), Charles Andrew Callaghan (Kyle), Alex Trow (Taylor), Patrick Barrett (Oakley), Danny Binstock (Patrick), Jessica DiGiovanni (Kendall). **Credits:** *Producer:* Randall Stone, Sam Duboff, Linda Berkeley. *Writer-Director:* Josh Duboff. **Comment:** Enjoyable program with good acting and production values and, although many TV series and movies have tackled the situation of friends reuniting after high school or college, *Twenty-Five* manages to find its own unique twist with the gay characters of Jimmy and Kyle and how they react with each other as well as Jimmy's straight friends. While the program does end unresolved, the doorway has been left open for additional episodes to follow.

Episode List: 1. The Only Normal Ones. 2. Cindy and Carl. 3. Kendall's Party. 4. I Forgot the Crab.

314 *Two Jasperjohns*. twojasperjohns.com /episodes. 2011 (Comedy).

Joel, Jonas, Joseph and Jude Jasperjohns are four of nine gay, red-headed dysfunctional brothers who were born in Ohio and have decided to pursue life's greater possibilities by moving to Brooklyn, New York. The brothers are not a bit alike, somewhat eccentric and have yet to adjust to life in a larger city. Each season is an overall look at one of a brothers' eccentricities and how they attempt to either deal with it or overcome it—without killing each other first.

Cast: Jim Noonan (Jude Jasperjohns), Vinny Lopez (Joseph Jasperjohns), Tim Harrington (Jonas Jasperjohns), Michael Hartney (Joel Jasperjohns). **Credits:** *Producer-Writer-Director:* Vinny Lopez. **Comment:** While the brothers are eccentric they also like to use foul language. The story arcs are amusing and the acting is very good. The program itself is well done and how they deal with life being gay is only a surface issue and not one that involves sexual situations.

Season 1 Episodes: "White Pants." Deals with Joseph's obsession with a pair of white pants that he believes are mystical and only good things can happen to him when he wears them.

Season 2 Episodes: "It." The problems the brothers face when they attempt to care for a gay dog.

Season 3 Episodes: "Personal Wealth." Jude contemplates his wealth; Joseph begins a quest to discover the meaning of life (his "Forever Love" philosophy) and Joel faces the fact that he is turning 52.

315 *Unicorn Plan-It.* unicornplan-it.com. 2011–2014 (Comedy).

Unicorn Plan-It is a Los Angeles–based planning organization run by a woman, who prefers women over men, named J ("The Boss Lady"). She is assisted by her lesbian staff: Keesha, "The emotionally promiscuous girl," Vick, "a lady getter," Bambi, a Lipstick Lesbian (and J's lover); Harmony, a woman who runs a meditation service called "Harmony Om" and the lone gay male of the group, Miguel. Stories follow the relationship each worker has with the other coupled with their individual pursuits to find happiness with that special someone.

Cast: Haviland Stillwell (Harmony), Sarah Croce (Keesha), Sherri D. Sutton (J), Catherine Wadkins (Bambi), Amir Levi (Miguel), Ashley Reed (Vick), Deborah S. Craig (Bree), Alexandra Grossi (Molly), Wendy Guerrio (June), Bruce Dern (Pitch), Idara Victor (Ariel). **Credits:** *Producer-Writer:* Sarah Croce, Ashley Reed, Haviland Stillwell. *Director:* Kim Rocco Shields, Ashley Reed, Haviland Stillwell. **Comment:** Although not a totally new idea, the concept of adding the lesbian touch does spice up the program. The acting is good, the characters likeable and the production values also very good. Veteran movie and TV actor Bruce Dern adds a nice touch to the series as Pitch.

Episodes:

1. VaGchat. The cast is introduced with an announcement that the bossy J and the sex kitten Bambi are getting married.

2. Bang.It.Out. Differences in opinions occur as the staff gathers to plan the upcoming wedding.

3. A Single Ceremony. Plans for the ceremony are disrupted when Keesha neglects to return the planning book after taking it home with her.

4. #OMmyGod. A shock awaits J when she catches Bambi with her ex-girlfriend (Harmony) and learns that Bambi still has feelings for her.

5. Hunting Bambi. J, hoping to win back Bambi's affections, begins a quest to find her.

6. Maybe Not Yet. J fails in her attempt but Bambi suffers a shock of her own when she catches Harmony in bed with Keesha.

7. And So It Is. Feeling they have both lost a love, J and Bambi comfort each other over what has transpired with Harmony.

8. Awkward/Awesome. Miguel, who despises women, bites the bullet and attempts to help a de-

pressed J get over her feelings for Bambi (whom she has apparently lost to Harmony).

9. Kiss Kiss Dang Dang. With the business suffering, Miguel appears to get J out of her self-pity mode when he tells her they need to plan five weddings (each of which costs $25).

10. Across the YOUniverse. It appears that Keesha and J have hooked up but all is not progressing well for Harmony, as Bambi has brought a third woman into their relationship (Bree) and has made her jealous as everything now revolves around Bambi.

11. Dinah Blow Your *Unicorn* Horn. Unable to figure out what has happened to Bambi, Harmony confronts her in an effort to get their relationship back on a one-to-one basis.

12. Come Together. Right Now. Over Me. The Unicorn Plan-It Ladies Party is held and Keesha finds instant attraction to Molly, Miguel's gorgeous lesbian roommate. All situations are left unresolved in the concluding episode.

316 *Vag Magazine.* vagmagazine.tv. 2010 (Comedy).

With a dream to start their own feminist magazine, three friends, Bethany, a lesbian, and straight girls Fennel and Sylvie, pool their resources (the revenue from their prior Etsy shop business) and purchase a bankrupt fashion magazine called *Gemma.* Felling the name is unsuitable, they change it to *Vag Magazine* and through its pages attempt to teach women how to become better women. The idea sounds good, but accomplishing that goal is not quite as easy and the program charts the comical pitfalls the staff encounters as they go about making a dream come true.

Other Staff Members: Meghan, a former staff member for *Gemma*; Heavy Flo, queen of the roller derby circuit; Reba, a legend of feminist pop culture journalism (author of the book *Activities with Celebrities*); and Kit. **Cast:** Nicole Drespel (Fennel), Sarah Clapsell (Meghan), Jocelyn Guest (Sylvie), Kate McKinnon (Bethany), Leslie Meisel (Reba), Veronica Osorio (Heavy Flo), Morgan Grace Jarrett (Kit), Shannon Coffey (Penny), Shannon Patricia O'Neill (Jaybird). **Credits:** *Producer:* Caitlin Bitzegaio, Leila Cohan-Miccio, Zach Neumeyer, Nicole Shabtai. *Director:* Zach Neumeyer. *Writer:* Caitlin Bitzegaio, Leila Cohan-Miccio. **Comment:** The story, though littered with references to problems faced by women (as well as gutter language for female body parts), is well acted and produced but has no adult situations or kissing scenes. It's basically the women simply trying to figure out what to do now that they have a magazine to publish.

Episodes:

1. Fumbling Toward Ecstasy. With the magazine purchased and the name changed, Bethany,

Sylvie and Fennel lay out their vision for the magazine during the first staff meeting.

2. Reject All American. As Meghan attempts to pitch a story about skirts and Kit, becoming less enthusiastic than when she was hired, tries to figure out what is happening. Bethany meets with a feminine products company called The Keeper about sponsoring the first issue.

3. Swamp Ophelia. As they seek a woman for the cover of their first issue, Bethany, Sylvie and Fennel believe they have scored a home run when they acquire Amaryllis Cross, lead singer of the indie pop group Forever Avonlea, unit they discover she is also slated to be on the cover girl on their rival magazine C**T.

4. Feminist Sweepstakes. The situation becomes a bit intense when Jaybird, the editor of the rival magazine (and Bethany's ex-girl friend) meet to discuss matters.

5. Living in Clip. Bethany's reunion with Jaybird has her feeling depressed (being together for 17 years before breaking up) and pondering whether or not to return to the dating scene; meanwhile when they learn that Jaybird has legal rights to use Amaryllis for her cover, Sylvie and Fennel decide to become the models for their magazine's first issue.

6. Revelling/Reckoning. At a party to celebrate the launch of *Vag Magazine* (33 pages with 10 pages devoted to The Keeper products) Jaybird's arrival shock's everyone, especially Meghan when Jaybird offers her a job at her magazine. The program's concluding episode.

317 *Vampire Killers.* vampirekillers.tv. 2008 (Drama).

The Half Moon Motel appears to be an ordinary, run-of-the mill motel. Looks can be deceiving as it houses thirteen alluring female vampires led by Charlotte Ross, a gorgeous lesbian creature of the night who thrives on the blood of young women. Charlotte, who plans to destroy the human race, has begun her attacks in Los Angeles but a small band of vampire hunters (John, Amy, Katrina, Orville) appear to be the only force that is capable of stopping her. The program charts the battle that ensues as good attempts to defeat evil with Charlotte just too clever and cunning to fall into the clutches of John and his hunters.

Cast: Ania Spiering (Charlotte Ross), Tim Fields (John), Katelyn Gault (Amy Madison), Nick Liam Heaney (Orville), Ginger Pullman (Katrina), Kalia Makaiau (Amanda Burrill), Carina Diaz (Karina Colon), Falda Helgadottir (Sirry Jons), Ming Li (Sasha Liu), Marco Mannone (Travis), Kit Paquin (Nicole), Audrey Farrow (Anna Ward). **Credits:** *Producer:* Doug Hutchison. *Director:* Tim Bladini. *Writer:* Tom Baldini, Doug Hutchison, Marco Mannone. **Comment:** Any program that involves vampires is sure to arouse interest. Add, however, a beau-

tiful vampire queen and her equally beautiful slaves and that interest is heightened. The first two aspects have been achieved, including a basic storyline but adding some background information would help. Other than being a vampire, who was Charlotte? How did she become a vampire queen? What set her on her path to destroy the human race? Who is John and how did he form his team? Why is this small army the only resistance Charlotte faces? Despite its short comings, the acting is excellent and the action moves quickly from one episode to the other. While all the action takes place at night (as Charlotte can be destroyed by daylight) some scenes are darkly lit and hard to see as to what is happening. It is also not in the proper aspect ratio (everything looks normal) as scenes are stretched a bit to fill the screen (giving everything a fat-like appearance). While Charlotte is extremely wicked and lives to feed on innocent young women, the program itself appears to be quite deceiving in what it actually delivers in Charlotte's encounter with the women on whom she feasts. The program was launched on YouTube and episodes 1 and 2 contain a warning of graphic violence that has been censored by YouTube due to its community standards policy. The episodes, however, can be viewed in its original format by logging on to vampirekillers.tv. The YouTube versions lead up to the graphic violence segment (apparently what Charlotte will do to her bound female meal) and the screen goes to black. Episodes 3, 4 and 5 run as originally produced. It appears, and it has been hinted that the graphic violence warning was a gimmick to get YouTube viewers to log onto the program's official site. Doing so, the viewer will find that the censored episodes do not exist and only episodes 3, 4 and 5 can be viewed. YouTube frowns on people who attempt fraud with their videos and the licensing deal that was struck is terminated. That may explain why the first two episodes are not on the official site but why are they still on YouTube with the false warning? Is it a clever scam?

Episodes:

1. Episode 1. At the Half Moon Motel a young woman fears for her life when Charlotte approaches her with fangs drawn.

2. Episode 2. The story from the prior episode continues with Charlotte killing the woman for her blood. Meanwhile John's team has traced Charlotte to the Half Moon Motel.

3. Episode 3. Charlotte, on the prowl for another victim, encounters John's team. In a plan to stop her, the team splits up with Katrina coming face-to-face with Charlotte.

4. Episode 4. Katrina's efforts to kill Charlotte fail and she becomes one of her victims.

5. Episode 5. As John's team arrives and sees that Katrina has been bitten, she pleads with John to kill her before she turns. John's hesitation fosters Katrina's transformation and, as the program ends, is about to attack John and Orville when a shot is

heard (possibly from Amy) and the screen goes to black. The program's concluding episode.

318 *Vanessa's Story.* outwithdad.com/ watch/vanessa. 2014 (Drama).

A spin off from *Out with Dad* (see entry) that continues to relate events in the life of Vanessa LeMay, a teenage girl who, after revealing that she is a lesbian, finds her world spinning out of control when her family refuses to accept her for who she really is. Distraught and feeling all alone, Vanessa leaves home and begins a desperate journey to find her place in the world. Vanessa is representative of real life teenagers who face the same circumstances and take to the streets (here in Toronto, Canada) to survive but face uncertain futures.

Theresa is Vanessa's mother, an overly strict Catholic woman who, in the *Out with Dad* series started Vanessa's downward spiral when she forbade Vanessa from seeing the girl she loved, Rose. Steven is Vanessa's father, a man who literally follows what his wife does. Jacob is Vanessa's younger brother. Matthew is Vanessa's older brother, who was "disowned" by his parents for going against their religion and marrying a Muslim girl (Fatima).

Cast: Lindsey Middleton (Vanessa), Wendy Glazier (Theresa LeMay), Robert Nolan (Steven LeMay), Jacob Ahearn (Jacob LeMay), Neil Silcox (Matthew LeMay), Afshan Golriz (Fatima LeMay). **Credits:** *Producer-Writer-Director:* Jason Leaver. **Comment:** The program was said to be "filmed in secret" during the production of its parent series. It is presented in black and white to effectively capture the despair Vanessa faces as she struggles to come to terms with what is happening in her life. The acting and production values are the same high caliber as in *Out with Dad.*

Episodes:

1. Vanessa Out. Unable to stand the rejection she faces at home for coming out as a lesbian, a teenage girl (Vanessa LeMay) runs away from home, taking to the streets of Toronto, Canada.

2. Vanessa Lost. Alone and wandering the streets, Vanessa meets a girl named Kayla (Katherine Fogler) whom Vanessa wrongfully trusts as someone who can help her.

3. Vanessa's Pain. Although Vanessa was given a place to stay for the night, Kayla saw Vanessa as a naïve girl from whom to steal her cell phone and sell it for drug money. Now, without a phone (and apparently no money), Vanessa, with a lesson learned (not to trust anyone) returns to the harsh streets.

4. Vanessa Runs, Part 1. Vanessa's efforts to find shelter lead her to a flop house where she fears for her life by a man who attempts to rape her.

5. Vanessa Runs, Part 2. Fighting off her attacker and escaping, Vanessa seeks shelter at the home of her brother (Matthew) and his pregnant wife (Fatima).

6. Vanessa's Calm. Although she now feels safe, Vanessa still has no idea as what to do next and is encouraged by Matthew to call home and tell their parents that she is safe. But Vanessa can't do that yet as she feels she needs more time.

7. Vanessa Meets Sera. Feeling that he can help his sister, Matthew introduces her to his friend Sera (from the series *Lesliville* [see entry]) who shared a similar situation.

8. Vanessa Goes Home. The program concludes with Vanessa building up the courage to return home and face the consequences of her actions.

319 *Venice the Series.* venicetheseries.com. 2010–2014 (Drama).

Gina Brogno is a beautiful interior designer living in Venice Beach, California. She is a lesbian, has an 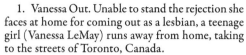 addiction to alcohol and is very devoted to her brother Owen, a bond that developed in their childhood as they struggled to deal with a father (John) who disapproved of everything they did. Because of her fear of commitment, Gina lost the girl she believed was the love of her life (Ani Martin, a photographer). Stories, presented like a daytime TV soap opera, relate events in the lives of the people that are close to Gina—and her efforts to navigate a love life that becomes complicated when she begins seeing a new woman (Lara) but discovers that a business asso-

Vanessa's Story. Title poster card (copyright JLeaver Presentations, 2014).

ciate from London (Tracy) has also become sexually attracted to her.

Cast: Crystal Chappell (Gina Brongo), Nadia Bjorlin (Lara Miller), Jessica Leccia (Ani Martin), Jordan Clarke (John Brogno), Galen Gering (Owen Brongo), Michael Sabatino (Alan Anders), Tina Sloan (Katherine Pierce), Hillary B. Smith (Guya), Harrison White (Jaime Smith), Adrienne Wilkinson (Adrienne), Michelle N. Carter (Michele King), Shawn Christian (Brandon), Aaron Hartzler (Drew), Gina Tognoni (Sami Nelson), Wes Ramsey (Van), Elizabeth Keifer (Amber), Peter Reckell (Richard), Judi Evans (Logan), Christian LeBlanc (Jake), Lesli Kay (Tracy Lansing), Annika Noelle (Sami Nelson).

Credits: *Producer:* Hillary B. Smith, Crystal Chappell, Kim Turrisi, Christa Morros, Maria Macina. *Director:* Susan Flannery, Karen Wilkens, Crystal Chappell, Albert Alarr, Hope Royaley, Maria Macina. *Writer:* Crystal Chappell, Kim Turrisi, Jill Lorie Hurst, Leslie N. Johnson, Erika Schleich, Lindsay Harrison, Janet Iacobuzio, Penelope Koechl.

Comment: The scenery is fabulous and the acting comparable to most television series. Venice is a continuation from the Otalia story line that was begun on the CBS series *The Guiding Light* right before its cancellation and delves more into the main character's relationships and is enhanced by sexually provocative situations.

Episodes:

1. Premiere. Gina and Ani are seen in bed indicating that, although they are intimate with each other, they have an emotional and troubled past. A mystery also begins when the body of a dead prostitute is mysteriously dropped off at a mortuary with no clues as to who she is or how or where she died.

2. Episode 2. Michele, Gina's assistant, and Guya, Gina's aunt, a tarot card reader, are introduced.

3. Episode 3. As Gina begins plans to decorate a hotel, she meets Tracy, the British interior decorator with whom she feels an immediate attraction.

4. Episode 4. As Tracy and Gina meet on the Rooftop Lounge, it appears that the two are becoming attracted to each other; meanwhile, Guya visits with Gina and Owens's father John (called The Colonel) hoping to get him to accept Gina for who she is (he cannot accept the fact that she is a lesbian).

5. Episode 5. While working out in a gym Gina is surprised to receive a phone call from her father, asking her to lunch. Although a bit unnerved, Gina agrees to do so as this is what her late mother (Katie) would want her to do.

6. Episode 6. Gina and Tracy are becoming closer (sharing an sensual kiss); Aunt Guya sets Owen up on a blind date (with Sami); Gina and Owen attend the luncheon arranged by Guya (but all does not go well as The Colonel not only belittles Gina, but Owen on his faltering acting career).

7. Episode 7. Feeling she needs someone to talk to, Gina calls Ani, who tries to tell her that she may never get her father's approval and should accept the situation and move on. As the two embrace, Gina admits to loving Ani but it is not quite sure if she loves her.

8. Episode 8. As Gina and Tracy continue with their plans for the hotel, it is becoming obvious they are more than just friends; later, with their Aunt Guya, Gina and Owen discuss past family relationships.

9. Episode 9. At a coffee shop Ani orders a coffee, realizes she left her money at home then meets Lara, a writer, who offers to pay for her coffee. They hit it off and agree to meet to have drinks.

10. Episode 10. Lara and Gina share a romantic dinner at a restaurant where each learns a bit about the other's past, including the fact that Lara is also a lesbian. As they talk, they also share a passionate kiss. Meanwhile, Owen and Sami, a Peace Corps worker, embark on their first date.

11. Episode 11. While Owen receives word that he has received a part in a movie, it becomes obvious that Gina and Ani have broken up as Gina is now with Tracy and Ani is with Lara.

12. Episode 12. The season 1 finale wherein Tracy and Gina's relationship is now on the line as Gina does not know if she can make the commitment Tracy wants; later, meeting with Ani, Gina tries to mend their relationship by hoping they can be friends (but Ani insists they go their separate ways).

13. Episode 13. Lara, upset with her editor over a book deal, finds comfort from Ani while Gina, alone, reflects on her life and her lost love (Ani). The second season begins.

14. Episode 14. Introduces the characters Catherine, Jamie and Van as Owen learns that his father has collapsed and is now in the hospital. Gina, now alone since Tracy has returned to England, finds that she still has feelings for Ani, made more so when she meets her on the beach.

15. Episode 15. As Ani learns about The Colonel, she and Gina embrace and both admit to missing each other (although Ani is still seeing Lara). Meanwhile, Guya tries to persuade The Colonel to accept the therapy he must endure to get well; Van, Guya's son pays her a visit.

16. Episode 16. As Guya finds a new love interest (Brandon), Lara attempts to conceal the fact that she has turned to alcohol. At the soup kitchen where Sami works, she meets Van, unaware of his connection to Owen (his cousin).

17. Episode 17. Guya tries to make Gina forget the past and help her father while Ani begins to notice Lara's strange behavior (caused by drinking). That night Guya's thoughts turn to her sister, Katie (Gina's mother).

18. Episode 18. Taking Guya's advice, Gina attempts to help her father with his rehabilitation while Ani catches Lara drinking.

19. Episode 19. Sami discovers that Van and Owen are related while Gina crosses paths with an old high school friend (Richard) but doesn't reveal the fact that she is a lesbian.

20. Episode 20. Owen suspects Van is seeing Sami behind his back; Gina is still struggling to get her stubborn father to do his needed exercises and Ani becomes concerned about Lara when she sees an e-mail from her editor about missed deadlines.

21. Episode 21. As Gina and her father seem to be becoming close, Owen admits to his friend Jamie that he lost the film role; Ani finds Lara passed out on the couch (from drinking) and Michele finds herself under pressure from Alan to finish the hotel designs.

22. Episode 22. As Owen attempts to explain his relationship with Sami to his father, Michele continues to work under pressure to complete the designs. Meanwhile Gina and Jamie learn that Brandon (Guya's boyfriend) is a detective and investigating the death of the deceased prostitute, who has been identified as Amber. Lara, continuing to drink, is saved by Gina and Ana after she falls into a swimming pool.

23. Episode 23. Katherine finds herself gazing at the beautiful women that surround her; Ani confronts Lara about her drinking; Owen sees Van and Sami kissing (but does not say anything).

24. Episode 24. Season 2 concludes with Lara and Ani attempting to come to terms with what is happening between them; Van telling Sami about Owen losing the movie roll; and The Colonel deciding it is time he became a part of Gina's life.

25. Episode 25. Season 3 begins with Gina having a sexy dream about Ani although Gina is not sure of her future with her. Gina later visits with her father to see that his health is improving and that he is actually happy to see her. Feeling that he and Sami are no longer a couple, Owen finds a new girl (Adrienne) although he still misses Sami.

26. Episode 26. Stella, The Colonel's nurse, plans a way to get him to continue therapy (challenge him to a game of arm wrestling. She wins as he continues). Owen approaches his father to tell him he lost the movie deal; Lara prepares to attend AA; Richard, still unaware that Gina is a lesbian, plans to reconnect with her.

27. Episode 27. Owen and Adrienne (the bartender at the Irish Mist Bar) spend the night together; Guya begins having visions of seeing her dead sister, Katie, and tells her she did her best to help raise Gina and Owen; Lara and Ani appear to be getting close again.

28. Episode 28. Gina discovers that, to help her in her time of need, Michele created designs and submitted them to Alan as Gina's. Brandon reveals that a household cleaning residue was found on the dead prostitute's skin and that she was wearing two different shades of nail polish, indicating that the killer painted them. Stella and The Colonel begin to bond; at The Irish Mist, Jamie (the owner) tells Gina he overheard Brandon discussing the case of the prostitute with Guya; Guya becomes panicked when, at the police station she sees a picture of the prostitute on Brandon's laptop.

29. Episode 29. When Katie's spirit appears to Guya she tells Katie that the dead prostitute looked just like her and explains that spirits can transfer if they died within the vicinity of each other (she believes the prostitute must have died in The Colonel's neighborhood). Richard and Gina meet at the Rooftop Bar and begin reminiscing about their past. It is here that Gina reveals she is a lesbian and hopes to have a lasting relationship with Ani. Guya begins her own investigation into the dead prostitute and, hoping to find information from The Colonel, spies an earring on the floor.

30. Episode 30. Guya's conversation with Brandon reveals that only one earring was found on the prostitute and it is being held as evidence; when Katie again appears to Guya, Guya tells her that she believes the prostitute died in The Colonel's home and that is how the prostitute acquired Katie's soul. Meanwhile Ani and Lara have gotten back together—but Lara is not the girl she once knew (Lara is now cold to her).

31. Episode 31. Lara and Ani discuss their situation with Ani telling Lara that she is proud of the fact that she is attending her AA meetings. As they talk their feelings for each other appear to be returning as they kiss and head for the bedroom. Guya questions Gina about the night of The Colonel's stroke hoping to learn what happened before he was taken to the hospital.

32. Episode 32. Guya receives another visit from Katie but they fail to figure out what the prostitute's connection was to The Colonel. Learning that a funeral has been planned for the prostitute (Amber), Guya also learns that Nurse Stella is accompanying The Colonel to the service. Meanwhile Brandon and his partner (Dana) have begun setting up surveillance equipment to record the people who show up for Amber's memorial service.

33. Episode 33. At the funeral, a mourner approaches The Colonel and tells him that Amber felt he was the father she never had. Gina, Owen, Richard and Amber's mother, Ms. Preston have also made an appearance. After seeing that Guya made an appearance at the funeral, Brandon approaches her to ask why. She reveals that Amber's spirit, manifesting itself through Katie, has been appearing to her in an effort to help her move on. Shortly after, Guya approaches Amber's mother to tell her that Amber never wanted to hurt her and had made the wrong choices. Guya then tells Brandon, off the record that Amber died in The Colonel's home.

34. Episode 34. Katie appears to be happy that Guya has Brandon but Guya wonders why Katie hasn't yet moved on. At a bar, where Lara and Sami discuss the book Lara is writing, Lara has a bit too much to drink and puts Sami in an awkward position when she becomes intoxicated.

35. Episode 35. The mystery surrounding Amber is revealed as dying of natural causes while with a client (The Colonel, who in turn panicked and

dropped her body off at the mortuary before fleeing). Brandon feels the case is closed and will no longer pursue it (and implicate The Colonel). Still at the bar, Lara tells Sami that she is going home to Ani and face the consequences. Gina is relieved that the situation has been resolved while Owen relishes the fact that his father actually did something illegal (dispose of a body).

36. Episode 36. The concluding episode that opens the story for additional episodes: Kate is revealed to have had an affair with a man named Tubbs (who could actually be Owen's father and not The Colonel); Richard finding out that he may have a daughter he never knew existed; Michele receiving help from Ani regarding her designs; problems entering Sami and Owen's relationship; Katie revealing the reason why she has returned as a spirit.

320 *The Vessel.* thevesselseries. com. 2012 (Comedy).

Mike and Rory are a gay British couple who seem to have it all. Or at least they thought they did until they realized they are not parents. Wanting a child of their own, but missing what they call a "vital component" they resolve their problem by asking their straight best friend Kim to become a surrogate (their "tummy mummy"). The program presents what happens as seen through Kim's eyes as she suffers all the traumas of pregnancy while at the same time helping prepare Mike and Rory to become parents. **Cast:** Lily Brown (Kim), Phillip Whiteman (Mike), Giovanni Bienne (Rory), Louise Jameson (Kim's mother), Robin Soans (Kim's father), Luke Courtier (Luke), Shazia Mirza (Doctor), Daphne Kouma (Midwife), Tim Pritchett (Tim), Rib Ostlere (Rob). **Credits:** *Producer:* Chloe Seddon, Philip Whiteman. *Director:* Tijmen Veldhuizen. *Writer:* Chloe Seddon, Phillip Whiteman, Giovanni Bienne. **Comment:** Delightful British-produced program that is well acted and flows smoothly from beginning to end. The program uses the clever First Person Singular method of filming that was developed in 1946 for the feature film *Lady in the Lake* (it was also encompassed in the 1951 DuMont TV series *The Plainclothesman*) wherein the camera lens becomes the eyes of a character and everything is seen from that perspective. Here the camera is Kim and, while she is not seen (except in the last episode), characters speak to her by talking directly into the camera.

What is the biggest favour   you could ask your best friend?

The Vessel ♀

fyrian films

The Vessel. Series poster art; left to right: Giovanni Bienne, Lily Brown and Phillip Whiteman (photograph and design by Vincent Whiteman, 2012).

Episodes:

1. A Mega Favor. Mike and Rory begin their journey into fatherhood by asking Kim to become a surrogate mother.

2. Not Actual Turkeys. The quest begins when Kim, Mike and Rory visit a surrogacy consultant and learn that (in England) a woman who has not had a child cannot become a surrogate mother. Two solutions are offered: have sex with one of the fathers or "do it yourself" via an ovulation kit and no actual sex. Kim chooses the latter.

3. A Bit Pregnant. Mike and Rory (but not so much Kim) are overjoyed when they learn Kim is pregnant.

4. God Didn't Give Either of Them a Womb. Kim's ponders the decision as how to tell her parents she is pregnant and who are the fathers of their grandchild.

5. The Teacher's a Psychopath. As Mike and Rory ponder names for the baby, they must also contend with Kim's hormonal changes.

6. The Third Dad? Kim seeks a way to tell her boyfriend Luke that she is pregnant and carrying a baby for her gay friends.

7. Damn That's My Ex.... Tim! An awkward situation arises when Rory, walking with Kim in a park,

meets his ex-boyfriend and stumbles around a way to tell him about Kim.

8. Stretch Marks. With the baby due shortly, Mike and Kim share their feelings about what is happening and change the course of their lives forever.

9. Ornithoscelidaphobia! A visit to the Natural History Museum finds Kim's water breaking and the big moment soon to arrive.

10. It Might Feel Like You're Having a Bit of Poo. The program concludes with Kim giving birth to a baby girl but also leaves Mike and Rory to fend for themselves as she accepted a job offer in New York City.

321 Vicky and Lysander. vickyandlysander.com/. 2012–2014 (Comedy).

Vicky and Lysander are a New York couple (married, although Lysander appears to be gay) who live in luxury on the Upper East Side of Manhattan. Lysander, a wealthy Southerner who inherited his money, is a jet-setting playboy, known by his signature turtleneck, who is the life of any party and a standout at art gallery openings. He is said to be "the type of guy every man wants to be and every girl wants to be with." Vicky, born in Houston and the daughter of an oil-rich family, is the woman who landed the flamboyant Lysander and has only one goal in life: climb the New York high society ladder with Lysander. The program charts the lives of two people, perhaps not the most readily recognized as being married, and the incidents that threaten to destroy their happiness as they seek to remain the king and queen of the wealthy New York society scene.

Cast: Damon Cardasis (Lysander), Shannon Walker (Vicky), Elizabeth Neptune (June), John Maybee (Jenny), Caitlin Zvoleff (Cecily), Brian Leider (Phil), Amanda Peters (Misfit), Tamara Daley (Lisa), Amy Driesler (Cass), Elizabeth Gray (Paula), Hillary Hamilton (Nancy), Alex Tonetta (Jethrob Barnaby). **Credits:** *Producer:* Damon Cardasis, Shannon Walker, Roxy Hunt, Lucian Piane, Tony Castle. *Director:* Tony Castle, Roxy Hunt. *Writer:* Damon Cardasis, Shannon Walker. **Comment:** Why isn't this series on TV could be the first thing that will pop into your mind as it has everything: excellent acting and production values, amusing, well-done stories, non-offensive situations and characters that are absolutely captivating. Yes, Lysander's moustache is fake, but it just enhances his character and makes the whole program work.

Episodes:

1. Newlyweds. Cecily and Phil, Vicky's sister and husband, must endure a not-so enjoyable dinner engagement with Vicky and Lysander.

2. Jaunt Through Central Park. Lysander tries to calm an upset Vicky when she learns her social enemy, Muffy, has acquired the services of her personal shaman, Tatanka.

3. Shopping with Jethrob Barnaby. Not satisfied with the flamboyant look he already has, Lysander seeks the help of his stylist (Jethrob) to improve his appearance.

4. Drinks with Jenny. Jenny, Lysander's transgender Cambodian fashion designer, is introduced as Lysander expresses his feelings that he and Vicky need to move downtown as that is where the coolness lies.

5. Crosby Street Breakdown. Vicky is in tears—she has not been invited to the Met Ball, a big social event. When Lysander discovers he too has not been invited, he suffers a complete meltdown.

6. Downtown. Although reluctant to leave the Upper East Side, Vicky joins Lysander in his move downtown to the Lower East Side where Lysander believes it has the people and atmosphere for him to survive and be himself.

7. Graphic Design. As Lysander immerses himself in downtown life, Vicky involves herself with an artistic group called Artists Against Inhumanity.

8. Surprise. Needing to get to an event but lacking transportation, Lysander seeks a way to get Vicky to take a cab—something she has never done before and refuses to start doing.

9. Big News. Vicky's thought personal phone call to Cecily to tell her she is upset with Lysander's bullying of her becomes a four way conversation when Phil and Lysander listen in.

10. Episode 10. Vicky's hosting of the Artists Against Inhumanity Gala Event (wherein Lysander is DJ-ing via his iPhone) gives Vicky the hope she needs to get her and Lysander back into the New York Society Circle.

11. Big News. At a dinner party Lysander announces that he has changed his image—he encompassed Jeans and proceeds to show how he will now look wearing them.

12. Jenny's Fashion Studio. At Jenny's studio, Lysander announces that he has created a new fragrance for men called "No Lie by Lysander" and plots his move to sell it.

13. New Endeavors. As Lysander approaches Skyway Capital Ventures to pitch "No Lie," Vicky begins taking art classes with an instructor (June) who is a bit too touchy with her female students.

14. No, No Lie. Vicky accepts an invitation to June's loft against Lysander's beliefs that June is not what she appears to be.

15. My June Lennon. As Lysander's doubts about June begin to haunt him he decides to investigate further while Vicky fails to see anything wrong with June (even her lesbian tendencies).

16. Give It to Me. At the Trinity Boxing Gym, Lysander attempts to work out his frustrations while Vicky, attending an art class, begins to realize that Lysander may be right about June.

17. Rise of the Falcon. June's influence over Vicky (turning her into a woman she calls Falcon) has little meaning to Vicky when Lysander reveals

that June is actually April McMillan, a mass murderer responsible for killing her art students.

18. The Plot Thickens. As Lysander sees that Vicky is about to leave him for June, he seeks Jenny's help in rescuing her from June's influence over her.

19. Super Heroes. Lysander and Jenny plot a way to save Vicky from June.

20. Battle Royale. Lysander and Jenny infiltrate June's studio wherein a fight ensues. June appears to be defeated and Jenny, Vicky and Lysander escape—only to be followed shortly after by June.

21. Back Uptown. As a car chase ensues, Vicky escapes June's grasp when Lysander drives back uptown—an area where June cannot enter (being a downtown resident) and escape. With the Lower East Side experience too much for either Vicky or Lysander to endure, they move back to the Upper East Side where, as the program concludes, they will live the society life they each crave.

322 Victors. facebook.com. 2013 (Drama).

Three young women (Tori, Hannah and Alley) each facing a real-life crisis (cancer patient, epileptic, abused child) are given a second chance at life when they are magically transformed into costumed super heroes, granted amazing powers and must now not only battle the forces of evil but learn how to adjust to their newfound abilities.

Cast: Christina Cusack-Curbelo (Danielle), Kyndalle Sheigh Allen (Hannah), Izzy Alexis (Alley), Krystle MacNeill (Tori), Jessica Benitez (Agent Leta), Jason Lewing (Josh), Maxon Hughes, Christy Mills, Thomas Summerford, Cecelia Kuhn, Kevin Gaddie. *Note:* The character of Alley is credited as both Izzy Alexis and Izzy Palag in text information. **Comment:** Although a teaser appears on line and text information is very vague, it appears, based on some information that *Victors* is a lesbian-themed series. The three leads (Tori, Hannah and Alley) and their equally gorgeous enemy, the evil Danielle, are not shown as such in what video information has been released (although Danielle's interaction with her nemeses hints at it). Also adding intrigue appears to be the dangerous and mysterious Agent Leta. There are a lot of promises made on Facebook (beginning in 2012) that the series is coming and that six episodes have been made, but other than the teaser and a behind-the-scenes video, no other episodes appear to have been released. The program itself appears action-oriented and has seemingly good special effects sequences based on what little can be seen.

Episodes:

1. Teaser. Highlights action scenes with virtually no introduction to the cast or who plays the roles (or who even produces, writes or directs it).

2. Victors' Interrogation Scene.

323 The Vines of Sauvignon Blanc. vine.com. 2013 (Comedy).

Doug, the gay owner of the Eleganza Winery vineyards is sitting at his desk when his secretary rushes in and tells him, "You have only two minutes and six seconds to live." His family has eagerly waited for this moment but Doug does not want the winery to go to his evil twin brother Duke. The program relates Doug's efforts to acquire a new heir by marrying a man he feels will care for his winery—all within the time he has left.

Cast: Reuchen Lemkuhl, Sue Galloway, Stephen Guarino, Jamie Lee, Leslie Meisel, Michael Hartney, Jarvis Derrell. Credits are not given. **Comment:** Called a "mini-sudser" as it is styled after a TV soap opera, the program does manage to tell a complete story in the time allotted. It is very fast moving and all episodes can be viewed as one complete story. The acting is very good and the editing expertly executed to prevent a smooth flowing story.

Episodes: 22 six-second episodes that tell the whole story in 132 seconds.

324 El Vlog de Greta (Greta's Vlog). elvlogdegreta.com. 2012 (Comedy).

Greta is a young woman enjoying life as a lesbian but also frustrated that she cannot connect with the perfect woman. She dates, has friends who are also lesbians but her frustrations always seem to overwhelm her. As Greta creates an Internet vlog to voice her opinions, the program relates those vlogs as Greta not only ridicules her own life but the travails of her friends.

Greta, the girl that holds the group together, previously worked as an economist before becoming a video artist. Sara is a theatrical props manager; Trinity, a video game designer, lives with Greta; Viv is a student and studying audio-visual communications; and Berenice is the landlady of the home wherein the girls live.

Cast: Esperanza Pedroza (Greta), Sara Casasnovas (Sara), Gemma Martínez (Trinity), Marina Salas (Viv) and Maru Valdivielso (Berenice, The Oracle). **Credits:** *Director:* Rhoda N. Wainwright, Karin Marzocchini. **Comment:** Depending on which sharing site you find, you will discover that some claim it is an Italian series while others maintain it is a Spanish series. *El Vlog de Greta* is Spanish and, while there is eye candy, the subtitles make it difficult to enjoy the series (it's not impossible, just hard). The acting is very good and, if you care to read, a smooth-flowing story with the girls interacting with each other as well as outside interests.

Episode List: Following is a list of the 10 videos that were produced:

1. Web Serie Lesbiana: El Volg de Greta: Teaser with English subtitles.

2. Web Serie Lesbiana: El Vlog de Greta: Teaser con sottotitoli in Italiano.

3. Web Serie Lesbiana: El Vlog de Greta: Part 1, English subtitles.

4. Web Serie Lesbiana: El Vlog de Greta: Que es Normal. English subtitles.

5. Web Serie Lesbiana: Felices Fiestas de Maru Valdivielso de El Vlog de Greta.

6. Web Serie Lesbiana: El Vlog de Greta: Part 1: Sous-titrage en Francais.

7. Web Serie Lesbiana: El Vlog de Greta: Part 1 con sottotitoli in Italiano.

8. Web Serie Lesbiana: El Vlog de Greta: Teaser.

9. Web Serie Lesbiana: El Vlog de Greta: Parte 1: Ring Ring. Subs, Eng/ESP.

10. Web Serie Lesbiana: El Vlog de Greta: Ring Ring. Subs, Eng/ESP.

325 *Wallflowers.* stage17.com. 2013–2014 (Comedy).

There is a support group run by a woman named Janice, a "modern master of love," that caters to the hopelessly and eternally single men and women of Manhattan, people who also happen to be gay, straight and bisexual but unable to make a connection. People who enter the support group are mostly in their thirties, social media shy and have not encompassed the possibilities of Internet dating. Members of the group feel comfortable in their new comfort zone but once leaving the support group find meeting someone a most difficult endeavor. The program focuses, in particular, on gay relationships, mostly those that are seen through the experiences of Bryce (and his later steady hookup with Alex).

Bryce, a former child star turned owner of the Hunter Casting Company, is openly gay but distrustful of people and enjoys drinking and smoking (sometimes to an excess).

Daisy, Bryce's best friend, is also his business partner but is his complete opposite and has a no-nonsense outlook on life (which she doesn't quite realize is complicating her romantic life).

Martin, almost 40 years old, is still looking to start a family but doesn't realize that his over-eagerness is preventing him from finding a woman that is compatible with him.

Janice, an advice counselor, was a former backup singer on a number of no-name bands. She feels her advice is indispensable and makes sure her followers know that.

Jane, a recently fired high-powered attorney, has just ended her affair with her married boss and has returned to the center after having successfully graduated.

Rhonda, a fun-loving girl with a positive outlook on life, is also the girl who constantly finds her heart broken by those who continually take advantage of her.

Linus, the newest member of the group, is a bar tender who has aspirations of becoming a comic book artist. Although he is attractive to others, he is inept at dating.

Victoria Pond, raised in a culture where women are seen as subservient, struggles to live above that distinction and feels the only way she can do so is by dating gay men.

Leslie is the office manager at Hunter Casting; Becca is a casting assistant (and Daisy's rival for everything); Wade is the Hunter Casting receptionist (replaced Todd); Alex is the musician who hooks up with Bryce; Fred is Janice's ex-husband, a band manager who eventually begins dating Jane (on Janice's insistence); Todd is Daisy's younger brother (a gay who secretly loves Bryce); Tina and Ricky are support group members. Mark is a filmmaker and Hunter Casting client with whom Daisy seeks to begin a relationship.

Cast: Sarah Saltzberg (Daisy Loeb), Chad Kimball, Lucas Near-Verbrugghe, Patch Darragh (Bryce Hunter), Gibson Frazier (Martin Parrish), Christianne Tisdale (Janice Ackerman), Susan Louise O'Connor (Rhonda), Ricky Dunlop (Ricky), Tina Hart (Tina), Marcia DeBonis (Leslie), Max Crumm (Linus), Angela Lin (Victoria Pond), Lisa Joyce (Nancy), Jillian Louis (Becca), John Gallbach (Alex), Gideon Glick (Todd), Brooke Davis (Brooke), Matt Dengler (Charlie), Wayne Wilcox, Mark Provencher (Mark), Tina Hart (Tina), Ricky Dunlop (Ricky), Robert Bogue (Fred). **Credits:** *Producer:* David Stoller, Ondine Landa Abramson, Kieran Turner, Michael Canzoniero. *Writer-Director:* Kieran Turner. **Comment:** Whether it is on TV or in feature films, gay and bisexual characters are often seen in a stereotyped light, not the people that they really are. *Wallflowers* attempts to change that image by presenting them as real people searching for love, not only on the fact that they are gay. The acting and production values are very good and stories, while they do have their amusing moments, also do not make the gay characters the total butt of the jokes.

Episodes: (all titles are based on TV series from the past).

1. Square Pegs. The story line is begun as Bryce, Daisy, Victoria and Martin decide to do something about their disastrous love lives.

2. Fridays. Believing that a support group may be the answer, the friends enroll in Janice's class for singles.

3. All-American Girl. As Daisy begins working for Mark, she finds herself in competition for his attention from Bryce and Victoria.

4. Hello, Larry. Bruce prepares for a blind date set up for him by Janice.

5. The Partridge Family. A Sunday afternoon finds the friends enjoying a relaxing time discussing events in their lives. Season one concludes.

6. The Invaders. Season two opens with Daisy and Mark making a connection and dating; Bryce setting his sights on a musician (Alex); Martin agree-

ing to become a Lamaze coach for a pregnant co-worker (Nancy); and Janice sets up Jane on a date with her ex-husband.

7. The Match Game. Bryce and Alex venture onto their first date while Jane hooks up with Janice's ex (Fred).

8. Super Friends. Feeling the need to be more of a companion to Nancy, Martin begins helping her around the house; Bryce hires a new assistant (Wade) when Todd leaves; Janice feels she needs to help steer Daisy and Mark's relationship in the right direction.

9. Misfits of Science. Bryce applies for the gay dating app "trickr" while Janice, discovering the prospect of Internet dating, believes her support group should also participate.

10. V. Nancy begins to have concerns about Mark's continual presence in her life while her husband is away; both Bryce and Jane are becoming a bit uneasy over their new relationships.

11. My Own Worst Enemy. As Janice attempts to ease the tension between Bryce and Alex, Martin, acting more like a husband than a friend, seeks the perfect gift for Nancy's soon-to-be born baby boy.

12. Roar. The concluding episode wherein it is revealed that Bryce was an actor who, after revealing he was gay, found his career over (but finds it may be reborn when a producer [Dan] offers him a role in his next project); Martin, purchasing what he believes will be the perfect gift for the baby (to be named Nate), a signed 1975 baseball, also finds it is time for him to move on when he meets Nancy's husband, who has returned to her.

326 Watchers: The Virtual Series. the watcherscouncil.net. 2003–2008 (Horror).

Buffy the Vampire Slayer spin off that continues to focus on the battle between good (The Watchers Council) and evil (demons, vampires and anything dispensed by a Hellmouth portal). In the original series Buffy Summers was a slayer of vampires watched over by Rupert Giles. They were assisted by Willow, a witch, Xander, her friend and Dawn, Buffy's younger sister. Willow was slowly revealed to be a lesbian with another witch (Tara) as her lover. *Watchers* picks up Willow's story with additional lesbian characters (Dawn, Faith, Rowena, Skye, Kadin, Serena and Kennedy) intertwined with straight character story lines.

The overall series re-introduces Rupert as a Watcher, a man from a long-line of such beings that train and protect female slayers like Buffy. When their Sunnydale, California–based Watchers Council is destroyed by the First Evil, Willow (who has discovered she was destined to become a Watcher) and Giles establish the New Watchers Council in Cleveland, Ohio, home to a second Hellmouth (a portal through which demons can pass from their realm into our world). Sunnydale was home to the first

Hellmouth). The program follows the Council members as they continue their battle against powerful demons, most notably The Presidium.

Principal Characters: Willow Rosenberg (High Priestess and head of the Coven Division of Witches); Rupert Giles (Council Advisor); Rowena Allister (Senior Watcher); Faith Lehane (Head of the Slayer Division); Kennedy Calendar (Lead Slayer); Dawn Summers (Watcher and Coven member) Xander Harris (Weapons Master); Robin Wood (Security Chief and Academy teacher); Andrew Wells (Coven High Priest); Jeff Lindquist (Watcher and Coven Member); Skye Talisker (Vampire and Dawn's lover); Grace Hatherley (a Watcher); Buffy Summers (Head of the Watcher Division); Kadin Van Helsing (Rogue Demon Hunter); Becca Giles (Bookstore owner and Giles' wife); Jason Felix (Head of Bureau Nine); Althenea Dimmons (London High Priestess); Lori Carew (Former Slayer and now Felix's assistant); Vi Joston (a Slayer); Tracey Hausser (Council member and college student); Ethan Rayne (Watcher and Magic Expert); Shannon Matthewson (Dawn's Slayer), Marsha (Slayer assigned to Willow).

Cast: Alyson Hannigan (Willow Rosenberg), Michelle Trachtenberg (Dawn Summers), Amber Benson (Tara), Eliza Dushku (Faith Lehane), Michelle Williams (Rowena Allister), Lacey Chabert (Skye Talisker), Lyari Limon (Kennedy Calender), Lindsay Felton, Michelle Rodriquez (Kadin Van Helsing), Anthony Stewart Head (Rupert Giles), Felicia Day (Vi Joston), Nicholas Brendan (Xander Harris), Sarah Michelle Gellar (Buffy Summers), Jennifer Connelly (Althenea Dimmons), Carly Schroeder (Marsha), Elijah Wood (Jeff Lindquist), Helen Shaver (Becca Montague-Giles), Christy Carlson Romano (Hope Lehane), Laura Prepon (Lori Carew), Caroline Dhavernas (Grace Hatherley), Gary Oldman (Jason Felix), Rachel Hurd Wood (Lorinda Sheparton), Steffani Brass (Shannon Matthewson), D.B. Woodside (Robin Wood), Tom Lenk (Andrew Wells), Thora Birch (Tracey Hausser), Robert Sachs (Ethan Rayne). **Credits:** *Producer:* CN Winters, Susan Carr, Dragon Writer 17 (as credited). *Writer:* CN Winters, Susan Carr, Kye Cook, Chris Cook, Dragon Writer 17, Dan Joslyn. *Director:* CN Winters, Susan Carr. **Comment:** The program began during the seventh season of *Buffy the Vampire Slayer* and remained loyal to the feel of the original series. The program incorporates regulars from the original series with excellent acting and production values. With the exception of teasers and fan-produced tributes to the series (available on YouTube), all the episodes have been taken off line.

Episodes:

1. Something Ventured, Something Gained. Establishes the premise as Willow discovers her true destiny (a Watcher) and she and Giles begin establishing the New Council.

326 • Watchers   200

2. Lake Eerie. The Council battles a demon that attacks boaters on Lake Erie.

3. Foreign Presence. Rowena is introduced as a Watcher from the Old Guard who is part of a move to dismantle the New Council.

4. Untimely Arrivals. Giles faces additional opposition to establishing the New Council when Old Guard members arrive in Cleveland.

5. Broken Allies. Seeing that she may have misjudged the New Council, Rowena sides with Giles and joins with him. Meanwhile, Willow becomes a Watcher to a new Slayer (Marsha).

6. Samhain. The Council must stop a demon bent on creating a zombie army.

7. Love and War. Dawn, Buffy's sister, is introduced and finds herself becoming attracted to a warlock named Jeff.

8. Another Year Old. Xander, from the original series, reunites with Willow to celebrate her birthday.

9. Love Hurts. Willow faces a crisis when her powers are temporarily lost after an encounter with The Presidium.

10. Dark Force Rising. Tara, from the original series (Willow's girlfriend), appears to Kennedy (Willow's current love interest) in a dream with information on how to restore Willow's powers. Meanwhile, Giles finds romance with Becca, a shopkeeper.

11. Blue Christmas. Anya, the demon girlfriend of Xander (from the original series), creates havoc by creating a demonic Santa Claus. Meanwhile as Willow and Kennedy's romance flounders, Giles and Becca's blossoms.

12. Modus Operandi. The Council attempts to stop a demonic Jack the Ripper type of killer.

13. Rash Decisions. A new demon, Sister Sin, becomes a threat to the city that the Council must destroy.

14. Family Ties. A fierce winter storm brings some unexpected calamity when family members of the New Council besiege headquarters and are forced to wait out the storm together.

15. About Last Night. Willow reveals to her parents that she is now a Watcher.

16. Restoration. A flash forward episode wherein a descendant of Willow in the year 2130 (a Colonel in the Military Watchers Council) reunites with a reincarnation of Tara (now a Slayer) as they attempt to stop an army of demons created by the New Council itself.

17. Scarecrow. Willow finds herself becoming attracted to Rowena as she, Giles and Rowena battle an evil Watcher/Magic abuser.

18. Gangland. Faith, a New Council member, tries to recruit a group of "lost girls" who acquire strength when they band together.

19. Lessons Learned. Mia, one of the "lost girls" becomes attracted to Kennedy as Faith and Giles begin their recruitment.

20. High Art. As Giles celebrates his 50th birthday, a painting he purchases at an auction becomes more than just that when he discovers it can reveal one's inner demons.

21. Child's Play. A hex, placed on Willow, Faith and Xander, returns them to a time when they were children.

22. May Day. As the Watchers and Slayers prepare for the celebration of Beltaine, The Presidium casts a spell that forces religious groups to attack the Council.

23. Another Day. Willow and Kennedy attempt to rescue Faith, who has been kidnapped by a demon.

24. Another Apocalypse. Season one concludes with the Council members combining their powers in an attempt to defeat The Presidium.

25. Everything New Again. Season two begins. Although the Council failed to defeat The Presidium, it has vowed to make its elimination their number one priority. A new demon, the Lover, from the kingdom known as Vor, rises and becomes a serious threat as it has the power to see what the Watchers are planning.

26. New Again. Willow begins mentoring her Slayer (Marsha) as demons plot to turn Faith into one of them.

27. Checkmate. Willow and Rowena engage in a game of chess, magically enhanced by the Witch's Coven, whose chess pieces come to life to reveal incidents from the women's past lives.

28. Swap Meet. Becca's attempt at casting spells backfires, causing Council members to switch identities.

29. True Colors. Becca learns that she is pregnant (by Giles) as Willow and Rowena become sexually attracted to each other.

30. Red Herring. The board game "Clue" becomes all too frightening when, at a costume party, Council members must defeat a killer who is playing the game for real.

31. Dream Warriors. A demon's spell has Council members dreaming they are in an arena battling a demon named Imbethit.

32. Hell Goddess. The Council battles a group of demons called Mizors, who have besieged Cleveland.

33. Time Out. Council member Tyrrell is exposed as manipulating a plan to eliminate the Council heads.

34. Real World. The Presidium's plan to recruit a human agent to kidnap Rowena and Mia backfires when he is killed and Rowena is wounded.

35. Blue Moon. In an attempt to cure a woman (Camille) of her vampirism, Troy (a werewolf) and Cassandra (a vampire) cast a spell that cures her but leaves them both werewolves.

36. Bad Blood. Although Camille believes she has left her past behind her, an unknown figure now threatens her—Kadin Van Helsing, heir to the Helsing legacy (vampire hunters) who has vowed to

kill her for killing her father (when she was a vampire).

37. In the Dark. Council members Vi and her twin sister Angie, try to help a disfigured, abused young man who is believed to be a monster.

38. Avatar. An encounter with a supernatural beast leaves Kennedy with super abilities—abilities that if used, could destroy demons—but damage the city as well.

39. Fire Eater. Becca and Giles face a Soul Stealer that is seeking Becca's unborn child.

40. Unfinished Business. Kadin teams with Kennedy to battle a seemingly unstoppable demon.

41. Chapel of Love. Having defeated the Soul Stealer, Giles and Becca set their sights on marrying.

42. Get a Life. A demonic incarnation of actress Jeri Ryan becomes the target of the Council when it begins killing fans at a comic book convention.

43. Rack and Ruin. Xander and Vi become closer while Kennedy and Mia face challenges to their relationship when Kennedy realizes she has deep feelings for Kadin.

44. Resistance. Willow, once turned evil on the original series, fears she may be returning to the dark side when continual nightmares appear to be leading her down that path.

45. Internal Affairs. A shape shifter, pretending to be a lover to both Vi and Xander, threatens to drain their life force while Dawn and Rowena seek a monster of their own—a dragon.

46. Wickerman. Faith and her Black Ops Squad attempt to stop The Presidium from masterminding a plot to invade the earth.

47. Ragnarok, Part 1. The second season concludes with the Council entering the Vor to battle Lover and The Presidium. Meanwhile Becca gives birth to a girl (Elizabeth) and Buffy becomes head of the Council.

48. Ragnarok, Part 2. The story continues with the battle against The Presidium.

49. War Zone. Now that he is a father, Giles elects to retire and places Rowena in the position of head of the Council. At this same time, the Council must battle a demonic sand worm that is threatening to wipe out U.S. troops in the Iraq desert. The third season begins.

50. Maternal Instincts. The Council seeks to stop a horde of demons that are seeking a human surrogate mother.

51. Both Sides Now. Rowena's first mission as the Council leader finds her attempting to clear Xander, Willow and Vi of charges that their negligence caused the death of several women and the fall of the Vancouver Watchers Council.

52. Just the Facts. A reporter (Robert Devlin) attempts to piece together the incidents that lead to the women's death and the fall of the council. His research uncovers startling evidence regarding the Watchers and their work.

53. Trial by Fury. A spell is put on Devlin to prevent him from revealing what he uncovered to the outside world. Meanwhile, Kadin must come to terms for killing a group of werewolves who had dedicated themselves to living peacefully with humans.

54. Luna. Rowena and Willow contemplate their relationship as the Council battles a series of strange occurrences during a full moon.

55. In the Balance. Rowena and Willow rekindle their stormy relationship as Kennedy and Kadin forge a new bond.

56. Loves Labors Lost. Rowena, Willow, Faith and Robin seek a way to bring an end to an ages-old feud between two families while Willow must also help uncover the source of ghostly occurrences at Giles' new home.

57. No Mercy. Rowena must decide if the mysterious Gregor Kalderash (Kennedy's uncle) is a candidate for the Council after he predicts an agonizing future for Willow and Faith. Meanwhile, Skye (a vampire) begins to raise suspicions about her mysterious activities.

58. Birthright. Assisted by Kennedy, Kadin seeks the other half of a medallion left to her by her father to claim her birthright as a member of the Helsing family. Meanwhile, Dawn becomes concerned over Skye's mysterious behavior.

59. Rule of Three. Vi attempts to come to terms with killing Gregor to save Willow and Faith; Dawn is rejected by slayer Shannon as her Watcher after Shannon befriends a deranged creature.

60. Roses Are Red. The Council must contend with the ghost of young girl (Rose) who has begun haunting the Cleveland Council. Skye turns renegade (killing a slayer) while Kennedy and Faith's relationship is apparently ending as Faith leaves the Council.

61. The Night in Question. Faith finds herself mysteriously transported to an alternate universe where she never achieved the status of a senior slayer with the Cleveland Council but that of a rogue slayer.

62. A Road Trip to Remember. A search is begun to find the rogue vampire, Skye. Dawn, shattered by Skye's death when she is found and destroyed, must come to terms that she has lost Skye and Buffy must realize that Dawn is no longer her kid sister, but a woman.

63. 59:23. The Council members ban together to defuse a mystical bomb that is set to detonate in less than one hour.

64. Skin Deep. Willow and Rowena must come to terms on the inherent differences in their relationship while Kennedy, reunited with Faith, must also choose to strengthen or abandon their relationship; and Xander and Vi appear to have progressed to a state where a relationship is now possible.

65. Strange Bedfellows. The Council must decide if Kadin is worthy of becoming a member (as she acts first and obeys orders later). Meanwhile, Dawn

seeks a way to restore Skye's soul and bring her love back to her; Kennedy is assigned the task of testing Kadin in the field—by helping her destroy a nest of vampires, lead by Harmony and Luna that were unleashed by the Hellmouth.

66. Very Bad Ideas. Dawn discovers a way to bring her lover back—by seeking the Witch's Coven's help in restoring Skye's soul.

67. Rules of Engagement. As a nest of demons appear, Rowena assigns Buffy to take her place while Dawn, acquiring the spell she needs, begins preparations to bring Skye back to her. Dawn succeeds but Sky is resurrected as a vampire.

68. Foucault's Pendulum. The Council learns (from a time traveler) that in 300 years Watchers and Slayers are doomed and that to protect that future, action must be taken now. As head of the Council, Buffy summons Council leaders from around the world to change the future.

69. The Secret Life of D.J. Tracy. Council member Tracy's college radio program provides the backdrop for a look at a week in the life of the Council as it deals with free lance vampire slayers and as Tracy deals with her own problems—from her encounter with a strange little boy to her work at school.

70. Ouroboros. Giles and Willow investigate the unearthing of a mysterious temple (Ouroboros) found on a construction site.

71. Shomer. Visions of what could happen if the Council were not created are brought to light when an angel appears to the Council to deliver a message: "For behold, I bring you things of great.... Doom."

72. Megiddo. The third season finale finds the Council faced with possible devastation as Hellmouth's from across the world start to open and dispense creatures that could destroy mankind. It appears that a temple in the lost City of Atlantis holds the key to destroying the enemy.

73. Better Days. The fourth season begins. The Council's battle against the demons from the prior episode makes them known to the world but also reveals to the public that demons really exist. Another organization, called Bureau Nine (led by Jason Felix) is revealed to also abolish demons—but for a substantial fee.

74. Unspoken. Rowena and Kennedy seek an ancient text that contains magic spells capable of banishing evil.

75. A Little Faith. Hope, Faith's younger sister becomes possessed by a demon seeking to use her to destroy Council members.

76. Based on a True Story. A screenplay, written by Council member Andrew, becomes a movie that is anything but the truth.

77. Withdrawal. Rowena experiments on Skye, hoping to cure her of her vampirism.

78. Hide 'n' Seek. Rowena, Faith, and Vi attempt to escape from a demon (Hell) after they are taken hostage and find themselves trapped in an amusement park fun house.

79. Collateral Damage. Kennedy seeks to help Kadin when she faces the wrath of a werewolf seeking to kill her for killing his werewolf family.

80. Revelation 9:6. Faith must contend with an anti-slayer—whose touch can take away the powers of a Slayer.

81. From the Bottom Up. Incidents in the lives of lesser known Council members are explored.

82. Trinity. The problems facing Council members Dawn, Skye and Shannon are explored.

83. Auld Lang Syne. Stories of the past are related by Giles, Rowena, Faith and Andrew on New Year's Eve.

84. Meiyo. Bureau Nine and its leader, Jason Felix, are profiled.

85. You Never Know. The Council must stop a pair of bungling demons before they can affect a plan to destroy the world.

86. Drawn Together. Willow and Andrew seek a way to escape a cursed comic book based on Faith's life when they are drawn into it.

87. Hidden. Kadin, Rowena, Faith, Buffy, Willow, Xander and Kennedy must overcome a curse that seizes their abilities to fight demons.

88. Lockdown. Amira, the Muslim Council member, seeks a way to end a fundamentalist Islamic takeover of the Council.

89. Alluvion. The Council clashes with Bureau Nine in an effort to acquire an ancient artifact.

90. Sacrifice. The demon Hell returns seeking to kill Council members with Kennedy determined to stop her. A confrontation forces Kennedy to kill Kadin in order to save Willow from her clutches.

91. Serena. Kadin, able to resurrect herself, returns to the Council—and to her lover, Serena.

92. Tokyo Knights. A lead to Hell's whereabouts brings Kennedy to Tokyo where she finally achieves her goal by killing Hell.

93. Bloodlines. Faith, feeling that she is becoming a less-effectual Slayer, finds her faith restored when she begins mentoring younger Slayers for the Council.

94. The Price. Kennedy's doubts about herself and what she has done to protect the innocent are brought to light when she is propelled into an alternate world without the protection of the Council.

95. Childe Roland. As Willow and Rowena plan to marry, the Council faces a crisis when Jason (of Bureau Nine) begins preparations to rid the world of magic to make it a better place.

96. The Dark Tower. The fourth season finale wherein the Council, helpless without magic, must find a way to stop Jason and the doorway he will open to let demons control the world.

Note: Episodes 97 through 123, which represent the series fifth and last season, have been taken off line. Flashbacks, coupled with flash forwards are incorporated to explore the past and future history of the New Council and its battle against a vicious demon called the Loathestone.

Fifth Season Episode Titles: *97:* Past, Present, Future. *98:* Home Sweet Home. *99:* Games. *100:* Time and Again. *101:* Orientation. *102:* Divination. *103:* Lorinda's Kiss. *104:* Triangle. *105:* Inside the Watcher's Council. *106:* The Unknown. *107:* Savage. *108:* Cone of Power. *109:* Webs We Weave. *110:* Reboot. *111:* Before I Wake. *112:* Turnabout. *113:* Tainted. *114:* Contingency. *115:* Unlikely Heroes. *116:* Underworld. *117:* Breaking Point. *118:* Last Tango in Cleveland. *119:* Asha. *120:* Unto the End. *121:* Generations. *122:* Generations II. *123:* Generations III.

327 *We Have to Stop Now.* youtube.com/user/wehavetostopnow. 2009–2010 (Comedy-Drama).

How to Succeed in Marriage Without Even Trying is a book written by Dyna and Kit, married therapists who are also lesbians. But, since the book was written, they have grown apart and even with the help of their own therapist (Susan) it appears that their marriage has ended. Unexpectedly, their book has become a number one best-seller and has stirred the interest of Guy, a film-maker who has contracted with them to produce a documentary based on their lives and the contents of their book. A breakup is now out of the question (as it could ruin their reputation and book sales) and the program follows their efforts to remain a couple despite the differences in their relationship.

Kit Janson is not always predictable in what she will do (sort of not sure if she sees a glass as half full or half empty). She is fun to be with, impulsive, honest and openly expresses her feelings. She maintains a strictly professional relationship with her clients (no matter how gorgeous one may be) and has come to realize that when she encounters a stumbling block to a relationship with another woman, she has a tendency to avoid facing the issues that are troubling her (or her lover).

Dyna Cella has a higher set of standards than Kit (classy and conservative). She prefers intellectual pursuits (such as reading books as opposed to surfing the Internet) and her high professional standards make her a more sympathetic when it comes to her patients. But like Kit, Dyna also has issues, the most personal being her tendency to conceal her loving and loyal side from those close to her (a situation that, if overcome, could possibly save her marriage to Kit).

Susan Dyson is Kit and Dyna's therapist, a compassionate woman with a knack for navigating her professional life, but just the opposite when it comes to her personal life, as she appears unable to maintain a steady relationship. She has been treating Kit and Dyna since the start of their breakup and has, in a way, changed her life: she is now prone to concealing her soft and compassionate side to focus on a straight forward, no-nonsense approach to counseling clients. She feels for Kit and Dyna and hopes that, through the documentary being made, she can

reunite them as the happily married couple they once were.

Cindy Janson is Kit's younger sister, a girl who loves to get high or drunk, can't keep an apartment or a job and always finds "a home away from home" by crashing at Kit and Dyna's home. Dyna puts up with Cindy despite her loss of personal time with Kit. Cindy enjoys flirting with both men and women (her idea of having fun) and thrives on people's misconceptions regarding her sexuality and her motives.

Guy, the film-maker, has become like a member of the family, recording every aspect of Kit, Dyna and Cindy's life but also finding complications as he has fallen for Cindy and become involved in all the awkwardness as Kit and Dyna pretend to be a happy couple.

Cast: Jill Bennett (Kit Janson), Cathy DeBuono (Dyna Cella), Ann Noble (Cindy Janson), Suzanne Westenhoefer (Susan Dyson), John W. McLaughlin (Guy), Meredith Baxter (Judy), Mary Frances Careccia (Dee Dee Cella), Shannan Leigh Reeve (Shauna), Maria Marini (Christy), Maia Madison (Sybil), Catherine O'Connor (Mandy). **Credits:** *Producer:* Jill Bennett, Cathy DeBuono, Ann Noble, Donna Rucks, Libbie Shelton, Robyn Dettman, Rebecca S. Katz. *Director:* Robyn Dettman, Jill Bennett, Cathy DeBuono. *Writer:* Ann Noble. **Comment:** Well-acted and produced program that tries not to be more than it actually is—two lovers trying to understand and overcome the problems that are plaguing their relationship. There are moments of tenderness, but no nudity or vulgar language and a well worth watching program with characters that are as real as people you may actually know.

Season 1 Episodes:

1. The Pilot. Establishes the fact that Kit and Dyna are in therapy and trying to become a couple again.

2. The Golden Rules. The rules of being a good therapist are explored.

3. The Sock Puppets. Susan, Kit and Dyna's therapist, attempts to use sock puppets as a form of therapy.

Note: The following Season 1 episodes have been taken off line: *A Day at a Time, Transfererntial, Who's Side Are You On* and *Carnal Knowledge, Parts 1, 2 and 3.*

Season 2 Episodes:

1. The Baby and the Bathwater. As Kit and Dyna continue their therapy counseling with Susan, it is suggested that a baby may be the key to solving their problems.

2. The Grass Is Always Greener. Hoping to get other opinions about their relationship problems, Kit and Dyna each seek the advice of a different therapist.

3. Sisterhood-Winked. DeeDee, Dyna's younger sister, comes to visit Dyna at a time when Dyna and Kit have taken the advice of their substitute therapists to date other women.

4. How Sweet It Is. To begin their new dating experience, Kit and Dyna, accompanied by Dee Dee, decide to embark on an ocean cruise (the Sweet Cruise) hoping to meet other women. Meanwhile, Shauna, Guy's younger sister, has accompanied them to chronicle their adventures, while Guy becomes attracted to Cindy, Kit's kid sister.

5. Celesbianism. As Kit and Dyna find some relaxation during the cruise, Susan attempts to solve her own romantic problems by venturing into the world of speed dating.

6. Q&A. Kit and Dyna, recognized by passengers as the celebrities they have become, hold a question-and-answer session aboard ship and recall some of their more interesting clients.

7. The Truthyness of the Matter. Meeting other women did not help, the question-and-answer session brought about hidden feelings and now Kit and Dyna feel they must return to therapy and seek out Susan.

8. It's Not a Game. The concluding episode that revolves around a poker game wherein truths are revealed that could reunite Kit and Dyna as a couple.

328 We're Getting Nowhere. afterellen. com. 2007–2008 (Comedy).

Three female hosts (called "The Terrible Three") recap and re-enact scenes from then current television programs, including lesbian themed series like *The L Word* and *South of Nowhere*. As the women sum up a program's episodes, they use whatever props are necessary (even sock puppets) to put their spin on the episode's story line. The program is presented like a vlog and was originally set in the bedroom of Jill Bennett's home in Los Angeles (later moved to her living room). Several episodes are also set in Dara Nai's living room. **Host:** Jill Bennett, Karman Kregloe, Dara Nai. **Credits:** *Producer:* Sarah Warn. **Comment:** Although it is not possible to present a comment based on viewing (as all episodes, including titles and descriptions have been taken off line) the program is historical in that it was the first series to air on afterellen.com and became the springboard for lesbian actors, writers and directors to express their opinions.

329 What's Your Problem? afterellen.com. 2008 (Reality).

Cathy DeBuono, a lesbian clin-ical psychologist, hosts a vlog wherein she and her guests discuss topics and issues relating to women both lesbian and bisexual.

Host: Cathy DeBuono. **Credits:** *Producer:* Cathy DeBuono. **Comment:** Candid program with a charming host and reverent topics that address problems with comical overtones. The first episode contains some technical problems (like on-air camera adjustments and poor lighting) but these improve from the second episode on.

Episodes:

1. What's Your Problem Pilot. Cathy appears and explains the overall format of her program.

2. Episode 2. Singer Janet Robin performs.

3. Three Lesbians, One Camera and a Bottle of Champagne. Guests JD Disalvatore (filmmaker) and Doria Biddle (radio talk show host) join Cathy for an overall look at lesbian life.

4. People and Blogs. Cathy and guest Suzanne Westenhoefer discuss love triangles.

5. Episode 5. Age differences, emotional maturity and figuring out if you are gay are discussed by Cathy and her guest Bridget McManus.

6. Episode 6. Homophobic mothers are discussed with guest Maeve Quinlan.

7. Episode 7. Actress Calpernia Addams joins Cathy for a look at the FTM (female-to-male) transgender.

8. Episode 8. First crushes and kisses are discussed by Cathy and her guest actress Marnie Alton.

9. Episode 9. Filmmaker Jane Clark and actress

What's Your Problem? **Series Poster Art (used by permission of Cathy DeBuono).**

Traci Dinwiddle guest to talk about the film *The Touch* and how it dealt with 19th century lesbian poet Renee Vivien.

10. Episode 10. A musical performance by Janet Robin highlights a program wherein Cathy responds to viewer questions.

11. Episode 11. A look at gay role models coupled with responses to viewer questions.

12. Episode 12. Comedian Erin Foley and Cathy discuss how they first met coupled with other remembrances of their pasts.

13. Episode 14. In a change of pace episode, Cathy introduces the audience to Dr. Jack, her veterinary friend.

14. Episode 15. Sociopaths and narcissists are discussed by Cathy and her guest singer Janet Robin.

15. Episode 16. Cathy and her guest Shannon Wentworth discuss a strange mix of subjects: traveling with your girlfriend, breasts, sex toys and toe puppets.

16. Episode 17. Calpernia Addams guests in a program designed to help lesbians open up when they are afraid of doing just that.

330 *Where the Bears Are.* wherethe bearsare.tv. 2012–2014 (Comedy).

Nelson, Reggie and Wood are gay roommates who live in the Silver Lake neighborhood of Los Angeles. Their lives appear to revolve around everything that is gay until circumstances beyond their control involve them in precarious situations that require their ingenuity to overcome and once again return to their comfort zones. Each season (three seasons produced as of December 31, 2014) involves the roommates, called "bears" in a murder-mystery that they must solve without themselves becoming victims or arrested as the culprits. Season one finds the bears seeking the killer of a man they find dead in their bathtub; solving the murder of a politician becomes their quest in the second season; while the third season follows their efforts to solve a series of murders that appear to be linked to Chunk Studios, a gay porn studio.

Cast: Rick Copp (Reggie Hatch), Joe Dietl (Wood Burns), Ben Zook (Nelson Dorkoff), Ian Parks (Todd "Hot Toddy" Stevens), Chad Sanders (Det. Chad Winters), George Unda (Det. Marcus Martinez), Loretta Fox (Susie Collins), Tim Hooper (Police Chief). **Credits:** *Producer:* Rick Copp, Joe Dietl, Ben Zook. *Director:* Joe Dietl. *Writer:* Rick Copp, Ben Zook. **Comment:** Bears, in the gay and bisexual culture, refers to a large, hairy man who projects a masculine image. Despite all the silliness and off-the-wall investigations, the program is a light-hearted spoof of straight-like characters that take it upon themselves to solve crimes. There are

Where the Bears Are. **Left to right: Rick Copp, Joe Dietl, Ian Parks and Ben Zook (copyright 2012 JayPG Photography).**

some intimate moments, numerous sight gags and very good acting and production values. There is some vulgar language and characters are a bit older than one would imagine gay men to be (sort of like *Murder, She Wrote* meets *The Golden Girls*) but that is where the program's charm lies—it is different and it can be enjoyed by anyone.

Episodes:

1. Bear Down. After a wild birthday party for Nelson the roommates wake up to find a dead body in their bathtub.

2. Bear in Mind. The deceased appears familiar to the bears but they are unable to place him. Meanwhile, the man Nelson spent the night with (Hot Toddy) begins acting suspicious.

3. Goldicop and the Three Bears. The deceased is revealed to be J. Cub (Julio Tello) and the bears face questioning from a police detective (Chad

Winters) about the mysterious death in the bath-tub.

4. Bear Essentials. Although the police investigation reveals that J. Cub's death has been ruled a suicide, the bears think differently and begin their own investigation into the case when the original report is reversed and the tragedy tagged as a homicide.

5. Bear on a Couch. The case begins with Wood seeking Susie Collins, his high school prom date who is now the Los Angeles County Coroner, for information on how J. Cub died. Complications set in when Susie, who still has feelings for Wood, reveals that J. Cub was poisoned and it could implicate him.

6. Bears of Interest. The bears join forces to trace the poison that was found on J. Cub's martini glass. Suspicion points to Hot Toddy when he claims he is too busy to be interviewed by the police.

7. A Bear and Honey. Without really thinking, Nelson decides to question Honey Garrett (Brooke Dillman), the chef who catered the party—and does so right in the middle of the taping of her reality TV show.

8. Bears in Heat. Figuring that Hot Toddy is the key to solving the case, the bears track him to Elysian Park, but must endure a grueling boot camp training exercise before they can see him.

9. Bear Fan. After questioning Hot Toddy, the bears learn that there was a party crasher at the birthday celebration and begin a search to find him.

10. Bear Cam. The party crasher is revealed to be George Ridgemont (George Sebastian), an obsessed fan of Wood's (from his days as a model) who only wanted to see his idol.

11. Bear on Stage. When Dickie Calloway (Tuc Watkins), Nelson's former comedy partner (in an improv act) is found to have known J. Cub, the bears discover the two were in a relationship.

12. Bear Reunion. Reggie and Wood learn from their friend Jackie Beat, a drag queen, that she witnessed a fight between J. Cub and his date the night prior to the murder.

13. Bear on a Date. Nelson feels Hot Toddy is somehow involved in the murder and seeks a way (through a romantic dinner) to get him to open up about J. Cub.

14. Bear Facts. Despite the suspicions that surround Hot Toddy, Nelson convinces Wood and Reggie that they should focus on Ramon Santiago, the leather bar owner who had a rocky relationship with J. Cub.

15. Bears Undercover. In an attempt to get close to Ramon, the bears go undercover—as a bouncer, a patron and a contestant in a bear chest contest being held at the bar.

16. Mr. Bear Chest. As Nelson competes in the Mr. Bear Chest Pageant of 2012 hosted by Hot Toddy, Wood and Reggie search the bar for clues.

17. A Bear in Need. The situation takes a turn for the worse when Wood is caught trying to break into Ramon's safe and Reggie is caught by Ramon's goons Thor and Hulk.

18. Bearnapped. Reggie, held hostage by Thor and Hulk, becomes the bargaining chip for Ramon (Mario Diaz) to recover evidence that Wood found that could implicate him in the murder.

19. Bears to the Rescue. Reggie, hoping to free Nelson teams with Detective Chad Winters to outsmart Ramon.

20. Stand Up Bear. With Reggie freed and Ramon not the guilty party, the bears next question Bruce Daniels (himself), a comedian who had an altercation with J. Cub.

21. Bear Fight. Nelson's insistence that Hot Toddy is not the killer infuriates Wood and Reggie who believe he is, but can't convince Nelson otherwise.

22. Bears in the Desert. As Nelson, who has chosen Hot Toddy over Wood and Reggie, leaves, Detective Winters reveals to Reggie and Wood that evidence was found that connects Hot Toddy to the murder. The problem: where are Nelson and Hot Toddy?

23. Bear Devil. While Wood and Reggie seek Nelson, Nelson, in Palm Springs with Hot Toddy finds that Wood and Reggie may be right when it appears Hot Toddy has set his sights on killing Nelson.

24. Bear Trap, Part 1. Wood and Reggie trace Nelson to Palm Springs, but it appears they have arrived too late as Nelson and Hot Toddy have already left their condo.

25. Bear Trap, Part 2. A showdown in the desert ensues when Wood and Reggie find Nelson and attempt to free him from Hot Toddy's clutches.

26. Christmas Special. The roomies celebrate Christmas in the program's season one finale.

Season 2 Episodes:

27. Party Bears. The second season begins with the bears becoming involved in the murder of Elliot Butler, Reggie's college fraternity brother, during his political fund raising party.

28. Truth or Bear. As the police begin to suspect Reggie as being the killer, Nelson believes he spotted a man (Cyril) at the fund raiser who is supposedly in prison while Wood encounters Hairy Potter (Pete Cincinato), an old crush.

29. Clear the Bear. Reggie, cleared of the charge by Detectives Winters and Martinez, vows to find Elliot's killer. Meanwhile the bears acquire a new roommate: Todd.

30. Bears in Chains. When clues lead to The Stockroom, a Silver Lake fetish club, the bears get more than what they bargained for when they meet the dominatrix Mistress Lena (Margaret Cho) and must "battle" her array of sex toys.

31. Leather Bears. Believing that Elliot's campaign manager, Mo Kapoor (Ray Singh) is connected to the murder, the bears track him to the Faultline, a Silver Lake leather bar.

32. Go Go Bear. Through his questioning of the bar's DJ, Reggie learns that Mo was seeing a personal trainer (Shannon Ward) and both are somehow connected to the murder.

33. Bear to Dream. Following a dream in which Nelson envisioned Cyril (Scott Beauchemin) escaping from prison, he learns that Cyril actually did escape and has been hiding under the radar ever since.

34. Blackmail Bears. After questioning the personal trainer, the bears come up empty, leading them to plot their next move: infiltrate Elliot's opponent's (Danny Pendleton) campaign headquarters.

35. Closet Bear. Suspecting that Danny's wife, Mary Ashley Pendleton (Becky Thyre) could have ordered a hit on Elliot to insure her husband wins, the bears infiltrate Danny's (Chris LeVoie) campaign headquarters.

36. Bear Movie Night. Without conclusive evidence, the bears return home and plan a movie night. The evening finds Nelson having trouble adjusting to Todd as his roommate while Reggie feels they need to get back into the game and find clues.

37. Break in Bears. With movie night over, the bears break into Danny's headquarters hoping to find evidence that Elliot's opponent was sleeping with his wife's personal trainer (Turbo) and seduced him into killing Elliot (and thus eliminating the competition).

38. Jail Bears. The bears are caught breaking and entering and arrested. When calls to Todd for bail money go unanswered, the bears find their only hope for release lies in the hands of George, Wood's obsessed fan, a strapped dentist with little money.

39. Bailed Out Bears. Jail time was not all that unproductive as Reggie found romance and Nelson gave acting lessons to inmates. But upon release, Nelson is shocked to learn that Todd spent the evening with Ivan (Howie Skora), his ex.

40. Bear on a Stakeout. Wood's decision to accompany detectives Winters and Martinez on a stakeout to find the elusive personal trainer Turbo leads to Wood revealing that he is not only involved with Detective Winters, but Martinez as well—and Winters and Martinez are partners in life.

41. Bear Interrogation. Turbo is caught and questioned and when Wood learns he has an airtight alibi for the night of Elliot's murder, the bears find they are back to square one.

42. Rugby Bears. As the bears continue seeking clues, they cross paths with Susie Collins, the now disgraced former county coroner (fired for sexual harassment) who is now coaching a man's rugby team.

43. Wine and Bear. When the bears discover that Jeremy Richards (Mark Rowe) had a fight with Elliot right before he was murdered, Reggie attempts to seduce him via a candle light dinner as a ruse to search for evidence to connect him to the crime.

44. Bear Audition. Nelson's initial intention to question Ivan, the casting director about the murder becomes secondary when he becomes distracted by auditions for a spokesman for Soak 'Ems (adult diapers) and sets his goal to become "The Face of Incontinence."

45. Crazy Bear. By pure accident, Nelson finds the murder weapon and leads the police to believe it belongs to Ivan; an APB (All Points Bulletin) is issued for the believed suspect, Ivan.

46. Hunting Bears. Feeling they need to get away from it all, the bears retreat to Big Bear for some needed rest, unaware they are being trailed by the real killer—Jeremy.

47. Bear in a Panic. Unaware that Jeremy is the killer, the roomies, especially Reggie (who has become attracted to him) accept him as one of their own; meanwhile, Wood becomes panicked when Detective Winters catches him in bed with his husband—Detective Martinez.

48. Bears in the Woods, Part 1. While alone with Reggie, Jeremy reveals that he is the killer and Reggie is next on his list. His motive: revenge (in college, Reggie, Elliot and Jeremy were fraternity brothers but Jeremy was an outcast—called "Dumbo" because of his large ears. He vowed to one day get even, and after having the world's first ear transplant, set out to eliminate those who made fun of him).

49. Bears in the Woods, Part 2. Reggie manages to escape Jeremy's clutches but a confrontation in the woods almost costs Reggie his life until he is rescued by Nelson, Wood and Detectives Winters and Martinez.

50. Thanksgiving Special. A celebration of the holiday—bear style.

Season 3 Episodes:

51. Model Bears. Wood begins his job photographing a reunion calendar for Chunk Studios and becomes a suspect in the murder of Cody Summers, the film company's cover boy.

52. Bears in the House. As Reggie learns that he is being considered as the host of a reality crime series on the Primitive Channel, he finds that his first story will be covering the Cody Summers murder.

53. Bad Bear Day. With Nelson hoping for a role as a small town Southern sheriff in a low budget horror movie called *Kick Ass Force*, he and Wood join Reggie in his investigation of Cody's murder but find that Detectives Winters and Martinez are reluctant to help them.

54. Dead Body Bears. As the bears continue their investigation, they learn that Susie Collins has not only been re-instated as the County Coroner (from first season episodes), but has hired a hunky new lab assistant (Big Ben, played by Piankhi Iknation).

55. Bear on a Table. Wood and Reggie devise a plan to search a chiropractor's office for clues in Cody's murder.

56. County Bear Jamboree. With the case becoming increasingly difficult to solve, the bears infiltrate a country-western bar known to be frequented by the Chunk Studios models.

57. Bedroom Bears. Detectives Winters and Martinez to step up their investigation by devising a plan to search the bears' home to see what clues they have uncovered.

58. Psycho Bear. As the mysterious killer still remains on the loose the bears seek the help of their old nemesis, Cyril (Scott Beauchemin) to help in making a profile for them to follow.

59. Teddy Bear. Nelson, posing as models manager Teddy Rose, attempts to get his client, Todd (Ian Parks), a job with Chunk Studios to spy for them; hoping the studio holds clues they may have overlooked.

60. Loaded for Bear. In an effort to get information, Wood, wearing a recording devise concealed in a pair of eye glasses, dines with Malcolm Lee (Pat Towne), the head of Chunk Studios while Reggie monitors the proceedings with his new assistant, George Ridgemont (George Sebastian).

61. Hollywood Bears. Nelson's jubilation over his first starring role as a sheriff in the movie is dampened by the casting of his acting rival, Dickie Calloway (Tuc Watkins) as his deputy.

62. Killer Bear. Nelson fails to notice that the actor playing the killer has been knocked unconscious and replaced by the real Chunk Studios killer.

63. Intensive Care Bears. Nelson, injured on the set of the movie, is taken to the hospital and unknowingly being observed by the Chunk Studios killer.

64. Peeping Bears. As the bears hit a dead end in their investigation, Reggie begins to fear he may lose his TV series before it even gets started.

65. Cover Bear. Believing that photographer Carla Cassidy (Mary Wachtel) may be the killer, Todd infiltrates a Chunk Studios photo shoot to uncover information. Meanwhile Reggie pits himself in a battle to solve the case before Mickey Swift (Adam Ridge), an Australian private detective who is not only gay, but out to solve the case.

66. Bear Scare. As the murders continue, Todd, Nelson and Wood believe Ashley (Brett Paisel), Chunk Studios make-up artist Alfie Cooper's (Sam Pancake) mentally unstable sister, may be the culprit.

67. Stripped Bear. As Todd continues his probe of Chunk Studios, he is unknowingly being stalked by someone who may just be the killer.

68. Dungeon Bear. Realizing that Todd may be in danger, Nelson and Wood rush to Chunk Studios to help him.

69. Bears in the Air, Part 1. During a flight to Australia (aboard Dingo Air Lines), Reggie gets an unsettling call from Detective Winters informing him that the case has not been solved and that the real killer is still on the loose.

70. Bears in the Air, Part 2. Believing that the killer may be on board the plane, Reggie begins questioning suspects with Wood using what he calls "Acute Ass Recognition" (can tell who anyone is by their butts) to help find the killer.

71. Bears in the Air, Part 3. The Bears uncover the killer—but face even a more harrowing situation when they discover the pilots have been poisoned and there is no one to fly the plane. The program's concluding episode.

331 *Who Knows Her Better?* onemorelesbian.com/tello/webseries/who-better-game-show/. 2012 (Game).

The format involves three people: a woman, her male partner and her gay or lesbian best friend. The woman is asked several questions and her responses recorded. Her male partner then best friend is asked the same questions and their responses must match what the woman said in order to score points. Who knows her best is determined by the partner or friend who matches the most answers with the woman.

Host: Elizabeth Keener, George Coleman. **Credits:** *Producer:* Christin Baker. *Director:* Jessica King. **Comment:** Interesting game show that borrows its format from a 1970s syndicated show called *Three's a Crowd* wherein a husband had to determine who knew him better—his wife or his secretary.

Episodes: Episodes are only available through a paid subscription service as tellofilms.com.

332 *Who the F##k Is Nancy?* webseries channel.com. 2014 (Comedy).

"Nancy" is softer terminology for gays who were termed "faggat" or "queer." "Nance" is a British effeminate variation on the term or slang for a "Nancy Boy." Alex and Jo, friends who are also gay, have always gotten along well together until Jo fanaticized about becoming famous as "The" Nancy, the one all gays will admire and adore. His endless efforts to achieve that goal have not only upset Alex, who has now taken second place in Jo's life, but an unknown entity (suggested as being an alien) who has sought that prestigious "Nancy" title. When the entity can no longer abide by Jo's attempts to displace it as "Nancy," it decides to rectify the situation by eliminating Jo and Alex in a live web cast execution that will insure it becomes "Nancy." The program follows the entity's efforts (by possessing earthlings) to stop Jo's progression and Jo, Alex and their drag queen friend, Judy, as they attempt to destroy it before it destroys them.

Cast: Alex Josselyn (Alex), Jo Primeau (Jo), Judy Virtago (Judy). **Credits:** *Producer-Director:* Alex Castor, Jo Primeau. **Comment:** Unusual program to say the least. Not only does it combine gays and drag queens but an alien "Nancy Boy." The production values are very good and the acting varies from very good to just hamming it up (especially with some of Jo and Alex's scenes). The producers assume you know what a Nancy, Nancy Boy or Nance is and they also assume you are aware of "The Legend of Bloody Mary" as aspects of that urban myth can be seen (saying the name of Bloody Mary three times in front of a mirror brings to life her evil spirit). In the series, Jo's constant winning about wanting to become "The Nancy" brings to earth a gay alien who is determined to destroy its evil (Jo and Alex) to achieve Nancy Boy fame. While first season episodes are basically Jo and Alex's efforts to comprehend what is happening as Jo strives for fame, the second season uses parodies based on horror feature films to bring Jo, Alex and drag queen Judy into encounters with the alien and a final confrontation wherein Judy literally saves their lives.

Episodes:

1. Celebrite. Jo has made a life choice: to become "The Nancy" displeasing all those who are close to him as all his energies are now devoted to that goal.

2. Just Nance! As Jo delves into his new life choice, he begins to realize that "famous partying" is a lot different from normal partying.

3. Call Me Nancy. Following the party, Jo posts its highlights on his website, Nancy Vision, only to find disappointment with one hit.

4. 1 Girl, 5 Gaysians. A party invitation by their friend Matt Barker to a Nancy Party, has Jo all excited until a glimpse of a drag queen appearing as actress Lindsay Lohan, gives him an uneasy feeling (possibly, but not stated, the alien's first encounter with Jo).

5. I Wanna Nance with Somebody. Jo and Alex prepare for the upcoming Nancy Party.

6. Mean Gays. Jo's continual infatuation with becoming "The Nancy" has taken its toll on Alex, who has become jealous of Jo's Nancy fame. As the first season ends, Jo and Alex appear to have broken up and gone their separate ways.

7. Nancy Screams. The second season of horror movie parodies begins with a take-off of the phone call scene from *Scream* wherein Jo receives a call from someone (the alien) who knows his every move. Unnerved, Jo makes the first attempt to reconnect with Alex and calls him for help.

8. Nancy's Nightmare. Alex confronts his friend Judy about his breakup with Jo while Jo has a *Friday the 13th*–like nightmare wherein he sees Judy turn into an angry alien with only these words for him—"Who the f##k is Nancy?" (apparently meaning Jo or the alien).

9. Nancy Knows What You Did Last Summer. Alex, back with Jo, discovers what is happening when the alien, taking over Judy's body, reveals it was summoned by Jo and he, in essence created her (as the alien now considers itself) and it can achieve Nancy fame by eliminating the competition—Jo (along with his friends Alex and Judy).

10. The Exorcism of Scarlett Bobo. As the trio tries to understand the situation they are now in, they find a strange DVD with the initial "N" on it and play it. It reveals that the alien will strike in seven days and there is no stopping it. The episode features excellent special effects.

11. Black XXXmas. With time running out, Jo, Alex and Judy figure they must come up with a plan of action to defeat the alien and save their lives.

12. Hellbound. Since the city's regular police force will not investigate cases involving Nancy Boys (or drag queens), Judy calls in the Vigilante Drag Police for help (which they receive little of).

13. Inside Ivory's Tower. With three days remaining and the trio no better off then they were seven days ago, they seek shelter in the home their drag queen friend Ivory Towers. It is here that a real woman (Morphine), a psychic, tells Jo that their enemy is an alien that has taken human form and it could be anybody.

14. The Silent Treatment. Feeling that Ivory's home is no longer safe, Jo, Alex and Judy make their way to another safe house.

15. Qrafty-ass Queen. With suspicions rising and not knowing who to trust, the trio heads to the home of a friend they feel they can trust. Unknowingly, they are being tracked by the alien.

16. The Evil Web. The concluding episode wherein a confrontation is held and Judy realizes she possesses the "weapon" that can defeat the alien. All her life Judy was teased and bullied for who she was and is. She tells the alien "You are a bully and you can kill me and the boys [Jo and Alex] but not their spirits. That is the essence of the Nancy Boys and you will never be them. You will never be a real Nancy." The alien begrudgingly disappears, apparently going back from where it came.

333 *Whoa Dude.* blip.tv. 2013 (Comedy).

A series of homoerotic clips created "by your favorite local frat boys, skaters, military men, jocks and naughty queens" and compiled from various Internet sites.

Host: Johnny McGovern. **Credits:** *Producer:* Johnny McGovern, James Pombo, Susan Wrenn, Lorna Paul, Bryan Douglas. *Writer:* Johnny McGovern, Linda James, Brandy Howard, Greg McKeon, Julie Goldman. **Comment:** Host Johnny McGovern appears in a setting based on late night talk shows and simply introduces the individual clips (such in a manner as Tom Bergeron on *America's Funniest Home Videos*). Due to their mature content, the episodes are age restricted on the YouTube sharing site (requires an e-mail account to view).

Episodes: 16 episodes were produced but only episodes 2, 3, 11 and 15 remain on line.

334 *Words with Girls.* youtube.com. 2012 (Comedy).

Partly scripted program to present an improvised look at the lives of Brittani and Hannah, twentysomething lesbians as they navigate the Los Angeles scene seeking to jump start their careers, hook up with women and, to give the program a documentary-like look, talk about themselves.

Cast: Sarah Croce (Sarah), Brittani Nichols (Brittani), Lauren Neal (Lauren). **Credits:** *Producer:* Sarah Croce, Brittani Nichols. *Director:* Sarah Croce. *Writer:* Brittani Nichols. **Comment:** Capable acting and standard production values in a non-offensive look at the lives of two women who happen to be friends, not lovers.

Episodes:

1. Semi. Brittani and Hannah discuss the prospect that if you are a lesbian, can you express attraction to a guy.

2. Gussy. The girls prepare to attend a party.

3. Token. At the party, Brittani becomes a bit apprehensive when she believes she is the only black person that has been invited.

4. Homophobic. Hannah relates her feelings about being uncomfortable about attending parties with gays and lesbians.

5. Mimicry. When Hannah spies a girl she would like to meet she finds competition from Brittani when she seeks the same girl.

6. Beard. Lauren, Brittani and Sarah's friend, seeks their help in ditching a man who just won't stop pursuing her. The program's concluding episode.

335 *Young N' Reckless.* youtube.com. 2013–2014 (Comedy-Drama).

The program is billed as "a raw, sexy, funny and semi-autobiographical riff on American soap operas." Four college students are profiled (Ashley and Chanel, bisexual; and straights Raven and Devan) with an intimate, if not humorous look at how they progress into adulthood and face the consequences of their reckless behavior before they reach that stage of development.

Cast: Aarika Trabona (Ashley), Talia Marrero (Raven), Kajuana Shuford (Chanel), Mark St. Cyr (Devan), Kiara McCarthy (Alana), Andre Jackson, Jr. (Victor), Shana Solomon (Melody), Andrew Rogers (Matthew), Marcos Sotomayor (Joshua), Rosalyn Coleman (Evelyn), Julia Tokarz (Wasted Girl), Arden Kelly (Ramona), Hugues Faustin (Hassan), Justin Hurtt-Dunkley (Jonathan), Collin Knight (Trey), Al Thompson (Tasean). **Credits:** *Producer-Writer:* Kajuana Shuford, William Alexander Runnels. *Director:* William Alexander Runnels. **Comment:** Although the program needlessly incorporates vulgar language, the story flows smoothly with good acting and production values. There are several sexual situations and the doorway has been left open for the program to continue.

Episodes:

1. The Morning After. The regulars are introduced: Ashley fears her long-distance relationship with Matt is interfering with her school work; Raven has been intimate with a married man (Hassan); Chanel, being Ashley's best friend, believes she should let Matt know how he is affecting her; and Chanel herself is seeking to re-connect with her ex (Devan).

Young N' Reckless. **Poster art from the series (used by permission).**

2. Scott Who? Although Chanel and Devan appear to be becoming a couple again, Chanel continues to see another man (Victor) and also finds complications when she is overcome with feelings for her long distance boyfriend Tasean.

3. Getting It. A look at Chanel, her background, and a phone conversation she has with Tasean.

4. Don't Seem Like the Type. Ashley, a bisexual, is torn between her girlfriend and Matt when Matt returns to her.

5. I Gotta Save My Money. As Chanel cuts class to have a rendezvous with another girl (Alana), Raven seeks a way to stay in school when she realizes her finances are low.

6. Birthday Burn, Part 1. A celebration of Raven's birthday has everyone preparing for a grand party—even an uninvited guest—Hassan.

7. Birthday Burn, Part 2. As the party gets underway, Hassan appears, seeking to know where his and Raven's relationship is headed.

8. Results Are In. Ashley's reunion with Matt resulted in them becoming intimate and now Ashley fears the worst: she may be pregnant.

9. After Math. The concluding episode: Ashley feels she has the right to choose and will decide whether or not to keep the baby; Melody, Hassan's wife, discovers he has been unfaithful; and Devan, unable to deal with Chanel, ends their relationship.

INDEX TO ENTRY NUMBERS

www.ingramcontent.com/pod-product-compliance
Lightning Source LLC
Chambersburg PA
CBHW080552060326
40689CB00021B/4833